www.wadsworth.com

wadsworth.com is the World Wide Web site for Wadsworth Publishing Company and is your direct source to dozens of online resources.

At *wadsworth.com* you can find out about supplements, demonstration software, and student resources. You can also send e-mail to many of our authors and preview new publications and exciting new technologies.

wadsworth.com
Changing the way the world learns®

The Role of Work in People's Lives
Applied Career Counseling and Vocational Psychology

NADENE PETERSON, Ed.D.

Our Lady of the Lake University

ROBERTO CORTÉZ GONZÁLEZ, Ph.D.

The University of Texas at El Paso

Brooks/Cole
Thomson Learning™

Australia • Canada • Denmark • Japan • Mexico • New Zealand • Philippines
Puerto Rico • Singapore • South Africa • Spain • United Kingdom • United States

Counseling Editor: *Eileen Murphy*
Assistant Editor: *Julie Martinez*
Editorial Assistant: *Annie Berterretche*
Marketing Manager: *Jennie Burger*
Project Editor: *Matt Stevens*
Print Buyer: *Stacey Weinberger*
Permissions Editor: *Robert M. Kauser*
Production: *Matrix Productions Inc.*
Designer: *Cynthia Bassett*
Copyeditor: *Patti Law*
Cover Designer: *Bill Stanton*

Cover Image: *© Boris Lyubner/SIS*
Frontispiece: *"The Role of Work in People's Lives," framed in a Moorish-style motif influenced by the famous, hand-carved Rose Window at the San José Mission, San Antonio, Texas. A wide range of work-related activities are depicted as performed by diverse peoples, not the least of which is a father actively involved in childrearing. —* artwork by Richard Arredondo
Compositor: *Scratchgravel Publishing Services*
Printer: *R. R. Donnelley & Sons, Crawfordsville*

Printed in the United States of America
1 2 3 4 5 6 7 03 02 01 00 99

**Library of Congress
Cataloging-in-Publication Data**
Peterson, Nadene.
   The role of work in people's lives: applied career counseling and vocational psychology/ Nadene Peterson, Roberto Cortéz González.
      p. cm.
   Includes bibliographical references and index.
      ISBN 0-534-34688-X
      1. Vocational guidance. 2. Work— Psychological aspects. I. González, Roberto Cortéz. II. Title.
   HF5381.P483 1999
   158.7—dc21   99-21251

Wadsworth/Thomson Learning
10 Davis Drive
Belmont, CA 94002-3098
USA
www.wadsworth.com

International Headquarters
Thomson Learning
290 Harbor Drive, 2nd Floor
Stamford, CT 06902-7477
USA

UK/Europe/Middle East
Thomson Learning
Berkshire House
168-173 High Holborn
London WC1V 7AA
UK

Asia
Thomson Learning
60 Albert Street #15-01
Albert Complex
Singapore 189969

Canada
Nelson/Thomson Learning
1120 Birchmount Road
Scarborough, Ontario M1K 5G4
Canada

Dedication

To my husband, Bob
                    —Nadene Peterson

To the memory of Rene A. "Art" Ruiz
and of Coystal Tabor Stone
                    —Roberto Cortéz González

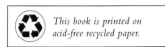
*This book is printed on
acid-free recycled paper.*

Contents

Preface

This book is designed for use in graduate level courses in life planning and vocational counseling. It represents the collaboration between two people of different ages, cultural backgrounds, and genders. We have attempted to provide a survey of historical development and theories that have been part of the field of vocational psychology and career counseling while including some of the latest thinking and influences on current practice. Several areas that we emphasize make this textbook unique, and we believe they will help students prepare for changes that are taking place in the world of work.

Basic to our approach are the importance of the changes in the role of work, rethinking work ethics and values, and a clearer understanding of where we have come from and where we are going. "Career" as we know it will no longer exist for most people, and job security will be in the hands of workers rather than companies.

Family life cycles have a profound impact on our thinking and planning. Long patterns of government assistance, hand-me-down family businesses, socioeconomic mindsets and definitions of success are changing. Too little has been written about these cycles that are based in family patterns. We attempt to increase awareness of this influential factor in thinking about work, career, and responsibility.

The global economy and a workforce that is more integrated in the United States and other countries are requiring that vocational practitioners (as we prefer to call career counselors) understand the different ethics and values that various cultures have as well as how to help workers deal with multiculturalism and diversity in a positive and collaborative way. Government programs increasingly mandate responsibility for self, regardless of socioeconomic status, physical limitations, or cultural influences. This sense of personal responsibility is a significant emphasis of this book.

Technology has been a major shaper of the workplace for many years. With the use of computers and the ability to store vast amounts of information on tiny disks, the role of the vocational practitioner is changing rapidly. Information that was hard to find is now readily available on the Internet, including standard sources such as the *Dictionary of Occupational Titles,* the *Occupational*

Outlook Handbook, and others that can be accessed in one's home or office. We note this developing field and propose a new understanding of the role of the vocational practitioner as a facilitator, counselor, advisor, and therapist.

We represent several years of teaching career counseling and development courses and have extensive clinical experience as vocational practitioners. Our own integrated approaches are presented in the Instructor's Manual and on the Web page for this book at http://counseling.wadsworth.com. The emphasis in this book has been on the actual practice and application of theories rather than on expansive discussion of all possibilities and research.

As a companion to this book we have edited *Career Counseling Models for Diverse Populations: Hands-On Applications by Practitioners.* Included are models across the lifespan from kindergarten to older adults. There are models for students at various levels, those with profound disabilities, cultural differences, athletes, and others. Résumé writing, genograms, the role of spirituality, and vocational groups each have models for practical use. Diverse adult groups such as prisoners, battered women in shelters, military personnel exiting the service, work rehabilitation for injured workers, career development in industry, job-locating skills, and creative aging in relation to work are all part of this book of models.

Three appendices are included: Appendix I is the *Code of Fair Testing Practices in Education* as disseminated by the American Psychological Association; Appendix 2 is the *National Career Development Association Ethical Standards;* and Appendix 3 is a list of resources for assessment instruments which are presented in the chapters.

We wish to thank Eileen Murphy for her faith in the project and her constant encouragement. We also thank the leaders and researchers in the field of vocational psychology who paved the way for this book and generously allowed us to use their findings and illustrations. Robert Peterson provided support, backup, editing, drafting, and coordinating details for the whole project.

From San Antonio, Texas, Nadene Peterson acknowledges the following persons and departments: Larry Golden, Ph.D. encouraged and aided in the early steps of developing this book. Dr. Peterson's students were a source of inspiration and information, and allowed her to test ideas on them. Research assistants Marjorie Kyle, Mary Gardner, Mark Enloe, Paul Gottschalk, and Amy Smith Doar exhaustively searched articles, books, and other materials. Rachel Nichols helped with the painstaking process of putting the manuscript on computer. Lyla Haggard provided writing suggestions. Our Lady of the Lake University Psychology Department provided research assistants and the library staff gave their generous support in obtaining materials through interlibrary loans, copying articles, and going out of their way to access various resources.

From El Paso, Texas, Roberto Cortéz González acknowledges several persons at the University of Texas at El Paso (UTEP), who assisted with resources and technical and moral support: Dennis J. Bixler-Márquez, Ph.D., Sally S. Blake, Ph.D., Helen Hammond, Ph.D., Norma G. Hernández, Ph.D., Pilar Herrera, Elena Izquierdo, Ph.D., Stephen Wesley Johnson, Ph.D., Sandra R. Lloyd, Ph.D., Duane A. Lundervold, Ph.D., Maricela Oliva, Ph.D., Arturo Pacheco, Ph.D., Susan Rippberger, Ph.D., and Wayne R. Sather, M.S.E.E., who saved me from many technical difficulties. Other very helpful people were Patricia T. Castiglia, Ph.D., Rebecca Salcido, J.D., Kathleen A. Staudt, Ph.D., Carolyn Kahl, and Deborah A. Morgan from UTEP's library. Elea A. Aguirre provided materials related to Foucault. Lance Choy, M.A., provided an extensive listing of Stanford CPPC library books on reserve. Mary Contreras, M.S., provided materials on welfare reform.

The following students from Dr. González's Fall 1996 "Lifestyle and Career Development" provided research assistance: Margaret Hill Acosta, Father Vicente Calderón, Ed Dominguez, Juan Enríquez, David J. Ferrell, Orlando González, Craig D. Kehrwald, Jeffrey Kuroiwa, Concepción Monrreal, Paul R. Petit, and Margarita R. Yetter.

We would like to extend our gratitude to our colleagues who reviewed the manuscript and provided valuable feedback: Nancy Betz, Ohio State University; Paul Blisard, Southwest Missouri State University; Alan Davis, Montana State University, Billings; Cass Dykeman, Oregon State University; Dennis Engels, University of North Texas; LeeAnn Eschbach, University of Scranton; Stephen S. Feit, Idaho State University; Marie E. Nowakowski, Hagerstown Community College; Lewis Patterson, Cleveland State University; Ann D. Puryear, Southeast Missouri State University; Howard Splete, Oakland University; and Zark Van Zandt, University of Southern Maine, Gorham.

Jeri Robison Turner read the manuscript and provided feedback, and Rance Molitor, massage therapist, removed stresses involved during the preparation of the book.

Significant work on this book was completed while on a pilgrimage with the St. Pius X chorus (El Paso, TX) to the Basilica of Our Lady of Guadalupe in Mexico City and at the formation house of the *Hermanos Menores Capuchinos,* Puebla, Mexico.

The sprawling public laundry works of Mumbai (formerly Bombay), India, are a far cry from the automated washers and dryers in the United States. However, the work gets done. Ordinarily, it is first come, first served, but an unwritten rule allows specific families that have used particular sinks consistently to go ahead of other families waiting in line. Some families hire a tradesman known as a *dhobi* to do their laundry.

Our look at the role of work in people's lives is not limited to paid employment located exclusively in the occupational structure, but includes work done in personal and familial domains (Richardson, 1993), such as laundry. Hence, we will see how even the most mundane work tasks can dramatically differ in form and procedure from country to country.

Photo by Nadene Peterson, January 1997

Current Perspectives on Work

What I object to, is the "craze" . . . for what they call labour-saving machinery.
[We] go on "saving labour" till thousands are without work and thrown on
the open streets to die of starvation. I want to save time and labour, not for a
fraction of mankind, but for all; I want the concentration of wealth, not in the
hands of a few, but in the hands of all. Today machinery merely helps a few to
ride on the backs of millions. The impetus behind it all is not . . . to save
labour, but greed. It is against this . . . that I am fighting with all my might.

—MOHANDAS KARAMCHAND *MAHATMA* GANDHI
(CITED IN AJGAONKAR, N.D., P. 36)

As in Gandhi's time, we are seeing the profound changes in the world of work as
a result of technology and its effect on individual workers. Gandhi helped India
to move at a deliberate pace toward independence, a modicum of industrial development, and limited occupational disruption for its citizens. Domestic production minimized the amount of corporate colonialism that could have made
India dependent on imports from foreign companies. So, for example, most auto-
mobiles, buses, motorcycles, motorized rickshaws, and bicycles that transport the
960 million Indians are manufactured within the country. Many people in India
need work; modern tools are, therefore, used judiciously. Road-building equipment in India is minimally used; instead, extended families are hired to manually
crush with hammers the rocks used to pave roads and highways. Genuinely

vocational psychology? Vocational psychology's relevance has been doubtful at best for women, racial and ethnic groups, persons with disabilities, gay/lesbian/bisexual persons, lower-income groups, the permanent under class, and international populations. The field is being challenged to dramatically transform into a practical source of assistance for people with vast arrays of life situations and work circumstances.

As a related term, **career counseling** is used to refer to "planning and making decisions about occupations and education" (Tolbert, 1980, p. 32). The term has evolved into being most applicable to white-collar, college-educated populations and the professional class. The word "career" is derived from the Latin *carrus,* meaning "chariot" (Super & Hall, 1978). Both *career* and *chariot* elicit a sense of movement through or progress over time, particularly emphasizing the element of competition, with the goal of placing first. Career also evokes the image of a corporate employee striving along the fast track to the top. A growing concern is that career counseling has developed élitist connotations that fail to capture and describe the work experiences of diverse populations. The world of work is changing rapidly, and theories of vocational development have barely kept pace. Old models of career development no longer apply.

From a Psychology of Careers
to a Social Analysis of Work

Richardson (1993) suggests some new directions for vocational psychology based on two serious problems with the field. The first problem is the time lapse between advances in developmental psychology and their incorporation into the career development literature. Too few aspects of social psychology and sociological methodology are integrated into vocational psychology, which has its roots in counseling psychology (Dawis, 1992). However, more aspects of political science, international relations, business, economics, women's studies, multicultural studies, and gay/lesbian/bisexual studies must be consolidated into occupational development. Richardson views the field of vocational psychology as resistant to new ideas, and questions why more vocational psychologists and theorists are not at the forefront of innovating approaches.

The second problem is that the theoretical and research literature in career development and vocational psychology is oriented toward the White middle class (Richardson, 1993). The **androcentric** foundations of the academic discipline have been attenuated since the 1970s by more focus on women's career development. Yet the almost total absence of literature from poor and lower-class populations of all races and ethnicities neglects a significant segment of the population. This demographic disregard perpetuates the **marginalization** of **oppressed groups** and upholds the implicit **classism, racism,** and **hetero-**

sexism of the external social structure. Richardson warns that vocational psychology's claims to the scientific validity of its research literature is undermined by the tacit tolerance for such disenfranchising practices.

A pioneer spirit marked the emergence of vocational psychology; this spirit may have calcified due to a desire to claim scientific legitimacy by the founding counseling psychologists (Richardson, 1993). The field's strict adherence to the scientific method has rendered it stale, with limited exploration of new developments, perspectives, questions, and populations. To remedy the situation, Richardson proposes that counseling psychologists—we would also add other clinical practitioners whose clients present work-related issues—entertain the following three possibilities: (1) focus on work in people's lives rather than on careers, (2) adopt an epistemology of social constructionism regarding work, and (3) view work in people's lives from the perspective of an applied psychology.

Richardson advocates shifting from the study of careers predominantly located in the occupational structure to examining work in people's lives. Work is a central human activity not exclusively located in the occupational structure. Reasons for this suggested shift are fourfold. First, career is inherently biased in favor of populations who have access to opportunities to develop occupationally and progress over time; work as a basic human function with multiple meanings would expand the vision of vocational psychology beyond a fixation on careers. Second, career fixation ties it too closely to the occupational structure, which marginalizes and ignores the work done outside this structure (e.g., the gendered nature of work, work done in personal and familial domains). Third, focusing on work in people's lives emphasizes the multiple contexts of an individual's life, whereas inquiry limited to employment within the occupational structure truncates what is known about people in their multiple and interacting contexts. Holistic practitioners consider clients' work across a full range of life's contexts. Fourth, work has social value and is not done only for individual success and satisfaction, to satisfy achievement needs, to earn a living, and/or to further ambitions. The relation of work to the social order makes explicit that working people exist in a larger community and live for others as well as themselves. Career, on the other hand, has become embedded in an ethos of self-centered individualism and an ethnocentric conception of the self that may actually undermine the fabric of society and culture. Notice how work has taken on a different meaning according to Richardson (1993) in contrast to Tolbert's (1980) traditional and limited rendition.

Richardson's second possibility for new perspectives on work—the adoption of the **epistemology** of **social constructionism**—would turn vocational psychology into more of an interpretive discipline. Knowledge of the world of work would consist of meaning making through subjective interactions between persons (Savickas, 1995). Epistemology addresses the origin, structure, and methods of knowing, and the standards of judging and validating knowledge about the world (Dervin, 1994; Peterson, 1970). Social constructionism "maintains that individuals' sense of what is real—including their sense of . . . their problems, competencies, and possible solutions—is constructed in interaction with others as they go through life" (De Jong & Berg, 1998, p. 226). Clients' problems become "a function of their current definitions of reality rather than as something that is objectively knowable" (p. 228). Vocational psychology would be based less on scientific objectivity and controlled empirical research, with greater emphasis placed on socially generated narratives.

Tinsley (1994) and Savickas (1994) responded to Richardson. Tinsley disagreed with Richardson's view that vocational psychology is theoretically stagnant and rigid. He perceives that theories are not threshed out for long enough periods of time. Instead, he sees the field as characterized by trendiness. Rather than being reluctant to try innovative, qualitative research approaches, few people are skilled in using these methodologies. This raises issues about the adequate training of graduate students and the feasibility of retraining practitioners in qualitative methods. Tinsley asserts that scholars focus on what is of intrinsic interest to them; vocational psychology will become relevant to minorities and working-class people only when a substantial number of persons with intrinsic interests and insights into these populations have been trained.

But Tinsley overlooks the external barriers that prevent such opportunities from occurring for persons with such insights and intrinsic interests (e.g., rising educational costs and decreasing financial aid, a lack of abundant numbers of mentors available in the field with similar intrinsic interests, entrenched mindsets in academia that overtly and covertly seek to prevent a focus on minorities and lower-income people). Tinsley also does not acknowledge what several recently trained individuals encounter upon their arrival into academic positions where they could make a difference: the self-seeking political behaviors of too many in higher education, which is partially reflected by their disregard for disenfranchised communities and disrespect for the missions of their social justice-oriented colleagues. Tinsley makes a valuable point when he states that sociologists, industrial and organizational psychologists, and management psychologists have contributed vast literature on the influx of women and minority groups into the workforce. However, each discipline seems unaware of the efforts of others.

Savickas (1994) more fully supports Richardson's (1993) proposal. He comments on the need to transcend from a *psychology of careers* to a *social analysis of work*. People can no longer build their lives around stable companies to develop their careers. The concept of career is outmoded and should be a subspecialty of the study of work. Others proclaim the traditional career a relic of the past (Hall & Associates, 1997). Savickas also calls for a change in research methodology. He promotes Richardson's idea of moving from general abstract principles about

Practical Applications

Clearly, vocational psychology needs to be transformed into a field that focuses on work in people's lives— this is the thrust of our text. As such, applied practitioners should be committed to (a) positioning themselves at the boundaries of core disciplinary and interdisciplinary sources, and (b) facilitating the development and enhancement of individuals who are clients and/or research participants (Richardson, 1993). Our sections on "Practical Applications" will reflect this perspective. In *Pedagogy of the Oppressed* (1993), the late Brazilian educator Paulo Freire [1921–1997] contended that in a racist and class-driven society, those in a dominant position can be oblivious to others' experience and thus to the unexamined effects of the impact of their own race and class privilege. Until the larger external structures of **power,** oppression, hierarchy, and privilege are examined, vocational psychology and career counseling will be remiss in addressing the occupational experiences of diverse groups. As a result, major blind spots will persist in what is known even about the White middle-class experience.

A Freudian legacy to vocational psychology has been to focus on pathologies or problems as residing in the individual and ignoring broader cultural factors, thus making society less accountable to its members (Pipher, 1996). In the twenty-first century, the transformation of career counseling and vocational psychology will entail an expanding vision of work and its influence on the quality of life for persons of various racial and ethnic groups, nationalities, sexual orientations, and socioeconomic classes. Practitioners must question how their own race, sexual orientation, educational training, and class privilege contribute to the way they view the role of work in people's lives, and how such views affect their intervention with clients' workplace issues.

individual careers to a socially situated, **localized knowledge** about how the world of work is differentially manifested in various communities. Any theory of occupational development will suffer from what Pipher (1996) calls a **zone of applicability,** limited by the "time, place, occupation, gender and income" (p. 29) of any given practitioner. We see a need for practitioners with varying experiences to update and focus their concerns about work-related issues in clinical practice.

MULTICULTURALISM AND DIVERSITY
The Multicultural Perspective

Throughout this text we emphasize considering **multiculturalism** and diversity in work-related issues in clinical practice. Multiculturalism is defined in two ways. Pedersen (1990) believes a **multicultural perspective** in clinical practice includes the following variables: demography (age, gender, place of residence) ethnography (ethnicity, nationality, religion, language usage), status (social, economic, educational factors), and affiliations (formal memberships, informal networks). Admittedly, a clear distinction between culture and ethnicity is lacking in Pedersen's definition. Sexual orientation and members of disabled communities also are not among the variables in his definition. Others have raised concerns that multiculturalism confounds race with culture (Helms & T. Q. Richardson, 1997). Nevertheless, when differences exist between a practitioner and a client among these recognized variables, the clinical encounter becomes a multicultural interaction. A client and a practitioner are unlikely to match up exactly along the above parameters.

Pedersen (1990) pointedly differentiates between **multicultural counseling** and the multicultural perspective. The latter term is relatively recent (Baruth & Manning, 1991). Multicultural counseling refers to a specialized aspect or subfield, while the multicultural perspective expands beyond all previously used terms (e.g., minority group counseling, pluralistic counseling, cross-cultural counseling) and is *a philosophical orientation* that encompasses the entire field of clinical practice.

The second definition of multicultural clinical practice is drawn from the **Multicultural Counseling and Therapy (MCT)** of Sue, Ivey, and Pedersen (1996). MCT contains six basic propositions. (1) MCT is a **metatheory,** or "theory of theories" (Sue et al., 1996, p. 12) that forms a means of understanding the numerous helping approaches developed by humankind. Both theories of counseling and therapy developed in the Western world and those helping models of non-Western cultures are judged neither right nor wrong, good or bad. Instead, each theory represents a different worldview. (2) The totality and interrelationships of experiences (individual, group, universal) and contexts (individual, family, cultural milieu) must be the focus of treatment. (3) Development of a cultural identity is a major determinant of clinician and client attitudes toward (a) self, (b) others of the same group, (c) others of a different group, and (d) the dominant group. **Dynamics of dominant-subordinate relationships** among culturally different groups also influence clinician-client attitudes. (4) MCT is most effective when the clinician uses modalities and defines goals consistent with the life experiences and cultural values of the client. (5) MCT theory emphasizes **multiple helping roles**—the one-to-one encounter aimed at remediation in the individual, larger social units, systems intervention, and prevention—developed by many culturally different groups and societies. (6) MCT theory emphasizes the importance of expanding personal, family group, and organizational consciousness into **self-in-relation, family-in-relation,** and **organization-in-relation;** the resulting clinical work is ultimately contextual in orientation, and allows for the use of traditional methods of healing from many cultures.

As a metatheory, one challenge facing MCT is pragmatic clinical relevance. "Metatheory is far removed from the realities of work with clients" (Berg & De Jong, 1996, p. 388). A second challenge is that MCT is only beginning to be multidisciplinary, and has barely incorporated the domains of vocational psychology, marriage and family therapy, group therapy—among other disciplines—into its approach.

With respect to diversity, "for helping activities to be effective with persons from diverse populations, those activities must also be unique. Therefore, to speak of the basic facets, or commonalities, in the professional preparation of persons intending to work with special groups is to raise an inherent contradiction" (Loesch, 1995, p. 340). No unique training methods are needed in working with diverse populations, but rather the unique applications of existing training methods. These unique applications can be developed by a substantial redefinition and innovation of existing training methods; that is, combining old and new helping activities that can be useful for diverse populations in specific contexts (González, 1997, 1998; Hollinger, 1994; Rosenau, 1992). More than ever before, practitioners are being confronted with the necessity of altering clinical approaches to respect a clients' culturally influenced family relationships (Schwartzbeck, 1997). Our concern is how such relationships impact the role of work in people's lives.

Multicultural clinical practice tolerates a diverse and complex perspective. Behavior is viewed as meaningful when it is linked to **culturally learned expectations and values.** Furthermore, **within-group differences** are significant for any particular ethnic or nationality group (Pedersen, 1990). Sue (1992) provides further elaboration. The methods, strategies, and goal definitions devised are consistent with life experiences and cultural values of the client. More than one solution to a problem and more than one way to arrive at a solution is acceptable. No one style of counseling, theory, or school is appropriate for all populations and situations. **Between-group differences** are also honored. The multicultural perspective provides the opportunity for two persons from different cultural perspectives to disagree without one being right and the other wrong (Pedersen, 1990; Sue, 1992).

In the United States the social environmental factors of racism and **prejudice,** economic disadvantage, and **acculturation** (Koss-Chioino & Vargas, 1992) cannot be removed from a clinical practice that addresses work-related concerns. Axelson notes that "prejudice is the emotional aspect of racism" (1993, p. 168). We define acculturation two ways: (1) as the process of accepting both one's original group values and the values of *at least one* other group (Olmedo, 1979), and (2) as the accumulation and incorporation of the beliefs and customs of at least one alternative culture (Mendoza & Martínez, 1981). What we call **"multi-culturation,"** with the acceptance of both one's own group and the elements of several other groups, is now more common than previous conceptualizations of two-way acculturation. A related construct is **ethnic identity development,** "one's sense of belonging to an ethnic group and the part of one's thinking, perceptions, feelings, and behavior that is due to ethnic group membership" (Rotheram & Phinney, 1987, p. 13). Ethnic identity development can be strongly related to how one perceives and effectively responds to racism, prejudice, and so-called acculturative stress in the workplace. These issues are discussed throughout our text and particularly in Chapter 14.

Sometimes social class differences may be more pronounced than cultural differences (Baruth & Manning, 1991). The topic of diversity is becoming increasingly divisive, and the debate over **affirmative action** has heated up. A recent *Wall Street Journal*/NBC News survey found that 2 out of 3 Americans oppose affirmative action (Roberts, Thornton, Gest, Cooper, Bennefield, Hetter, Seter, Minerbrook, & Tharp, 1995). The assault on affirmative action is gathering strength from a slow-growth economy, stagnant middle-class incomes, and corporate downsizing, all of which make the question of who gets hired or fired more volatile.

Similar to the assertions of Sue and Sue (1990) about counseling and psychotherapy, we contend that occupational development does not take place in a vacuum isolated from the larger sociopolitical influences of our society. Axelson (1993) writes, "Career development in today's society is more appropriately seen as a complex personal process in interaction with cultural, political, and economic forces over a lifetime of experiences" (p. 225). **Historical context** can play a key role in the development of work-related behaviors and trends. We attend to the interaction of all these forces as they pertain to an applied vocational psychology.

Diversity of the U.S. Population The United States of America is a nation of immigrants, although at times it is politically expedient to ignore this historical reality. An example of its increasing diversity is revealed in the population figures for the 1990 U.S. Census presented in Table 1.1.

Increases in numbers of **Asian American/Pacific Islander** and **Hispanic** population have been the most dramatic. Between 1980 and 1990, the Asian

TABLE 1.1 1990 U.S. Census

	1990	% OF 1990 POPULATION
Total population	248,709,873	100.0 %
White	177,332,011	71.3 %
African Americans	29,986,060	12.1 %
Hispanics	22,354,059	9.0 %
Asian American/ Pacific Islander	7,273,662	2.9 %
American Indian/ Eskimo/Aleut	1,959,234	0.8 %
Other Race	9,804,847	3.9 %

SOURCE: U.S. Bureau of the Census (1992, November)

American/Pacific Islander population grew by 107 percent ("Asian population doubles," 1991). Since 1990, the Asian American/Pacific Islander population has grown about 4.5 percent every year (Bennett & Martin, 1995). Much of this growth (about 86 percent) is accounted for by immigration. By the year 2000, this population is projected to reach 12.1 million people, or about 4 percent of the total U.S. population. As a whole, Asian Americans/Pacific Islanders have high **educational attainment.** In 1994 nearly 9 out of 10 males and 8 out of 10 females age twenty-five and over had at least a high school diploma. But among Asian American/Pacific Islander ethnic groups, high school graduation rates vary widely. Data from 1990 shows a graduation rate of 31 percent for **Hmongs,** 88 percent for Japanese. The Hmongs are among the most recent group of Asian American immigrants (Tapp, 1993), while most Japanese have been in this country for several generations. The 1993 **median income** of Asian American/Pacific Islander families ($44,460) resembled that of White families ($41,110).

Despite high educational attainment and similar median family incomes, the 1993 **poverty rate** for Asian American/Pacific Islander families, at 14 percent, was higher than the 8 percent for White families (Bennett & Martin, 1995). Furthermore, Leong and Gim-Chung (1995) note that while education is highly valued in Asian and Asian American cultures, it is not universal, stating that "Access to education is mediated by immigrant status and class background. Even though education may be valued, some families and individuals may not be able to invest in education nor afford to wait for delayed income. Awareness of these divergent levels of educational attainment within the Asian American/ Pacific Islander population smashes the **'Model Minority'** stereotype" (Suzuki, 1989, p. 209).

Practical Applications

The population growth of Asian Americans/Pacific Islanders and Hispanics has practical applications for workplace diversity. M. Ray Perryman, business economist-in-residence at the Edwin L. Cox School of Business at Southern Methodist University, reports that the labor force is expected to increase 12 percent by the year 2005, and many males entering the labor market in 2005 will be minorities (Perryman, 1996). He cites U.S. Department of Labor statistics that project nearly one-third of such males will be non-White, largely from foreign-born Hispanic and Asian populations. By 2005, considering both males and females, the growth of labor is expected to increase from Asian Americans/Pacific Islanders by 39 percent, from Hispanic populations by 36 percent (due partly to high birth rates and few retirees), and from **African Americans** by 15 percent. Because

of the current education levels of many minority workers, the jobs available to them are liable to be low-wage positions unless vocational training, academic planning, and corporate support of training programs step in to make a difference.

Although Asian Americans/Pacific Islanders are the fastest-growing minority group in the United States, little research has been conducted regarding occupational development in this population (Leong & Serafica, 1995). Available information on Asian American/Pacific Islanders is sparse and fragmented, lacks a critical mass of studies on a particular topic, and is devoid of any history of theoretically based, programmatic research. Likewise, Hispanic occupational development has received little attention in the theoretical and empirical literature (Arbona, 1995).

Equal access to occupational opportunities for racial and ethnic

The Hispanic population increased 50 percent between 1980 and 1990 ("Asian population doubles," 1991). Since 1990, the Hispanic population has increased to 29.7 million people ("Hispanic population nears 30 million," August 7, 1998). The Hispanic population is "younger" than the White population: the **median age** of Hispanics in 1993 was 26.7 years, approximately 9 years less than that of the White population (35.5 years) (del Pinal, 1995). Despite significant progress, the educational attainment of Hispanics remains

minorities will become a greater issue in the twenty-first century. Tuition at public universities is increasing, financial aid decreasing. A college education is moving further beyond the reach of lower-income students (Associated Press, 1996e; New York Times News Service, 1997). More than 80 percent of all college students in the U.S. attend public universities. Research conducted by the Education Trust, a nonprofit research organization, found the gap in educational opportunities that narrowed from 1970 to 1990 between White students and racial/ethnic minority students is widening again (New York Times News Service, 1996). This trend does not bode well for the long-term occupational development of racial and ethnic minorities.

To help reverse this course, brochures using **racial and ethnic role models** that contain culturally relevant occupational information for minorities are effective (Rodriguez, 1994). Based on the National Career Development Association's *Guidelines for the Prepa-ration and Evaluation of Career and Occupational Information Literature* (1991), Rodriguez clearly and concisely presents the creation process of occupational information brochures. She emphasizes the need to establish a partnership between counseling professionals and sponsors, since minority members of a sponsor group can bring vital first-hand information and experience to the brochure content. Several basic elements are evaluated for inclusion in the brochures: an introductory series of interest-sparking questions to motivate minorities to continue reading the brochure; a question-and-answer format to facilitate reading and defining points for future review; and content written in non-technical, standard English at the eighth- to tenth-grade reading level. Rodriguez states that role-model life stories provide influential motivational information crucial for career decision-making. Few materials currently exist which help racial and ethnic minorities to expand their awareness and knowledge of career options.

well below that of the rest of the population. In 1993 the proportion of Hispanics with low educational attainment—less than a fifth-grade education—at 11.8 percent, was 14 times greater than that of Whites (0.8 percent). Moreover, in 1993 the proportion of Hispanics twenty-five years and older with a high school education, at 53.1 percent, was also less than Whites (84.1 percent). Data from 1992 indicate that about 39.9 percent of Hispanic children under eighteen were living in poverty, compared with 13.2 percent of White children (del Pinal, 1995).

RELATIONSHIP OF WORK
TO THE GLOBAL ECONOMY

Global Competition

Corporate mergers and acquisitions reached a record high in the United States during 1995: more than 8,700 of them, valued at more than $460 billion (Associated Press, 1996d). Corporate executives predict more buyouts in the U.S. and abroad. A survey of 150 senior executives of Fortune 1,000 companies conducted during January/February 1996 revealed that two-thirds of the respondents expected to buy other U.S. businesses in the next twelve months and 39 percent said they expect overseas acquisitions. Among the survey respondents, 36 percent plan to buy companies in Western Europe, 28 percent plan to buy in South America, and 26 percent plan to buy in Asia. Respondents indicated that **global competition** is the single most important issue facing corporate America. More than half of the executives said cultural differences remain the strongest challenge for companies that acquired foreign businesses.

Chinese leader Deng Xiaoping's death (February 19, 1997) provided concrete meaning of the **global economy** for many in the U.S. Deng's most important legacy was to enable tens of millions of his compatriots to raise themselves from poverty by removing the stigma that Mao Tse-tung (1893–1976) had placed on personal gain (Associated Press, 1997b). In Chairman Mao's time there was no trade with the U.S. China's economic transformation under Deng made the U.S. its biggest foreign market. Sixty percent of all the shoes sold in the U.S. are made in China (Associated Press, 1997a). Seventy-five percent of all toys in the U.S. are made in foreign countries, and 60 percent of those toys are made in China (Associated Press, 1996b). Other major goods imported into the U.S. from China include clothing, telephones and other telecommunications equipment, household appliances and television sets, and computers, computer chips, and other office equipment (Associated Press, 1996a). China is poised to displace Japan as the country giving the U.S. its largest trade deficit. Meanwhile, the Chinese are playing hardball when it comes to granting American companies access to its huge market of 1.2 billion people. The U.S. is being pressured to move jobs onto Chinese soil in return for access to the latter's marketplace (Sanger & Lohr, 1996). In the immediate years ahead, this could create layoffs in the U.S.

Globalization happens slowly, but the consequences for workers are very real. Naturally companies want to manufacture near their buyers while taking advantage of low wage rates in so many countries. Cheap labor forms one of the few "comparative advantages" that countries like China offer in the race toward global competitiveness. In the aerospace factories,

Practical Applications

A person's success in the emerging global economy will depend on many factors, flexibility being most important. According to Herr and Cramer (1996), the elements of personal flexibility are **basic academic skills** (e.g., the ability to read, follow directions, and use mathematics and computers) and **adaptive skills** (e.g., problem recognition and definition, handling evidence, human relations, and the ability to learn, analyze, and implement). A recent report (Prospect Centre, 1991) funded by the Department of Employment describes the attributes needed by innovative and flexible workers: creative and forward planning (Murray, 1993); as the number of people who are self-employed or operate a small business is increasing, entrepreneurial and creative thinking are required.

> Entrepreneurial behavior, which consists of acquiring understanding of systems, risks, and change, will be an important ingredient in the future in many aspects of the global economy, as well as in government, in service industries, in manufacturing, . . . in education . . . [and] will be critical to many nations in both domestic and international economic development (Herr & Cramer, 1996, p. 134).

Organizations that downsize will find those workers who think like entrepreneurs more valuable, while the world of work will be looking for people who can deal with change and find new solutions to problems.

An estimated 84 percent of world trade wealth flows to the richest fifth of the world's population while less than 1 percent goes to the poorest fifth ("Matters of Scale," *World Watch,* 1994, cited in Michelozzi, 1996). Even though being able to make money is essential to survival, more people are searching for occupations in business or industry that not only provide an adequate income, but also are committed to the betterment of the local community.

Michelozzi (1996) observes that "in our rush to the future, we have disrupted communities; depleted centuries-old resources; polluted once-pristine air, water, and earth; and littered the world with our castoffs" (p. 120). There are many things that money cannot buy, but having enough money is essential. More and more people are using their time, energy, and talents to find careers in business or industry that promote a vital local community as well as provide an adequate income. Others (e.g., Brown, Flavin, & Postel, 1992) express concern that we are destroying our very life support systems. Choices regarding work which contribute positively to the world as we leave it for the next generation are critical now more than ever before.

workers make the equivalent of $50 a month or 35 cents an hour; they live in barracks in secure military facilities. . . . [A]s a country bursting with potential buyers, China offers foreign firms an enormous market; in fact, beating their international competitors is the real reason that many American companies are ready to give away their technology and sacrifice their workers. (Tolchin, 1996, p. 64)

INTERDEPENDENCE OF THE SOCIAL, ECONOMIC, AND EDUCATION SYSTEMS

Vocational practitioners are confronted with assisting clients to make occupational decisions and face the job market at a most uncertain time in history. Each practitioner must be aware of interdependent social, economic, and education systems—as well as the role politics plays throughout. Employment in today's workplace will require specific updated skills, and millions of unemployed workers with obsolete skills may create a national crisis (Krannich, 1989). Individuals must become self-reliant and effective in dealing with the job market because they may not be able to turn to the government or corporations for help. Morrison (1990) suggests two major changes that play key roles in forming the future job market: the "maturing" of America and the restructuring of the workforce as more women/mothers become fully employed.

A 1990 United Way Strategic Institute article forecasted nine forces that would drastically affect the future job market: (1) *The maturing of America* phase begins with the aging of the "babyboom" generation. (2) *The mosaic society* will move away from the "mass society" of today—increased levels of education, diverse ethnic groups, more elderly persons, increased number of single-person households, and legal and illegal immigrants are segmenting America. The labor force is multicultural and multilingual. (3) *A redefinition of societal and individual roles*, because over half of all U.S. companies will offer remedial education for employees by the year 2000, and individuals will take more responsibility for their own futures. An emphasis on wellness will see individuals take more responsibility for their own health, instead of relying only on medical technology. (4) *The information-based economy* will rely heavily on technological advances in communication. Information overload and decreasing quality of information will affect everyone. (5) *Globalization* will increase foreign ownership of U.S. industries and the presence of U.S. firms in other countries. (6) *Quality of life issues* (e.g., individual health and well-being, energy conservation, ozone depletion, the link between personal behavior and disease risk) will become a major concern. (7) *Mass economic restructuring* will occur as American producers and consumers become more global. (8) *Roles of family and home will be redefined* (e.g., home shopping, work-at-home employees). (9) *Social activism will experience a rebirth.* "After a decade of concentration on business and economic growth, the public agenda pendulum is swinging decisively in the direction of social concerns" (p. 16). It is interesting to observe at the end of the 90s how accurate the United Way Strategic Institute was in identifying the forces shaping our society as we enter the twenty-first century.

Social Systems

The "Babybuster" Generation People currently in their twenties are making an impact on the world of work. This group is known as **"babybusters"** and is so diverse and so different from other generations that it is interesting to study their lifestyles, work attitudes, and life philosophies. Gross and Scott (1990) estimate that 40 percent of people in their twenties were children of divorce. Even more were latchkey kids—the first to experience the downside of the two-income family. This may also explain why the only solid commitment they seem willing to make is to their own children. The biggest sense of resentment and anger in the babybusters is that they had little time with their parents, who spent so much time with the job.

This younger generation has grown up in a vastly different environment than children have before and has yet to find a niche (Deutschman, 1990). They live in the shadow of the babyboomers and reject the many extra hours of work that generation puts in. While babybusters understand the value of a college education, they appear to be choosing jobs more for their own satisfaction rather than for prestige. Companies are discovering that this generation desires more flexibility, access to decision-making, and time to enjoy their weekends. Because of the differences in work values, older managers have difficulty appreciating these younger workers' assertiveness about their choices. When workers in their forties and fifties retire, there will be a strong demand for anyone with skills to replace them; babybusters are confident their skills and educational level will meet the demands of the workplace. "This 'knowledge is power' mentality makes them feel unbound, free to pursue unpredictable paths" (Deutschman, 1990, p. 47).

The Science/Technology Connection The science/technology connection is a critical challenge for nearly everyone faced with making a living (Michelozzi, 1996). Who will benefit from the dramatic science/technology explosion? African Americans, Hispanics, and low-income persons may be more spectators than true participants in America's technological renaissance (Hernandez, 1998; Young, 1989). When it comes to computer literacy education in the schools, there may also be a difference between the "haves" and the "have nots" (Poole, 1996), which limits opportunities for children in poorer school districts to learn the necessary skills.

Societal Forces Drummond and Ryan (1995) identify societal forces that influence perceptions of what is acceptable in an occupation. (a) *Family socialization* influences work preferences and values of children, as well as educational attainment and occupational achievement. (b) *Socioeconomic level* is also a factor. Higher-income families prepare their children for entering a profession, not unskilled or less prestigious occupations. Such preparation is unavailable for children from low-income families. (c) *Employers* are also influential. They define acceptable work roles for their workers. (d) *Governmental bodies* make laws and regulations that affect individuals (e.g., safety standards and minimum wage).

Economic Systems

Inequity and Inequality Two major concerns for most people are making enough money to live on and having a job they can live with (Michelozzi, 1996). But **inequity** and **inequality** continue to be realities. Women need 66 weeks to earn the same amount as men earn in 52 weeks, according to the National Organization of Business and Professional Women (Armendariz, 1997). The U.S. Census Bureau reports that, for every dollar earned by a man, a woman earns 71 cents—a wage gap of $8,999 annually, amounting to $250,000 over an entire career. O'Toole (1993) writes that, "In 1991, when median full-time pay was $30,000 for White men and $21,000 for White women; it was $19,000 for African American women and $16,000 for Hispanic women. At those levels, the daily mission is survival. Options are few" (p. 96). A 1992 MS. Foundation/Center For Policy Alternatives survey (cited in O'Toole, 1993) intentionally polled more **Women of Color** than Whites, and noted that low pay and discriminatory hiring practices were deep concerns. This caused incredible financial strain and was a source of their fear of unemployment and not being able to meet financial obligations.

In the U.S. the rise in income inequality remains clear (Boroughs, Guttman, Mallory, McMurray, & Fischer, 1996). Demographics have played a big role in the growth of poor families, particularly in the rise in single-parent families. The proportion of children living in mother-only families has grown from 8 percent in 1960 to 22 percent in 1995, and single parents account for half of all families earning less than $10,000 a year. Among more prosperous U.S. workers, of all the income gains made from 1977 to 1990, 79 percent fell into the pockets of the top 1 percent of families, a group that is expected to earn an average of $438,000 in 1996. Within that top 1 percent, inequality is also growing because the top tenth of 1 percent appears to be getting the lion's share of the economic rewards.

The "widening disparity in the fortunes of American workers is becoming an entrenched fixture of the economy" (Holmes, 1996, p. A18). Census Bureau figures show that the income disparity between the richest and poorest is at its widest gap since World War II. Average income for the top 20 percent of households went from $73,754 in 1968 to $105,945 in 1994, an increase of 44 percent when adjusted for inflation. Average income of the bottom 20 percent of households went from $7,202 in 1968 to $7,762 in 1994, an increase of 7 percent when adjusted for inflation. Contributors to this income disparity appear to be fourfold: (1) the economy's shift away from relatively low-skilled manufacturing jobs that paid high wages, (2) the decline in the number of unionized workers, (3) an increased reliance by business and industry on computers and computer-assisted technology which requires higher skills and education, and (4) the increased use of part-time workers.

Wage Stagnation Wage stagnation is another factor that has impacted our current economic basis (Roberts, Friedman, Sieder, Schwartz, & Sapers, 1996). Median household income has been flat for 20 years, and workers' real weekly wages have dropped $23 or almost 5 percent. The combination of high profits and low wages is feeding the perception that working hard and going nowhere threatens the American Dream.

Educational Systems

The indisputable gender inequality in the U.S. workplace is evident from kindergarten through twelfth grade (Gaskell & Willinsky, 1995; Gilligan & Noel, 1995; Orenstein, 1994; Pipher, 1994; Sadker & Sadker, 1994; Taylor, Gilligan, & Sullivan, 1995). Girls and boys, adolescent women and men, are differentially reinforced in many school systems. This differential treatment has grave implications for the career development of women in particular. The soundness of the future workforce in general, resulting from inequities in school district funding, is laid bare by Jonathan Kozol in his powerful book, *Savage Inequalities: Children in America's Schools* (1991). Federal policies continue both to reinforce and increase the existing gulf between rich and poor school districts. This means that differences in the availability of educational supplies and resources, in teacher salaries and school morale, and in the expectations conveyed to children about what society believes they can achieve, have an incalculable and often tragic impact on the occupational development of children in poorer districts. We discuss gender and social class factors throughout this text.

From an international perspective, Blossfeld and Shavit (1993) summarize and synthesize results from a study of change in educational opportunities for cohorts who attended school before and after major educational reforms in thirteen industrialized countries. Research participants were from Western capitalist countries (the United States, the former West Germany, the Netherlands, Sweden, Great Britain, Italy, and Switzerland), Western formerly socialist countries

(Poland, Hungary, and the former Czechoslovakia), non-Western capitalist countries (Taiwan and Japan), and Israeli Arabs. In most of these countries, unequal access to educational opportunities has remained stable, despite educational reform and educational expansion. Educational expansion is defined as "an increase in the proportions of successive cohorts who [achieved a given level of schooling]" (p. 14).

Educational reform efforts have had a negligible impact on changes in educational attainment. In all the countries Blossfeld and Shavit (1993) studied, the average level of education has risen across cohorts at the primary level and at the lower secondary level. In some countries the transition from primary to secondary education is a major branching point between continuing and discontinuing in school. In the former West Germany, Switzerland, Sweden, and Poland, vocational education serves as an alternative to continuing in secondary and tertiary (i.e., higher) education. Vocational education attracts students from lower socioeconomic classes because it provides rapid access to a skill, and allows for the absorption of disadvantaged groups at the secondary level without disturbing the interests of advantaged groups at higher levels. But vocational education ultimately can lead to dead-end jobs where a lack of opportunity or challenge can become a significant contributor to psychological distress (Barnett & Rivers, 1996), and often continues the cycle of low-income/poverty mentality.

TAKEOVERS, MERGERS, AND CORPORATE CLIMATE

Many middle-class families experience an "end of optimism" when they are "forced to work two to three jobs to pay the bills" (Tolchin, 1996, p. 51). Seventy-five percent of those polled agree with the statement that "middle class families can't make ends meet," and 57 percent regard the economy as "stagnating."

> Two-thirds of those surveyed worried that their children wouldn't live as well as they did, and a majority believed that the American dream was now out of reach for most families. Most respondents did not see the vaunted economic recovery showing up in their household budgets, and by 1995 signs were beginning to appear that indicated people were beginning to accept the economic ceiling as a condition unlikely to change. (p. 51)

By most indications, the rich are getting richer, the poor are getting poorer, and the middle class seems to be losing ground economically. Even though the middle class has worked hard, studied hard, and tried to do all the right things to climb the traditional career ladder, they are experiencing job loss, falling or stagnating wages, insecure pensions, and reduced home ownerships. The middle class realizes they may not be keeping pace financially, and their children will most likely fall even farther behind (Tolchin, 1996).

"[R]ecent polls and studies show that . . . a growing number of Americans are beginning to shift the anger and frustration they once directed at the government to corporate America. This shift is occurring despite . . . the wave of mergers [that are making] big [corporations] get bigger. Profits are up and unemployment is down" (Yates, 1995, p. 6J). Frank and Cook (1995) draw attention to an increasing resentment on the part of the average worker toward executives with huge salaries. Feller (1996) writes that "the pay ratio of chief executives to average workers in big corporations has gone from 41:1 in the mid-1970s to 187:1 in 1995" (p. 145). More recent reports calculate these pay ratios at even higher proportions (Kadlec & Baumohl, 1997; Reingold, 1997). Other industrialized societies such as Japan and the reunited Germany do not tolerate these exorbitant pay ratios (Sanger & Lohr, 1996), while the French have long used "savage capitalism" to describe American economics (Bellah, Madsen, Sullivan, Swidler, & Tipton, 1992, p. 91).

Another kind of anger and frustration results from uncertainty about how a merger or takeover will affect an individual. When workers hear of massive layoffs caused by these changes they become concerned with their own security. Many of the mergers are promoted in positive terms, but often workers find out later that they may be laid off or forced to retire with the concomitant loss of benefits and health insurance and little prior notice. On a more positive note, Greenwald (1997) reports that despite frequent downsizing, more than 11 million new jobs have been created since 1991, reflecting a fundamental shift from manufacturing to services and technology. Fifteen of the hottest fields are presented in Table 1.2.

In Table 1.2, three of the top six fields—teacher, nurse, and social worker—are traditionally female-dominated professions. In the United States, public and private elementary and secondary school enrollment is expected to climb to 55.9 million by the year 2005, surpassing the 51.3 million "babyboomers" in class in 1971 (Associated Press, 1996c). The public school teaching force will grow from 2.8 million in 1991 to a projected 3.3 million by the year 2002, with *half the teachers in the year 2005 being hired in the next ten years.* Not revealed in Table 1.2 is that the need for some workers—especially lawyers, physicians, and paralegals—is likely to be stronger in smaller towns and rural areas than in larger cities already having an excess of such workers.

Over the past thirty years, the accelerating pace of technological change has created new boomtowns and job opportunities for so-called "gold-collar"

TABLE 1.2 Fifteen of the Hottest Fields

FIELD	PROJECTED GROWTH IN NUMBER OF JOBS, 1994–2005	ANNUAL SALARY (1994 MEDIAN)
Teacher	606,000	$34,000
Nurse	473,000	$35,600
Executive	466,000	$40,000
Systems analyst	445,000	$44,000
Truck driver	271,000	$24,300
Social worker	187,000	$26,500
Lawyer	183,000	$58,000
Financial manager	182,000	$37,000
Computer engineer	177,000	$44,000
Accountant	120,000	$32,000
Physician	120,000	$54,000
Marketing manager	114,000	$43,800
Physical therapist	81,000	$33,300
Product designer	76,000	$30,700
Paralegal	64,000	$25,800

SOURCE: U.S. Bureau of Labor Statistics, cited in Greenwald (1997)

workers whose vocational training is grounded in math and science, computer literacy, and basic writing and speaking skills (Greenwald, 1997). Fifteen of the hottest places to find employment are presented in Table 1.3.

Interestingly, none of these fifteen locations are in the Midwest or the Northeast, but instead are largely in the West, Southwest, Northwest, and South.

Continued learning will be vital for survival in the future world of work. Greenwald (1997) warns that many individuals who live in inner cities and who lack basic education already do not have the skills or credentials to land a good job initially. A *Time*/CNN telephone poll of 657 currently employed adult U.S. citizens revealed that 37 percent of respondents would like to change jobs if they could, 41 percent prefer to stay employed where they are now if they could, and 22 percent were unsure if they would like to change jobs or stay employed where they are now. In addition, when asked about the likelihood that they would change jobs within the next five years, 45 percent of respondents believe their own job change was likely, 51 percent believe it was unlikely, and 3 percent were unsure. Nowadays, a basic educational foundation is vital for individuals, coupled with a flexible ability to add new work skills to one's repertoire and to adjust to the demands of a constantly permutating work environment.

Most workers whose wages have stagnated have had little opportunity to upgrade their skills, either on the job or on their own (Kramer, 1997). Improv-

TABLE 1.3 Fifteen of the Hottest Places

CITY	JOB GROWTH, 1994–1996 (PERCENTAGE)	KEY AREAS
Las Vegas, NV	8.0%	Casinos
Phoenix, AZ	5.8%	High-tech, small manufacturing
Austin, TX	5.6%	High-tech, manufacturing
Salt Lake City, UT	5.5%	Bio-tech, construction
Boise, ID	5.0%	High-tech, retail
Atlanta, GA	4.8%	Business services, retail
Portland, OR	4.5%	Semiconductors
Albuquerque, NM	4.4%	High-tech, services
San Jose, CA	4.1%	High-tech
Dallas, TX	4.0%	Financial services, communications
Fort Lauderdale, FL	3.7%	Data processing
Mobile, AL	3.7%	Telemarketing, financial services
Orlando, FL	3.4%	Software design, entertainment
Seattle, WA	2.8%	Aviation, high-tech
Raleigh, NC	2.8%	Pharmaceuticals, high-tech

SOURCE: DRI/McGraw-Hill, local chambers of commerce, cited in Greenwald (1997)

ing one's job prospects is contingent upon additional job training. The majority of businesses do not invest in upgrading their workers' job skills because then workers are free to take their improved marketability to other employers. At best, upgrading is provided for those workers at the top, with the assumption that the workers they supervise will produce higher returns as a result. Few workers in the lower echelons receive any enhanced training. Two solutions have been proposed that give businesses economic incentives to invest in upgrading their workers' skills: (1), a tax-free compensation program for companies to train all employees or the company loses tax advantages for training only some employees, and (2), contracts for employees receiving training that insure they remain a specified time so that companies could reap the benefit of their investment. These proposals would be in the economic self-interest of the U.S. government and businesses alike.

Downsizing in the United States

When a large American steel company began closing plants in the early 1980s it offered to train the displaced steel workers for new jobs. But the training never "took"; the workers drifted into unemployment and odd jobs instead. Psychologists came in to find out why and found the steelworkers suffering from acute identity crises. "How could I do anything else?" asked one of the workers. "I *am* a lathe operator." (Peter Senge, *The fifth discipline,* cited in Bridges, 1994, p. 76)

An analysis by *The New York Times* of U.S. Department of Labor numbers showed more than 43 million jobs have been eliminated in the U.S. since 1979, yet there has been a net increase of 27 million jobs in the U.S. over that period, enough to absorb easily all the laid-off workers plus the new people starting off in the world of work (Uchitelle & Kleinfield, 1996). Many of the job losses came from stores failing and factories moving; increasingly, the disappearing jobs are those of higher-paid, white-collar workers, many at larger corporations, women as well as men, many at the peak of their careers. Only about 35 percent of laid-off, full-time workers end up in jobs that pay the same or better. Reductions in the armed forces and in civilian Defense Department employees have been proportionally higher than even in the public sector (Bradford, 1996). In Western Europe, which like the United States has had an ingrained cultural expectation of lifelong employment (Sanger & Lohr, 1996), shareholder pressures to downsize are complicated by an already existing 11 percent unemployment rate, which is double that of the U.S. (Tagliabue, 1996).

Tolchin writes:

> The unemployment rate may be the lowest that it has been in years, but tens of thousands of middle-aged Americans have been thrown out of work thanks to downsizing, outsourcing, exporting jobs abroad, and other recent phenomena loosely attributed to the post industrial world. Many have supplanted their lost jobs with new jobs—another reason the unemployment rate looks so bright—but the problem is that most of the new jobs pay lower wages and offer far fewer benefits. (1996, p. 50)

A recent poll by *The New York Times* (Uchitelle & Kleinfield, 1996) reveals that nearly 75 percent of all U.S. households have had an encounter with layoffs since 1980. In 33 percent of all households, a family member has lost a job. Another 40 percent more know a relative, friend, or neighbor who was laid off. Permanent layoffs are occurring in large numbers even during an economic recovery that has lasted five years and even at companies that are doing well. One in ten adults—approximately 19 million people, a number matching the adult population of New York and New Jersey combined—stated that a lost job in their household had launched a major crisis in their lives. Workers with at least some college education make up the majority of people laid off, outnumbering those with no more than a high school education, a reversal from the 1980s. Better-paid workers—those earning at least $50,000—account for twice the number of lost jobs than in the 1980s. While 2 million people are affected by violent crime each year, nearly 50 percent more people, about 3 million, are affected by layoffs each year.

During these upheavals some dispossessed employees experience a diluted sense of self-worth and shattered confidence (Uchitelle & Kleinfield, 1996) through painful and demeaning job changes. Assurances from employers that a pink slip is "nothing personal" may be pointless for the worker whose identity has been based largely on one's work life (Bragg, 1996b). But for many it is personal. One worker states, "It's like the company telling you that you're no damn good" (Bragg, 1996a, p. A17).

Families of downsized workers also can experience emotional strain. Deprivations and disappointments can predominate in the home (Bragg, 1996a). The divorce rate is as much as 50 percent higher than the national average in families where one earner, usually the father, has lost a job and cannot quickly find an equivalent one (Uchitelle & Kleinfield, 1996). Some parents angrily regret the late evenings and weekends they gave to their jobs when they realize that "company loyalty" was all one-sided (Bragg, 1996b). After downsizing has occurred the workplace becomes altered, amid "ghost town" environments, motivation and risk-taking decreases (Kleinfield, 1996). Community and civic life often become fragmented, too. Churches and service organizations lose members (Rimer, 1996; Uchitelle & Kleinfield, 1996). In their civic and work lives, people may seem unwilling to give as much of themselves as they did before. Employees show less desire to be absorbed into their workplace culture, and workers do not give 100 percent anymore (Kleinfield, 1996). One solution is to draw a line beyond which the incursions and compromises of business become too much, and be ready to walk away (Johnson, 1996).

Corporate downsizing replaces team spirit and camaraderie with internal competition. Employees compete for their positions with their own coworkers and with younger prospects. Information sharing between team players becomes information hoarding in an effort to have an edge. Organizational employees also are competing against themselves. Blinded by the fact that downsizing has often meant adverse working conditions, employees tend to blame themselves when they are unable to meet impossible demands. Thus, they push themselves hard to improve the quantity and quality of the work they produce, leading to longer hours at the workplace. Not surprisingly, employees suffer from tremendous stress and subsequent physical and mental health problems. Bennett (1990) further predicts that the typical employee of the future will have different priorities other than settling into an organization for a career life. These people will seek smaller companies in which to work, choose work that is interesting, and expect the corporate environment to be more flexible to individual needs.

Diversity in the Era of Downsizing

Daniel Yankelovich, president of the polling firm DYG, Inc., asserts that African Americans, immigrants, and women are among the diverse targets of scapegoating as a consequence of job insecurity in the face of downsizing (Uchitelle & Kleinfield, 1996). Other experts say that part of the growth in membership of so-called hate groups can be traceable to disaffected downsized workers. Employer commitment to diversity has eroded in the current environment of uncertainty. Women and minorities express concern that they are more vulnerable. In some instances, women have been eliminated from jobs disproportionately (Kleinfield, 1996). However, minorities appear to have been most adversely affected. U.S. Department of Labor statistics indicate that employment and earnings of African Americans relative to Whites have unquestionably declined since the 1970s (Uchitelle & Kleinfield, 1996). Diversity becomes a delicate issue in the era of downsizing because the Federal Equal Employment Opportunity Commission sees a red flag whenever the make-up of a downsized workplace deviates more than 3 to 4 percent from the original demographics (Kleinfield, 1996).

Ironically, now that the American White middle class is experiencing what African Americans have dealt with all along—job insecurity and unemployment—the word coined is "**downsizing**" (Carter, 1996). The term itself has been called a middle-class concept by Lloyd Lewis, Jr., an Ohio state representative (Rimer, 1996). Lewis, an African American, graduated from the University of Dayton with a business degree in 1948. At that time, National Cash Register offered jobs to all his White classmates, but not to him. He notes that job losses and economic uncertainty have now affected the White middle class, middle management, where no one ever thought it would happen. Lewis also points out that while many African American middle-class workers have also been hurt by downsizing, their sense of betrayal is not as pronounced as that felt by Whites. Social and behavioral scientists can appear élitist by focusing on the effects of downsizing now that it has hit the White middle and upper classes. For years, blue-collar workers have been laid off when business was bad, with less attention paid to their plight at the time. The difference now is that there are fewer and fewer call-backs; millions of blue-collar workers have been laid off forever (Bragg, 1996b). The reality is that when the White middle class starts feeling anxious and aggrieved, responses are needed from the political system ("Downsizing and its discontents," March 10, 1996), from business, and even from social and behavioral scientists.

"JOB SHOCK" AND THE
INFORMATION REVOLUTION

Downsizing, layoffs, and restructuring of corporations have created what Dent (1995) identifies as **"job shock."**

- Job shock creates pain. Layoffs and restructurings hurt people at the basic survival level, . . . [threaten their] . . . ability . . . to provide shelter, food, and comfort for themselves and their families. . . . [T]oday, white-collar jobs as well as blue-collar jobs are being lost.

- Job shock rattles consumer confidence. . . . [P]eople without jobs stop spending except for basic needs. . . . [Those] who have kept their jobs feel insecure enough to curtail spending as they see their neighbors and coworkers being laid off. This dampens the robustness of the economy and retards any movement toward recovery.

- Job shock terrorizes people you know. You do not need a news item or even a futurist to tell you individual horror stories about job shock. You probably know somebody who has been thrown out of a job. You may have a recent college graduate still living at home because it is so tough to break into the job market.

- Job shock points the finger, creating bad guys in the business community. You may even think that all the ills of job shock are merely the results of corporate downsizing and re-engineering, something that big business is doing to the workforce for the sake of making a buck. (p. 6)

Job shock is only the tip of the iceberg for fundamental changes that will continue to occur even as we see sustained economic growth right into the next century. Jobs are going to be redeployed, automated, eliminated, and regenerated in forms we haven't yet imagined. (Dent, 1995, pp. 6–7)★

Organizations are going to continue to experience more radical and rapid changes than most leaders ever imagined. In many cases these changes are not going to be gradual, but rather fast and comprehensive. Talk to anyone who has been through a corporate takeover (merger) and he/she can attest to the overwhelming pace of change within that organization.

Toffler (1970) predicted that we as a society would be affected by the Information Revolution, with the computer providing the technology that would move us in that direction. Nearly thirty years later his prediction has proven true. A natural progression from an agricultural society to a factory/assembly line/manufacturing society, to a streamlined, automated society is taking place

★ © 1995 by Harry Dent from Job Shock. Reprinted by permission of St. Martin's Press.

Practical Applications

Multicultural and diverse clientele who aspire to upward mobility would benefit by understanding that there is something new and disturbing about the current economic woes. The White middle and upper classes—those very groups that have benefited most from the education and training that have for decades provided the main path to upward mobility—are experiencing massive losses of jobs for the first time ("Downsizing and its discontents," March 10, 1996). Practitioners are strongly urged to explore clients' expectations of anticipated economic and material gains to be derived from the world of work. Clients must realize that the old certainties about work no longer apply (Kleinfield, 1996). A common attitude is that no corporate entity owes anybody a career. Clients entering the job market can learn from

more experienced, adaptable workers who are now accepting without sentiment the fact that their company does not owe them as much as people used to expect (Uchitelle & Kleinfield, 1996). These workers figure out the best angles to job security by mastering tasks, developing new skills, and cultivating political ties.

Top performers at jobsites nevertheless have been laid off because they had the weakest political bonds (Uchitelle & Kleinfield, 1996). David H. Ponitz, the President of Sinclair Community College in Dayton, Ohio, has put it quite plainly: "You have to understand what the new reality is. The new reality is that you have to know something that somebody else doesn't know, but that is not enough. You have to keep growing dramatically if you're really going to

before our eyes. Downsizing of the white-collar workforce is a clear indication that the revolution is under way, with the traditionally more secure and best paid jobs in jeopardy. This phenomenon is a first in our society and has garnered much media attention. Yet it happened to blue-collar workers during the 1970s and early 1980s. At that time many towns that relied on steel and iron industries became ghost towns, and few have recovered.

"Work revolutions begin in times of crisis and emerge in the decades following the introduction of new technologies when people finally realize they can no longer resist the inevitable change and must radically re-engineer the workplace," says Dent (1995, p. 22). He further observes that we are reluctant to accept the inevitable and need to see it as an ally, not a threat. Even though the work revolution appears to be producing a stronger economy, higher personal

keep a job" (Rimer, 1996, p. A18). Once employment has been obtained, upwardly mobile multicultural and diverse clients may need to sharpen skills to enhance their careers. Clients who minimize their expectations about guaranteed, long-term security are less likely to become disillusioned by current trends in the mainstream U.S. workforce.

Linguistic minority clients may need reinforcement about what they can gain by being fluent in their non-English language. Fluency here means basic writing, reading, and conversational skills. Fluency levels required for scholarship or business often can only be achieved through formal training and / or immersion in the second language (Vidueira, 1996). The economic importance of languages other than English remains largely unrecognized in the United States. On the West Coast, for example, several Asian languages, in addition to Spanish, are valuable for conducting business. "[The United States] isn't doing enough to prepare our kids for the emerging global economy," says Elena Izquierdo, Ph.D., Assistant Professor of Teacher Education at the University of Texas at El Paso. Regarding the economic value of being bilingual, Dr. Izquierdo explains, "Bilingual students enter the job market with a tremendous advantage" (quoted in Vidueira, 1996, p. 16).

Besides linguistic skills, Dent (1995) suggests other skills will be needed:

> Problem-solving skills [will require that employees] (a) become results-oriented, (b) be proactive, and (c) think creatively. People skills [will challenge workers to] (a) know [themselves], (b) become sensitive to the needs of others, and (c) increase [their] tolerance level. Integrative skills [will emphasize the need for personnel to] (a) expand [their] ability to communicate, (b) sharpen business skills, and (c) get a grasp on information technologies. (pp. 191–92)

standards of living, and more quality and choice for some, what most people are experiencing is the need to work twice as hard just to keep up with the basics.

Concurring with Dent's (1995) assertion and Toffler's (1970) prediction that the workforce will move to outer suburbs and smaller towns, Walberg (1996) reports on the growing interest in home-based businesses, specifically in the face of downsizing, restructuring, or the gentler euphemism, "right-sizing." Because of these changes, loyalty to the employer has been lost and security for the employee is much less certain. If a workplace revolution occurs in this country, it will be because people have the freedom to be creative and resourceful. People with **entrepreneurial skills** are finding that operating a full or part-time business out of the home can be an alternative to the corporate world of insecurity and stress. Estimates for 1996 indicate that a new home-based business is started in the U.S. every 11 seconds, generating $382.5 billion annually in revenues (Walberg, 1996). Home-based businesses now command respect from those in the marketplace, and can be started and operated on a shoestring budget, and have unlimited growth potential. But there is little or no job security with home-based business, and the individual(s) have to pay high dollars for health insurance and retirement benefits.

It is essential that practitioners encourage their clients to develop linguistic skills, problem-solving skills, people skills, and informational retrieval skills. These are indispensible to survival in a global economy. Mastery of such skills can reduce gender inequality in the workplace and enhance equal access to occupational opportunities for historically disenfranchised and marginalized people. A transformed vocational psychology will advocate for skill development as never before. The computer, especially, will dictate how we conduct business in the future. But before leaping into the future, it is beneficial to pay attention to past valuable contributions to the role of work in people's lives. Thus, we examine values, ethics, and meaning in the workplace in Chapter 2.

Values, Ethics, and Meaning
in the Workplace

Work is the way we tend the world, the way people connect. It is the
most vigorous, vivid sign of life—in individuals and civilization.

LANCE MORROW (CITED IN MICHELOZZI, 1996, P. 123)

Work has multiple definitions based on both internal factors (e.g., a person's
culture, psychological make-up) and external factors (e.g., the times in which
the person lives, the economic situations of that era). In the United States work
is central to most people's lives. This chapter is divided into four sections. First,
we discuss values and ethics in general. Second, we explore work values in particular. Third, we consider work ethics from an historical, cultural, and postmodern perspective. Fourth, we examine the concept of meaning in work/job
satisfaction and lesiure/avocational activities.

VALUES AND ETHICS

Definition of Terms

Frequently, **values** and **ethics** are used interchangeably, but they are not identical and have distinctions (Corey, Corey & Callanan, 1993). The word *value* is
derived from the Latin *valere,* meaning "strong, brave, courageous" (Raths,
Harmin & Simon, 1966). As a noun, *value* means (a) "worth" in terms of usefulness, such as a principle, (b) "that which is of importance to the possessor," such

as a standard, and (c) "utility" or "merit," such as a quality. As a verb, *value* means "to regard highly, to esteem, or to prize." Ethics represent an objective inquiry about **behavior.** Behavior refers to overt actions such as driving a car or playing a guitar (Van Hoose & Paradise, 1979). The goodness or badness of a behavior is the provenance of **morality.** Pipher (1996) broadly defines morality as choosing wisely and decently how one will be in the universe. Morality concerns itself with action that is purposeful and for the good of all.

Ethics address behavior, but not all behavior equally. Ethics deal with **conduct,** or when a person voluntarily chooses between alternative courses of action. Whenever a person asks, "What ought I to do?" or "Is it wrong for me to do this?" that person is dealing with matters of ethics (Van Hoose & Paradise, 1979, p. 9). We define **work ethics** as the principles of conduct that govern a person's work-related behaviors. We see clients who seek guidance and meaning when struggling to make well-reasoned and ethical choices about work-related issues, and/or who have questions dealing with the work ethics of their coworkers.

The Nature of Values The nature of values is extremely complex. Considerable argument among philosophers has produced a considerably broad definition of values (Peterson, 1970; Raths et al., 1966). Given that a simple and generally agreed upon definition of value is difficult to formulate, three common principles help to understand the nature of values. Values (1) are hypothetical constructs, (2) represent what one "ought" to do or what one perceives is the "right" thing to do, and (3) are motivational forces. With respect to the first principle, values must be objectively inferred by the justification of choices made regarding goals or objects; values are subjectively evident by responses involving elements of belief, interest, wants, and desires. Regarding the second principle, values concern themselves with ethics, behavior, conduct, and morality. For the third principle, values influence the role of work in people's lives.

Constructing a Value In a classic work, Raths et al. (1966) proposed seven standards for constructing a value (see Table 2.1).

In Table 2.1, choosing a value relies on a person's cognitive abilities. The person must choose without submitting to externally imposed pressures. Prizing a value emphasizes the emotional level. The key is to refrain from imposing one's declared value upon others. Acting on a value concerns external behavior and moving beyond lip-service. A person must be willing to act on the choice in some repeated pattern over time. If all seven standards are unmet the result is a **value-indicator,** or a value in the process of "becoming."

TABLE 2.1 Seven Standards for Constructing a Value

CHOOSING (1st principle)	1. freely
	2. from alternatives
	3. after thoughtful consideration of the consequences of each alternative
PRIZING (2nd principle)	4. cherishing, being happy with the choice
	5. willing to affirm the choice publicly
ACTING (3rd principle)	6. doing something with the choice
	7. repeatedly, in some pattern of life

SOURCE: Raths et al., 1966, p. 30.

Raths et al. (1966) mention several types of values, including:

familial	professional	economic	spiritual
social	cultural	political	individual
artistic	educational	material	institutional

Likewise, there are several types of value-indicators. Positive value-indicators include:

goals or purposes	aspirations	feeling
attitudes	interests	beliefs
activities		

Negative value-indicators include:

| worries | problems | obstacles |

Cultural Values. We object to the singling out of any cultural value as a primary explanation for behaviors that benefit or impede educational attainment and its related occupational achievement for any multicultural group. Such singling out gave rise to terms like **"culturally deprived"** and **"culturally disadvantaged."** Culturally deprived suggests an absence of culture and culturally disadvantaged means a person is at a disadvantage because he or she lacks the cultural background of the dominant social and political structure (Atkinson, Morten & Sue, 1993). The implication is that if the cultural heritage one possesses is not the right one, that person is deficient.

The real issue is **ethnocentrism,** where one culture's values matter more than those of another culture (Atkinson et al., 1993). These two terms ignore society's external structures—political and economic. These external structures strongly contribute to adverse conditions said to reflect cultural values. We see within-group differences, developmental considerations, external structures, and contextual factors (e.g., family background, access to technology) as salient variables for persons who enact educational and work-related plans.

Cultural Values vs. Family Values. In *The Shelter of Each Other: Rebuilding Our Families*, Pipher (1996) writes that families are ancient institutions with whom our culture is at war. The entertainment media is an electronic village raising consumers, as children are taught drastically different values from what parents say they value.

Admittedly, the media and the broader culture are at fault for conveying flimsy values (Pipher, 1996). The electronic village has created "a home without walls" (Pipher, 1997). Parents must be vigilant about protecting their children from junk values. Children also learn to be consumers from their peers (Pipher, 1996) and by watching their parents' behavior. Many parents unwittingly model consumerist values, and pursuit of material possessions affects parents' work lives. When work becomes the first priority everything else caters to it. Kids learn that being a successful consumer equals working long hours and living at a hectic pace. Many parents get so busy that they take no time to stop and think about what they are doing.

One's occupation cannot be artificially separated from other parts of one's life (Pipher, 1996, 1997). Families are struggling against external structures that shape the quality of life both at home and at work. The role of work in people's lives needs to include the familial domain (M. S. Richardson, 1993). A tranformed vocational psychology will (a) take external structures into greater consideration, (b) search less within families or individuals for the sources of their suffering, and (c) recognize and respect the multiple environments in which families of varying socioeconomic classes currently live.

WORK VALUES

Values are central to an individual's self-definition and motivation (Rokeach, 1973). Values maintain and enhance self-regard by helping a person to adjust to society, defend oneself against threat, and test reality. Although people in all cultures work, people's valuing of and motives for work reflect the nature of a culture at a given time (Axelson, 1993). Biological survival is a primary imperative. Beyond that, the status of work has been based upon (a) social, economic, and religious beliefs; (b) values; and (c) practices in an historical context.

Attitudes toward work have varied over the centuries. Ancient Hebrews viewed work both as painful drudgery, a punishment for moral transgressions, and as self-fulfilling and satisfying, a positive act of redemption that restored one's

Practical Applications

Vocational practice requires assisting clients in identifying their (1) basic survival needs, (2) wants or choices that involve moral reason and judgment, and (3) values (Michelozzi, 1996). Making value decisions is not always easy. They may involve choices between the better of two goods or the lesser of two evils. "But in time a true value will become a comfortable part of your life pattern. Values are what you *do* and not what you *say* " (Michelozzi, p. 16, italics in original).

Becoming aware of one's values is an intrinsic part of each person's life and it includes occupational choices. Each occupational choice changes a person's lifestyle. The person must learn "new skills, change behaviors to fit your new role, make new friends, and learn a new vocabulary" (Michelozzi, 1996, p.17).

Clients may need a friendly reminder from practitioners that they do have choices (Pipher, 1996). They may have internalized values because at a certain time they were the only ones possible. External pressures from parents, economic circumstances, and institutional practices can result in values that are truly not one's own. These would best be described as value-indicators. Externally imposed value-indicators have to be reevaluated. Exploring alternative possibilities about what is good, what one ought to do, and what makes for client happiness

offer promising opportunities for both personal and occupational growth.

To aid practitioners, Simon, Howe, and Kirschenbaum (1995) offer literally hundreds of values-clarification questions. In Chapter 4 we identify several values-clarification surveys useful for clients.

Practitioners who assist clients to sort out their values also help them develop their **character,** strengthen their **will,** and prioritize their **commitments** (Pipher, 1996). Character is that which makes an individual wise and kind (i.e., moral) choices. Will is an individual's ability to act on one's values. Commitment is being available when it is neither convenient nor easy. Character takes a lifetime to develop. Behavior that accords with one's value system shows character through **self-regard,** which implies hard-won self-knowledge and should not be confused with **narcissism,** which implies self-absorption and self-preoccupation (Pipher, 1996). In the workplace, a well-developed character is unlikely to adopt the opinions of the last person one has talked to. A strong sense of self-regard reduces conduct such as backstabbing, gossiping, spying, discrediting others' efforts, and pettiness towards co-workers.

Practitioners can help clients to strengthen their will by encouraging them to consider as victories those

Continued

Continued

times when clients behave according to what they value the most. Commitment has suffered in many workplaces. Pride in a job done well has been undermined in workplaces hit by downsizing and layoffs (Bragg, 1996a, 1996b) and workers may no longer trust the integrity of their supervisors. Practitioners can help clients to discern what they are willing to be steadfast about when change and crisis occur (Pipher,

1996), and when they need to cut their losses and move on.

Regarding character development and education, Pipher (1996) believes one of the best gifts that parents can pass on to their children is how to work. Several authors have presented a set of ethical values which schools and parents can teach to children. A comparison of some of these sets of ethical values is presented in Table 2.2.

TABLE 2.2 A Comparison of Ethical Values that Can Be Taught to Children

DOSICK (1995)	TEXAS EDUCATION AGENCY (1996)	THE LEAGUE OF VALUE-DRIVEN SCHOOLS (BASED ON FRYMIER ET AL., 1995, 1996)
respect	honesty	learning
honesty	responsibility	honesty
fairness	compassion	cooperation
responsibility	perseverance	service
compassion	loyalty	freedom
gratitude	justice	responsibility
friendship	self-reliance	civility
peace	self-discipline	
maturity	integrity	
faith		

relationship with God (Axelson, 1993; Borow, 1973). Self-fulfillment through work was a moral obligation firmly rooted in the Judean tradition transmitted to the Christian church in the first centuries C.E., and later transformed during the Protestant Reformation in Western Europe in the sixteenth century. This transformation and its enduring legacy are discussed later in this chapter.

From the worker's perspective, work today is very different from any time before. In the United States today, mergers and takeovers rise from the value placed on the profit motive or the "bottom line." The early American values of self-restraint, self-control, hard work, and frugality created a more desirable moral climate than what we have today (Pipher, 1996). People's desire for work as a social experience has changed very little, but with the emphasis on cutting

Continued

Dosick's (1995) ten ethical values shown above are for families, but his book is applicable to adult character development. The Texas Education Agency's (TEA, 1996) curriculum is for elementary schools and has a host of resources listed—activities, films, books. The League of Value Driven Schools bases its values education program on the research of Jack Frymier and colleagues (Frymier, Cunningham, Duckett, Gansneder, Link, Rimmer & Scholz, 1995, 1996). Character development and values education are crucial components to the preparation of our future workforce and cannot be separated out from occupational education activities with children and youth. Of course, the best way for parents, teachers, and other adults to teach children and youth these ethical values is to model them in their conduct both at home and at work.

Work gives structure to people's lives (Pipher, 1996). Independently wealthy people risk having less reason for getting up out of bed in the morning and can experience aimlessness and a lack of purpose. But even with the loss of privilege and position, work can give a person something for which to live. Work in the personal and familial domains (M. S. Richardson, 1993) combine with historical context in the case of Nicholas II [1868–1918], last Tsar of Russia. His diary poignantly records the chores he devised for himself and his children in their months of captivity immediately following his abdication in 1917. His captors permitted the family to cultivate a kitchen garden and to gather winter's fuel by chopping down trees and sawing wood (Maylunas & Mironenko, 1997). Growing vegetables and stockpiling firewood gave them dignity and purpose, occupied their days, and gave meaning to their existence during their imprisonment.

staff size and outsourcing to small businesses, many people are not finding their need for affiliation met, and experience alienation from peers as more are working out of their homes (Licht, 1988). Nearly one quarter of the workforce already works full time or part time out of their homes. Some positive outcomes from this trend are the higher motivation that occurs from working for oneself and the possibility of having more time to spend with the family. Conversely, family members potentially can be treated more as coworkers.

Work hours per week are increasing (Schor, 1991). Americans are working an estimated sixty hours a week, fifty weeks a year. Workers dream of owning their own homes and cars, paying college tuition for their children, and having enough leisure time. Unfortunately, to maintain the dream, many homes with dual wage earners have children who are looking after themselves. Family life is thus affected, as workers cannot provide the parenting children need.

As for the work values traditionally espoused by vocational psychology, Osipow and Fitzgerald (1996) question their relevance to multicultural and diverse populations.

> Possibly the most profound challenge to the generalizability of career development theories is posed by the assertion that many racial/ethnic minority individuals do not share the value systems on which the traditional explanations are based. Virtually every discussion of minority career development contains the assertion that racial/ethnic minority group membership is associated with a more collectivist, group-oriented value system, whereas non-ethnic white Americans are thought to share a highly individual-centered white culture whose values are reflected in the theories used to explain their career behavior. To the degree that such an assertion is correct, it constitutes a profound limitation on the validity of vocational development theories, suggesting that they may not be applicable to many minority individuals. (p. 275)

Collectivist societies presumably include most traditional preindustrial societies, the predominantly Catholic countries of Southern Europe and Latin America and most Asian and African cultures (Ross & Nisbett, 1991). In **collectivism,** "in-group norms and role relations provide both the motivating force that drives the individual and the compass from which the individual takes direction" (p. 181). The emphasis is on family and community-based relations and values. Individualistic societies are presumed to include most of the nations in Western Europe—which gave rise to the **Protestant Reformation**—and North America. In **individualism,** the "emphasis [is] on personal goals, interests, and preferences. Social relationships are dictated by commonality of interests and aspirations and are therefore subject to change as those interests and aspirations shift over time" (p. 181). An individual's choices of dress, diet, friends, occupation, or spouse are relatively free of family dictates or from others to whom one might be linked by traditional roles.

Collectivism is most similar to other-oriented values (Raths et al., 1966). Individualism most closely resembles self-oriented values. Current workplace cultures can be a combination of collectivist and individualist values. Mission statements usually provide a value-indicator of workplace aspirations, but a collectivist-sounding mission statement may disguise an individualistic work environment. Familial values are often collectivist in nature and are most likely to collide with professional values that are predominantly individualistic. We discuss this clash of values later in this chapter and in Chapter 8.

Practical Applications

Individualistic/collectivistic dichotomies across cultures frequently overlook some key points. We offer three cautionary notes to practioners.

1. *Retain sight of within-group differences, including variations within "non-ethnic" White Americans.* Even within the same family, a range of orientations from individualistic to collectivistic can occur. Broad statements about any group having an individualist or collectivist value system are dangerous, especially where work-related behavior is concerned. From a multicultural perspective, within-group differences for any particular racial, ethnic, or nationality group are significant (Pedersen, 1990; Sue, 1992), including the dominant, White majority group. Within-group differences such as "psychological orientation, family structure, socialization, sex, generation, social class, situations, and technological and economic developments seem to influence the formation and selection of various value preferences or expressions" (Carter, 1991, p. 170). Remaining mindful of such differences minimizes false dichotomies across cultures and enriches vocational psychology interventions for all clients.

The literature on **Black Cultural Learning Styles (BCLS)** (Frisby, 1993; T. Q. Richardson, 1993) is one attempt to use cultural values as a primary explanation for behaviors that benefit or impede educational attainment and occupational development for African Americans. BCLS asserts that African-American students' learning styles are fundamentally incompatible with those of European-American students. The idea behind BCLS is that **Afrocentrism** (i.e., behaviors based on an African cultural heritage) accounts for behavior differences between Black and White students. African Americans presumably value interconnectedness, cooperative learning situations, and community possessions. BCLS also presumes an African-American emphasis on spiritual values and a flexible orientation towards time. European Americans presumably value separateness, competitive learning situations, and private ownership. BCLS also presumes a European-American emphasis on material values and a precise orientation towards time. Frisby notes, however, that BCLS was devised by Western African-American scholars who attempted to describe the behaviors of Western African-American students, so the European influence on BCLS cannot be discounted. BCLS perpetuates false dichotomies and fails to recognize within-group differences. The "hoop dreams" of literally thousands of young African-American males belie an emphasis

Continued

Continued
on cooperative learning situations that BCLS upholds. Hoop dreams are as inherently competitive as any other athletic activity.

Another multicultural example is the attempt to use differences in cognitive styles of Mexican-American students to explain behaviors that benefit or impede educational achievement (Buenning & Tollefson, 1987; Saracho, 1989) and occupational development. Presumably, the cognitive styles of Mexican Americans are cooperative and collectivist in learning situations. Again, insufficient attention is given to within-group differences that recognize contextual, as opposed to cultural, aspects of collectivist and individualist orientations.

2. Be alert for when individualistic values and collectivistic values develop in the worldview of a single person, dependent on context. A **worldview** is "the frame of reference through which one experiences life. It is the foundation for values, beliefs, attitudes, [and] relations" (Fouad & Bingham, 1995, p. 335). Failure to understand or accept another worldview can have a detrimental consequence in terms of clinical outcome (Pedersen, 1990; Sue, 1992). While we agree with Ibrahim (1991) that persons from different cultural backgrounds perceive the world differently, social psychology persuades us that individualism and collectivism are, more often than not, situational rather than dispositional within a given client. When various work-related issues arise for clients, those with largely collectivistic personal and social histories may begin struggling with individualistic wants and a desire to place their own interests first. Such clients may perceive that in the past, their personal needs and wants have been neglected or set aside in deference to others' interests. Both developmental and contextual factors would form part of such clients' new-found individualistic yearnings.

3. Consider the developmental role of acculturation—indeed, the role of "multiculturation"—in assessing the individualistic/collectivistic role orientation of their clients, especially minority group clients. This can both expand and enhance the validity of vocational development theories and their applicability to many minority individuals. For all clients, an added dimension can be incorporated into occupational counseling when work-related issues are examined in the context of one's own culture, the broader culture, and one's work culture.

WORK ETHICS

Work ethics are the principles of conduct that govern a person's work-related behaviors. Work ethics form a part of the Judeo-Christian tradition. Included in this tradition are scriptural views of work. For example, the apostle Paul wrote, "Whatever you do, work at it with all your heart, as working for the Lord, not for men, since you know that you will receive an inheritance from the Lord as a reward" (Colossians 3:23–24). The value of working hard, its divine mandate, and its positive consequences are common themes in the Judeo-Christian tradition.

Axelson (1993, pp. 227–28) presents a range of attitudes toward a work ethic:

"Work is the medicine for poverty."
—Yoruba (Afro-Cuban) proverb

"Work with the rising sun, rest with the setting sun."
—Chinese proverb

"Work alone makes life bearable, keeps away boredom, vice, and need."
—François Marie Arouet de Voltaire (1694–1778), French writer and philosopher

"Work consists of whatever a body is *obliged* to do, and play consists of whatever a body is not obliged to do."
—Mark Twain (1835–1910), American writer and humorist

"Life is work."
—Henry Ford (1863–1947), American automobile manufacturer

"I do the thing which my own nature drives me to do."
—Albert Einstein (1879–1955), German-born American physicist

The Protestant Work Ethic

Of the variety of work ethics, the most powerful one in the United States and in the world's predominantly Protestant countries is the **Protestant work ethic**. Misunderstood by many who tend to view it as a single amorphous entity, in fact, the origins of the Protestant work ethic are more complex than most people realize. No vocational psychology textbook we know of addresses in depth the Protestant work ethic. This omission ignores a major influence on vocational psychology. The Protestant work ethic has both sociological and historical perspectives.

Weber's Sociological Perspective *The Protestant Ethic and the Spirit of Capitalism* (1958) is the most widely known work of sociologist Max Weber (1864–1920). This landmark analysis was originally published in 1904. Weber's controversial thesis is that the religious upheavals resulting from the Protestant Reformation, especially Calvinism, produced the psychological conditions which made possible the development of capitalist civilization (Tawney, 1958).

Weber understood Calvin's disciples to believe they could avoid damnation by doing "good works." "The social activity of the Christian in the world is

solely activity *in majorem gloriam Dei"* [Latin for 'to increase the glory of God']"
(Weber, 1958, p. 108). Social activity should be understood to mean simply
activity within the church, politics, or any other social organization (Weber,
1958). Weber implied that Calvin's perception of divine order entailed participation in strenuous, exacting enterprise which individuals must choose and
pursue with a sense of religious responsibility (Tawney, 1958). The fulfillment of
duties in worldly affairs became the highest form of moral activity a person
could assume (Weber, 1958).

Weber's thesis was that capitalism became the social counterpart of Calvinist
theology. (a) Labor became an economic means to a spiritual end; (b) covetous-
ness was less a danger to one's soul than was sloth; and (c) diligence, thrift, so-
briety, and prudence became virtues of both God's "elect" and the commercially
prosperous (Tawney, 1958). Western capitalism was conducted by unremittedly
devoted businessmen who pursued maximum money profit through non-
violent, legal, and honest means (Lessoff, 1994). Work became an opportunity
and a challenge to make use of God-given resources, both in oneself and in the
environment (also known as **responsible stewardship**). Each person would be
divinely called to use one's talents and abilities for the greater good of all. From
this divine calling derives a sense of vocation.

Critique of Weber's Thesis. Quite plausibly, Weber's outlook reflected in part his
early years. Weber had a wealthy background; his family enjoyed considerable
political and social connections (Miller, 1971). He wrote during Imperial
Germany's military and intellectual preeminence (Andreski, 1983). Weber's Germany was characterized by an intense **jingoism**—a pronounced chauvinism
and nationalism marked by a belligerent foreign policy, in this case an arms race
between the British and German empires. Not blind to his own country's shortcomings, Weber wanted to see Germany achieve full status as a world power. He
saw the need for exceptional leaders to rise above tradition and bureaucracy to
cope with the dangerous European tensions of the day (Wrong, 1970). In other
words, Weber's thesis is bound by his personal upbringing and by the social,
cultural, and political milieu of his time. Yet his charisma and moral and intellectual integrity cannot be denied; probably only Marx and Freud are more
widely known and respected as social thinkers by the general Western intellectual public (Wrong, 1970). Few historical arguments have produced a greater
wealth of intellectually fertile, subtle, and often deeply disturbing responses
(Leuthy, 1970). Most relevant here are ethics and the world of work.

Weber (1956, 1978) acknowledged that capitalism existed in the ancient
civilizations of Greece, Rome, India, and China; in the Islamic empires of the
eighth through nineteenth centuries; in fourteenth-century Venice and Florence,
and in the Antwerp of the fifteenth century, but argues that the capitalist enterprise had to wait until religious changes had produced a capitalist spirit (Tawney,

1958). Critics charge that instead of Calvinism producing the spirit of capitalism, both with equal likelihood could be regarded as different effects of other large-scale historical changes. For example, the Black Death of the fourteenth century dramatically altered the composition and political influence of Western Europe's workforce; the Spanish influx of New World gold and silver into Europe during the sixteenth century produced skyrocketing inflation. Historically, one tremendous change in societal structures—the broader intellectual movement of the Renaissance of the fourteenth through sixteenth centuries—removed many conventional restraints in Western Europe (Tawney, 1958).

Weber (1976) acknowledged that the political and economic characteristics of ancient societies, not spiritual deficiencies within a group of people, hindered their full-fledged capitalistic development. But Weber ignored the changes that had occurred in the Roman Catholic Church, which by then had incorporated many of Martin Luther's original protests (Severy, 1983), and which no longer served as a barrier to the emergence of capitalism (Miller, 1971). Others contend Weber does not show any logical connection, from a religious point of view, between the work ethic and the profit motive (Lessnoff, 1994). Weber's thesis is also attacked because, while capitalism apparently began as the practical idealism of an aspiring bourgeoisie, it ended up as excessive materialism (Tawney, 1958), originally one of the major complaints of the Protestant reformers about Catholicism (Wrong, 1970). Thus, the impact of drastic transformations in social and economic systems, as opposed to the superior cultural and religious values of one of several multicultural groups, stands as an equally powerful alternative explanation to Weber's thesis.

Similarly, the present-day global economy is primarily responsible for the abundance or shortage of work opportunities. Infrastructural factors (i.e., social, political, and economic transformations), instead of being deficient in individuals or cultures, play a more significant role in influencing occupational developments. Too often, vocational psychology's bias is on the individual and ignores broader contextual trends. Examining the historical origins of work-related behaviors, such as the Protestant work ethic, helps to clarify how external factors impact individual lives.

Historical Perspectives on the Protestant Work Ethic
The British North American Colonies. The **Puritan work ethic** is a more accurate term for Protestant work ethic in the U.S. An historical and contextual awareness of Puritanism puts into perspective both the Protestant work ethic and vocational psychology. By the late sixteenth century, Puritans had strength and position in English society in far greater proportion to their numbers (Smith, 1971), which predated their later dominance in the British North American colonies. The Puritans were radicals. They contended that, as a means of containing corruption, the secular branch of the government should be held

accountable to the spiritual branch of the church. For Puritans, the purpose of life was a spiritual one, with the duty of the church to serve God, not the Crown or governmental institutions. In this respect Puritans resembled their contemporary polar opposites, the Jesuits of the Catholic Counter-Reformation (Fuentes, 1992).

British colonial expansion during the seventeenth century occurred largely because of capitalistic and industrial growth. Money was available to finance pioneering energies of the 1600s and all English settlements were commercial in their inception, with an understanding that long-term investments and confidence in the future were necessary to realize a return on the original capital. It required all the accoutrements of civilization to initiate and sustain these business ventures. Thus, "Of all the great [European] powers, only England exported her peoples. Spanish imagination was caught by the glitter of gold and the anguish of [Native American] souls crying for salvation [and whose conversion made up for souls lost to Protestantism in Northern Europe]; France sought trade and raw materials" (Smith, 1971, p. 224).

Puritans were one of four waves of Protestant immigrants who colonized British North America (Fischer, 1989). Historically relevant to vocational psychology are two Puritan **folkways** pertaining to work and time. Folkways are "the normative structure of values, customs, and meanings that exist in any culture" (Fischer, 1989). **Work ways** refer to "work ethics and work experiences; attitudes toward work and the nature of work" (Fischer, 1989, p. 9). **Time ways** refer to "attitudes toward the use of time, customary methods of time keeping, and the conventional rhythms of life" (Fischer, 1989, p. 9). Each of the four waves of British North American immigrants had diverse modal characteristics related to work and time. These modal characteristics are presented in Table 2.3.

As Table 2.3 shows, the Puritan migratory wave was the first to occur. They originally came from the east of England between 1629 and 1640 and settled the Massachusetts Bay Colony. Their religious denomination was Congregational. The Puritan élites consisted of ministers and magistrates. Their work ethic was based on the idea that every Christian had two callings—a general calling and a special calling (Fischer, 1989). The Puritan's general calling was to live a Godly life on earth; their special calling was to vocation. While the Puritans did not believe that success in one's calling insured salvation, they did believe that a sense of vocation was the way to serve God in the world. Work was virtuous; poverty was the result of one's own lewdness; no virtuous person required charity (Whitmore, 1971).

Puritans invested time with sacred meaning, "God's Time" (Fischer, 1989). An obsession with "improving the time" originally had spiritual connotations that were later transformed into secular and materialist ends. Around 1680, the English Puritan Ralph Thoresby invented the alarm clock to better measure the

TABLE 2.3 Four British Migratory Waves to North America: Modal Characteristics Related to Work Ethic and Time Ethic

Region of origin:	East Anglia[1]	South and West[2]	North Midlands[3]	Borderlands[4]
North American destination:	Massachusetts	Virginia	Delaware Valley	Backcountry[5]
Migration Period:	1629–1640	1642–1675	1675–1715	1717–1775
Religion of migrants:	Congregational	Anglican	Friends	Presbyterian and Anglican
Origin of immigrant élites:	Puritan ministers and magistrates	Royalist younger sons of gentry and aristocracy	Quaker traders, artisans, and farmers	Border gentry and statesmen
Work ethic:	Puritan	Leisure	Pietistic	Warrior
Time ethic:	Improving the time	Killing the time	Redeeming the time	Passing the time

[1]East Anglia consisted of the east of England, especially the counties of Norfolk, Suffolk, Essex, Hertfordshire, Cambridgeshire, and Huntingdonshire—plus parts of Bedfordshire and Kent.

[2]The South and West consisted of Cornwall, Devonshire, Somersetshire, Dorsetshire, Wiltshire, Hampshire, West Sussex, Surrey, Berkshire, Oxfordshire, Middlesex, Buckinghamshire, Northamptonshire, Leicestershire, Staffordshire, Warwickshire, and Gloucestershire.

[3]The North Midlands consisted of Yorkshire, Lancashire, Cheshire, Derbyshire, Nottinghamshire, Lincolnshire, Shropshire, Herefordshire, Worcestershire, and the latter four named counties listed under the South and West above.

[4]The Borderlands consisted of the north of Ireland, the lowlands of Scotland, and the northern counties of England—Northumberland, Cumberland, Westmorland, and Durhamshire.

[5]The Backcountry consisted of southwestern Pennsylvania, the western parts of Maryland and Virginia, North and South Carolina, Georgia, Kentucky, and Tennessee.

SOURCE: Adapted from Fischer (1989). Reprinted by permission of Springer Publishing Company.

passage of time. Even Benjamin Franklin [1706–1790], in his 1748 essay *Advice to a Young Tradesman, Written by an Old One*, admonished: "Remember that TIME is Money" (cited in Fischer, 1989, p. 159, capitals in original). (Franklin also invented daylight saving time.)

Other Anglo-American colonists were not occupied with work and time in quite the same way. The colonial Virginians originally came from the south and west of England between 1642 and 1675. Their religious denomination was Anglican. Their élites consisted of Royalist (i.e., supporters of the Crown) younger sons of the gentry and aristocracy whose older brothers inherited the family property back in England. These younger sons made their own way in the New World. In British Colonial North America, they were among the most socially prominent families of their day. In colonial Virginia, most White slave owners worked harder than they cared to admit while attempting to keep up appearances of gentility. "Wealth was regarded not primarily as a form of capital or a factor of production, but as something to be used for display and consumed for pleasure. . . . The economic consequence of this attitude was debt" (Fischer, 1989, p. 367). Time ways were less strict. "The people of Virginia were less obsessed than New Englanders with finding some godly purpose for every passing moment, but their lives were more tightly controlled by the rhythms of a rural life" (Fischer, 1989, p. 369). Tobacco was the main crop. It required unremitting care once planted, and consumed the lives of all Virginians with alternate periods of "killing the time."

The Quakers of the Delaware Valley originally came from the North Midlands between 1675 and 1715. Their religious denomination was the Friends. Their élites consisted of traders, artisans, and farmers. The Quakers encouraged industry and condemned idleness. Their pietistic work ethic reinforced the idea of serving God with one's best talents. Also prominent in the Quaker worldview were discipline, integrity in business dealing, and austerity. Spiritual exercises were prescribed to enhance discipline and to acquire absolute dominion over one's acts. Business integrity was vital; disciplinary hearings for "dishonest dealing" had both economic and moral implications. Austerity meant that money was not to be indulged via conspicuous consumption or vulgar displays of wealth, but rather to be saved, invested, and turned to constructive purposes. That venerable banking institution, Lloyd's of London, was founded by Quakers.

The men and women of the Backcountry originally came from the British Borderlands between 1717 and 1775. Their religious denominations were Presbyterian and Anglican. Their élites consisted of Border gentry and statesmen and they had their share of social prominence. But the backsettlers had a different lifestyle from the established settlements of the other British colonies. They settled what was then the frontier and initially served as a buffer between the Quakers and the Native Americans. A stereotype arose that their strong warrior ethic made for a weak work ethic (Fischer, 1989). A reliance on farming and herding meant that work was seasonal. Fieldwork was backbreaking: hoe-husbandry was the main system for crop farming (axe, broad hoe, narrow hoe); plows were seldom used. The people of the Backcountry perceived the rhythms of life as something that could not be avoided, shaped, or resisted. Hence, the backsettler's belief that they were powerless to change events was demonstrated in their idea of "passing the time."

The Industrial Revolution to the Early 20th Century The Protestant-based concepts of human nature and work endured until the Industrial Revolution of the late eighteenth century, when the "spiritual man" was replaced by the "economic man" (Herzberg, 1966, p. 53). Hand tools were replaced by machine and power tools, resulting in yet another change in social and economic organization and the development of large-scale industrial production. Contemplation of the soul was replaced by empirical study of the body. The worker was viewed primarily as a creature of physical needs, a creature of comfort. During this time of great industrialization, there was a drive for better production. Out of this pursuit, the principles of scientific management were born which led to industrial engineering (Herzberg, 1966).

The essence of industrial engineering is individual differences, one of the prime laws of psychology (Dawis, 1992). The emphasis is on eliminating variability in individual differences. This limits the work task so that the one talent held in common will be used, thus minimizing the possibility of error . . . but at the cost of wasted human talent. To justify this denigration of workers, industry developed the myth of the "mechanistic man." This new myth viewed humans' overriding desire as that of wanting to be used efficiently with a minimum of effort. People were considered to be happiest when they were replaceable parts of replaceable machines that manufactured replaceable parts (Herzberg, 1966). Presumably, people were delighted when they did not have to make decisions.

Upon researching low worker motivation it was found that an additional myth was needed to keep morale up and production high. The concept created was the "social man." People were defined essentially as social animals primarily in search of social gratification; their prevailing desire was to be acceptable to fellow workers. Following in the wake of the "social man" was the idea of the "emotional man," who was in need of and searching for psychotherapeutic environments (Herzberg, 1966).

Today industry has turned to the "instrumental man." In the wake of technological development, the level of human activity that serves industry is a person's higher capacities. Workers' intellectual talents must now be organized in the same way that their motor skills were organized for assembly-line operations.

By the 1900s the Protestant work ethic was summarized in a sermon: "Business is religion and religion is business. The man who does not make a business of religion has a business life of no character" (Herzberg, 1966, p. 52). In this context virtue was defined as economic success, and economic success was defined as virtue. This circular worldview is a legacy of Calvinism's emphasis on the individual's predestined fate: the "elect" are known by their economic success. Hence, the fashion tradition known as "Sunday best" equates Godliness with economic success.

Critique of the Protestant Work Ethic Upholding any type of work ethic in the context of changing cultural values and economic patterns in our society has profound implications. Cultural perspectives arise independently of objective situational forces (Ross & Nisbett, 1991). Values, beliefs, and modes of interpreting events characterizing a given culture or subculture can take on a life apart from the situations that launched them. Cultural artifacts can survive well beyond the demise of those situations. The Protestant work ethic is one cultural artifact, a deliberate contrivance of the cultural élite (Fischer, 1989). It has been severely abused and has endured beyond its usefulness. Too often it has been used to mask greed. Too frequently profit motives are not based on honesty, respect for the law, or worker well-being.

Other weaknesses make the Protestant work ethic outmoded: (a) The ethic is historically based on intentional misrepresentations and calculated exaggerations for political purposes, which has bequeathed an inherently distorted legacy. (b) It has limited multicultural applicability. (c) It is anti-woman and anti-feminist. (d) The Protestant work ethic is a basis for a "Blame the Victim" belief system. (e) It cannot be readily applied to the working habits of many immigrant populations. Each of these points is explored below.

An Inherently Distorted Legacy. The Protestant work ethic is outmoded because it is the legacy of a religious wing that sought to purify an already reformed church. The Puritans would have done away with all vestiges of Catholic ritual in the Church of England, including wedding rings and ecclesiastical vestments (Ashley, 1980). The severity of such measures is as evident now as it was then. The distortions inherent in such a worldview persist despite the adaptations and secularizations of the work ethic that have occurred through the centuries. A lack of wellness and an unhealthy lifestyle can result when such a distorted worldview goes unexamined.

Limited Multicultural Relevance. A second reason the Protestant work ethic is outmoded is its limited (at best) multicultural relevance. The ethic omits explicit acknowledgment of the debt owed to the Jewish ancestral part of its Judeo-Christian heritage. Jewish peoples' work ethic (Herz & Rosen, 1982) has contributed substantially to the economic, cultural, and social development of the United States (Goren, 1980). The first recorded instance of divine calling appears in Genesis 12, when God called on Abraham in approximately 2000 B.C.E. to lead his people from ancient lower Babylon to Canaan located several hundred miles west. Martin Luther, a precursor of John Calvin, disrespected Jewish people's industriousness. In *About the Jews and their Lies* (1543), he stated, "we do not know to this day which devil has brought [the Jews] here . . . a plague, pestilence, pure misfortune on our country" (quoted in an exhibit panel, "Why the Jews? The Patterns of Persecution," El Paso Holocaust Museum and Study Center, 1997). **Anti-Semitism** was well entrenched by Luther and Calvin's time. The Gospel of John (18:38–40) says that Jesus Christ was crucified by "the Jews," while Matthew (27:24–26) wrote of Jesus as crucified by "the crowd."

The El Paso Holocaust Museum and Study Center quotes John Chrysostom of the fourth century condemning the Jews for killing Christ. By refusing to give credit where it is due regarding divine calling, the overt anti-Semitism of the Protestant work ethic reveals its limited multicultural relevance to an historically valuable segment of the workforce in the United States and elsewhere.

Bowman (1995) notes that the Protestant work ethic teaches that work should be the main focus, if not the defining focus, of one's life, but also presumes that everyone has equal access to occupational opportunities. The ethic appears to ignore the message that African Americans and members of other ethnic minority groups hear on a daily basis; namely, that only certain careers are open to multicultural populations because of their race and/or ethnicity. This message becomes evident when African Americans: (a) seek same-race role models in various careers where there end up being few, if any, available role models (i.e., engineers, computer scientists, researchers); (b) receive negative feedback about careers that their peers, elderly, or respected members of other racial groups indicate are inappropriate career choices; (c) enter a career that has few racial or ethnic minorities and learn that their hiring occurred mainly to fill a quota, implying that the employee was not really qualified; and (d) find themselves in a position that forces them to interact with a system that is often alien, sometimes even hostile, to achieve status.

It is hardly surprising, then, that many African Americans tend to select occupations where other members of their community appear to congregate, **"protected" careers** (e.g., education, social work, and the social sciences) where less racial discrimination is perceived to occur (Murry & Mosidi, 1993). Both current circumstances and historical context demonstrate that external factors are integral in the career development of *any* client. Thomas Jefferson [1743–1826] recognized in his later years that "the opportunities for the development of [African Americans'] genius were not favorable" (Will, 1997, p. 6A).

Some Asian-American students excel academically because they adhere to a **Confucian work ethic.** The Confucian work ethic requires them to do well because they owe it to their parents (Butterfield, 1990). Doing well academically brings honor to the family, although diversity within the Asian-American population reflects a range of academic achievement (Hsia & Kirano-Nakanishi, 1989). Asian Americans are not the "Model Minority" (Suzuki, 1989). The Protestant work ethic neither honors nor respects those Asian Americans who adhere to the Confucian work ethic.

An Anti-woman, Anti-feminist Ethic. The Protestant work ethic, with its patriarchal posturing, is implicitly anti-woman and anti-feminist. It ignores **gender stratification** in the world of work. Gender stratification refers to "the hierarchical distribution by gender of economic and social resources in a society" (Andersen,

1983, p. 77). The Protestant work ethic ignores women's past and present participation in the labor force; the economic mobility of women workers; how gender issues at work become complicated by race, ethnicity, and social class; and the differential access to social and economic resources (Andersen, 1983). The Protestant work ethic bolsters a sense of male entitlement that has perpetuated an imbalance in the gender division of domestic labor, and affects personal relationships as well as domestic and international policies (Baxandall & Gordon, 1995).

A Basis for a "Blame the Victim" Belief System. In his book, *When Work Disappears: The World of the New Urban Poor,* sociologist William Julius Wilson describes the dominant American belief system concerning poverty and welfare: "it is the moral fabric of individuals, not the social and economic structure of society, that is taken to be the root of the problem" (1996, p. 164). The U.S. welfare debate of recent years painted the non-working poor as "immoral freeloaders disdainful of work" (Cose, 1996, p. 47).

Victim-blaming used to be cloaked in kindness and concern, most often obscured by a perfumed haze of humanitarianism (Ryan, 1971). But social policies in the United States have become increasingly punitive (Wilson, 1996). The welfare law passed in 1996 ended unlimited assistance for the poor, set time limits on benefits, and turned public assistance over to the states (Associated Press, 1997). Critics of welfare reform contend that "plunking once-dependent people into jobs won't succeed in the long term if new hires lack education and skills—and the private sector cannot bear the burden of training them alone" (Associated Press, 1997, p. 5A). The persistent and disturbing signs of inequality and the high level of **distress** in the U.S. is inconsistent with our professed ideals and enormous wealth (Ryan, 1971). These inconsistencies create a state of tension, a "dissonance" (Festinger, 1957; Festinger, Schacter & Back, 1950) that must be resolved. One contradictory situation or the other must be changed to restore the balance.

An ideal, almost painless evasion, as a means of satisfying one's conscience as well as one's patriotism, is to blame the victim. Given that we cannot comfortably believe that *we* deliberately contrive and are the cause of that which is socially problematic, we are almost compelled to believe that *they*—the problematic ones—are the cause and this immediately prompts us to search for deviance (Ryan, 1971). To blame the victim, identification of the deviance as the cause of the problem has been a simple step that ordinarily did not require the methodical collection of scientific evidence. The pathologizing of women in traditional psychology literature exemplifies how scholarly research has long participated in victim-blaming (Atkinson & Hackett, 1993, chapter 1; Fitzgerald & Nutt, 1986).

In the United States, **belief in a just world** is the tendency to view victims as the cause of their own misfortune. While this belief may maintain a sense of order and reduce fears, the failure to recognize the power of the situation is known in social psychology as the **"fundamental attribution error"** or bias (Gilbert & Jones, 1986; Jones, 1979; Nisbett & Ross, 1980; Ross & Nisbett, 1991). Indeed, **"self-serving bias"** often occurs when people invoke situational causes to justify their own conduct, minimizing traits and dispositional causes, especially in circumstances viewed negatively by others. Consequently, persons living in poverty or formerly hardworking individuals who have been downsized may have to maintain their dignity just when they are likely to be told that their misfortune is caused by their own character deficits.

In the collectivistic cultures of the East, the presumption is that situational factors play more of a role in determining behavior than in the individualistic cultures of the West (Ross & Nisbett, 1991, chapter 7). Collectivist people may be less susceptible than individualist people to the fundamental attributional error. Immigrants to the United States from largely collectivist cultures may have a work ethic where they see themselves as less the focal point of attention in their dealings with their peers than their more individualist North American counterparts.

A Disrespect for Immigrant Work Habits. A fifth reason the Protestant work ethic is outmoded is its disrespect for immigrant work habits. Politicized during the 1996 U.S. Election Year when the anti-immigrant issue raised its ugly head, anti-immigrant sentiments are nothing new. For over a hundred years, U.S. constitutional law has been shaped by anti-immigrant bias rooted in racism, particularly against Asians (Koh, 1994). Sixty percent of American citizens believe that current levels of immigration are too high. The economic impact of immigrants and their effect on American culture are increasingly worrisome for the average worker. Three themes run through the modern U.S. Supreme Court's decisions regarding immigration. First, an obsession with sovereignty and governmental power, with the power to exclude aliens, especially those likely to become "public charges" (Koh, 1994, p. 74). Second, an unwillingness to scrutinize the immigration decisions of government officials, with no specified constitutional limitations on the power of Congress to regulate immigration. Third, contempt for international law and indifference to the due process and equal protection claims of foreigners seeking entry to the U.S.; undocumented workers who have physically entered the U.S. remain legally outside it, which deny longtime but unofficial residents of the U.S. meaningful constitutional protection.

Lipset (1990) concluded that the Protestant ethic, which has evolved into the work ethic, is not part of the lack of motivation and productivity that is seen now in the workplace. His conclusion opposes that of the American Management Association survey, which stated that the direct cause of the nation's declining productivity is the erosion of the "traditional work ethic." Lipset offers two statistics to validate his opposition: Americans are working more hours now

Practical Applications

Even though the Puritan work ethic included a sense of calling or vocation about one's work (Packer, 1994), a major Puritan legacy to vocational psychology and the role of work in people's lives is the secular meaning attached to "improving the time." Alarm clocks and daylight saving time are two cultural artifacts from Puritan folkways. This value placed on "improving the time" is seen today in attempts to schedule **"quality time"** into family life. Quality time is a way to compensate for work's encroachment into the familial domain. We momentarily address whether quality time actually improves the time.

The Virginian gentlemen farmers were the ones who lived beyond their means and who would have maxed-out their credit cards if such things had existed in those days. The need for credit/consumer counseling is hardly new. Like their later counterparts in the deep South, behind their facade of gentility and manners, the Virginian gentleman farmers also had a vested interest in maintaining slavery, the legacy of which is enduring racism and **discrimination** against African Americans (Hacker, 1992).

We find the Quakers' philosophy to be the most attractive, and would gladly do business with them. Their notion of serving God with one's best talents is especially appealing.

Employment, employment opportunities, and all that we consume and use in our everyday lives thereby become God-given gifts for which to be thankful and not taken for granted. The Quakers' integrity also draws us to them. Their scrupulousness exemplifies the kind of coworkers we want for ourselves.

The **myth of rugged individualism** is a legacy of the Backcountry people that still pervades America's work ethic. We propose that this myth be replaced with the **reality of rugged collectivism.** Men hardly settled the Backcountry one by one; they could never have settled the Backcountry without the help of women. In those rare instances when plows were used in the Backcountry, it was often the wife who pulled the plow if they could not afford oxen. She used what we now call her lower center of gravity to pull the plow; her husband used his upper-body strength to steer the plow. These wives returned to fieldwork as soon as possible after childbirth, sometimes within hours of delivery. Baxandall and Gordon (1995) present an absorbing documentary of the history of working women's contributions to the founding of the U.S. before 1820. The authors shed light on the collective, community-based values that contributed to the settling of the frontier.

Discarding the myth of rugged individualism and recognizing the reality of rugged collectivism would go a long way towards changing the role of work in people's lives today. Expectations would be more realistic. Work environments would be healthier places. Job satisfaction would rise. Work and leisure would be better balanced. Needless stress would be eliminated. The "bottom line" could be achieved without downsizing and sacrificing employee wellness.

Being alert to the historical origins of White Protestant work-related behaviors in North America illuminates within-group differences through examining attitudes toward work and the use of time among the **Anglo** population. These days, the term "Anglo" is a gross misnomer and its usage perpetuates racism. Less than 20 percent of the U.S. population has British ancestry today (Fischer, 1989); indeed, 40 percent of the total U.S. population is of German ancestry. Regardless, the Protestant work ethic has exerted so much influence on our educational, social, political, and economic systems that it is hardly ever thought about and its values are rarely challenged (Axelson, 1993).

Clients can trace the beginnings of their own work ethic by answering the following questions.

Questions for Examining Clients' Work Ethic

1. Can clients tell a story about the exact origins of their work ways? of their time ways?

2. Who taught them about work ways? about time ways?

3. What explicit messages have clients received about work ways? about time ways?

4. In what context (e.g., time and place) were these messages imparted to them?

5. Are these messages useful for clients now?

6. Do they wish to retain such practices as part of their behavior?

7. What kinds of coworker conduct do clients deplore and seek to avoid? admire and seek to emulate?

8. How would clients prefer to use their "spare time"? What, if anything, prevents them from using their "spare time" as they would like?

9. Do clients take vacations? If so, how regularly? If not, why not?

10. What are clients' opinions about charity? about welfare?

11. Have they ever received charity? been on welfare?

12. Under what circumstances would they accept charity? welfare?

Practitioners should periodically ask themselves the questions cited above. The need to enhance one's clinical awareness makes it incumbent upon practitioners to remain alert to how their own work ethic influences their interactions with clients.

than in the past decade, contradicting predictions of decreased productivity, and they are working out of a desire to work rather than a need (85 to 87 percent of the workforce claims they are satisfied with their jobs).

> Not everyone subscribes to the American Work Ethic. Senator Edward
> M. Kennedy recounts how, during his first campaign for the U.S. Senate,
> his opponent said scornfully in a debate that this man has never worked a
> day in his life. Kennedy says that the next morning he was shaking hands
> at a factory gate and one worker leaned toward him and confided, "You
> ain't missed a goddamned thing!" (Morrow, 1981, p. 94).

A transformed vocational psychology will allow for multiple work ethics. Socially generated narratives of the role that work takes in people's lives needs to occur. The balance between feeling pressure to work and finding meaning in life is a personal responsibility confronting each individual.

The Myth of "Quality Time" One way workers with families cope with workplace demands on their lives is to set aside quality time to spend with their spouses and children. Quality time is a legacy from the Puritans' preoccupation with improving the use of time. In *The Time Bind: When Work Becomes Home and Home Becomes Work,* sociologist Arlie Russell Hochschild (1997) argues that long-hour work cultures have absorbed increasing amounts of family time. The underlying workplace political issue is whether workers are judged mainly on the excellence of their job performance—their **productivity**—or on their actual amount of time present in the workplace, called **face visibility.** For most employers, face visibility matters more.

Family-friendly policies that would allow for more of a healthy balance between work and family by means of flex time, job sharing, unpaid paternity leave, and part-time work do not find widespread implementation, as appealing as such policies may seem. Hochschild (1997) reviews several possible explanations for why little use is made of these policies. First, working parents cannot afford shorter hours. Second, workers are afraid of being laid off if they work shorter hours. Third, workers are unaware of the existence of family-friendly work policies, or if they do know of such policies, workers do not know how to get them. During her three years of field research at a Fortune 500 company in the Midwest that she calls Amerco, Hochschild interviewed employees from the executive suite to the factory floor. She learned that for many, life at work was more pleasant and rewarding than life at home. The more that "work in the public realm is valued or honored, . . . the more private life is devalued and its boundaries shrink" (p. 198). Moreover, "some workers may feel more 'at home' at work . . . [because] they feel more appreciated and competent there" (p. 200). Lastly, "the takeover of the home by the workplace is certainly an unacknowledged but fundamental part of our changing cultural landscape" (p. 203).

Practical Applications

Former U.S. Secretary of Labor Robert Reich reflects: "Quality time? Forget it. As the father of two teenagers, I've learned that you can't 'pencil in' parenting" (1997, p. 9). His words are uncomfortably true for many. "Quality time," with its origins in workplace deadlines, cycles, pauses, and interruptions, is the antithesis of **child time.** Child time is a pace that is flexible and mainly slow, and entails patiently making allowances for "over-see[ing] the laborious task of tying a [child's] shoelace, [tolerating] a [child's] prolonged sit on the potty, [and listening] to the scrambled telling of a tall tale" (Hochschild, 1997, p. 5). Many parents' expectations are thwarted when they schedule "quality time," only to find one or more of their offspring peevish, grumpy, sleepy, clingy or aloof, absorbed in a television program or computer game, or preferring the company of a friend to that of their parents'. When offspring are not at their best during the precious time set aside for quality relating, frustrations abound for both parent and child. Parents often make "quality time" mainly to attend their child's performance-based activities. "If you regard your children only as 'pride-producing machines' . . . they will measure their worth by *what they do,* not by *who they are*" (Dosick, 1995, p. 14, italics in original).

Practitioners can help clients sort through the relation to work and personal/family responsibilities. A major issue is the extent to which workers can live the values that they say are important to them as parents. Too often parents are forced by workplace politics to act against their better selves in performing their jobs (Pipher, 1996). Family and work roles are discussed more fully in Chapter 8.

The ensuing time bind has contributed to the myth of "quality time" (Hochschild, 1997). Parents who consciously or half-consciously know they are shortchanging their families and home life end up scheduling (for all intents and purposes, into their appointment books) the "quality time" they spend with their children. In Hochschild's field study, of the 130 Amerco employees she interviewed, one-fifth of the workers openly admitted to a pattern of neglecting family life for their work life, and one-half of the workers voiced a theme that indicated a similar type of neglect. "Quality time" presumes that the time workers devote to family relationships can be separated from ordinary time, with the hopes that scheduling intense periods of family togetherness will compensate for lost hours devoted to work, in the belief that parent-child relationships will suffer no loss of depth. "Instead of nine hours a day with a child, [parents] declare [themselves] capable of getting the 'same result' with one more intensely focused total quality hour" (Hochschild, 1997, p. 50, quotations in original). Thus, unless a child's medical emergency forces parents to take time off from work to tend to them, many parents operationalize "quality time," making a point to attend their children's performance-based activities such as sporting events or music/dance recitals. "Quality time" appears intended to assuage the guilt many parents feel for putting work before family.

A Postmodern Work Ethic for the 21st Century

In Chapter 1 we called for a transformation of vocational psychology. Issues that confront vocational theorists and practitioners include the need to (a) become more interdisciplinary, (b) attend to external structural factors and their impact on the world of work, and (c) expand one's vision on how work affects the quality of life for diverse groups. In this chapter, we have thus far examined how values, work values, and work ethics are influenced by the present-day media, historical context, and other social and cultural trends. Vocational psychology's challenge is to keep pace with the broader cultural shift into the Information Revolution of the post industrial age.

With the unprecedented demands on work and family life, Mark L. Savickas (1993) tentatively proposes a postmodern work ethic for the twenty-first century. He is vocational psychology's leading proponent among a relatively small but growing cadre of postmodern social scientists and clinical practitioners. **Postmodernism** is an intellectual movement with its roots in art and architecture, philosophy, literature, and cultural studies. It questions and rejects the fundamental assumptions of **modernism** (Burr, 1995). Modernism is based on **logical positivism,** a twentieth-century philosophical movement which contends that all genuine knowledge can be discovered through scientific method. Thus, observation and experiment—**empiricism**—are the only valid means of adding to the knowledge base.

The world of work in the modern era was characterized by **industrialism.** Positivistic inquiry guided the rise of industries and manufactured products, particularly by the assembly line method. "Job Shock" and the Information Revolution, corporate downsizing, multiculturalism in the U.S., and the burgeoning global economy are creating a paradigmatic shift. A **paradigm** is "a central overall way of regarding phenomena . . . [and] may dictate what kind of explanation will be found acceptable" (Flew, 1984, p. 261). Within the field of vocational psychology the paradigm shift is from modern objectivity to postmodern perspectivity (Savickas, 1993, 1995b). A proposed list of these shifts is presented in Table 2.4.

**Table 2.4 The Paradigm Shift from Modern Objectivity
to Postmodern Perspectivity**

MODERN	POSTMODERN
Positivism	Postmodernism
industrial age	information age
printing press	electronic media
Newtonian physics	Quantum physics
demand singular truth	appreciate multiple realities
principles	particulars
empiricism	interpretivism
objectivity	perspectivity
reason	relationships
procedural rationality	interpretive community
concepts	constructs
language reflects reality	language produces reality
definitions describe	definitions inscribe
discover meaning	invent meaning
goal—accurate	goal—useful, interesting
clients receive predefined services	clients agentic in interpreting and shaping their own lives

SOURCE: Savickas (1993), p. 209. Reprinted by permission of Springer Publishing Company.

"Our society is taking a fundamental step beyond postivism, objectivistic sciences, and industrialism. The question of what we are moving toward, however, remains unanswered" (Savickas, 1993, p. 208). Postmodernism is one possible paradigm shift for vocational psychology. As shown in Table 2.4, postmodernism departs from modernism. Modernism embodies the time from the Industrial Revolution to the early twentieth century. Postmodernism embodies the Information Revolution. The printing press/print media is the major means of mass communication in modern times, the electronic media in postmodern times. Modern Newtonian physics (i.e., natural order or concrete predictability within the universe) is replaced by postmodern quantum physics (i.e., natural chaos or mathematical complexity within the universe). Modernism demands a singular truth that is scientifically verifiable: universal principles, empiricism, objectivity, reason, and procedural rationality are used to confirm or disconfirm hypotheses. Postmodernism appreciates multiple realities that are subjectively constructed: contextual particulars, interpretivism, perspectivity, relationships, and interpretive communities create **localized knowledge.** Modernism is characterized by concepts presumed to exist independently of the knower. Postmodernism is characterized by constructs intersubjectively created. Language reflects modernism's independently knowable world and definitions describe

objective reality. Language produces postmodernism's community of understanding and definitions inscribe subjective reality. With the scientific method as
the foundation of modernism, meaning is discovered and the goal is achieving
accurate descriptions. With the **contextual interpretation** that is the hallmark
of postmodernism, meaning is invented and the goal is attaining that which is
socially useful, relevant, and viable. In modernist approaches to clinical practice,
clients receive pre-defined services. In postmodern approaches to clinical practice, clients are agentic in interpreting and shaping their own lives. **Agentic
behavior** involves action and independence (Barnett & Rivers, 1996). Client
expertise plays a greater role in postmodernism more than in modernism.

In summary, postmodern contextual interpretation replaces discovering
truth in objective reality with understanding truth as a subjectively constructed
version of reality. The scientific method sought to objectify and decontextualize
phenomena and maximize explained variance by controlling for confounding
variables. It is exactly these confounds that postmodern qualitative research and
clinical practice seeks to particularize and contextualize. Given the changing
role in people's lives, Savickas (1993) presents his twenty-first-century postmodern work ethic by comparing it with the work ethics of the nineteenth and
twentieth centuries. These comparisons are presented in Table 2.5.

In Table 2.5, the nineteenth century "vocational ethic" was a secular version
of the Puritan work ethic. Independent effort, self-sufficiency, frugality, self-discipline, and humility were valued. Typically, occupational choice followed family
traditions like taking over the family business or staying on the family farm. To
this day, craftspeople, farmers, and small business operators retain much of this
vocational ethic. The vocational ethic fit with Romantic "conceptualism" which
encouraged passion, genius, and creativity as an outward expression of one's in-

Table 2.5 Comparisons of Work Ethics

19th CENTURY VOCATIONAL ETHIC	20th CENTURY CAREER ETHIC	21st CENTURY DEVELOPMENT ETHIC
Self-employed farmers	Employed by organizations	Work in teams and craftspeople
Romantic conceptualism (Meaning in the person)	Logical positivism (Meaning in the world)	Postmodern interpretivism (Meaning in the word)
Value feelings	Value facts	Value perspectives
Be creative	Be rational	Actively participate in the community
Success through self-expression & individual effort	Success through moving up someone else's ladder	Success through cooperation & contribution

SOURCE: Savickas (1993), p. 210. Reprinted by permission of Springer Publishing Company.

Practical Applications

The postmodern method of inquiry asks, "What perspective is most useful for this particular context?" (Savickas, 1993, pp. 207–208). Instead of one scientific best truth, the postmodern ethic would be based on a **dialogic community** where language is the primary vehicle for creating meaning in the workplace. Employees would be more proactive in drawing their own vocational path, speaking and acting for themselves, and relating the work-role to other parts of their lives—relationships, children, residential environments (M. S. Richardson, 1993; Savickas, 1993). Work would no longer be separated or compartmentalized in people's lives. Subjective perspectives would take on increasing significance, and clinically speaking, one's life story would incorporate work into other facets of one's existence and life theme.

Q. What prevents an open dialogue and an exchange of ideas in the workplace?

A. Coworkers' current jealousy, past dishonesty, reputations for territoriality, vindictiveness, and controlling behavior.

A rule of thumb for initiating and maintaining a dialogic community is, "Keep in mind that negative connotation, or the invalidation, of any major participant is destructive to the process of opening space for conversation" (Anderson & Goolishian, 1991, p. 7). Experience has taught both of us that this is much easier said than done. Initial encounters with postmodernism can be jarring for practitioners trained in the modernist tradition. For the moment, we offer no critique of the postmodern paradigm. We first need to acquaint our readers more with postmodernism. Postmodernism is definitely an acquired taste. We explore it further in our discussion of leisure and avocational activities below. Postmodern methods of assessment are briefly considered in Chapter 3. Postmodern approaches to vocational psychology are discussed in Chapter 5. The postmodern family is presented in Chapter 8.

---

ner being. This idea of an inner being predates the Romantic age of the late eighteenth century and early nineteenth century and originates in ancient Greece. The apostle Paul was strongly influenced by Greek culture. He uses the term "inmost being" (Ephesians 4:23). Modernism views the self as an autonomous, isolated being; postmodernism views the self as constructed in relationship (Becvar & Becvar, 1996).

As the United States entered the twentieth century, with the emergence of large organizations workers began having careers (Savickas, 1993). Career workers received little reinforcement for self-expression and individual effort. The challenge for working for someone else and moving up their corporate ladder replaced self-employment in small businesses and on farms. Career counseling used the scientific method to determine vocational choice. Interests, values, and abilities became objectively quantifiable entities that existed in the world "out there." A scientifically based psychometric instrument helped to discover the best fit between a person and a work environment. With this matching achieved, the question of career selection was settled. Such career counseling approaches reflected the age in which they were used. These approaches also have ancient roots, which we discuss at the end of Chapter 4. The changing spirit of the current age makes the career ethic less relevant. Given the dramatic transformations in the world of work and in the broader society and culture, vocational psychology's reliance on logical positivism as a foundation for the discipline is engendering increasing ambivalence.

MEANING IN WORK / JOB SATISFACTION

Juliet Schor observes that:

> We've lost a balanced attitude toward time. And the irony of it is that, in the end, many of the people who run around harried and frenzied end up having less time. . . . [Many writers approach this] from a psychological angle—that individuals are working too hard because of a psychological deficit. (cited in an interview by Stone and Taylor, 1991, p. 43)

Although some people are unable to balance time issues, Schor notes they are relatively few. A bigger problem exists in "the competitive labor market" where employers demand long hours. People are being overworked, but not by their own choice.

Aside from being overworked by their employers, some workers find comfort in the workplace when there is conflict at home. Work has become comfortable and the worker feels alienated from the family. "Home is where the real stress is" (Barnett & Rivers, 1996, pp. 35–36). People look for happiness at work rather than face the problems waiting outside of work. When work becomes too time consuming, single people may lose personal connections and social support (Schor, cited in Stone & Taylor, 1991).

Americans today work one month longer per year than they did in 1970, with more time on the job than any other industrialized country except Japan (Stone & Taylor, 1991). The corporate world believes that to remain competitive with Japan we need to work more hours. But Japan is not the only model for success. Many Western Europeans have managed to maintain their standard of living, keeping wages even and taking six weeks of vacation per year.

While the standard of living increases for those working longer hours, what is the cost? Studies indicate that possession of material things has not engendered any deeper sense of meaning and satisfaction in our lives. Schor suggests that:

> if you look at all of the cases of companies that have changed their work week from forty hours to, say, thirty-eight, thirty-seven or thirty-six without reducing pay, workers are happier. They tend to show up for work on time. They don't quit as frequently. They go to the doctor on their own time. They do their work in a shorter amount of time. (Stone & Taylor, 1991, p. 102)

And according to O'Toole:

> in the 1950s, it was marriage; in the 1960s, it was changing the world; in the 1970s, it was career advancement; in the 1980s, it was money; in the 1990s, it's personal fulfillment—anyway you can get it. Under the new rules for defining success, anything goes, but certain themes recur. A successful life has many parts: it offers opportunities to contribute to colleagues, company and community, it has flexibility, and time for family, friends and personal interests, and it proceeds at a sustainable pace. (1993, p. 49)

Evidently, ideas of financial success are also shifting. A five-year study conducted at the University of California at Los Angeles Higher Education Research Institute found that the "percentage of U.S. college freshmen who consider it important to be 'very well-off financially' has dropped, while the percentage interested in 'developing a meaningful philosophy of life' has risen" (O'Toole, 1993, p. 52).

Earlier in this chapter we explored the influence of the Protestant work ethic with one's primary concern being one's work and that each job had a calling. Yet the changes occurring in the work force are causing a reevaluation of the meaning of work in one's life. For many, the workplace has little sense of community and competition has replaced teamwork, especially in middle and upper management positions. Now that women comprise 47 percent of the work force, they can address the meaning of work in a different manner. If a shared sense of community is important in all aspects of life, what type of paradigm shift is necessary to reintroduce interpersonal communication at work? Perhaps reframing meaning in work and shifting focus to relational activities, such as family and community involvement, forms the basis for such a shift.

Practical Applications

Most people would choose to work rather than live comfortably for the rest of their lives without working, (Macoby & Terzi, 1981; Vecchio, 1980a). As the rise in the proportion of women and minorities in the workforce indicates, more people are trying to gain access to work, and the demand for paid employment of all types continues to grow. In most of the work that people do we find a confrontation of the individual with the organization. The results of this confrontation yield satisfaction or dissatisfaction, feelings of competence or inferiority, and motivation to be productive or work alienation.

Corey and Corey (1997) present a self-inventory that practitioners may find useful when clients are dealing with issues related to meaning in work. These items are presented in Exercise 2.1.

The self-inventory in Exercise 2.1 is a useful point of departure for conversations with clients. Specific means by which clients desire to express themselves through work can be explored, expectations and beliefs regarding job longevity can be examined, and particular needs that clients seek to have fulfilled by work can be discussed.

EXERCISE 2.1 Self-inventory on Meaning in Work

Directions: Use the following scale to respond:

4 = this statement is true of me *most* of the time;

3 = this statement is true of me *much* of the time;

2 = this statement is true of me *some* of the time;

1 = this statement is true of me *almost none* of the time.

_____ 1. I wouldn't work if I didn't need the money.

_____ 2. Work is a very important means of expressing myself.

_____ 3. I expect to change jobs several times during my life.

_____ 4. A secure job is more important to me than an exciting one.

_____ 5. If I'm unhappy in my job, it's probably my fault, not the job's.

_____ 6. I expect my work to fulfill many of my needs and to be an important source of meaning in my life.

_____ 7. I want work to allow me the leisure time that I require.

SOURCE: Corey and Corey (1997), p. 139.

Lack of identification with job titles, functions, one's role in the company mission can reduce meaning in one's work and create job dissatisfaction (Berger, 1990). Work can be satisfying, neutral, or threatening. Most jobs do not allow us to avoid pain or help us grow—two necessities for satisfaction. Employers need to be more honest with prospective workers about dealing with work without meaning, and to emphasize productivity, not face visibility.

Job Satisfaction

A worker is likely to have seven job changes over a lifetime (Berger, 1990), with job satisfaction being related to these changes. Job satisfaction is not a singular term and has been defined in many ways, with two direct components: (1) "overall satisfaction" with the entire job situation, and (2) "facet satisfaction" with certain aspects of the job. A worker can be dissatisfied with a certain part of one's job (e.g., pay, working conditions, coworkers) but have an overall sense of satisfaction. **Equity theory** adds other factors relevant to job satisfaction: personal fairness, justice, and equity (Pritchard, 1969). Equity theory relates to what is obtained versus what is desired in relation to other people.

CASE EXAMPLE

Catherine had been working for a small, private organization where decisions were made based on specified criteria, personal fairness, and equity. A change of leadership resulted in a shift in workplace "rules." Decisions at Catherine's workplace were now made based on the new leader's subjective likes and dislikes, with little regard for employees' years of experience or abilities. Sexual favoritism became part of Catherine's workplace politics. Those who did not participate in the after-hours sexual encounters had their own sexuality besmirched by the leader. For Catherine and those of her coworkers who did not take part in such office politics, job satisfaction plummeted, despite having loved their jobs. Salaries and promotions were now based on whatever the new leader deemed "competitive." The men and women who indulged the leader's sexual politics were deemed most competent. Turnover at Catherine's workplace increased as she and her coworkers who had other employment opportunities regretfully departed. Coworkers who benefited from the inequitable arrangement retained their jobs.

Factors Related to Job Satisfaction Job satisfaction is directly related to nine factors:

1. prestige of the job;
2. autonomy–control over the conditions of work;
3. cohesiveness of the work group, which facilitates interaction;
4. challenge and variety of job tasks;
5. employer concern and involvement of employees in decision-making;
6. wages with respect to both amount and one's perception of adequate wages compared to others performing similar tasks;
7. mobility potential of the job (workers want to feel there is potential for upward movement through the skill hierarchy, the occupational hierarchy, the organizational structure in which the work is performed, or any combination of the three);
8. satisfactory working conditions; and
9. job security (O'Toole, 1993).

People in different cultural settings vary in the way they learn problem solving and in the patterns of skills they acquire. Cultures vary in the salience attached to certain skills, in the combination of basic cognitive processes that are called upon in any given context, or in the order in which specific skills are acquired. Work will have different meanings for diverse populations.

Leisure and Avocational Activities

The cycle of all work and no play can be ameliorated by affordable **leisure activities.** Factors affecting leisure time include available discretionary income, time, and learning opportunities. Social, physical, intellectual, and creative activities are available that do not require much money. Some of these are joining a community theater group, tutoring or volunteering with children or older adults, enrolling in adult education classes, or organizing a volleyball team. Participating in sports, rather than being a spectator, helps relieve work stress and refocuses our work perspective.

An alternative possibility for satisfying self-expressive needs and meaning in work can occur through leisure and **avocational activities.** Avocational activities are pursued systematically and consecutively for their own sake; the objective is something other than monetary gain, which may incidentally occur (Super, 1976). Leisure and avocational activities can be especially rewarding when other parts of one's life are not going as smoothly as one would like. Persons who put all their eggs in one basket, so to speak (whether work, an intimate relationship, or parenthood) risk an imbalance that can adversely affect their well-being as well as persons around them. Leisure is hardly "goofing off." Leisure provides a respite from work responsibilities and pressures.

Practical Applications

Clients may be second-guessed by spouses, family members, and friends about spending money on avocational activities that yield no financial profit. Clients who perceive a lack of support from significant others for avocational activities may benefit from some explicit values clarification for themselves. Practitioners can also help clients to strengthen their self-regard—that centered, knowing sense of who one is (Pipher, 1996)—as a means of remedying any self-doubts about the worth of leisure or avocational pursuits. Clients who pursue avocations are likely to value personal growth and development. Practitioners may have to reinforce clients' desires to "explore the choices available to them in significant parts of their lives" (Corey & Corey, 1997, p. vii). They also may have to remind clients that lifelong learning via avocational pursuits is an extremely valuable skill that can be transferred back into the world of work.

Leisure can be consumed unwittingly by two habits: indiscriminant television viewing/channel surfing and regular "happy hour" participation. Conversely, physical therapists tell of the springtime emergence of **"weekend warriors"** (usually men more than women), who engage in athletic activities while out of shape, thereby injuring knees or rotator cuffs. These weekend warriors are not using their leisure time efficiently while trying to recapture youthful self-images (whether accurate or not) which they can no longer replicate. This kind of leisure, intended as a relaxation from work, can be no fun at all. Physical limitations due to age, or injuries due to biomechanics or being out of shape, can prevent some athletic activities and require a readjustment of how leisure is spent. Practitioners working with clients' adopting realistic physical expectations may encounter clients' grief and mourning as their leisure is renegotiated. Leisure and avocation may be assessed by the questions in Exercise 2.2.

Some clients may prefer to compartmentalize their lives and keep leisure and avocational activities separate from their jobs. Their paycheck may serve to provide some of life's pleasures away from the job. Leisure and avocational activities—athletic, artistic, musical, creative—can be more enjoyable and rewarding when one has mastered them early in life. We encourage

Continued

Continued

EXERCISE 2.2 Personal Reflections on Leisure and Avocation

1. How do you typically spend your leisure time?

_____

_____

2. Are there ways that you'd like to spend your leisure time differently?

_____

_____

3. What nonwork activities have made you feel creative, happy, or energetic?

_____

_____

4. Could you obtain a job that would incorporate some of the activities you've just mentioned? Or does your job already account for them?

_____

_____

5. What do you think would happen if you couldn't work? Write what first comes to mind.

_____

_____

SOURCE: Corey and Corey (1997), pp. 168–169.

practitioners, teachers, and parents involved with young children to be mindful of the life-long significance of this foundation setting. The quality of life and work can be enhanced by well-developed (cultivated over a period of time), respectably accomplished (a level of accomplishment that one can respect in oneself) leisure and avocational activities.

Other Contributing Factors Among the other factors contributing to the meaning of work and leisure are a person's age and socioeconomic class. Postmodernism can also provide a perspective on such meanings.

Age. Sometimes the vocational psychology literature, the popular press, and certain research findings give the impression that processes of self-understanding and finding meaning in achievement or choice are important only during the exploration or anticipation phases of youth. Efforts to help people deal successfully with such needs are most frequently available in schools and colleges, places primarily occupied by youths, rather than in settings primarily occupied by adults (Herr & Cramer, 1996). Adults who have always wanted to try something, but have not had the chance to do so until now, may need to be encouraged by prac-

CASE EXAMPLE

With support and guidance from Señor Ildefonso Ibarra, a retired gardener, his sons Manuel and Miguel, with Roberto Cortéz González, cultivate a flower garden dedicated to San Francisco de Asís (1182–1226) at a Franciscan chapel in El Paso, Texas. Gardening is a healing activity, an ancient tradition that transcends the practical need for food (Pipher, 1996) and allows for "a powerful and unique expression of human personality" (Strong, 1992, p. 7). As part of the landscaping team, González is enriched on many levels by this leisure activity. Parishioners also derive pleasure from watching the flowers grow from spring through fall.

The Chapel of San Francisco de Asís, El Paso, TX. Photograph by Roberto Cortéz González.

titioners, family, and friends. Other adults who have substantial work histories may begin to seek meaning in something other than occupational achievement; values change, and "doing" becomes less important than "being."

Socioeconomic Class. Class bias is an ever-present threat to the widespread applicability of the meaning of work and leisure. Work and achievement are the main driving forces of most middle class individuals (Payne, 1995). Much of the preceding discussion seems most relevant for such a population. Persons living in poverty are more apt to be driven by subsistence concerns, survival, relationships, and entertainment as a means of momentary relief from the grind of daily life (Payne, 1995; Zucchino, 1997). The wealthy are more likely to emphasize the maintenance and cultivation of financial, political, and social connections (Payne, 1995). Practitioners are reminded that a client's self-expressive needs and quest for meaning will be influenced by their socioeconomic status.

A transformed vocational psychology includes making it relevant to lower-income populations. Persons living in poverty may espouse concrete values over abstract ones. A present-time orientation may predominate, the future existing only as a word (Payne, 1995). Emotional significance may be used to assign importance to time, not its actual measurement. Work is about making enough money to keep one's head above water. A job is not about a career. A lower-income person's worldview is reflected in the statement, "I was looking for a job when I found this one" (Payne, 1995, p. 109). Practitioners could explore meaning in work with clients for whom a job hunt matters more than career development. Raw economic necessity may be the predominant theme for persons on fixed incomes and those in the lower socioeconomic classes.

Meanings of work and leisure may be qualitatively different from those of higher socioeconomic classes. Higher income and independently wealthy persons may have existential concerns of another sort. CEOs whose salaries may be 200 times more than their employees (Kadlec & Baumohl, 1997; Reingold, 1997) are likely to experience unique challenges to justify their earnings.

Postmodernism. Meaning in work is imminently suitable for a postmodern vocational psychology. Multiple meanings of work and leisure can be constructed through both personal and social narratives. **Narrative approaches** focus on the stories clients tell about themselves and others in attempts to make sense out of the world around them (Penn, 1991; Sarbin, 1986). Personal narratives exemplified by **constructivism** actively construct their personal realities and create their own representational models of the world (Meichenbaum & Fong, 1993). Social narratives typified by **social constructionism** view meanings and understandings of the world as developed through social interaction (Gergen, 1985). Both personal and social constructions of reality are subsumed under **constructivist epistemologies** (Feixas, 1990; Lyddon, 1995; R. A. Neimeyer, 1993b). Constructivist epistemologies conceptualize human beings as "active agents who, individually or collectively, co-constitute the meaning of their experiential world" (R. A. Neimeyer, 1993a, p. 222).

Postmodern meaning-making about work and leisure respects individualism and collectivism. Many possible understandings of behaviors, interactions, or events in a client's workplace would be determined by social, political, and cultural contexts. In postmodern vocational psychology, language used in stories creates meaning, with as many possible stories to tell as there would be clients (Corey, 1996). Client stories require **narrative viability.** That is, the story has to cohere into the larger system of personally and socially constructed realities into which it is incorporated, and the consequences of the story have to be practical (Granvold, 1996). Whereas a modernist objective reality is observed and systematically known, a postmodernist subjective reality is revealed through language as a function of the situations in which people live and work.

The language process used by practitioner and client to explore meaning in work and leisure is called **discourse.** Discourse is "a system of statements, practices, and institutional structures that share common values" (Hare-Mustin, 1994, p. 19). In personal constructivist discourse, the paramount question would be one of personal consequence. In social constructionist discourse, the paramount question would be one of social consequence. Multiple discourses (i.e., the client's, the practitioner's, the client's employer, any relevant subcultures plus that of the dominant culture's) form the basis for postmodern vocational psychology. The goal is to allow clients to find new meanings in their work and leisure, and to "restory" these meanings in a way that frees clients from the mesmerizing power of the dominant culture (Doherty, 1991).

Dominant socially constructed discourses can serve to oppress those not of the majority culture, perpetuate the status quo for those who have political and economic power, and marginalize those who do not share in the co-creation of currently popular and widely accepted stories (Foucault, 1970). For example, women sometimes suspend parts of themselves in the workplace when the socially constructed realities there are at variance with their personal, first-hand experience (McKenna, 1997). Practitioners need to be mindful of not buying into dominant discourses that socially construct workplace realities in a way that negate clients' personal experiences of reality. "Client stories . . . have a vital *intra*personal function—namely, to establish continuity of meaning in the client's lived experience" (Neimeyer, 1995a, p. 233, italics in original). The practitioner helps the client to nurture rather than suppress deeply personal narratives. First-person narratives are vital to prevent the disenfranchisement of clients who encounter a discrepancy between their personal experience and what is socially constructed by others. This can be done in the form of a work autobiography. Since the workplace is becoming increasingly diverse, it is important that practitioners encourage students/clients to explore their own work values and work ethic so they can better understand how to deal with co-workers who may not have the same commitment to values and ethics. The next chapter expands on the role of the counselor/vocational practitioner and incorporates ethical considerations.

3

Perspectives on the Vocational

Practitioner's Role

The vocational practitioner/career counselor role frequently has been misunderstood. Graduate students often perceive it as helping a client find a job, a task that seems less important than dealing with emotional and mental health. Allied health professionals sometimes have this same misunderstanding. Vocational/career counseling is a major specialty within counseling psychology. It is impossible to separate vocational concerns from emotional factors, family interactions, and social well-being. Consequently, this chapter is separated into three separate sections. First, we identify specific roles and competencies for vocational practice and career counseling. Second, we provide suggestions for evaluating counselor effectiveness and career programs. Third, we discuss assessment in vocational psychology and career counseling.

PROFESSIONAL PRACTICE AND
VOCATIONAL COUNSELING

Standards and goals for career counseling are found in a publication by the **National Career Development Association** (NCDA), *The Professional Practice of Career Counseling and Consultation: A Career Resource Guide* (1994, 2nd edition) edited by Dennis Engels. The following information is reproduced by permission of the NCDA, 5999 Stevenson Avenue, Alexandria, VA 22304.

Roles of the Career Counselor

Services of career counselors differ depending on the counselor's level of competence, the setting, and the clientele. **National Certified Career Counselors,** other professional career counselors, career facilitators, and several other types of clinical practitioners help clients to make and carry out decisions and plans related to both lifestyle and career directions. Practitioner strategies and techniques are tailored to the specific work-related needs of the client.

Career counselors do one or more of the following:

1. Conduct individual and group personal counseling sessions to help clarify life/career goals.

2. Administer and interpret tests and inventories to assess abilities, interests, and other factors, and to identify career options.

3. Encourage exploratory activities through assignments and planning exercises.

4. Utilize career planning systems and occupational information systems to help individuals better understand the world of work.

5. Provide opportunities for improving decision-making skills.

6. Assist in developing individualized career plans.

7. Teach job hunting strategies and skills and assist in the development of resumes.

8. Help resolve potential personal conflicts on the job through practice in human relations skills.

9. Assist in understanding the integration of work and other life roles.

10. Provide support for persons experiencing job stress, job loss, and career transition (Engels, 1994, p. 21).

These services are available to students from K–12, colleges/universities, and adults in the community. The vocational practitioner/career counselor can also be in private practice. NCDA has a booklet entitled *The Nuts and Bolts of Private Practice Career Counseling* (1991).

Ethical Responsibilities

Career development professionals must only perform activities for which they "possess or have access to the necessary skills and resources for giving the kind of help that is needed. . . . If a professional does not have the appropriate training or resources for the type of career concern presented, an appropriate referral must be made. No person should attempt to use skills . . . for which he/she has not been trained" (Engels, 1994, p. 14). The *National Career Development Association Ethical Standards* is presented in Appendix 2.

Career Development Specialities

There are several areas of specialization in career development. These are: (1) *Career counselors* (private and public settings) possess basic skills in consultation, program development, and program evaluation. (2) *Human resource, career development, and employee assistance specialists* (in-house organizational setting or contract services) participate in the design and implementation of systems for employee development and career management. (3) *Career and employment search consultants* (private setting) offer job search assistance for clients who possess career direction. (4) *Cooperative education instructors* (educational setting) secure supervised work experience that is consistent with the curricular activities, needs, and abilities of students. (5) *Employment agents* (private setting) obtain employment for clients on a contractual basis where the fee is paid by the employer. (6) *Outplacement consultants* work for firms whose services are retained by corporations and other organizations. (7) *Job placement specialists* (public setting) develop effective working relationships with employers. (8) *School counselors, community college and college counselors and counselors in postsecondary technical institutes* develop and implement developmental counseling program based on models such as the National Career Development Guidelines (NOICC, 1989), which include attention to career development throughout the lifespan (Engels, 1994, pp. 26–27).

Career Counselor Training and Credentials

The designation "National Certified Career Counselor" signifies that the career counselor has achieved the highest certification in the profession. It also means that the person has: (1) earned a graduate degree in counseling or a related professional field from a regionally accredited higher education institution, (2) completed supervised counseling which included career counseling, (3) acquired a minimum of three years of full-time career development work experience, and (4) successfully completed a knowledge-based certification exam. Professional career counselors may also be trained in a graduate-level, counselor preparation program that specializes in career counseling. They may be licensed by state agencies or certified by national or state professional associations (Engels, 1994, p. 21). The National Occupational Information Coordinating Committee (NOICC), in conjunction with NCDA, has developed a curriculum for career development facilitator for para-professionals who work under the supervision of a career counselor. The curriculum is administered by the Career Development Institute at Oakland University in Rochester, Michigan.

Considerations for Practitioner Training To prepare for the future, a comprehensive study is needed of graduate training programs for vocational practitioners/career counselors/consultants. Blustein (1992) identifies a number of suggestions for "reinvigorating" the vocational emphasis in counseling psychology. The list includes:

1. [The need] to develop a means of understanding how career and mental health issues interact in assessment and treatment.

2. The need to develop a theoretically driven way of conceptualizing work-related problems in counseling and psychotherapy. Currently, practitioners may use some sort of individualized synthesis of a career theory . . . in conjunction with the primary theoretical orientation that guides their thinking about psychotherapy. . . . [A]n alternative . . . ought to develop a means of understanding work-related problems in a manner that links these issues explicitly to the concerns that clients experience in other domains of their lives.

3. A renewed agenda for vocational psychology would be to understand more about the process of working with clients in career-related interventions.

4. The area of occupational mental health . . . represents another important means of enhancing the vocational realm . . .

5. The growing interest in consultation [in business and industry] . . . offers yet another aspect of a renewed agenda.

6. A number of lines of inquiry have emerged in recent years that have direct relevance. . . . [These include] a . . . public debate on the relative merits of adolescent employment, . . . the relationship between vocational behavior and family functioning and the interrelationship between career development and collateral lines of development, . . . [and] addressing some of the more complex social issues that pertain to vocational behavior.

7. The important role of culture in human behavior and development has become a significant aspect of contemporary thought in counseling psychology. . . . [V]ocational psychologists have initiated some highly creative work . . . on the role of culture . . . and gender . . . in vocational behavior. (pp. 716–720)

A recent study surveyed 290 counseling psychology graduates from twelve counseling psychology training programs (Heppner, O'Brien, Hinkelman and Flores, 1996). "Results indicate that trainees' most negative experiences were disparaging remarks about career counseling from faculty and supervisors and their formal course work in career development. Conversely, trainees reported that the most positive influences on their attitudes were experiences obtained by working with career clients" (p. 105). Perceived emphasis in counseling training was on "social-emotional counseling" rather than career/vocational counseling. "The question of how some trainees received degrees from intensive graduate programs in counseling psychology without gaining interest or sufficient skills in career counseling is a critical one" (p. 119). Many students indicated that the quality of the vocational psychology training was a greater problem than the amount of course work available. Students lacked understanding of how career counseling activities affected their view of the field. The most negative influence came from faculty and supervisors. One student said "her vocational psychology teacher express[ed] her boredom with the topic at each class session, or in more subtle ways, such as being ill-prepared or presenting boring lectures in career development classes" (p. 120). On the other hand, "trainees wrote of their excitement in working with supervisors who had a passion and excitement and who integrated personal and career counseling in effective ways" (p. 121). Trainees found positive changes in the lives of their "social-emotional" clients' mental health when occupational concerns were addressed.

A career counseling practicum can produce changes in conceptualizing work-related issues in clinical practice. Supervisees can gain understanding about (a) international cultural differences, (b) relating career issues to a counseling theory basis, (c) demystifying career counseling, (d) moving from psychopathology to developmental concerns, and (e) working with group process in a classroom, and (f) integration of personal/career information through use of assessments and technology (Warnke, Kim, Koetzlow-Milster, Terrell, Dauser, Dial, Howie & Thiel, 1993).

A person who wants to pursue the field of career counseling should contact NCDA to obtain a list of available graduate schools that offer specific programs in career management, career/vocational psychology, or programs that offer a general degree in counseling with an emphasis in career/occupational counseling.

The vocational practitioner/career counselor role is complex and varied. Training, credentials, and ethical standards are clearly stated. But the historical role of vocational development in counseling psychology needs to be reasserted. Our collective experience is that separating vocation from the rest of life is not possible and can often be counterproductive.

COUNSELOR AND PROGRAM EVALUATION

Evaluating career counseling is difficult. An experimental approach is not possible for ethical reasons, and clarity and agreement on the outcomes of the counselor's work are difficult to define (Kellett, 1994). Evaluation is usually overlooked in counselor training and there is little agreement on the instruments to evaluate outcomes. "In the absence of some definitive information on the contribution that career and employment counseling can make and [are] making, there is a real danger that counseling, which is not now well integrated with other career and employment programming, will be pushed further to the side, with even less resources given to it" (p. 351).

In career and employment counseling circles program evaluation is an effectiveness and accountability issue. Although counselors frequently lament that they are vulnerable in the face of growing accountability concerns and often approach program evaluation with a negative attitude, they do not view evaluation as a solution. An evaluation course is only an optional part of many training programs. Counselors rarely evaluate their programs and services. They acknowledge that accountability is important, but few models exist for helping counselors. Most counselors report receiving an annual performance appraisal; however, little firsthand observation of their work with clients is conducted (Conger, Hiebert & Hong-Farrell, 1993) and rarely are clients asked to give feedback regarding the services.

An evaluation framework is needed that is user-friendly, provides both formative and summative evaluation, and offers counselor feedback regarding their interactions with clients (Hiebert, 1994). **Formative evaluation** refers to program evaluation activities that are conducted during the course of a program. **Summative evaluation** refers to program evaluation activities that are conducted at the end of a program. Both types of evaluation can be conducted on a given program. Formative evaluation is somewhat more flexible in that adjustments and corrections can be made to evaluation procedures during their ongoing activities.

Few counselors regularly review programs or client services (Hiebert, 1994). If a program review is conducted, often clients are not consulted regarding the process. Counselors report feeling that the attention and administration of time given to program review, evaluation, and improvement is inadequate. But recognition of these concerns does not provide sufficient incentive to change them.

A framework is necessary that includes outcome and process as equal partners in the counseling enterprise (Hiebert, 1994). Process without outcome is not counseling any more than is outcome without process. When counseling is successful, counselor and client processes will lead to client-learning outcomes. These learning outcomes will impact motivation, self-awareness, capacity for self-direction, personal agency, and other skills necessary for the global changes. If counseling is to survive reduced resources and increased accountability, a new approach for the role of evaluation needs to be developed. An attempt to evaluate career and employment counseling must begin with the question: What are the legitimate processes and outcomes of counseling? When is career counseling effective, with whom, under what conditions, and on which outcome dimensions?

Another approach to evaluation is a study of cost benefits as an indicator of effectiveness. This requires a different mindset for most vocational counselors and is complicated to achieve. However, "if the economic benefits to individuals or to society exceed the cost of career guidance or career counseling one can argue that counselors are generators of resources, not simply consumers of them" (Herr & Cramer, 1996, p. 712). Although there is an expectation that counseling should produce results that have a direct socioeconomic impact, often the more legitimate outcomes of counseling are the learning outcomes (Kileen & Kidd, 1991; Kileen, White & Watts, 1993). For instance, when a client has learned effective coping skills regarding financial challenges, family conflict, and lack of support, counseling should be considered successful, even if the immediate result is not job placement.

In his 1994 article, Flynn discusses approaches to the evaluation of the effectiveness of career counseling. He cites the work of Fretz (1981); Spokane (1991); Kirschnes, Hoffman, and Hill (1994); and Nevo (1990), among others, as resources for implementing evaluative processes. Through the interchange with a counselor, a client ideally learns about him/herself, discovers information about jobs and occupations, builds a network of social support, and receives feedback and positive reinforcement. Understanding how personal dynamics can interfere with career decisions is important.

Flynn summarizes Spokane's (1991) hypotheses about the nature of the career-counseling process and the reasons why clients appear to benefit in important ways.

1. The career counseling process can be validly represented by a model composed of three states (beginning, activation, and termination) and eight subphases (opening, aspiring, loosening, assessment, inquiry, commitment, execution, and follow-through).

2. Each substage of the process involves a key therapeutic task, a counselor process and technique needed to achieve the task, and an expected client reaction to its successful completion . . .

3. Before career counseling intervention can begin, clients need to clarify (with the help of the counselor) the nature of the decisions and conflicts they face.

4. Effective career counseling instills a sense of hope in the client that a reasonably congruent career option will be found and implemented. (p. 275)

These processes can provide the basis for the development of an evaluation model of career counseling, and the authors cited above give a variety of ideas for developing evaluation procedures.

Approaches to Evaluation Using Existing Models

Evaluation models developed in schools have broader application to vocational counseling. Comprehensive guidance programs provided to local districts allow counselors to respond to data specific to state and national concerns. Counselors and counselor educators can use the subject matter (Gysbers, Hughey, Starr & Lapan, 1992) of comprehensive guidance programs to develop practical means of gathering such needed outcome data. They can also develop evaluation scales that are easy to use and link student-perceived mastery of both career and personal guidance competencies to critical educational outcomes (Multon & Lapan, 1995).

Competencies and Indicators

Competencies and indicators form a Texas model called Texas Evaluation Model for Professional School Counselors (TEMPSC). TEMPSC evaluates school counselors' performance based on the seven core roles and competencies described in Texas Counseling Association's job description for the professional school counselor: program management, guidance, counseling, consultation, coordination, assessment, and professionalism. Each *role* on the TEMPSC Performance Evaluation Form is described by *competencies,* competencies are described by *indicators,* and indicators are detailed by *descriptors.* All seven roles and role sublevels described in the TEMPSC are not all equally applicable to every counselor. If a guidance director wanted to develop a program and get specific feedback on the performances of the counselors in a certain role, there are particular subscales that can be used to address that area. Much of the information here can be applied to outcomes for all vocational counselors. Examples of TEMPSC roles for guidance, counseling, and assessment—their competencies, indicators, and descriptors—follow:

ROLE: GUIDANCE

Competency 2.3: Guides individuals and groups of students through the development of educational and career plans

Indicator 2.31: Involves students in personalized educational and career planning.

DESCRIPTORS:

Helps students establish goals and planning skills

Assists students in determining their abilities, achievements, interests, and goals

Makes effective use of consultation skills as needed in guidance process

Encourages parental input into student planning

Interprets tests results to students in a meaningful manner allowing them to focus on their strengths and improve on their weaknesses

Guides groups of students in the application of their test results to their educational and career plans

Correctly assesses student's educational and career aspirations and information needs

Makes recommendations based on appropriate criteria

Uses appropriately sized groups

Indicator 2.32 Presents relevant information accurately and without bias.

DESCRIPTORS:

Makes no significant errors

Presents information so that students can process/internalize it

Uses vocabulary appropriate to the students

Explains content clearly

Presents appropriate amounts of information

Stresses important points

Clarifies students' misunderstanding

Uses accurate terminology

Makes up-to-date educational and occupational information resources available/accessible to students

Uses materials effectively

Is knowledgeable about the range of education and career alternatives and the values of each (p. 17)

ROLE: COUNSELING

Competency 3.1: Counsels individual students with presenting needs/concerns

Indicator 3.11 Provides counseling systematically.

DESCRIPTORS:

Responds appropriately to students at their maturity levels in kindergarten through the twelfth grade.

Responds to the identified needs of students, such as but not limited to career and educational development issues (p.18).

ROLE: ASSESSMENT

Competency 6.2: Interprets test and other appraisal results appropriately

Indicator 6.23 Interprets tests and other appraisal results to students and their parents.

DESCRIPTORS:

Interprets tests and other appraisal results to students in a meaningful manner, assisting them to focus on their strengths and improve upon their weaknesses.

Interprets test and other appraisal results to parents, assisting them to better understand their student's scholastic abilities, achievement, aptitude, interests, and career development (p. 24)

The Missouri Comprehensive Guidance Program (MCGP) is based on three content domains: (1) knowledge of self and others, (2) career planning and exploration, and (3) educational and vocational development. In this program, counselor duties should include:

- implementing curriculum
- counseling individuals and groups with respect to educational and career plans
- consulting with teachers and parents
- referring students to appropriate agencies
- coordinating, conducting, and being involved with activities that improve the operation of the school
- evaluating and revising the guidance program
- continuing professional growth (Gysbers et al., 1992).

A schematic presentation of this evaluation program, which contains both formative and summative evaluation, is presented in Table 3.1.

Focus Groups Bloch (1992) proposes a model for using focus groups to evaluate career development programs. Focus groups provide the opportunity to appraise the knowledge and experiences of a variety of people with a common interest. Through carefully structured questions, materials, and planned interactions within the group a focused situation is created to yield the desired information in a relatively short period of time. Career Information System of Iowa

**Table 3.1 Personnel Job Description, Supervision
and Evaluation Procedures**

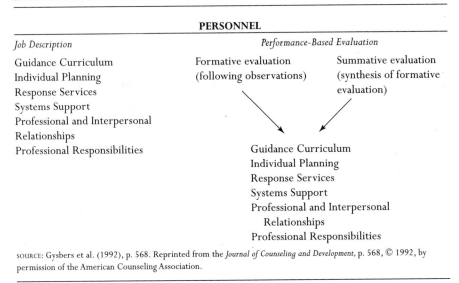

PERSONNEL	
Job Description	*Performance-Based Evaluation*

Guidance Curriculum
Individual Planning
Response Services
Systems Support
Professional and Interpersonal
Relationships
Professional Responsibilities

Formative evaluation   Summative evaluation
(following observations)   (synthesis of formative
                              evaluation)

Guidance Curriculum
Individual Planning
Response Services
Systems Support
Professional and Interpersonal
Relationships
Professional Responsibilities

SOURCE: Gysbers et al. (1992), p. 568. Reprinted from the *Journal of Counseling and Development*, p. 568, © 1992, by permission of the American Counseling Association.

(CISI) uses focus groups to evaluate the system's effectiveness for the various populations who use it.

Advantages of focus groups include expediency, since within one session, opinions can be gathered from a variety of people; cost effectiveness; and group interaction processes (e.g., brainstorming, role-playing, image projection). Focus groups can be used in a variety of settings. They are helpful for program evaluation, modification, planning, and development (Bloch, 1992). However, a focus group cannot replace quantitative studies.

Performance Assessment Another way to evaluate programs is performance assessment. "In performance assessments, students are active participants, creating answers, products and performances to demonstrate what they have learned. Performance assessment tasks are often based on real-world problems" (Hutchinson, 1995, p. 3). Techniques include group projects, interviews, demonstrations, role-plays, and portfolios. One constructivist model of performance assessment, Pathways, consists of five modules:

1. "Knowing about Yourself, Knowing about Careers"

2. "Succeeding with the Résumé and the Application"

3. "Succeeding with the Interview"

4. "Solving Problems on the Job"
5. "Anger Management on the Job" (Hutchinson, 1995, p. 4).

The American School Counselors Association (ASCA) and National Occupational Information Coordinating Committee (NOICC) portfolio system uses a performance assessment, "Get a Life: Your Personal Planning Profile," and contains sections on self-knowledge, life roles, educational development, and career exploration.

In performance assessments, students are motivated, teachers are more accountable to students for teaching concepts and skills that are transferable to the real world; and teachers and counselors gain current information about what students are learning in the classroom. However, performance assessments have never shown that students generalize concepts to more global outcomes.

While many of the evaluation programs cited have come from schools, they provide the seeds that vocational counselors can use in any setting to evaluate their work. More research needs to be done to develop outcome studies and evaluation of the process in which the individual counselor and the client participate.

ASSESSMENT IN CAREER COUNSELING

Assessment has a long-established tradition in career counseling and vocational psychology. Students and practitioners need to be aware of the uses and abuses of assessment. A complete discussion of assessment procedures is beyond the scope of our text. However, Kaplan and Saccuzzo (1997) is a well-written, comprehensive source for further discussion of such procedures. Another valuable resource is the **Code of Fair Testing Practices in Education** (1988) (see Appendix 1), written to be understood by the general public, especially test-takers and/or their parents or guardians. An overview of the basic principles of assessment is presented, with relevance to multicultural and diverse populations.

Basic Principles

Assessment refers to a procedure used to evaluate an individual in terms of current and future functioning (Kaplan & Saccuzzo, 1997). The general public, as well as graduate students studying to become clinical practitioners, often confuse the terms "assessment" and "testing." Tests are one of the specific tools of the overall assessment procedure. **Tests** are measurement instruments that quantify behavior, and are sometimes called an **assessment tool**. A **test battery** is a collection of tests whose scores are used together in appraising an individual.

Tests and inventories can serve a number of functions in career counseling. Tests can motivate people by exploring previously unconsidered career options; but tests can limit, as well, by discouraging lower-income minorities from pursuing academic areas that appear out of their reach, or by indicating that women are best suited for traditional careers. Interpretation of test results requires that the counselor possess a thorough knowledge of the test—including its psychometric properties—the clinical background to understand the test-taking client, and the ability to communicate test results in a straightforward, understandable fashion (Brown, Brooks & Associates, 1991). Tests do not measure intrinsic qualities, but rather qualities that are learned and that may vary from situation to situation.

There is continued interest in both the use of tests and descriptions of tests. For instance, ten million copies of the Self-Directed Search (SDS) have been administered.

> Walsh (1990) estimated that in 1988 1.5 million people took the Myers-Briggs Type Indicator (Myers & McCaulley, 1985), and 1.0 million the Strong Interest Inventory (Hansen & Campbell, 1985). The Armed Services Vocational Aptitude Battery (ASVAB: U.S. Department of Defense, 1992) purports to test 1 million a year and the ACT Assessment (American College Testing, 1988) 1.5 million. The United States Office of Technological Assessment (1992) report "Testing in American Schools" asserts that since 1970, sales revenue from Kindergarten to 12 standardized tests has doubled, while enrollment has declined approximately 10%. (Zytowski, 1994, p. 220).

Not only are assessment instruments being used to a greater extent, the number of books published on the role of testing in counseling has also increased. *The Journal of Career Assessment* is devoted solely to the topic. Kapes, Mastie, and Whitfield (1994) have written *A Counselor's Guide to Career Assessment Instruments*, already in its third edition. *Using Assessment Results,* by Zunker and Norris (1997), is now in its fifth edition. A plethora of instruments are also available with new ones being developed annually. Not all assessment procedures are tests. Strictly speaking, an assessment device is a test when its procedures for administration, scoring, and interpretation are standardized.

Test Administration Test administration refers to the act of giving a test (Kaplan & Saccuzzo, 1997), and to the procedures surrounding the giving of a test. The test administrator is the person who gives the test (Kaplan & Saccuzzo, 1997). This person must be qualified. A graduate student obtaining supervision at a practicum and/or internship site should have, at the very least, relevant course work and an on-site supervisor qualified to administer any tests that the supervisee is expected to administer. A supervisee, much less a clinical practitioner, should not administer any test for which they have not received adequate educational training, practice, and supervision. The prioritizing of politics and economics over ethics when it comes to clinical practice and client welfare is simply unsupportable. These ethical issues are discussed further in the *Standards for Educational and Psychological Testing* (1985), by the joint committee of the American Education Research Association, the American Psychological Association, and the National Council on Measurement in Education.

A **standardization sample** (also known as a **normative sample**) is a comparison group consisting of individuals who have been administered a test under standard conditions; the instructions, format, and general procedures are usually outlined in the test manual for the **standardized administration** of a test (Kaplan & Saccuzzo, 1997).

Types of Tests An **individual test** can be given to only one person at a time by a test administrator; **group tests** can be given to more than one person at a time (Kaplan & Saccuzzo, 1997). A **norm-referenced test** evaluates each individual relative to a normative group (Kaplan & Saccuzzo, 1997) or standardization sample. **Norms** summarize the performance of a group of individuals on which a test was standardized, and usually include the **mean** and **standard deviation** for a reference group and information on how to translate a raw score into a percentile rank. (A mean is the arithmetic average of a set of scores on a variable. A standard deviation is the square root of the average deviation around the mean, and is used as a measure of variability in a distribution of scores.) The standard deviation squared equals the **variance. Percentile ranks** refer to the proportion of scores that meet or fall below a particular score.

Ability tests "measure skills in terms of speed, accuracy, or both" (Kaplan & Saccuzzo, 1997, p. 11). When taking an ability test, faster or more accurate responses mean a better score on a particular characteristic. For example, on a Scholastic Aptitude Test (SAT) or Graduate Record Examination (GRE), the more mathematics problems one can solve in the amount of time allotted on such subtests, the higher one's score on the ability to solve such problems.

There are three types of ability tests: **achievement tests, aptitude tests,** and **intelligence tests.** Achievement tests measure previous learning. For instance, a test that measures how many words one can correctly spell is a spelling achievement test (Kaplan & Saccuzzo, 1997). Aptitude tests measure the potential for acquiring a specific skill. With a certain amount of training, education, and experience, one's aptitude for a given pursuit can be developed. For example, music aptitude refers in part to how well one might be able to play a musical instrument, or how accomplished one might become, given a certain number of lessons. A further example would be cultivating an aptitude for math and science among adolescent females, which is crucial for their current personal and academic well-being (Orenstein, 1994) and for their long-term occupational prospects. Often there is a gap between young people's confidence and their ability and aptitude. Intelligence tests measure the potential to (1) solve problems, (2) adapt to changing circumstances, and (3) profit from experiences (Kaplan & Saccuzzo, 1997).

Achievement, aptitude, and intelligence tests are not always easy to distinguish from one another because they are highly interrelated. Attempts to separate prior learning from the potential for learning have met with little success. Given the considerable overlap among achievement, aptitude, and intelligence tests, all three concepts now are encompassed under the term **human ability tests** (Kaplan & Saccuzzo, 1997).

Personality tests measure overt and covert traits, temperaments, and dispositions (Kaplan & Saccuzzo, 1997). For instance, the tendency to remain aloof from others, while not requiring any special skill or ability, reflects the varying preferences of some people who typically prefer or are disposed to remain isolated. **Structured** or **objective personality tests** are based on self-report statements where the test-taker answers "true" or "false" or "yes" or "no." **Projective personality tests** provide ambiguous test stimuli where response requirements are less clear. "Rather than being asked to choose among alternative responses, as in structured personality tests, the individual is asked to provide a spontaneous response" (Kaplan & Saccuzzo, pp. 10–11). As part of any vocational counseling activity it is essential to be familiar with different types of tests, what test results can and cannot indicate, and how to incorporate this information into the client's total profile.

Unlike the assessment tools mentioned above, **interest inventories** and **values clarification activities** are unique to vocational psychology and career counseling. Interest inventories usually result in a profile where clients' responses to questions about interests in activities, competencies, and occupations are matched with interests of persons already working in various occupations who report that they enjoy their work. Interest inventories do not tell the client what to do for a living, but rather expands their options of occupations to consider. There are values scales inventories available as well as values clarification activities, usually based on the seven standards for constructing a value (Raths, Harmin & Simon, 1966) presented in Table 2.1. We include values clarification activities when we teach Master's level courses in life planning and career development. Many of our students who do such an activity for the first time as a class exercise say they wish they had had the chance to do so earlier in their lives. Both interest and value inventories are included in a vocational assessment test battery, as well as personality and skills inventories.

Reliability and Validity Two of the most fundamental concepts of standardized assessment are reliability and validity. **Reliability** refers to "the accuracy, dependability, consistency, or repeatability of test results. In more technical terms, reliability refers to the degree to which test scores are free of measurement error" (Kaplan & Saccuzzo, 1997, p. 12). Classical test theory assumes that each person has a true score on an ability or characteristic that would be obtained if there were no errors in measurement. Since assessment instruments are imperfect, the observed score that is obtained for each person may differ from the person's true score on an ability or characteristic. The index of the amount of error in a test or measure is known as the **standard error of measurement.** Classical test theory assumes that errors of measurement are random errors that will be the same for all people. The standard error of measurement tells how much a score varies on the average from a true score. The standard deviation of an observed score and the reliability of the test are used to compute estimates of the standard error of measurement. Types of reliability are presented in Table 3.2.

Validity refers to "the meaning and usefulness of test results . . . [and] the degree to which a certain inference or interpretation based on a test is appropriate" (Kaplan & Saccuzzo, 1997, p. 12). **Inferences** are logical deductions made from evidence about something that one cannot observe directly. Given that validity is the evidence for inferences made about a test score, there are three types of evidence, or validity. These three categories of validity are devised by the joint committee of the American Education Research Association, the American Psychological Association, and the National Council on Measurement in Educa-

TABLE 3.2 Types of Reliability

test-retest reliability	a method for estimating how much measurement error is caused by administering the test at two different points in time; test-retest reliability is usually estimated from the correlation between performance on two different administrations of the test
alternate forms/parallel forms reliability	the method of reliability assessment used to evaluate the error associated with the use of a particular set of items; equivalent forms of a test are developed by generating two forms using the same rules; the correlation between the two forms is the estimate of alternate forms' reliability
split-half reliability	a method for evaluating reliability in which a test is split into two halves; the correlation between the halves of the test, corrected for the shortened length of the halves, is used as an estimate of reliability

SOURCE: Kaplan & Saccuzzo (1997)

TABLE 3.3 Types of Validity

1. **content validity**	the extent to which the content of a test represents the conceptual domain it is designed to cover
2. **criterion validity** (aka **empirical** or **statistical validity**)	the extent to which a test score corresponds to an accurate measure of interest; the measure of interest is called the criterion
a. **predictive validity**	the extent to which a test forecasts scores on the criterion at some future time
b. **concurrent validity**	a form of criterion validity in which the test and the criterion are administered at the same time
3. **construct validity**	a process used to establish the meaning of a test through a series of studies; to evaluate construct validity, a researcher simultaneously defines some constructs and develops the information to measure it; in the studies, observed correlations between the test and other measures come to define the meaning of the test
a. **convergent validity**	a form of construct validity whereby evidence is obtained to demonstrate that a test measures the same attribute as do other measures that purport to measure the same thing
b. **discriminant validity**	a form of construct validity whereby evidence is obtained to demonstrate that a test measures something different from what other available tests measure

source: Kaplan & Saccuzzo (1997)

tion, and appear in *Standards for Education and Psychological Testing* (1985). The three types of validity and their subcategories are presented in Table 3.3.

Another type of test and two other types of validity deserve mention. A **criterion-referenced test** describes the specific types of skills, tasks, or knowledge of an individual relative to a well-defined mastery criterion. The content of criterion-referenced tests, therefore, is limited to a set of well-defined objectives. **Differential validity** is the extent to which a test has different meanings for different groups of people, such as a test that may be a valid predictor of college success for White students but not for Black students. **Face validity** is the extent to which items on a test appear to be meaningful and relevant; face validity is actually not a form of validity, since face validity is not a basis for inference (Kaplan & Saccuzzo, 1997).

One can have reliability without validity. But it is logically impossible to demonstrate that an unreliable test is valid. If the test is not reliable, attempts to demonstrate the validity of a test will be futile.

Relevance for Multicultural and Diverse Populations

Stages of the Assessment Process. The practitioner's role is to consider multicultural worldviews (Fouad, 1993). Many trainees, as well as seasoned professionals, can

Practical Applications

The terms we have just defined may be familiar to readers who have taken courses in statistics, measurement and evaluation, or testing and assessment. As faculty members, we have heard graduate students complain about why they have to take such courses, especially since some students do not anticipate that they will be conducting standardized assessments after graduation as part of their future employment. These complaints are short-sighted. The practitioners' role is to retain a solid understanding of the basic principles of assessment for several reasons. Among them: to be cognizant of the standardized assessments available to clients, to make appropriate referrals if they are not adequately trained to administer such assessment instruments themselves, and to be professionally conversant with their colleagues who do administer and score such tests. Sometimes the practitioner may have to explain in everyday language to their clients the reasons for an assessment referral, the purpose of the assessment procedure, and the results of the assessment, particularly if the client has not had the test results clearly explained to them by the test administrator.

fall into the trap of disrespecting their clientele's lifestyles. Clients' racial and ethnic backgrounds, culture, language usage(s), socioeconomic status, gender, sexual orientation, and religious affiliation can impact self-images and the opportunity structure of the world of work. Consequently, the initial problem clarification stage between practitioner and client (Walsh & Betz, 1990) can result in barriers to effective practitioner-client communication. At this stage, for example, clients' individualistic and collectivistic orientations need to be discerned by the practitioner for the assessment procedure to be viable.

During the second stage of the assessment process, information-gathering (Walsh & Betz, 1990) expectations need to be clarified, especially since most clients will be unfamiliar with the need to self-disclose and the limits of confidentiality (Fouad, 1993). Sue and Sue (1990) remind us that various assessment procedures have been used to maintain the status quo and to keep minority individuals in their place. This abuse of power may have been experienced by multicultural clientele in past situations, and so the vocational practitioner needs to be mindful not to stereotype clients.

Understanding the information obtained is the third stage of the assessment process (Walsh & Betz, 1990). Data interpretation and theoretical conceptualization occur at this point. If rapport was not established during the information gathering stage, the information subsequently obtained may be incomplete, marked by careless responses, or by socially desirable responses. Current theories of vocational development inadequately consider the impact of race and social class on career development (Fouad, 1993) and are biased toward an individualistic orientation.

The fourth and final stage of the assessment process is coping with the problem (Walsh & Betz, 1990). Practitioners' ongoing challenge is to allow clients to self-define which solutions are compatible with their worldview. Practitioners must avoid imposing their own mindset on clients who do not share their background.

Understanding Gender Dynamics. More than an awareness of gender differences, the practitioner's role is to understand gender dynamics (Hackett & Lonborg, 1993). For example, a **gender role analysis** assesses the potential costs and benefits for women and men in terms of adopting traditional and nontraditional gender role behavior. These measures are presented in Hackett and Lonborg, pages 210–211. In addition to understanding basic principles of assessment, practitioners need to (a) be well versed in literature on the career development of women, (b) view assessment as an integral component—not a discrete activity—of career interventions, (c) be aware of possibilities for one's own bias, (d) use a gender role analysis as part of assessment, (e) consider qualitative alternatives to standardized testing, and (f) continually examine and work on one's own gender-related issues to assure maximum effectiveness and ethical practice in occupational counseling with women.

Limited Consideration of Cultural Factors. In a review of *The Clinical Practice of Career Assessment* (1991), Bowman (1995) searched the table of contents, the index, and the chapters and examples provided, but found no mention of racial and ethnic issues in assessment. She further warns that unawareness on the practitioner's part of the **potential biases in career assessment instruments** can lead to the dissemination of misleading information to minority clients at best, and potentially damaging information at worst. At issue is an etic perspective versus an emic perspective in assessment methods. **Etic** perspectives emphasize universal human behaviors; many cultures are examined and compared, presumably from a position outside those cultures. **Emic** perspectives are culture-specific, examining human behavior from criteria related to the internal characteristics of the culture, presumably from a position within that culture (Dana, 1993).

Another way to look at this issue is the three types of **test bias** by Walsh and Betz (1990). **Content bias** occurs when test items are more familiar to one racial or ethnic group than another. Experience has shown that it can include familiarity of objects and terms based upon one's geographical region. Individuals from non-Judeo-Christian, mainstream, American cultures also may encounter content biases. **Internal structure bias** pertains to the relationship among items of a test and the manner in which test takers perceive the items. **Selection bias** occurs when a test's predictive validity is differential across groups.

Similarly, Suzuki and Kugler (1995) summarize concerns about the androcentric tradition in intelligence and personality assessment with multicultural populations. These concerns include (a) inappropriate test content, (b) inappropriate standardization samples, (c) examiner and language bias, (d) inequitable social consequences, (e) measurement of different constructs, (f) differential predictive validity, and (g) differences in test-taking skills.

Values held by multicultural clients can impact vocational test taking and career decision-making (Fouad, 1993). Little empirical evidence exists to guide the practitioner's role. Like gender role analysis, measuring acculturation can correct for cultural differences when multicultural clients are not from a White American cultural background (Dana, 1993; Grieger & Ponterotto, 1995; Paniagua, 1994; Suzuki & Kugler, 1995). Acculturation as a moderator variable helps to reliably "estimate . . . the potential contribution of cultural variance to an assessment procedure" (Dana, 1993, p. 113). A host of acculturation indexes are presented in Dana (1993, chapter 7) and in Paniagua (1994, chapter 8).

We advocate that it should become common practice to administer acculturation indices whenever multicultural populations are participants in career-related research and when vocational assessment instruments are re-normed. This would entail a commitment throughout the academic discipline, from scholars and practitioners of both the dominant cultural background and those of other racial and ethnic origins. Tackling the complexities of occupational preferences/abilities/aptitudes as moderated by acculturation could transform vocational psychology into an academic discipline that truly mirrors diversity. The issue of whether acculturation is of intrinsic interest to scholars (Tinsley, 1994) would be transcended. Acculturation has mainly been the interest of racial and ethnic minority scholars and practitioners. If everyone in the field started adding acculturation indices to re-norming activities and other career-related research, this would show the respect due for diversity of the U.S. population. The results of such a change could show up in the academic discipline within ten to fifteen years. By vocational psychology's 100th anniversary—that is, the year 2009—the field could be well on its way to becoming more relevant to a broader range of persons than ever before!

African Americans. The research literature has a long way to go in developing normative samples using African Americans (Bowman, 1995). Normative samples will have to encompass within-group differences for any career assessment instruments to be reliable and valid. With African Americans, if norms on various assessment tools are not available, Bowman contends that it is the practitioner's responsibility to assist in the development of such norms.

Cultural variables that may affect assessment and treatment of African-American clients include racial labels, **familism** and **role flexibility,** religious beliefs, **healthy paranoia,** and the language of African-American clients (Paniagua, 1994). The following discussion of such variables pertains to vocational and career assessment.

1. *Racial labels.* These have varied historically over time and included *Colored, Negro, Black,* and *African American.* Colored and Negro are now considered derogatory and are inappropriate for practitioner use. Black emphasizes skin color while African American emphasizes cultural heritage. Practitioners are advised to ask clients directly how *they* identify themselves in terms of racial labels.

2. *Familism and role flexibility.* The extent to which nuclear and extended families are an influence in African-American clients' lives should be assessed. Familism among African Americans can include both biological and nonbiological members. Collectivism is more likely to be valued than individualism, but this is contextual. A **genogram** is a useful tool for practitioners to compile for illustrating the extended family tree and highlighting the role of work in the familial and personal domains (Richardson, 1993). Patterns of educational attainment, employment in "protected careers," and work histories of individual family members can influence African-American clients' perceived occupational opportunities. In Chapter 8 we present a work-related genogram of five living generations of one family.

   Role flexibility refers to who is the head of the family or a parental figure at any given time, and also to competencies in performing work tasks that have traditionally been part of the gender division of labor. Role flexibility can impact educational attainment and occupational development of individuals and families. Rigidity in terms of gender roles and work tasks can limit individuals and families.

3. *Religious beliefs/church affiliations.* This should not be automatically assumed. Within-group differences will be evident here. If an African-American client is an active church member, practitioners should ask if the client has discussed vocational and career concerns with anyone in church. Inclusion of these third parties in occupational exploration activities is a possibility.

4. *Healthy paranoia.* A legacy of past slavery and continued racism, healthy paranoia may be part of some African Americans' social and psychological development. A suspicion of others of different races and values can impact client-practitioner interaction and client occupational development.

Non-African-American practitioners should not be surprised if they encounter some healthy paranoia among their African-American clients from time to time. Healthy paranoia, not unique to African Americans, can characterize any individual or subgroup that has experienced oppression. A lack of awareness and respect for this phenomenon can make a practitioner appear racist at worst, or give the impression of **privileged complacency** at best.

5. *Language.* The use of Black English and street talk among subgroups of African Americans may not be understood by some practitioners and should be dealt with in a matter-of-fact request for clarification/translation. A very real, if uncomfortable, issue is the extent to which some African-American clients can speak Standard American English (SAE). One's mastery of SAE will impact educational attainment and occupational opportunities among African Americans as well as other minorities, as controversies about Black English and bilingual education in recent years have shown (Associated Press, 1996a, 1996b; "'Black English' is stumbling block for black children," December 27, 1996).

Asian Americans. Leong and Gim-Chung (1995) offer guidelines on conducting and using career assessment with Asian Americans:

1. Use of career assessment instruments needs to be undertaken with caution, since there are a lack of cultural norms and empirical research demonstrating the cultural validity of such instruments.

2. Probable sources of bias within theories of career choice (such as the North American emphasis on individualism versus the Asian emphasis on collectivism) may turn up as multiple sources of bias in the assessment process.

3. Certain elements in Asian-American test-taking attitudes may be important to keep in mind. Asian Americans socialized into an authoritarian family may be less likely to question or challenge the practitioner who is viewed as an authority figure. Thus, when an Asian-American client is referred for assessment, the reason and goals for the assessment procedure may need to be carefully explained to such clients.

4. The test interpretation/feedback session with Asian Americans is likely to be influenced by cultural factors. Two important interpersonal dimensions are **"maintaining face"** and preventing **"loss of face,"** the violations of which can interfere with effective use of the assessment results. There may also be a need for more structured approaches to test interpretations with Asian Americans than would be the case with other clients.

Hispanics. Several concerns of assessing other multicultural populations relate to Hispanics as well. The practitioner's role is to evaluate Hispanic clients' proficiency with English, especially if a Spanish language version of the instrument is available and more appropriate. Appropriate norms are another concern, and whether White norms will be used if Hispanic norms are unavailable (Cervantes & Acosta, 1992; Dana, 1993; Fouad, 1993). The wide range of career assessment instruments may not have the same meaning and interpretation for Hispanics (i.e., differential validity, internal structure bias, selection bias); further research is needed on the affects of acculturation, language proficiency, socioeconomic status, geographic location, and generational status (Fouad, 1995). Recent immigrant status may have a particular impact on psychosocial stressors among Hispanics and can affect assessment results, especially client's reason for immigration (i.e., political refugee versus seeking work), and socioeconomic and educational levels (Cervantes & Acosta, 1992).

We currently work in predominantly Hispanic cities. Many of our counseling graduate students come from the public school teaching profession. From what our students, our clinical supervision of counselors within the schools, and our own client caseloads tell us, we know that strict attention to the issues of language proficiency, appropriate norms, and acculturation does not always occur. Nor is due consideration given to differentiating the effects of income level and ethnicity. Beyond concerns of the content of our Master's students' academic training and the appropriate use of various assessment instruments with Hispanics, we are especially mindful that internal politics within educational institutions continues to impinge upon the educational attainment of many Hispanic children and youth with whom our graduates work. Our impression is that the value of developing occupational awareness among Hispanic children and youth and their families does not appear to be a high priority among educational administrators, teacher educators, and a substantial number of school counselors already in the field.

Native Americans. Martin (1995) discusses five moderating variables relevant to developing an assessment plan with Native Americans:

1. *Language Usage.* Use of native language and proficiency in English can have intervening affects on the assessment process. An informal determination of the client's level of English proficiency may be necessary. A native-speaking interpreter may be needed. A developmental history of language usage may be in order. Word recognition, word meanings, spelling, comprehension, narrative analysis, oral language skills, receptive language skills, and those skills that will be most important in the work setting all need to be considered. For those clients who have English usage skills, conventional career assessment instruments are considered appropriate.

2. *Cultural orientation*. It will be useful to determine the extent that home, family, and community figure into the worldview of Native Americans. Varying levels of acculturation will also impact how similarly to the American mainstream Native Americans will view occupational issues. A case study process is helpful in understanding how culture impacts career decision-making. Essential elements to include are (a) family structure, (b) client perceptions of the acculturative process, (c) client involvement in traditional ceremonies, (d) client financial role within the family structure, (e) client short- and long-term goals related to living on one's reservation, and (f) client work-related values (e.g., academic achievement, professional status, income, work independence, job-related and upward mobility).

3. *Home community*. Environmental context, especially for those living on or near reservations, is vital to enhancing a Native-American person's career decision-making. The client's history on and off the reservation, work experiences, and vocational training need to be clarified. Family occupational history and that of close friends is useful information to gather. Career developmental tasks and their relation to social networks and traditional value systems also need to be considered.

4. *Family system*. The extent of involvement in nuclear and extended families will vary by individual. A traditional, extended family orientation may mean that individual decision-making may be subordinated to group decision-making, since decisions may impact the family, not just the individual. A full exploration of values pertaining to family, homeland, tribal traditions, and community provides a more comprehensive view of the consequences of career decision-making. Other factors to consider are: how decisions are made within the family system, who the major decision-makers are, client's family roles and responsibilities, family members' expectations for the client's career pursuits, and family willingness to support the client in career planning, vocational training, job searches, placement, and retention.

5. *Communication style*. Maximizing informal interactions during the assessment process with Native American clients can decrease any perceptions of the test administrator as an adversary. The attending, influencing, and focusing microskills of Allen E. Ivey and his colleagues (Ivey & Gluckstern, 1984; Ivey, Gluckstern & Ivey, 1982) are proposed as minimizing misunderstandings created by differences in language, culture, environment, or lifestyle.

Gay, Lesbian, and Bisexual Persons. Basic career assessment procedures need to be modified to take sexual orientation factors into account when the client is gay/lesbian/bisexual (Gelberg & Chojnacki, 1996). Oftentimes, linkages to sexual orientation are not considered in the make-up of various career assessment instruments and the meaning of their results (e.g., differential validity). Sexual orientation does affect career and life planning. Heterosexism and homophobia are rampant in the workplace (Woods, 1994). **Heterosexism** refers to the culturally conditioned bias that heterosexism is intrinsically superior to homosexuality (Rochlin, 1985), while **homophobia** refers to an irrational dread and loathing of homosexuality and homosexual people (Weinberg, 1972, cited in Rochlin, 1985).

To counter the shortcomings of heterosexist-based assessment instruments, Gelberg and Chojnacki (1996) suggest a semi-structured interview as a starting point with gay, lesbian, and bisexual persons before proceeding on to the conventional vocational assessment route. But two major problems will persist: (1) Current methods of assessment may be biased and/or incomplete in assessing a gay/lesbian/bisexual client's interests, values, experiences, or skills. (2) Career counseling models for gay, lesbian, and bisexual persons fail to consider the full repertoire of career developmental tasks and processes.

People with Disabilities. Career development can be curtailed among people with disabilities. They may have had limited opportunities for social and vocational experiences (Curnow, 1989), which can show up on test results. The practitioner's role is to consider the unique problems and needs of people with disabilities that require specialized services.

Regarding secondary special education students, "*Appropriate* assessment relates primarily to asking the 'right' questions (validity), and *competent* assessment pertains primarily to the issues of how well the questions are asked (reliability)" (Clark & Kolstoe, 1995, pp. 104–105, italics in original). The "right" questions come out of the domains of values, attitudes, habits, human relationships, occupational information, and job and daily living skills. This perspective expands the assessment emphasis beyond academic and cognitive performance or on work and vocational outcomes to include other critical concern areas.

Intelligence tests should be used with great caution and only by test administrators who are sensitive to the specific applications of these test results for decisions regarding vocational training or employment (Clark & Kolstoe, 1995). Furthermore, information obtained from intelligence tests should be but one part of the information gathered. Academic achievement tests are of questionable use for some special-needs youth. A functional, life-career development and transition approach may be more relevant. Achievement tests are unlikely to answer questions such as: Can the adolescent read directions, measure flour, make change, handle his or her own income? These criterion-referenced approaches can provide discrete bits of information that have some predictive utility.

While aptitude tests generally are not used in secondary special education programs, performance aptitude tests that measure manual and finger dexterity, speed, ability to follow directions, and persistence, do have some direct applicability. Interest inventories should be used selectively as gross screening devices and for structuring a process for self-study and guidance activities. Self-study can include formal and informal explorational activities to allow students an opportunity to become acquainted with unfamiliar work activities and environments. Direct interviews are a useful guidance tool towards the goal of better decision-making and goal-setting through self-awareness. Little effort has been expended on administering personality tests to youths with mental and educational handicaps, with more attention given to behavior observations, self-report devices, and interviews.

A comprehensive, ongoing vocational assessment is a necessary and prerequisite condition in creating any vocational education or training program for persons with mental retardation (Levinson, Peterson & Elston, 1994). Typically, this comprehensive assessment entails an evaluation of (a) mental ability, (b) academic achievement, (c) sensory processes and motor skills, (d) vocational aptitudes, (e) adaptive behavior and social skills, (f) functional living skills and appropriate work habits. Data on each of these areas includes information derived from interviews, paper and pencil tests, performance tests, work samples (i.e., tasks common in a number of jobs within an occupational area that are performed by a client under the supervision of a trained observer), simulated work experiences (i.e., real jobs performed by a client in a highly sheltered, supervised situation), and actual on-the-job work experiences. Naturally, the data-gathering techniques emphasized within an assessment program frequently depend on the philosophical approach taken when conducting vocational assessments. Nevertheless, a comprehensive vocational assessment program makes use of all of the above data-gathering techniques and involves a variety of personnel.

Traditionally, the assessment of individuals with mental retardation has focused on vocational aptitudes and interests, as well as functional living skills and appropriate work habits (Levinson et al., 1994). Results from such assessments have then been used to predict vocational potential. But there are two problems with traditional assessment when used with people with mental retardation. First, there often is a minimal, direct relationship between the behaviors sampled by a test and those behaviors required for successful job performance. Using test behaviors to predict work behaviors is inappropriate. Second, traditional assessment focuses on products of past learning. This approach assumes that an individual's previous experiences have been sufficient for such learning to occur. Given the limited range of vocational and life experiences of many of these persons, this approach is likewise inappropriate. A more useful, contemporary alternative approach to traditional assessment is to focus on actual competencies and skills required for the successful performance of specific jobs. Assessment outcomes directly relate to program planning and include the instructional processes needed to acquire specific competencies and skills.

The assessment of functional living skills represents one contemporary, alternative approach to traditional assessment with persons with mental retardation (Levinson et al., 1994). Assessment of functional living skills typically includes:

1. evaluation of self-help skills such as dressing, eating, or toileting

2. consumer skills, including money handling, banking, and purchasing

3. domestic skills, such as household maintenance

4. health care

5. community knowledge, including travel skills and telephone usage

6. job readiness skills, such as interviewing skills and on-the-job information

7. vocational behavior, including job performance and productivity, work habits and attitudes, and work-related skills

8. social behavior on the job, including interactions with coworkers and supervisors. It is precisely the comprehensive and ongoing nature of vocational assessment for persons with mental retardation that makes it so challenging.

Recognition of Attention Deficit Disorder (ADD) in adults is recent and not yet widespread. Consequently, little empirical evidence exists to guide practitioners who serve adults newly diagnosed with ADD (Nadeau, 1995). In a comprehensive model for career counseling with adults with ADD the practitioner's role is to integrate test results from evaluations of ability, achievement, interests, personality traits, and specific problematic learning disorder (LD) and ADD concerns. When administering any test, the individual's attention difficulties should be taken into account. Among these difficulties are impatience, distractibility, motor restlessness, a tendency toward careless errors, and inattention when reading. All of these can affect test reliability and validity. Test administrators can accommodate the strong tendency of adults with ADD from making careless errors by allowing clients to mark their answers next to the questions in question booklets, instead of requiring them to transfer answers onto an answer sheet. The test administrator or a technician/assistant can transfer the answers to any answer sheets at a later time to facilitate computer or template scoring. Paper-and-pencil tests may highlight the reading difficulty of an adult with ADD. Frequent breaks may improve performance for those who have difficulty concentrating. Clients with an accompanying LD that contributes to reading problems may benefit by having the questions read aloud to them. Breaking a test into one-hour segments may help counteract restlessness, mental fatigue, and distractibility. By all means, testing should take place in a quiet, nondistracting environment.

Assessment Traditions of the 20th Century

Several influences contributed by a number of cultures over the centuries have affected the current status of vocational assessment. These include (a) the use of test batteries during Imperial China's Han dynasty (206 B.C.E.–220 C.E.); (b) the work of Sir Francis Galton (1822–1911) and his origination of statistical concepts of regression to the mean and correlation, derived from the theory of evolution articulated by his relative Charles Darwin (1809–1882); and (c) the experimental and practical study of individual differences by James McKeen Cattell (1860–1944) at Columbia University (Kaplan & Sacuzzo, 1997; Sattler, 1988). Most of the major developments in testing have occurred in the early twentieth century. Watkins (1992) categorized these developments into four assessment traditions: vocational guidance, psychometric, mental hygiene, and Rogerian.

The Vocational Guidance Tradition Watkins's (1992) first category, the vocational guidance tradition, is traced back to the pioneering efforts of Frank Parsons [1854–1908]. Parsons, an individual of unflagging energy, served as a teacher, counselor, lawyer, political activist, reformer, and author (Zytowski, 1985). The impetus for Parson's contributions and the vocational guidance tradition can be traced to three trends occurring at the beginning of the twentieth century: a wider variety of careers due to increasing industrialization, secondary school enrollment growth, and difficulties experienced by young men and women in the labor market. These trends combined to create new conditions of educational opportunity and occupational choice. Parsons's views on vocational counseling were published in *Choosing a Vocation* (1909). In conceptualizing the vocational choice process Parsons said that one must consider three broad factors: (1) a clear understanding of yourself, your aptitudes, abilities, interests, ambitions, resources, limitations, and their causes; (2) a knowledge of the requirements and conditions of success, advantages and disadvantages, compensations, opportunities, and prospects in different lines of work; and (3) true reasoning on the relations of these first two factors. To facilitate vocational exploration, he relied on interviewing, assessment procedures, and a diagnostic method.

With some modifications, Parsons's approach to vocational guidance led to the development of the **trait-factor theory** of career counseling. This approach, sometimes referred to as "test 'em and tell 'em," or "three interviews and a cloud of dust," regards diagnosis, testing, and assessment as central to the counseling process (Crites, 1981). These three activities were aided substantially by the development of interest tests and related measures.

Though the trait-factor approach to counseling is said to be on the decline, the central Parsonian assumption of matching people and jobs continues today to underlie the most prominent vocational assessment tools and concepts. This seems to be especially true in regard to the congruence model. This model is very much in evidence today in both career assessment and counseling practice, as reflected in John Holland's work, and some of the career inventories (particularly the Strong Interest Inventory and the Career Inventory Assessment, CAI).

The Psychometric Tradition Watkins's (1992) second category is the psychometric tradition. In France, Alfred Binet (1857–1911) and Theodore Simon (1873–1961) developed an intelligence scale to assess a variety of mental functions; one result of their work, the diagnosis of mentally retarded individuals (Sattler, 1988), stimulated the psychometric tradition in the United States. In the 1930s people involved in the vocational guidance and psychometric traditions combined their efforts and attempted to identify methods by which they could assist the unemployed to find employment. The Stabilization Research Institute (1931, cited in Watkins, 1992) was pivotal in combining the two traditions. The Institute developed psychological tests and methods for the assessment of the abilities and interests of the unemployed, researched the reeducation potential and problems of the unemployed, and demonstrated retraining and reeducation methods. The work at the Institute and the contributions of the psychometric tradition provided the vocational guidance tradition with a substantive philosophical and psychological base. The seminal contributions of Strong and Kuder are further examples of the way in which vocational guidance and psychometric traditions were combined.

The psychometric tradition also contributed to the development of personality tests, including The California Psychological Inventory (CPI; Gough, 1957), The Minnesota Multiphasic Personality Inventory (MMPI; Hathaway & McGinley, 1943), and The 16 Personality Factor Questionnaire (16PF; Cattell, 1949). These instruments, among others, show the increasing psychometric sophistication that has been applied to test development over the years.

Each of these instruments have continued to be used with recent revisions on CPI (Gough, 1990), MMPI-2 (Butcher, Dahlstrom, Graham, 1989), and 16PF (Institute for Personality and Ability Testing, 1995). The Adult Personality Inventory (Krug, 1991) and the Millon Clinical Multiaxial Inventory (MCMI) are other examples of the increase, development, and use of personality assessments. In vocational assessment one can also see this reflected in the Strong Interest Inventory (SII), the Kuder Occupational Interest Survey (KOIS), the Career Assessment Inventory (CAI), and other highly useful and usable career/interest inventories. These are but a few illustrations of the evolution of the psychometric tradition and its continuing effects on the assessment tools that counseling psychologists and other practitioners currently use in their work.

The Mental Hygiene Tradition The mental health tradition is Watkins's (1992) third category of major developments in testing. Mental health and assessment instruments were illustrated in Beers (1908, cited in Watkins, 1992) who focused on two issues: (1) concern over the need to improve the care and treatment of patients hospitalized for serious personality disturbance, and (2) concern over how to prevent such disorders. Although Beers's contributions were more indirect in terms of assessment, his humanizing influence may well have spilled over into how mental health professionals think about assessment, its purposes, and how different assessment methods are used.

The Rogerian Tradition Watkins's (1992) fourth category of assessment traditions, the person-centered (Rogerian) tradition, gave us some of our most fundamental ideas about assessment methods and their utilization. This tradition has six guiding ideas:

1. Assessment methods can be used by and for clients.

2. Clients can use their assessment results to their own benefit.

3. Assessment should be a collaborative effort between counselor and client.

4. Clients can benefit most from assessment when they are actively involved in the entire assessment process.

5. Clients can benefit most from assessment information when it is considered in a facilitative, non-threatening atmosphere.

6. Through providing information that stimulates self-examination, self-exploration, self-understanding, and insight, assessment methods can be facilitative to the client during the counseling process.

The influences that have affected our current use of assessment methods are quite diverse, but are bound by one unifying theme: the desire to assist clients in better helping and understanding themselves (Watkins, 1992). Either directly or indirectly, these traditions in relation to assessment have had humanizing effects upon our views about clients and provided us with means by which client self-exploration, self-understanding, and insight could be facilitated. Some very powerful assessment tools, if used ethically, responsibly, and in an informed manner, can be of considerable value to clients.

Assessment has experienced a renaissance of sorts. It is alive, well, and thriving, and is a diverse and rich area of practice. It is much more important and relevant to the counseling profession than may have been realized during the 1970s and 1980s. Different assessment tools provide objective data to a counseling process that is primarily subjective. The balanced combination of information from both the assessment tools and the person's self image allows the counselor to help the client integrate these various aspects of the whole person into the career decision-making process.

Postmodern Approaches to Assessment

Traditional twentieth-century vocational assessment is whole-heartedly modernist. Clients without a Eurocentric worldview have been pathologized, caricatured, or dehumanized (Dana, 1993). The practitioner's role is not to take for granted the assumption that assessment procedures are universally reliable and valid for all clients—an etic perspective. Without the development of culture-specific norms—an emic perspective—an assessment instrument developed on a given standardization sample is of limited use for a non-member of the cultural group of that normative sample. Lack of culture-specific norms has not prevented the use in the past of a given assessment tool with a client for whom norms do not exist. This type of sloppy scientific method led to postmodern approaches toward assessment.

Other shortcomings of the scientific method have contributed an increased emphasis of postmodernism in vocational psychology and career counseling. Research on job satisfaction and workaholism is incomplete, fragmented, and has not reached the level of empirical refinement that the scientific method demands. Androcentrism and heterosexism have kept the logical positivist ideals of assessment from being met. Postmodern approaches to vocational assessment therefore merit consideration as a viable alternative to traditional approaches.

New assessment methods and measures for use by vocational practitioners/ career counselors give more attention to the client's subjective experience which is an addition to, not a substitution of, the objective observations yielded by standardized assessment instruments (Savickas, 1992). Contextual interpretation becomes part of a larger, objective test battery. Using a **phenomenological perspective,** counselors "seek to comprehend the meaning of clients' interests and abilities as part of a life pattern" (p. 337). A modern approach to interests and abilities as quantifiable characteristics can unintentionally treat clients as objects. A postmodern approach deals with interests and abilities by helping clients discern what they intend to do with assessment results to fashion a career. Modernism would treat assessment results in terms of predictive accuracy, postmodernism in terms of expressed interests.

Traditionally objective assessment results have entailed "the delivery of authoritative guidance and concentrate[d] exclusively on the client's role as a worker" (Savickas, 1992, p. 337). Subjective assessment allows for looking at the role of work in people's lives and removes the artificial distinction between personal and career counseling. Early recollections, occupational daydreams, **life**

themes, autobiographies, and the multiple roles and tensions in a client's life, become legitimate areas for collaboration between practitioner and client.

Client narratives about their education, employment history, and occupational aspirations can reveal characters, plots, and recurring situations. The practitioner's role is to listen for themes, tensions, and connections in their clients' lives and place the role of work into context with other roles. Practitioners and clients collaborate on the meanings of client life experiences. The practitioner's reading between the lines and making explicit connections between loosely attached ideas takes subjective assessment to another level. While **narrative approaches** have been a part of clinical psychology for many years (Jones & Thorne, 1987; Savickas, 1992), they are new to vocational psychology. An infusion of postmodern contextual interpretation in assessment and occupational development holds some promise to invigorate and transform vocational psychology.

As with standards and goals for career counseling, quality assurance issues in program evaluation and vocational assessment will need to be further addressed in the future. Thus far, we have addressed broad concerns in career counseling and vocational psychology. We have looked at current perspectives, historical trends, and professional certification concerns. In the next chapter we begin to discuss specific approaches to career counseling/vocational development.

4

Approaches That
Rely Principally on
Assessment Instruments

In this chapter we begin our formal discussion of vocational psychology theories. Four approaches rely strongly on the use of assessment instruments: (1) Trait-Factor Theory, (2) Holland's Typology, (3) the Myers-Briggs Type Indicator, and (4) the Theory of Work Adjustment. We conclude this chapter with some of the historical antecedents to vocational psychology from 2,500 to 500 years ago.

TRAIT-FACTOR THEORY

Evolution of Vocational Guidance

Frank Parsons (1854–1908) developed the idea of choosing a vocation rather than hunting for a job. Originally trained as an engineer, he proposed a set of objective standards and assessments to guide a person vocationally. In his landmark, posthumous book, *Choosing a Vocation* (1909), he proposed three steps to vocational development:

> First, a clear understanding of yourself, your aptitudes, abilities, interests, resources, limitations and other qualities. Second, knowledge of the requirements and conditions of success, advantages and disadvantages, compensation, opportunities, and prospects in different lines of work. Third, true reasoning on the relations of these two groups of facts. (p. 5)

RALPH

"We think he'll either be a dentist
or a lion trainer."

Reprinted by permission of King Features Syndiate, Inc.

Sharf (1996, chapter 2) describes each of these steps, including assessment instruments for each step.

Williamson (1939) describes a six-step career counseling process: (1) analysis, (2) synthesis, (3) diagnosis, (4) prognosis, (5) counseling, and (6) follow-up. The first three steps involve gathering and synthesizing clinical information to determine client strengths and weaknesses. Conclusions are based on those strengths and weaknesses. These steps help the counselor to identify how well such strengths and weaknesses match client adjustment to available conditions or choices (Chartrand, 1991). At the same time, vocational psychologists at the University of Minnesota developed special aptitude tests, personality inventories, and other devices elaborating and expanding Parsons's three steps, mostly in response to employment problems created by the Great Depression.

All these developments became part of Trait-Factor Theory. **Traits** are learned, which makes them viable for change through lifelong learning. This raises questions about traits' stability and endurance. Traits of greatest interest to vocational practitioners—interests, special aptitudes, and scholastic aptitudes—seem relatively stable (Hogan, DeSoto & Solana, 1977). When a vocational practitioner administers an interest inventory to a client, the practitioner

Practical Applications

Trait-factor views career choice as a straightforward cognitive process (Williamson, 1965). Sharf (1996) summarizes the process as:

Step 1—Gaining Self-Understanding: (a) Aptitudes, (b) Achievements, (c) Interests, (d) Values, and (e) Personality.

Step 2—Obtaining Knowledge about the World of Work: (a) Types of Occupational Infor-

mation, (b) Classification Systems, and (c) Trait and Factor Requirements.

Step 3—Integrating Information about Oneself and the World of Work, including identifying occupational options and developing a plan of action.

Trait-Factor Theory approaches are a useful place to *start* an occupational counseling process.

---

is interested in how well the inventory predicts job choice and subsequent satisfaction (**predictive validity**). The practitioner is equally interested in how the same score can help the client identify values, preferences for work activities, decision-making style, and way of being perceived by others (Brown, Brooks & Associates, 1991).

Reviews of trait-factor research have varied. Klein and Weiner (1977) conclude: (1) Each individual has a unique set of traits that can be measured reliably and validly. (2) Occupations require that workers possess specific traits for success, although a worker with a rather wide range of characteristics still can be successful in a given job. (3) The choice of an occupation is a rather straightforward process, and matching is possible. (4) Brown et al. (1991) emphasized that the closer the match between personal characteristics and job requirements, the greater the likelihood of success—productivity and satisfaction.

Assessment Instruments based on Trait-Factor Theory Trait-factor approaches to test interpretation focus on predicting the likelihood of success based on similarities of responses between the client taking the test and persons already in the occupation who report that they enjoy their work. These approaches do not tell clients what job they should have. No attempt is made to predict long-term success.

Clients find occupations that match their current abilities and needs. The practitioner's role is to teach clients how to obtain information from existing sources since few occupational materials contain the full range of information that clients need. Clients determine a tentative occupational choice, then the practitioner directly helps clients implement that choice. The practitioner may find a suitable preparation experience, identify employment opportunities, and teach the skill needed to secure the job and hold it. The final step is follow-up. It involves determining whether the course of action established by counseling is correct in the client's view. With satisfactory results, no further steps are necessary. With unsatisfactory results, the process may have to be reinitiated.

A list of assessments follows.

Aptitude Tests. These aptitude measures were generally normed on high school and college populations:

- American College Testing (ACT)
- APTICOM
- Armed Services Vocational Aptitude Battery (ASVAB)
- College Board Scholastic Aptitude Tests (SAT)
- Differential Aptitude Tests (DAT)
- School and College Ability Tests (SCAT)
- United States Employment Service General Aptitude Test Battery (GATB).

These tests measure learning potential in various environments.

Interest Inventories. These assessment tools assist in determining a client's range of work interests.

- Campbell Interest and Skills Survey
- Career Assessment Inventory
- Career Occupation Preference System Interest Inventory (COPS)
- Interests, Determination, Exploration & Assessment System (IDEAS)
- Jackson Vocational Interest Survey (JVIS)
- Kuder Occupational Interests Survey (KOIS)
- Self-Directed Search (SDS)
- Strong Interest Inventory (SII)
- Vocational Preference Interests (VPI)
- Wide Range Interest-Opinion Test (WRIOT).

Values clarification inventories include:

- Minnesota Importance Questionnaire (MIQ)
- Rokeach Values Survey

- Study of Values (SV)
- Values Scale (VS)
- Work Values Inventory (WVI).

Personality Tests. The most frequently used ones are:
- California Psychological Inventory (CPI)
- Career Decision Scale (CDS)
- Edwards Personal Preference Schedule (EPPS)
- Career Factors Inventory (CFI)
- Eysenck Personality Inventory (EPI)
- Myers-Briggs Type Indicator (MBTI)
- Personal Research Form (PRF)
- Salience Scale
- Vocational Identity Scale (VIS)
- Sixteen Personality Factor Questionnaire (16PF) (PCD Profile Form)
- Neuroticism, Extraversion, and Openness Personality Inventory, Revised (NEO-PI-R).

Publishers of each test are listed in Appendix 3.

Evaluation of Trait-Factor Theory Trait-Factor Theory works best with clients who are clear on their **self-concept,** aware of options, and have had various life/work experiences. Assessments used with this theory assume that clients can differentiate between their likes and dislikes, and their preferred activities, coworkers, and lifestyle.

For several decades, the trait-factor approach enjoyed considerable success. Until the 1950s it was the major theory used for career counseling. This preeminent position faded as client-centered psychotherapy permeated the counseling field and developmental and social learning approaches to career counseling matured. The current status of Trait-Factor Theory is debatable. Its contribution to vocational psychology continues to be acknowledged, but its viability as a specific counseling approach is sometimes dismissed.

Both the model and the counseling approach that it spawned have been carefully scrutinized. Some interpretations of the model's underlying assumptions are disputable, but have been widely cited ... [including] the belief that occupational choice is a single event, that a single type of person works in each job, that there is a single right goal for every career decision maker, and that occupational choice is available to everyone. (Chartrand, 1991, p. 519)

Counselors who used trait-factor approaches were often criticized for being too directive and forceful in their recommendations. The trait-factor model includes "(a) diagnosis of the client's problem and assignment of multiple tests, (b) interpretation of the test results, and (c) selection of a career alternative based on test results" (Chartrand, 1991, p. 519).

A New Model for Trait-Factor Theory

The trait-factor approach was updated by Chartrand and Bertok (1993), who described a cognitive-interactional view. Their very comprehensive assessment paradigm included attention to client's cognitions, personality and interpersonal relations. Including the client's interests, abilities, values, and the characteristic of the client's work environment, the paradigm is meant to apply to a variety of counseling situations, whether one is trying to fit a person to an initial occupational choice or to facilitate adjustment at a later point in career development. A three-dimensional model guides persons doing cognitive-interactional assessment: (1) attention to problem type—choice, implementation, performance, adaptation; (2) problem focus—person, environment, or their interaction; (3) timing of the assessment—early, middle, late. Also, a client's perceived level of self-knowledge or knowledge of occupations, perceived work and nonwork stressors, and personality needs to be assessed.

Person by Environment (PxE) Fit

The trait-factor approach has evolved into the **Person by Environment (PxE) Fit,** which is described in Table 4.1.

PxE is based on three assumptions. First, people are capable of making rational decisions, which illustrates the appropriateness of cognitive interventions. Second, people and work environments differ across various situations, thus, identifying patterns could be helpful in organizing people and environments. Third, the greater the congruence between personal traits and requirements on the job, the greater the possibility of finding job satisfaction (Chartrand, 1991). In addition there is a reciprocal process between individuals and the environment (Rounds & Tracey, 1990).

Relevance to Multicultural and Diverse Populations

African Americans. No specific test of the Trait-Factor Theory pertinent to African-American populations has been uncovered (Brown, 1995). To understand the diverse life experiences of African Americans, the domain of potential

TABLE 4.1 Comparisons between the Trait-Factor and PxE Fit

TRAIT-FACTOR	PXE FIT
Theoretical Assumptions	
■ Humans are capable of rational decision-making. ■ Reliable and meaningful individual and environmental differences can be assessed. ■ Matching person and environments increase the probability of positive outcomes.	■ Humans are capable of rational decision-making. ■ Reliable and meaningful individual and environmental differences can be assessed. ■ Matching persons and environments increase the probability of positive outcomes. ■ Individuals seek out congruent environments. ■ PxE fit is reciprocal and ongoing.
Theoretical Framework	
■ Empirically based formulations that apply matching principle	■ Theoretical formulations that address both structure and process
Counseling Diagnosis	
■ Differential diagnosis of career choice difficulties	■ Differential diagnosis of career choice, planning, and adjustment difficulties
Counseling Process	
■ Williamson's (1939, 1950) six-stage problem-solving sequence	■ Rounds & Tracey's (1990) four-step information processing sequence
Counseling Outcome	
■ Two levels: specific goal attainment and learning decision-making skills	■ Two levels: specific goal attainment and learning decision-making skills
Counselor Style	
■ A supportive teaching style	■ Typically a supportive teaching style ■ Congruence between counselor behavior and client needs
Psychometric Information	
■ Psychometric instruments can be used to predict relevant criteria. ■ Interpretations are made within the broader context of counseling, are based on actuarial and clinical information, and are used to enhance self-understanding.	■ Psychometric instruments can be used to predict relevant criteria. ■ Interpretations are made within the broader context of counseling, are based on actuarial and clinical information, and are used to enhance self-understanding. ■ Client involvement in the assessment process is actively sought.

SOURCE: Chartrand (1991), p. 519. From the *Journal of Counseling and Development*, p. 519, © 1991, by permission of the American Counseling Association.

factors salient to the career behavior of these persons needs to be adequately defined, operationalized, or investigated. Dismissing Trait-Factor Theory as irrelevant to the career behavior of African Americans may be premature; better-designed research is needed to test its validity for African Americans.

Gay, Lesbian, and Bisexual People. Gelberg and Chojnacki (1996) modify the trait-factor approach to include sexual orientation and level of sexual identity development as personal variables that need to go beyond the traditional consideration of vocational interests, values, and abilities and aptitudes. The degree to which a work environment is either affirmative or hostile to gay, lesbian, and bisexual persons needs more attention because incongruence results when a gay, lesbian, or bisexual person is in an overtly or covertly discriminatory work environment.

Hispanics. Available research on the assessment of interests of Hispanics indicates that the interest patterns and structures of interests is not different than for Whites (Fouad, 1995). More study is needed to determine if acculturation, the number of generations in the United States, socioeconomic status, and geographic location modifies the similarity of results across cultures.

Asian Americans. Assessment of career interests with Asian Americans using psychometrically valid instruments remains sparse (Leong & Gim-Chung, 1995). Representative, normative samples of Asian Americans are needed from across the United States.

Native Americans. Of particular concern with Native-American populations is whether such persons grew up on a rural reservation, in an urban area, or both. PxE Fit becomes especially relevant because this approach considers an individual's inherent differences, and thus allows Native Americans an opportunity to integrate personal, environmental, and cultural characteristics into the career development process (Johnson, Swartz & Martin, 1995). Awareness of the world of work, characteristic of both trait-factor and PxE approaches, is vital with Native Americans whose knowledge about vocations and careers is limited. Use of local norms for any standardized assessment instruments is strongly recommended. In many reservation communities where job opportunities are limited, an accurate person-job match is facilitated by the trait-factor approach (Johnson et al., 1995; Martin, 1995).

HOLLAND'S TYPOLOGY

John L. Holland's typology has probably driven more empirical research since its initial appearance in the 1950s than any other theory of career behavior. A revision of his theory and its current status reflects a number of significant refinements and improvements (Holland, 1992), and he has become more explicit in explaining the theory in terms of PxE considerations. Four working assumptions comprise the core of his theory: (1) In American culture, most persons can be categorized as one of six types: **realistic, investigative, artistic, social, enterprising,** or **conventional.** (2) There are six correspondent model environments. (3) People search for environments that will let them exercise their skills and abilities, express their attitudes and values, and take on agreeable problems and roles. (4) Behavior is determined by interaction between personality and environment.

Five secondary assumptions moderate and explain the differences in the outcomes (Holland, 1992). (1) **Consistency** is the degree of relatedness between personality types or between environmental models. (2) **Differentiation** is the degree to which a person or environment is well defined. (3) **Identity** estimates the clarity and stability of a person or environment's identity. (4) **Congruence** means that different types require different environments. (5) **Calculus** is the relationship within and between types or environments, and it can be ordered according to the hexagonal model where the difference in the distance between types or environments is inversely proportion to the theoretical relationship between them.

Figure 4.1 shows a hexagonal model for Holland's typology. This is known within the vocational psychology and career counseling field as the "RIASEC Hexagon."

Personality types and work environments adjacent to each other are presumed to be most similar. Types and environments opposite each other are presumed to be most dissimilar. To further elaborate, a number of principles seem plausible.

> The choice of a vocation is an expression of personality.
>
> Interest inventories are personality inventories.
>
> Vocational stereotypes have reliable and important psychological and sociological meanings.
>
> The members of a vocation have similar personalities and similar histories of personal development.
>
> Because people in a vocational group have similar personalities, they will respond to many situations and problems in similar ways, and they will create characteristic interpersonal environments.
>
> Vocational satisfaction, stability, and achievement depend on the congruence between one's personality and the environment in which one works. (Holland, 1992, pp. 7–10)

Holland's original model has developed over the years with refinements based on Staat's (1981) theory of social behavior and Krumboltz's (1979) social learning theory of career decision-making. How types develop is shown in Figure 4.2.

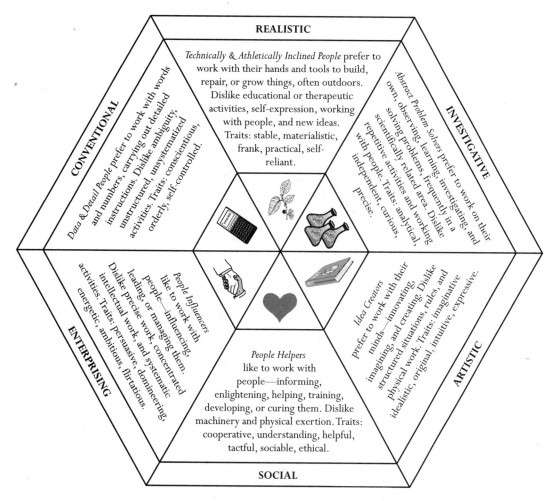

FIGURE 4.1 A Hexagonal Model for Defining the Psychological Resemblances Among Types and Environments and Their Interactions

SOURCE: Holland (1992), p. 29.

Formulations of the Types

The hexagonal model visually represents the theory, assists one to identify the amount of consistency in one's personality patterns and environments, and enhances awareness of the congruency or incongruency between personal traits and work environments. We have gone to the original source to describe formulations of the types (Holland, 1992).

The Realistic Type

The development of a Realistic pattern of activities, competencies, and interests creates a person who is predisposed to exhibit the following behavior:

1. Prefers realistic occupations or situations—electrician—in which one can engage in preferred activities and avoid activities demanded by social occupations or situations.

2. Uses realistic competencies to solve problems at work and in other settings.

3. Perceives self as having mechanical and athletic ability and lacking ability in human relations.

4. Values concrete things or tangible personal characteristics—money, power, and status (p. 19).

The demands, opportunities, and people of the Realistic type create a characteristic atmosphere that operates in the following way:

1. It stimulates people to perform realistic activities such as using machines and tools.

2. It fosters technical competencies and achievements.

3. It encourages people to see themselves as having mechanical ability and lacking ability in human relations; it encourages them to see the world in simple, tangible, and traditional terms.

4. It rewards people for the display of conventional values and goods, money, power, and possessions (pp. 36–37).

The Realistic person is apt to be:

Asocial	Materialistic	Self-effacing
Conforming	Natural	Inflexible
Frank	Normal	Thrifty
Genuine	Persistent	Uninsightful
Hard-headed	Practical	Uninvolved (p. 19)

The Investigative Type

This development of an Investigative pattern of activities, competencies, and interests creates a person who is predisposed to exhibit the following behavior:

1. Prefers occupations or situations in which one can engage in preferred activities and competencies and avoid activities demanded by enterprising occupations and situations.

2. Uses investigative competencies to solve problems at work and in other settings.

3. Perceives self as scholarly, intellectual, having mathematical and scientific ability, and lacking in leadership ability.

4. Values science (p. 20).

The demands, opportunities, and people of the Investigative type create a characteristic atmosphere that operates to produce the following outcomes:

1. It stimulates people to perform investigative activities.

2. It encourages scientific competencies and achievements.

3. It encourages people to see themselves as scholarly, as having mathematical and scientific ability, and as lacking leadership ability; it encourages them to see the world in complex, abstract, independent, and original ways.

4. It rewards people for the display of scientific value (p. 37).

The Investigative Person is apt to be:

Analytical	Helpful	Responsible
Cooperative	Idealistic	Sociable
Patient	Empathetic	Tactful
Friendly	Kind	Understanding
Generous	Persuasive	Warm (p. 20)

The Artistic Type

This development of an Artistic pattern of activities, competencies, and interests creates a person who is predisposed to exhibit the following behavior:

1. Prefers artistic occupations or situations in which one can engage in preferred activities and competencies and avoid the activities demanded by conventional occupations or situations.

2. Uses artistic competencies to solve problems at work and in other settings.

3. Perceives self as expressive, original, intuitive, nonconforming, introspective, independent, disorderly, having artistic and musical ability, and ability in acting, writing, and speaking.

4. Values aesthetic qualities (p. 20)

The demands, opportunities, and people of the Artistic type create a characteristic atmosphere that operates to produce the following outcomes:

1. It stimulates people to engage in artistic activities.

2. It fosters artistic competencies and achievements.

3. It encourages people to see themselves as expressive, original, intuitive, nonconforming, independent, and as having artistic abilities (acting, writing, and speaking). It encourages people to see the world in complex, independent, unconventional, and flexible ways.

The Artistic person is apt to be:

Complicated	Imaginative	Intuitive
Disorderly	Impractical	Nonconforming
Emotional	Impulsive	Original
Expressive	Independent	Sensitive
Idealistic	Introspective	Open (p. 21)

The Social Type

This development of a Social pattern of activities, competencies, and interests creates a person who is predisposed to exhibit the following behavior:

1. Prefers social occupations and situations in which one can engage in preferred activities and competencies and avoid the activities demanded by realistic occupations and situations.

2. Uses social competencies to solve problems at work and in other settings.

3. Perceives self as liking to help others, understanding others, having teaching ability, and lacking mechanical and scientific ability.

4. Values social and ethical activities and problems (p. 21).

The demands, opportunities, and people of the Social type create a characteristic atmosphere that operates to produce the following goals and outcomes:

1. It stimulates people to engage in social activities.

2. It fosters social competencies.

3. It encourages people to see themselves as liking to help others, understanding of others, cooperative, and sociable; it encourages them to see the world in flexible ways.

4. It rewards people for the display of social values (p. 38).

The Social person is apt to be:

Ascendant	Helpful	Responsible
Cooperative	Idealistic	Sociable
Patient	Empathetic	Tactful
Friendly	Kind	Understanding
Generous	Persuasive	Warm (p. 21)

The Enterprising Type

This development of an enterprising pattern of activities, competencies, and interests creates a person who is predisposed to exhibit the following behavior:

1. Prefers enterprising occupations or situations in which one can engage in preferred activities and avoid the activities demanded by investigative occupations and situations.

2. Uses enterprising competencies to solve problems at work and in other situations.

3. Perceives self as aggressive, popular, self-confident, sociable, possessing leadership and speaking abilities, and lacking scientific ability.

4. Values political and economic achievement (p. 22).

The demands, opportunities, and people of the Enterprising type create a characteristic atmosphere that operates to produce the following goals and outcomes:

1. It stimulates people to engage in enterprising activities such as selling, or leading others.

2. It fosters enterprising competencies and achievements.

3. It encourages people to see themselves as aggressive, popular, self-confident, sociable, and as possessing leadership and speaking ability. It encourages people to see the world in terms of power, status, responsibility, and in stereotyped, constricted, dependent, and simple terms (p. 39).

The Enterprising person is apt to be:

Acquisitive	Energetic	Optimistic
Adventurous	Exhibitionistic	Self-confident
Agreeable	Excitement-seeking	Sociable
Ambitious	Extroverted	Talkative (p. 21)
Domineering	Flirtatious	

The Conventional Type

This development of a Conventional pattern of activities, competencies, and interests creates a person who is predisposed to exhibit the following behavior:

1. Prefers conventional occupations or situations in which one can engage in preferred activities and avoid the activities demanded by artistic occupations or situations.
2. Uses conventional competencies to solve problems at work and in other situations.
3. Perceives self as conforming, orderly, and as having clerical and numerical ability.
4. Values business and economic achievement (p. 22).

The demands, opportunities, and people of the Conventional type create a characteristic atmosphere that operates to produce the following goals and outcomes:

1. It stimulates people to engage in conventional activities, such as recording and organizing data and records.
2. It fosters conventional activities and competencies.
3. It encourages people to see themselves as conforming, orderly, non-artistic, and as having clerical competencies; it encourages them to see the world in conventional, stereotyped, constricted, simple, dependent ways.
4. It rewards people for the display of conventional values: money, dependability, and conformity (p. 40).

The Conventional person is apt to be:

Careful	Inflexible	Persistent
Conforming	Inhibited	Practical
Conscientious	Methodical	Prudish
Defensive	Obedient	Thrifty
Efficient	Orderly	Unimaginative (p. 23).

Holland (1985) suggests that:

types produce types through parental endowment of physical and psychological potential and provision of environmental opportunities. These influences lead individuals to acquire preferences for some kinds of activities and aversions to others at an early stage in their vocational development. These initial preferences are subsequently reevaluated as a result of participation in environmental settings (e.g., schools, colleges, employment), and the interaction among these multiple sources presumably creates a characteristic disposition or personality type that is predisposed to exhibit characteristic behavior and to develop characteristic personality traits, attitudes, and behaviors that in turn form repertoires or collections of skills and coping mechanisms (p. 16).

Assessment Instruments Used with Holland's Theory The following assessment instruments are used with Holland's Theory:

1. Self-Directed Search (SDS)
2. My Vocational Situation (MVS)
3. Strong Interest Inventory (SII)
4. The World-of-Work map (American College Testing, 1990)
5. Vocational Preference Inventory (VPI)
6. Career Assessment Inventory—primarily for post-high school
7. Harrington/O'Shea Systems—Career Decision Making Revised (CDM-R)

Evaluation of Holland's Model Holland's theory has been extremely well researched, with continual refinements and improvements. Each time revisions are made, nine empirical studies are conducted to further test aspects of his theoretical hypotheses. Throughout the research, most findings corroborate the theory's vitality and validity. The model serves a useful purpose in the field of vocational psychology.

While this theory attempts to explain considerations of the PxE fit, Schwartz (1992) questions the validity of the concept of congruence. There is no clear evidence that congruence is associated with achievement or stability. Occasionally positive associations between congruence and satisfaction are an artifact of an uninvestigated common association between role-choice clarity and both congruence and satisfaction.

Differences in needs, interests, values, abilities, experiences, and psychological state between those who are most and least satisfied as well as accomplished in their respective occupations could develop PxE fit tests that are more valid than the inventories used today. "Comparatively, little vocational psychology research is devoted to the development of occupation-specific, occupational-specialty specific or occupational-group specific tests. Is Holland's work worthy of so much attention or should vocational psychology move on?" (Schwartz, 1992, pp. 185–186). Holland (1996) points to several studies, primarily Helms and Williams

Practical Applications

Various instruments are used to assess personality types. Most common is the Self-Directed Search (SDS), a self-completed, self-scored look at an individual's occupational daydreams, activities, actual occupations, and self-estimates across several abilities and skills areas. The total score adds up to the relative strength of each area in the RIASEC hexagon. The three highest scores become the three-letter code. This code and others closely related to it become the basis of matching the individual and the occupation. Other instruments used are the Strong Interest Inventory (SII), Career Assessment Inventory (CAI) and the Vocational Preference Inventory (VPI). The Occupations Finder (1994) is an excellent resource that can be used with the SII, CAI, VPI, and SDS results.

A client's hexagon location has many practical applications:

1. Using the three-letter code for occupational groups on the hexagon clients can find occupations close to their own hexagon locations. For example, clients with an SAI code will see that occupations with SAE, SIA, IAS, and ASE codes also are nearby. Clients may wish to broaden career exploration by looking into those occupations as well.

2. When an interest test is used, such as the SII, determine whether a client's preferred occupation and measured interests have similar (congruent) hexagon locations. To the extent that the locations are similar, the preferred occupation will be supported by measured interests and the client will generally have many occupations available to choose from.

3. Compare the hexagon locations of a client's interests and abilities.

There are several practical implications of the congruence theory, mainly for those who happen to be incongruent in their occupational choice. Some solutions are:

1. Replace their working unit with a more congruent working unit while remaining in the same occupation and specialty.

2. Replace their specialty within their occupation with one that is more congruent for them.

3. Choose an avocational activity that is congruent with their interests (with the option of making it their occupation after a sufficient period of experience and training).

Continued

4. Play down the importance of the job and its environment as sources of satisfaction and other measures of well-being, and compensate by enhancing the importance of other kinds of congruence, such as skill congruence, avocational congruence, or congruence with the ideas of the other's in one's environment.

5. Change one's occupation and/or environment to a more congruent one. (Meir, 1989, p. 229)

According to Holland (1992), "maladaptive career development equals the failure to develop a personality pattern that is consistent and differentiated or a clear sense of vocational identity, or a failure to establish a career in a congruent occupation" (p. 137).

Maladaptive career development can occur if a person has had

(a) "insufficient experience" to understand interests and/or competencies and has learned little knowledge of occupational environments; (b) "ambiguous, conflicting or depreciative experiences" or information regarding abilities, personal traits or work environments; (c) lack of personal, educational and/or financial resources to explore the occupation of his/her choice; (d) economic or social or cultural barriers that affect job opportunities. Economic hard times can reduce both job opportunities and career exploration possibilities (p. 137).

In contrast, adaptive vocational behavior can develop as a result of the following:

(a) acquiring well-defined interests and competencies;

(b) observing/evaluating accurately one's interest, abilities, and personal characteristics;

(c) compiling an array of occupational information based on experience that has validity and objectivity;

(d) acquiring a sufficient identity in a vocation, self-confidence, interpersonal capabilities, cultural awareness, and resources to make vocational decisions as the need occurs and to deal with other common job problems;

(e) creating ways to finding the necessary personal, educational, and financial resources to reach his/her goals;

(f) being able to track one's course without allowing cultural, economic, social, or technological influences to be negative (Holland, 1992, p. 138).

These well-delineated concerns are areas where practitioners need to put substantial effort into helping clients create conditions that lead to these outcomes and provide vocational assistance.

(1964) and a reexamination by Helms (1996) that demonstrate strong support for the congruency hypothesis. Holland cites studies by Carson and Mowsesian (1991) and Gottfredson and Holland (1990) that found a sense of vocational identity more valuable in predicting job satisfaction than congruency of interests and job, and that expectation of job satisfaction was a better predictor of actual job satisfaction than the congruency of interests and job.

The existence of traits and their predictive power merits reexamination. In social psychology the debate is whether dispositionism or situationalism explains people's behavior (Ross & Nisbett, 1991). **Dispositionism** is the layperson's belief "that individual differences or traits can be used to predict how people will behave in new situations" (p. 3). **Situationalism** refers to the belief that the ability to predict how people will react in certain situations is actually quite limited. Quantitative (i.e., modernist-based) research has shown a maximum correlation of .30 between a measure of individual differences on a given trait and subsequent behavior in a new situation where that trait is hypothesized to be strongly predictive. This leaves .70 of the variance unexplained. Many laypeople and researchers fail to realize how the power of situations in general, and the power of subtle situational factors in particular, determine people's responses to their social environment more than quantifiable measures of traits. This failure to recognize the power of the situation is called a **fundamental attribution error** (Gilbert & Jones, 1986; Jones, 1979; Nisbett & Ross, 1980).

Trait-factor and PxE approaches will only predict so much. Vocational psychologists are advised that these approaches will probably not break the .30 ceiling that social psychologists have encountered when attempting to demonstrate that stable personal attributes can accurately predict the behavior of particular people in particular situations. An unexplained variance of .70 accounts for long-term occupational adjustment, satisfaction, and success. We wonder how vocational psychology and career counseling would have evolved differently if its scholars and researchers had been in dialogue much earlier with the social psychologists. Perhaps postmodern, **contextual interpretation** would have become a central component much sooner in the vocational guidance and assessment tradition.

Relevance to Multicultural and Diverse Populations Interest inventories require a client to be introspective, something not encouraged among subcultures with predominantly collectivist values (Prince, Uemura, Chao & Gonzales, 1991). External structural factors also can influence the way multicultural persons view occupations. The RIASEC hexagon's accuracy and meaning across cultures has not been extensively researched. The subtle values with which a practitioner evaluates significant between-group differences on measured interests, especially when one of those groups is the dominant White population, also should be monitored. Traditional models of assessment may need to be adjusted for multicultural and diverse populations.

African Americans. The historic experience of many African Americans is one of restricted work options; yet Holland did not address the long-term implications of this historical reality on the development of work personalities (Brown, 1995). Empirical support does exist for African Americans in different occupations having different patterns of interests. Likewise, empirical support exists for person-environment fit/congruence, where African Americans of a particular Holland code are found in occupations with similar classification codes. More research is needed that addresses the concepts of congruence, consistency, differentiation, and identity for validity with African Americans.

Hispanics. Substantial research attention has been given to career interests with diverse Hispanic subgroups using different RIASEC-based assessment instruments (Arbona, 1995). Hispanic high school and college students' view of the world of work is similar to that of the majority White culture. The Holland scales may be considered appropriate for assessing Hispanic students' interests. However, the general fit between personality and environment among Hispanic populations remains to be tested empirically.

Asian Americans. Marked occupational segregation apparently characterizes the Asian-American population (Leong & Serafica, 1995). **Occupational segregation** refers to an overrepresentation of specific population groups in some occupations while being underrepresented in others. Generally speaking, occupational segregation can be the result of differential access to various occupations, including restricted access. Asian Americans are overrepresented among physicians (e.g., five times more than expected, given their proportion of the U.S. population; three times more than expected among medical scientists, physicists, astronomers, and biological and life scientists; and twice as often among engineers, architects, accountants, and auditors (Hisa, 1988, cited in Leong & Serafica, 1995). Congruence studies are needed to clarify whether occupational segregation reflects vocational choice on the part of Asian Americans—in the sense that Holland conceptualizes choice—or whether segregation results from other factors such as parental pressure, occupational stereotyping, or discrimination.

Native Americans. The absence of occupational knowledge or experience can skew the results for respondents of any RIASEC-based instrument. Careful consideration needs to be given to this fact when assessing Native Americans (Johnson et al., 1995).

Gay, Lesbian, and Bisexual Persons. Heterosexual bias is always a risk with any career assessment instrument. Career aspirations of gays/lesbians/bisexuals may differ from heterosexual men and women, and these differences may show up in RIASEC-based instruments (Gelberg & Chojnacki, 1996). Gay men, for example, tend to score higher in the Artistic and Social domains than do heterosexual men. What remains unclear is whether interest inventories are measuring intrinsic differences between gay, lesbian, and bisexual persons and heterosexual persons, or whether external factors such as social expectations to conform are exerting pressure on response patterns.

People with Disabilities. Holland's emphasis on testing and the provision of occupational information to clients is of limited utility for individuals with mental retardation (Levinson, Peterson & Elston, 1994). Without adequate opportunities for developing the skills upon which vocational potential is measured, testing can become one of the least desirable forms of assessment to use with persons with mental retardation. A heavy reliance on self-direction in Holland's approach also restricts its usefulness for such individuals. A clinical modification of this approach can occur, but only in terms of identifying practical occupational options for persons with mental retardation.

Women. Gender differences in interest inventories have been noted by several scholars (Betz, 1994; Betz & Fitzgerald, 1987; Hackett & Lonborg, 1993; Walsh & Betz, 1990). Sex-restrictiveness in results can occur when uninformed practitioners use interest inventory results to reinforce gender stratification in the world of work. Inventory results that perpetuate occupational stereotypes by gender are still a danger. For women, within-group differences in sex-role socialization can influence the response patterns and reflect differences due to experience, not interests.

THE MYERS-BRIGGS TYPE INDICATOR

The **Myers-Briggs Type Indicator (MBTI)** is not designed as a career development tool but is used in conjunction with other instruments. Research on the MBTI primarily has been done through the Center for the Application of Psychological Type. The MBTI is closely related to Trait-Factor Theory (Sharf, 1996). Based on a theory of personality devised by Swiss psychologist and psychiatrist Carl Gustav Jung (1875–1961), for career counseling purposes the MBTI is used primarily with interests and aptitude assessments. The MBTI manual (Myers & McCaulley, 1985) lists preferred work environments by psychological types and can be applied to career adjustment as well. We have gone to the original source for these descriptions.

The essence of Jung's comprehensive theory . . . [of] . . . psychological types is . . . that everyone uses four basic mental *functions* or *processes* . . . [:] . . . sensing (S), intuitive (N), thinking (T), and feeling (F). Everyone uses these four essential functions daily . . .

To understand Jung's theory, it is essential to appreciate the uses of the terms *perception* and *judgment*. Perception includes the many ways of becoming aware of things, people, events, or ideas. It includes information gathering, the seeking of sensation or of inspiration, and the selection of the stimulus to be attended to. Judgment includes all the ways of coming to conclusions about what has been perceived. It includes decision-making, evaluation, choice, and the selections of the response after perceiving the stimulus.

Jung divided all perceptive activities into two categories—sensing and intuition. He called these *irrational functions* . . . [in] . . . that these functions are attuned to the flow of events and operate most broadly when not constrained by rational direction . . .

Sensing (S) refers to perceptions that are observable by the senses. Sensing establishes what exists. Because the senses can bring to awareness only what is occurring in the present moment, persons oriented toward sensing perception tend to focus on the immediate experience and often develop characteristics associated with this awareness such as enjoying the present moment, realism, acute powers of observation, memory for details, and practicality.

Intuition (N) refers to perception of possibilities, meanings, and relationships by way of insight. . . . Intuition permits perception beyond what is visible to the senses, including possible future events. Thus, persons oriented toward intuitive perception may become so intent on pursuing possibilities that they may overlook actualities. They may develop the characteristics than can follow from emphasis on intuition and become imaginative, theoretical, abstract, future oriented, or creative.

Jung used the terms *thinking* and *feeling* . . . to refer to the *rational functions* that are directed toward bringing life events into harmony with the laws of reason.

Thinking (T) is the function that links ideas together by making logical connections. Thinking relies on principles of cause and effect and tends to be impersonal. Persons who are primarily oriented to thinking may develop . . . [:] analytical ability, objectivity, concern with principles of justice and fairness, criticality, and an orientation to time that is concerned with connections from the past through the present and toward the future.

Feeling (F) is the function by which one comes to decisions by weighing the relative values and merits of the issues. Feeling relies on an understanding of personal and groups values; thus, it is more subjective than thinking. . . . [P]ersons making judgments with the feeling function are more likely to be attuned to the values of others . . . , [have] a concern with the human as opposed to the technical aspects of problems, a need for affiliation, a capacity for warmth, a desire for harmony, and a time orientation that includes preservation of the values of the past. (p. 12, italics in original; boldfaces added)

While the functions or processes are included in the above, Jung was very interested in the complementary attitudes or orientations to life embodied in **extraversion** and **introversion.**

In the extraverted attitude **(E),** attention seems to flow out, or to be drawn out to the objects and people of the environment. . . . [C]haracteristics associated with extraversion [are]: awareness and reliance on the environment for stimulation and guidance; an action-oriented, sometimes impulsive way of meeting life; frankness; ease of communication; or sociability.

In the introverted attitude **(I),** energy is drawn from the environment, and consolidated within one's position. The main interests of the introvert are in the inner world of concepts and ideas. . . . [Introverts have the following] characteristics . . . : interest in the clarity of concepts and ideas; reliance on enduring concepts more than on transitory external events; a thoughtful, contemplative detachment; and enjoyment of solitude and privacy (p. 13).

While Jung did not deal with the importance of judgment and perception directly, Isabel Myers and Katharine Briggs formulated these concepts as a way of describing attitudes and behaviors to the outside world. Furthermore, in relation to the EI attitude, the defining of judgment/perception orientation helps identify which of the two functions, E or I, is the dominant and which is the auxiliary. These help indicate whether thinking-feeling or sensing-intuition are more prominent.

In the **perceptive (P)** attitude, a person is attuned to incoming information. For sensing-percepting (SP) types the information is more likely to be the immediate realities. For intuitive-perceptive (NP) types the information is more likely to be new possibilities. But for both SP and NP types the perceptive attitude is open, curious, and interested. Persons who characteristically live in the perceptive attitude seem in their outer behavior to be spontaneous, curious, and adaptable, open to new events and changes, and aiming to miss nothing.

In the **judging (J)** attitude, a person is concerned with making decisions, seeking closure, planning operations, or organizing activities. For thinking-judging (TJ) types the decisions and plans are more likely to be based on logical analysis; for *feeling-judging* (FJ) types the decisions and plans are more likely to be based on human factors. But for all persons who characteristically live in the judging (J) attitude, perception tends to be shut off as soon as they have observed enough to make a decision. . . . Persons who prefer J often seem in their outer behavior to be organized, purposeful, and decisive. . . . It is important to make sure it is understood that judgment refers to decision-making, the exercise of judgment, and is a valuable and indispensable tool (p. 14).

Each of these preferences combines to create sixteen different personality type descriptions. These are described in Table 4.2.

Considerable research on the MBTI has been in conjunction with the Strong Interest Inventory (SII) (Levin, 1990; Miller, 1988, 1992; Dillon & Weissman, 1987). Results of the MBTI and the SII combine to form a career development plan (Hammer & Kummerow, 1993). Figure 4.2 outlines this process.

Evaluation of the Myers–Briggs Typology The MBTI has been used by many counselors but has not had universal acceptance. A thorough analysis of many studies involving the MBTI questions the instrument's validity (Pittenger, 1993). It is one of the most researched tests around. Herr and Cramer (1996) indicate over 200 studies between 1991 and 1994. However, it is a source of controversy among academics. There are questions about its limitations in counseling, its tendency to make people feel good, and the lack of psychological training of its developers. Yet many counselors believe the information and understanding gained from the instrument have been useful. Our recommendation is that practitioners use it with a full understanding that other instruments may be as effective. To pull together current thinking, a model developed by Chartrand and Bertok (1993) and a new scale developed by Holland and Gottfredson (1994) to assess a person's attitudes and strategies about careers give practitioners some idea of the directions toward which trait-factor thinking is developing.

The NEO Personality Inventory-Revised (NEO PI-R) An important personality instrument which measures the "big five" personality indicators—neuroticism, extroversion, openness, agreeableness, and conscientiousness—is the NEO PI-R. The instrument was used by Holland and Gottfredson, who developed the Career Attitudes and Strategies Inventory (CASI) (1994) to assess how work and nonwork environments affect career change, work performance, and job satisfaction. These scales include: Job Satisfaction, Work Involvement, Skill Development, Dominant Style, Career Worries, Interpersonal Abuse, Family Commitment, Risk-Taking Style, and Geographical Barriers. In comparing Vocational Identity (Holland, Daiger & Power, 1980) with several scales in the

TABLE 4.2 Effects of the Combinations of All Four Preferences in Young People

CHARACTERISTICS FREQUENTLY ASSOCIATED WITH EACH TYPE

	SENSING TYPES		INTUITIVE TYPES	
INTROVERTS	**ISTJ** Serious, quiet, earn success by concentration and thoroughness. Practical, orderly. matter-of-fact, logical, realistic and dependable. See to it that everything is well organized. Take responsibility. Make up their own minds as to what should be accomplished and work toward it steadily, regardless of protests or distractions.	**ISFJ** Quiet, friendly, responsible and conscientious. Work devotedly to meet their obligations. Lend stability to any project or group. Thorough, painstakingly accurate. May need time to master technical subjects, as their interests are usually not technical. Patient with detail and routine. Loyal, considerate, concerned with how other people feel.	**INFJ** Succeed by perseverance, originality and desire to do whatever is needed or wanted. Put their best efforts into their work. Quietly forceful, conscientious, concerned for others. Respected for their firm principles. Likely to be honored and followed for their clear convictions as to how best to serve the common good.	**INTJ** Usually have original minds and great drive for their own ideas and purposes. In fields that appeal to them, they have a fine power to organize a job and carry it through with or without help. Skeptical, critical, independent, determined, often stubborn. Must learn to yield less important points in order to win the most important.	**INTROVERTS**
	ISTP Cool onlookers—quiet, reserved, observing and analyzing life with detached curiosity and unexpected flashes of original humor. Usually interested in impersonal principles, cause and effect, how and why mechanical things work. Exert themselves no more than they think necessary, because any waste of energy would be inefficient.	**ISFP** Retiring, quietly friendly, sensitive, kind, modest about their abilities. Shun disagreements, do not force their opinions or values on others. Usually do not care to lead but are often loyal followers. Often relaxed about getting things done, because they enjoy the present moment and do not want to spoil it by undue haste or exertion.	**INFP** Full of enthusiasms and loyalties, but seldom talk of these until they know you well. Care about learning, ideas, language, and independent projects of their own. Tend to undertake too much, then somehow get it done. Friendly, but often too absorbed in what they are doing to be sociable. Little concerned with possessions or physical surroundings.	**INTP** Quiet, reserved, impersonal. Enjoy especially theoretical or scientific subjects. Logical to the point of hair-splitting. Usually interested mainly in ideas, with little liking for parties or small talk. Tend to have sharply defined interests. Need careers where some strong interest can be used and useful.	
EXTRAVERTS	**ESTP** Matter-of-fact, do not worry or hurry, enjoy whatever comes along. Tend to like mechanical things and sports, with friends on the side. May be a bit blunt or insensitive. Adaptable, tolerant, generally conservative in values. Dislike long explanations. Are best with real things that can be worked, handled, taken apart or put together.	**ESFP** Outgoing, easygoing, accepting, friendly, enjoy everything and make things more fun for others by their enjoyment. Like sports and making things. Know what's going on and join in eagerly. Find remembering facts easier than mastering theories. Are best in situations that need sound common sense and practical ability with people as well as with things.	**ENFP** Warmly enthusiastic, high-spirited, ingenious, imaginative. Able to do almost anything that interests them. Quick with a solution for any difficulty and ready to help anyone with a problem. Often rely on their ability to improvise instead of preparing in advance. Can usually find compelling reasons for whatever they want.	**ENTP** Quick, ingenious, good at many things. Stimulating company, alert and outspoken. May argue for fun on either side of a question. Resourceful in solving new and challenging problems, but may neglect routine assignments. Apt to turn to one new interest after another. Skillful in finding logical reasons for what they want.	**EXTRAVERTS**
	ESTJ Practical, realistic, matter-of-fact, with a natural head for business or mechanics. Not interested in subjects they see no use for, but can apply themselves when necessary. Like to organize and run activities. May make good administrators, especially if they remember to consider others' feelings and points of view.	**ESFJ** Warm-hearted, talkative, popular, conscientious, born cooperators, active committee members. Need harmony and may be good at creating it. Always doing something nice for someone. Work best with encouragement and praise. Little interest in abstract thinking or technical subjects. Main interest is in things that directly and visibly affect people's lives.	**ENFJ** Responsive and responsible. Generally feel real concern for what others think or want, and try to handle things with due regard for other person's feelings. Can present a proposal or lead a group discussion with ease and tact. Sociable, popular, sympathetic. Responsive to praise and criticism.	**ENTJ** Hearty, frank, decisive, leaders in activities. Usually good in anything that requires reasoning and intelligent talk, such as public speaking. Are usually well-informed and enjoy adding to their fund of knowledge. May sometimes be more positive and confident than their experience in an area warrants.	

SOURCE: Myers & McCaulley, 1985, pp. 20–21.

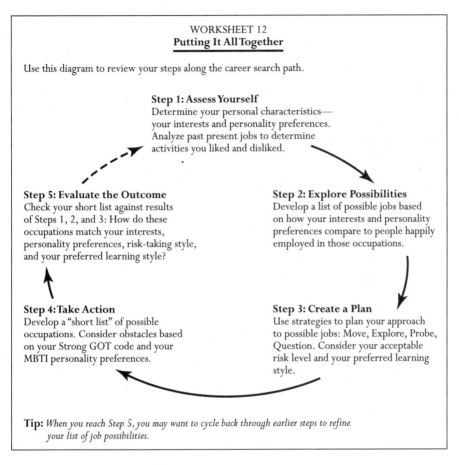

WORKSHEET 12
Putting It All Together

Use this diagram to review your steps along the career search path.

Step 1: Assess Yourself
Determine your personal characteristics—
your interests and personality preferences.
Analyze past present jobs to determine
activities you liked and disliked.

Step 5: Evaluate the Outcome
Check your short list against results
of Steps 1, 2, and 3: How do these
occupations match your interests,
personality preferences, risk-taking style,
and your preferred learning style?

Step 2: Explore Possibilities
Develop a list of possible jobs based
on how your interests and personality
preferences compare to people happily
employed in those occupations.

Step 4: Take Action
Develop a "short list" of possible
occupations. Consider obstacles based
on your Strong GOT code and your
MBTI personality preferences.

Step 3: Create a Plan
Use strategies to plan your approach
to possible jobs: Move, Explore, Probe,
Question. Consider your acceptable
risk level and your preferred learning
style.

Tip: *When you reach Step 5, you may want to cycle back through earlier steps to refine your list of job possibilities.*

FIGURE 4.2 Using the SII and the MBTI for a Career Development Program

SOURCE: *Hammer & Kummerow (1993).*

CASI, clearer definitions were found with a high correlation between Vocational Identity and Job Satisfaction and a negative correlation between Vocational Identity and Career Worries or Interpersonal Abuse. When compared with the NEO-PI-R, the correlations between Vocational Identity, the scales on the CASI and the five personality factors of the NEO-PI-R indicate much better predictive possibilities for job satisfaction, the ability to change, and possibly even work performance.

THE THEORY OF WORK ADJUSTMENT

As an outgrowth of better rehabilitation services for vocationally disabled clients, René Dawis, Lloyd Lofquist and their associates at the University of Minnesota

---

Practical Applications

With use of the booklet, *Introduction to Type and Careers* (Hammer, 1993), the MBTI can foster career development in several ways. A client can be directed to:

- Use the identified traits and write a composition that describes oneself.
- Describe an ideal work environment based on one's traits.
- Divide a group of clients into subgroups based on type and discuss the similarities and traits.
- Divide a group of clients into subgroups by diverse types, identify differences, and discuss the implications for a learning environment.
- Choose an occupation, describe the personal traits that would be helpful in that work, and compare their own traits and occupational aspirations.
- Have clients write self-descriptive adjectives.
- Using MBTI results, project their lifestyle five and ten years from now.
- Ask clients to describe how personal traits influence career development and choices.
- For dual-career couples, have each describe traits and the effect on work environments and interactions at home.
- Ask individuals who are considering a career change how personal traits contribute to seeking a career change.

---

developed concepts of Trait–Factor Theory into the **Theory of Work Adjustment (TWA).** Work adjustment is a "continuous and dynamic process by which a worker seeks to achieve and maintain a correspondence with a work environment" (Dawis & Lofquist, 1984, p. 237). Other theories related to career development are primarily concerned with vocational choices. TWA is more associated with the relationship of the person to the job and to the occupational setting. Hershenson's (1993) work adjustment theory is related more to developmental concerns than trait–factor ideas. Although TWA describes factors that influence an individual's adjustment to the work environment, it also works to define a good career choice as one in which individuals are both satisfactory and satisfied (Fouad, 1993).

An important aspect of the work adjustment theory and its related research is the relationship between the individual's needs and the reinforcement systems of those needs that are present in the work setting. Murray (1938) defined needs

and Holland (1973) speaks to the tolerability of the work situation and its congruence with the worker's needs. Lofquist and Dawis (1989) listed twenty different reinforcers that can possibly be found in a work setting. These are reduced to six categories: safety, comfort, status, altruism, achievement, and autonomy. Different individuals will have needs that match with the reinforcers of any given occupation or setting. The match between needs and reinforcers will be a likely indicator of job satisfaction and the length of time an individual will work in that particular setting. Job satisfaction and tenure will vary according to closeness of fit or match with needs and reinforcers.

TWA theorizes that each individual seeks to achieve and maintain a sense of **correspondence** with the environment. Correspondence is present when the individual and the environment are attuned and when work meets the needs of the individual and the individual meets the demands of the work environment. Correspondence is a dynamic process because both the needs of the individual and the demands of the job change. However, if the correspondence continues, job tenure is extended.

TWA consists of eighteen propositions and corollaries (Dawis & Lofquist, 1984). Current theory is based on research that modified their earlier work (Dawis, England & Lofquist, 1964; Dawis, Lofquist & Weiss, 1968; Lofquist & Dawis, 1969). These can be summarized in four major points. (1) The personality of the worker and the work environment must be in basic agreement. (2) The individual's needs are the primary concern for how he/she will fit into the work environment. (3) To achieve stability and tenure, the individual's needs must correspond to the reinforcer system of the work environment. (4) Job placement works most effectively when the worker's traits match the requirements of the work environment.

Two basic concepts predict work adjustment: *satisfaction* and *satisfactoriness*. Satisfaction is related to the worker and one's adjustment to the work environment. Satisfactoriness refers to the employer and whether the needs of the work environment are being met by the worker. TWA concerns itself with (a) turnover, absenteeism and tardiness; (b) job morale; (c) commitment to the job; and (d) productivity as indicators of work adjustment. TWA differs from Trait-Factor Theory in that it makes use of clearly defined concepts and follows an articulated theoretical model.

Hershenson's (1993) model of work adjustment contains three interacting subsystems within the person that intervene with the work setting to facilitate work adjustment. His model is presented in Figure 4.3.

In Figure 4.3, Hershenson conceptualizes three interacting personal subsystems: work personality, work competencies, and work goals. Work personality refers to the person's work-related self-concept, motivation, needs, and values and is presumed to begin developing during the preschool years. Work

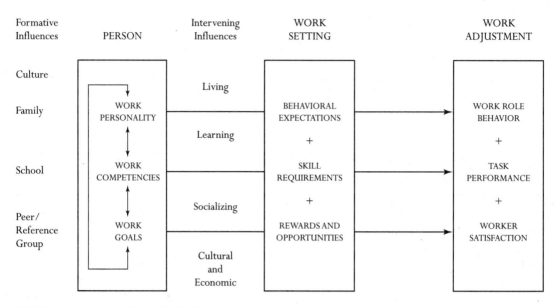

FIGURE 4.3 Hershenson's Model of Work Adjustment

SOURCE: *Hershenson (1993), p. 445. Reprinted from the* Journal of Counseling and Development, *p. 445, © 1993, by permission of the American Counseling Association.*

competencies refer to the person's work-related habits and physical, mental, and interpersonal skills that develop during the school years. Work goals refer to the person's development upon leaving school and entering the work world. Formative influences on the person include culture, family (especially on work personality), school, and peer and reference groups (especially on work goals). Intervening influences (e.g., living, learning, socializing, cultural, and economic factors) are carried into the work setting, where behavioral expectations, skill requirements, and rewards and opportunities come into play. These all affect work role behavior, task performance, worker satisfaction, and work adjustment.

Hershenson's (1993) model is contextually based. It allows consideration of many external structural factors. For example, peer and reference group determine if many high schoolers see themselves as college material and apply for college admission, scholarships, and other financial aid. Family influence can be quite subtle, yet many young people mimic the behaviors and attitudes toward work that they see in the adults around them. Behavioral expectations are another factor: many schools and workplaces have middle-class values that have to be made explicit to individuals from lower-income backgrounds (Payne, 1995).

Assessment Instruments Used with Work Adjustment Theory

Abilities. Abilities include pervasive attitudes, predicted skills as opposed to acquired skills, and a necessary way to help conceptualize the wide variety of

---

Practical Applications

TWA is useful for conceptualizing the types of problems that an individual may have in adjusting to a particular job. It helps clients with problems with coworkers and supervisors, an inability to meet the demands of a work situation, and pre-retirement/retirement issues. For instance, an individual's skills may not be developed sufficiently to meet the requirements of the job. Furthermore, the job may require skills that the individual is unable to develop due to lack of education or ability. An individual's values and needs are not met by the work environment. Another concern could be that the individual does not understand the reinforcer patterns of the work involved. Sometimes dissatisfaction with the job may be due not to the job itself but to problems outside of work. When a client complains of problems at work, the initial approach is to assess the client's work personality and environment. Assessing the work values and needs of a client can be done by using the MIQ, or if this is not possible, using the conceptual schema of the MIQ along with other measures of adjustment and personality.

---

work skills (Dawis & Lofquist, 1984; Sharf, 1996). The General Aptitude Test Battery (GATB) and the Occupational Ability Patterns, both developed by the U.S. Department of Labor, describe the important abilities that are required for a great variety of jobs.

Needs and Values. The Minnesota Importance Questionnaire (MIQ; Rounds et al., 1981) identifies twenty needs:

ability utilization	compensation	security	supervision (technical)
variety	recognition	authority	company policies/ practices
advancement	moral values	social service	
coworkers	activity	working conditions	supervision-human relations
responsibility	creativity		
achievement	independence	social status	

Job Satisfaction. The Minnesota Satisfaction Questionnaire is another part of the system of assessment used in TWA. These instruments are available from Vocational Psychology Research, Department of Psychology, University of Minnesota.

Interests are not part of the usual assessment procedure for TWA, since they are defined by abilities and values. TWA uses the Minnesota Occupational Classification System which has as component parts the Occupational Ability Patterns and the Occupational Reinforcer Patterns to help place clients in appropriate work settings.

Evaluation of Work Adjustment Theory TWA has been carefully developed with rigorous care to devise appropriate assessment instruments, test hypotheses, and codify a useful tool for fitting people with work environments. Most people work in a situation rather than spend their time making vocational decisions. Practitioners will face many issues related to work situations and person-environment fit. TWA approaches the subject in a systematic manner. More recent findings concerning learning theory need to be incorporated into the research on TWA (Hesketh, 1993). Concerns about the thoroughness of study of gender and ethnic groups have been noted (Tinsley, 1993).

Relevance for Multicultural and Diverse Populations TWA emphasizes individuals, not groups. Therefore, "gender, ethnicity, national origin, religion, sexual orientation, and disability status are seen as inaccurate and unreliable bases for estimating skills, abilities, needs, values, personality styles, and adjustment style of a particular person ... [the current functioning of a person is dependent on] opportunity or its absence" (Dawis, 1994, p. 41).

HISTORICAL ANTECEDENTS TO VOCATIONAL PSYCHOLOGY

Now that the reader is acquainted with foundational approaches to vocational psychology, some of the historical antecedents to the academic discipline can be appreciated. One's theory and practice of vocational psychology can be truncated by historical ignorance (Dumont & Carson, 1995). Historical "myopia" can contribute to a rigid, "unicultural" perspective (p. 371). The philosophy of vocation did not arise from twentieth-century psychological and sociological theories, but actually predates written history. Only in the mid-1990s did scholars present documentation that revealed the ancient roots of vocational psychology and guidance. Recent scholarship shows that 2,500 to 500 years ago, precursors to Parsons's (1909) work as well as current theory and practice already existed. Predicates of vocational psychology can be unearthed from ancient Egypt, Greece, and China, as well as from the age of classical Islam to the multicultural society of late medieval Spain.

Ancient Egypt and Greece

In the Western world, two of the earliest literate peoples lived in ancient Egypt and Greece, whom Dumont and Carson (1995) refer to collectively as the Eastern Mediterranean civilizations. The following discussion, based on their article, explores Western antecedents to vocational psychology practice.

Ancient Egypt As early as 10,000 B.C.E., fixed-location agriculture flourished in the Middle East and southeast Africa. Economics in these areas initially were dependent on the seasonal work of planting and harvest. As the population grew, cities formed and governments evolved that eventually led to the development of several Egyptian empires along the banks of the Nile River. The economy gradually branched out to include land and sea-trade routes. A proliferation of occupations arose—architecture, engineering, construction work, seamanship, interior and exterior design—and work by artisans and craftsmen, including what is now called mortuary science. Ancient Egyptian empires, among others, developed what is now called military science. A strong army and navy enabled them to maintain their civilization and expand Egyptian influence throughout the Eastern Mediterranean to encompass Greek and Semitic peoples. Most important for the ancient Egyptians was a writing technology that allowed for record keeping and communications. Predicates of vocational psychology include the division of labor; the use of sociopolitical mechanisms to channel persons into appropriate occupational roles; and the allocation of resources for educating, skill training, and socializing persons into the workforce.

Ancient Greece From approximately 1000 B.C.E., the ancient Egyptians contributed to later Greek civilizations, especially many cultural and religious customs. The ancient Greeks shaped modernist thinking about a wide range of topics, including architecture, drama and athletic competition, politics and ethics, philosophy and psychology, logic and geometry, epic narrative, and mythology. To support the rich civilization and the complex mercantile economy of the ancient Greeks that superseded that of the ancient Egyptians, sociopolitical mechanisms were necessary to allow young people the opportunity to develop requisite skills.

Hesiod, writing towards the end of the eighth century B.C.E., advocated that people engage in occupational activities according to aptitude and emphasized the virtue of earning an honest living. Avocational activities also were encouraged while crops awaited maturation. Thus, amateur seafaring, public debates and oral recitation of epic poetry, boxing competitions, and craft activities filled their leisure time. Later, those who excelled at such avocational activities became professionals at them.

Solon, the great "lawgiver" of the seventh century B.C.E., recognized aptitudes and interests. In central Greece, Attica developed beyond a land-based agricultural economy to include fishing, the manufacture of weapons and bronze and steel armor, the importation of raw materials and the exportation of finished products, public administration, and education. Citizens of all classes in Attica were accorded the right to progress in their work. Those who became highly accomplished were respected.

The Athens of Pericles in the fifth century B.C.E. also supported an individual's right to achieve what their capabilities allowed without interference from the state. A meritocracy prevailed. The work culture was exclusively male. Captives brought back from foreign wars (mostly women and children; men were usually executed at battle sites) became servants and slaves and were compelled to assimilate into the Athenian underclass, much as immigrants in the West today are pressed to assimilate into their new country's political economies starting from the underclass. Then as now, some members of the underclass became wealthy through commerce and mercantile activities.

Person by Environment Fit originated in ancient Greece, a legacy of the classical developmentalism of the Greek philosophers. Plato (c. 427 B.C.E.–c. 327 B.C.E.) wrote that the development of vocation begins in childhood. He recognized that a child's education determines success as an adult, and proposed an admirably balanced curriculum of aesthetics and athletics, literary and cognitive endeavors. For one to be good at anything one would have to practice it from their youth onwards. In what sounds like a prescient warning of the evils of television, Plato admonished exposing children to stories that only shaped a lazy or dangerous character. One's competence would determine their status in the republic. Plato remarked on the desirable qualities for certain occupations. His multimethod screening for police candidates included (a) the extent to which the interests of the republic would rule candidates' lives, (b) tests of judgment from youth onwards, and (c) assessment of candidates' vulnerability to bribery and other corrupting influences. Physicians who had known illness themselves were deemed more able to understand their patients' ailments, but judges need not have committed evil acts to be qualified to condemn those whom they judged.

Marketplace demand was a recognized basis for diversification of vocational opportunities and occupational choices in ancient Greece. The need for specialization, with a natural aptitude for one's work, placed heavy emphasis on training and education. Changing occupations was discouraged by the sociopolitical system. One was expected to spend one's entire life reaching for the highest skills of their occupation.

Ancient China

At the same time that Greece evolved the role of work in people's lives, ancient China transformed from an emphasis on feudalism to a new and efficient centrally administered imperial government. The following discussion is based on Dumont and Carson (1995).

In the twelfth century B.C.E, China made the transition from a Bronze Age to an Iron Age, which occurred in the Eastern Mediterranean civilizations at roughly the same time. By the sixth century B.C.E., the first formulations of Chinese philosophy appeared, resulting in what is traditionally known as the "Hundred Schools." Taoism and Confucianism are the best known of these schools.

Taoism Taoism purportedly is derived from the writings of a government-employed scribe later referred to as Lao-tzu, "old one." Taoism asserts that one must be true to one's nature in order to live a fulfilled life and follow an occupation consistent with one's true nature. It was believed that propitious events occurred to those pursuing a proper vocation, and one was enabled to pursue a choice of work. Thus, a version of Person by Environment Fit originated in ancient China concurrent with ancient Greece. These events find their present-day counterpart in vocational psychology when career choice is casually attributed to chance "accidents." Taoism conceived of government as a self-perpetuating disorder (Lao-tzu sounds like he was discontented in his work) which placed limits on what we refer to now as personal growth and self-actualization. Government only served to structure and stylize social conditions to meet its own needs at the expense of the individual. The Taoist notion of excessive government can be generalized to the risks of excessive "rational" and "willful" control over one's occupational decision-making. Imposing a rigid, systematic method of occupational decision-making on oneself or others risks violating one's true nature and fosters a lack of job satisfaction and productivity.

Confucianism In contrast to Taoism, Confucianism held that a wisely administered government had moral integrity. Confucius was an actual historical person, K'ung Ch'iu, thought to have been an itinerant private tutor and teacher in the China of sixth century B.C.E. He advocated leadership by good example and treating others as one would treat oneself. His faith in the possibilities inherent in wise government predated Plato. Wise government was defined as the orderly concentration of power in the hands of those most capable of administering it. From this basic Confucian philosophy arose the first civil service testing programs.

Classical Islam

In addition to the precursors of vocational psychology in ancient Egypt, Greece, and China, other historical roots of vocational theory come from classical Islam. Islam was founded in 622 C.E. in present-day Medina, Saudi Arabia, by the prophet Mohammed (c. 570 C.E.–632 C.E.). He proclaimed himself the latest in a long line of prophets that included Moses, Elijah, and Jesus Christ. In the centuries immediately following Mohammed's death, the Muslim religion spread from North Africa and Spain in the West to Persia (Iran) and India in the East. The Islamic empire extended further than that of the Greek empire established by Alexander the Great in the third century B.C.E. Classical Islam reached its zenith in the eleventh century with caliphates—great religious capitals and cultural centers—established in Cordobá, Spain and Damascus, Syria.

Predicates of vocational psychology are mentioned in a tenth-century Iraqi text (Carson & Altai, 1994). The discussion that follows is based on their article.

The text, *Rasa'il Ikhwàn al-Safá wa-Khulln al-Wafa* (commonly translated as **Treatises of the Brothers of Purity,** or *TBP*), was written around 955 C.E. by what is believed to be a group of five to ten Muslim reformers from the Basra region of what is now southern Iraq. The group collectively called themselves **Ikhwàn al-Safá** to hide their individual identities for fear of reprisal by Islamic fundamentalists. The initial goal of the authors of the *TBP* was to compile all the known sciences into one work, regardless of the cultural origins of such knowledge. This was a radical concept at the time because only knowledge of Islamic origin was seen as valid and trustworthy. The authors compiled information from Greek, Jewish, Christian, Persian, and Indian sources. Various sciences were classified as traditional or foreign. Traditional sciences were disciplines based on the Koran (the Islamic holy book) and included grammar, poetry, history, theology, and law. Foreign sciences were disciplines based on human intervention and were discovered through the use of reason. Traditional sciences had the weight of divine authority behind them, foreign sciences did not, so it was more acceptable to criticize and correct them. Islamic fundamentalists were threatened by foreign sciences and tried to suppress them whenever possible.

In the *TBP,* ideas related to vocational psychology fall under the classification of foreign sciences. Three tenets are discussed: (a) information in decision-making, (b) congruence, and (c) the components of congruence. These topics are touched upon throughout the *TBP.* As described in the *TBP,* information in decision-making was the ruler's prerogative. One usually followed family tradition in terms of work. However, the ruler was expected to be knowledgeable of occupations and to reassign occupational roles when dictated by workforce needs. An appropriate match between people and their jobs was based on the behaviors and mental abilities required to perform job tasks.

Job descriptions mentioned in the *TBP* include musicians, painters, and jugglers. Musicians were expected to be both composers and performers, with emphasis on the nature of the job and the way audiences were affected. Some musicians would only have limited audience appeal, while other musicians would enjoy wide popular appeal. Differences in abilities among musicians were acknowledged. Painters were expected to imitate that which appears in nature, including things, persons, and animals. As with musicians, vast differences in acquired skills among painters were acknowledged. Jugglers were expected to possess speed and to make actions appear invisible to the naked eye. Social class differences were noted in response to jugglers' acts—uneducated people laughed, intelligent people were surprised and amazed. Entry into these occupations, the subsequent work path, and aspects of job satisfaction were rarely mentioned by the *Ikhwàn al-Safá*. Ostensibly, many occupations described in the *TBP* were open to both men and women, but one occupation was specifically identified as suitable for women only: "weeper" at funerals.

Congruence assumes that a person is best capable of one line of work. Long before Parsons (1909), the *Ikhwàn al-Safá* linked presupposed compatibility between a person's individual characteristics to certain occupations. Workers were classified into seven broad groups: (1) artisans and craftsmen; (2) businessmen and traders, (3) construction engineers and workers; (4) kings, rulers, sultans, politicians, and soldiers; (5) employees, servants, and daily workers; (6) the disabled, the unemployed, and the idle; and (7) men of religion and scholars. These broad groups were further subdivided into occupations, with descriptions of the appropriate character, personality type and traits, and relevant goals and prerequisite motivations associated with each occupation. Similar to Holland's (1985) concept of the effects of a vocational environment on an individual's vocational personality, the *TBP* assumed that an occupation would have characteristics that would force workers into certain behaviors while on the job.

The ability of a worker to properly perform a given occupation's responsibilities in the *TBP* was based on four factors: (1) intellective factors and education, (2) temperament and physique, (3) natural environment and chance, and (4) astrological factors.

Intellective factors and education entailed the content of the domain of knowledge needed for competent performance of the occupation, suitably diverse methods for learning skill acquisition, perceptual ability as grounded in one's sensory organs themselves, and particular features of occupations. The way a person's native intelligence and potential lent themselves to occupational mastery resembles many present-day theories of adult career development. *Temperament and physique* referred to what are known today as a person's intellectual, academic, and occupational interests; innate personality traits; body type; and mental abilities. *Natural environment and chance* could have been "chance" events of either natural or human origin, and resemble the investigation of the role of chance factors which are of increasing interest to present-day theorists of occupational development. *Astrological influences* determined personal characteristics. Astrology was not of Islamic origin and therefore considered a foreign science.

Like Dumont and Carson (1995), Carson and Altai (1994) conclude that gaining an historical perspective on vocational psychology helps to put the academic discipline into context. The historical relevance for multicultural and diverse populations becomes evident in both articles, which helps minimize the apparent twentieth-century androcentric foundations of the field. These androcentric foundations are further eroded when one examines the ideas of occupational choice published in late medieval Spain.

Late Medieval Spain

Medieval Spain was the most multicultural society in Europe. When the rest of the continent was in the Dark Ages that followed the fall of the Roman Empire, in early medieval Spain Islamic Cordobá shone as a brilliant beacon of intellectual and cultural light in an otherwise grim and harsh European civilization. Christians, Jews, and Muslims intermingled and frequently intermarried. Professions such as government administrator, musician, scholar, sailor, merchant, and the medical and apothecary arts were enriched by the integration of practices derived from the multiple coexistent religious groups. This vibrant society produced one of the earliest comprehensive compilations of occupational descriptions, *Speculum Vitae Humanae* (*Mirror of Human Life*), published by Bishop Rodrigo Sánchez de Arévalo in 1468. Sánchez de Arévalo's book is the subject of an article by Chabassus and Zytowski (1987), upon which the following discussion is based.

The Mirror of Human Life was published when printing with movable type was perfected by Johann Gutenburg (died 1467). Over the next 125 years, the book went through many editions in its original Latin, and also in Spanish, French, and German. Based on a public debate Sánchez de Arévalo witnessed in his youth, he subtitled his book *The Advantages and Disadvantages, the Satisfactions and Bitterness, the Consolations and Miseries, the Favorable and Unfavorable Things, the Flattery and Danger of All States of Life.*

Book I describes the pros and cons of secular occupations: kings and princes, knights, consorts by marriage (the latter being the only occupational account to mention women), judges and mayors, weavers, blacksmiths, carpenters, hunters, animal caretakers, actors, and physicians ("the most honorable of crafts for it is essential to human life"). One of the drawbacks of being a physician: "They glory in the highly esteemed name of doctor for the sake of profit!" The advantages and disadvantages of the liberal arts as a field of study also are discussed: grammar, logic, rhetoric, sciences, astronomy, music, arithmetic, and geometry.

Book II examines the pros and cons of religious vocations: popes (including the stressors that made so many of them short-lived), cardinals, archbishops, bishops, priests, deacons, cantors (i.e., singers—a Jewish legacy), stewards, schoolmasters, and monks. He does not seem to mention mother abbesses and nuns.

Despite the fact that Sánchez de Arévalo's *Mirror of Human Life* focused only on occupations for men, his work was the most detailed description of available occupations published to date. Like the Islamic *Treatises of the Brothers of Purity,* he lists three fundamental concepts that are especially relevant to present-day applied career counseling and vocational psychology: information in decision-making, congruence, and the components of congruence.

Regarding information in decision-making, Sánchez de Arévalo wrote that occupational choices could not be made without information gathered in advance. A failure to choose well would result from "not sufficiently know[ing] the pleasant and unpleasant . . . , the advantages and disadvantages of various states and ways of life" (cited in Chabassus & Zytoski, 1987, p. 170).

Similar to the cultures of ancient Greece and classical Islam, the society of late medieval Spain recognized that congruence—choosing an occupation compatible with an individual's characteristics—was optimal. "Each has to consider what nature makes him inclined for" (cited in Chabassus & Zytoski, 1987, p. 170), wrote Sánchez de Arévalo. He quoted several ancient Roman philosophers to support his argument, including: "Cicero (106–43 B.C.E.): 'All deliberation needs to encompass one's nature.'" Also, "Seneca (5 B.C.E.–65 C.E.): 'Forced pursuit is unfruitful, for in opposition to nature, virtue is taken from labor'" (p. 170). These statements echo the Person by Environment Fit and Holland's typology that desires to match personality traits to workplace environments.

Sánchez de Arévalo expounded on Seneca and the ideas that natural aptitude and inclination (e.g., interests, values, and/or personality) are essential to consider in occupational choice. "Study yourself, measure your forces, consider your fragility, your makeup, your nature, your habits" (cited in Chabassus & Zytoski, 1987, p. 170)—good advice through the centuries, now a guiding influence in modern approaches to vocational psychology.

Fundamental precepts of vocational psychology are usually presumed to have been devised in the twentieth century (Dumont & Carson, 1995). But the above exposition of the historical antecedents to vocational psychology illustrates a venerable ancestry that predates Parsons (1909) by thousands of years. No student who reads of these earliest ideas could ever again call vocational psychology a dull subject. The history of the academic discipline is lavish in its multicultural and multidimensional contributions to the role of work in people's lives.

5

Foremost Counseling Theories
Applied to Careers

Several preeminent counseling theories are applicable to vocational psychology. This chapter ranges from the most classic modernist theories to the newest postmodern approaches to the role of work in people's lives. We first focus on psychodynamic approaches to work. Then we discuss the person-centered or humanistic, existential approaches to vocational counseling. Next we address reality therapy and consider cognitive behavioral therapies. Finally, we present the postmodern epistemologies of social constructionism and constructivism as they relate to vocational psychology.

Before we begin, let us say a few words about the difference between counseling and psychotherapy. Often the terms are used interchangeably because there is no consensus among clinical practitioners about when counseling ends and psychotherapy begins (Sharf, 1996). Without entering this debate, we use the terms interchangeably. Vocational psychology is a useful part of any clinical practitioner's repertoire. The boundaries between vocational psychology and personal counseling and psychotherapy are artificial (Brown, 1985). Others differentiate between vocational researchers and career counseling practitioners (Hackett & Lonborg, 1993). Many work-related issues concern clients of counselors, social workers, marriage and family therapists, psychologists, psychiatrists, as well as those who seek help from teachers, coaches, and clergy. Frankly, there are not enough specialists in vocational psychology to accommodate all the clients who have work-related concerns.

PSYCHODYNAMIC THEORY

The degree to which you can make your work playful, [is the measure
that] you've got it made.
—Edward S. Bordin (cited in Goodyear, Roffey, and Jack, 1994, p. 571)

Traditionally speaking, the term *psychoanalysis* refers to: "(1) a theory of personality and psychopathology, (2) a method of investigating the mind, and (3) a theory of [clinical] treatment" (Wolitzky, 1995, p. 12). The various forms of psychoanalytic theories and therapies trace their origins back to Sigmund Freud (1856–1939), whose original writings comprise twenty-three volumes (Wolitzky, 1995). Most theories of counseling and of marriage and family therapy are reactions against traditional Freudian psychoanalysis. Yet Freud is an intellectual giant of the twentieth century, whose principles have been applied to work, society and the family, music and art, literature and religion (Simpson, 1987).

To discuss traditional psychoanalysis and its variants, often called **psychodynamic approaches,** is beyond the scope of this book. Corey (1996) provides a comprehensive introduction, and the video *Freud under Analysis* is an excellent overview (Simpson, 1987). We confine our focus to psychodynamic theory as it pertains to the role of work in people's lives. Beginning with Alfred Adler (whom we discuss in Chapter 8), Carl Gustav Jung, and Karen Horney (also known as neo-Freudians), several of Freud's original disciples broke with him over the issue of libidinal drives in childhood as the primary determiners of mental life and behavior. Libidinal drives are but one example of the **mechanistic model** adopted by Freud and other psychoanalytic and psychodynamic practitioners. Mechanistic models aim to discover scientifically the processes that describe the true mechanisms underlying the explanation of a phenomenon (Flew, 1984). Freud, a quintessential modernist, posited that **unconscious motivation** was the mechanism that determined human behavior. Unconscious motivation occurs out of one's awareness but is revealed clinically through free association and in daily life through slips of the tongue and the jokes one finds amusing.

Edward S. Bordin's psychodynamic approach proposes that play is the basis for the role of personality in work and career. The need for play is fused with the requirements of work to find a satisfying vocation. This approach addresses the decision process made during the quest for an appropriate vocation as well as how individual differences affect "the kinds and styles of satisfactions sought" (Bordin, cited in Brown, Brooks & Associates, 1990, p. 104).

The spirit of play is caught in the term *spontaneity*, which is used to refer to the elements of self-expression and self-realization in our responses to situations. Spontaneity is a major key to differentiating work from play. What marks the essence of play is its intrinsically satisfying nature. Although we may engage in play for extrinsic reasons—status, achievement, admiration, even money—what distinguishes play from work is the satisfaction gained from simply engaging in the activity (Bordin, cited in Brown et al., 1990, p. 105, italics in original).

Bordin's theory contains seven propositions: (1) All people in all parts of their lives want feelings of completeness and the opportunity to experience profound happiness. (2) Compulsion and effort as part of one's development find expression in combining work and play. (3) One's attempt to find an "ideal fit between self and work" is characterized by "striving for career decisions." (4) "Developmental conceptions" of lifestyles or character expressions provide the basis for finding occupations that satisfy intrinsic motives. (5) Early developmental experiences and feelings provide the basis of the individual's unique career development. (6) "Personal identity" consists of one's unique features, but also incorporates features of each of the parents. (7) When there are unresolved aspects of the self, the effects of doubting and lack of satisfaction will most likely be manifested in difficulty with career decision-making (Bordin, cited in Brown et al., 1990).

Bordin wanted "counseling to represent something other than the mechanized testing approach. People have different facets that can be expressed in different ways, in different work roles. . . . [O]ne facet is an emphasis on precision or thorough, systematic thought" (Goodyear et al., 1994, pp. 568–569). Bordin believed his two greatest contributions to the vocational psychology field were his ideas on personality and work, because of their importance to the clinical understanding of a person's potential and their function in "assessing the resources and orientations that a person uses in coping with life's challenges," and his idea of the "working alliance," which can be a potent "means of integrating our various ideas about how to bring about change. . . . [W]ithin that conception is a core for what will amount to the basic science of psychotherapy" (Goodyear et al., p. 570).

If vocational choice is an integral expression of a person's personality, then the same constructs used to understand personality development should be helpful in understanding vocational choice (Segal, 1961). Psychoanalytic concepts such as **identification** (relating to another person or idea by adopting on aspects of that person or idea), development of **defense mechanisms** (coping strategies to fend off unpleasant ideations and/or feelings), and **sublimation** (substituting hostile, aggressive or sexual impulses into a more socially accepted form) can provide insight into personality characteristics of individuals' specific vocational choices.

Practical Applications

Applications of the model include: (1) individual vocational counseling, (2) general developmental programs, (3) modification of work to permit more expression of self, and (4) potential application in connection with the closely related concerns of aging and retirement (Bordin, cited in Brown et al., 1991).

Diagnosing career-concerned clients at major decision points in their lives has received limited attention (Miller, 1993). Vocational psychology often is seen as responding solely to career-related problems by applying definite techniques or knowledge to resolve them. Miller combines Bordin's model of diagnostic constructs with an orthogonal model offered by Matre and Cooper (1984) to form the following diagnostic constructs.

> *Dependence*—dependent clients have difficulty solving their problems, are dependent on others to help them, and come to the practitioner for help. It is common for them not to accept responsibility for their own situations. *Lack of information*—because they lack the information necessary to make a choice they face, these clients often seek help. As a rule they are responsible for themselves. *Self-conflict*—when inner conflicts regarding self-image and behavior are incongruent or even when aspects of self-image are at war, these clients seek help. *Choice anxiety*—feelings of being

trapped between two less-than-pleasant choices can lead to procrastination, which is anxiety producing in itself, and the inability to organize one's life. Clients with this no-win situation usually experience stress, tension, lack of sleep, and a draining anxiety. *No problem*—these clients are in tune with themselves and their environment and check in for a "tune-up" or a way of finding reinforcement for choices they have made (Miller, 1993, pp. 36–37).

Matre and Cooper (1984) identify two primary dimensions that impair career decision-making: decided-undecided state and decisive-indecisive trait. **Decided-undecided state** is the temporary indecision that accompanies many decision-making tasks. Salamone (1982) believes that indecision is a normal, rational-cognitive issue, and can be alleviated through accurate information that helps a person make the decision. **Decisive-indecisive trait** is a more permanent trait that is a part of decision-making tasks. Indecisiveness derives from psychological issues and is associated more with a person experiencing personal problems (Miller, 1993).

Combining the works of Bordin (1946) and Matre and Cooper (1984) results in the following propositions. The **decided-decisive client** could be treated through support since this is not a diagnosable problem. The **undecided-decisive client** needs more information and would most benefit from assessment and/or career counseling. The **undecided-indecisive client** is experiencing choice anxiety. These clients suffer from anxiety, low self-concept, immaturity and other negative personality traits that impair career counseling. Personal *and* career counseling are recommended. The **decided-indecisive client** is in self-conflict. They have formed a temporary decision, but are unable to make an actual choice and experience conflict as they want to pursue one career, but have an interest in a dissimilar career (Miller, 1993, pp. 38, 40). An illustration of these theoretical relationships is presented in Figure 5.1.

As shown in Figure 5.1, dependent clients are lodged in the decided-indecisive and the undecided-indecisive quadrants. Lack-of-information clients are lodged in the undecided-decisive quadrant. Self-conflicted clients are firmly lodged in the decided-indecisive quadrant. Choice-anxiety clients are lodged

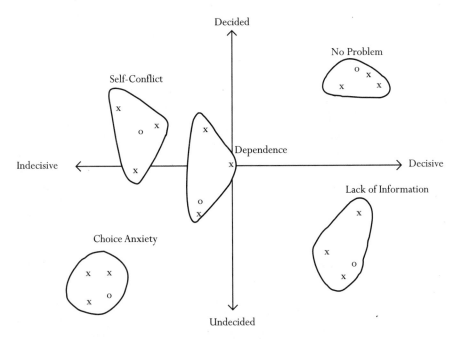

FIGURE 5.1 Theoretical Relationship Between Matre and Cooper's Indecision/Indecisive Paradigm and Bordin's Diagnostic Concepts

SOURCE: Reprinted by permission of the publisher from the Journal of Employment Counseling, *1993, p. 39.*

in the undecided-indecisive quadrant, while no-problem clients are lodged in the exact opposite, decided-decisive quadrant.

Practitioners should form a "working alliance" to diagnose the client's conflict before offering a counseling strategy (Meara & Patton, 1994). This alliance uses the theoretical underpinnings of psychoanalytic process. The client must bring to the alliance: (a) a dissatisfaction with where they are emotionally, (b) a recognized need for assistance, (c) the willingness to accept assistance, (d) the ability to create a rational working relationship with the practitioner, (e) an understanding of the difference between observation and experience, and (f) an ability to want to know more about themselves (Greenson, 1967, cited in Meara & Patton, 1994, p. 164). Meara and Patton further discuss client's fears of the counselor, the process, and change, and cite Bordin's model of dealing with the confusions a client may develop, such as goal confusion, task confusion, and bond confusion.

An essential component for counseling success is positive collaboration between practitioner and client (Horvath & Symonds, 1991; Horvath & Greenberg, 1994). Based on Bordin's approach, the *Working Alliance Inventory (WAI)* was devised to assess the quality of the interaction between practitioner and client (Horvath & Greenberg, 1989). The *WAI* could be a useful quality assurance/program evaluation measure for practitioners, even if they do not use a psychodynamic approach to their vocational guidance.

Evaluation of the Psychodynamic Approach In vocational psychology, psychoanalytic theory has played a minor role (Osipow, 1983). Psychodynamic theory will probably continue to have limited impact because of the length of time it takes for a client to understand the unconscious motivation that can be a compelling factor in their career selection. Psychopathology may account for many of the vocational problems that individuals have, and difficulty in career decision-making may be related to identity problems in youth. A psychoanalytic conceptualization of career choice emphasizes the impulse gratification and anxiety reduction that a particular career offers rather than the interests and abilities that a career may require.

Relevance for Multicultural and Diverse Populations Renowned psychiatrist Thomas Szasz asserts that one can accept many of the clinical methods and techniques of psychoanalysis without embracing its ideology (Simpson, 1987). In this respect, adaptations of psychodynamic approaches have potential application for multicultural and diverse populations. For example, clients may experience both transference and countertransference reactions to bosses and coworkers. By **transference** we mean that a client may react toward a boss or coworker in a manner similar to a significant person in the client's past or present. By **countertransference** we mean that a boss or coworker may react toward a client in a manner similar to a significant person in the boss's or coworker's past or present. Transference and countertransference reactions are especially likely in an increasingly diverse workforce. The distortions that occur in transference/countertransference reactions can also occur when misunderstandings inevitably arise among diverse coworkers.

Clinically, all psychodynamically-oriented approaches have a built-in, individualistic, Western bias in which the presenting problem is presumed to reside within the client. Clients' social and environmental contexts may come into direct conflict with the presumption that the problem in intrapsychic (Corey, 1996). Oftentimes, systemic approaches that focus on the client's immediate and extended families and network of friends may be more appropriate. A given multicultural client may be both individualistic and collectivistic contingent upon context or issue. To the extent that psychodynamic approaches pathologize populations that have already been oppressed—those who live in poverty, the working poor, persons with limited educational and occupational opportunities, persons with alternative lifestyles—we do not endorse the application of psychodynamic theory. However, if psychodynamic theory is used to assist the client to better understand the self in the context of social and cultural realities, then it can be an effective tool.

PERSON-CENTERED APPROACHES

Like psychodynamic approaches, there are a variety of **person-centered approaches** (Bohart, 1995). Also known as humanistic psychology, it was founded by Carl Rogers (1902–1987). In this section we review some of the studies on person-centered approaches to vocational development.

C. H. Patterson described the core conditions for a therapeutic relationship. First, understand the client; practitioners must empathize to see the world through the client's eyes. Any vocational decision is based on the world as the client sees it, not on the world as somebody else sees it. Second, respect the client, even when the client's behaviors are unlikable. Third, be genuine; whatever the practitioner says to the client is an honest response, not a facade. The practitioner is not playing a role, but is a real person with the client. Finally, be concrete; practitioners need to focus on specific rather then general ideas and behaviors that the client communicates (Freeman, 1990).

Practical Applications

Our experience shows that understanding the client's needs aids in making a career change. A young woman sought counseling after having several unpleasant job experiences, which contributed to her negative self-concept. She had an accounting degree and was a skilled accountant but disliked her work. Results of an Edwards Personal Preference Schedule (EPPS) demonstrated high needs for affiliation and achievement. She had not experienced much interaction with others in her jobs. Nor did she advance in the field as she had envisioned. Through counseling she decided to use her skills to further her education, pursue work in the social sciences, and eventually pursue an administrative position.

Brown (1985) suggests that the distinction between career and personal counseling should be minimized. Manuele-Adkins (1992) recommends that counselor training programs incorporate more career counseling techniques in coursework and practica. Imbimbo (1994) concludes that a career counselor needs to be able to alternate between active and directive approaches to be more facilitative and explorative in his/her role. An eclectic style frees the counselor from the strictures of any narrowly defined theory or technique. "Eclectic career counsel-

ing is in some ways harder and requires more broadly based skill and information than either strictly personal or career counseling. The challenge for counselors is to be able to provide a comprehensive service to clients who have comprehensive needs" (p. 58).

Another aspect of applying career counseling to the whole person is emphasized in the term "occupational wellness." Wellness concerns expressed in terms of physical, emotional, and spiritual health need to be translated into the workplace (Dorn, 1992). There is every reason to believe that career concerns affect one emotionally, spiritually, and physically, and the relationship of career and personal identity is a recurring theme in vocational psychology. Another area practitioners need to consider is the link between family and work—the role of work in the familial domain (Richardson, 1993). Work is an "extension of family drama . . . [and] . . . interactional problems and interpersonal dynamics are sometimes translated into the work environment" (Chusid & Cochran, 1989, cited in Dorn, 1992, p. 177). The reverse is also true: emotions may advance or hinder career options and impact wellness, just as emotions generated by work affect family and home.

In vocational guidance, the practitioner does not relieve the client from responsibility. Nor does the practitioner lead or direct the client to make a choice the practitioner believes is best. The practitioner's role is to aid the client to obtain more information about interests and the world of work. Assessment may be part of that process, but the tests used are based on the client's interest. The practitioner interprets test results to the client and presents test results in a way the client can understand. The client has the freedom to agree or disagree, and must be allowed enough time to interact with the results. The client must understand that any vocational choice is not a lifetime decision, because most people change jobs an average of seven times over the course of a lifetime. Throughout this process, responsibility and control are left to the client.

Sometimes a client will reveal personal problems that may appear to have little or no relationship to career issues. However, the practitioner needs to be attentive to personal problems, since emotions are involved in making occupational choices. The goal, however, is to present occupational choices as logical, cognitive, and rational. "Client-centered counseling is always just that, in career counseling as well as in therapeutic counseling—the client is the center of the process, and the determiner of the content of the process and its outcome" (Patterson, interviewed in Freeman, 1990, p. 300).

There are three important principles to keep in mind: (1) build client belief in self, (2) pace the therapy at the client's rate, and (3) build on a succession of short-term goals (Wrenn, 1988). Practitioners relate to clients as "the same complex whole person that you know yourself to be" (p. 340.).

Manuele-Adkins (1992) expands the client-centered consideration to include developmental issues, and suggests the following tripartite approach based on Patterson (1964) and Super (1951): "(a) the developmental nature of the career choice process, (b) the concept of career development as an implementation of the self-concept, and (c) the importance of factors that influence clients' concepts of themselves and the world of work" (pp. 314–315). To integrate career and personal counseling more successfully the practitioner must assess the client's differing psychological needs and understand how specific occupations may not meet particular needs.

Evaluation of the Person-Centered Approach The supportive tone of the client-centered approach sets an appropriate mood or environment for counseling to occur, but practitioners need more techniques than the client-centered approach alone can provide. These can include work and autobiographical information questionnaires that assist clients in developing a list of traits that describe them, such as the Adjective Checklist (ACL) and the Adjective Self-Description (ASD).

EXISTENTIAL APPROACHES

Although [human beings] cannot always select their life circumstances, they can . . . choose their attitudes toward their circumstances. By taking a positive stance in tragic or unfavorable situations people can recover and be revitalized. They can grow rather than perish. (McIlroy, 1979, p. 351)

Existentialism is rooted in the perception that people control their own destiny. Applied to vocational counseling, client growth is based upon one's chosen philosophy, which can be altered. Everyone has a unique view of life through which one tries to understand the world by interpreting one's experiences. McIlroy (1979) observes that

the person who continues to grow psychologically and spiritually possesses a different philosophical framework. This growing individual will

---

Practical Applications

Koehn (1986) offers several suggestions for practitioners.

- Listen carefully for attitudes that indicate the client's beliefs about either meaninglessness or meaningfulness.
- Observe how the client is experiencing his or her world—is he or she cynical or optimistic?
- Do not force a meaning on to a struggling client.
- If a client appears to interpret work as totally self-serving, assist the client to reevaluate beliefs using values clarification activities.
- Use the client's interpretation of meaningful work as the basis for occupational choice.
- Use the theme of death to help client's search for meaning.

- Ask "What do you want to have accomplished in life?" or "What are five words you want to be true about you before you die?"
- Give the client the task of writing two epitaphs, one he/she thinks others would write, and one he/she would like to have written about them. Discuss the differences and how to work towards the one the client would choose. Be aware, however, that any discussion of death can raise anxieties.
- Encourage the client to make authentic choices.
- Use "focusing" techniques as an experiential exercise to help the client get in touch with the affective responses to a particular situation.

- Use guided fantasy to imagine a typical day at work with all its interactions, duties, and feelings about the activities. This can help clients understand their positive or negative responses to the work situation and help them reexamine the authenticity of their career/job choice. "This deeper inquiry into the 'givens' of existence promote authentic decision-making, commitment, goal-setting, and engagement in work." (Koehn, 1986, p.184–85, quotations in original)

Clients who displace responsibility and insist on blaming others for their misery are not viable candidates for effective intervention (Yalom, 1980). This is especially true when they have been fired and portray themselves as the innocent victim, complain about their current job but do nothing to change the situation, or hop from job to job. However, if these issues are addressed early in counseling, clients can get beyond blaming others and move to a more proactive stance in their job search.

We would add these practical suggestions. Help clients

- View "career" in a full sense with the long range goal being the development of a meaningful lifestyle.
- Assess the quality of their current lifestyles—the degree of psychological and spiritual aliveness they experience.
- Periodically reassess their philosophies and life experiences.

Practitioners can also

- Incorporate the concept of an ongoing life process as part of healthy human development.
- Integrate both philosophical and experiential strategies into the counseling process.
- Clarify philosophical assumptions underlying therapeutic interventions.

accept internal potency, be response-able, and view life as a challenge. . . . Life is not meaningless; instead, the meaning of life becomes fuller and clearer for the individual. . . . The degree of satisfaction is viewed as a by-product because satisfaction is not a goal in itself; rather, satisfaction ensues when meaning is discovered. (p. 352)

From this **existential approach,** McIlroy outlines a four-dimensional model for a high-quality occupation and meaningful lifestyle: (1) career was once viewed as a ladder one climbed, mostly with one employer and similar jobs; (2) career is now viewed as a lifestyle, including work, social life, family life, physical health and leisure; (3) transcendence is best learned through personal experience—rising above a current situation to a new level of awareness and imagination—and (4) the spiritual realm is defined by the nonphysical part of our person, the human spirit.

One must find one's own meaning in life, and through this discovery one will find happiness (McIlroy, 1979). Vocational practitioners need to assist clients to find meaning, understanding, and an ability to deal with uncertainty in lifestyle and in work.

Koehn (1986) also suggests that existential beliefs can be used to enhance career decision-making. There are three existential concerns—meaninglessness, death, and responsibility that can be examined in vocational counseling. Clients can discover the ability to move toward someone or something rather than having oneself be a basis for meaning and satisfaction.

Frankl (1967) defined a life devoid of meaning as an "existential vacuum" or an "existential frustration." Meaningful living is characterized by feelings of involvement, fulfillment, and a powerful sense of doing something worthwhile. The "vacuum" is characterized by feelings of inner emptiness, boredom, and apathy. A person experiencing these frustrations will often appear cynical, lacking in direction, and unwilling to put much effort into various activities. Frankl suggests this vacuum is a spiritual state that is pathological in nature. Discussions regarding the meaning of life can be a powerful source of dialogue can incorporate a spiritual perspective in career counseling.

Regarding the existential motif of death, this philosophy embraces death as a motivator for the need to accomplish something while living. Each of us is going to die. This is a continuous theme throughout one's life. "Through awareness of death, we can strive to make our lives worthwhile" (Koehn, 1986, p. 181).

Responsibility as an existential motif can best be described as "the buck stops here" approach with "here" being the client. Each of us is responsible for (a) our own attitudes and actions, (b) fulfilling our potential, and (c) discovering our own meaning in life. Yalom (1980) defines responsibility as "authorship." "To be aware of responsibility is to be aware of creating one's own self, destiny, life predicament, feelings and, if such be the case, one's own suffering" (p. 218).

Evaluation of the Existential Approach The existential approach to the role of work in people's lives relies on the maturity and age of the client seeking help. It requires a client to be willing to enter into a process to learn about one's own potential. Time to accomplish the process may be too lengthy and the practitioner may not seem directive enough if there is pressure to obtain work soon.

Relevance for Multicultural and Diverse Populations Clients from diverse backgrounds can be encouraged to weigh alternatives and explore the consequences of choices they make in their lives (Corey, 1996). While external oppressive forces beyond their control may seriously impinge on clients' quality of life, clients need not allow themselves to be passive victims of circumstances. Clients can be helped to examine their role in the creation of their problems while at the same time be taught ways to counter their external

CASE EXAMPLE

Work-family issues are existential in nature. Parents often confront hard choices between spending more time with the family or earning more money to spend (Pipher, 1996). McKenna (1997) describes the experience of realizing that the corporate workplace has been traditionally geared toward men with full-time wives at home. This image may be out-of-date, given the numbers of dual-career couples, but the male provider role is still the presumption behind many workplace cultures. For many men, the **male provider role** means his sense of self-worth is derived from occupational status and income. Long hours on the job (face visibility) indicate that one takes work seriously, is a serious "player" (Hochschild, 1997) and is a contender for promotion. Anything less signals a lack of commitment to the job, including **flex-time, job sharing, maternity leave**—or, Heaven forbid, **paternity leave** (Melvin, 1998). For both men and women in such work cultures, one's identity becomes largely a factor of what one does for a living, not who one is and how one lives—human doings not human beings. Pervasive downsizing and a decrease in corporate loyalty mean that both men and women have begun questioning the myths that long hours and hard work will ensure permanent employment and a secure retirement. Face visibility does not equal productivity. Nor does productivity ensure job security.

Although the women's movement and the civil rights movement helped women to enter the corporate workplace, the definition of success in these workplaces was and largely remains based on a masculine culture, according to McKenna (1997). The rules for corporate success were set by men long before women arrived on the scene. Babyboomer women have demonstrated that they are as capable and competent as men, but at the expense of compounding their lives by adding male-defined success identities to their female identities. Many women who were determined to break down sexist barriers (e.g., exclusivity, discrimination, bias) did not know what they were in for when they broke into the higher occupational ranks. Across income brackets, women whose personal confidence and clarity of perspective have been gained from occupational accomplishment and years of experience are beginning to question work structures that value work first and family a distant second.

From an existential standpoint, the role of work in people's lives appears on the verge of a turning point, but for this to happen both men and women must reassess their definitions of success. Broader structural factors in the workplace will be compelled to respond when a critical mass of workers begins to press for more balance in their lives. Babyboomers hitting middle age who have been betrayed by a work system that downsized them without a second thought are at the head of an increasing groundswell that is demanding a more humane lifestyle.

circumstances. Practitioners can advocate for their clients (Grevious, 1985) without taking over clients' tasks and hindering the development of feelings of competence. But existential approaches may be excessively individualistic and assume that a multicultural client can make all changes internally (Corey, 1996). External realities of power and hierarchy, discrimination and **oppression,** are often dismissed. Clients with a strong sense of collectivism may feel invalidated by having all the responsibility for their condition placed upon themselves. There is also a likelihood of "blaming the victim" should a client not exhibit sufficient levels of self-determination. Practitioners with an existential theoretical orientation can come across as too nondirective for those clients desiring answers and concrete solutions to their immediate problems. Structured, problem-oriented approaches to vocational counseling are antithetical to existential approaches.

COGNITIVE BEHAVIORAL APPROACHES

Cognitive vocational counseling is an approach that helps clients challenge their **vocational irrational beliefs** so they can attain their career and personal goals. Work and personal problems are often inseparable and interactive. Cognitively oriented practitioners, therefore, believe there is an "advantage of providing a methodology which can address individuals' beliefs about their personal and work lives within the realistic expertise of the various helping disciplines and the reality of external conditions" (Richman, 1993, p. 91). When using cognitive approaches, the client can be taught to deal with pervasive thought patterns, concomitant behaviors, and emotional factors that affect all of life, including work.

Albert Ellis (1962) outlined the basis for **Rational-Emotive Therapy (RET).** RET posits an A-B-C model where emotional, behavioral, and physiological disturbances are most likely the result of beliefs about the activating events (A) in people's lives. By disputing irrational beliefs (B) about activating events, the undesirable consequences (C) will lessen. Work and cognitions can easily become intertwined, and the changes in career development "lend support to the premise that identifying and modifying cognitions can influence an individual's ability to deal effectively with the unexpected, uncontrollable changes and events in the work world" (Richman, 1993, p. 96).

Cognitive Information Processing (CIP)

Sampson, Peterson, Lenz, Reardon (1992) use a **Cognitive Information Processing** (CIP) perspective to describe the career development of individuals. A pyramid divided into four sections on three levels visually represents important domains in CIP. The base of the pyramid is divided into two kinds of knowledge.

Practical Applications

RET theorists have not suggested their techniques for vocational counseling, but they have definite applications. If a client clings to any irrational ideas about him/herself, it is very possible that the client's occupational development will be less effective. For instance, the belief that a person must be competent, adequate, and achieving in all areas to be worthwhile makes career choices difficult. Also, the belief that events from the past determine present behavior can inhibit career advancement and success. Little attention has been given to clients' thoughts regarding work and how these thoughts contribute to client frustration and indecision (Lewis & Gilhousen, 1981). Career myths also can lead to faulty development (Borman & Dickson, 1991).

The practitioner who intervenes using RET would help clients "modify their nonproductive beliefs about uncontrollable negative external events in their work and personal lives, . . . [and] address the cognitive barriers that impede their . . . goal attainment" (Richman, 1993, p. 93). Clients and practitioners would benefit by recognizing society's irrational beliefs about work. Thus, "clients may more readily gain awareness and accept the reality that establishing and maintaining a career requires planning, hard work, taking risks, and experiencing discomfort without any guarantees about the future. . . . Transitions and up-and-down cycles are part of the human condition. Helping clients to accept and deal with this reality is essential for mental health in all areas of life" (p. 95). Richman recommends a technique of having clients draw a picture of where they see themselves in their current situation, followed by one where they would like to be. The first can help them identify and question negative attitudes and beliefs about themselves and why they are not where they think they should be. The second drawing helps them begin to clarify goals and reformulate beliefs that may interfere with reaching their goals. Focusing on vocational irrational beliefs helps clients to identify the thoughts that may keep them from attaining goals. Even learning that one does not want to work is a positive process. Clients often need help realizing that some goals (i.e., financial independence, freedom to live as they please) may require work as a means of achieving that goal.

Lack of information, unclear interests, limited experience, deficient job skills, and a poor economy are just some of the obstacles individuals face in their career development. Thus, assessing the information, resources, skills, and interests of clients along with cognitions about themselves, others, and the job market enables practitioners to help increase the probability that clients will take appropriate behavioral steps toward achieving their goals (Richman, 1993).

The first domain, **self-knowledge**, includes values, interests and skills. The second domain, **occupational knowledge,** forms the other half of the base of the pyramid and includes information about individual occupations and a schema for organizing occupations. The third domain, **decision-making skills,** is in the center section of the pyramid and entails understanding and mastering the decision-making process. The fourth domain, **metacognitions,** forms the top of the pyramid and involves self-talk, self-awareness, and the monitoring of cognitions.

CIP encompasses a cycle of generic career-problem-solving and decision-making skills, and this is called the **CASVE Cycle.** The CASVE cycle includes: (1) *communication*—understanding the external demands and internal states that signal the need to begin problem-solving; (2) *analysis*—clarifying or obtaining knowledge about self, occupations, decision-making, or metacognitions; (3) *synthesis*—elaborating and synthesizing alternatives; (4) *valuing*—prioritizing alternatives and making tentative choices; and (5) *execution*—formulating a plan for implementing a tentative choice that includes a preparation program, reality testing, and employment seeking. "The cycle is a **recursive process:** individuals move backward and forward through the cycle in response to their emerging decision needs and the availability of information resources" (Sampson et al., 1992 p. 68). Assumptions that underlie CIP appear in Table 5.1.

For a thorough discussion of CIP, we highly recommend Peterson et al. (1991).

TABLE 5.1 Assumptions Underlying the Cognitive Information Processing (CIP) Perspective of Career Development

ASSUMPTION	EXPLANATION
1. Career choice results from an interaction of cognitive and affective processes.	CIP emphasizes the cognitive interaction of an interaction domain in career decision-making, but it also acknowledges the presence of an effective source of information in the process (Heppner & Krauskopf, 1987, Zajonc, 1980). Ultimately, commitment to a career goal involves an interaction between affective and cognitive processes.
2. Making career choices is a problem-solving activity.	Individuals can learn to solve career problems (that is, to choose careers) just as they can learn to solve math, physics, or chemistry problems. The major differences between career problems and math or science problems lie in the complexity and ambiguity of the stimulus and the greater uncertainty as to the correctness of the solution.

Continued

TABLE 5.1 Assumptions Underlying the Cognitive Information Processing (CIP) Perspective of Career Development *(continued)*

ASSUMPTION	EXPLANATION
3. The capabilities of career problem solvers depend on the availability of cognitive operations as well as knowledge.	One's capability as a career problem solver depends on one's self-knowledge and on one's knowledge of occupations. It also depends on the cognitive operations one can draw on to derive relationships between these two domains.
4. Career problem solving is a high-memory-load task.	The realm of self-knowledge is complex; so is the world of work. The drawing of relationships between these two domains entails attending to both domains simultaneously. Such a task may easily overload the working memory store.
5. Motivation	The motivation to become a better career problem solver stems from the desire to make satisfying career choices through a better understanding of oneself and the occupational world.
6. Career development involves growth and change in knowledge structures.	Self-knowledge and occupational continual knowledge consist of sets of organized memory structures called *schemata* that evolve over the person's life-span. Both the occupational world and we ourselves are ever-changing. Thus, the need to develop and integrate these domains never ceases.
7. Career identity depends on self-knowledge.	In CIP terms, career identity is defined as the level of development of self-knowledge memory structures. Career identity is a function of the complexity, integration, and stability of the schemata comprising the self-knowledge domain.
8. Career maturity depends on one's ability to solve career problems.	From a CIP perspective, career maturity is defined as the ability to make independent and responsible career decisions based on the thoughtful integration of the best information available about oneself and the occupational world.
9. The ultimate goal of career counseling is achieved by facilitating the growth of information-processing skills.	From a CIP perspective, the goal of career counseling is therefore to provide the conditions of learning that facilitate the growth of memory structures and cognitive skills so as to improve the client's capacity for processing information.
10. The ultimate aim of career counseling is to enhance the client's capabilities as a career problem solver and a decision maker.	From a CIP perspective, the aim of career counseling is to enhance the client's career decision-making capabilities through the development of information-processing skills.

SOURCE: *Career Development and Services: A Cognitive Approach,* by Gary Peterson, James Sampson, and Robert Reardon, pp. 8–9. Copyright 1991 by Brooks/Cole Publishing Company. Reprinted by permission.

Assessments Used with Cognitive Theory

1. Career Decision Scale
2. Cognitive Differentiation Grid

Perspectives on the Cognitive Behavioral Approaches Cognitive behavioral approaches evolved from experimental findings in cognitive psychology to include the interaction of behavioral therapy principles (Beck, 1993). More "purist" cognitive therapy approaches continue to evolve (Robins & Hayes, 1993). Three metaphors explain the role of cognitive and affective processes in behavior change: cognition as (1) a form of conditioning, (2) information processing, and (3) narrative construction (Meichenbaum, 1993).

As a form of conditioning, cognition attends to client self-statements and images that are "viewed as discriminative stimuli and as conditioned responses that come to guide and control overt behavior" (p. 202). Rehearsing adaptive coping skills (i.e., participant modeling, mental imagery) helps change clients' overt behaviors, thoughts, and feelings. As information processing, cognition views the mind as a computer (Meichenbaum, 1993). Cognitions (e.g., preattention and attention, decoding, encoding, retrieval, attributional biases) and cognitive errors (e.g., beliefs, schemata, current concerns, tacit assumptions) are what clients bring to situations. Clients' information processing—even when inadvertent, unwitting, and unknowing—is evidence for how they view the world. Depression results from errors in thinking (i.e., dichotomous thinking, overgeneralization, personalization, magnification) which RET calls irrational beliefs and which cognitive therapy calls cognitive distortions. Cognitive behavioral approaches help clients to become aware of these processes and to develop competing responses that are more adaptable for coping with their lives. Cognition as narrative construction represents the most current, unfolding metaphor. Narrative constructions are a hallmark of the perspective known as constructivism.

> The constructivist perspective is founded on the idea that humans actively construct their personal realities and create their own representational models of the world. . . . [T]he human mind is a product of constructive symbolic activity, and that reality is a product of personal meanings that individuals create. It is not as if there is one reality . . . [that] clients distort . . . , thus contributing to their problems; rather, there are multiple realities [and thus multiple meanings], and the [practitioner's] task . . . is to help clients become aware of how they create these realities [and meanings] and of the consequences of such constructions. (Meichenbaum, 1993, p. 203)

The practitioner becomes a co-constructivist to help clients alter their stories as part of an ongoing meaning-making activity. Stories that clients construct become a central component to adaptation. Client strengths, resources, and coping abilities are emphasized; pathologizing of behaviors is minimized. Exceptions to the problem are built upon, which give client stories a contextual nature (i.e., times when they cope effectively, times when they do not). The practitioner helps the client to construct narratives that fit the client's present circumstances. The story is coherent. It captures and explains client difficulties. Most modernist-trained practitioners take issue with constructivism's aim for narrative viability over historical accuracy (Bruner, 1986; Sarbin, 1986, Part IV; Polkinghorne, 1988; Spence, 1982). But historical accuracy is difficult if not impossible to achieve. A practitioner can never know exactly what happened when a client tells a story about an incident at work. Clients from the same workplace would have different stories to tell about the same incident. **Narrative viability** requires the story to cohere into related, larger systems of personally or socially constructed realities; the consequences of the story for an individual or a group have to be practical (Granvold, 1996). Clinical encounters become opportunities for narrative transformations and changes in meaning to take place in client lives. Narrative transformations challenge the assumptions of traditional cognitive therapies because pluralistic belief systems undermine the objectivist equation of mental health with accuracy of reality contact (Neimeyer, 1993). Constructivist models are postmodern with their emphasis on multiple meanings as equally valid.

Constructivist practitioners are less likely to impose their values on clients (Corey, 1996). Clients become active agents in making meaning out of their experiential world. Constructivism has begun to impact vocational psychology as evidenced by the recent flurry of publications (Forster, 1992; McAuliffe, 1993; Richardson, 1993; Rockwell, 1987; Savickas, 1993, 1994; 1995a, 1995b).

POSTMODERN APPROACHES

[Work]is about a search . . . for daily meaning as well as daily bread.
—Studs Terkel, *Working* (1974, p. xiii)

In Chapter 2 we introduced postmodernism in regard to a work ethic for the twenty-first century. Postmodernism questions and rejects logical positivism (the scientific method as the only basis for genuine knowledge) and asserts that there are valid alternatives to empiricism (observation and experiment) as a means for adding to the realm of knowledge. Modernism and the idea of an autonomous, isolated self dates back to ancient Greece. In contrast, many postmodern approaches view the self as constructed in relationship (Becvar & Becvar, 1996).

O'Hara and Anderson (1991) write in "Welcome to the Postmodern World":

Without quite noticing it, we have moved into a new world, one created by the cumulative effect of pluralism, democracy, religious freedom, consumerism, mobility and increasing access to news and entertainment. This is the world described as "postmodern" to denote its difference from the modern world most of us were born into. A new social consciousness is emerging in this new world and touching the lives of all kinds of people who are not the least bit interested in having a new kind of social consciousness. We are all being forced to see that there are many beliefs, multiple realities, an exhilarating but daunting profusion of worldviews to suit every taste. We can choose among these, but we cannot choose not to make choices. (p. 20)

Gergen (1991b) contends that the technological advances of the late twentieth century—computers, electronic mail, satellites, faxes—mark an accelerating social connectedness leading to a state of multiphrenia, where the individual is split into a multiplicity of self-investments. This **social saturation** of the self changes the coherent and unified sense of self, inherent in modernist conceptualizations, into a multiphrenic, postmodern condition where an individual swims in a sea of drowning demands.

Rather than an objectively detected modernist reality, the subjectively created postmodernist reality is part of what is clinically known as the constructivist epistemologies. Constructivist epistemologies view human beings as active in the individual and collective co-creation of their experiential world (Neimeyer, 1993). The emergence of constructivism represents one of the most profound developments within cognitivism (Granvold, 1996). The practical contrasts between traditional cognitive and emergent constructivist approaches to therapy are presented in Table 5.2.

As shown in Table 5.2, cognitive approaches attend to specific disorders. Automatic thoughts or irrational beliefs are isolated to correct present dysfunctions (Neimeyer, 1993). Constructivist approaches attend to more comprehensive belief systems or personal accounts that have developed over time to form present fundamental assumptions about one's self and one's world. Thus, styles of therapy differ.

Cognitive approaches are highly directive to promote a systematic revision of one's beliefs (Neimeyer, 1993). The individual is the sole focus of cognitive treatment. Client verbalizations are subject to tests of empirical validity. To paraphrase Aaron T. Beck, a cognitive practitioner may ask a client, "What evidence do you have for that belief?" Constructivist approaches are less structured and more exploratory. Both the individual and broader systems (family, workplace) are the focus of treatment, with the practitioner as co-author of the client's

TABLE 5.2 Practical Contrasts Between Traditional Cognitive and Constructivist Approaches to Psychotherapy

FEATURE	TRADITIONAL COGNITIVE THERAPIES	CONSTRUCTIVIST THERAPIES
Diagnostic emphasis	Disorder-specific	Comprehensive, general
Target of intervention and assessment	Isolated automatic thoughts or irrational beliefs	Construct systems, personal narratives
Temporal focus	Present	Present, but more developmental emphasis
Goal of treatment	Corrective; eliminate dysfunction	Creative; facilitate development
Style of therapy	Highly directive and directional	Less structured and more exploratory
Context of therapy	Individualistic	Individualistic to systemic
Therapist role	Persuasive, analytical, technically instructive	Reflective, elaborative, intensely personal
Tests for adequacy of client beliefs	Logic, objective validity	Internal consistency, consensus, personal viability
Interpretation of client's meanings	Literal, universal	Metaphoric, idiosyncratic
Interpretation of emotions	Negative emotion results from distorted thinking, represents problem to be controlled	Negative emotion as informative signal of challenge to existing constructions, to be respected
Understanding of client "resistance"	Lack of motivation, dysfunctional pattern	Attempt to protect core ordering processes

SOURCE: R. A. Neimeyer (1993), p. 225. © 1993 by the American Psychological Association. Reprinted by permission.

newly emergent narrative. The new story has to have narrative viability. To paraphrase Mark L. Savickas, a constructivist practitioner may ask a client, "How is your belief useful or meaningful for this particular circumstance/context?"

Cognitive interpretations of client meanings are presumed to be literal and universal in nature, constructivist interpretations metaphorical and idiosyncratic to that client (Neimeyer, 1993). Cognitive approaches view client negative emotion as a distorted appraisal of situations. Distortions need to be controlled or eliminated. Constructivist approaches view client negative emotion as a warning sign, a challenge to a client's attempts to make personal meaning of their current experiences. Client "resistance" is seen by cognitivists as a lack of motivation or a dysfunctional pattern that the practitioner actively disputes, and by constructivists as self-protection of core ordering processes with which clients make sense of their world.

"The boundaries distinguishing traditional cognitive approaches from constructivist approaches are not well defined" (Granvold, 1996, p. 347). The picture is complicated by constructivist approaches that look at personal versus social constructions of reality. **Social constructionism** views meanings and understandings of the world as the result of interactions with others (Berger & Luckmann, 1966; Gergen, 1985), with several possible understandings of behaviors, interactions, or events determined by the cultural and social contexts in which a person is interacting. Language is the primary vehicle for the transmission of meanings and understandings (Anderson & Goolishian, 1988). Historical context can play a key role in how one constructs an interactional experience (Osbeck, 1991). Social constructionist practitioners explore the client's perceptions and understandings about clinical issues, including lifestyle and work. Practitioners do not have preconceived notions about the universal nature of psychological problems, diagnoses, or change.

Social Constructionism

Taylor Rockwell's Approach In an early example of the social construction of careers, Rockwell (1987) considers influences that significant others have on one's thoughts and feelings about the career options one is considering. Development of work roles is influenced by parents, teachers, peers, siblings, coaches, and neighbors. "A person's self-perceived profile of talents, skills, and competencies" (p. 97) are socially constructed as a consequence of the way a person is steered and rewarded by important people in their life. Approval expectancy for a given occupational choice is constructed by those with whom a person has significant emotional ties. Using the scientific method to provide empirical evidence of socially constructed realities, Rockwell shows that the career decision-maker's expectation of approval from significant others strongly influences certain occupational choices.

The Rockwell Occupational Approval Grid (ROAG), developed by Rockwell (1986), with an accompanying manual for counselors, is an assessment instrument to be used with this approach. As of this text's publication, they are available from Taylor Rockwell, Brownlee Dolan Stein Associates, Inc., 90 John Street, New York, NY 10038.

Mark L. Savickas's Approach "Vocational psychology is a product of modernity" (Savickas, 1995b, p. 17). The scientific method was and is the primary basis for explaining career choice. Scientifically based assessment instruments predominate as a way to discover the best fit between a person's traits and a work environment. Career counseling approaches have always reflected the historical context of the age in which they appeared. Dramatic transformations are happening in the world of work because of changing economic patterns and cultural values across the globe. This means that sole reliance on logical positivism as a foundation for vocational psychology is the discipline's Achilles heel. Incorporating additional ways of knowing has become more urgent than ever. Working one's way up the career ladder was a common metaphor used throughout most of the twentieth century to describe mainstream careers. But large organizations that support long-term employment rapidly are disappearing, and the concept of career—and certainly, career ladder—is relevant for fewer people. In this sense, Richardson (1993) advocates that career counseling becomes a specialty within vocational psychology, and that the role of work in people's lives is more representative of the advent of the twenty-first century. Career counseling needs to keep up with society's progression into the postmodern era; postmodernism has propagated, if not converged with, six innovations that have emerged in career counseling (Savickas, 1993):

"No more experts" (p. 210). Savickas sees a second-order change in the way career counselors practice. Rather than being expert interpreters of interest inventories and possessing privileged information about occupations, vocational practitioners are validating clients' efforts to actively and independently shape their own lives. Career counselors are moving from (sometimes unwittingly) acting as agents of the dominant culture to opening a space for conversations that have a range of occupational possibilities.

"Enable rather than fit" (p. 211). Postmodern approaches to career foster **deconstruction** of the Person by Environment Fit (PxE) paradigm. Multicultural and diverse discourse is moving from marginal status to center stage. An enablement paradigm is replacing PxE and encourages clients to express and devise their own life plans.

"Rewrite the grand narrative" (p. 211). The **Grand Narrative** of the twentieth century emphasizes new advances in human productive capacities founded upon reason and freedom. The role of work in people's lives provides a key link to the reality of the Grand Narrative and one's social identity within that Narrative. Yet, multiculturalism and diversity undermine the coherence of and conformity to the Grand Narrative. A legacy of the Puritan work ethic, one's work role and career is central to the Grand Narrative. The multiple perspectives of postmodernism make work one of many roles in a person's life, but not always the

central role. Life design will become the overarching construct of career counseling in the postmodern era, with occupational choice as but one aspect of such a design.

"Career is personal" (p. 212). Part of this refers to the artificial concept that places career counseling as separate from personal counseling. The subjective and personal meanings that clients construct to make sense of life and work have often been ignored up to now. Intersubjective concerns will become an added part of objective methods of vocational assessment and career guidance.

"Career development theory is not counseling theory" (p. 212). Overreliance on objective assessment put the original focus on how clients choose occupations and develop careers. Vocational guidance has been the focus more than the career counseling process. In this sense career development theory has never been counseling theory. Postmodern approaches to career become activities where the practitioner and client co-construct or socially construct the meaning of the client's direction in life. This quest for sense is one of invention, not discovery. **Hermeneutical activity,** with its emphasis on the methodological principles for interpreting the meaning of a literary passage in a text, becomes central. The literary qualities of a client's story become primary.

"Stories rather than scores" (p. 213). The singular focus on objective career with its concepts like PxE Fit is a legacy of modernism, with remote ancestry in ancient Greece and ancient China. Postmodernism views clients as concerned with life purpose, not job positions; with subjective meanings to solutions in growing up, not the meanings of interest inventory scores that tell clients their stronger than average preferences for an occupation when compared to a normative group. Objective developmental tasks become subjective social expectations or existential themes. Objective identity becomes subjective striving for establishing inner continuity of lived experiences (Neimeyer, 1995b). Values become the expression of a central life theme (Savickas, 1993).

In the postmodern approach to career counseling described by Savickas (1993), the influence of social constructionism is apparent. Enablement gives clients the chance to deconstruct by freeing themselves from the mesmerizing discourse of the dominant culture (Doherty, 1991), and allows them to define for themselves the meaning of success, the role of work in their lives, and what else matters as much as, if not more than, work. The same can be said for practitioners who help clients rewrite their part in the Grand Narrative of the twentieth century. Many workers who uncritically bought in to the Grand Narrative found themselves in an unrewarding Rat Race (see Pipher, 1996; Hochschild, 1997; McKenna, 1997). Several scholars and practitioners, whether or not self-identified postmodernists, have not felt comfortable with artificial, arbitrary distinction between career counseling and personal counseling. Savickas's notion of the career as personal is similar to feminism in career counseling and the idea of the personal as political (Brooks & Forrest, 1994). The practitioner and client's co-construction of the meaning of the client's direction in life is fine as long as narrative viability is maintained. It is no use encouraging a client to believe that he will be a member of the U. S. polo team in the next Olympics if that client has no horsemanship skills, cannot swing a mallet, and does not have the financial means to train for the Olympic team. Hermeneutic activity will come most easily to practitioners with extensive backgrounds in English or other literature, Bible studies, or narrative histories.

The emphasis on stories over scores is paramount. Both of us have long been appalled by unskilled career counselors who simply give a student computer-scored results and computer-generated reports of vocational assessment instruments without really taking the time to listen whether a computer-generated profile coheres with the meaning making of the student, or how it matches with what one knows about oneself. Savickas (1992) writes that the boredom many career counselors feel when doing the same old thing can be alleviated by adopting more intersubjective approaches that actively engage the client in a quest for meaning. This whole different way of doing things is one of the most refreshing aspects of a postmodern approach to occupational development. Clients can benefit enormously by a practitioner's infusion of some of these approaches into their clinical work.

Career has been deconstructed by postmodern discourse (Savickas, 1995b). Burr (1995) defines discourse as "a systematic, coherent set of images, metaphors and so on, that construct an object in a particular way" (p. 184). Furthermore,

> discourses offer a framework to people against which they may understand their own experience and behavior and that of others, and can be seen to be tied to social structures and practices in a way which masks power relations operating in society. (Burr, 1995, pp. 71–72)

Historically, career has mainly meant work in the occupational structure by degreed professionals. Work performed at home and in the community has been marginalized (Richardson, 1993), and persons who performed such work have been disempowered. Dominant discourses often mask inequitable social arrangements that support the interests of relatively powerful groups in society (e.g., males, the upper class). In vocational psychology, the focus on women and work-family issues confronts the privileged position of many males in the workplace.

From a postmodern perspective, work is more than an occupational role. It is but one of many contexts in people's lives. The fracture of the modern career ethic (Savickas, 1993, 1995b) potentially could be replaced by a postmodern work ethic rooted in a new perspective on the occupational role, one that emphasizes connectedness and social contribution. Correspondingly, vocational psychologists are being challenged to revise their core philosophy of science and to reform their field into an interpretive discipline (Savickas, 1995b, p. 18).

Six issues debated between logical positivists versus contextual interpretivists over which philosophy of science vocational psychology should use are presented in Table 5.3.

The debate summarized in Table 5.3 is unlikely to be resolved anytime soon. We hope to see a middle road evolve where instead of either/or, both logical positivism *and* contextual interpretivism are used in vocational psychology without any contradiction in the duality of such an existence. This would really honor and respect multiple perspectives. Epistemic collectivism means that a person's thoughts and beliefs as expressed through epistemic individualism become situated knowledge when communities socially legitimate those thoughts and beliefs. However, a counterpoint is provided by the late Russian constructivist Lev Vygotsky (1896–1934), who noted that a child's cognitive development occurs on the social level first—i.e., interpsychologically, between people—and on the personal level second—i.e., intrapsychologically, within the child (1978). In other words, the individual still constructs a personal meaning even after a community socially legitimates situated knowledge. This is a recursive process where a personal construction of reality (epistemic individualism) is legitimated through a social construction of reality (epistemic collectivism) and then idiographically understood as yet another personal construction of reality (a "second draft", if you will, of epistemic individualism). Both epistemic individualism *and* epistemic collectivism go through endless "multiple drafts" of reality construction.

Both universality *and* particularity can have practical applications to the role of work in people's lives. Beginning with universality, a practitioner could say to a client, "When a lot of people feel job stress, [and then utter the results of generalizable research findings, such as symptoms]." To tailor for particularity, the practitioner can then ask, "Do any of these [generalizable objective research findings] seem like they fit for you?" The same principle applies to the issue of validation versus legitimation. Beginning with validation, the practitioner could say, "When a lot of people are burned out from work, [then impart singular truths validated in reference to theory]." To make it legitimate for the client, the practitioner can then ask, "Does any of this sound like something you are going through?" Many practioners probably particularize and legitimate without using these terms.

Essence is losing ground to context because of broad external factors beyond the control of logical positivists and contextual interpretivists. Yet, concepts

TABLE 5.3 The Debate over Which Philosophy of Science Vocational Psychology Should Use: Logical Positivism vs. Contextual Interpretivism

LOGICAL POSITIVISM	CONTEXTUAL INTERPRETIVISM
1. Epistemic Individualism individual as principal agent of knowledge production; knowledge already exists separately from the individual in an objectively knowable world	Epistemic Collectivism communities as primary agents of knowledge production; knowledge is mediated through discourse, socially constructed subjectivity
2. Objectivity scientific method is universal method because it controls biases and leads to knowledge, prediction, and control	Perspectivity scientific method is only one method, not "the" method; behind the facade of value-free objectivity is a commitment to technical rationality; multiple perspectives produce richer, deeper, more complex knowledge
3. Universality generality of testing principles; theoretical; design experiments	Particularity examine locally situated practices that seem useful in specific circumstances; seek stories of individual's experiences and problem descriptions
4. Validation knowledge validated in reference to theory; seek universal properties that govern human conduct (e.g., singular truths)	Legitimation knowledge legitimated by its usefulness when implemented; seek diverse interpretive communities that share a local perspective (e.g., multiple realities)
5. Essence essentialized selves; context, culture is a variable; vocational behavior is a pure category	Context social context and unique circumstances; culture as the context of meaning; vocational behavior is part of a complex of coherent interrelationships within which it is embedded
6. Concepts concept as something already existing in nature that was discovered and named; directly reflect reality through the filters of self-chosen vocabulary	Constructs constructs as personal and cultural component of meaning making; linguistically invent reality through lived experience

SOURCES: Best and Kellner (1991), Harding (1993), Savickas (1993, 1995b)

continue to be a fact of daily life for most people. O'Hara and Anderson (1991) and Savickas (1993, 1995b) temper their enthusiasm by acknowledging that modernism and its counterpart, the scientific method, are alive and well.

Constructivism

Personal Construct Psychology Personal construct psychology (PCP) offers a philosophical rationale that has a well-articulated foundation and a methodology that was developed during years of study (Kelly, 1955). PCP is one form of constructivism. Evolutions of PCP are discussed in Feixas (1990, 1995). Various forms of constructivism are examined in Lyddon (1995).

PCP makes the case for having the career explorer determine the dimensions used to foster self-understanding. The methodology is based on the Role Construct Repertory Tests (Reptest), a structured exercise developed by Kelly (1955) and subsequently modified by many PCP practitioners to address various domains of study. The Goals Review and Organizing Workbook (GROW) (Forster, 1992) is a structured exercise designed to facilitate career-related self-understanding using a PCP rationale. GROW is based on the premise that career explorers benefit from articulating their own dimensions when they see increased understanding of themselves. In PCP terms, the dimensions are called constructs. A person's goals are equivalent to desired anticipations. The personal construct can be used as the primary conceptual unit for investigating the elicitation and articulation of a person's goals (Forster, 1992).

Constructivism and Career Indecision Most vocational psychologists and career counselors have relied on logical positivism as a basis for studying and treating **career indecision** (Savickas, 1995a). Frank Parsons scientized vocational guidance and made it an objective enterprise by concentrating on "true reasoning" as a way of making it a legitimate science for the twentieth century. Career counselors "abstracted career indecision from its context and objectified it with reliable and valid measurement procedures" (p. 364). Subsequently, career indecision as an objective phenomenon evolved over three phases.

1. Indecision as a dichotomy categorized career clients as decided or undecided, and implied that indecision was symptomatic of a personality problem or defect. The decided/undecided dichotomy prevailed from the 1930s until the late 1980s. The Parsonian concept of well-developed aptitudes and interests as a personal perquisite for a reasonable vocational choice implied that indecision was symptomatic of immaturity or psychopathology. Practitioners tried to cure underlying causes (i.e., defects in one's inner being) of indecision. "Intrapersonal anxiety, interpersonal conflict, cultural differences, lack of skill, [and] limited self-knowledge" (Savickas, 1995a, p. 364) were presumed to be defects of self that could be objectively detected and treated.

Practical Applications

The Goals Review and Organizing Workbook (Forster, 1986) has been used in a variety of settings, including high schools and college counseling centers. Client evaluations indicate it is useful for clarifying and organizing personal goals. GROW gives four guidelines for facilitating the articulation of personal goals: First, participants begin this sequential process by remembering and designating several personal events that are meaningful and easily differentiated from other past events.

Second, participants use those events to elicit personal constructs that allow them to differentiate these events from other events. Third, when differentiating among events, the nature of the elicited personal constructs is framed by the potential use that is specified. Fourth, after a variety of constructs have been elicited and used to describe aspects of the self, they are prioritized and then tested for usability.

GROW has five steps that facilitate the participant's articulation of several goal statements. (1) Take an inventory of your Daily Activities and Identify Constructs. This step is initiated when participants complete the One-Week Activity Inventory, which can be recalled from the previous week or completed as a record of the current week. (2) Recall Special Events and Identify Possible Reasons. Participants identify seventeen additional events. (3) Write Goal Statements Using Personal Constructs or Reasons. The main activity is to use ideas or constructs elicited in the previous steps to make goal statements. (4) Prioritize Your Goal Statements. Participants are asked to list their goals statements by choosing between two goals at a time, and continuing this paired-comparison process until choices have been made for all possible combinations. (5) Use Your Top Goals To Rate Representative Activities from Your Past Week. Participants try out their prioritized goal statements by using them to evaluate representative activities randomly selected from their One-Week Activity Inventory (Forster, 1992).

Assessments Used with Personal Construct Psychology

In addition to GROW, two other PCP-based instruments have been designed to facilitate self-understanding:

1. The Job Attribute Clarifier (JAC) (Forster, 1982) elicits personal constructs used by participants when they differentiate among jobs that they know about. Prioritized job attributes can be used to write and ideal job description.

2. The Dependable Strengths Articulation Process Short Form (DSAP-S) (Haldane & Forster, 1988) guides participants through a sequence of exercises that lead to the articulation of personal strengths considered by the participant to be dependable and valuable. DAP-S is based on practices developed by Haldane (1988). A description of an intervention using the DSAP-S and its effects on self-esteem has been reported by Forster (1991).

2. Indecision as a universal continuum replaced the decided/undecided dichotomy and was popularized by John L. Holland and Samuel H. Osipow. During the 1970s each developed scales to assess a client's position on the indecision continuum. Indecision from this perspective is discussed in Chapter 7.

3. Indecision as a multidimensional concept recognizes the heterogeneity of undecided persons. In the late 1980s and early 1990s several scales were developed to assess the multidimensionality of indecision, which we present in Chapter 7.

From a constructivist perspective, the subjective experience of indecision has not been fully explored (Savickas, 1995a). Because of the overwhelming objectification and decontextualization that has occurred from the positivist perspective, indecision has largely been operationally defined from objective test scores. The constructivist approach switches this definition to "subjective stories told by a client" (p. 365). Indecision for a constructivist is normal, not pathological. Indecision is a transformation in progress that occurs when a person appears to be on the verge of losing their place in the world (or at work) and is confronted with resolving a **wavering** doubt (Cochran, 1991). Unsettled wavering is movement toward meaning and a life-shaping decision that can alter the course of a person's life. "We think and represent life in story" (Cochran, 1991, p. 20). Thus, narrative becomes an inherent part of the experience of indecision. Decision-making is a settling of one's orientation to life, the narrative one strives to realize. The narrative a person attempts to clarify and refine is called a **life theme.**

Csikszentmihalyi and Beattie (1979) define life theme as "an affective and cognitive representation of existential problems which a person wishes to resolve. It becomes the basis for an individual's fundamental interpretation of reality and a way of coping with that reality" (p. 45). Indecision occurs because a person has not recognized his or her life theme (Savickas, 1995a). One cannot voice one's own life project when one has not yet thought it through. A constructivist practitioner concentrates on how a client's indecision is embedded within an ongoing pattern of meanings being lived by the client.

Practical Applications

Savickas (1989, 1995a) presents a five-step model of constructivist counseling for career indecision.	1. Practitioner collects client stories that reveal client's life theme. Literary criticism is relied upon for

what makes a good story. "A life theme is like a plot in literature" (Savickas, 1995a, p. 367). The client's plan of action is composed of various plots. Meaning is inscribed into events that form part of an integrated whole. The interaction between life events and the plan of action form the life themes. Two kinds of stories, (a) those that focus on the client's central life concern, and (b) those that focus on the career indecision, are useful for the practitioner to elicit. The practitioner's attention is given to troubles, imbalances, or deviations that client stories accentuate. A good place for practitioners to start is to ask about stories regarding the client's family.

We think it is telling whenever clients' faces light up as they tell their story, and we attend to moments when clients beam with delight as well.

2. As a "reality check," the practitioner narrates the theme back to the client, who then has a chance to edit the practitioner's feedback narrative. In addition to family stories, stories about client identity will help to reveal the narrative goal by addressing the "gap between what is and what ought to be" (Cochran, 1991, p. 12). Any heroes or heroines the client had growing up, the way the client puts meaning to his or her experiences, recalls events that led to the crystallization of the client's self, and rehearses ways to cope with life, will also provide the practitioner with identity stories (Savickas, 1995a).

3. The meaning of the client's current indecision is discussed with the counselor in relation to the life theme. Several questions can be asked here: (a) Under what circumstances did you recognize your indecision? (b) What does it feel like to be undecided? (c) Does this feeling remind you of anything else from your life? (d) Tell me another story about a time when you had this same feeling. (e) Is there anything that haunts you? (f) From what you have told me about your life, what part of the story is most related to your indecision? (Savickas, 1995a).

4. Practitioner and client jointly extend the life theme into the future. Interests and occupations are named that clients might have hesitated about before. Client interests are used by the practitioner to guide story construction and become "future solutions to old problems" (Savickas, 1995a, p. 372). Occupational choices can help clients deal with unfinished business, settle old scores, or compensate for something missing from childhood.

5. Practitioner and client use behavioral counseling methods to specifically identify and put into place the plan to achieve a particular occupational choice.

The intersubjective reality of the client is quite evident in Savickas's (1995a) constructivist counseling for career indecision. McAuliffe (1993) adds a developmental component when constructivism is used to address career transition.

Constructive Developmental Theory and Career Transition McAuliffe (1993) explores **constructive developmental theory,** or an individual's meaning-making framework, for career transitions. "In psychological terms, career can be an act of meaning construction" (p. 23). Most adults' meaning making can be characterized by three balances.

1. *The Interpersonal Balance.* "I am my relationships" rather than "I have relationships" (McAuliffe, 1993, p. 24, quotations in original). This person (a) is entirely embedded in relationships, (b) has no center to author a story of "how things should be" (p. 24, quotations in original), (c) cannot generate a perspective separate from the relationships in which they live, and (d) has insufficiently individuated and does not have a coherent identity. This person's occupational choices—if choices they be called—are often based on unquestioned assumptions or uncritical acceptance of the line of work appropriate for someone of his or her reference group (i.e., family, peers, ethnicity, socioeconomic class, religion). Blind adherence to the Interpersonal Balance can stifle one's own voice and lead one to miss one's calling. The limits of the Interpersonal Balance are reached when the environment challenges the individual to generate his or her own point of view.

2. *The Institutional Balance.* "I am my occupation" rather than "I have an occupation" (McAuliffe, 1993, p. 24, quotations in original). This person becomes thoroughly identified with a particular life role (a sole job title or position) and cannot self-correct to connect to the larger purposes (a workplace mission statement) of which he or she is merely a current expression. Such rigidity or single-mindedness can blind one to one's larger occupational potentials. Meaning making becomes enhanced when one can reflect on a broader, future perspective and can see possible occupational roles into which one can evolve. The limits of the Institutional Balance are reached when one recognizes that he or she has been conserving a product (a job title or position) rather than cultivating a process (potentially multiple positions or occupations).

3. *The Interindividual Balance.* "Who am I becoming and how shall I express this emerging self?" rather than "What does my community, my family, my ethnic or religious group expect of me?" [Interpersonal Balance] or "How do I maintain the current form I am in?" [Institutional Balance] (McAuliffe, 1993, p. 25, quotations in original). This person is open to new information that may challenge the occupational choice made, is able to hear dissonant and even contradictory voices, and is not preoccupied with "preserving its own coherence at all cost" (p. 24). These persons have developed flexibility to negotiate life choices and transitions and have maximized their options to respond to both their internal

Practical Applications

The developmental level of the client's meaning-making system is assessed to clarify whether surface adjustments or cognitive transformations occur. Surface adjustments are similar to first-order change. **First-order change** is "any change in a system that does not produce a change in the structure of the system" (Lyddon, 1990, p. 122). Cognitive transformations are similar to second-order change. **Second-order change** is "a type of change whose occurrence alters the fundamental structure of a system" (p. 122). Surface adjustments or first-order changes would be like a lateral move that a worker makes between similar positions within the same occupational field. Cognitive transformations, or second-order changes, would be like a revision that a worker makes by leaving one occupational field for another. First-order change in the world of work would include a student transferring from one school to another, a worker relocating across town or leaving one corporation for another, or a person in a religious vocation going from one assignment to another within the religious order. Second-order change in the world of work includes the transition from school to work, becoming a new parent and hunting for childcare, relocating to a different town, a downshift from the corporate world, and the departure from the secular world to enter a religious vocation.

Practitioners can elicit cognitive developmental information by questioning clients about the costs to clients for changing fields and how clients know when a decision is correct for them. Clients' responses will reveal their primary emphasis on Interpersonal or Institutional Balances as the meaning making which currently predominates. Sometimes first-order change is all that is needed, especially if the client's meaning making appears adequately calibrated within a given Balance. The practitioner uses "reflective clarification, information giving, encouragement, and . . . *rational* decision-making" (McAuliffe, 1993, p. 25, italics added).

At other times second-order change is needed, especially if the client's meaning making in response to environmental demands is inadequately calibrated within a given Balance. Second-order change is called for when there is a challenge to the major assumptions of a client's self-definition or what he or she knows about the world of work. The way one defines self and occupation is transformed. The practitioner helps the client obtain more information about the self and the world of work. Further practical applications of constructive developmental theory are found in McAuliffe (1993). For more in-depth understanding of second-order change we recommend the classic Watzlawick, Weakland, and Fisch (1974).

needs and the external environment. The Interindividual Balance accepts incompleteness, and thus is most desirable for managing career transition.

Constructive developmental theory posits that most people's meaning making will be characterized by two of the above balances, with one of the balances predominating. Within each balance is the maintenance of an equilibrium between the poles. There is a presumed developmental progression from Interpersonal to Institutional to Interindividual Balance. An authentic occupational/vocational quest is most likely to occur when the Interindividual Balance predominates.

Evaluation of Postmodern Approaches Postmodern approaches are in their nascent stages in vocational psychology. They are very much works in progress. The literary quality of clients' clinical statements is emphasized over scientific properties. Practitioners who can see all sides of a story will find postmodern approaches congenial. Others may have a harder time letting go of their modernist training.

Social Constructionism. Similar to Thomas Szasz's assertion that one can accept many psychodynamic clinical methods without adopting the ideology (Simpson, 1987), a vocational practitioner can use social constructionism without abandoning modernism completely. Vocational practitioners may want to take advantage of what social constructionism has to offer without becoming a casualty of its excesses (Rosenau, 1992).

Constructivism. "Constructivism is more highly developed philosophically than methodologically" (Granvold, 1996, p. 349). The efficacy of constructivist approaches has not been fully established (Gonçalves, 1995; Guidano, 1995; Neimeyer, 1995a). Internal tensions exist within the constructivist movement between proponents of the individualistic perspective and proponents of the communally defined language perspective (Neimeyer, 1995b). Lyddon's (1995) attempt to incorporate social constructionism into a larger constructionist taxonomy are likely to be resisted by those who prefer to keep social constructionism separate from constructivism. Constructivist clinical practitioners acknowledge arbitrary boundaries between psychotherapy and counseling and between separate therapy traditions. Critical scholarship is a provisional solution to the challenge of internal tensions within the constructivist movement (see Neimeyer, 1995b).

Critics of the constructivist epistemologies include Held (1990), who writes, "the view that we cannot, under any circumstances, know an independent reality is itself, paradoxically, a reality claim" (p. 181). Coale (1992) writes, "The emphasis on language as *the* mechanism for changing meaning is a contradiction of the constructivist position that all reality is non-objective and, therefore, that there is room for many ways of understanding and doing anything" (p. 23, italics in original). Rosenau (1992) and Burr (1995) are two good places for readers to learn for themselves about postmodernism and social constructionism, respectively.

Postmodern interventions hold the most promise with clients whose occupational life has been disrupted to such an extent that their core assumptions about reality, self, and the role of work are no longer functional (Lyddon, 1990; Richardson, 1993). When a client has been downsized, laid off, fired, passed over for promotion, or reached a saturation point that looks like overwork and exhaustion, then we see the value of attending to both personal and social constructions of reality. We also remain vigilant about postmodern conversational artistry degenerating into plain old con artistry (Efran & Fauber, 1995): at present there is no system of checks and balances that prevents postmodern approaches from being used in an unscrupulous manner and as a cover for deceit and dishonesty. "Constructivism allows for a retention of personal responsibility that can balance social constructionism from deteriorating into political manipulation and/or oppressive conspiracies of silence" (González, 1997, p. 379).

In the workplace, a profound difference between what is said and what seems to be can contribute to employee disengagement, stress, and wavering. An overemphasis on the social construction of reality can eclipse individual employee rights and fail to acknowledge the existence of work that takes place outside the formal occupational structure (Fisher, 1995; Richardson, 1993).

Relevance for Multicultural and Diverse Populations Not everyone lives in a postmodern world. "Pockets of postmodernism exist, as do pockets of appalling premodern poverty" (González, 1997, p. 378). Practitioners need to stay mindful of how their own class privilege (Freire, 1993) and education levels can sway them into uncritical acceptance of the idea that we have uniformly entered a postmodern age. Proclamations that the modern world is rapidly waning (Srivastva, Fry, & Cooperrider, 1990) or dead (Hoffmann, 1991) are premature at best, elitist at worst. At first glance the pluralism espoused by multiculturalism and the multiple perspectives espoused by postmodernism appear to be compatible, but closer inspection reveals issues of classism, sexism and elitism that simply will not go away. The modern world that postmodernism reacts against was not the world of multicultural peoples (Johnson, 1991). Feminism and postmodernism are not necessarily conceptual and political allies (Benhabib, 1992). Nor is postmodern discourse frequently heard among construction laborers or public housing residents (Russell & Gaubatz, 1995).

Objectively detectable social and political realities of oppression DO exist outside the realities created—or glossed over—by language. Socially constructed, dominant discourses can serve as smokescreens to disguise inequality (Hare-Mustin, 1994). At other times, indirect talk—coded, politically laden, and sarcastic language—is a socially constructed reality that aims to silence others (Capper, 1995). González (1998) is concerned about postmodernism being foisted on multicultural and diverse clients without their informed consent. Many of these clients will not match their practitioners' familiarity with the postmodern literature, which makes consensual co-creations of reality quite unlikely. González is concerned about postmodernism as part of a hidden agenda, to be insinuated into clinical dialogues with unsuspecting and unaware clients. It is not the practitioner's place to disabuse any lower-income or immigrant client from pursuing a part in the Grand Narrative of the twentieth century. For many racial and ethnic minority persons, fine words from persons of the dominant culture can quickly lose their credibility unless supported by actions (Sue & Sue, 1990).

Confrontations between cultures have brought home the fact that people see the world differently (Smith, 1989). But the pendulum has swung too far in the direction of multiplicity. "Multiple views, yes; multiple realities, no. . . . Even if reality were no more than the sum of all . . . multiple realities . . . , that sum would stand as the inclusive reality which would not itself be multiple" (pp. 234–235). Moreover, "it is impossible that any one system has all the truth" (p. 240).

With the above statement, we close our look at foremost counseling theories. Postmodern strands represent the most recent perspectives, but all of these important movements have broadened our understanding of mental health interventions. While none of them was designed to specifically address the issues involved in career counseling, we have attempted to clarify the ideas and techniques that can be useful to career counselors. Individuals cited in the chapter, such as Bordin and others, Koehn, Sampson, and Savickas, have developed workable applications of these major theories for use by vocational practitioners.

Another strong sphere of influence of career counseling comes from those theories that see career choice as an integral part of one's development across the life span. Chapter 6 is devoted to the major ideas of developmental theorists.

6

Developmental Perspectives

Mom and Dad always say, "Edith just be yourself." Even though
they criticize everything about me. And then when I am being
myself, they say, "Stop doing that." They never seem to get what
I was doing was just being myself. Either they don't know who
I really am or I'm really not who they had in mind.

—EDITH ANN
(WAGNER, 1994, P. 21)

Edith Ann, a character created by comedienne Lily Tomlin and her partner,
writer Jane Wagner, is a five-year-old girl who expounds on life from the vantage point of her oversized rocking chair. One can always count on Edith Ann
for a perceptive remark on what it is like to be a kid. As the quotation above
makes clear, kids receive all sorts of mixed messages, especially from adults,
which can make the choices about what they want to be when they grow up
even more challenging.

In this chapter we survey different **developmental perspectives** on vocational psychology. Developmental perspectives presume that one's self-concept,
how an individual sees oneself, changes over time as a consequence of age and
life experience (e.g., a child's self-concept can be muddled by mixed messages
from adults). Developmental perspectives also presume that the role of work in

people's lives begins in childhood as a reflection of expectations placed on children by adults who regularly interact with them. These adults include parents and other relatives, teachers, coaches, and school counselors, as well as neighbors, family friends, and other caregivers. The media also powerfully impacts the self-concept and related occupational development of children, especially by promoting values claiming that having the money to consume products equals the good life (Pipher, 1996).

ERIKSON: PSYCHOSOCIAL DEVELOPMENT APPROACH

Erik Erikson's (1950) identity theory is well researched. "Although most contributors to the career development literature have acknowledged Erikson as the intellectual father of the construct of identity, none have succeeded in formulating a construct of identity that is more than a caricature of his thinking" (Vondracek, 1991, p.130). Recent theories of identity rest upon Erikson's original theory (1950, 1959, 1963, 1968). In *Identity: Youth and Crisis* (1968), he states:

> The wholeness to be achieved at this stage . . . [is] a sense of inner identity. The younger person, to experience wholeness, must feel a progressive continuity . . . between that which he conceives himself to be, and that which he perceives others to see in him and to expect of him. Individually speaking, identity includes, but is more than, the sum of all the successive identifications of those earlier years when the child wanted to be, and often was forced to become, like the people he depended on. Identity is . . . a crisis to be solved only in new identifications with age mates and with leader figures outside of the family. (p. 87)

Embedded within Erikson's (1950) eight stages of life-span growth and development is the stage that mainly occurs during adolescence and post-adolescence. Each of the stages plays a major part in career development. Erikson focused on the importance of a person's ability to be successful at work within the sociocultural and interpersonal environment. His stages are presented in Table 6.1.

Erikson's theory focuses primarily on three identity domains—vocation, ideology, and family. Archer and Waterman (1983) expand these domains to include vocational planning, religious beliefs, political ideologies, sex-role orientation, values, and family roles (Vondracek, 1992). There has not been much interest in directly applying or expanding Erikson's theory to vocational psychology. However, his ideas influence developmental psychology and life-span thinking in career and vocational counseling.

TABLE 6.1 Erikson's Eight Stages of Psychosocial Development

STAGE 1. BASIC TRUST VERSUS BASIC MISTRUST

Successful resolution: the person likes or trusts work associates, friends, relatives; feels essentially optimistic about people and their motives; has confidence in self and in the world in general.
Unsuccessful resolution: the person distrusts people; prefers to be alone because friends "get into trouble"; dislikes confiding in anyone; distrusts both self and the world in general.

STAGE 2. AUTONOMY VERSUS SHAME AND DOUBT

Successful resolution: attitudes and ways of doing things are his or her own and are not followed because others expect them; is not afraid to hold own opinions or do what he or she likes.
Unsuccessful resolution: is self-conscious about own ideas and ways of doing things, preferring to stay within tried and trusted ways; avoids asserting self against group; emphasizes how much like others he or she acts and feels.

STAGE 3. INITIATIVE VERSUS GUILT

Successful resolution: takes pleasure in planning and initiating action; plans ahead and designs own schedule.
Unsuccessful resolution: lets others initiate action; plays down success or accomplishment.

STAGE 4. INDUSTRY VERSUS INFERIORITY

Successful resolution: likes to make things and carry them to completion; strives for skill mastery; has pride in production.
Unsuccessful resolution: is passive; leaves things undone; feels inadequate about ability to do things or to produce work.

STAGE 5. EGO IDENTITY VERSUS ROLE DIFFUSION

Successful resolution: has strongly defined social roles; feels at home in work, family, affiliations, sex role; enjoys carrying out role behavior; has sense of belonging; takes comfort in style of life and daily activities; is definite about self and who he or she is; feels continuity with past and present.
Unsuccessful resolution: is ill at ease in roles; lost in groups and affiliations; does not enter into required role behavior with much conviction; may have radical switches in work or residence without meaning or purpose.

STAGE 6. INTIMACY VERSUS ISOLATION

Successful resolution: has close, intimate relationship with spouse and friends, sharing thought, spending time with them, and expressing warm feelings for them.
Unsuccessful resolution: lives relatively isolated from friends, spouse, children; avoids contact with others on an intimate basis; is either absorbed in self or indiscriminately sociable; relations with people are stereotyped or formalized.

Continued

TABLE 6.1 Erikson's Eight Stages of Psychosocial Development *(continued)*

STAGE 7. GENERATIVITY VERSUS STAGNATION

Successful resolution: has plans for future that require sustained application and utilization of skills and abilities; invests energy and ideas into something new; has sense of continuity with future generations.

Unsuccessful resolutions: seems to be vegetating; does nothing more than routines of work and necessary daily activities; is preoccupied with self.

STAGE 8. INTEGRITY VERSUS DESPAIR

Successful resolution: feels satisfied and happy with life, work, accomplishments; accepts responsibility for life; maximizes successes.

Unsuccessful resolution: feels depressed and unhappy about life, emphasizing failures; would change life or career if had another chance; does not accept present age and mode of life, emphasizing past; fears getting older; fears death.

SOURCE: *Early and Middle Adulthood,* 2nd ed., by L. E. Troll. Copyright 1985, 1975 by Wadsworth, Inc. Reprinted by permission of the publisher and by Dr. Walter Gruen.

GINZBERG: A DEVELOPMENTAL APPROACH

Human development has been central to theory and practice in career counseling for the past fifty years. Ginzberg, Ginsburg, Axelrad, and Herma (1951)—an economist, a psychiatrist, a sociologist, and a psychologist, respectively—speculated that career development is a process culminating in occupational choice during one's early twenties. They further assert that "Occupational choice is a developmental process; it is not a single decision, but a series of decisions made over a period of years. Each step in the process relates to those that precede and follow it" (p. 185). Four sets of factors influence vocational choice: (1) individual values, (2) emotional factors, (3) amount and type of education, and (4) the effect of reality through environmental pressures (e.g., geographic location, employment opportunities, etc.). These factors influence the formation of attitudes, which in turn shape occupational choice. Ginzberg et al. view choice as a process motivated by life stages, in which preadolescents and adolescents face certain tasks. As these tasks are confronted, compromises between wishes and possibilities can have an irreversible effect on one's decisions and options (Ginzberg et al., 1951, cited in Herr and Cramer, 1996). These stages are presented in Table 6.2.

Ginzberg et al. (1951) recognize individual variations in the career development process. Two primary causes for these individual variations have been suggested (Zunker, 1994). First, developing occupational skills early often leads to

TABLE 6.2 Ginzberg et al.'s Stages of Career Development

PERIOD	AGE	CHARACTERISTICS
Fantasy	Childhood (before age 11)	Purely play orientation in the initial stage; near end of this stage, play becomes work-oriented.
Tentative	Early adolescence (ages 11 to 17)	Transitional process marked by gradual recognition of work requirements; recognition of interests, abilities, work reward, values, and time perspectives.
Realistic	Middle adolescence (ages 17 to young adulthood)	Integration of capacities and interests: further development of values; specification of occupational choice; crystallization of occupational patterns.

SOURCE: Zunker (1994), p. 28.

earlier than usual career patterns. Think of teenage world-class athletes—professional tennis players, Olympic gymnasts and swimmers—nearly all of whom are "past their prime" by age 30. Some artists and performers also begin their life's work earlier than usual. Then there are those who began working as children and have identified themselves as workers ever since. Second, the timing of the realistic stage may be delayed if factors such as emotional instability, various personal problems, and financial affluence are present.

Vocational behavior is rooted in the early life of the child and develops over time (Ginzberg et al., 1951). However, Ginzberg reformulated his theory in 1971 to include three premises: (1) occupational choice is a process that remains active as long as one is making decisions about work and career; (2) decisions made during the early period (ages 5–17) will help shape career choices, but changes occurring in a person's own work and life will also influence career choices and patterns; and (3) decisions about jobs and careers are attempts to find a better match between personal needs/desires, and work opportunities/constraints.

By 1984 Ginzberg had modified his theory even further, noting that people periodically reassess their satisfactions with work, so that occupational choice becomes a lifelong process. Early decisions restrict later ones when people seek to improve their changing career goals and fit them into the changing realities of the world of work.

Ginzberg and his associates introduced the concept of career development as an active, dynamic process that spans an individual's working life. From this, other developmental career theorists emerged.

Evaluation of Ginzberg's Theory   Seligman (1994) offers two major criticisms of Ginzberg's theory. First, it is a descriptive theory that does not provide much direction to the process of facilitating career development or offer many suggestions for career counseling. Second, the research participants were mostly White males, with questionable generalizability to diverse populations.

SUPER'S LIFE-SPAN, LIFE-SPACE APPROACH

"Few disciplines have the good fortune to have a prodigious scholar at work on its problems for over six decades. Such is vocational psychology's debt to [the late Donald] Super" (Borgen, 1991, p. 276). Super brought comprehensive scholarship to the field of career behavior and development, and in his later years he synthesized much of his theory and research. For Super (1980), career is embedded in both the **life-span** and the **life-space.** The current status of his work is a loosely unified set of theories dealing with specific aspects of career development, taken from developmental, differential, social, personality, and phenomenological psychology and held together by self-concept or personal construct theory (Super, 1990).

Super's theory serves as a model for several reasons. First, it covers the entire life-span. Second, he developed inventories to validate the constructs of his theory, giving counselors assessment instruments that cover many aspects of career/job/occupation, including work adjustment, mid-career concerns, and the relationship of job to person. Third, an impressive amount of research has been done in conjunction with the concepts of his developmental theory. Fourth is the integration of the self-concept into the decision-making process.

Super proposed the following fourteen propositions.

Propositions of Super's Life-Span, Life-Space Approach

1. People differ in their abilities and personalities, needs, values, interests, traits, and self-concepts.

2. People are qualified, by virtue of these characteristics, each for a number of occupations.

3. Each occupation requires a characteristic pattern of abilities and personality traits, with tolerances wide enough to allow both some variety of occupations for each individual and some variety of individuals in each occupation.

4. Vocational preferences and competencies, the situations in which people live and work, and, hence, their self-concepts change with time and experience, although self-concepts, as products of social learning, are increasingly

stable from late adolescence until late maturity, providing some continuity in choice and adjustment.

5. The process of change may be summed up in a series of life stages (a "maxicycle") characterized as a sequence of growth, exploration, establishment, maintenance, and decline. . . . A small (mini) cycle takes place in transitions from one state to the next or each time an individual is destabilized by a reduction force, changes in type of manpower needs, illness or injury, or other socioeconomic or personal events. Such unstable or multiple-trial careers involve new growth, reexploration, and reestablishment (recycling).

6. The nature of the career pattern—that is, the occupational level attained and the sequence, frequency, and duration of trial and stable jobs—is determined by the individual's parental socioeconomic level, mental ability, education, skills, personality characteristics . . . , and **career maturity,** and by the opportunities to which he or she is exposed.

7. Success in coping with the demands of the environment and of the organism in that context at any given life-career stage depends on the readiness of the individual to cope with these demands . . . (on his or her career maturity). *Career maturity* is a constellation of physical, psychological, and social characteristics; psychologically, it is both cognitive and affective. It includes the degree of success in coping with the demands of earlier stages and substages of career development, and especially with the most recent.

8. Career maturity is a hypothetical construct. Its operational definition is perhaps as difficult to formulate as that of intelligence, but its history is much briefer and its achievements even less definitive. Contrary to the impressions created by some writers, it does not increase monotonically, and it is not a unitary trait.

9. Development through the life stages can be guided, partly by facilitating the maturing of abilities and interests and partly by aiding in reality testing and in the development of self-concepts.

10. The process of career development is essentially that of developing and implementing occupational self-concepts. It is a synthesizing and compromising process in which the self-concept is a product of the interaction of inherited aptitudes, physical make-up, opportunity to observe and play various roles, and evaluations of the extent to which the results of role playing meet with the approval of superiors and fellow workers (interactive learning).

11. The process of synthesis of or compromise between individual and social factors, between self-concepts and reality, is one of role playing and of

learning from feedback, whether the role is played in fantasy in the counseling interview or in such real-life activities as classes, clubs, part-time work, and entry jobs.

12. Work satisfactions and life satisfactions depend on the extent to which the individual finds adequate outlets for abilities, needs, values, interests, personality traits, and self-concepts. They depend on establishment in a type of work, a work situation, and a way of life in which one can play the kind of role that growth and exploratory experiences have led one to consider congenial and appropriate.

13. The degree of satisfaction people attain from work is proportional to the degree to which they have been able to implement self concepts.

14. Work and occupation provide a focus for personality organization for most men and women, although for some persons this focus is peripheral, incidental, or even nonexistent. Then other foci, such as leisure activities and homemaking, may be central. (Social traditions, such as sex-role stereotyping and modeling, racial and ethnic biases, and the opportunity structure, as well as individual differences, are important determinants of preferences for roles such as worker, student, homemaker, and citizen (pp. 206–208, italics in original)

Super's life-span, life-space approach to career counseling synthesizes theories and models into three graphic representations. The first graphic representation, life stages and substages of developmental tasks, is shown in Figure 6.1.

In Super's Life Career Stages, transitions are mini-stages in which important events take place. If one skips a step in moving from stage to stage, it may cause a negative impact (i.e., if one skips from growth to establishment without exploration, the result could be poor career/job choice and dissatisfaction). While the stages of growth, exploration, establishment, maintenance, and decline apply to the whole life, these same stages are enacted in a mini-version within each age group.

Super's stages provide a framework for vocational behavior and attitudes called **developmental tasks**. A developmental task is a new accomplishment or responsibility to be faced at a certain point in an individual's life, the successful achievement of which leads to happiness and success. Five developmental tasks are presented in Table 6.3.

In conjunction with the five vocational development tasks are thirteen metadimensions of the self-concept (personal construct): (1) self-esteem, (2) stability, (3) clarity, (4) abstraction, (5) refinement, (6) certainty, (7) realism, (8) regnancy, (9) harmony, (10) structure, (11) scope, (12) flexibility, and (13) idiosyncrasy (Zunker, 1994). **Self-esteem** can be key to decision-making, but

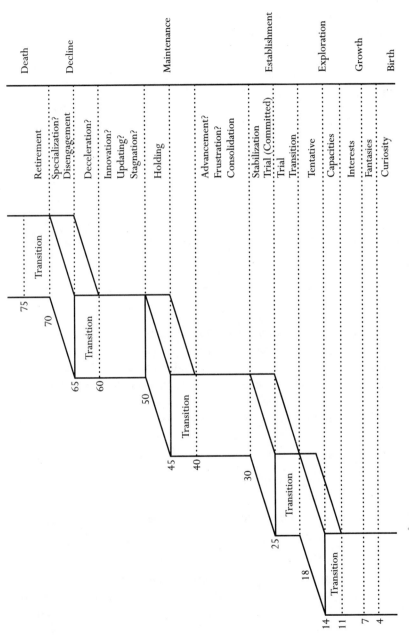

Death

Decline

Maintenance

Establishment

Exploration

Growth

Birth

Retirement

Specialization?
Disengagement

Deceleration?

Innovation?
Updating?
Stagnation?

Holding

Advancement?
Frustration?
Consolidation

Stabilization
Trial (Committed)
Trial
Transition

Tentative

Capacities

Interests

Fantasies

Curiosity

Transition

Transition

Transition

Transition

Transition

75

70

65

60

50

45

40

30

25

18

14

11

7

4

Note: Each transition, whether psychogenic, sociogenic, econogenic, or all of these, has its own minicycle of growth, exploration, establishment, maintenance, and decline: its recycling.

FIGURE 6.1 Life Stages and Substages Based on the Typical Development Tasks, with Focus on the Maxicycle

SOURCE: Super in Brown, Brooks and Associates (1990), p. 214.

TABLE 6.3 Super's Vocational Development Tasks

VOCATIONAL DEVELOPMENT TASKS	AGES	GENERAL CHARACTERISTICS
1. **Crystallization**	14—18	A cognitive process period of formulating a general vocational goal through awareness of resources, contingencies, interests, values, and planning for the preferred occupation
2. **Specification**	18—21	A period of moving from tentative vocational preferences towards a specific vocational preference
3. **Implementation**	21—24	A period of completing training for vocational preference and entering employment
4. **Stabilization**	24—35	A period of confirming a preferred career by actual work experience and use of talents to demonstrate career choice as an appropriate one
5. **Consolidation**	35 onwards	A period of establishment in a career by advancement, status, and seniority

SOURCE: Zunker (1994), p. 31.

research yields conflicting results (Betz, 1994). Women with high self-esteem are better able to successfully implement other aspects of their self-concepts. Fixedness of stages seems to be relevant in women's lives. Women who saw these stages as age-related did not feel the stages applied to their life sequence. The recycling idea has helped the theory pertain more to women. The study of women's careers has focused not on stages and patterns, but on what determines a women's career (Freeman, 1993).

Four other concepts help to understand the breadth of Super's theory.

1. Career maturity (see Proposition 8 above) is when one's career is at a peak. There may be several peaks or no peaks.

2. **Salience** is the importance of a role in a person's life.

3. Career determinants in the Archway Model (Figure 6.2) include what we know about person–environment interactions.

4. **Career adaptability** describes the balance an individual attempts to maintain between the work world and personal environment (Super & Knasel, 1979). Goodman's (1994) survey of adaptability cites several definitions (Ashley, 1984; Gelatt, 1991; Hall, 1986; Herr, 1992; Pratzner & Stephan, 1989). Career adaptability applies more to adults who have already found career maturity but are faced with changes, the need for learn-

ing how to deal with uncertainty and ambiguity in a positive manner, and
the acceptance of inconsistency. Ways to deal with life-long developmental
issues include risk-taking, being open to unexpected opportunities, overcoming barriers, overthrowing the status quo, and personal flexibility. Career adaptability requires that practitioners develop a better understanding
of the career transition process and to provide adaptability training; adaptability needs to be incorporated into the training with children, adolescents, and adults in the early stages (Goodman,1994). Savickas (1997)
writes that

> adaptation seems like a particularly appropriate construct for bridg-
> ing theory segments because of its great relevance. . . . This shift in
> attention from the individual to the individual-in-situation coin-
> cides with contextual and multicultural perspectives on work. . . .
> I propose that career adaptability replace career maturity as the
> central construct in the career development theory segment.
> (pp. 253–254)

Savickas further suggests that adaptability has a continual application throughout the life-span. He also recommends Susan D. Phillips' (1977) construct—
adaptive decision-making—as a critical dimension in career adaptability.

The second graphic representation of Super's approach is called the **Archway Model,** as seen in Figure 6.2.

Super's Archway Model integrates various aspects that contribute to development of the total self-concept (personal construct). The left column represents
psychological and personal characteristics and includes needs, intelligence,
values, interests, aptitudes, personality, and role self-concepts related to these attributes. The right column represents societal characteristics and includes community, school, family, society, labor market, and role self-concepts related to
these aspects of a person's life. While not part of the illustration, the columns
interact and are not always separate and independent from each other. The
doorstep between the two columns represents the biological-geographical foundations of development. The arch across the top is the career that results from
the foundation and the pillars. The keystone of the arch is the person who is the
decision maker, in whom all the influences converge from below.

The concept of roles is integral to Super's career development theory. A
second visual model of life-span development is Super's **Life-Career Rainbow**
design to describe the various roles one plays during one's life, as shown in Figure 6.3.

Super's Life-Career Rainbow shows that roles may vary during a lifetime. In
adolescence, exploration is paramount, leading to career decisions. In the early
adult years, becoming established in a career and finding one's way is major. In

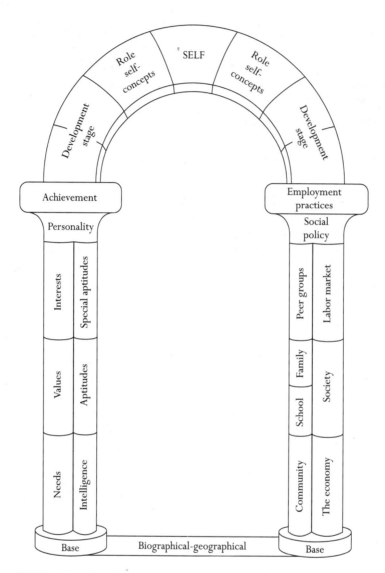

FIGURE 6.2 Super's Archway Model

SOURCE: *Super in Brown, Brooks and Associates, 1990, p. 200.*

the middle adult years, maintenance, job satisfaction, and adjustment to work changes are the focus of attention. In later adult years, slowing down and adjustment to different career concerns occur. As one scans the rainbow with each of the roles, changes in the importance of roles become apparent. The over-arching concern is the changing emphasis in career concerns and relationship of career

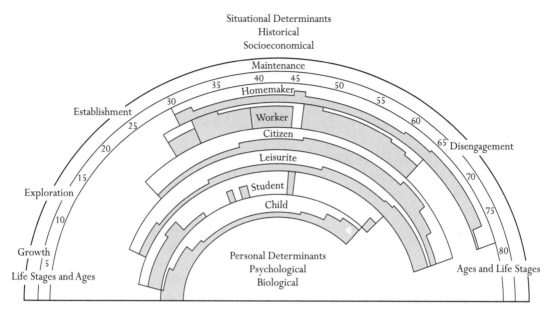

FIGURE 6.3 The Life-Career Rainbow
SOURCE: Super (1990), p. 212.

to roles. Of increasing importance are Super's ideas about life-space. Since an individual's work is in the context of a whole life, it is one of many roles across the life-span.

> Individuals make decisions about work-role behavior (such as occupational choice and organizational commitment) within the constellation of social positions that give meaning for two individuals who live in different situations. For example, dedication to work may differ between two individuals in the same job because one is also active as a spouse, parent, and Girl Scout leader while the other is also active as a daughter, sister, and swimmer. (D. E. Super, Savickas, and C. N. Super, 1996, p. 128)

Assessments Used with Super's Theory Super's measurement instruments are designed to measure an individual's concerns, values, and beliefs instead of measuring personality traits or aptitudes. Thus, his instruments are consistent with his theoretical ideas, and include:

1. The Adult Career Concerns Inventory (ACCI)
2. The Career Development Inventory (CDI)

3. The Salience Inventory (SI)

4. The Values Scale (VS)

5. The Work Values Inventory (WVI)

6. Thematic Extrapolation Method (TEM)

7. Career Maturity Inventory (CMI)

8. Career Adjustment and Development Inventory (CADI)

Relevance for Multicultural and Diverse Populations There is limited empirical evidence available about the relevance of Super's developmental theory for multicultural and diverse populations. Examining the extent to which racial and ethnic identity development affects career development could make Super's theory more relevant to minorities (Fouad & Arbona, 1994). We encourage both logical positivist *and* contextual interpretivist approaches to learn more. New ground could be broken with the development of multicultural norms on the Career-Development Assessment and Counseling model (C-DAC) to include an appropriate measure of acculturation. This would greatly enhance what is known about the occupational development of multicultural populations.

African Americans. The relationship between the self-concept and career behavior has not been systematically investigated with African Americans (Brown, 1995). Nor has the role of socioeconomic status and discrimination on occupational/self-concepts been investigated. Definable stages of career development, and variable implementation of the self-concept as a function of the developmental stage, have not been validated with African Americans. The concept of career maturity may need revision because it is correlated with socioeconomic status, and most African Americans are lower-income. Differences in the nature of African-American self-concepts, and the way in which it is implemented vocationally over time in the way that Super proposed, remain unknown.

Hispanics. "Neither theoretical formulations nor empirical research to date have elucidated which specific aspects of SES or ethnicity impact which aspects of career development for specific populations. . . . [T]here is very little empirical information related to the validity of the instruments and the theory among people of low-socioeconomic resources (White and non-White) and among ethnic minorities" (Arbona, 1995, pp. 47–48).

Native Americans. Johnson, Swartz, and Martin (1995) review three vocational psychology approaches with Native Americans, but Super's developmental approach is not among them. Nor does Martin (1995) specifically mention Super's approach in Native-American occupational development. The Archway Model would be relevant for Native Americans, especially given the model's consideration of the economy, community, school, family, peer groups, and social policy that appear on the right column of the arch (see Figure 6.2 above). These factors have not been fully fleshed out for applicability to Native Americans. Economic conditions are especially salient because they are affected by the maintenance of native language and customs (Johnson et al., 1995). The Life-Career Rainbow also has the potential application for widespread application to Native Americans.

Asian Americans. "Research on Asian Americans to date lacks a developmental perspective" (Leong & Serafica, 1995, p. 86). We wonder if some of Super's approach is individualistic for Asian Americans with a strong collectivistic orientation. To the extent that Asian-American parents "exert direct influence on the career aspirations and choices of their children" (Leong & Serafica, 1995, p. 71), their youth may have to submit "to the wisdom of the elderly" (p. 71). The Life-Career Rainbow has applicability to Asian Americans (Leong & Serafica, 1995). Asian-American college students show less career maturity than their White American counterparts (Leong, 1991), but these results may be considered preliminary at best. Within-group differences (career maturity of college-bound and non-college bound Asian Americans) would be more telling.

People with Mental Retardation. Little research has been conducted on the application of Super's developmental theory to persons with mental retardation (Levinson, Peterson & Elston, 1994). More broadly, since developmental theories target the nonhandicapped population, the complete application of such theories to individuals with mental retardation seems inappropriate. Persons with mental retardation generally have been limited in terms of both vocational exploration and range of experiences, so progress through developmental stages may be slowed and nonsystematic, if at all. A modified developmental approach can be adapted for use with individuals with mental retardation, beginning with setting age ranges aside. Degree of retardation and previous range of occupational and life experience will differentially impact the stages that entail (a) increasing self- and occupational awareness, (b) facilitating occupational exploration, (c) implementing an occupational choice, and (d) enhancing adjustment within a given occupation.

Gay, Lesbian, and Bisexual Persons. Modifying traditional developmental theories can contribute to effective career counseling with gay/lesbian/bisexual persons (Gelberg & Chojnacki, 1996). The person's level of sexual identity development has to be incorporated into life-span approaches.

Practical Applications

Super's developmental model presents some specific guidelines for practitioners to understand and evaluate clients' life-stage in order to define relevant counseling goals. Clarifying self-concept and finding appropriate experiences to determine the client's life stage would be essential for a practitioner to accomplish. Super does not talk about specific counseling procedures, but his thinking suggests a nondirective approach to clients. Since the process involves identifying the client's life-stage and level of career maturity, an immature client would need to focus on orientation and exploration. Mature clients could concentrate on decision-making and understanding the reality of their situations, leading to implementation. Using the tasks listed in Table 6.3, techniques that can be used include problem definition, deciding issues, working to-

wards understanding, using reflection and processing, and using assessments to gain more awareness about work with specific career and occupational information.

Client stages, needs, and level of understanding will differ. For example, when working with adolescents, Zunker (1994) cites Super's (1974) outline of six dimensions.

Orientation to vocational choice (an attitudinal dimension determining if the individual is concerned with the eventual vocational choice to be made); Information and planning (a competence dimension concerning specificity of information individuals have concerning future career decisions and past planning accomplished); Consistence of vocational preferences (individuals' consistencies of preferences);

Cass (1979) presents a six-stage model of sexual identity development that is applicable to gays, lesbians, and bisexuals (see Table 6.4).

The stage of a gay, lesbian, or bisexual person's sexual identity development can influence willingness to enter work environments where homophobia prevails. Self-esteem of gay/lesbian/bisexual persons can be affected by the interaction of their sexual identity development and workplace homophobia. In addition, "coming out of the closet" can be a central developmental transition for many gay, lesbian, and bisexual persons. This transition is inevitably intertwined with occupational development. Woods (1994) defines "in the closet" as knowingly misrepresenting one's sexuality to others by encouraging (or at least permitting) others to draw a conclusion one knows is false. "Coming out of the closet" is an ongoing process that can have enough salience to form

Crystallization of traits (individual progress toward forming a self-concept); Vocational independence (independence of work experience); and Wisdom of vocational preferences—dimension concerned with individual's ability to make realistic preferences consistent with personal tasks. (Zunker, 1994, pp. 33–34)

Of particular interest is Super's Career-Development Assessment and Counseling model (C-DAC) (Super, Osborne, Walsh, Brown, and Niles, 1992). The assessment tools in this battery include the Strong Interest Inventory (SII), The Values Scale (VS), The Career Development Inventory (CDI), The Adult Career Concerns Inventory (ACCI), and the Salience Inventory (SI). Two basic sequences of tests follow after a general orientation to the purpose and nature of the battery. Sequence A: (1) CDI/ACCI, (2) SII, (3) VS, (4) SI. Sequence B: (1) SII, (2) VS, (3) CDI/ACCI, (4) SI. An additional sequence is adapted to special cases and uses other instruments.

The ideas behind the sequences include the following: (1) The CDI is used if the client is a student, the ACCI if the client is an adult. (2) Sequence A is used to look first "at the developmental stage, the tasks, or concerns the individual faces" (Super et al., 1992, p. 77). (3) Sequence B "begins with the client's interests, as some people come to counseling seeking to find or to confirm an occupational choice" (Super et al., p. 77).

No aptitude tests are used since most institutions already screen a person for that. If there has been no screening, then the authors recommended the Differential Aptitude Test (DAT), the Armed Services Vocational Aptitude Battery (ASVAB) or the Miller Analogies Test (MAT), depending on the situation and the age of the client (Super et al., 1992).

a third pillar or column in Super's Archway Model. As part of developmental approaches to occupation, first romantic relationships, leaving home for the first time, and job promotions are also developmental transitions of gay, lesbian, and bisexual persons. A recognition that work role and sexual orientation cannot be completely detached from each other—given the social nature of work—makes life-span, life-space approaches to occupations relevant for sexual minority persons.

Evaluation of Super's Career Decision Theory Super's legacy is designed to be flexible enough to adapt to new conditions. Refinements of Super's theory can evolve as research is conducted to determine how the economic and occupational changes taking place around the world affect and modify the

TABLE 6.4 Sexual Identity Development of Gay/Lesbian/Bisexual Persons

STAGE 1: IDENTITY CONFUSION

"Who am I?" "My behavior may be called [gay, lesbian, or bisexual]." "Does this mean that I am [gay/lesbian/bisexual]?" With self-labeling of one's own behavior, the realization that feelings, thoughts, or behavior can be defined as gay, lesbian, or bisexual presents an incongruent element into a previously stable situation.

STAGE 2: IDENTITY COMPARISON

"Where do I belong?" "I may be [gay/lesbian/bisexual]." Social alienation, sense of "not belonging" can arise. Loss of self-concept of future heterosexual identity is not yet replaced by another sexual identity. "I do not want to be different."

STAGE 3: IDENTITY TOLERANCE

"I am probably [gay, lesbian, or bisexual]." Any sexual identity turmoil ceases when social, emotional, and sexual needs are acknowledged. Growth occurs when person attempts to resolve inconsistency in view of self, others' view of self.

STAGE 4: IDENTITY ACCEPTANCE

"I am a [gay/lesbian/bisexual] person." Sexual identity validated, normalized. There is acceptance rather than tolerance of sexual self-identity. The nonlegitimizing policy of heterosexuals produces tension.

STAGE 5: IDENTITY PRIDE

Commitment to gay, lesbian, and/or bisexual persons is strong. "These are my people." There is awareness of incongruence between self-acceptance and society's rejection. Devaluation of heterosexual others.

STAGE 6: IDENTITY SYNTHESIS

Dichotomy between heterosexual and gay/lesbian/bisexual world decreases. Similarly, dissimilarity between gay, lesbian, bisexual self, and heterosexual others is recognized. Sexual identity honored as one of many aspects of the self.

SOURCE: Adapted from Cass (1979).

theory and concepts such as the "meaning of work, work identity, and for new or emerging career patterns in many nations" (Herr, 1997, p. 241). Because women "are occupying leadership roles in traditional and nontraditional occupations, greater attention to gender issues in role salience and career decision-making needs to be applied to life-space, life-span perspectives" (p. 241). The

Work Importance Study in several nations is seminal in its work toward understanding national cultural differences (D. Super, Sverko & C. Super, 1995). Studies using more than two of Super's constructs—values and work-role salience—are needed (Herr, 1997). There is also a need to focus more directly on the various "obstacles, barriers, reinforcements, received messages, and other variables affecting the career behavior of women, racial and ethnic groups, persons with disabilities, and people of alternative sexual orientations" (p. 243).

OTHER CAREER DEVELOPMENTAL THEORISTS

Tiedeman and O'Hara

Tiedeman and O'Hara's approach to career development is basically self-development and includes cognitive development and the subsequent decision-making process of the individual (Tiedeman & O'Hara, 1963). Career development unfolds as one resolves ego-relevant crises, as the evolving ego identity is a crucial part of career development. The evolving self-in-situation develops from the earliest awareness of the self. Evaluating experiences, anticipating and imagining future goals, and storing experiences in memory for future reference are part of the evolving ego identity (Tiedeman & O'Hara, 1963).

Tiedeman and O'Hara's theory is based on Erikson's eight psychosocial crises and from the work of Ginzberg and Super. The theory focuses on ego development, the self-in-situation, and the self-in-world. From this theoretical basis they proposed a two-stage model of career development with appropriate substages.

1. Anticipation or preoccupation period:
   - Exploration—awareness of options develops
   - Crystallization—options are explored, narrowed
   - Choice—decisions are made
   - Clarification—plans are implemented
2. Implementation or adjustment period:
   - Induction—entry into the world of work
   - Reformation—modification of goals and environment
   - Integration—becoming an established member of the workforce (Seligman, 1994).

From this model a person can assess and define vocational/career direction while gaining a better understanding of the basics for the chosen direction. This process forms the basis for career identity. Tiedeman and O'Hara suggested career connections with each of Erikson's eight stages of the life-span (see Table 6.1 above).

Tiedeman and Miller-Tiedeman

Influenced by phenomenological and existential ideas, later termed **"constructive-developmentalism"** by Savickas (1989), Miller-Tiedeman (1988) developed a life career theory: Life is a learning process and, from experiences, one constructs one's own reality and meaning. Miller-Tiedeman's work is often viewed as a decision-making model. The approach promotes the development of self-awareness, meaning-making, and choices, helping people lead more "self-directed, decision-guided" lives. "This approach views career development as only one aspect of the process of development, and emphasizes the importance of individuality and taking control of one's life" (Seligman, 1994, p. 12).

Recently, Miller-Tiedeman and Tiedeman (1990) have developed a life career theory based on self-organizing systems, process, and decision theory—they are sometimes listed with the decision-making theorists. Life career theory emphasizes the need for career choices to come from one's internal frame of reference. A person searches from within to first find career direction, and then applies various strategies to make a career decision. From this theory comes the following philosophy: "Don't push life in your direction for you to learn; learn from life, and let life teach you" (Wrenn, 1988, p. 340). Miller Tiedeman (1989) emphasizes LIFECAREER, the need to teach young and older adults how to live life as a process. Life decisions and career decisions are integrally related. (Decision-making theories will be discussed further in Chapter 7.)

Gottfredson's Theory of Circumscription and Compromise

In her approach, Gottfredson (1996) combines trait-factor and developmental theories. Major tenets include: (a) self-concept—one's self perception; (b) occupational images—similar to occupational stereotypes but without the negative implications of stereotypes; (c) a cognitive map of occupations—based on dimensions such as sex type, occupational prestige level, and field of work; (d) compatibility—assessing different occupations with images of themselves and looking for congruence; (e) social space—range of alternatives in the cognitive map of occupations; (f) circumscription—how individuals narrow the territory or alternatives; and (g) compromise—relinquishing some alternative for the less compatible but more accessible ones.

Practical Applications

There are five criteria that assess an individual's career success. Failure to meet a criterion indicates a problem(s). (1) Can the client name one or more occupational alternatives? If not, is there a lack of self-knowledge to judge compatibility? Are there internal or external conflicts in the goals? (2) Are the client's interests and abilities a match for the occupation(s) selected? If not, are there external pressures from parents or misperceptions of self? (3) Is the client satisfied with the alternatives identified? If not, was client's choice an unacceptable compromise of interests, sex type, family concerns? (4) Has the client left any alternatives open? If not, why have alternatives been restricted? (5) Is the client aware of opportunities and realistic about obstacles for implementing the chosen occupation? Is the client failing to overcome obstacles? (Gottfredson, 1996). Since much of her theory and research concentrated on gender issues, it would seem important to incorporate this in our work with women.

Gottfredson outlines the following underpinnings for her theory. (1) "Career choice is an attempt to place oneself in the broader social order" (p. 181). "Social" aspects of self (gender, social class, intelligence) are emphasized more than personal ones (values, traits). (2) Cognitions of self and occupations develop early. Career development needs to begin as early as in the preschool years. (3) Vocational choice assists a person in eliminating options and narrowing choices. (4) Individuals compromise their goals as they face the reality of implementing their aspirations.

MULTICULTURAL DEVELOPMENTAL PERSPECTIVES

Vocational psychology can adapt itself to multicultural populations by considering minority identity development (Atkinson, Morten & Sue, 1989). A model is outlined in Table 6.5.

To date, no theory of occupational development accounts for identity stage of minority development (Osipow & Littlejohn, 1995). This missing information

TABLE 6.5 Summary of Minority Identity Development Model

STAGES OF MINORITY DEVELOPMENT MODEL	ATTITUDE TOWARDS SELF	ATTITUDE TOWARDS OTHERS OF THE SAME MINORITY	ATTITUDE TOWARDS OTHERS OF DIFFERENT MINORITY	ATTITUDE TOWARDS DOMINANT GROUP
Stage 1: Conformity	self-depreciating	group-depreciated	discriminatory	group-appreciating
Stage 2: Dissonance	conflict between self-depreciating and appreciating	conflict between group-depreciating and group-appreciating	conflict between dominantly held views of minority hierarchy and feelings of shared experience	conflict between group-appreciating and group-depreciating
Stage 3: Resistance and immersion	self-appreciating	group-appreciating	conflict between feelings of empathy for other minority experiences and feelings of culturo-centrism	group-depreciating
Stage 4: Introspection	concern with basis of self-appreciation	concern with nature of unequivocal appreciation	concern with ethnocentric basis for judging others	concern with the basis of group depreciation
Stage 5: Synergetic articulation and awareness	self-appreciating	group-appreciating	group-appreciating	selective appreciation

SOURCE: Donald R. Atkinson, George Morten, and Derald Wing Sue, *Counseling American Minorities* (3rd edition). Copyright 1989 by William C. Brown Publishers, Dubuque, Iowa. All rights reserved. Reprinted by permission.

is crucial: an individual's stage of minority development determines conformity to mainstream societal norms. Many racial and ethnic minority persons face the dual challenge of minority identity development combined with general development. A triple challenge occurs when racial and ethnic minority persons also face questions of gay/lesbian/bisexual identity development and occupational development.

A racial and ethnic minority person in Stage 1 of the model shown in Table 6.5 would have unequivocal Conformity to the dominant group (Atkinson et al., 1989). In a work setting, a Stage 1 individual would feel deficient in perceived desirable characteristics of the dominant culture. These individuals may rely on affirmation from White males (being the dominant group in this country), regardless of the talent or ability that they possess. Not until a breakdown in one's denial system occurs does a racial and ethnic minority person experience the Dissonance of Stage 2. Breakdown of denial can be gradual or abrupt. Denial system breakdown can occur in many ways. One can have a new co-worker of the same racial or ethnic background but at a different Stage in the Minority Identity Development Model, whose worldview makes for a different reading of workplace politics. Blatant racism in the workplace, especially racism that is rewarded or goes unpunished, can jolt somebody out of Stage 1 and into Stage 2.

Growing awareness of inequity and inequality, and a realization that not all dominant cultural values serve the best interests of a racial and ethnic minority person (Atkinson et al., 1989), can nudge a person on to the Resistance and Immersion of Stage 3. Until a person passes beyond at least Stage 3 of the Minority Identity Development Model, the development of a stable self-concept can be prolonged and the expression of that self through the role of work can be delayed. Issues of oppression in the workplace are also confronted in Stage 3.

Decision-making processes can be most effective with clients in the Introspection of Stage 4 (Atkinson et al., 1989). Cultural constraints and personal freedom vie with each other at this stage. The racial or ethnic minority person has to resolve these inner tensions. By Stage 5, the person has enough internal skills and knowledge to exercise the desired level of personal freedom (Atkinson et al., 1989). One's sense of minority identity is balanced with an appreciation for other cultures. More psychological resources are present to deal with intractable issues of discrimination and oppression.

With affirmative action as a simmering topic in reference to equal access to occupational opportunities, vocational psychology will be remiss until multicultural and diversity issues are solidly at the center—not a subspecialty—of any theory of occupational development. In the next chapter we explore social learning and decision-making models and address their relevance for multicultural and diverse populations.

7

Social Learning and
Decision-Making Approaches

"We know what we are, but we know not what we may be."
—WILLIAM SHAKESPEARE
HAMLET, ACT IV, SCENE V

Social learning approaches to vocational psychology focus on the genetic and socially inherited attributes that people bring to their work environments. These
attributes and environments interact to produce self-views that influence a
person's work-related behaviors. Work-related behaviors, in turn, are modified by
both natural and programmed reinforcers and punishments (Osipow, 1983). This
chapter is divided into four parts. First, we present the concept of **self-efficacy**,
which forms the foundation for social learning theory. Second, we examine social learning approaches to the role of work in people's lives. Third, we consider
social cognitive career theory, a recent innovation in vocational psychology that is
influenced by self-efficacy and social learning. Fourth, we look at occupational
decision-making models, also influenced by self-efficacy and social learning.

BANDURA: SELF-EFFICACY THEORY

Social learning theory is based in part on the idea of self-efficacy. Self-efficacy
refers to perceived judgments of one's capacity to successfully perform a given
task or behavior (Bandura, 1977, 1984, 1986). The basic phenomenon centers on

people's sense that they exercise some personal control over events affecting their lives. With self-efficacy, successful performance is the vehicle for change.

Expectations of personal efficacy are derived from four principle sources of information: (1) performance accomplishments, (2) vicarious experience, (3) verbal persuasion, and (4) emotional arousal. Performance accomplishments are based on personal mastery experiences. Mastery expectations are raised depending upon successes and lowered based on failures, particularly early repeated failures. Repeated successes produce strong efficacy expectations and reduce the negative impact of occasional failures. Performance accomplishments are induced by participant modeling, performance desensitization, performance exposure, and self-instructed performance. Vicarious experience relies on inferences from social comparisons (which are a less dependable source of information about one's capabilities than the direct evidence provided by performance accomplishments), and is induced by live and symbolic modeling. Verbal persuasion is induced by suggestion, exhortation, self-instruction, and interpretive treatments. People rely on emotional arousal to judge self-perceived anxiety and vulnerability to stress. High arousal usually debilitates performance. Efficacy expectations increase in the absence of aversive arousal (e.g., tension, visceral agitation). Emotional arousal is reduced by attribution relaxation, biofeedback, symbolic desensitization, and symbolic exposure. Direct mastery experiences and modeling can also reduce arousal.

Cognitive appraisal mediates the impact information has on efficacy expectations. Social, situational, and temporal circumstances enter into such appraisal. Expectation alone does not determine behavior; if competent capabilities are lacking, expectation alone will not produce successful behavior to bring about desired outcomes. The provision of appropriate skills and adequate incentives facilitate efficacy expectations. Bandura's model of perceived self-efficacy is graphically depicted in Figure 7.1.

Figure 7.1 shows the sources of efficacy information on the left: performance accomplishments, vicarious learning, emotional arousal, and verbal persuasion. Qualities of the resulting behavior are shown on the right: the choice to approach or avoid certain situations, competency of performance, and persistence in the face of obstacles.

A social cognitive perspective for career development has been researched by Krumboltz and Mitchell (1984) and Hackett and Betz (1981). Krumboltz and Mitchell used Bandura's theory as a basis for their own social learning theory of career decision-making. Hackett and Betz focused on incorporating career behavior into self-efficacy theory. **Intrinsic interests** show themselves in a person's "enduring interest in activities that engage their feelings of personal efficacy and satisfaction" (Lent, Larkin & Brown, 1989, p. 280). **Task interest** gives a person more motivation to interact with the task, which in turn offers

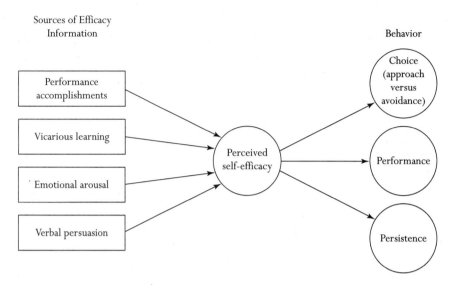

FIGURE 7.1 Bandura's Model of Perceived Self-Efficacy

SOURCE: Betz (1992), p. 23.

more of a chance for "personal and vicarious success experiences, and further self-efficacy enhancement" (Lent et al., p. 287). The reciprocal interaction of interests and perceived efficacy greatly affect one's educational/career choice and performance.

Self-efficacy expectations refer to beliefs in one's ability to successfully produce required outcomes. Efficacy expectations affect career decisions and personal achievements. Take, for example, the process of career decision-making. Individuals' beliefs about their ability to decide on an appropriate career choice can be summed up in **career decision-making self-efficacy.** As the theory continues to develop, more research is needed on how to treat low career decision-making self-efficacy (Lent & Hackett, 1987; McAuliffe, 1992; Maddux, Stanley & Manning, 1987).

Relevance for Multicultural and Diverse Populations

Gender differences. Self-efficacy theory is relevant to the occupational development of women (Betz, 1992, 1994; Betz & Fitzgerald, 1987; Betz & Hackett, 1981, 1983). Mathematics self-efficacy, a crucial factor in the selection of a college major, has long-term implications for women's occupation and earning power. In a prime example of how vocational psychology can enrich itself through interface with other academic disciplines, theories of cognitive development and learning teach that (1) girls and boys have the same natural ability in math, and (2) girls get better grades than boys in math (Byrnes, 1996). The general public, numerous parents and educators, and several counselors and academic advisors remain largely unaware of these research findings. Too many girls and young women have long been told that they naturally have no mathematical ability. Furthermore,

> (3) gender differences favoring boys are only likely to emerge if the math test requires problem-solving *and* the students taking the test are either older than 14 or gifted. Gender differences favoring girls are likely to emerge in two situations: (a) when the math test requires computational skill *and* the students are below the age of 15 or (b) when the math test contains items that require knowing when you have enough to answer *and* the students are gifted. (Byrnes, 1996, p. 176, italics in original)

Males and females have similar natural ability but different levels of confidence in the fields of education (Sadker & Sadker, 1994), women's studies (Bingham & Stryker, 1995; Orenstein, 1994), and parenting (Elium & Elium, 1994; Marone, 1988). Pipher (1994) thinks teacher education needs to focus on equity training to eradicate even subtle forms of classroom discrimination. She also advocates all-girl math and science classes. We think such all-girl classes should be taught by women. Vocational practitioners, school counselors, allied helping professionals, parents, teachers, and school administrators share an interest in rectifying differences in mathematics self-efficacy.

Beyond the elementary school level, Bingham and Stryker (1995) suggest the following prerequisites for girls to succeed at math. First, girls must see themselves as successful at math. Performance accomplishments matter. Second, support and high expectations need to be conveyed to girls from family, teachers, and peers. Third, girls need to understand what math offers them and why it is important to future success and life satisfaction. The long-term implications for women's occupations and earning power can be affected by many people in a variety of positions and disciplines. Vocational psychologists can help by being aware of the approaches other disciplines take toward mathematics self-efficacy.

African Americans. Self-efficacy theory relevance for African Americans remains largely unknown. Brown (1995) states:

> We need to know ... to what extent do efficacy expectations effect the perceived range of academic and occupational options, the effectiveness of career decision-making, and academic achievement? If self-efficacy is found to play a major role in the career behavior of African Americans, then another set of important questions concerns whether and to what extent the self-efficacy expectations of African Americans are modifiable through career intervention. (p. 17)

Occupational self-efficacy has been scarcely researched with African Americans.

Hispanics. Few studies have examined occupational and academic self-efficacy with Hispanics (Arbona, 1995). For Hispanic students, occupational and academic self-efficacy are predictive of career choice and academic achievement, respectively. For those seeking to understand the relation between career-related behaviors of Hispanics and various sociocultural forces (i.e., economic background, minority status, acculturation level), the concept of **collective self-efficacy** holds promise. Collective self-efficacy is predicated on the idea that immigration histories vary for Hispanic ethnic subgroups, with differential socioeconomic and political consequences as well. An Hispanic individual will likely have a sense of both collective and personal self-efficacy, which would be wise to take into account when making occupation-based interventions. Varying rates of academic achievement for Hispanic ethnic subgroups (del Pinal, 1995) make academic self-efficacy relevant to Hispanics (Arbona, 1995).

The College Self-Efficacy Instrument mentioned earlier has been validated successfully on Hispanics (Solberg, O'Brien, Villarreal, Kennel & Davis, 1993). Two subscales show strong relationships to college adjustment: (1) course efficacy pertains to writing papers, performing well in classes, and time management; (2) roommate efficacy pertains to interpersonal aspects of communal living and managing household management issues. Self-efficacy expectations as a determinant of college adjustment seems useful to measure at two- and four-year colleges where Hispanics and other minorities form a substantial part of the student body. Self-efficacy's role in persistence and retention of minority college students is another research area that remains largely unexplored.

Asian Americans. Collective self-efficacy has potential relevance for Asian Americans when acculturation is assessed as a moderating variable. Asian Americans who are less acculturated to the individualistic American mindset will likely show more collective self-efficacy than personal self-efficacy. Career decision-making self-efficacy holds promise for Asian Americans (Leong & Serafica, 1995).

Native Americans. Occupational self-efficacy can be limited among Native American youth with restricted exposure to the world of work (Martin, 1991). Yet performance accomplishments have a natural relevance for many Native Americans who have learned their traditions and customs through behavioral modeling and experiential-based learning (LaFromboise, Trimble & Mohatt, 1990).

Gay, Lesbian, and Bisexual Persons. Because of societal **homophobia** and heterosexism, gay/lesbian/bisexual persons in the early stages of their sexual identity development may have low occupational self-efficacy and can eliminate occupation options even when their actual abilities in those eliminated occupations are quite high (Gelberg & Chojnacki, 1996). Self-efficacy expectations in job searches as linked to sexual orientation remain unexplored (Gelberg & Chojnacki, 1996).

Practical Applications

Many career decision-makers are helped only partially by traditional information-oriented approaches. Practitioners can increase their awareness of the personal-emotional barriers that hinder clients from making and implementing sound occupational plans. Self-efficacy theory can challenge negative expectations (McAuliffe, 1992). Self-efficacy can be valuable in short-term interventions that often happen in occupational guidance situations, ensuring that personal-emotional issues around occupational decisions receive the attention they deserve. "Assessment of the client's specific career decision-making self-efficacy expectations should precede interventions" (p. 27). Three recommended instruments for this approach are the Career Decision-Making Self-Efficacy Scale (CDMSES; Taylor & Betz, 1983), the Career Confidence Scale (CCS; Pickering, Calliotte & McAuliffe, 1990), and the Career Search Self-Efficacy Scale, which refers to an

"individual's degree of confidence that they can successfully perform a variety of career explora-

tion activities, including their judgments about their ability to successfully explore personal values and interests, effectively network with professionals in a field of interest, [and] successfully interview for a job" (Solberg, Good, Fischer, Brown & Nord, 1995, p. 448).

After determining where a client demonstrates the least confidence, the practitioner can employ a combination of counseling strategies taken from social-cognitive principles (Bandura, 1977, 1986) and cognitive restructuring techniques (Mitchell & Krumboltz, 1990). Once a client's interests have been determined, various interventions can help develop efficacy expectations.

1. The most powerful intervention would involve the structuring of successful performance accomplishments.
2. The second source of efficacy information—vicarious or observational learning—would require the counselor to find role models of success in the client's feared area.

Continued

Continued

3. In the area of emotional arousal, techniques of anxiety management may be useful.

4. Next, the counselor can show the client how to become aware of negative self-talk and to stop it and replace it with task-focused cognition—for example, self-statements—focusing on the characteristics of the problem.

5. Verbal persuasion and encouragement are tools that are strengths of the counselor—the counselor can be the reinforcer and can strengthen beliefs of self-efficacy by expressions of belief in the person's potentially underused capabilities. (Betz, 1992, p. 25)

The practitioner's support is crucial as clients proceed with steps they hope will advance their careers. Clients' goals may take them into unknown areas, making the practitioner's encouragement valuable.

Another area of practical application is the development of the Career Counseling Self-Efficacy Scale (CCSES) (O'Brien, Heppner, Flores & Bikos, 1997). The CCSES has been used to train graduate students in vocational counseling and has established reliability and validity. The CCSES can be incorporated into coursework in career counseling and into program evaluation procedures to enhance practitioners' vocational counseling effectiveness and to aid therapeutic outcome.

Evaluation of Self-efficacy Theory Betz (1992) writes:

> The particular usefulness of Bandura's original self-efficacy model is that the elements for treatment were explicitly contained in the theory—because it is a social learning model, the causes of the problem, that is, deficits in the information needed to develop strong expectations of personal efficacy, are also the means for the cure. (p. 24)

This can affect both men and women when their low self-efficacy perceptions limit their career options, especially if these options are associated with jobs held by the opposite sex.

Self-efficacy theory has plenty of practical applicability and the potential to be empirically verifiable for a variety of research participants. However, some discrepancies appear in the theory. First, without any personal mastery, experiences, it can be virtually impossible for both clients and research participants to initially appraise their self-efficacy with accuracy (González, 1990).

Second, self-efficacy theory is inexact.

> For some people, feelings may constitute the dominant basis for making judgments about self-efficacy. For other people, rational and considered

appraisals may predominate. Assessing self-percepts of efficacy to perform a given task or behavior is highly subjective in nature. Accounting for such subjectivity has not been done in research on self-efficacy ... [in] ... various domains. (González, 1990, p. 217)

Empirical evidence is inconclusive as to whether increases in self-efficacy entirely reflect behavioral attainment/performance mastery. Ethnographic, qualitative research could tell what influences self-efficacy estimates, in addition to cognitive appraisal.

Third, it can be difficult to distinguish between efficacy expectations and outcome expectations (Bandura, 1984; Eastman & Marzillier, 1984; Marzillier & Eastman, 1984). Bandura (1977) originally defined outcome expectations as a person's estimate that a given behavior will lead to certain outcomes. He defined efficacy expectations as the conviction that one can successfully execute the behavior required to produce the outcomes. Ostensibly, a person's efficacy expectations allow for behavior which gives rise to outcome expectations that produce desired it is not easy to show that people's estimation ask or behavior is not influenced by their con-

dure is developed which measures and em- xpectations and outcome expectations do controlling for any external motivators that efficacy assessment, the validity of self- a certain amount of healthy skepticism.

es generally, discrimination and other forms omes and/or a minority individual's expec- the adequacy of that minority individual's lt, both efficacy and outcome expectations ent effects on career behavior for racial and sexual-orientation minorities as well. This acy theory. The theory could be expanded erceived presence of adequate incentives to ader contextual and external structural fac- centives. Until then, the question remains implies a belief that a particular behavior

generalizability of the research on career derations (Church, Teresa, Rosebrook &

Szendre, 1992). Gender differences in self-efficacy have relied largely on categorical distinctions between occupations (male-dominated versus female-dominated), whereas more valid research results could occur if gender dominance of an occupation were treated as a continuous variable. Vocational interests, incentives, and aptitudes have had a limited integration into career self-efficacy studies. College students have been most often studied, with little attention given to underachieving and ethnic minority individuals. Reid (1993) refers to college students as **populations of convenience.** Using college students as research participants has always been easy, especially for academic researchers who are pressured to publish, but such populations of convenience make for weak, restricted results and ignore the economic and political realities more representative populations face.

KRUMBOLTZ: SOCIAL LEARNING APPROACH

Krumboltz's (1979) social learning approach to vocational counseling focuses on the self-system and emphasizes behavior and cognitions in making career decisions. Four factors interact to produce movement along one career path or another: (1) **genetic endowment** and special abilities, (2) **environmental conditions** and events, (3) **learning experiences**, and (4) **task approach skills**. While other theories of career development also are concerned with inherited abilities and environmental considerations, social learning focuses particularly on learning experience and task approach skills. Genetic endowment refers to the innate aspects rather than those that are learned. These include (a) physical appearance, (b) race, (c) sex, (d) intelligence, (e) musical ability, (f) artistic ability, (g) muscular coordination, and (h) predisposition to certain physical illnesses.

Environmental conditions refers to (a) the number and nature of job opportunities; (b) the number and nature of training opportunities; (c) social policies and procedures for selecting trainees and workers; (d) rate of return for various occupations; (e) labor laws and union rules; (f) physical events (i.e., earthquakes, droughts, floods, hurricanes); (g) availability of and demand for natural resources; (h) technological developments; (i) changes in social organization; (j) family training, experiences, and resources; (k) educational systems; (l) neighborhood and community influences, and other social, cultural, political, and economic considerations (Krumboltz, 1979).

Learning experiences are of two basic types. First, **instrumental learning experiences** occur when the individual acts upon the environment in such a way as to produce desirable consequences. There are three components to the instrumental learning experience: antecedents, behavior, and consequences. Second, **associative learning experiences** occur when an individual pairs a situation that has been previously neutral with one that is positive or negative. Two types of associative learning experience are: (1) observation, and (2) classical conditioning (Krumboltz, 1979).

An important part of career decision-making is understanding how an individual approaches a task. Task approach skills include (a) goals setting, (b) values clarification, (c) generating alternatives, and (d) obtaining career information. Interactions among genetic endowment, environmental conditions, and learning experiences lead to skills in doing a variety of tasks (Sharf, 1997).

Social learning theory is grounded in the following constructs: (a) reciprocal determinism, (b) observational learning, (c) extrinsic/intrinsic/vicarious learning, and (d) self-reinforcement. Self-observational generalizations and task approach skills result from the process of reciprocal determinism and learning experiences. An individual can observe his or her performance in relation to the performance of others or his or her past performance and make generalizations about it (Bandura, 1986).

Task approach skills are defined as cognitive, and along with performance abilities and emotional predispositions for coping with the environment, allow for interpreting a task in relation to self-observational generalizations and making covert or overt predictions about future events. Career selection is a natural process influenced not only by decisions made by each individual involved but also social forces that affect occupational availability and requirements. People select, and are selected by, occupations.

Krumboltz's theory has been extended to social learning theory of career decision-making (SLTCDM). This theory has two parts: (1) "explain the origins of career choices" and (2) "explain what career counselors can do about many career-related problems" (Mitchell & Krumboltz, p. 233). Current research is being conducted by Krumboltz et al. regarding the concept of planned happenstance.

Assessments Used with Krumboltz's Model

1. Career Beliefs Inventory (CBI)
2. Values Scale (VS)
3. Strong Interest Inventory (SII)
4. Campbell Interest and Skill Survey (CISS)
5. Self-Directed Search (SDS)
6. DECIDES
7. Myer's-Briggs Type Indicator (MBTI)

Practical Applications

Krumboltz's social learning theory (1979) pertains to a lifelong process, not a one-time decision. Practitioners help clients learn how to make wise career decisions by using different techniques—including assessment—to integrate genetic factors, learning experiences, and cognitive and emotional responses. After completing the career counseling process, a client should be able to modify current career plans or make entirely new choices depending on their new learning experiences.

DECIDES, a social learning model of career counseling (Krumboltz & Hamel, 1977; Sharf, 1997), is a behavioral approach which provides for reinforcements and consequences. Essentially, it is a problem-solving model of decision-making. The seven steps of DECIDES form the acronym which is used: (1) define the problem, (2) establish an action plan, (3) clarify values, (4) identify alternatives, (5) discover probable outcomes, (6) eliminate alternatives systematically, and (7) start action. Although these steps are presented sequentially, they are flexible in that the individual may backtrack to a previous step and begin the process again.

The first step should be very specific and agreed upon by both practitioner and client. The second step involves putting in written form each action to be taken in each step of the DECIDES process, including written time deadlines. The third step involves identifying and recognizing

what the client believes to be important in a career. The client should have an understanding of what is important to him or her based on previous job experiences. At this stage, it is helpful to administer Super's Values Scale (VS). The fourth step involves evaluating the client's beliefs of self-observation, and generalizations about their interests or capabilities. Interest inventories such as the Strong Interest Inventory (SII), Holland's Self-Directed Search (SDS), and the Campbell Interest and Skill Survey (CISS) may be used to illuminate the client's interests and to suggest occupations consistent with those interests. Brainstorming may be used as a client makes a list of occupations which sound interesting.

The fifth step involves discovering probable outcomes of career choices. The client compares the information obtained about the various occupations with his or her identified values, abilities, and interests, and then decides which jobs would bring more satisfaction. Once the client has prepared a comprehensive list of possible occupations to consider, the sixth step is to eliminate the least desirable alternatives. The practitioner should be aware of possible faulty beliefs and/or stereotypes that a client may rely on to eliminate options. The final step in this process is to take action. This is the step in which the client actually engages in job-seeking or school-seeking behavior. This includes making a résumé, getting and filling out applications to schools and for jobs, signing up to take college entrance exams, and going on interviews (Sharf, 1997).

The most important underlying issue in the DECIDES program is whether the client is able to apply wise decision-making skills rather than simply achieve the beginning goal. If this process has been successfully undertaken it should be applicable to any problems the client encounters, not just career-related ones. The practitioner helps the client learn how to learn.

As a practitioner using the social-learning model, it is very useful to understand client self-observational generalizations and task approach skills used in the past. Consistent with this model, it would be important to teach the client how to evaluate the personal consequences of learning experiences and then arrange an appropriate sequence of career-relevant exploratory learning experiences. The client needs to learn a rational sequence of career decision-making skills.

Krumboltz (1991a) published an important assessment tool called the Career Beliefs Inventory (CBI) to help people identify career beliefs that could be hindering them from achieving their career goals. "The fundamental premise upon which the CBI is based is that people make assumptions and generalizations about themselves and the world of work based on their limited experiences" (p. 1). The CBI does not intend to suggest that beliefs are good or bad, but may simply obstruct a client's ability to set or reach goals. The basic areas that the twenty-five scales in the assessment cover are: (1) My Current Career Situation, (2) What Seems Necessary for My Happiness, (3) Factors that Influence My Decisions, (4) Changes I Am Willing to Make, and (5) Effort I Am Willing to Initiate. This assessment can be used effectively in the DECIDES program.

Occupationism

The first thing we do, let's kill all the lawyers.
—William Shakespeare, *Henry VI, Part Two,* Act IV, Scene ii

Another area of recent interest to Krumboltz (1991b) is **occupationism**, discrimination against individuals based solely on their occupation. Occupationism falls into the same category as racism, sexism, and religious bigotry, and is just as universal. Krumboltz urges practitioners "to launch a campaign" (p. 311) that would make occupationism become as intolerable as sexism and racism. Krumboltz believes this campaign would eventually lead to major changes in the profession of career counseling. Three properties of occupationism are

discriminability, **consequentiality**, and **unjustifiability**. Discriminability occurs when people make judgments which are based on the relative position of a person's occupation within "an almost universally agreed upon [occupational] prestige hierarchy" (Krumboltz, 1991b, p. 310). An act cannot be labeled occupationist unless it is potentially harmful or helpful to a person's interests, called consequentiality. "The effects of occupationist acts may be either harmful or beneficial to an individual's interests, depending on the circumstances" (Carson, 1992, p. 492). Unjustifiability occurs when "a property of occupationism is related to the degree of knowledge an individual has of the quality of work performed by another" (Carson, 1992, p. 492).

Occupational prestige is the relative standing, or status, among occupations. The term also refers to how various occupations are perceived and esteemed by different populations. "Anthropologists have noted that different cultures seem to esteem different sorts of occupations" (Carson, 1992, p. 494). Krumboltz (1991b) concludes that part of the work of vocational practitioners is to "convert insights into beliefs used to guide actions" (p.314). The intent of this is to examine, evaluate, and advocate. Some occupations are unanimously agreed upon as being horrible while others are esteemed as admirable and honorable. "For other occupations, one might say that the jury is still out, that collective opinion and debate have not yet resolved the level of desirability of the occupation" (Carson, 1992, p. 496).

Krumboltz (1991b) believes that to engage in shallow occupationism with clients could affect their dignity and self-respect. Deep occupationism is associated with widely shared beliefs about the desirability of various occupations, reflects a common vision of what we most care about as people, and provides a statement about the kind of society we want to be (Carson, 1992).

"A central question . . . is this: How can one help people to identify with the kind of work they believe is consistent with the kind of life they wish to lead?" (Carson, 1992, p. 501). According to Krumboltz (1991b), society needs to confront the issue of which types of employment will be held in high esteem and which will not. There may be times when to remain neutral in the face of a client's consideration of either particularly worthy or particularly reprehensible career options would be both unprofessional and unethical (Carson, 1992).

CASE EXAMPLE

Legitimate News Photographer or *Paparazzi*? To Some Segments of the General Public It's All the Same.

In one of the most extreme instances of hurtful occupationism in recent years, news photographers across the United States and throughout the world experienced a backlash in the weeks following the death in a car crash of Diana, Princess of Wales. In places as diverse as Hollywood, Atlantic City, Memphis, Dallas, and as far afield as New Zealand, news photographers have been the targets of heckles, harassment, and physical attack (Associated Press, 1997).

Discriminability became evident when some segments of the general public in these various locales made judgments against legitimate news photographers solely on the basis of their occupation. Apparently, this segment of the general public lumped news photographers in with the *paparazzi*. The *paparazzi* often obsessively stalk celebrities and other public figures and deliberately intrude upon their privacy in the hopes of taking a photograph that will earn them hundreds of thousands of dollars. Some people worldwide have blamed the *paparazzi* for the princess's death. To help cooler heads prevail, former *Washington Post* publisher Katharine Graham wrote, "One point we all have to keep clear is that the *paparazzi* are different from the news

media and most other photographers" (Graham, 1997, p. 69).

Consequentiality was manifested in the occupationist act where a New Zealand newspaper photographer was physically attacked. Her physical well-being was threatened and her dignity was adversely affected. Even those photographers who had been verbally abused had their professional interests harmed.

Unjustifiability became apparent when certain members of the general public ignored the quality of work performed by the news photographers they harassed. For those persons who disregarded the legitimate status of their occupation, it would be interesting to know if these same individuals had ever purchased the publications that paid big money for *paparazzi* photographs of Diana. Rather than segments of the general public facing up to their own culpability in reinforcing the media's hounding her to death, it is easier to scapegoat news photographers instead. Alter (1997) writes, "The same people who are ranting about 'the *paparazzi*' will be the first to buy all of the special issues of Diana—full of pictures taken in years past by *paparazzi*" (p. 62). This illustrates the type of issues involved in occupationism.

Relevance for Multicultural and Diverse Populations

Native Americans. Given the limited frequency with which Native Americans enter technical or scientific fields (Johnson, Swartz & Martin, 1995), the availability and accessibility of occupations is an issue. If Native Americans are not seen in certain occupational roles, young people from similar backgrounds may not see such occupations as an option.

Asian Americans. "Research is needed as to whether Asian Americans who possess . . . [task approach skills relative to career decision-making] . . . to a greater degree than their peers arrive at a career choice more readily and with a higher degree of career certainty" (Leong & Serafica, 1995, p. 97). Further research is needed in the areas of career decision-making, career certainty, and maintenance of career choices.

African Americans. Research is sparse on the career decision-making processes of African Americans (Brown, 1995). Gender differences and opportunity structure need to be considered for social learning theory's relevance for African Americans (Griffith, 1980). Wilson's (1996) analysis of the disappearance of work opportunities in the inner city poses a formidable challenge for social learning theory and other career counseling approaches to become more tenable for multicultural and diverse populations.

Hispanics. Similar to the extremely limited research among Asian Americans and African Americans, the acquisition of occupational knowledge and awareness for Hispanics is an area to which social learning can be applied (Fouad, 1995). Like Native Americans, Hispanics are underrepresented in technical and scientific fields. There is not extensive research literature on programs that promote math and scientific achievement.

Gay, Lesbian, and Bisexual Persons. Social learning theory is relevant for gay/lesbian/bisexual persons (Gelberg & Chojnacki, 1996). Occupational stereotyping can impact the degree to which a gay, lesbian, or bisexual person values certain occupations and believes that occupational success is possible. Without sexual orientation minority role models in the workplace, the desirability of those occupations can diminish for gay, lesbian, and bisexual persons. Feelings of isolation and negativity can also result for sexual orientation minorities without mentors or role models.

People with Disabilities. Social learning theory has its greatest utility in training persons with mental retardation to function within a previously identified appropriate job training program (Levinson, Peterson & Elston, 1994). Behavioral and learning principles can be applied to necessary skill acquisition for completing vocationally appropriate developmental tasks.

Evaluation of Social Learning Theory The complexity involved in acquiring career preferences, choice, and decision-making skills (Leong & Serafica, 1995) exceeds social learning theory's capacity to explain through empirical, quantitative research methods alone. Ethnographic, qualitative research methods might be more useful for comprehending such complexity (Polkinghorne, 1984, 1991).

We want to see greater emphasis placed on Krumboltz's second factor, environmental conditions and events, which produces movement along one career path or another. Number and nature of both job and training opportunities; social policies and procedures within educational systems; and social, cultural, political, and economic considerations may most heavily impact multicultural and diverse populations. Social learning theory has yet to fully develop its potential along these lines. Ogbu (1992) discusses the nature of the relationship between a given minority culture and the dominant White American culture and the implications on minority education. Differential school success among various minority groups is intimately related to long-term occupational achievement and cannot be artificially separated out from research questions regarding vocational development. Societal and community educational policies and practices have denied multicultural and diverse populations equal access to good education (Kozol, 1991; Sadker & Sadker, 1994).

Even in those instances when educational accomplishments have occurred, many minorities have been denied "adequate and/or equal rewards with Whites . . . through a job ceiling or other mechanisms" (Ogbu, 1992, p. 7). Social learning theory needs to exert itself to examine how "the meaning and value students associate with school learning and achievement . . . [determine students'] efforts toward learning and performance" (Ogbu, 1992, p. 7).

Minority groups vary according to cultural differences and social or collective identities (Ogbu, 1992). **Voluntary minorities** immigrate to a country to improve their economic situation (Traindis, 1993) and are inclined to **primary cultural differences.** Primary cultural differences "existed before two groups came in contact, such as before immigrant minorities came to the United States" (Ogbu, 1992, p. 8). **Involuntary minorities** immigrate to a country through forced slavery, political expulsion from their homelands, or other economic or military developments beyond their control (Triandis, 1993) and are inclined to **secondary cultural differences.** Secondary cultural differences "arose after two populations came into contact or after members of a given population began to participate in an institution controlled by the dominant group, such as the schools controlled by the dominant group" (Ogbu, 1992, p. 8) and develop when one cultural group dominates another. The subordinate group copes with its position by reinterpreting its primary cultural differences or showing the emergence of new types of cultural norms or behaviors. Involuntary minorities are more apt to evidence secondary cultural differences via cognitive, communication, interaction, and learning styles, as well as **cultural inversion.** With cultural inversion, involuntary minorities are apt to consider certain behaviors, events, symbols, and meanings as inappropriate for themselves because these characterize White Americans.

Voluntary minorities retain a sense of who they are without developing a nonoppositional social identity in reference to White Americans (Ogbu, 1992). The primary cultural differences of voluntary minorities do not erect insurmountable cultural and language barriers between such minorities and White Americans. Voluntary minorities show an equivalent sense of security and self-worth to White Americans so that such minorities do not perceive a threat to their own culture, language, and identities. Voluntary minorities accommodate, but do not assimilate. They play by the rules of the game for school success because of long-term gains and payoffs and "tend to be enthusiastic about education" (Triandis, 1993, p. 51).

Involuntary minorities develop an oppositional social identity when they are subordinated by White Americans in economic, political, social, psychological, cultural, and language domains (Ogbu, 1992). Secondary cultural differences of involuntary minorities are more likely to erect insurmountable cultural and language barriers between such minorities and White Americans. Involuntary minorities do not show an equivalent sense of security and self-worth and thus perceive a threat to their own culture, language, and identities by White Americans. Involuntary minorities maintain their cultural and language differences as indicators of their collective identities and regard school success as trying to act like the Whites. Involuntary minorities tend to have "anti-establishment attitudes . . . and less interest in education" (Triandis, 1993, p. 51).

Both voluntary and involuntary minorities have to adjust to the dominant culture. Yet, voluntary minorities do not equate academic success with adopting the White cultural identity, involuntary minorities do.

Social learning approaches to the role of work in people's lives have the capacity to articulate the environmental conditions and events that characterize the educational and occupational opportunities of both voluntary and involuntary minorities. But social learning theory has yet to do this. Natural and programmed reinforcers and punishments for voluntary and involuntary minorities have not been closely scrutinized as they pertain to occupational development. This closer scrutiny would enrich and elaborate upon learning experiences, task approach skills, and occupationism as they occur among diverse populations. Voluntary minorities are more likely to measure success according to within-group differences. Involuntary minorities are more likely to measure success according to between-group differences. Thus, given two members of the same minority group, the first may assume voluntary status while the second may assume involuntary status as a minority.

SOCIAL COGNITIVE CAREER THEORY

Lent, Brown and Hackett (1996) propose a new approach that combines the ideas of Bandura and Krumboltz with Hackett and Betz (1981). Social Cognitive Career Theory (SCCT) makes four basic assumptions:

1. interests are strongly related to one's self-efficacy and outcome expectations;

2. performance accomplishments in a specific endeavor will lead to interests in that endeavor to the extent that they foster a growing sense of self-efficacy;

3. self-efficacy and outcome expectations affect career-related choices largely (though not completely) through their influence on interests; and

4. past performance affects future performance partly through people's task mastery abilities and partly through the self-efficacy percepts they develop, which presumably help them to organize their skills and persist despite setbacks. (p. 400)

SCCT can expand the interests of clients and help facilitate their choices, aid in dealing with barriers to decision-making and success, and improve their perspective regarding their own self-efficacy (Lent et al., 1996). Self-efficacy, outcome expectations and personal goals are not purely objective constructs, but are interpreted in a contextual framework. SCCT uses the client's own experiences as well as other variables, such as "gender, race/ethnicity, physical health/ ability, genetic endowment, and socioeconomic status" (Lent et. al, 1996, p. 386) as a means of identifying the interplay between the concepts. SCCT adopts ideas from various career theories, including self-efficacy, social learning, cognitive processing, and can include assessments used in trait-factor approaches. The contextual emphasis allows for cultural and gender differences by emphasizing individual experiences as a basis for career development. SCCT is a recent advancement in ever-growing convergence of ideas from various theories into more practical applications.

DECISION-MAKING MODELS

Delays have dangerous ends.
—William Shakespeare, *Henry VI,* Part One, Act III, Scene ii

Several models for decision-making have been proposed. All are designed to aid clients to come to a decision armed with self-understanding and a rational means of choosing vocations and jobs. We have chosen to focus on three specific models with further ideas on indecision and indecisiveness.

Gelatt Model

The **Gelatt decision-making model** illustrates the cyclical nature of decision-making and the sequence of the decision-making process. This model provides: (a) a framework from which methods and techniques can be derived as guidelines in career-counseling programs; (b) a system to determine values that are a significant part of the decision-making process; and (c) a concept of a series of decisions—immediate, intermediate, and future—pointing out that decision-making is a process.

Gelatt's model has five steps to complete the process. The individual: (1) recognizes a need to make a decision and then establishes an objective or purpose; (2) collects data and looks at possible courses of action; (3) uses the data to determine possible courses of action, outcomes, and probability of outcomes; (4) focuses attention on his/her value system; and (5) evaluates and makes a decision that can be a terminal decision or investigatory decision (Zunker, 1990).

Gelatt's (1991) later model of career decision-making is called **Positive Uncertainty,** a "whole-brained approach to planning your future" (p. vi). "*Uncertainty* describes the condition of today's river of life. The successful decision-maker navigating the river needs to be understanding, accepting, even *positive* about that uncertainty" (p. 1, italics in original).

> The two factors, the unpredictability of the future and the limited rationality of people, make organizational and personal planning unfeasible—*unless we change how we plan and make decisions.* First, we must accept, even embrace, two facts: the need to change our approach from predicting the future to creating it, recognizing that the future is our present responsibility. Finally, we need to dislodge the superiority of rational over intuitive decision-making because we need both strategies equally to make good decisions. (Gelatt, 1991, p. 2, italics in original)

Gelatt further explains the **two-by-four process,** two attitudes and four factors. The attitudes are: (1) accept the past, present, and future as uncertain; and (2) be positive about uncertainty. The four factors to consider are: (1) what you want, (2) what you know, (3) what you believe, and (4) what you do (p. 6).

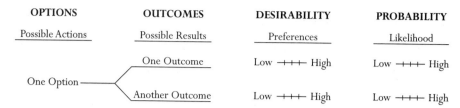

OPTIONS	OUTCOMES	DESIRABILITY	PROBABILITY
Possible Actions	Possible Results	Preferences	Likelihood

FIGURE 7.2 Gelatt's Decision Tree Imagery

SOURCE: *Gelatt (1991), p. 60.*

His theory uses these attitudes and factors to provide flexibility within the model. This model also differs from traditional decision-making models in that he proposes four "paradoxical principles" which are based on creativity: (1) Be focused and flexible. (2) Be aware and wary. (3) Be objective and optimistic. (4) Be practical and magical (p. 6). These variations, from the four factors and two attitudes, are the basic principles of Positive Uncertainty. "Following each principle is an example of a traditional decision maker who needs to become balanced in his or her decision-making approach" (p. 6).

Gelatt (1991) developed the decision tree model, which encourages clients to "think through their uncertainties using both rational and intuitive processes and make their own decisions as to how to decide" (p. 60). This model is presented in Figure 7.2.

Practical Applications

The practitioner can ask: Is the client aware of the need to make a decision? Does the client possess the resource skills necessary in the decision-making process? Readiness should be considered in the initial exploratory interview conducted by the counselor. A second counseling consideration involves the client's self-knowledge. Does the person possess sufficient self-knowledge of interests, abilities, values, and relevant past experiences? Does he/she have the skills to apply this knowledge to the consideration of alternatives? An adequate prediction-system strategy requires both self-knowledge and the ability to apply this knowledge in the choice process. In addition, the practitioner should consider the individual's knowledge of educational training opportunities, as well as occupational environments, requirements, and demands. The more informed individual has a greater probability of a desired outcome. Finally, the client needs to understand the process of decision-making, including knowledge of the decision-making steps and of the flexibility required to weigh alternatives (Zunker, 1994).

The model in Figure 7.2 allows the client to use both rational and intuitive methods to make their own decisions based on their readiness. These steps offer the client the means to develop a whole-brained decision style (Gelatt, 1991). No attempt is made by Gelatt to estimate the combined value of probability and desirability; these will be idiosyncratic to the client. Two questions clients can ask themselves as they use this model are "What else could I do?" and "What else could happen?" (Gelatt, 1991, p. 60).

Gati: The Sequential Elimination Approach

In 1986 Gati advanced a new model for career decision-making based on Tversky's (1972) theory of choice. Gati's model used the idea that each occupational alternative has a series of aspects and that at each stage of the selection process, the importance of the aspect becomes the criterion for keeping or eliminating the alternative. He called this the **sequential elimination approach.** It is considered to be a rational manner to approach career decision-making, especially when many alternatives are present. The sequential elimination approach identifies various career options that prove compatible to the client's preferences. This goal is achieved by gradually eliminating the options that are not compatible with the individual's preferences.

Gati, Fassa, and Houminer (1995) propose nine steps involved in sequential elimination. (1) Define and structure the decision problem by clarifying the goal of the decision and determining the alternatives from which to choose. (2) Identify relevant aspects—it is not possible to consider all possibilities. The client will need to choose those on which he/she wants to concentrate. This is important because the outcomes depend on the choices made at this time. (3) Rank aspects by importance—this activity is also crucial since importance is a major criterion for selection. (4) Identify optimal and acceptable levels of compromise one is willing to make. (5) Eliminate occupations with incompatible preferences—each aspect is considered as to its importance, with a careful and thoughtfully worked-through elimination of options to seven or fewer. (6) Test sensitivity to changes in preferences—after reducing the options to a few, it may be wise to reexamine the earlier stages in order to "reduce the probability of missing a potentially suitable option" (p. 214). (7) Collect additional information—used to compare the alternatives that still remain after the previous steps. (8) Rank alternatives by overall desirability—this involves steps toward deciding which alternative the client will decide to try out first, second, etc. Focusing on the possible advantages and disadvantages will help in this process. (9) Outline steps to actualize the most preferred alternative—the last stage should focus on planning the actions to be taken to act upon the individual's choices. "These may also include actions aimed at increasing the chances of realizing the most desired alternative" (Gati et al., 1995. p. 216).

Practical Applications

The sequential elimination approach can be incorporated into the career counseling process in five sessions (Gati et al., 1995). During the first session the client's situation can be defined in terms of a decision that needs to be made, with an outline of the alternatives developed. The practitioner explains to the client what will occur in the following sessions. The focus of the second session helps the client evaluate and compare the different alternatives, including pointing out aspects the client may have overlooked. After this, the client will be able to assess the importance of each aspect through ranking them. At the end of this session the client can be told to think about his/her preferences within each of the ranked aspects, and realizing the importance of compromising. "The counselor may help the client explicate his/her preferences by suggesting that he/she recall relevant past experiences" (p. 217).

The sequential elimination process actually begins during the third session. A rank order of importance is assigned to each aspect under consideration, identifying those that meet the optimal level. Then the levels considered acceptable are ordered. The practitioner provides feedback as to the alternatives this order of choices eliminates. The client takes the list of remaining alternatives and compares them with what he/she feels intuitively would be acceptable.

During the fourth session, the practitioner goes over the preceding stages with the client and explains their outcomes. In doing so, the client might identify alternatives that are still worth further consideration. At the end of this session, the client should collect information about the remaining alternatives.

Once the client has comprehensive information, he/she can decide which alternative is the most suitable as well as desirable. During the final session, the considered alternatives can be ranked on the basis of all the available information. The practitioner can help the client outline the steps to be taken to promote the best alternative. "Finally, the nine steps of the process may be reviewed to increase the prospect that the individual will be able to apply them in future career decisions" (Gati et al., 1995, p. 217).

Dinklage: Eight Decision-Making Strategies

Instead of a process, Dinklage (1968) describes eight strategies for making decisions. Four of the strategies are ways of *not* making a decision: (1) being fatalistic, (2) delaying, (3) compliant, or (4) paralytic. Being fatalistic is a way of letting others make the decision for oneself and thus, not choosing. By delaying, the individual postpones making the decision until it is made by others or by circumstance. When compliant, someone else is allowed to decide for oneself. Paralytic is when individuals feel unable to make a decision because they are frightened or anxious. The common link of these four strategies is that the client is *not* making a decision.

There are four different strategies in which people *decide not to decide*: (1) intuitive, (2) impulsive, (3) agonizing, and (4) planful. Here, intuitive means making a decision based on feelings rather than thoughts. Intuitive decisions are often very reliable, but should be followed up with an analysis of a person's strengths. An impulsive individual makes quick decisions without looking at alternative possibilities with careful thought. An agonizing individual sorts constantly through information about oneself and occupations, but has problems reaching a decision. A planful individual makes a decision based on both feelings and a knowledge of one's abilities, interests, and values (Sharf, 1997).

Career Indecision

The world is full of uncertainty. One domain where uncertainty plays a significant role is that of career decisions. Feeling positive about uncertainty (Gelatt, 1989) is not enough; individuals have to incorporate uncertainty into their career decisions as they do any other relevant information. Disregarding uncertainties may lead one to choose an option that is inferior to others. Sometimes one option is clearly better than or even dominates others. Dominance refers to the case when one option is better than another in at least one of the aspects, and is at least as good as the other, for each of the other relevant aspects (Gati, 1990).

Savickas (1990) concludes that personal counseling may be an option for indecisive clients so that they can deal with the psychological blocks to decision-making, reduce their fears, and increase their competence in problem solving. Krumboltz (1992) suggests that being undecided is not bad, but a welcome challenge to our linear cultural assumptions that one must make a decision and get on with it. Yet, being undecided is bad if it creates psychological distress and nurtures unproductive **irrational beliefs** (Fouad, 1993).

Newman, Fuqua and Seaworth (1989) address the issue of anxiety in **career indecision.** They define career indecision as a "state of being undecided about a career" and point out that often the practice of career counseling is less than adequate when indecision is involved, since it is much more complex than it is usually perceived to be. Several factors can be part of career indecision: (a) anxiety, (b) external locus of control, (c) problems in self-perception, (d) interpersonal difficulties and dependency, (e) interests, (f) ability levels, and (g) cognitive styles.

There is a difference between indecision and indecisiveness. Heppner and Heindricks (1995) conducted a process and outcome study of these two factors in career decision-making. Undecided clients are more likely to respond quickly to the tasks of vocational search and career decision-making. Indecisive clients appear to have issues that override the basic career decision, and may often need a more intensively therapeutic intervention. This may involve time to resolve personal issues that may create indecision (such as parental pressures and expectations or fear of failure). This study provides a carefully monitored outcome from which to hypothesize. Too often career indecision is seen as a distinct issue *from,* instead of *in* career counseling.

Czerlinsky and Chandler (1993) use a structured interview for vocational career decision-making. Although this instrument is designed for people with physical disabilities, it applies to several settings, including schools. This type of interview attempts to provide assistance for making a vocational decision and dealing with the implications for training or education needed to implement the decision. One of its strengths is that it faces the problem of career indecision and the obstacles with which individuals are confronted, especially those with physical disabilities. This is called the Vocational Decision-Making Interview Revised (VDMI-R) and can be ordered from Pro Publishing Associates, P.O. Box 35526, Dallas, Texas, 75235-0526.

Assessments for Decision-Making

1. Career Decision Scale
2. Assessment of Career Decision-Making
3. Harrington O'Shea Career Decision-Making System
4. My Vocational Situation
5. Career Decision Profile

Relevance for Multicultural and Diverse Populations

People with Disabilities. The Gelatt model's heavy reliance on self-direction would seem ineffective to use with persons with mental retardation (Levinson et al., 1994). However, decision theory can be adapted to apply to mentally retarded individuals. Incorporating a developmental framework, decision theory can be appropriately applied at logical decision points during the vocational counseling of persons with mental retardation. These logical points include the time when decisions need to be made about (a) which occupational areas should be explored further, (b) which occupations are realistic options, and (c) which options should be pursued. One clinical modification of this approach would be for the practitioner and the client to collaborate during the decision-making process. Another practical adaptation would be to integrate data derived from any previous trait-factor assessment at the logical decision point when realistic occupational options are being considered.

Gay, Lesbian, and Bisexual Persons. Sexual orientation has been little considered in career decision-making research (Gelberg & Chojnacki, 1996). Among the issues that can arise for gay/lesbian/bisexual persons in career decision-making is how to handle (a) workplace discrimination, (b) work relationship issues, (c) gender role issues when making career decisions, (d) coming out of the closet in a particular work environment, and (e) the level of gay, lesbian, and bisexual affirmation in a given city or geographical region. A client's stage of sexual identity development will influence the way these issues are handled.

Other Multicultural Populations. Harrington (1991) writes about the cross-cultural application of the Harrington-O'Shea Career Decision-Making System (CDM). For cross-cultural adaptation within the same country, the CDM was translated for usage among the U.S. Spanish-speaking population. In an example of the kind of multidisciplinary efforts we would like to see in vocational psychology, personnel at the National Assessment and Dissemination Center for Bilingual Education assisted in producing the Spanish version of the CDM. The CDM has been translated for usage among the Canadienne Quebeçois French-speaking population, with assistance from the Ontario Institute for Studies in Education. English language versions of the CDM also have been produced for use in Canada and Australia. In each instance, construct and concurrent validity of the CDM has remained intact.

The regular use of My Vocational Situation with college students who have not selected a college major has been reported by the Career Center (CPPC) at the University of Missouri-Columbia (Candrl & Heinzen, 1994; McDaniels, Carter, Heinzen, Candrl & Weinberg, 1994). CPPC staff purposely avoid using the term "undecided," which has negative connotations and implies that something is wrong with a student undecided about a college major. Instead, they use the term "deciding" to normalize the process, especially for freshmen and sophomores, and to emphasize that "deciding" students are not alone and have plenty of company in terms of focusing on a career path.

Evaluation of Decision-Making Models Most career decision-making has focused on high school and college populations. An inherent weakness in the career decision-making research is an excessive reliance on **populations of convenience,** largely college students (a) from introductory psychology classes (Cohen et al., 1995; Solberg et al., 1995; Temple & Osipow, 1994), (b) from other courses (Solberg et al., 1995), or (c) recruited from flyers posted on bulletin boards (Blustein & Phillips, 1990). Career decision-making research can be immeasurably strengthened by more sophisticated sampling techniques that tap more representative populations whose occupational struggles are of a qualitatively different nature from that of undergraduates. Career decision-making research suffers from incipient **classism.** We encourage more occupational decision-making research to be done on (1) non-college bound populations, (2) students in poor junior high and high schools who already are underserved by school counselors and who would benefit by research and intervention on occupational decision-making, (3) welfare recipients who are mandated by reform measures to get a job and achieve a means for a long-term livelihood, (4) displaced blue collar workers, and (5) reentry women and immigrants with high school educations or less.

Social learning theory and the related emphasis on career decision-making has added to the perspective of the role of the counselor. Krumboltz and his associates have attempted to put more emphasis on the activities of the counselor. To help determine actions to be taken in the context of the client and his/her strengths and weaknesses that go beyond genetic endowments, the practitioner can offer services that encourage effective and efficient decision-making. The issues of indecision and indecisiveness are often indicative of life themes that encompass more than career concerns.

These problems can relate to family situations and influences, which we explore in depth in Chapter 8. While the foremost counseling, developmental, and social learning and career decision theories have influenced vocational psychology practice, less attention has been given to family and parental influences. We will attempt to discover the effects family has on career paths and choices.

8

Family and Systemic Influences
on Occupational Choice

JUST THINK: Your family are the people most likely to give you the flu.
—EDITH ANN
(WAGNER, 1994, P. 126)

In Chapter 6 we met Edith Ann, the little girl who dispenses pearls of wisdom from her oversized rocking chair like a guru perched on a mountaintop. Edith Ann is an astute observer of family life. Families can give you more than just the flu. Sometimes, families inspire us to go into a particular line of work. Family influences on occupational choice are receiving greater attention in vocational psychology, although the notion that the role work plays in people's lives is affected by their family-of-origin is hardly new. We begin this chapter with an exploration of the theoretical models of Alfred Adler (1870–1937) and Anne Roe (1904–1991). Second, we present traditional family systems approaches to occupational development. Third, we look at work-family conflict, dual-career families, and single-parent families. Fourth, we examine the recent phenomenon known as the postmodern family as it applies to the workplace, touching upon the myth of workplace as family. Finally, we offer some observations on incorporating a systemic approach into vocational psychology.

Certain family background factors are linked to a child's occupational development, including parents' socioeconomic status/educational level and one's own genetics (Penick, 1990). Freisen (1986) believes a child's **educational at-**

tainment is a result of the father's occupation. Educational attainment ultimately effects the child's occupational achievement. Sibling dynamics also affect a person's occupational goal-setting abilities (Bradley, 1982). Family, school performance, and life experiences contribute more to occupational choice than do attitudes toward self or society (Owens, 1992).

The nuclear family was once the predominant type in the United States. Today, the breadwinner father and stay-at-home mother comprise less than 3 percent of American families, with 60 percent of them being dual-earner couples (Barnett & Rivers, 1996). Given these changes in our families and in the role of work, we have developed this chapter to help practitioners realize the influence families have in occupational development.

THEORETICAL MODELS OF ADLER AND ROE

Adler: Life Tasks of Vocation

Adler contends that there are five major life tasks that humans must meet: (1) vocation—giving by working, (2) society—interpersonal and intrasocietal relationships, (3) love—intimacy and family, (4) spirituality—relating to Higher Beings and/or the universe, and (5) self—dealing with the personal self. Adlerian-oriented vocational research typically has revolved around **birth order, lifestyle, early recollections,** and social interests (Watts & Engels, 1995). Birth order is thought to affect the child's place in his or her family, and on a larger scale, the child's future place in society.

> Different ordinal positions (e.g., first-born, only child, among others) each entail a distinctive, developmental experience in relation to various family members. From this experience, the child learns diverse coping patterns and behaviors . . . and . . . a means of establishing a place in the family system. Such learnings are believed to crystallize into a coherent, consistent and unitary perceptual adaptational set: the lifestyle. Once developed, the lifestyle serves as a stable frame of reference for the individual, providing a method for both organizing and interpreting internal and external events. (Watkins, 1984, p. 29)

Lifestyle, although self-sustaining, is supported by a person's early recollections. Children's memories, usually those prior to age eight, coincide with the individual's lifestyle pattern. The manner in which memories are retained is purposeful and deliberate. Early recollections are an integral part of a lifestyle's maintenance. Since work is a way of one contributing to the community, a person's social interests are a part of work. Work gives an individual a sense of "belongingness," that the individual matters to others (Watkins & Savickas,

1990). Family relationships, in turn, influence an individual's work approach and social interests.

In Adlerian theory a person's life and behavior is determined by an intrinsic goal. To achieve this goal, which involves the well-being of the person, the individual decides a life plan. Out of this life plan evolves a lifestyle empowered by the goal. Difficulties arise when the goal is self-defeating. Therefore, it is necessary to discover what the goals are to eliminate self-defeating behaviors and to facilitate self-enhancing behaviors.

Four stages of Adlerian counseling are (1) relationship, (2) psychological investigation, (3) interpretation, and (4) reorientation. Relationship is based on an "equalitarian quality" with cooperation. Psychological investigation is an attempt to understand the underlying motivations of the client. It is a non-evaluative process by which the practitioner attempts to formulate a work picture of the individual. Interpretation is the opportunity for the practitioner to make "tentative inferences" which are descriptive of the client and may involve finding ways for the client to meet life tasks. Reorientation depends on the client's desire to bring about change and to attempt new behavior. The practitioner encourages the client to work through such changes (Sweeney, 1989).

Assessment Used with Adlerian Vocational Counseling

- BASIS: An Inventory (Basic Adlerian Scales for Interpersonal Success—Adult)

Multicultural Applications of Adlerian Concepts to Vocational Counseling In a symposium on multicultural career counseling, Hartung (1992) presented a case study and the responses to the case were made from developmental, person-centered, and Adlerian perspectives. The Adlerian response, provided by Powers and Griffith (1993), began with a brief description of Adler's three life tasks that confront all human beings and that define the requirements for successful adaptation: (1) the social task of friendship—making one's place in the community, (2) the task of love and sexuality, and (3) the task of work. In career counseling, Adlerians address all three.

The authors comment further on Adlerian assumptions that guide their work (Powers & Griffith, 1993). **Individual psychology (IP)** conveys an awareness of the human being as indivisibly embedded in the social world. IP considers each individual's lifestyle as based on convictions and attitudes initially assumed in childhood and rehearsed and refined thereafter in an unself-conscious manner. A sufficiently discouraging failure or pattern of failures in a person's lifestyle may demand a reexamination of values and a reorientation of direction. IP understands the line of individual movement as a person striving from a subjectively felt inferiority toward a fictional finalism of superiority and security, and it can be understood only in its social context. Social interest, the basic feeling of belonging and engagement in securing and enhancing one's life by contributing to the security and enhancement of the common good, is the measure of a person's mental health. Failure is seen as originating in an individual's lack or loss of courage, which dictates a hesitating attitude in the face of life tasks. In this pattern of discouragement, the individual consciously or unconsciously may erect further obstacles to excuse and explain failure as a means of retaining some remnant of self-esteem.

The goal of self-understanding is reached through engaging clients in the Psycho-Clarity Process (Powers & Griffith, 1987, cited in Powers & Griffith, 1993). The **Psycho–Clarity Process** helps clients understand (a) what they are doing; (b) what their purpose is in doing these things; (c) what costs are involved in doing them; and (d) what else is open to them to do. The client is sovereign in considering matters of change. Clients cannot change their minds until they know their minds; clients cannot know their minds until they speak their minds. As they struggle to make sense of their troubles to the practitioner, clients are forced to cast their problems in the language of common sense, revealing their private perception of things. Until clients speak their minds, they cannot share ideas and solve problems.

Clients describe their family's influence on their vocational choice. Family atmospheres are described in terms of emotional exchanges, and give the Adlerian practitioner clues as to client expectations about the way people relate to each other, and how clients expect people to relate to them. The ways clients have encountered certain governing images of social life in childhood situations provide the key to understanding current client errors. Family values are presumed to be upheld by both parents. Clients' personal code and standards are guided by such values. Adlerian practitioners understand the limits of their clients' social interest by their sense of ethnicity or religious, social, or economic particularities. Clients' birth order alert the practitioner to the orientation from which they work out their personal visions of the world. Presumably clients subconsciously revert to birth order vantage points in all social situations. Clients' accounts of their environmental opportunities give the Adlerian practitioner a measure of the way in which they evaluate the openings for advancement that they believed, and may still believe, to be open to them.

Regarding the social task of friendship and making one's place in the community, the Adlerian practitioner helps the client to see the antisocial implications of one's ambitious striving for superiority, which requires those around the client to be inferior to the client, a requirement that those around the client are likely to resent and resist. Data are gathered about the gender and relative ages of the client's siblings and the client's assessment of the meaning of his or her psychological birth order vantage. To what extent was the client trained to get along by going along? Regarding the task of love and sexuality, the practitioner uncovers the client's convictions about gender. The focus is on the client's subjective evaluations that arose with the awareness of the separate identities of mother and father, even in situations where there was one parent present. Client convictions about gender provide clues about client's perceived destinies. Formation of attachments with anyone of the other sex, and the client's dreams of marriage, are of interest because work can fill in lonely time until the client's dreams come true. Regarding the task of work, when does the client hesitate in the face of life tasks, especially as a means of staving off a possible defeat of one's vocational ambitions? These hesitations are often privately arranged on the basis of messages, real and imagined, that clients received growing up. The client is encouraged to expose and to give voice to these heretofore private arrangements that are no longer working for the client.

Strengths of the Adlerian approach uniquely applicable to multicultural populations include the following. Parents not of the U.S. mainstream can be helped to understand how they influence the directional striving of their children. Parents who reinforce cooperative behaviors among their children ("be good in school") send a different message than parents who reinforce competitive behaviors among their children ("do well in school"). These messages also relate to a second consideration, perceptions of child and adolescent striving. A child who is an outstanding student can get criticized within the family for "thinking they are better" or "trying to be like the Whites," as is likely to happen when families have the worldview of involuntary minorities (Ogbu, 1992). The successes of a child from a multicultural family are more likely to be celebrated when families are voluntary minorities (Ogbu, 1992). Culturally learned expectations and values are useful for an Adlerian-oriented vocational practitioner to assess. It is crucial not to confound socioeconomic class with race/ethnicity. Adlerians will be pressed to determine the appropriateness of their counseling style for a diverse clientele. Such determination is vital when labeling "errors" in life scripts or when considering how multicultural clients evaluate openings for advancement.

One limitation is Adler's concept of the task of love and attachment to the opposite sex. The presumption of heterosexuality may be misplaced and can perpetuate heterosexism in the workplace.

Roe: A Needs Approach

Roe's (1957) theory of vocational choice is usually included in a section with Holland's theory of vocations, since both are based on psychological needs and development of personality. We place Roe's theory in this chapter because so much of her research explored the relationship of parental/family influence on the vocational choices of their children, and how early childhood experiences reinforce or weaken higher order needs, thereby influencing the child's occupational development. Roe based her theory of personality development primarily on Maslow's (1954) hierarchy of needs and the relevance of occupational choice to these needs. From most to least important, these needs are: (1) physiological; (2) safety; (3) belongingness and love; (4) importance, respect, self-esteem, and independence; (5) information; (6) understanding; (7) beauty; and (8) self-actualization (Roe & Lunneborg, 1990).

Roe describes her theory in five propositions:

1. Genetic inheritance sets limits to the potential development of all characteristics but the specificity of the genetic control and the extent and nature of the limitations are different for different characteristics.

2. The degrees and avenues of development of inherited characteristics are affected not only by experiences unique to the individual but also by all aspects of the general cultural background and the socioeconomic position of the family.

3. The pattern of development of interests, attitudes, and other personality variables with relatively little or nonspecific genetic control is primarily determined by individual experiences, through which involuntary attention becomes channeled in particular directions.

4. The eventual pattern of psychic energies in terms of attention-directedness, is the major determination of interests.

5. The intensity of these needs . . . their satisfaction . . . and their organization are the major determinants in the degree of motivation that reaches expression in accomplishment. (Roe & Lunneborg, 1990, pp. 75, 78)

Roe (1990) goes on to state that, "In our society, no single situation is potentially so capable of giving some satisfaction, at all levels of basic needs, as the occupation" (p. 69).

Occupational selection is based on psychological needs developed through parent-child interaction (Roe, 1957). Because parental attitudes towards the child are more important than any actual parental behaviors, Roe developed three classifications to fit a range of attitudes:

1. *emotional concentration on the child:* ranges from overprotection to overdemandingness

2. *avoidance of the child:* two extremes are rejection and neglect

3. *acceptance of the child:* two extremes are casual acceptance and loving acceptance. (Sharf, 1997, p. 310)

In Figure 8.1 the inner circles describe the range of attitudes towards children and the influence these have on occupational choices as the circles widen.

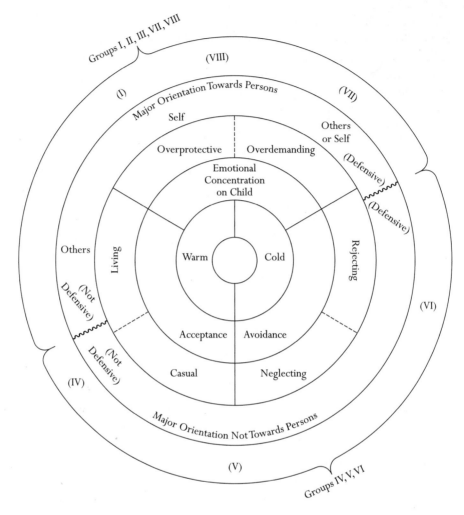

FIGURE 8.1 Hypothesized Relations Between Major Occupations,
Occupational Choice, and Parent-Child Relations

SOURCE: Roe and Lunneborg (1990), p. 79.

Starting with the idea of warm or cold response from parents, branching to the
three attitudes listed above, this figure illustrates how the person arrives at a vocational decision as postulated by Roe.

Roe's eight occupational groups differ from the groupings used in the
Dictionary of Occupational Titles. She believed these groups better describe the
types of occupations, especially considering that parental influences are a major
factor in occupational choice. The eight groups are:

1. *Service:* occupations concerned with catering to and serving the personal tastes, needs and welfare of other people. Occupations include social worker, guidance/career counselor, domestic and protective services (e.g., house manager, executive housekeeper, waiter, waitress).

2. *Business Contact:* occupations concerned with sale of commodities, investments, real estate and services with persuasion as a basic task.

3. *Organization:* occupations concerned with organization and efficient functioning of commercial enterprises and governmental agencies, such as administrative and management positions.

4. *Technology:* occupations concerned with production, maintenance, and transportation of commodities and utilities (e.g., engineering, crafts, machine and tool operators, transportation and communication).

5. *Outdoor:* occupations concerned with cultivation, preservation, and gathering of items which grow in the earth's environment for food and use in other products (e.g., farmers, fishermen, foresters, harvesters of all kinds).

6. *Science:* occupations concerned with scientific theory and its application (e.g., natural scientists, social scientists, physical scientists, physicians, psychologists, chemists, physicists).

7. *General Culture:* occupations concerned with preservation and transmission of cultural heritage, with interest in human activities rather than individuals (e.g., educators, journalists, law specialists, religious functionaries, linguists, people who function in the humanities).

8. *Arts and Entertainment:* occupations concerned with the use of special skills in the creative arts and entertainment (e.g., painters, writers, musicians, dancers, poets, entertainers). (Roe & Lunneborg, 1990; Roe & Klos, 1972)

Children develop attitudes, interests, and capacities based upon the situation experienced with their parents. They select an occupational category based upon their need structure; however, the level of attainment within that category is based more on their ability and socioeconomic background. This led Roe to develop a model to explain level of attainment that has little relationship to parental influence, but based more on abilities with socioecomonic circumstances added (see Roe & Lunneborg, 1990).

The six levels of occupational attainment are:

1. *Professional and Managerial 1*—Independent responsibility. This level includes those who innovate and create new ways to take leadership, who have independent responsibility, and who have the highest authority in the social group (i.e., responsibility for decisions, policymaking, education).

2. *Professional and Managerial 2*—Similar to level 1, but differs primarily in degree. They may be involved in responsibility with some autonomy, for interpreting policy and education at a somewhat lower level.

3. *Semiprofessional and Small Business*—These individuals have little responsibility for others, apply policy to themselves and have less responsibility for education. They may manage a small business.

4. *Skilled*—These are individuals for whom training is required, whether in the form of an apprenticeship or vocational education, at either a technical school or a high school.

5. *Semiskilled*—These individual require less training, but less than level four. They have much less autonomy and are permitted little initiative.

6. *Unskilled*—Little special training is need for these individuals. Rather, they tend to rely on directions given to them, and work in repetitive jobs. (Roe & Lunneborg, 1990)

Assessments Used for Roe

1. The Parent-Child Relations Questionnaire I & II
2. California Occupational Preference System (COPS)
3. Vocational Interest Inventory
4. Ramak and Courses (used primarily in Israel)

Evaluation of Roe's Theory Most research on Roe has tended to discount her theory's validity. However, she has contributed much to the field of vocational psychology with her classification system and circular model, which explains how influential early childhood experiences can be to a person's vocational decisions. In fact Peterson believes her original classification system was the basis for Holland's further development and refinement of these classification codes. Hartung and Niles (1997) found little observable correlation between family variables and work-role salience or vocational identity. They go on to generalize these findings to the role of family-of-origin dynamics by suggesting that "the current data thus raise questions about the role of family-of-origin dynamics in career development. Practitioners need to focus less on clients' family backgrounds and more on clients' individual traits, states, and goals, when examining their work-role and vocational identity development" (p. 9). As the remainder of this chapter shows, Hartung and Niles's conclusions, to focus exclusively on the individual client, are simplistic and premature when the larger family context is considered.

TRADITIONAL FAMILY SYSTEMS APPROACHES TO OCCUPATIONAL DEVELOPMENT

Numerous laypersons seem to know intuitively that their decisions, conflicts, priorities, and outlooks have been heavily influenced by their families-of-origin.

Practitioners are well aware of family influences on self-esteem, maturity, motivation, and resources. For many of us, whether layperson or practitioner, our most significant others are our families. But what is the best way to address family influence in vocational psychology?

Family systems approaches are fundamentally different from traditional vocational psychology approaches. Systemic approaches to clinical practice focus on interactions *between* individuals. Traditional vocational psychology approaches focus on interactions *within an* individual. A full discussion of theories of marriage and family therapy is beyond the scope of this chapter. However, if a vocational practitioner wants to explore systems theory further, von Bertalanffy (1968) is the classic work, and the list of primary references in Becvar and Becvar (1996) are another useful resource. In this section, we explore several categories of family systems: family-of-origin, family life cycle, family configurations, socioeconomic effects on family functioning, genograms, dual-career and single-parent families, work/family conflict, and postmodern families.

Family-of-Origin

Family-of-origin is used by psychodynamic family theorists and therapists to examine interactions between couples, but has been rarely applied to relationships at the workplace (Weinberg & Mauksch, 1991). Family-of-origin can have a very strong influence on all aspects of life. The rules that govern what behaviors are appropriate in a given setting are learned at a young age and can be determined in part by socioeconomic status, sex-role socialization, and ethnicity. In terms of occupational development, culturally learned expectations and values and family-of-origin influences can be great or small. Workers can play certain roles in their jobsites that they played in their families while growing up. Especially intriguing is the idea of **"organizational transference,"** where a boss or coworker represents an important family member to an employee (Weinberg & Mauksch, 1991) and consequently, unresolved issues with that family member can be projected by the employee onto the boss or coworker.

The manner in which issues were dealt with in the family-of-origin will be determined by cultural influences on the family, which may be traditional, modern, or even postmodern. Traditional family lifestyles emphasize close ties to family and community throughout life. Modern family lifestyles emphasize individual competition, and science is given great importance in explaining the mysteries of life. Postmodern family lifestyles emphasize each member in a different groove, with no sense of the family moving together in a common direction (discussed at the end of this chapter).

Family-of-origin and expectations are closely related. What is modeled and expected by one's family, parents' educational levels, and the importance of a career or vocation versus a job all impact the young person beginning to think in terms of life planning. Parents who are interested and involved in their child's life obviously will have a different kind of influence than those who are not. When parents are interested in their own career and life planning they are influencing their children to place importance on these issues as well. Parental and peer influences are powerful. They shape ambitions more directly and with greater impact than any other source, more than one's scholastic aptitude, previous academic achievement, or social origin (Spencer & Featherman, 1978), and this remains true today.

While peer pressure is one of the most influential factors in a child's life, researchers have found that the family has an even greater impact. Parents have more influence on their child's occupational and educational aspirations than do their friends. Children who perceive that their parents have high aspirations for them will be more successful than those whose parents have low aspirations, especially adolescents who base their self-perception on their parents' perception of them (Davies & Kandel, 1981). Significant others' aspirations also directly influence a child's own aspiration.

Family background is a factor in a person's lack of vocational aspiration and inability to make a decision. When faced with this situation, practitioners need to assess the sources that impede motivation (e.g., family atmosphere, relationships). A person's relationship with parents and/or siblings can have a negative impact on vocational aspirations. If possible, a practitioner should consult with at least one family member of the client to corroborate a client's report on family situations.

Young and Friesen (1992) described ten categories of **parental intentions**: (1) skill acquisition, (2) acquisition of specific values and beliefs, (3) protection from unwanted experience, (4) increased independent thinking or action, (5) decreased sex role stereotyping, (6) moderation of parent–child relationships, (7) facilitation of human relationships, (8) enhancement of character development, (9) development of personal responsibility, and (10) achievement of parent's personal goals. The parent's side of the parent/child interaction sequence is particularly appropriate to the study of parental influence on the occupational development of their children. The parent(s) interacted with the child or intervened on the child's behalf with intention. Several parent programs reflecting these intentions are developed further in Chapter 9.

Family Life Cycle

Intact or Nuclear Families Pipher (1996) captures the essence of the traditional, intact nuclear family with the Irish proverb, "It is in the shelter of each other that people live." The family life cycle is the primary context for individual human development (Carter & McGoldrick, 1989). Practitioners' views of family problems and strengths can be deepened by looking at the connectedness of the family as a natural, multigenerational system that moves through time. Several family life cycles have been classified. Carter and McGoldrick begin with a model related to American middle-class families as presented in Table 8.1.

We limit ourselves to comments regarding Table 8.1 in relation to occupational development. Each stage of the family life cycle has second order changes required to proceed developmentally. **Second order change** occurs "when the generations can shift their status relations and reconnect in a new way [so that] the family can move on developmentally" (Carter & McGoldrick, 1989, p. 14). In Stage 1, item C of the second order changes, the young adult is faced with establishing a work life and financial independence as a partial means of shifting to adult-to-adult status with parents. Single young women may have a more difficult time of achieving adult-to-adult status with their parents, because the daughter (more so than the son) still does not often achieve full adult status until she marries. Yet, statistically speaking, "the more education a woman has and the better her job, the less likely she is to marry. Just the reverse is true for men" (McGoldrick, 1989b, p. 211).

In Stage 2, among the second order changes to be renegotiated by newly-married couples is the role of work in their lives. Sooner or later, work responsibilities in the occupational domains, and the division of labor in the familial and personal domains (Richardson, 1993), will be addressed by couples. Financial dependence on either spouse's extended family can become an issue in marital adjustment. This is where occupational stability and gainful employment matters. "[L]engthy educational . . . [requirements] for many professionals may also complicate the adjustment to this phase of the life cycle by setting up the problem of prolonged dependence on parents" (McGoldrick, 1989b, p. 232). When both spouses are equally successful and achieving in their work lives, with the ability to function independently both economically and emotionally, achieving marital adjustment can be problematic.

At Stage 3, item B, families with young children will have to arrange for childcare when both parents work full time. Most marital conflict at this stage revolves around childcare for dual-earner couples (Carter & McGoldrick, 1989). More often than not, responsibility for arranging for childcare falls upon the wife. Couples who jointly undertake this responsibility are in the distinct minority. Childcare arrangements for two-paycheck marriages are most often seen as a "women's issue." Childcare arrangements will continue to be a "women's issue" until fathers realize that their own emotional health suffers when they fail to see childcare as a "men's issue" as much as a "family issue," and until they begin to speak up in the workplace requiring satisfactory provision for family needs (Barnett & Rivers, 1996). It is little wonder that the highest rate of divorce occurs at Stage 3 (Carter & McGoldrick, 1989).

TABLE 8.1 The Stages of the Family Life Cycle

FAMILY LIFE CYCLE STAGE	EMOTIONAL PROCESS OF TRANSITION: KEY PRINCIPLES	SECOND ORDER CHANGES IN FAMILY STATUS REQUIRED TO PROCEED DEVELOPMENTALLY
1. Leaving home: Single young adults	Accepting emotional and financial responsibility for self	a. Differentiation of self in relation to family of origin b. Development of intimate peer relationships c. Establishment of self regarding work and financial independence
2. The joining of families through marriage: The new couple	Commitment to new system	a. Formation of marital system b. Realignment of relationships with extended families and friends to include spouse
3. Families with young children	Accepting new members into the system	a. Adjusting marital system to make space for child(ren) b. Joining in child-rearing, financial, and household tasks c. Realignment of relationships with extended family to include parenting and grandparenting roles
4. Families with adolescents	Increasing flexibility of family boundaries to include children's independence and grandparents' frailties	a. Shifting of parent-child relationships to permit adolescent to move in and out of systems b. Refocus on midlife marital and career issues c. Beginning shift towards joint caring for older generation
5. Launching children and moving on	Accepting a multitude of exits from and entries into the family system	a. Renegotiation of marital system as a dyad b. Development of adult-to-adult relationships between grown children and their parents c. Realignment of relationships to include in-laws and grandchildren d. Dealing with disabilities and death of parents (grandparents)
6. Families in later life	Accepting the shifting of generational roles	a. Maintaining own and/or couple functioning and interests in the face of physiological decline b. Support for a more central role of middle generation c. Making room in the system for the wisdom and experience of the elderly, supporting the older generation without overfunctioning for them d. Dealing with loss of spouse, siblings, and other peers and preparation for own death. Life review and integration.

From Betty Carter and Monica McGoldrick, *The Changing Family Life Style*, p. 15. © 1989 by Allyn & Bacon. Reprinted by permission.

At Stage 4, the transformation of the family system in adolescence, one's occupational self-concept can be vulnerable to negative feedback and needless neglect, especially for teenage females (Gilligan & Noel, 1995; Orenstein, 1994; Pipher, 1994; Sadker & Sadker, 1994; Taylor, Gilligan & Sullivan, 1995). Common adolescent symptoms (drug and alcohol abuse, teenage pregnancy, delinquency/gang membership) also need to be assessed and addressed (Carter & McGoldrick, 1989). These symptoms cannot be artificially separated out from occupational development. Midlife career changes of parents with adolescent children can be extremely stressful due to forced layoffs and downsizing (Bragg, 1996b).

Stage 5 is the most problematic because it is the newest and longest phase (Carter & McGoldrick, 1989). The "empty nest syndrome" can leave one or both parents at a loss for what to do with themselves. Mothers who have focused most of their energies on their children may have to change their lifestyle but feel unprepared to face the world of work. Fathers who have focused most of their energies on work may regret not spending enough time with their now departing children. A good twenty years of worklife can remain for both parents. The potential is for disruption and disintegration of the parental couple or for moving into uncharted possibilities—new careers, continued education, hobbies, travel, and a more "balanced" lifestyle.

Stage 6, families in later life, entails adjustments to retirement (Carter & McGoldrick, 1989). This can create a vacuum for the retired worker and can strain previously existing balances in marriages. Financial insecurity and dependence are another set of issues to be dealt with, and can be particularly difficult for those who have been long accustomed to self-reliance during their working years. In family-owned businesses, elderly parents may sometimes be reluctant to hand over the reigns of power. At the other extreme, some formerly industrious parents may become completely dependent on their grown children. Status changes as a result of aging can affect men and women differently and should be closely monitored.

Vocational psychology can transform itself in part by giving increased consideration to a family life cycle perspective. Even the corporate world is showing belated signs of recognizing the importance of families (Associated Press, 1997a). It will be interesting to see the extent to which CEOs will advocate for work-family issues.

Divorced Families A major dislocation in the family life cycle can occur with divorce (Carter & McGoldrick, 1989). Additional steps are required to restablize and proceed developmentally. These phases related to divorce and the postdivorce family are shown in Table 8.2.

Regarding Table 8.2 in relation to occupational development, our remarks pertain to divorce phases 2 (developmental issue A) and 3 (developmental issue

TABLE 8.2 Dislocations of the Family Life Cycle Requiring Additional Steps to Restabilize and Proceed Developmentally

PHASE	EMOTIONAL PROCESS	DEVELOPMENTAL ISSUES OF TRANSITION: PREREQUISITE ATTITUDE
Divorce		
1. The decision to divorce	Acceptance of inability to resolve marital tensions sufficiently to continue relationship	Acceptance of one's own part in the failure of the marriage
2. Planning the breakup of the system	Supporting viable arrangements for all parts of the system	a. Working cooperatively on problems of custody, visitation, and finances b. Dealing with extended family about the divorce
3. Separation	a. Willingness to continue cooperative coparental relationship and joint financial support of children b. Work on resolution of attachment to spouse	a. Mourning loss of intact family b. Restructuring marital and parent–child relationships and finances; adaptation to living apart c. Realignment of relationships with extended family; staying connected with spouse's extended family
4. The divorce	More work on emotional divorce: Overcoming hurt, anger, guilt, etc.	a. Mourning loss of intact family; giving up fantasies of reunion b. Retrieval of hopes, dreams, expectations from the marriage c. Staying connected with extended families
Postdivorce family		
1. Single parent (custodial household or primary residence)	Willingness to maintain financial responsibilities, continue parental contact with ex-spouse, and support contact of children with ex-spouse and his or her family	a. Making flexible visitation arrangement with ex-spouse and his[/her] family b. Rebuilding own financial resources c. Rebuilding own social network
2. Single parent (noncustodial)	Willingness to maintain parental contact with ex-spouse and support custodial parent's relationship with children	a. Finding ways to continue effective parenting relationship with children b. Maintaining financial responsibilities to ex-spouse and children c. Rebuilding own social network

From Betty Carter and Monica McGoldrick, *The Changing Family Life Style*, p. 22. © 1989 by Allyn & Bacon. Reprinted by permission.

B) and postdivorce phases 1 (developmental issue B) and 2 (developmental issue B). Work performance can suffer for both men and women during the divorce and its aftermath. Homemakers who are financially compelled to re-enter the workforce may have issues related to low self-confidence, "rusty" job-related skills, lack of knowledge of job search and decision-making skills, and reactions of family and friends (Betz, 1994). Our clinical experience has shown that a woman re-entering the workforce is more vulnerable to sexual harassment, especially if it is known that she is recently separated or divorced. Child support and custody issues can take a heavy emotional and financial toll, the latter of which can distort the role of work in one's life. Because the man's potential earning power is often greater than the woman's, states with no-fault divorce can contribute to the so-called feminization of poverty.

Step Families Divorce is not the only instance when the family life cycle requires restabilization to proceed developmentally. Remarriage and the blending of families have their own prerequisite attitudes and developmental issues. The remarried family life cycle is presented in Table 8.3.

Relevant to our discussion of Table 8.3 are the plan for maintaining a cooperative financial relationship with the ex-spouse (Step 2, developmental issue B) and the realignment of financial arrangements (Step 3, developmental issue B). Remarried families can take either a step up or a step down in socioeconomic level. When both parents remarry, children have to learn two sets of rules and navigate two sets of lifestyles as they travel back and forth between mom's house and dad's house. Refusal to cooperate on financial arrangements can have an adverse impact on children caught in the middle. Our clinical experience has taught us that when academic and behavioral problems develop out of children's response to divorce and remarriage, these problems should be attended to immediately because they can have long-term implications for educational attainment and occupational development.

Low-Income Families

The Family Life Cycles of Low-Income Families and Professional Families. Fulmer (1989) has developed a model comparing the family life cycle of the American middle class with low-income families, presented in Table 8.4.

Table 8.4 implicitly refers to the daughters of professional and low-income families. When a first pregnancy occurs to an adolescent daughter from a low-income family, her educational attainment and occupational development can be adversely affected. A second teenage pregnancy bodes even more unfavorably for upward mobility. A daughter from a professional family who concentrates on pregnancy prevention is free to focus on earning an undergraduate and graduate degree, while continually gaining more independence from her parents and developing a professional identity of her own. In contrast, the teenage mother from a low-income family is more likely to (a) acquire adult status at an earlier age, (b) marry and divorce, (c) maintain connections with her kinship network,

TABLE 8.3 Remarried Family Formulation: A Developmental Outline

STEPS	PREREQUISITE ATTITUDE	DEVELOPMENTAL ISSUES
1. Entering the new relationship	Recovery from loss of first marriage (adequate "emotional divorce")	Recommitment to marriage and to forming a family with readiness to deal with the complexity and ambiguity
2. Conceptualizing and planning new marriage and family	Accepting one's own fears and those of new spouse and children about remarriage and forming a stepfamily Accepting need for time and patience for adjustment to complexity and ambiguity of: 1. Multiple new roles 2. Boundaries: space, time, membership, and authority 3. Affective Issues: guilt, loyalty conflicts, desire for mutuality, unresolvable past hurts	a. Work on openness in the new relationships to avoid pseudomutuality b. Plan for maintenance of cooperative financial and coparental relationships with ex-spouse c. Plan to help children deal with fears, loyalty conflicts, and membership in two systems d. Realignment of relationships with extended family to include new spouse and children e. Plan maintenance of connections for children with extended family of ex-spouse(s)
3. Remarriage and reconstitution of family	Final resolution of attachment to previous spouse and ideal of "intact" family; Acceptance of a different model of family with permeable boundaries	a. Restructuring family boundaries to allow for inclusion of new spouse-stepparent b. Realignment of relationships and financial arrangements throughout subsystems to permit interweaving of several systems c. Making room for relationships of all children with biological (non-custodial) parents, grandparents, and other extended family d. Sharing memories and histories to enhance stepfamily integration

From Betty Carter and Monica McGoldrick, *The Changing Family Life Style*, p. 24. © 1989 by Allyn & Bacon. Reprinted by permission.

and (d) become a grandmother at an earlier age than her female counterpart from a professional family. She is also likely to experience ongoing financial stress. Helping young people and adults from low-income families to maximize their occupational achievement remains a largely unmet challenge for vocational psychology. Ironically, low-income families could benefit most from occupational guidance and information. Such attention would both refine and revise

TABLE 8.4 Comparison of Family Life Cycle Stages

AGE	PROFESSIONAL FAMILIES	LOW-INCOME FAMILIES
12–17	a. Prevent pregnancy b. Graduate from high school c. Parents continue support while permitting child to achieve greater independence	a. First pregnancy b Attempt to graduate high school c. Parent attempts strict control before pregnancy. After pregnancy, relaxation of controls and continued support of new mother and infant
18–21	a. Prevent pregnancy b. Leave parental household for college c. Adapt to parent–child separation	a. Second pregnancy b. No further education c. Young mother acquires adult status in parental household
22–25	a. Prevent pregnancy b. Develop professional identity in graduate school c. Maintain separation from parental household d. Begin living in serious relationship	a. Third pregnancy b. Marriage—leave parental household to establish stepfamily c. Maintain kinship network
26–30	a. Prevent pregnancy b. Marriage—develop nuclear couple as separate from parents	a. Separate from husband b. Mother becomes head of own household with kinship network
31–35	a. First pregnancy b. Renew contact with parents as grandparents c. Differentiate career and child-rearing roles between husband and wife	a. First grandchild b. Mother becomes grandmother and cares for daughter and infant

From Fulmer, in Betty Carter and Monica McGoldrick, *The Changing Family Life Style*, p. 551. © 1989 by Allyn & Bacon. Reprinted by permission.

traditional theories of vocational "choice" for applicability to a broader population. And yet in many inner city schools, relatively few resources are available for students to learn about occupations through modeling, mentoring, computer-based information, or life experiences.

Hidden rules and **unspoken cues** characterize different socioeconomic classes (Payne, 1995). Patterns of thought, social interaction, and cognitive strategies are part of hidden rules. Given that schools and businesses operate from middle-class norms, students from poverty must be explicitly taught those middle-class habits to help them succeed in school and in the world of work. **Generational poverty** refers to families that have lived in poverty for two or more generations. Situational poverty refers to families that have lived in poverty for a shorter time due to circumstances such as death, illness, or divorce.

Major differences, based on more than money, exist between those in generational poverty and the middle class. Payne defines poverty as "the extent to which an individual does without resources" (p. 15), and identifies these resources as financial, emotional, mental, spiritual, physical, support systems, role models, and knowledge of hidden rules.

Financial resources, having money and purchasing power, when taken alone fail to explain why some individuals leave or remain in poverty. **Emotional resources**—the ability to exercise self-control and possessing the stamina to weather negative situations and feelings—are most important of all to move up from one class to the other. **Mental resources**, having the abilities and skills (e.g., reading, writing, computing) to process information and use it to negotiate daily life, lead to self-sufficiency. **Spiritual resources,** believing in a higher power that provides guidance and an understanding for life's purpose, help one from seeing oneself as hopeless but rather as capable, worthy, and valuable. **Physical resources,** being able-bodied and mobile, lead to self-sufficiency. Another resource, **support systems,** having friends and family who have valuable knowledge to share and who will back up a person in times of need, are external in nature. **Role models,** knowing and having access to adults who are nurturing and appropriate in their behavior towards children, and who do not demonstrate habitually self-destructive behavior, are particularly helpful in teaching one how to live one's life emotionally. **Knowledge of hidden rules,** having an awareness of the unspoken understandings and cues that allow a person to fit into a certain group, is essential if one wishes to survive in a particular socioeconomic class. The major hidden rules among the classes of generational poverty, the middle class, and the wealthy are presented in Table 8.5.

In Table 8.5, hidden rules about money, personality, social emphasis, time, education, destiny, language, and driving force are most relevant to the world of work. The following discussion is based on Payne (1995). In the interest of brevity, we do not focus on the wealthy.

Among the hidden rules of the middle class, money management is vital. A stable, achievement-oriented personality is desirable. Self-governance and self-sufficiency in social interactions is attractive. A future time-orientation with decisions made against future ramifications is preferred. Education for climbing the ladder of success is crucial. Good choices made now to impact future destiny are considered wise. The language of negotiation is valued. Work and achievement are the driving forces that characterize the middle-class lifestyle. Notice the legacy from the Protestant work ethic in these hidden rules (e.g., self-discipline, self-regulation of one's conduct) which make for good business sense and for reliable employees.

In contrast, the hidden rules of those who live in poverty do not seem to emphasize self-discipline and self-regulation. Money is to be spent, but then, an

TABLE 8.5 Major Hidden Rules Among the Classes of Poverty, Middle Class, and Wealth

	POVERTY	**MIDDLE CLASS**	**WEALTH**
POSSESSIONS	People	Things	One-of-a-kind objects, legacies, pedigrees
MONEY	to be used, spent	to be managed	to be conserved, invested
PERSONALITY	is for entertainment A sense of humor is highly valued.	is for acquisition and stability. Achievement is highly valued.	is for connections Financial, political, social connections are highly valued.
SOCIAL EMPHASIS	Social inclusion of people they like.	Emphasis is on self-governance and self-sufficiency.	Emphasis is on social exclusion.
FOOD	Key question: Did you eat enough? Quantity important.	Key question: Did you like it? Quality important.	Key question: Was it presented well? Presentation important.
CLOTHING	Clothing valued for the individual style and expression of personality.	Clothing valued for its quality and acceptance into the norm of middle class. Label important.	Clothing valued for its artistic sense and expression. Designer important.
TIME	Present most important Decisions made for the moment based on feelings or survival.	Future most important. Decisions made against future ramifications.	Traditions and past history most important. Decisions partially made on basis of tradition/decorum.
EDUCATION	Valued and revered as an abstract but not as a reality.	Crucial for climbing success ladder and making money.	Necessary tradition for making and maintaining connections.
DESTINY	Believe in fate. Cannot do much to mitigate chance.	Believe in choice. Can change the future with good choices now.	Noblesse oblige (an obligation to display charitable conduct)
FAMILY STRUCTURE	Tends to be matriarchal.	Tends to be patriarchal.	Depends on who has the money.
WORLDVIEW	Sees the world in terms of local setting.	Sees the world in terms of national setting.	Sees the world in terms of international view.
LOVE	Love and acceptance unconditional, based upon whether or not an individual is liked.	Loved and acceptance conditional and based largely on achievement.	Love and acceptance conditional and related to social standing and connections.
LANGUAGE	Casual register Language is about survival.	Formal register Language is about negotiation.	Formal register. Language is about connections.
DRIVING FORCE	Survival, relationships, and entertainment	Work and achievement	Financial, political, and social connections.

SOURCE: Payne (1995), pp. 91–92. © 1995 RFT Publishing Co. Reprinted by permission of Ruby K. Payne, Ph.D.

Practical Applications

Students from poverty need to be taught the hidden rules of the middle class without having their own life-styles denigrated (Payne, 1995). This leaves students the choice to use middle-class rules if they desire. But middle-class solutions should not be imposed on students and adults from poverty when alternative, feasible solutions can be found. Practitioners can learn to become aware of the hidden rules of poverty and lessen the anger and frustration educators feel at times when working with students and adults from poverty. Greater awareness of the hidden rules of poverty can also reduce the classism that pervades much of voca-tional psychology. A common attitude of those living in generational pov-erty is that society owes them a liv-ing. Those living in situational poverty tend to have pride and a disdain for accepting charity. Clients in situ-ational poverty usually have more resources, including knowledge of the formal register, than clients in generational poverty.

With a tendency to focus on cur-rent feelings instead of long-term outcomes, students and adults from poverty who get angry are apt to quit if they do not like the teacher or boss. These same students and adults will work hard if they like the teacher or boss. Conflict resolution skills may need to be taught as part of the hid-den rules of the middle class, which values negotiation. Students and adults from poverty have learned to distrust organizations as basically dishonest, and require a demonstra-tion of integrity from the teacher, the boss, or the management. Physically hard work is more the norm among men from generational poverty. This differs from the male provider role of the middle class.

Payne (1995) summarizes that, at school, students from poverty are more apt to: (a) be disorganized—lose papers, lack required parental signatures; (b) do homework less often, even when they are capable of doing well in school; (c) use physical aggression to settle conflicts; (d)

insufficient amount to meet expenses makes money management difficult. A per-sonality that focuses on entertainment and humor is highly prized, which helps to deal with the frustrations, restrictions, and deprivations of poverty. The social inclusion of people they like makes for two difficulties. First, kids from poverty who do not like their teachers are less likely to do their homework. Second, adult employees from poverty are more prone to quit their jobs if they do not like their bosses. A present-time orientation, with decisions based on feelings or survival, can appear as a lack of foresight to the middle class and the wealthy. But in the context of poverty, a present-time orientation often makes sense. Educa-

focus on part of an assignment or part of what is on the written page; (e) not start a task or monitor their own behavior; (f) laugh inappropriately when disciplined; (g) use the casual register; and (h) be unaccustomed to or not know how to use middle-class courtesies. Without intervention by a school counselor or other practitioner, these behaviors do not bode well for the development of desirable work habits on the job.

Adults from poverty who have managed to work their way into the middle class are nevertheless likely to retain vestiges of their earlier background. But then, the point is not to eliminate behaviors that characterize living in poverty, but to augment behaviors which characterize living in the middle class. Persons who get out and stay out of generational poverty most often do so through education. Four motivators help people leave poverty behind: (1) a goal, vision, or something they want to be, have, or accomplish; (2) a painful situation where anything would be better; (3) an educator, spouse, mentor, or role model who "sponsors" them, shows

them a way, or convinces them that a different lifestyle is feasible; and (4) a specific talent or ability that provides a way out of poverty (Payne, 1995).

Practitioners teach more about hidden rules and provide resources through program development, program evaluation, clinical intervention, and research. More cohesive research is needed on mentoring students and adults from poverty. Kuehr's (1997) review of the literature reveals a lack of uniformity in research regarding mentoring at-risk youth to reduce school dropout rates. Most of the studies she reviews come from the field of educational leadership, school counseling, and child and family studies. Clinical intervention and research with low-income populations is a far cry from the populations of convenience obtained by using college students from introductory psychology courses as research participants. Vocational psychology could be transformed if it were more available and amenable to populations that truly need occupational information and related interventions.

tion is often valued by parents who live in poverty. Naturally, many of these parents want a better life for their children than they had. But because many of these parents do not know how to guide their children through the school years, education is valued in abstract, not concrete, terms. The belief in fate and that one cannot do much to mitigate chance can appear as passive submission to destiny. This worldview is hardly conducive to instilling progress. The language of survival is also not predictive of success. Survival, relationships, and entertainment as the driving forces that characterize the lifestyle of poverty emphasize a collectivist orientation where reliance on interconnected others is paramount.

The casual register of the language of poverty and the formal register of the language of the middle class need further explanation here. Joos (1967, cited in Payne, 1995) describes **casual register** as that language which (a) is used between friends, (b) with a general, non-specific word choice, (c) is dependent upon nonverbals for assistance in conveying meaning, and (d) with often incomplete sentence syntax. **Formal register** is language which (a) is used in work and school, (b) with a specific word choice, and (c) with complete sentences and standard syntax. Students from low-income and racial and ethnic minority backgrounds often have no access to formal register in the home. These students are at a severe disadvantage in the world of school and work, where "ability to use formal register is a hidden rule of [the] middle-class" (Payne, 1995, p. 63). An ability to use the formal register enables one to perform well academically, score high on standardized tests, and make a good impression in job interviews.

Welfare Reform A consideration of low-income families and their influence on the occupational development of its members would not be complete without mention of the U.S. welfare reform of 1996. Welfare reform actually refers to **House Rule (HR) 3734, the Personal Responsibility and Work Opportunity Reconciliation Act,** passed by both Houses of Congress in August 1996. HR 3734 replaced (1) **AFDC—Aid to Families with Dependent Children** which expired in October 1996, (2) **JOBS—the Job Opportunities and Basic Skills** training program, (3) Emergency Assistance programs, and (4) ended entitlements to cash assistance (Hard & Schoenmakers, 1997). **TANF—Temporary Assistance for Needy Families** was created in October 1996 and replaced the AFDC and JOBS programs. Block grants are provided to each state in the form of cash assistance and employment services for TANF recipients.

TANF aims to (1) provide in-home care for children of needy families; (2) end dependency on the government by promoting job preparation, work, and marriage; (3) prevent out-of-wedlock pregnancies; and (4) encourage two-parent families (Hard & Schoenmakers, 1997). Time limits for TANF recipients depend on client's education and/or work experience. These time-limited benefits are a labyrinth of requirements that are going to entail the guidance of well-informed practitioners. Vocational psychologists—the majority of whom were conspicuously silent during the public debates on welfare reform—can transform their academic discipline by contributing to the job preparation and work-related aspects of TANF through program development, program evaluation, clinical intervention, and research. TANF recipients will have a five-year maximum eligibility. Job training is a vital part of the welfare to work transition (The Center for Public Policy Priorities, 1997).

Mead (1992) provides a highly readable analysis of the nonworking poor in America before welfare reform. His book places current welfare reform measures into historical context. When it comes to discussing poverty in America, both conservative and liberal political thinking take a view of human nature which Mead calls "the competence assumption." The **competence assumption** takes for granted "that the individual is willing and able to advance his or her own economic interests. . . . Americans are in motion toward *economic* goals" (p. 19, italics in original). He explains that "competence here means all the qualities that allow a person to get ahead in economic terms—not only intelligence, but foresight, energy, discipline, and the ability to sacrifice for the future" (p. 19).

The competence assumption places work as the central role in people's lives. Work in the occupational domain is given precedence over work in the familial and personal domains (Richardson, 1993). The competence assumption's emphasis on foresight, discipline, and delayed gratification resemble the hidden rules of the middle class (Payne, 1995). Political issues of social regulation are operating here (Foucault, 1977, cited in Rabinow, 1984). Welfare recipients have been judged by standards that do not characterize their lifestyles, and they have not been consulted as to whether or not such standards are even relevant. The competence assumption also echoes the limitations of the Protestant work ethic and the historic work ways of the British American colonists (Fischer, 1989). In addition, the competence assumption ignores the growing trend among parents in the middle and professional classes, who are now more "willing to sacrifice on-the-job advancement for time with their children" (Barnett & Rivers, 1996, p. 84). Thus, the underlying premise of the competence assumption is flawed in many ways. But, that's politics.

Here is yet another example of how vocational psychology can make itself more responsive to the pressing issues of the day. We encourage vocational psychologists to enter, if belatedly, into the dialogue on welfare reform and to add their perspective, especially to point out how the competence assumption is misguided.

Genograms

Another useful means of analyzing the family's influence on occupational development is to devise a **genogram** of the client's family. A genogram is a family assessment process that clients seem to enjoy and rarely find threatening. McGoldrick and Gerson (1985) write:

> A genogram is a format for drawing a family tree that records information about family members and their relationships over at least three generations . . . [and] display family information graphically in a way that

provides a quick gestalt of complex family patterns and a rich source of hypotheses about how a clinical problem may be connected to the family context and the evolution of both problem and context over time. (p. 1)

To obtain data on the occupational patterns of a client's family, the practitioner begins by simply asking the client to name family members and to identify each family member's occupation. The practitioner usually starts with the family-of-origin and proceeds back through the grandparents, aunts, uncles, and cousins. The client is asked to tell what they know about the occupational development process of various relatives (e.g., level of education, employment history, reasons for any job changes, current occupational status, work ethic). Graphic depictions form the backbone of any genogram (McGoldrick & Gerson, 1985). Each graphic depiction or symbol denotes the biological and legal relationships among family members from one generation to the next.

Genogram symbols help practitioners grasp client occupational development issues from the purview of family structure dynamics (McDaniels & Gysbers, 1992) (see Figure 8.2). Genograms in occupational counseling can help clients understand work-family roles and responsibilities. Okiishi (1987) suggests that the genogram is a tool for recording information as the client and practitioner make written notes about persons in the client's family-of-origin. The client's uniqueness is emphasized when seen in the context of the family. Mitchell and Krumboltz (1984) suggest four major assessment areas to be examined when a client's career decision-making problem is believed to be related to inaccurate or dysfunctional self-observation and/or worldview generalizations: (1) the content of the client's self-observation and worldview generalizations; (2) the processes by which they arose; (3) whether these beliefs and generalizations truly create problems; (4) whether stated beliefs disguise more fundamental but as yet unarticulated beliefs. Okiishi (1987) integrates these four assessments into areas of discussion to include client perceptions of (a) the family member's success as a spouse, parent, employee, friend, and relative; (b) the increased or decreased mobility associated with being a member of the family; (c) the way time, space, money, and relationships were managed in and outside of the family; and (d) each person's integration of various life roles, including work.

A genogram could help practitioner and client determine the individuals in the client's family who may have been significant to the formation of the client's career expectations. Practitioners gain a better understanding of the client's view of the world of work. Possible barriers posed by significant others or perceived by the client to be restrictions could be identified. Sex role stereotypes could be pinpointed. Questions that could be asked include: "At what age did each relative begin working? How often were jobs changed? What kind of emotional or financial assistance was offered and accepted? What kinds of satisfaction did the client perceive as gaining from various work experiences? What are the disadvantages in the relatives' work experiences?" (Okiishi, 1987, p. 139).

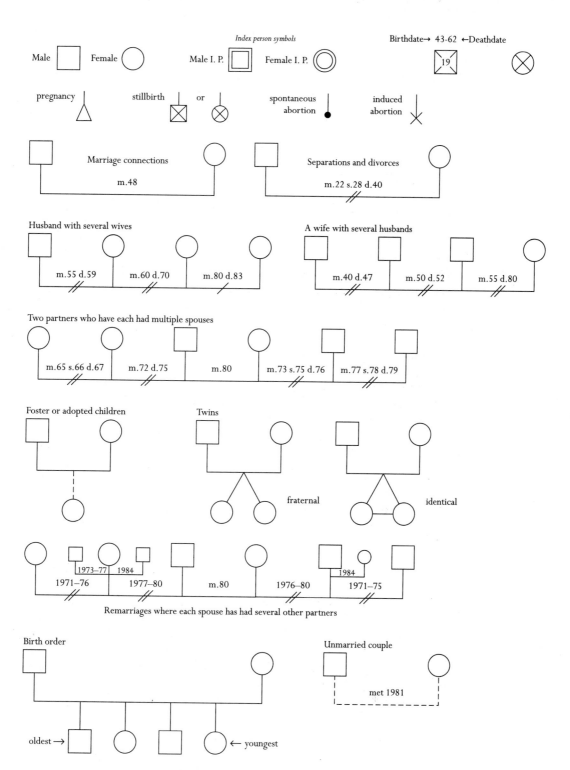

FIGURE 8.2 Genogram Symbols and Procedures

SOURCE: *McGoldrick and Gerson (1985), pp. 10–14.*

Practical Applications

Genogram use in occupational counseling involves at least three steps: (1) at the client's direction, the practitioner constructs the genogram; (2) the practitioner documents with the client the occupations of relatives mentioned on the genogram; (3) the practitioner explores with the client the relatives mentioned on the genogram, noting especially the role modeling as the client perceives it and the reinforcement provided to the role model (Okiishi, 1987).

Some possible areas to investigate with the client are: (a) Multigenerational themes concerning education, careers, work values, work ethics, and gender roles. (b) Multigenerational family decision-making patterns. (c) Family rules about the "acceptable" range of employment possibilities, and locations. (d) Changing career patterns across several generations of the family. (e) The influence of larger social changes or historical events on the family members' career choices. (f) The career patterns of various family members—Who did what when? How do family members play out their leisure role? Their citizen role? How many roles are family members expected to carry? (g) The emotional charge around career issues in the family—loyalty issues, aborted dreams, achievement expectations (Moon, Coleman, McCollum, Nelson & Jenson-Scott, 1993).

Family influence on occupational development is usually not confined to one generation. This influence is substantial across three generations (McGoldrick & Gerson, 1985). One way to examine this is to construct a work-related genogram of at least three generations that depicts the occupations of as many family members as possible. This genogram would be useful in generating ideas and understanding of family influence, and understanding one's view of the world of work.

CASE EXAMPLE

"The Most Hated Women in America"

Figure 8.3 presents a work-related genogram of five living generations of the Boone and Williams family, featured in Pulitzer Prize winning journalist David Zucchino's book, *Myth of the Welfare Queen* (1997). Between July 4, 1995 and January 1, 1996, Zucchino followed the lives of several unmarried welfare mothers residing in the ghetto of North Philadelphia,

Pennsylvania. He quotes community activist Cheri Honkala that welfare mothers are "the most hated women in America" (p. 62). Unwed mothers are stereotyped as the primary drain on the U.S. welfare system. In fact, before the welfare reform measures of 1996–1997, one-third of all welfare mothers were women in their thirties, not the unwed teen mother of popular stereotype. The Boone and Williams genogram portrays the family as of 1995, before welfare reform took place. We use "work-related genogram" to describe this family, since "career genogram" would hardly be appropriate.

The **index person** in Figure 8.3 is 56-year-old Odessa Boone, shown as a circle (for her female gender) with the lines doubled (for her status as index person). Her late father is Shellmon Boone, shown as a box (for his male gender) with an X inside (for his deceased status). Her mother is Bertha Hill, age 81.

Shellmon Boone sharecropped in Georgia's red dirt country. He labored at one farm until there was no more work, then moved on to the next farm where work was available. His wife Bertha and their three children accompanied him on his job moves, "always hungry, always on the bottom edge of poverty" (Zucchino, 1997, p. 32).

Bertha Hill grew up in a sharecropper's shack. Both her parents worked the fields. From the time Bertha could walk she also worked the fields, earning up to $1.25 a day chopping cotton and pulling green beans.

Odessa Boone began working the fields at age 5, adding to the family income.

Shellmon and Bertha separated in 1950 (as indicated by the double slash //) after his drunken rages and physical abuse became intolerable. She and the children moved to North Philadelphia to live with her sister and brother-in-law. Bertha found work as a farmworker in southern New Jersey and occasionally earned extra money as a seamstress and housekeeper. Odessa, age 11 when the move occurred, spent her summers as a farmworker alongside her mother. Odessa spent the school year living with relatives in Georgia, where she had contact with her father. Bertha's two severely handicapped sons, Junior and Charles, lived year-round with Bertha's sister.

Bertha went on welfare in 1967, age 53. After nearly fifty years of farm work, and nearly twenty-five years of lifting and bathing her two handicapped sons by herself, Bertha's health began to fail. She had never seen herself as dependent on anyone else. She had always shunned any sort of charity. Bertha Hill was a worker. She went on welfare as a last resort because it was available and after so many years of backbreaking work she felt entitled to government benefits. In 1967, those benefits were $90 every two weeks.

Odessa began taking care of herself at age 13. That year, a racial incident happened at school in Georgia: Odessa refused to call a White girl the same age "ma'am." The fathers of both girls agreed the White girl was old enough to be shown this kind of respect due a White woman in the South. Odessa's refusal earned her a death threat from the White girl's

Continued

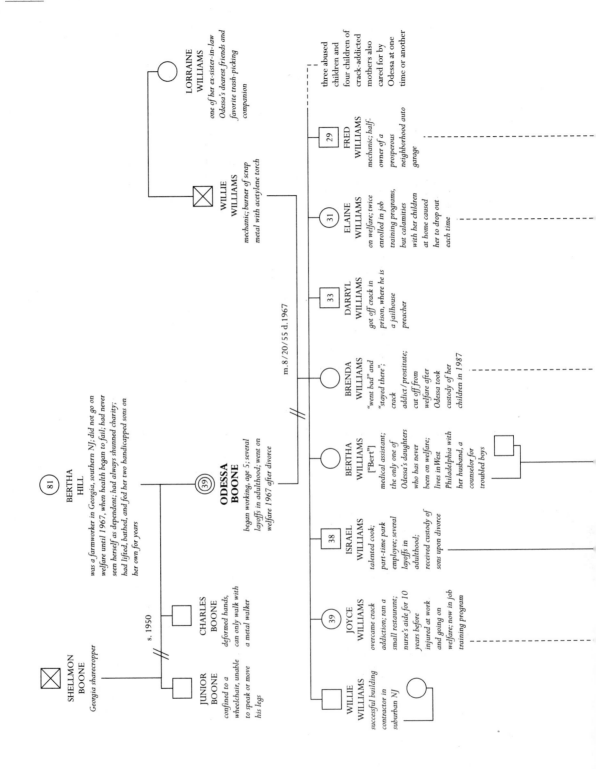

SHELLMON BOONE
Georgia sharecropper

BERTHA HILL
was a farmworker in Georgia, southern NJ; did not go on welfare until 1967, when health began to fail; had never seen herself as dependent; had always shunned charity; had lifted, bathed, and fed her two handicapped sons on her own for years

LORRAINE WILLIAMS
one of her ex-sister-in-law Odessa's dearest friends and favorite trash-picking companion

s. 1950

JUNIOR BOONE
confined to a wheelchair, unable to speak or move his legs

CHARLES BOONE
deformed hands, can only walk with a metal walker

ODESSA BOONE (39)
began working, age 5; several layoffs in adulthood; went on welfare 1967 after divorce

WILLIE WILLIAMS
mechanic; burner of scrap metal with acetylene torch

m. 8/20/55 d. 1967

WILLIE WILLIAMS
successful building contractor in suburban NJ

JOYCE WILLIAMS (39)
overcame crack addiction; ran a small restaurant; nurse's aide for 10 years before injured at work and going on welfare; now in job training program

ISRAEL WILLIAMS 38
talented cook; part-time park employee; several layoffs in adulthood; received custody of sons upon divorce

BERTHA WILLIAMS ["Bert"]
medical assistant; the only one of Odessa's daughters who has never been on welfare; lives in West Philadelphia with her husband, a counselor for troubled boys

BRENDA WILLIAMS
"went bad" and "stayed there"; crack addict/prostitute; cut off from welfare after Odessa took custody of her children in 1987

DARRYL WILLIAMS 33
got off crack in prison, where he is a jailhouse preacher

ELAINE WILLIAMS 31
on welfare; twice enrolled in job training programs, but calamities with her children at home caused her to drop out each time

FRED WILLIAMS 29
mechanic; half-owner of a prosperous neighborhood auto garage

three abused children and four children of crack-addicted mothers also cared for by Odessa at one time or another

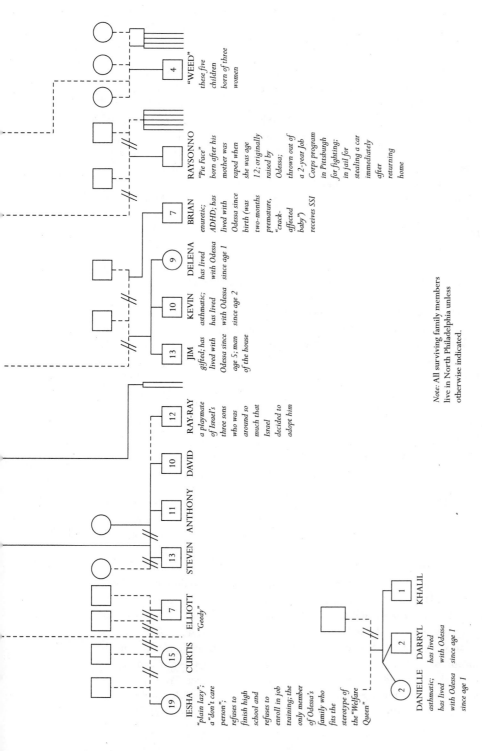

IESHA
"plain lazy";
a "don't care
person";
refuses to
finish high
school and
refuses to
enroll in job
training; the
only member
of Odessa's
family who
fits the
sterotype of
the "Welfare
Queen"

CURTIS

ELLIOTT
"Geedy"

STEVEN   ANTHONY   DAVID

RAY-RAY
a playmate
of Israel's
three sons
who was
around so
much that
Israel
decided to
adopt him

JIM
gifted; has
lived with
Odessa since
age 5; man
of the house

KEVIN
asthmatic;
has lived
with Odessa
since age 2

DELENA
has lived
with Odessa
since age 1

BRIAN
enuretic;
ADHD; has
lived with
Odessa since
birth (was
two-months
premature,
"crack-
affected
baby")
receives SSI

RAYSONNO
"Pie Face"
born after his
mother was
raped when
she was age
12; originally
raised by
Odessa;
thrown out of
a 2-year Job
Corps program
in Pittsburgh
for fighting;
in jail for
stealing a car
immediately
after
returning
home

"WEED"
these five
children
born of three
women

DANIELLE
asthmatic;
has lived
with Odessa
since age 1

DARRYL
has lived
with Odessa
since age 1

KHALIL

Note: All surviving family members
live in North Philadelphia unless
otherwise indicated.

FIGURE 8.3 Work-Related Genogram of the Boone and Williams Family, 1995

source: Adapted from Zucchino, 1997.

Continued

father. Odessa's school days ended. For safety's sake her father sent her to live with relatives in the Georgia countryside, where she worked the fields for $3 a day. Here she met sharecropper Willie Williams. They married on August 20, 1955 (as shown above the solid line that connects them in the genogram), when Odessa was eight days past her fifteenth birthday.

Willie and Odessa moved to north Philadelphia in 1956 to be near her mother. Willie found work as a mechanic and later as a burner of scrap metal with an acetylene torch. Odessa Boone considered herself a worker. She completed an eighteen-month mechanics course and then worked two-and-a-half years repairing cars at a garage in north Philadelphia before being laid off and then worked various jobs.

Five critical incidents in the life of our index person deserve mention: (1) Odessa accidentally sliced open her ankle as a young woman. Without access to proper medical care, the wound never healed properly. Sometimes the ankle collapses. She has taught herself to move slowly and to balance herself on her good ankle to keep from toppling over. (2) In 1957, 1962, and 1967, Odessa had nervous breakdowns. She is currently on Valium. (3) In 1968, Odessa broke her pelvis in a car accident, but the fracture went undiagnosed until she had an x-ray in 1991. She has lived in chronic pain all these years. (4) In 1986, she suffered a mild stroke. (5) Currently, Odessa weighs 240 pounds. She is asthmatic and always carries an inhaler. At home, she has a nebulizer. She has high blood pressure.

Odessa went on welfare in 1967 out of desperation. Willie had grown increasingly jealous and physically abusive. She was unable to find work and by then she had eight children to feed. As with most women in abusive situations, the violence increased when she actually tried to leave. Willie threatened to kill her. She managed to get out alive, but she suffered her third and most severe nervous breakdown in the process. Welfare was the only option available to her at the time.

Her mother taught Odessa that "you make do with what you have" (Zucchino, 1997, p. 17). One way Odessa makes do is by trash picking. She calls it her "trash therapy" (p. 18). The way Odessa sees it, being on welfare does not mean she is helpless or dependent. Trash picking is not stealing—that would be against Odessa's sense of decency: she allows no cursing in her home and reads half a chapter of the Bible every night at bedtime. Besides, people foolishly throw away a lot of good things.

Among Odessa's trash picking finds are an entire china set, unopened and still in its original packing box. Some newlyweds probably received the china as a wedding gift, disliked the pattern shown on the box, and threw it away intact. Another one of Odessa's prized trash picks is a nearly new king-size mattress and box spring. She has trash-picked perfectly usable appliances. Trash-picked luggage, curtains, adults' and children's clothes—including a child's snowsuit—have all contributed to making Odessa's house a home. When Odessa finds something she already has, she trash picks it anyway to sell later. Each trash-picked item is not income for which welfare would penalize her. As she puts it, "I'm not ashamed to go after what I need" (Zucchino, 1997, p. 41).

By 1995, Odessa's eight children are grown and have extremely divergent occupational paths:

The eldest son, also named Willie Williams (age not mentioned), is a successful home building contractor in southern New Jersey. He often helps his mother and grown sisters with repairs at their homes. He also repairs and maintains Odessa's trash-picked appliances.

The second child and eldest daughter, Joyce Williams, 39, started well. A serious, determined person with an entrepreneurial spirit, she decided to become a successful career woman while still in high school. She ran a small restaurant in north Philadelphia before becoming a casualty of the crack epidemic that hit her neighborhood in the mid-1980s. The readily available money in her restaurant cash register facilitated her drug use. Joyce overcame a crack addiction through her own willpower. She then worked for ten years as a nurse's aide before injuring her back trying to lift a heavy patient. The injury left Joyce unable to perform her job's physical demands and she had to quit. By then she had four children to feed, including Iesha, Curtis, and Elliott— nicknamed "Geedy" for his greedy appetite (as shown in the genogram by the dashed line leading vertically

down from Joyce; one child's name, gender and age not mentioned). Currently, Joyce receives AFDC, food stamps, and cash assistance for her three youngest children. Joyce's children were born of four different fathers (as shown in the genogram by the four boxes and dashed lines that appear below Joyce), none of whom has ever provided child support. Joyce is on welfare reluctantly. She is not accustomed to depend on others and is humiliated that she can no longer rely on herself. Her welfare caseworker helped Joyce enroll in a JOBS program, a business administration course in northeast Philadelphia where Joyce is learning all the latest computer programs, including Windows 95 (not yet commercially available at the time of our genogram). Joyce hates being on welfare; to her it's like taking charity. Of her self-image, she says, "I'm a person who *needs* to work" (Zucchino, 1997, p. 26, italics in original).

Israel Williams, 38, is a divorced father with custody of his four sons: Steven, Anthony, David, and one adopted son, Ray-Ray (as shown in the genogram by the dashed line leading horizontally to the right from David). In Odessa's family, the men are not expected to marry the mothers of their children, but it is important for men to economically support those children. Israel is an outstanding example of an honorable man who provides for his children. A talented cook who helps his mother prepare huge family dinners at Thanksgiving and Christmas, he has held several jobs as a cook, being laid

Continued

Continued

off each time. His later employment has included furnace repair work, occasional auto mechanic, temporary jobs at a computer chip factory and the post office, and part-time scrap metal burner. At times, Israel relies on Emergency Assistance for food stamps to feed his four sons.

Bertha Williams (age not mentioned), nicknamed "Bert" by Odessa, is a high school graduate and has worked her entire adult life. "Bert" is the only one of Odessa's daughters married to the father of her children (number, names, genders, and ages not mentioned) and the only daughter never on welfare. "Bert" works as a medical assistant and her husband (unnamed in the book) is a counselor for troubled boys. They live in a fine house in west Philadelphia. Odessa's 1984 Chevrolet Caprice Classic was a gift from "Bert" and her husband. The Caprice is Odessa's only transportation: she is too heavy to comfortably navigate the public bus system; with her bad ankle, she risks toppling over and being prey to crack addicts who would willingly rob her. Odessa earns extra cash by driving grocery shoppers home from the store. She can judge who is safe and trustworthy and has made many acquaintances among the shoppers. They are always glad to pay for a ride home to avoid being vulnerable on the bus, their arms full of grocery bags.

Brenda Williams (age not mentioned), in Odessa's words, "went bad" and ". . . stayed there" (Zucchino, 1997, p. 27). Brenda was a sweet and respectful little girl. At age 13 her behavior changed and she began talking back and staying out late at night. She got addicted and became a prostitute to earn money to buy more crack. She had a series of drug-addicted boyfriends, one of whom fathered her three eldest children: Jim, Kevin, and Delena; another man fathered Brenda's fourth child Brian (as shown in the genogram by the dashed line leading vertically down from Brenda and by the two boxes and dashed lines that appear below Brenda). Brenda lost custody of her children to Odessa in 1987, who ended up on welfare a second time to care for them. Odessa receives AFDC, food stamps, and cash assistance for Brenda's four children. Odessa also receives Supplemental Security Income (SSI) for Brian, born a "crack-affected baby." Currently, Brenda is a prostitute who lives in crack houses and turns up at Odessa's from time to time. Crack is easy to find. From her front porch, Odessa can see crack dealers plying their trade on the street corners at both ends of the block.

Darryl Williams, 33, is currently in the State Correctional Institution at Graterford, PA, fifty minutes away from Odessa. A crack addict, he figured that "prison would be the best place to clean himself up" (Zucchino, 1997, p. 15), so he deliberately broke his probation on charges of drug possession and of breaking and entering. He has found Jesus and is a jailhouse preacher. Two part-time jobs await him upon parole: one with eldest brother Willie's home building business, one with youngest brother Fred's auto garage.

Elaine Williams, 30, Odessa's youngest daughter, lives in a row house at the opposite end of the block from her mother. Elaine is a good-natured woman who takes life as it comes. She had six children (as shown by the dashed line leading vertically down from Elaine; names, genders, and ages not mentioned in the book). As with Joyce and Brenda, Elaine receives no child support from the biological fathers of her children, but receives AFDC, food stamps, and cash assistance for her five youngest children. Elaine enrolled twice in JOBS training programs, but each time a calamity at home with her children caused her to drop out. During those times of crisis, Elaine put her children first. Strict attendance policies at the JOBS programs did not permit any leave of absence, and she had to quit. Although welfare pays for childcare, Elaine feels her children are not properly taken care of and wishes she could be at home with them. Elaine believes that children need their mother at home. With her case manager's help, she is scheduled to enroll in a third JOBS program (enrollment in two JOBS programs is usually the maximum limit allowed) at a trade school in northeast Philadelphia, studying hotel management and food services. Given Joyce's progress in her business administration and computer JOBS program, Elaine is feeling family pressure to start and finally complete her third JOBS program.

Fred Williams, 29, Odessa's fourth son and youngest child, is a mechanic and half-owner of a prosperous auto garage in the neighborhood. He has five children by three women (as shown in the genogram by the dashed line leading vertically down from Fred and by the three circles and dashed lines that appear below Fred;

names, genders, and ages of four of the children not mentioned in the book). At one point, the three women and their children all lived under one roof! Like Israel, Fred does the honorable thing: he provides for his children, and that is what counts.

In addition to rearing her own eight children and Elaine's eldest son Raysonno, Odessa took in seven other children at one time or another as a certified foster parent for the Department of Human Services (three abused children and four children of crack-addicted mothers, as shown on the genogram by the dashed line leading horizontally to the right from Fred). Including the six children who currently live with Odessa—daughter Brenda's four children and granddaughter Iesha's twins, Danielle and Darryl—Odessa has reared twenty-two children at one time or another from three different generations. With spiritual resources and an extended family support system (Payne, 1995), Odessa makes do.

Iesha, 19, Odessa's granddaughter, is the only member of the extended family who comes anywhere close to fitting the stereotype of the Welfare Queen. A social construction of politicians, their speechwriters, and the media, the stereotypical Welfare Queen is an African American, unwed teenage mother living in the inner city. She is a product of generational poverty. The Welfare Queen uses multiple (a) aliases, (b) Social Security cards, and (c) addresses to cheat the welfare system out of thousands of dollars. With Medicaid providing health benefits, on her tax-free income the Welfare Queen is a Cadillac

Continued

Continued

owner and lives a lavish, big-spending lifestyle (Zucchino, 1997). The Population Reference Bureau reports that most welfare recipients are actually White, reside in suburbs or rural areas (Associated Press, 1996a), and live in situational poverty with nearly one-third lifting themselves out of it within a year (Associated Press, 1998). Of the 38 million poor people in the U.S., 40 percent are children not of legal age to work and 10 percent are 65 or older. Less than half of the nation's poor received any cash assistance from the government. In 1996, the government's definition of poverty was a household income of $16,036 or below for a family of four (Jones & Belton, 1997).

Iesha is described by her mother Joyce as "just plain lazy" (Zucchino, 1997, p. 26) and by Odessa as a "don't care person" (p. 340). Iesha has no interest in finishing high school or enrolling in any job-training program. She lives with her aunt Elaine and the latter's children. Welfare is a way of life for Iesha, who collects $248 in cash every two weeks and $288 in food stamps once a month. Some of this cash and food stamps she must give to Odessa, who houses Iesha's two-year-old twins. Iesha simply refuses to take care of her babies. As with Joyce, Brenda, and Elaine, Iesha receives no child support from her children's biological father. Rumor has it that he became a crack addict and is serving prison time for armed robbery.

Among Odessa's other grandchildren is Brenda's son Jim, 13, a gifted and talented youth who has lived with Odessa since age 5. Up to now, Jim's being the man of the house has not weighed too heavily upon him. Our concern about Jim's future is whether the environment will wear down his stamina and defeat his ambitions (Kozol, 1991). Jim is the age his mother was when her behavior changed irreparably for the worst.

Jim's half-brother Brian, 7, born a "crack-affected baby," may have the duration of his SSI benefits limited by stricter standards for disability mandated by Congress. Any termination of SSI benefits may be accompanied by a lack of readily available information on the right to appeal the cutoff of funds (Los Angeles Times, 1997). Families like Odessa's often do not understand that they must act quickly—request a continuance within ten days to continue receiving benefits during the first level of appeal, and appeal the termination within sixty days. Information on appeals is often buried deep within termination letters and is not clearly understandable to many recipients.

Elaine's son, Raysonno, likewise has an uncertain future. Expelled from a two-year Job Corps program in Pittsburgh for fighting, he ended up in jail for stealing a car immediately after returning home. Raysonno typifies the person from generational poverty whose conflict-resolution skills and emotional resources are inappropriate to middle-class expectations for conduct on the job (Payne, 1995).

For Odessa and many of her family, TANF will change their lifestyles in ways that cannot even be calculated. Especially remarkable are the varied employment routes taken by Odessa's children. Why did the eldest child (Willie), the fourth child ("Bert"), and the eighth child (Fred) become middle class when their five siblings did not? Perhaps Willie, "Bert," and Fred mastered the hidden rules of the middle class (Payne, 1995). By the third generation of the above genogram, generational poverty does not persist in all branches of the family. The range of occupational achievement among Odessa's eight children points to within-group differences.

In one family, whatever the cultural/racial background or socioeconomic origins, individual needs and talents combined with parental dispositions (Clark, 1983), life experiences, and opportunities will influence educational attainment and occupational development. Odessa's parental disposition and interpersonal relationships probably differed with each child in her household. She never dreamed that Brenda, her sweet and respectful little girl, would grow up to become a drug addict and a prostitute. Odessa did not come from this kind of family. From a dislocation of the family life cycle perspective (Carter & McGoldrick, 1989), as a postdivorce family, Odessa did not receive co-parenting support in rearing Brenda from her ex-husband, the noncustodial parent. Nor did Willie maintain financial responsibilities to his ex-wife and children.

Even the effects of the crack epidemic on the Williams family show within-group differences. Joyce overcame her addiction through her own determination. Darryl detoxed in prison. Brenda is still an addict and is all but homeless. The crack invasion of north Philadelphia and elsewhere in the late 1980s is a practical and unpleasant, if lucrative, example of the global economy in action, through drug smuggling into this country and drug dealing in this country.

Similar to systems approaches, family-of-origin, and various models of the family life cycle, genograms offer a rationale and interventions useful to the practitioner whose major goal is to help clients make decisions with full awareness of all important factors of self, family influences, and family work patterns.

WORK-FAMILY CONFLICT, DUAL CAREERS, AND SINGLE-PARENT FAMILIES

Work-Family Conflict

As the nature of work changes, recent research has focused on **work-family conflict** and the negative effects on an individual's health. There are three forms of work-family conflict: (1) **time-based conflict**—time can only be spent on one role which neglects the other roles; (2) **strain-based conflict**—stress from

Practical Applications

Much of the current research has focused on the problems associated with young women in the realm of career and family plans. But these concerns are as applicable to young men. Young men are still not as influenced by the decision to have a family, but they are faced with the changing traditional expectations about career development. Harmon (1989) reports data in which younger women plan to work most of their lives without lengthy periods of unemployment. Baber and Monaghan (1988) document this desire to have everything when they sampled female undergraduates and 73 percent agreed with the statement "I want it all, to be a parent, a spouse, and career person, and am determined to manage it all and do it well."

Adolescents are also expecting a future where they combine career and family roles. Weitzman (1994) cites several underlying factors to consider when involved in the process of "multiple-role planning."

Decisions about life roles are extremely complex ones. Variables that affect this process (e.g., socioeconomic status, racial/ethnic background, individual personality characteristics) are important to consider when attempting to categorize the development of multiple-role plans. Following the first assumption, it is the belief that multiple-role planning will be informed and influenced by personal values, interests, and

one role effects all areas of performance; and (3) **behavior-based conflict**— behavioral styles are not compatible throughout all roles (Greenhaus & Beutell, 1985).

Most of the past research focused on women, since they were considered the primary caretakers of a family. However, as men become more involved in the family, more study is needed on how work–family conflict affects men (Barnett & Rivers, 1996). "With the increasing numbers of single parent employees and dual-career couples, and the rising expectations regarding both quality work and family involvements, it becomes crucial to assist individuals in achieving balance in their work and family demands" (Loerch, Russell & Rush, 1989, p.307).

Conflicts arise when a person's values are in direct opposition to one another. For example, women's dilemma is often that they want to work in order to help support the family, but not at the cost of caring for and nurturing the children. Men's dilemma is often that they realize the importance of their family,

goals; individual differences in these areas will, thus, result in the development of various constellations of life-role plans. A third assumption is that one's orientation toward multiple-role planning will influence future satisfaction and the experience of stress associated with combining career and family roles. Less well-developed plans and overly optimistic attitudes are likely to result in greater amounts of stress and conflict and reduce life satisfaction. Finally, although the focus is on the individual who is planning for career and family roles, it is important to recognize that other people will be involved in this process. Romantic partners, family, friends, and future employers will all have an influence on the kinds of multiple role plans that are developed. (p. 16)

Multiple-role realism is "the recognition that multiple-role involvement is a complex and potentially stressful lifestyle, paired with awareness of the need for careful planning and consideration of the interface between work and family roles" (Weitzman, 1994, p. 16). This differs from career maturity, which focuses on career development.

The work-family interconnection is a basic part of women's and men's vocational development. As adolescents and young adults work to combine career with family, it is imperative that this interconnection be continuously addressed. "A better understanding of realism in multiple-role planning can provide the basis for a satisfying and workable multiple-role lifestyle, as opposed to one where unrealistic attempts to fulfill role obligations result in unwanted personal sacrifices" (Weitzman, 1994, p. 23).

but they also have to deal with the values of success associated with the male identity (Voydanoff, 1988). In recent studies related to marital and job satisfaction, flexibility, skills in negotiation/compromise, a couple's joint self-esteem, and ability to assess problems were all important variables (Derr, 1986; Meeks, Arnkoff & Glass, 1986; Rachlin & Hansen, 1985). These variables suggest several strategies for the practitioner.

Dual-Career Families

In this section we examine in more depth (a) dual-career families, (b) single-parent families, (c) couples living together, and (d) singles. The term "typical family" has multiple meanings in today's society. In the United States, and, increasingly elsewhere, most people will experience many types of family systems throughout their lives.

The increase in numbers of **dual-career families** suggests an even greater need of systemic attention and focus on the part of vocational practitioners. Today working couples have to develop new ways of living and relating to each other and to the world. One of the greatest challenges facing dual-career families is finding adequate childcare. Increases in the number of women working outside the home, particularly mothers with children still at home, is one of the most dramatic social changes in American history. Organizations have been slow to respond to the needs of dual-career families. Dual careerism will continue to be a major factor altering the family for years to come.

How do couples engage in dual careers and integrate parenting and childcare? Richter, Morrison and Salinas (1991) make these observations about the ways couples deal with the issue. If a couple puts **career first, then family**, the issues they will experience are (a) the woman's biological time clock, (b) the man's physical degeneration and lowering of stamina, (c) age differences between parents and children, and (d) ambivalence about having children. If a couple puts **family first, then career**, the issue becomes (a) less affluence, money, and options for having material things; (b) shorter or lessened career opportunities; (c) less guilt feelings for neglect of family-oriented values; (d) more marital satisfaction; and (e) one stays at home for a few years while the other works, then they trade off. If a couple **shares career and family together**, each can (a) share the problem of task overload and emotional overload, and (b) have the best of both worlds. If a couple considers **childcare options**, the possibilities become (a) staggered parental care, (b) care by extended family member, (c) family daycare, (d) group daycare, (e) full-time babysitter/housekeeper/nanny, (f) both parents dovetailing their work schedules, (g) taking a child to work, (h) a parent cooperative, (i) children in charge of themselves, (j) drop-in centers, (k) working from home, and (l) a combination of the above. If a couple concerns itself with **parenting issues**, they will need to decide (a) how it will be done, (b) who will do it, (c) who will be responsible for discipline, and (d) what will be the shared responsibilities—quality time with children, physical needs, security, recreation/leisure time, allowing autonomy for children, delegation of household chores.

Another concern is that of equity or the sense of fairness that exists in the dual-career couple's relationship. Since there are household and family responsibilities to share, considerations of each other's career and the decisions as to time commitment and job requirements must be balanced. Rachlin and Hansen (1985) found that women tend to take more responsibility (because they have been socialized to do so), and it is likely that the scenario has not changed drastically since that time.

The dual-career couple is also faced with the demands of their respective careers. Conflict between work and family demands often appear to force choices of which job is the most important. While values may play an important part in the day-to-day decisions, the overall concern is the marriage relationship itself. Balancing career, home, family, and relationship is a daily task. **Negotiation** is an important "art" in the dual-career marriage. Couples that know how to negotiate see conflict in a different way. The focus is on resolving an issue in the most mutually satisfactory manner possible, rather than on changing the other spouse's point of view (Hall, 1989).

As a society, people have been focusing on changing organizations so that women can have a career and a family, but recent research on dual-career couples shows that men share the same problems. "We do know that some men make career accommodations for the sake of a career, wife, or the family, but the question is, how many men make career accommodations, and how much accommodating do they do?" (Hall, 1989, p. 7).

Hall (1989) uses the term **invisible daddy track** to refer to men who are not vocal about childcare concerns, so the public is unaware of the strain on fathers. Oftentimes men who use paternity leave or flexible work schedules are viewed as not being serious about their careers, which leads them to stay silent about child-related concerns. Many men sacrifice aspects of their career for their family, but do it quietly. There are at least five ways to approach the problem of work/family balance for men. (1) Restructure work arrangements for more flexibility. (2) Women who regularly note their career accommodations can keep them private the way some men do. (3) Women who want flexibility can consider part-time work or other ways to find time away from work. (4) Consider home-centered work for one spouse or both. (5) Consider any work/family choices as a one-time career decision (Hall, 1989).

Unfortunately, many corporations do not allow the type of flexibility needed to promote work/family balance. As the threat of downsizing and restructuring increases, employees are being pushed to produce more, work harder, stay longer, and work on weekends to keep their jobs. This leads to an inevitable paradox: employees are placing more importance on their families at the same time the unstable job market is causing them to spend more time on their jobs. As the number of dual-career couples increases, practitioners will need to help women and men explore how work and family issues influence their career choices. Lesbian dual-career couples receive even less external support than their gay or heterosexual counterparts (Fassinger, 1996). We discuss these issues further in Chapter 13.

Single-Parent Families

Of the 9 million single-parent families in the United States, 8 million are single mothers and 1 million are single fathers (Kaplan, 1993). About one out of five single mothers have never been married. In 1990, 61 percent of African-American families were single parent, compared with 33 percent among Hispanics and

23 percent among Whites. Single-parent families have increased substantially, from about 2.4 million in 1960 to 10.1 million in 1991, and about 1 million children each year are affected by divorce. Married-couple families numbered an estimated 53.2 million in 1994 (Rawlings, 1995).

The single-parent family is a growing phenomenon, often subject to extreme economic problems. Most single parents experience difficulties with role identity, social stigma, providing financially for the family, and balancing work/ family responsibilities. The lack of formal education and job skills limit access to occupations that provide income for an acceptable standard of living. Women socialized into traditionally low-paying "female" occupations face even greater difficulties (*ERIC Digest,* No. 75, 1988).

Poverty is a major issue for single-parent households, especially those led by women. Inability to find appropriate childcare at a reasonable cost affects a single parent's employability. Sometimes it is cheaper for mothers not to work than to work and pay the exorbitant cost of childcare. Often these single mothers are uneducated and of a cultural minority—many being displaced homemakers and teenage mothers (Burges, 1987).

Single motherhood can cause decline in psychological well-being due to the stressors of living in near poverty. If these women have never been a part of the workforce, they are especially prone to depression. Single fathers also find it difficult to be a competent wage earner and parent. Single-parent pressures make it difficult to make time for personal development. "As a result overload and interference with necessary tasks often occur. Single-parent families lack the personnel to fill all the roles expected of a family in our social structure" (*ERIC Digest,* No. 75, 1988).

Given the link between poverty and unemployment, occupational planning is imperative. For the single parent, the benefits of receiving vocational counseling and learning a skill are twofold, (1) increased job opportunities and income, and (2) a greater sense of self-esteem. For women the economic security of a job often will motivate them to leave abusive situations.

To achieve effective job training and placement, the following aspects need to be considered: emotional support, job-seeking skills, basic skills instruction (especially literacy skills), outreach and recruitment, childcare, gender role analysis, self-concept building, skills assessment, the challenges of combining work and family responsibilities, nontraditional job skills, and parenting education.

Multicultural Implications of Work-Family Conflict, Dual-Career Families, and Single-Parent Families Multicultural dual-career couples may be vulnerable to acculturative stress from the lifestyle they lead and the struggle to retain their original group values while attempting to incorporate the mainstream values of their work cultures. Politically induced workaholism perpetuated by their jobsites may be especially difficult to manage. Like many workers, multicultural dual-career couples may perceive that they are putting in too many hours on the job because they have to, not because they want to. Values clarification and assessment of leisure activities may be useful. Working twice as hard to appear at least as competent as coworkers from the dominant culture is a struggle faced by many multicultural dual-career couples. For clients originally from the lower socioeconomic classes, the meanings they attach to work may require exploration. Practitioners can ask clients, "Is this your idea of upward mobility?"

Because 61 percent of African-American families are headed by a single parent (Kaplan, 1993), it is crucial to develop programs for African-American adolescents to inform, educate, and train them so they can be financially better prepared to deal with the stressors of this lifestyle. From the single parent's perspective, children need to find role models and mentors to assist them in the occupational process. What are the values, work attitudes, and goals in these families and how does the socioeconomic system affect their decisions? (Clark, 1983). What support systems are available from, say, extended family, community, or church?

To what extent do African-American and Hispanic single parents have the same needs as Whites? Are the structures we have in place meeting the needs of these varying cultural groups? If not, what needs to be developed? How much flexibility is there in tailoring programs and models to suit the needs of individuals and particular individuals within families?

Among Hispanics, it is useful to surmise how many extended family members take responsibility for child rearing and providing financial assistance. However, not all Hispanics have extended family nearby to lend a hand, and even for Hispanics with extended family members nearby, social support may not be available for a variety of reasons. It is dangerous to stereotype that, among Hispanics, extended family are willing and able to help. More broadly, lack of education and skills predominates among the U.S. Hispanic population. Many do not finish high school, with the consequence of fewer job opportunities available and, if they do find work, it is for minimum wage (McDaniels & Gysbers, 1992).

THE POSTMODERN FAMILY AND VOCATIONAL PSYCHOLOGY

With increased attention on dual-career and single-parent families, vocational psychology has yet to attend to the postmodern family. Gergen (1991a) describes a scene from the postmodern family's daily life:

> Tommy needs to eat at 6:00 because of a school function at 7:00. His
> sister, Martha, must be picked up from her field hockey game at 7:15.
> Both children are upset because their mother, Sarah, has an office func-
> tion and can't get home until after 8:00—thus, no dinner and no trans-
> portation. Sarah asks her husband, Rick, to come to the rescue, but he has
> to work late to prepare for a flight to Dallas the next morning. It is also
> Sarah's mother's birthday the next day, but Sarah is not prepared. Urgent
> messages await on the answering machine, one from a longtime friend of
> Rick's, in town for a day and wanting to drop by, and another from a
> close friend of Sarah's in tears because of her floundering marriage. (p. 29)

Rick and Sarah experience more dread, guilt, and anxiety that they should be
spending the evening helping their children with their homework, planning for
their family vacation, paying long-neglected bills, or spending "quality time"
together.

The postmodern family is likely to feel scattered by the intensifying busy-
ness of their lives. Social saturation has shrunk the family's physical world while
their cultural and social worlds have expanded and grown more complex. In
addition, rising divorce rates and remarriages, as well as other variations in living arrangements (homosexual couples, housemates) have muddled the definition of "family." This blurring of boundaries has given rise to what is now called
the "floating family."

The Floating Family

The **floating family** transcends the boundaries of traditional family units related by blood, common residence, and shared surnames (Gergen, 1991a), and
consists of relationships that can be in a more continuous state of flux than with
one's family of origin. Floating-family networks are based on affectional ties of
choice rather than blood ties of chance, and often occur when traditional family
members withdraw from the family's orbit through connections established by
the technologies of social saturation. An individual's most important relationship
may be with an unrelated person who lives far away, the connection largely
maintained by electronic mail and/or long-distance telephone calls, with only
occasional visits. The floating-family network fluctuates and shifts with circumstances and time.

The "Formed Family"

What Gergen (1991a) calls the floating family, Pipher (1996) calls the **"formed
family,"** although she does not use the term "postmodern." Similar to the floating family, the formed family evolves for those persons who do not have access

Practical Applications

Several issues acknowledged by Gergen (1991a) can guide practitioners working with clients from saturated and floating families. Some clients may initially feel disconcerted when they begin to notice extensions of familylike relationships with coworkers on the job. It is not unusual for some clients to feel more at home during a Monday lunch with a longtime working comrade than the traditional family members with whom the client shared a Sunday dinner the night before. Are practitioners willing to normalize their clients' coworker floating-family connections? The practitioner can help clients determine whether such connections are mutual; one-sided floating-family feelings towards coworkers can set the client up for disappointment.

When floating-family feelings among coworkers are mutual, some clients may feel guilty or confused about the connections, believing that such primary relationships should only be reserved for spouses, romantic partners, and/or traditional family members. At such times the practitioner can explore with the client whether nostalgia and sentimentality are present, and whether upon closer inspection the idealized safe, secure, nurturing, stable, traditional family was not also oppressive, sexist, inflexible, and emotionally stultifying. Another issue related to the real losses involved in the client's traditional family transformation is what ideals coworkers as floating family can offer as compensation. Practitioners can listen for the value clients place on having a broader understanding of the world provided by coworkers as floating family. Practitioners can collaborate with clients in weighing whether traditional family relationships are being taken for granted. With clients who see themselves in a saturated world, practitioners have to decide whether to knowingly adopt a moderate postmodern stance and support the idea that there are many aspects to the self—if not actually many selves—and whether emotional sustenance for the client can be derived from various coworker, floating-family members. Another possibility is for practitioners to actually give clients O'Hara and Anderson (1991) and Gergen (1991a) to read as a bibliotherapy intervention for further discussion.

to a supportive biological family or for those who prefer a community of friends to the families into which they were born. The staying power of a formed family is contingent upon whether its members stay together despite disagreements, lend each other money when one member loses a job, or visit one another in a convalescent center after one has been paralyzed in a car crash. Pipher also notes that some immigrants become formed family members to help each other in a new country. Formed families also occur when biological families do not stick together during a crisis. Requisite social skills are needed to be in a formed family: dull, abrasive, and shy people can be left out of formed families.

Practical Applications

To help clients discern the reliable members of their biological or formed families, among the questions practitioners can ask (Pipher, 1996) is: If you lose your job, who will lend you money to pay the rent? Our concern is whether it is wise to establish a formed family with co-workers. What are the political risks of establishing such relationships at work? Will certain information be used against you (e.g., fighting with your mate, going through a period of depression) when it comes time for job-performance evaluations, pay raises, or promotions? Clients may need to think through the pros and cons of making coworkers part of their formed families.

The Myth of Workplace As Family

Floating-family networks are based on affectional ties of mutual choice rather than blood ties of chance. This can mean that, given the number of hours co-workers can spend in each other's company at the workplace, it would hardly be surprising for some employees to have familylike feeling with coworkers on the job (Gergen, 1991a). In fact, some workplaces may encourage employees to feel as if they are part of "one big happy family." This is a myth that can lull one into a false sense of security. Unstated assumptions go along with the myth of workplace as family.

Thomas (1990) writes that viewing the workplace as family "suggests not only that father knows best; it also suggests that sons will inherit the business, that daughters should stick to doing the company dishes, and that if Uncle Deadwood doesn't perform, we'll put him in the chimney corner and feed him for another 30 years regardless" (p. 115). Such unstated assumptions have their constituencies and defenders. If Uncle Deadwood was told he did good work for ten years, but the last twelve years or so were unproductive and it was time to help him find another chimney, then shockwaves would travel through the workplace. Every family-oriented employee would draw their swords in defense of the sanctity of guaranteed jobs.

Another outgrowth of the myth of workplace as family is unchallenged paternalism (Thomas, 1990). If father knows best, then managers will seek employees who will follow their lead and do as they do. If the managers cannot find employees who are exactly like themselves, then they will seek people who aspire to be exactly like themselves. Employees become extensions of managers' hands and minds, responsive to every unspoken cue and compliant. But what happens to the workplace as family when there is a shake-up in management?

Relevance for Multicultural and Diverse Populations Workplace as family is dishonest mythology (Thomas, 1990). Father does not always know best; in fact, sometimes he is completely out of touch. Managers cannot buy into the "father knows best" concept, seek employees exactly like themselves, and create a workplace that is truly hospitable to multicultural and diverse populations. These populations can learn from the experiences of members of the dominant culture who have been burned by their workplaces that posed as families.

INCORPORATING A SYSTEMIC APPROACH INTO VOCATIONAL PSYCHOLOGY

For vocational psychology to incorporate a more systemic approach, closer attention will have to be given to family practice in the twenty-first century. Three major movements represent an overall epistemological shift in the marriage and family therapy fields: feminism, social constructionism, and multiculturalism (Hardy, 1993). These three movements are also shaping the vocational psychology field. Both fields could gain immeasurably by entering into a dialogue on how these three movements affect issues of mutual interest, particularly as the full impact of these movements has not been realized in either field.

Practitioners will need a knowledge of "how the dynamics of power affect all levels of human functioning, particularly with regard to differences related to race, ethnicity, gender, and class" (Pinderhughes, 1995, p. 139). Power is "the capacity to influence for one's own benefit the forces that affect one's life space and/or as the capacity to produce desired effects on others" (p. 133). Dynamics of power clarify the value society assigns to a multicultural group's status and how such status influences between-group differences. To avoid an abuse of power and exploitation of clients, practitioners need to be aware of their own "internalized responses to power in relation to racial, ethnic, gender, and class differences" (p. 138).

This concludes our discussion of career/vocational theories and family influences that form the basis for the practice of career counseling. The next four chapters address programs and resources that can be used with various age groups across the life span.

9

❖❖

Career Counseling
in the Schools

Here is something adults always say that I do not like:
"Edith, what do you want to be when you grow up?"
As if what I am right now is not enough.

—EDITH ANN

(WAGNER, 1994, P. 20)

Many of us can remember being asked, "What are you going to be when you grow up?" We probably felt proud when we had a ready answer to give, or confused or worried when we could not give a definite response. As Edith Ann so aptly puts it, the question can make a child feel inadequate, as if enjoying childhood were not enough. In this chapter we begin by examining the National Career Development Guidelines. Second, we look at the National Occupational Information Coordinating Committee's competencies for elementary, middle, and high school students. Third, we consider the school counselor's role in career development. Fourth, we present programs, techniques, assessments, and resources for career counseling for students K–12. Fifth, we address an often-overlooked aspect of occupational guidance programs—the involvement of parents.

THE NATIONAL CAREER
DEVELOPMENT GUIDELINES

Before discussing the application of career counseling to various age groups and populations we want to mention a major resource that details the national standards for career development, starting with kindergarten through adulthood. In 1996 the National Occupational Information Coordinating Committee (NOICC) published the *National Career Development Guidelines,* a handbook of information for anyone responsible for career development in any setting for any age group. The purpose of the handbook is "to strengthen and improve comprehensive, competency-based career counseling, guidance and education programs" (p. i). It explains its standards, including national, state and local roles, discussing organizational commitments, structure, and support; presents a proven implementation process to establish new programs or enhance existing ones; discusses marketing the program and the Competencies and Indicators for elementary, middle school, and high school; provides information for getting started, with examples of lesson plans and activities; and presents the Competencies and Indicators, as well as information on building career development programs for adults in various settings. To obtain the *National Career Development Guidelines* and other publications of the NOICC contact your state OICC, State Supervisor of Guidance, the NOICC, or the NOICC Training Support Center (NTSC).

NOICC
2100 M Street, NW, Suite 156
Washington, DC 20037
202-653-7680

NTSC
OK Dept. of Vocational and
Technical Education
1500 West Seventh Avenue
Stillwater, OK 74074-4364
405-743-5197

SCHOOL GUIDELINES:
NATIONAL OCCUPATIONAL INFORMATION
COORDINATING COMMITTEE

The NOICC (1996) defines the National Career Development Guidelines Competencies and Indicators for elementary, middle school, and high school. Factors pertaining to self-knowledge, educational and occupational exploration, and career planning are presented in Tables 9.1, 9.2, and 9.3.

In 1997 the American School Counselor Association (ASCA) changed its national standards for school counseling programs. In career development, students learn to "employ strategies to achieve future career success and satisfaction . . .

TABLE 9.1 Self-knowledge

ELEMENTARY	MIDDLE SCHOOL	HIGH SCHOOL
Knowledge of the importance of a positive self-concept	Knowledge of the influence of a positive self-concept	Understanding the influence of a positive self-concept
Skills to interact positively with others	Skills to interact positively with others	Skills to interact positively with others
Awareness of the importance of growth and change	Knowledge of the importance of growth and change	Understanding the impact of growth and development

SOURCE: NOICC (1996), pp. 1–8.

TABLE 9.2 Educational and Occupational Exploration

ELEMENTARY	MIDDLE SCHOOL	HIGH SCHOOL
Awareness of the benefits of educational achievement	Knowledge of the benefits of educational achievement to career opportunities	Understanding the relationship between educational achievement and career planning
Awareness of the relationship between work and learning	Understanding the relationship between work and learning	Understanding the need for positive attitudes towards work and learning
Skills to understand and use career information	Skills to locate, understand, and use career information	Skills to locate, evaluate, and interpret career information
Awareness of the importance of personal responsibility and good work habits	Knowledge of skills necessary to seek and obtain jobs	Skills to prepare to seek, obtain, maintain, and change jobs
Awareness of how work relates to the needs and functions of society	Understanding how work relates to the needs and functions of the economy and society	Understanding how societal needs and functions influence the nature and structure of work

SOURCE: NOICC (1996), pp. 1–8.

TABLE 9.3 Career Planning

ELEMENTARY	MIDDLE SCHOOL	HIGH SCHOOL
Understanding how to make decisions	Skills to make decisions	Skills to make decisions
Awareness of the interrelationship of life roles	Knowledge of the interrelationship of life roles	Understanding the interrelationship of life roles
Awareness of different occupations and changing male/female roles	Knowledge of different occupations and changing male/female roles	Understanding the continuous changes in male/female roles
Awareness of the career planning process	Understanding the process of career planning	Skills in career planning

SOURCE: NOICC (1996), pp. 1–8.

[and] understand the relationship between personal qualities, education and training, and the world of work (Campbell & Dahir, 1997, pp. 17, 19). Table 9.4 provides an example of delivery-system activities in a program that represents compliance with a state comprehensive guidance program with the counselor's role in each activity defined.

Below is an example of a career and technology department program that implements the career education process for a school district. The program was developed and implemented by Linda Catherine in the East Central Independent School District (ISD) in San Antonio, Texas, and reprinted here by permission. The Career Education Design is illustrated in Figure 9.1.

At East Central ISD all education is viewed as career education. The classroom becomes the workplace, the student's first job. From K–12, experiences and activities at each level provide readiness for the next level. Although the means and methods of instructional emphasis may shift, learners will encounter career education from Pre-Kindergarten through grade 12. Academics and work ethics combine to teach lifelong skills such as teamwork, attendance, problem solving, technology, and product excellence. East Central gives each student the opportunity to achieve his or her highest potential.

Table 9.5 outlines the specific components of each of the steps in the Career Education Design.

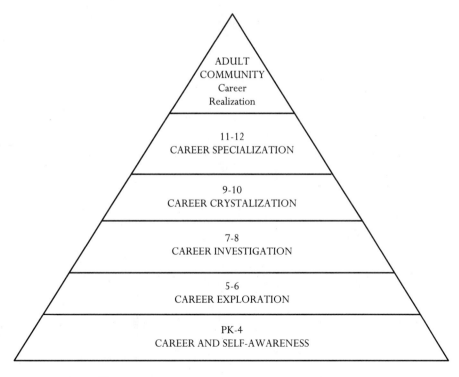

FIGURE 9.1 Career Education Design

TABLE 9.4 Facilitating Students' Career Development Through Comprehensive Guidance Programs: Delivery System Activities

GUIDANCE CURRICULUM	INDIVIDUAL PLANNING SYSTEM	RESPONSIVE SERVICES	SYSTEM SUPPORT
Provides guidance content in a systematic way to all students Pre-K–12	Assists students in planning, monitoring, & managing their personal & career development	Addresses the immediate concerns of students	Includes program staff, and school support activities and services
Self-Understanding Educational & Work World Information Decision-making skills Goal-setting skills Planning skills	Educational Planning & Decision-Making Career Planning & Decision-Making Assessment for Self-understanding Information Resources for Exploring & Planning the Work World Student Advisory Program Parent Involvement	Small Group Counseling Parent Consultation Individual guidance Individual counseling	Advisor Consultation Administrator/Consultation
Counselor Role: Group Guidance Consultation	Counselor Role: Assessment Guidance Consultation Coordination	Counselor Role: Counseling Consultation Coordination	Counselor Role: Professionalism Program Management Consultation

SOURCE: Patricia Henderson, Ed.D., Northside Independent School District, San Antonio, TX.

TABLE 9.5 East Central Independent School District Career Education Design

ADULT COMMUNITY		(CAT LAB) Shadowing/Mentorships Business Panel Discussion and Speakers Mock Interviews Teacher/Counselor Inservice Vocational Student Organizations Coops School To Work Articulation Tech Prep College/Career Day, College Visits Internships
Career Realization and Employment 11–12+ Career Specialization	(CAT LAB) Assessment Instruments Database Colleges and Careers Business Partnerships 1–1 Career Counseling Portfolio/Career Pathways update—Grades 8–14 Employment Information Resource and Referral Center Financial Aid SAT/ACT/TASP Information College Representatives and Recruiters Scholarships, Grants	
9–10 Career Crystalization	Career Pathways Update Grades 8–14 Career Search and Research Career Instruction Portfolio/Resume Assessment Instruments and Inventories Database College and Careers Teacher/Counselor Inservices	
7–8 Career Investigation 5–6 Career Exploration	Database College and Careers Career Pathways (8th) Interest Inventory (8th) Career Pathways Brochure (Doors) Career Resource Libraries Career Days Career Instruction 6th and 8th Grades Presentations	Vocational Biographies Business & College Field Trips Second Step 6 & 6 Social Skills Career Investigation Course for All 8th Graders
PK–4 Career and Self-Awareness	Career Resource Libraries Career Instruction 1st and 4th Grade Presentations Hands-on Career Activities Guest Speakers Field Trips Career Integrated Curriculum and Resources (CASA) Career Guidance in the Classroom Career Fairs/Career Pathways	Second Step (Social Skills) Career Interviews

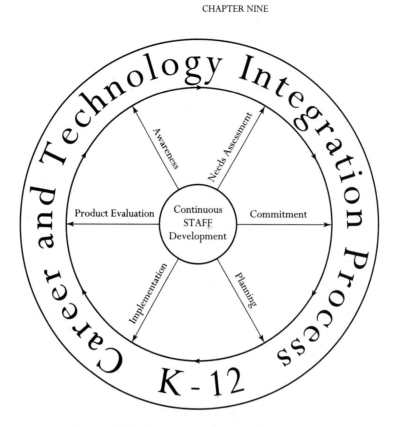

FIGURE 9.2 Career and Technology Integration Process

Figure 9.2 is a graphic representation of the Wheel-Hub Model of the Career and Technology Integration Process.

Two considerations of the model in Figure 9.2 are (1) career and technology integration K–12 is a comprehensive systematic and developmental process involving all ECISD staff and students, and (2) through the career and technology integration process, students will develop the SCANS skills and competencies necessary to be successfully employed in the global workforce of the new millenium. The pervasive integration of career thinking and relevance throughout the school program can prepare students for the lifelong task of finding suitable and satisfying work.

THE SCHOOL COUNSELOR'S ROLE
IN CAREER DEVELOPMENT

An essential role of the school counselor is to facilitate students' career development from pre-K through grade 12 using comprehensive guidance programs, as illustrated in Table 9.4. The role of the school counselor should be one of collaboration, systems expert, colleague, options creator, and career goals advocate (McCharen, 1997). Career connection counselors need to (a) offer career awareness and explanation at the earliest possible age; (b) help students identify interests, goals, and career majors and job options (including nontraditional jobs traditionally held by persons of a given gender, race, or ethnicity); (c) help develop a plan of study; and (d) provide rigorous academics for all students. Parents and students should participate in determining academic and career options, high school courses, shadowing experiences, summer internships, service (volunteer) learning, apprenticeships, financial and school-based enterprises.

Hansen (1993) offers suggestions for schools to prepare students for work in the future. First, devise career development programs using the curriculum in conjunction with work so that students are better able to experience the world of work. Second, bring attention to gender bias in the classroom in order to end harmful career stereotyping. School counselors need to take a more proactive role in the student's career decision-making process rather than just be a part of the administrative aspect.

> Counselors truly will need to be change agents, help democratize the school as a work organization, be willing to create innovative models and strategies, and clearly link national and/or local career development competencies to the various forms of outcome-based education to assure that career development and counselors are an integral part of new school reforms. Schools must develop strategies to meet the occupational development needs of every population, including minority and low-income students. Students need to be computer literate to survive in the twenty-first century. Therefore, "Counselors and career development specialists will need more training in both the potentials and limitations of computer-assisted career guidance." (Hansen, 1993, p. 20)

Use of Career Assessment in the Schools

If one wishes to gauge the extent of career assessment in school counseling practices, Freeman's (1996) study of high school counselors' use of standardized paper-and-pencil and computer-assisted tools is enlightening. Sixty-nine percent of those who use career assessment tools use more than one, and 44 percent use both computer and paper-and-pencil tools, indicating that there is no clear preference of any one tool. Thirty percent of high school counselors never use any career assessment tool, and nearly half do not use a computer in assessment. This may indicate a low priority given to career-planning activities, even at a time when the world of work is so rapidly changing. Perhaps greater priorities within some schools revolve around (a) scheduling, (b) increasing standardized achievement test scores, (c) gang/drug/alcohol-related issues, (d) crisis management, (e) academic failure, and (f) remedial problems. The emphasis on career development goals in the American School Counselor Association guidelines, coupled with the results of surveys by the National Career Development Association (Brown, Minor & Jepsen, 1992)—which reported that the public highly supports career development in the schools—show a need for more career development activities in the schools.

Given the increased pressure for career guidance in the schools on one hand, and the apparent lack of use of assessment tools on the other, the disparity between goals and practice needs to be addressed. Freeman (1996) asks several pertinent questions:

> Are the roles of school counselors too fragmented to allow for systematic career development activities? Do counselors prefer not to use assessment tools? Do school counselors perceive career assessment activities to be a lower priority than working with at-risk students? Are the tools inappropriate for the school setting? Have school counselors been trained to use career counseling computer-assisted and paper-and-pencil systems? (p. 194)

In a review of twenty-nine national reports on educational reform, increased attention to career guidance, with education as preparation for the world of work, was identified as the most important function of school counselors (Hoyt, 1989). The school counselor's role in educational reform has highlighted the need to understand the counselor's role, with administrative support as vital towards countering negative stereotypes and facilitating shared decision-making and multidisciplinary efforts (Allen, 1994).

The Issue of Administrative Support

School counselors often find their roles to be more like administrative assistants than counselors. This raises the issue of administrative support for school counselors. Are principals and administrators aware of the ASCA guidelines for school counselors? Do school counselors get placed in the role of paper pusher or disciplinarian? Do principals give career and occupational development high priority? Lack of support from their administration leaves school counselors in the dilemma of wanting to provide counseling and guidance but having their time delegated to mundane tasks, with little time or energy for guidance. Nonetheless, school counselors must take responsibility for informing administrators of the scope and value of their services and skills.

Much research has been done on the ambiguity of a counselor's role and job tasks. "In hypothesizing about the reasons school counselors appear to underutilize career assessment tools, some school counselors may perceive career counseling as a lower priority than other roles. Others may perceive career guidance as a high priority, but are plagued with a severe lack of time or support" (Freeman, 1996, p. 194). A time/task analysis helps school counselors appropriately devote ample time to each required task (Fairchild & Seeley, 1994). Yet, some school counselors may place a higher importance on counseling for personal development and negate the importance of career counseling. The truth is that by practicing career counseling a school counselor may help a student find his or her own niche in the world of work, which would positively affect a student's personal development.

Career Education As a Course Requirement for All Teacher Education and Educational Administration Majors

A current challenge to vocational psychology is for practitioners to increase their dialogue with school administrators at all levels regarding the importance of continuous, ongoing education of students about the world of work. Even schools in the same district vary dramatically in the time and attention administrators allow school counselors to devote to career and work-related educational activities. A once-a-year "career day" is not enough, particularly if school counselors get so busy booking speakers and coordinating exhibits that students in personal crisis are ignored (we have seen this happen repeatedly). And while career-related information may be included in curricula pertaining to math, science, social studies, and languages, teachers may have to receive constant reminders about opportunities that exist in the world of work that are relevant to the subjects they teach. Teachers who have never worked in any other profession may especially benefit from in-services on educating their students about the work world, expanding beyond the vocational education tracks available in many school district programs. Optimally, a required course in career development for all teacher education majors would transform how opportunities in the world of work are taught in the schools. It could change the way teachers think about their subject matter's relevance, and help school counselors whose hands are often tied by administrative responsibilities.

In addition, a required career education course for all educational administration majors, including those on the graduate level who plan to become principals and superintendents, would reinforce the importance of career education in the schools. If educational administrators took such a course, they would be more aware, supportive, and respectful of school counselors' and teachers' efforts to inculcate their students with knowledge of the work world. Administrators, teachers, and school counselors all need to be informed about ways to incorporate occupations/careers into the learning process. Dialogue between their respective state and national professional organizations would be useful in coordinating career education efforts among all school personnel and extend the discussion to broader levels.

PROGRAMS, TECHNIQUES, ASSESSMENTS, AND RESOURCES FOR CAREER COUNSELING K–12

Elementary Schools

The American School Counseling Association (ASCA) realizes the importance of career guidance in the schools for students from pre-K through grade 12. According to Hoffman and McDaniels (1991):

> This developmental approach to career guidance is highly consistent with the developmental philosophy of contemporary elementary school counseling programs and their goal of helping children to experience healthy intellectual, social, emotional, and career development for success in the present and future. In view of the current definitions of career development as self-development and career as encompassing all roles, settings, and events in the life of the individual, the overall elementary guidance and counseling program may well be perceived as a life career development program. (p. 163)

A career development program should be appropriate to the child's developmental age, and activities should be planned so a child can meet specific developmental milestones that:

> (a) develop self-understanding and a realistic, positive self-concept;
> (b) acquire the knowledge, understanding, attitudes, and competencies to function effectively in their current life roles such as son or daughter, family member, sibling, student, classmate, worker at home and school, friend, peer group member, team member in sports and games, and "leisurite"; and (c) develop an awareness of the career development options available to them in school and the community. (Hoffman & McDaniels, 1991, p. 164, quotations in original)

Career guidance materials are available for use in the classroom to incorporate an effective career development program, including: guidance kits, video and audiotapes, books, films, games, and puppets.

Most states have an education agency that sets parameters and guidelines for programs of career education in the curriculum. Oftentimes there are separate agencies; one for career education and one for vocational education including career technology and school-to-work. These agencies determine the types of information and competencies that are required for each age group. In many situations, sad to say, these mandates are not followed, or they are merely recommendations that are not enforced. Whether mandated or recommended, these guidelines can help obtain funds for implementing various special programs through Work Force Development and School to Work allocations.

Other Programs and Considerations As an example of a realistic understanding of work, Catlett (1992) devised a two-week unit on work that offers third graders a broad view of the world of work and explores the actual meaning of work. "The goals of the unit are to foster a respect for all jobs, to increase the children's understanding of the importance of work itself, and to nurture an appreciation of school as their work" (p. 151). The unit includes:

1. *People at Work* features a slide show called *Learning about Work* which was produced by the Communications Workers of America and gives children a diverse view of different work places. Children also interview their parents to discover the requirements needed for different jobs as well as their parents' level of happiness.

2. *Children at Work* offers a look at how the world has changed for children since the time they used to work instead of going to school. Questions such as why it was necessary for children to work and what would it be like if it was still that way augment cultural and historical perspectives.

3. *The Pontiac Motor Company* unit simulates an assembly line making paper cars. Children experience the world of work firsthand as they fill out job applications, agree to abide by work rules, and actually operate their own store.

Children need to appreciate the value of work; this happens through giving them an understanding of work (Catlett, 1992). A goal of this particular program is to teach children that work can give dignity to one's life, whether the worker's job is attending third grade or presiding over a nation. "Labor is not an abstract concept, an ingredient to be mixed with others to produce certain economic results. Labor is people, and we don't want children to be dispassionate about people" (p. 154).

Helpful to counselors is information regarding differences based on gender, ethnicity, and socioeconomic status. Phipps (1995) investigated the following questions:

1. What are the career dreams of 8–11-year-old children and how do they vary by student demographic characteristics?

2. What do children of this age range understand about the requirements for attaining their career dreams, and how does this knowledge vary by student demographic characteristics? (p. 20)

She found that these children were able to choose a career and explain their choice, and that gender, ethnicity, and socioeconomic status were related to what children chose as a future occupation, and the educational requirements for that position. For more specifics on this research, we suggest the Phipps article.

Practical Applications

A series of books for elementary school girls encourages them to consider nontraditional occupations. Astronomer (Ghez & Cohen, 1995) and cardiologist (Redborg & Cohen, 1996) are explored in English-language books. Architect (Siegel & Cohen, 1992a, 1992b), engineer (Cohen, 1992, 1995), marine biologist (1992a, 1992b), paleontologist (Gabriel & Cohen, 1993a, 1993b), and zoologist (Thompson & Cohen, 1992, 1993) are explored in both English- and Spanish-language books. These innovative books raise occupational possibilities for little girls before they reach an age where they are told they can't do something. The Berenstain Bears (Berenstain & Berenstain, 1974) also convey a "can-do" attitude that encourages girls to remain confident in their capabilities to accomplish various tasks.

As we will discuss, the confidence gap that widens between adolescent females and males in middle and high school can be minimized by a solid foundation set for girls during their elementary school years. "By sixth grade . . . both girls and boys have learned to equate maleness with opportunity and femininity with constraint" (Orenstein, 1994, p. xiv). Canfield and Wells (1994) provide teachers with 100 ways to enhance children's self-concept, which can only maximize occupational potential for all students. (See chapters 1 and 2 in Peterson and González's *Career Counseling Models for Diverse Populations,* which are designed for elementary school.)

Assessments of Elementary School Students' Career Interests and Preferences

1. Information interviews of teacher to assess interests
2. The E-WOW
3. Job-O
4. The Murphy-Meisgeier Type Indicator for Children
5. Early School Personality Questionnaire

Middle School

Career counseling for middle school students is relatively unresearched. Middle school is defined as sixth, seventh, and eighth grades, which usually covers ages 11–13. These early years of adolescence are a confusing time for many students.

Their primary focus is on self-definition, finding out who they are and what they like and dislike. During this stage students are only beginning to develop more mature social relationships, striving for independence, and creating their own set of values. For a career guidance program to effectively target this age group it must take into account developmental needs of early adolescence and provide assistance in the transition from elementary school into high school. Counseling should focus on helping these students develop a clear understanding of their competencies, identities, and relationships with others, and provide opportunities for career exploration. Impressionable adolescents often experience defining moments in their middle school years that can have lifelong implications. The career exploration process is one defining moment.

In many industrialized countries the transition from primary to secondary education includes a major branching point where continuance or discontinuance in school is determined (Blossfeld & Shavit, 1993). For example, in Sweden, Switzerland, and Poland vocational education is an alternative to continuing in secondary and higher education. Lower-income students are especially attracted to vocational education because it provides rapid access to a marketable skill. Vocational education absorbs disadvantaged groups at a secondary level without threatening the interests of advantaged groups.

Grant (1997) identifies goals counselors must consider when dealing with middle school students: (a) reinforce each student's resiliency strengths and relate them to the world of work; (b) get students involved in extracurricular activities; (c) develop and identify a student's relationship with a significant adult in his or her life or community; and (d) be aware of the drastic developmental differences that run the gamut between concrete and abstract reasoning. With this in mind career guidance must expose adolescents to the world of work and address their developmental needs.

Belvis, Rodriguez, and Fellan (1996) present the following career counseling program by grade level.

Sixth Grade Most sixth-grade students are usually between the ages of eleven and twelve. Since these students' exposure to the work world comes only from observing family members or their teachers, coaches, and clergy, the counselor's task is to widen their knowledge base by acquainting them with many different occupations and not simply direct them towards any particular career. The following six-week curriculum module presents an example of a program that can be integrated into the last six weeks of school, allowing students to continue researching various occupations during the summer break.

Week One focuses mainly on widening the student's knowledge of work and job opportunities through two assignments that involve making a list of all the occupations the student has ever heard of or dreamed about. Through group discussion, students exchange various ideas and add more occupations to their list. Students can make a poster or collage by drawing or cutting out pictures from magazines of people doing jobs that appeal to them, offering an artistic outlet for researching their interests. In Week Two students narrow their list to four or five occupations that seem especially appealing. This should be completed individually so students do not collaborate and end up with identical lists. Students learn how to gather information about a wide range of careers and understand the dignity of each worker, regardless of the prestige connected with the job. The teacher is integral at this stage, making sure that there are no duplications. During Week Three the students research each of the four or five jobs they chose in order to find the requirements necessary to obtain these particular jobs. Included in this research should be such items as educational requirements, salary, job duties, responsibilities, uniforms (if needed), working conditions, and job outlook for the twenty-first century. This information can be obtained from the library, interviews with people who currently work in the desired positions, and in-class research. In Week Four students write a brief description for each of their jobs, including a paragraph on the reason each job was chosen for further study and discussion of some positive and negative aspects of the job. The teacher must remain impartial to all descriptions regardless of status. During Weeks Five and Six students share their job descriptions with other class members. Each student chooses one occupation and makes a short oral presentation on it. In this way the class learns of twenty or so different occupations.

The goals of this curriculum inclusion are to enable students to broaden their perceptions of occupations as well as learn about diverse job opportunities. The interaction of teacher/counselor and peers is crucial to this knowledge. Though the students will not be expected to focus on a particular future job, their ability to make appropriate career decisions will be greatly increased through this practice.

Seventh Grade Seventh-grade students, who are usually between the ages of twelve and thirteen, are experiencing emotional and physical changes. Peers are becoming more important in their lives. Therefore, a seventh grade career counseling program needs to (a) increase a student's self-awareness and confidence through learning and experiencing both personal and group success, and (b) offer hands-on experience by observing and/or shadowing different people at work. By the seventh grade, a student should have a basic knowledge of the world of work and build on that knowledge to make academic choices.

Two types of hands-on experiences involve (1) trips to various occupational settings and (2) opportunities for people from different occupations to come into the classroom to explain what they do and how they do it. These experiences give students the chance to question workers about their jobs and or careers. Interaction and participation of the students is vital to this process. The counselor can also develop a plan for students to visit different work environments so they can observe people working. Using groups of four or five students effectively provides more opportunities for experiences to be shared with the entire class. Group discussions, led by the teacher or counselor, can provide important situations for the students to consolidate their thinking and begin the task of incorporating their individual interests and abilities into their awareness.

Another activity to promote career awareness in the seventh grade is for students to develop their own career center. The career center can grow as the students' knowledge grows. Included in this center are the students' job descriptions and reports from their respective field studies, and information gathered from teachers and counselors. Each student should contribute to the center an entire file with at least five job descriptions. Parents and community can also be asked to contribute books and any information that they have about occupations and the world of work. By the end of the year the career center will be started, offering incoming students the opportunity to contribute to and learn from the work of the previous students. At the seventh grade level, the primary objective of career exploration is to acquaint the student with the world of work and learn more about various occupations that interest them, rather than decide on a particular occupation. Broader knowledge will be valuable as the students grow and change as individuals.

A six-week curriculum for seventh grade could include the following:

In Week One students review the twenty or so occupations they learned about in sixth grade and select six of them to pursue further. Two occupations should have a field trip involved to allow the students to see firsthand what is involved. The other four occupations could be explored by having workers in those occupations come speak to the class. During Week Two speakers continue to come to class and students write one-page summaries of what they learn. By Week Three, the two field trips have been completed. Students again write a one-page summary of what they have learned. Beginning in Week Four, students start to organize all the information into a career center. By Week Five each student contributes four new job descriptions to the career center files (different occupations will be assigned to each student). In Week Six students bring in books, pamphlets, and any other information they have collected for the career center. If a computer is available, all the information can be entered for ready access. The goal for the year is to continue to gather information about as many occupations as possible and to organize it into a career center.

Eighth Grade Eighth-grade students are usually between the ages of thirteen and fourteen. They need a basic knowledge of the world of work and various occupations. The eighth-grade curriculum should build on the knowledge acquired in sixth and seventh grades. The goal of this curriculum is to give the students information that will become a basis for decision-making during high school and beyond. Eighth-grade students have reached a higher level of maturity and self-understanding and are ready to explore occupations in greater depth. Their abilities to think in abstract terms and to introspect help them be aware of and realize their capabilities and explore their interests.

In the eighth grade the career program needs to include biweekly classroom visits by people from different occupations who discuss their career and its educational requirements, training, and apprenticeships. These speakers should represent a variety of occupations and levels from the surrounding community, allowing students to see the skills required for many kinds of jobs and to understand that dignity and pride can come from any line of work. Presenters need to be males and females from diverse ethnic backgrounds. It is imperative that students see that they have the capabilities to achieve goals regardless of gender or ethnicity. This in-depth interchange with workers provides students a clearer understanding of different occupations and allows them to interact with the presenters.

By the end of the first semester, all eighth grade students should have taken an interest and personality assessment. At least two jobsite visits should be arranged so students can observe workers in their environment. In doing so, the students are able to evaluate the situation, answering questions such as "Is this really the kind of work that interests me?" and "Does the work environment match my personality?" Asking questions of various people in the workplace and even being allowed to use equipment involved helps students see whether their career dreams are appropriate and if they should pursue their goal further or reprioritize their list of options.

Counselors can provide classroom presentations and role-play situations. Students can be put in small groups so they can develop skills working within a group or team. One goal for eighth graders would be that they had obtained enough information regarding self and occupations to assist in course selection in high school, particularly when choosing electives and the classes they need to pursue their occupational dreams.

Report Card Paycheck Grant (1997) designed an activity to convey the idea that school is work for middle school classes. It is particularly effective with at-risk students. The model is seen in Box 9.1.

BOX 9.1

Report Card Paycheck

Guidance/Small-Group Lesson Plan
Report Card Paycheck
Objective(s):

- identify needed qualities for a good report card
- identify needed qualities for a good paycheck
- relate report card to paycheck
- identify connection between learning now and career opportunities in the future
- apply report card paycheck to a monthly personal budget
- adjust budget to fit paycheck
- identify ways to improve either budget or paycheck by adjusting budget or report card
- name ways to improve report card

Materials:
Copies of report cards
Report Card Paycheck Worksheet—½ sheet
Report Card Paycheck conversion sheet
Computer
TV/VCR or large-screen projector
T-view

Lesson Sequence:
Stage 1: (one class period)
1. Ask students:
   - Why do people work? Write answers on board.
   - What do employers look for in an employee? List on the board.
   - Identify those traits that are also helpful in school and have students state the area of the report card that reflects that trait.
2. Ask students: What is your job now as a _____ grader? Make list.
   What is your "pay" for doing job now? (How do you know how you're doing?)
   How is your report card like a paycheck?
3. Use the Career Pyramid illustration for discussion of how their years of education build the foundation for their career.

Continued

Continued

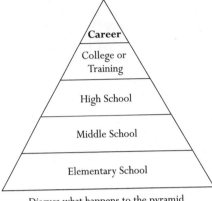

Discuss what happens to the pyramid
when a level is not as strong

Stage 2: (one class period)
1. Pass out report card copies; have students circle last nine weeks' grades,
   conduct, and attendance.
2. Using report card, fill in Report Card Paycheck Worksheet.
3. Using RCPW, fill in Report Card Paycheck conversion sheet; do
   calculations.
4. Take monthly net income and place on Budget spreadsheet.
5. Discuss budget, e.g., how to adjust amounts realistically and other options
   of improving report card.
6. Goal Setting: Take students through the goal-setting process to achieve the
   needed changes discussed in #6 on their report card.

Name: _____

Report Card Paycheck Worksheet

Number of :

(Grades)	(Conduct)	(2nd Period Absences)
_____A's	_____E's	_____
_____B's	_____S's	_____
_____C's	_____N's	_____
_____D's	_____U's	_____
_____F's		

SOURCE: Grant (1997). For more information regarding this project, contact Grant directly at dcgrant@stic.net.
(Chapter 3 in Peterson and González's *Career Counseling Models for Diverse Populations* is a program for middle
school.)

Name: _____

Report Card Paycheck Worksheet

(Grades)	(Conduct)	(2nd Period Absences)
_____A's	_____E's	_____
_____B's	_____S's	_____
_____C's	_____N's	_____
_____D's	_____U's	_____
_____F's		

Report Card Paycheck

Number of:

Grades

	A's	×	$250	=	_____	
_____	B's	×	$175	=	_____	
_____	C's	×	$125	=	_____	
_____	D's	×	$75	=	_____	
_____	F's	×	−$100	=	_____	**Total Grades: $**_____
			Total:	$	_____	

Conduct

	E's	×	$50	=		
_____	S's	×	$25	=		
_____	N's	×	−$25	=		
_____	U's	×	−$50	=	_____	**Total Conduct: $**_____
			Total:	$	_____	

Second period absences (place a "1" in the appropriate blank)

_____	0–2	$300	
_____	3–6	$150	
_____	7–more −$100	_____	**Total Absences: $**_____
	Total:	$ _____	

Total Monthly Paycheck: $_____

Yearly Salary: (Total Monthly × 12) $_____

Continued

BUDGET

	PROJECTION	AUG.	SEPT.	OCT.	NOV.	DEC.	JAN.	FEB.	MARCH	APRIL	MAY
Income:											
Net Income											
Expenses:											
House:											
mortgage/rent/taxes	$450.00										
electric/gas/water	$80.00										
phone	$25.00										
long distance	$25.00										
Total	$580.00										
Laundry/Dry cleaning	$50.00										
Food	$250.00										
Entertainment	$100.00										
Gas	$100.00										
Vacation	$75.00										
Storage	$25.00										
Christmas	$80.00										
Auto Insur./Deductible	$175.00										
Auto Repair	$40.00										
Medical/Dental insurance & bills	$75.00										
Clothing	$40.00										
Gifts	$17.00										
Total	$1,027.00										
Loan payments	$200.00										
Total	$200.00										
Totals	$1,227.00										
Surplus/Deficit											

Assessments for Middle School

1. Interest, Determination, Exploration, and Assessment System (IDEAS)
2. Career Assessment Inventory (CAI)
3. EXPLORE
4. Myers Briggs Type Inventory (MBTI) for adolescents

This information is used to assist in scheduling classes for high school.

At-Risk Students Because there are students in increasing numbers who are "at-risk" of dropping out of school, we address the particular situations of these students. Basic to the success of any program for at-risk students is addressing the students' basic needs (see Maslow), to get them motivated and interested in career development activities. For a variety of reasons, some students may not finish high school; earlier intervention may encourage the completion of high school requirements. Walz and Bleuer (1992) report low self-esteem as a common factor in at-risk students. Other contributing factors are substance abuse, underachievement (may be learning or emotionally disabled), teen pregnancy, and violence and crime (Kuczynski, 1997).

An eight-week program by Kuczynski for at-risk students in the eighth grade includes a workbook and other materials and is outlined briefly here. Beginning in Week One, complete demographic information about the students, including information about living situation, educational level of parents, grandparents, or guardians. Read and discuss *Dropping Out of School*. Complete IDEAS Survey. In Week Two go over test results of IDEAS. Research five occupations in which they have interests in the *Occupational Outlook Handbook* (hard copy or disk). Start exercises in the workbook *What Do You Want to do When You Grow Up?* Complete Interest Inventory Checklist. In Week Three go to a Career Resource Center to examine college catalogues, including vo-tech schools, community colleges, colleges and universities, financial aid programs, entrance requirements. Complete information sheet on the above data. Plan a visit to one of the institutions. In Week Four emphasize motivational considerations. Several possibilities, such as a video like "You Deserve It" and others show role models for various populations. Discuss motivation, training, education, work ethics, and goals. In Week Five read a two-page summary of the film or other resource used in the previous week and complete the questionnaire "What Can You Do Now to Get Where You Want to Be? In Week Six complete parts two and three of the workbook. Complete the interview sheet for the next week. In Week Seven discuss the information from the interviews. Complete the Happy/Success exercise. In Week Eight schedule a field trip to a state prison for a program called Project Reality, a look at the consequences of dropping out of school and engaging in a life of crime.

Practical Applications

Gender Differences
Academic performance cannot be artificially separated from future occupational considerations for adolescents, especially for young women. Research in cognitive development and learning shows that as early as the first grade, females perform better than males on reading comprehension and writing tests; by adolescence, males perform better on math, science, and most social studies tests (Byrnes, 1996). Even when ability in math and science is the same for adolescent females and males, confidence levels are often higher for males than for females (American Association of University Women [AAUW], 1991; Orenstein, 1994). This confidence gap also is apparent in higher career aspirations expressed by adolescent males than females:

> There is a circular relationship between liking math and science, self-esteem, and career interests. . . . Because of the differences in the ways adolescent women and men think about math and science, the influence of teachers on young women and their self-esteem and careers is particularly strong. (AAUW, 1991, p. 15)

The AAUW's observation regarding teacher influence on young women's career aspirations reinforces our opinion that *all* teacher education majors should take a required course in career development. Boys' dominance in the classroom can create a

---

Additional resources for this program include Goldentyer (1994), the Interest Determination, Exploration, and Assessment System (IDEAS) (1990), and Sagor (1993). (Chapters 4 and 5 in Peterson and González's *Career Counseling Models for Diverse Populations* are a program for at-risk students.)

Rural Students To offer descriptive data on the differences in career interests between adolescents at the beginning and end of the fourth stage of vocational development (e.g., knowledge of skills necessary to seek and obtain jobs [see Table 9.2]), Hall, Kelly, and Van Buren (1995) studied eighth-grade students, primarily from rural settings. Research participants consisted of 986 students (508 female, 478 male; 592 rural, 394 urban).

Results suggest concern for the future personal and economic well-being of rural students. These students exhibit relatively low interest in investigative and

kind of passivity on the part of girls' class participation, especially in the middle school years, so that young women become passive observers to the learning process rather than competent participants (Orenstein, 1994).

An increased awareness on the part of teachers, especially math and science instructors, about how young men are reinforced more than young women to participate in class, even disruptively, could have a dramatic impact on how our youth are educated and their related occupational paths, since many adolescent young women do not pursue occupations that require math and/or science.

Parents will find practical assistance about how to enhance their daughters' confidence and self-esteem in Bingham and Stryker (1995), Elium and Elium (1994), and Marone (1988). Brzowksy (1998) provides information on how parents can prevent their daughters from being shortchanged when it comes to computers and technology, which are nontraditional occupations for women.

Ethnic Differences
Academic performance also impacts the occupational achievement of multicultural populations. Research on cognitive development and learning shows that, across all subject areas—reading, writing, math, science, and social studies—"White students perform substantially better than both African-American and Hispanic students, and Hispanics perform slightly better than African-American students" (Byrnes, 1996, p. 266). Among adolescent females, African Americans show more pessimism "about both their teachers and their schoolwork than . . . [White or Hispanic] girls" (Orenstein, 1994, p. xvii).

social occupations, areas of significant job growth in the next decade. The relatively high interest of rural students in realistic occupations is a sector of the labor market in which no job growth is expected (Berman & Cosca, 1992). Given this combination of individual interests and labor market growth, rural students are most likely to find future employment opportunities in enterprising and conventional occupations in the service sector, where the greatest number of jobs will be created. Most of these jobs, with the exception of managerial positions, do not pay as much as those that will be created in the investigative and social interest areas. Rural students will be economically disadvantaged in tomorrow's job market relative to students from urban areas. There needs to be further study on the fourth stage of vocational development. Particularly intriguing are questions of when compromise begins and how economic and labor market realities are reflected in personal interests (Hall et al., 1995).

Post, Williams, and Brubaker (1996) conducted a study in which gender differences in rural eighth grade student's curricular, career, and lifestyle expectations were examined. Boys and girls both have equal interest in careers, plan to work, expect success, and take science courses with about the same regularity. A larger number of girls, however, plan to go to college, want to work with people instead of things, expect to make allowances in their work life in order to have children, are more likely to consider nontraditional occupations, and are more strongly influenced by their mother's work life.

High School

The U.S. Department of Labor's (1991) Special Commission on Achieving Necessary Skills (SCANS) lists the competencies necessary to prepare students with the skills for transitioning into the world of work after high school or college. The goal of SCANS is for teachers and counselors to incorporate these skills into the curriculum so that students will learn to reason and think on their own.

The skills identified by the SCANS report comprise five competencies and a three-part foundation of skills and personal qualities needed for solid job performance. The five competencies include:

1. *workers' productive use of resources*—that is, allocating time, money, materials, space, and staff;
2. *interpersonal skills*—working on teams, teaching others, serving customers, leading, negotiating and working well with people from culturally diverse backgrounds;
3. *information*—acquiring and evaluating data, organizing and maintaining files, interpreting and communicating, and using computers to process information;
4. *systems*—understanding social, organizational and technological systems, monitoring and correcting performance, and designing or improving systems; and
5. *technology*—selecting equipment and tools, applying technology to specific tasks, and maintaining and troubleshooting technologies (United States Department of Labor, Special Commission on Achieving Necessary Skills, 1991, Appendix B).

The three-part foundational skills and personal qualities include:

1. *basic skills*—reading, writing, arithmetic, and mathematics, speaking and listening;
2. *thinking skills*—thinking creatively, making decisions, solving problems, seeing things in the mind's eye, knowing how to learn and reasoning; and

3. *personal qualities*—individual responsibility, self-esteem, sociability, self-management and integrity (U.S. Department of Labor, Special Commission on Achieving Necessary Skills, 1991, Appendix C).

While much of the research and many of the programs developed for high school have focused on college-bound students, recent emphasis has included students who do not go on to college. We have three major concerns. First, that occupational and career planning become an integral part of the curriculum in schools. Second, that curricula have the flexibility to allow students to follow most closely matched career goals and opt for the training that meets those goals, including postsecondary education of all types if applicable. Third, that an occupational/career center primarily for students going from school to work be established to aid in the planning and transition involved in this process.

Basic Occupational/Career Counseling Tasks in High School Each academic year should include specific units that prepare high school students for occupational goals. Wood (1990) describes a four-day career preparation unit for ninth graders that involves completing a self-scoring interest survey and interpretation of the results, choosing careers to research further, and planning a tentative schedule of classes for the next three years. The advantages of this program would acquaint counselors and students with available resources and help students and teachers clarify goals and how to meet them in the classroom.

Tenth grade provides the opportunity for students to broaden their understanding of a life plan. The PLAN program from ACT, Inc., is one of the computerized programs that systematically guides the student through curriculum and training. Family influences, parental involvement, and timelines are helpful to high school sophomores. Eleventh grade is typically when students take precollege tests such as the ACT or SAT to determine further educational goals. Additional help can come from personality and values assessments. Volunteering, firsthand observations, shadowing, and part-time jobs are possible learning tools for this age group. Seniors are at the decision-making point, whether it be college, vo-tech training, on-the-job training, or work. Guidance in decision-making is an integral part of the counselor's role, and skills to implement plans need to be emphasized. Information from knowledge and understanding gained each year should be organized so students can develop a beginning profile that includes ability, interests, values, and personality factors.

School to Work The William T. Grant Foundation's Commission on Youth and America's Future makes policy recommendations from existing research regarding the problems students currently are facing. The commission has found that students planning to enter the workforce with a high school diploma and no specific training or skills have fewer economic opportunities available to them. This lack of opportunity has created many problems for students, for which several programs have been developed, two of which are the Job Training Partnership Program and the Youth Opportunities Demonstration Act. Both offer students opportunities not previously available. "Society needs to recognize the important role which youth can play as good citizens by providing opportunities for them to give needed services in the community" (Haggerty, 1989, p. 321).

Herr (1995) specifically suggests approaches and activities that counselors can use with "employment bound" youth. He expresses concerns that most systems (parents, schools, peers, and media) tend to work more with college-bound students at the expense of students who will need or want to find employment upon completion of high school. These latter students particularly need to learn the basic skills described in the SCANS report. Gray and Herr (1995) observe the "mismatch between projected demand and supply of credentialed college graduates when one looks at data from selected occupations" (p. 74). Table 9.6. demonstrates this.

Table 9.6 shows more future openings in fields other than professional. To facilitate planning for the school-to-work student, we have included current thinking regarding possibilities, an example of programs, and considerations for special groups.

The K-Mart Employment for Youth (KEY) program was evaluated to ascertain if the curriculum developed proved to be helpful in the confidence level of the participants, especially as it related to job skill competencies. "The curriculum consists of the following components: (a) attaining a job, (b) dressing for success, (c) job-interviewing skills, (d) job-retention skills, (e) assertiveness training, (f) career planning, (g) team building, (h) conflict management skills, (i) merchandise strategies, and (j) store operational procedures" (Lingg, 1996, pp. 264–65). The purpose of the program was to teach skills to chronically unemployed minority teenagers. Results demonstrated that the students who completed the ten-week course were more confident about planning and developing their careers to find a job than students who did not complete the course. While this involved minority youth, it also has implications for a type of training that is needed by any teenager who is chronically unemployed and can be targeted as an at-risk student in high school.

The Southern Regional Education Board's (SREB) High Schools That Work program is the nation's largest and fastest-growing effort to combine academic courses and modern career/technology studies to raise the achievement of high school students in general and career/tech studies. The program is based on the belief that students and career/technology programs of study can master complex academic and technical concepts if schools create an environment that encourages students to make the effort to succeed.

TABLE 9.6 Projected Average Annual Job Openings: 1990–2005

	OPENINGS	NUMBERS OF CREDENTIALS AWARDED	NET OPENINGS
Professional Managerial			
Executive, Administration	436,000	506,830	−70,830
Construction Managers	7,000	825	+6,175
Marketing, Advertising, and			
Public Relations Managers	23,000	66,416	−43,416
Professional Specialty	*623,000*	*1,120,063*	*−497,063*
Physical Scientists	8,000	35,163	−27,163
Lawyers	52,000	85,611	−16,308
Technical			
Technicians	183,000	212,767	−29,767
Health	79,000	71,804	+7,196
Engineering	52,000	85,611	−33,611
Blue-Collar, Technical			
Craft, Precision Metal, and			
Specialized Repair	455,000	133,057	+321,943
Mechanics, Installers, Repairers	160,000	91,758	+68,242
Service Occupation	*882,000*	*237,062*	*+644,938*
Operators, Laborers	*447,000*	*41,504*	*+435,496*
Farming, Forestry, Fishing	*90, 000*	*14,547*	*+75,453*

SOURCE: Gray & Herr (1995), p. 75.

Another program, "Counseling for High Skills: Vo-Tech Career Options," which is funded by the DeWitt Wallace Readers Digest Fund, is administered by Kansas State University. "The overriding basic goal of this project is to increase significantly the percentage of high school students not bound for four-year colleges who (a) enroll in some kind of postsecondary vo-tech educational program, and (b) secure employment in the primary labor market in jobs related to the educational programs they pursued" (Hoyt, Hughey & Hughey, 1995, p. 11). The success of this program will depend on helping high school counselors use the data and they in turn assisting high school students make decisions to attend post-secondary vo-tech educational programs.

Apprenticeship Programs Hoyt (1994) suggests that as America's occupational society moves from secure lifetime jobs to flexibility,

the popularity of both work-based learning in general and youth apprenticeship in particular is growing rapidly. . . . The need to counsel persons
regarding a variety of forms of postsecondary education is growing rapidly. The counseling profession should become actively involved in meeting this need with respect to all forms of work-based learning. The challenges are especially great with respect to youth apprenticeship programs.
(p. 216)

Mentoring programs are a challenging new idea (Hoyt, 1994), while youth
work-based learning is increasingly affecting the field of career development.
The changing nature of work and the need for better-educated workers have
led the charge for both work-based learning and youth apprenticeships. Clearly,
in order for the U.S. to compete in the global economy, shifting from low-skills/
low-wages to a highly-skilled/high-wages population is critical. However, such
a shift, which undoubtedly causes worker displacement, necessitates a more active and earlier involvement for career development practitioners in this decision-making process.

Nontraditional Vocational Education McKenna and Fererro (1991) found
that nontraditional vocational education is still not widely accepted and suggest
ideas for alerting more high school students to the possibilities in vocational
education by (a) finding ways to make the public more aware of nontraditional
programs, (b) incorporating information into the curriculum, (c) encouraging
school districts to develop programs for nontraditional work as a means of improving income levels in the community, (d) promoting visits by workers in
nontraditional jobs, and (e) encouraging all teachers and counselors to present
information in nonstereotypical gender terms.

Relevance for Multicultural and Diverse Populations

Women. **Sexism** in the schools remains a formidable barrier to occupational
development. Sadker and Sadker (1994) pinpoint the dilemma faced by young
women in high school.

> Many . . . [young women] think that being bright is in conflict with be-
> ing popular. To go to the prom with the right date, to be a cheerleader, to
> be chosen as most popular, to be elected class officer—such is the stuff of
> high school dreams. High academic success is not always congruent with
> these new priorities. (p. 101)

At this age, a young woman's intellectual achievement may intimidate her peers,
particularly young men. No one wants to be perceived as uncool, and such pressure to be popular pushes too many young women out of advanced math and

Practical Applications

Practitioners need to assist youth to participate in mentoring and apprenticeship programs, thereby encouraging younger adolescents (tenth graders) to be aware of career options. Dialogue with business and community leaders could lead to developing cooperatives to make job apprenticeships available upon high school graduation. Practitioners should realize that students are more likely to make decisions based more on what mentors say than what counselors advise (Hoyt, 1994). Regardless of community participation, educators must focus on students' acquisition of several kinds of skills including "(a) . . . adaptive skills that will enable them to change with change, . . . (b) work skills identified in the SCANS Report (1991), and . . . (c) . . . work values . . ." (Hoyt, p. 222).

High school counselors should organize career counseling activities that assist students in moving from an explicit setting of values to an implicit use of those values in evaluating alternatives. Career activities also need to stimulate thoughts about the person's own particular decision-making style. One practical way of accomplishing this task would be to develop instruments that would provide feedback to students on how they frame a decision (Cochran, 1983b), with the understanding that families remain a powerful influence on career decisions.

science courses. Curricular choices made at this stage may prevent later access to further training in science and technology, or as Sadker and Sadker note, "[Young women in] high school . . . who avoid these courses are making their first career move, and most of them don't even know it" (p. 101).

Ethnic Differences. Mau (1995) studied minority students' ideas about educational planning, aspirations, and achievements. Regarding educational planning he found African–American students generally were more active than White students in using counselors to plan for careers. It was unclear if this was counselor-initiated or student-initiated. More significantly, the study found that students were much more likely to go to peers for career planning and information than to counselors or teachers. The need for counselors to include peers in the counseling process becomes obvious.

Practical Applications

The Understanding Adolescence Study (Taylor, Gilligan & Sullivan, 1995) of multicultural young women at risk for early motherhood and school dropout has practical applications for the occupational development of such populations. Broadly speaking, the researchers' goal was to bring young women "into psychology as first-person narrators so that women's and girls' voices can directly inform theories of human development" (p. 6). More specifically, the researchers found that, across different racial and ethnic groups, when the young women imagine their future, "they describe job or career goals first and mention marriage, family, or other significant relationships second, or not at all" (p. 177). Obstacles to future career plans were said by many young women to take the form of relationships.

The specific relationships they refer to are those with a spouse or male partner and with children. While a few . . . [young women] cite "money" or "grades" as potential problems, the most common answers to the question of what might get in the way [of future plans] are "kids," "a boy," "getting married too soon," or simply "getting married." Obstacles to future career plans include not only the obvious one of pregnancy but also relationships formed too soon after high school, before careers and jobs are well under way. (p. 177, quotations in original)

Aspirations are more likely to part company with expectations for poor and working-class young women than for middle-class and

---

In the area of educational aspirations, Mau (1995) found that Hispanic and Native American students generally had lower aspirations. Students who had better academic achievement, regardless of race or ethnicity, also had higher aspirations. The importance of recognizing within-group differences—whether ethnic, gender, or achievement levels—is emphasized as well. Understanding external barriers of bias, stereotyping and discrimination, and internal barriers of aspirations, motivation, and self-esteem will add to the effectiveness of counselors (Mau, 1995).

Youth with Disabilities. Lichtenstein (1998) writes about high school work experience and later success in the workforce or in college.

The relationship between high school work experience and later success in the labor force or in college is being debated in the popular press, at

affluent young women. Poor and working-class young women are more likely to see a dichotomy between "relationships or 'being single with a job'" (p. 186, quotations in original).

Taylor et al. (1995) note that to listen to young women requires adults' learning how to do so and recognizing resistance to do so. The learning part entails adults' overcoming limited understandings of the meanings of cultural and class experiences as they impact a young woman's family life, relationships, education, and future opportunities. The recognizing resistance part entails adults' willingness to deal with a young woman's questions and statements that adults would prefer not to hear. Young women who are "socially marginalized because of their class, race, ethnic background, or sexual orientation" (p. 193) are most apt to have their voices stifled or negated by adults who would

rather not deal with painful realities. We wonder if this is why vocational psychology has not launched a strong and authoritative response that addresses the occupational development of adolescent females, especially poor and working-class young women.

Women often lack job skills and occupational information (Rea-Poteat & Martin, 1991). A ten-day summer career exploration program, "Taking your place: Exploring technology and tomorrow," emphasizes career possibilities and self-image for adolescent girls. Using visits to women at work in a nontraditional setting, hands-on opportunities, and counseling, the program has been effective in opening these young women's minds to occupational possibilities. A workbook titled *CHOICES: A teen woman's journal for self-awareness and personal planning* (Bingham, Edmonson & Stryker, 1994) was used in the program.

school board meetings, and even in the academic literature. The debate centers on the time constraints that are imposed on students who combine school and work. The concern is that jobs held by youth and young adults results in less time devoted to studying and homework, and thus in lowering academic performance and postsecondary education aspirations. (p. 15)

Work during high school most often becomes a problem when a young person is employed more than twenty hours a week. For youth with disabilities, obtaining employment opportunities during high school is even more difficult. The greatest obstacles await young women with disabilities. Compared to young men with disabilities, young women with disabilities are less likely to finish high school, less likely to find jobs if they do finish school, and more likely to have jobs in low-wage service occupations. Furthermore, the wage gap between disabled young women and disabled young men is greater than their nondisabled counterparts.

Syzmanski (1998) proposes an ecological approach to assist youth with disabilities from diverse backgrounds in the transition from school to work. "According to the ecological model, career development is determined by the dynamic interaction of individual, contextual, mediating, environmental, and outcome constructs with congruence, decision-making, developmental, socialization, allocation, and chance processes" (p. 127). Among the ecological considerations for transitioning, *individual constructs* include aptitudes, abilities, and interests. *Contextual influences* on occupational development include family background, socioeconomic status—especially poverty and poor schools, limited work opportunities, and war. Individual and social *mediating constructs* include work personality, self-efficacy, outcome expectations, acculturation, and racial identity. *Environmental constructs* refer to (a) work environment (e.g., skill requirements and reinforcers, employee's work interests, occupational structure, workplace organizational structure, the labor market), and (b) the physical nature of the workplace (e.g., architectural design, job accommodation). *Outcome constructs* include **job satisfaction, work adjustment, job stress, discrimination,** and prejudice. The process of *congruence* refers to the person by environment fit (PxE). *Career decision-making* especially needs to be nurtured during the school-to-work transition for youth with disabilities. *Developmental process* refers to career maturity. The *socialization process* is "important to examine [so as to assess] the extent to which [disabled] students have been socialized to expect or pursue less than their potential" (p. 135). *Allocation* refers to the gatekeeping process/role played by parents, teachers, counselors, and personnel directors. *Chance processes* include unforeseen events and the importance of planning skills for disabled students to capitalize on chance.

Hanley-Maxwell, Pogoloff, and Whitney-Thomas (1998) consider families to be at the heart of the school-to-work transition process for youth with disabilities. Several barriers to family involvement exist. (1) There can be a family lack of knowledge, personal resources, authority and power, and communication. (2) Practitioners' perceptions of appropriate family involvement can be limiting. (3) It can be useful to determine the extent to which the family has been discouraged in the past regarding involvement in educational decisions. (4) Confused expectations can complicate matters. (5) Other demands and commitments can limit a family's opportunity to participate. (6) Usual family stresses can impede involvement in a disabled student's transition. Family involvement in transition can be supported through relationship building (including the highlighting of family expertise), getting to know the family (including characteristics, life cycle stage), restructuring role (including parents and families as collaborators, assessors, and policy makers), and through exchanging information (including information resources).

Practical Applications

Rusch and Millar (1998) offer the following critique of transitioning practices. "Complete consensus has not been achieved within our society on what constitutes desirable postschool outcomes for all youth as a result of an effective education" (p. 42). The authors add "Although numerous . . . [vocational education programs for youth with disabilities] have been attempted, few have been rigorously evaluated or researched to determine effective practices or their impact on student postschool outcomes" (p. 52). The School to Work Opportunities Act of 1994, which was intended to aid transitioning, is reviewed by Cobb and Neubert (1998). The Act's implementation is further discussed by Seigel (1998). Comprehensive transition assessment and evaluation of students with disabilities is examined by Thurlow and Elliott (1998).

PARENTING PROGRAMS FOR CAREER AWARENESS

Parents are an important force in the career development process of adolescents (Trusty, Watts & Crawford, 1996). Penick and Jepsen (1992) found family functioning variables to be stronger predictors of career development than gender, socioeconomic status, and educational achievement. Parents, therefore, may be high school students' most valuable career development resource. Formal programs can be developed to assist parents of minority students in communicating to teachers and counselors their academic expectations for their sons and daughters (Atkinson, Morten & Sue, 1993). These programs can be used by counselors to encourage parents to view educational choices in a realistic fashion, to help parents communicate these views to their children and understand the curricular options and consequences of various academic choices (Commission on Precollege Guidance and Counseling, 1986).

Deciding what to do with one's life can be very frightening when it is first encountered in adolescence (Yost & Corbishley, 1987). As adolescents begin to gain a concrete sense of who they are, they enter a critical period. The development of ego identity is crucial to normal maturation, as inadequate identity formation results in self-doubt and role confusion (Erikson, 1963). A central aspect of ego identity development, particularly in our culture, involves answering the question, "What work will I do in my life?" The primacy of vocation is evident when new acquaintances immediately ask what it is that we "do" after learning our name. The maturity that adolescents need to choose a career direction and obtain secure employment requires integrating the self into a fused identity (Marcia, 1966). Certainly parents often provide a valuable and positive influence in helping their children decide what to pursue in the work world. There may also exist a negative aspect of parental influence when parental encouragement is overzealously applied and becomes a pressurized demand for success (Grotevant & Cooper, 1988). And parental encouragement may only focus on a limited range of acceptable alternatives that can thwart an adolescent's career exploration and choice.

Just as awareness of positive parental involvement has implications for career counselors, so does awareness of potential negative parental involvement. The discovery of incompatible wishes, goals, and choices between adolescents and parents presents an extremely sensitive situation requiring high-level skills and understanding by the counselor. The immediate priority is to provide the adolescent with support for the difficult, uncomfortable, and perhaps anxiety-producing situation. The adolescent can be led to understand that confusion is a normal and understandable reaction to such a predicament. At this point, the task is to inquire about the student's wishes. Does he or she want to confront or avoid parental demands or overinvolvement concerning his or her career decision-making process? Would family counseling be appropriate? The counselor's primary role is to help the adolescent decide on what is right for him/her. These sometimes painful but maturing decisions assist the adolescent in his/her transition into adulthood.

Another concern pertains to the parents who are not presently involved in assisting their adolescents with career decision-making. Can they be significantly motivated to become involved? Are there specific factors that are influential in motivating parents to become involved? In what ways might parents be most effective facilitators of their adolescent's career development?

An impressive amount of career growth and maturity is possible when parents work together with their adolescent children with the added value of the parents clarifying their own career concerns and improve family communication. Adolescents want and need guidance for their future (Middleton & Loughead, 1993).

The Effect of Family Interactions   There is no doubt about the relationship between family interactions and children's career development. Parents often want to assist their children in career decisions, but frequently do not have the knowledge and skills to encourage effective career decisions. Otto and Call (1985) have found that involving parents in the career-decision process is a visible way to respond to the public expectation that schools assist young people in making career plans.

Kush and Cochran (1993) tested the effectiveness of a "Partners Project" for parents to help their adolescent children develop increasing responsibility regarding a career. By providing a situation that is accepting and encouraging, parents can help (1) adolescents understand motives; (2) develop goals based on that understanding; (3) formulate plans based on the goals; (4) work to accomplish them over time; and (5) keep a sense of responsibility, "taking ownership for motives, goals, plans, actions, and consequences" (p. 435). They applied this to a standard career counseling strategy, emphasizing self-responsibility in an encouraging environment. In comparison with a control group, students who completed the "Partners Project" showed "an enhanced sense of agency regarding career. More certainty in career direction and less indecision indicate greater confidence. More career salience and crystallization of ego identity indicate more meaningful motivation, a basis for self determination in career" (p. 437).

Whiston (1989) describes a group for parents with a focus on maximum parental involvement in their children's career development. The group is designed to be a blend of traditional career exploration and family dynamics techniques. Parents who participated in this group report that they gain insight into the complexity of effective career decision-making and communication patterns within their families. Often the parents report that this group assists in a better overall relationship with their children.

The focus is on maximum involvement by parents in their children's career exploration. Family interactions are strengthened when parents understand from the beginning that the emphasis will be on parental expectations and behaviors. When parents identify their own interests and then indicate what are their children's interests; this is a worthwhile exercise for increasing the parent's insight about themselves and their children. From a **family systems** orientation, exploration of family values can lead to an analysis of roles, boundaries, values, traditions, and messages that have a bearing on their children's abilities to look at career options. A caution for parents is that even though they want to be sure their child selects the correct career, their emphasis should be on supporting their gathering of information, allowing them autonomy in taking responsibility for the search. Parents often are unfamiliar with the process of career search and may have unrealistic expectations about career decisions (Whiston, 1989). It is easier to encourage parents to become involved in family counseling when the concerns are centered on their involvement in their child's career concerns. An interesting side benefit is that some parents have been able to clarify their own career concerns in the process.

Parent Intentions Young and Friesen (1992) studied the intentions of parents when they attempt to influence the career development of their children. They developed ten categories of intentions.

Practical Applications

Hoare (1991) and Ramirez (1991), in concurrent studies, state that parents of public school seniors appear to regard schools, school counselors, and people working in their teen's particular field of interest as their best sources of career development information, especially if they have been contacted at least once by the school. Evidence seems to point toward a greater reliance on particular personal resources— spouse/partner, person working in the field, or peers for higher SES groups, and a greater reliance on public resources and relatives for lower SES groups. Parent's perceptions of career information resources differ by race—parents from non-White cultures tended to rely more on family and friends.

The studies cited indicate that the school and the school counselor are influential career information sources, which provides an important opportunity to impact families, especially those of minority and low-income backgrounds. Given the many demands on counselor's time, a group or seminar approach for parents may be the most effective strategy. Moreover, professionals need to be accessible, knowledgeable, and current regarding career information and should be able to lead parents to other available resources. School counselors should pay special attention to parents of students interested in the military and self-owned occupational groups because these parents rate school counselors lowest (Trusty & Watts, 1996).

1. skill acquisition such as a mother monitoring the study habits of her teenage son to help him develop study skills or a father teaching his daughter photography as a possible occupational choice,

2. acquisition of specific values or beliefs,

3. protection from undesirable experiences,

4. increase independent thinking or action,

5. decreased sex role stereotyping among boys and girls,

6. foster good parent-child relationship by discussing their relationship with their children, by changing ground rules between the parent and child as the child matures,

7. facilitation of human relationships (getting along with others, encouraging helpful relations among siblings),

8. enhancement of character development (including child's self image and self confidence),

9. development of personal responsibility, and

10. achievement of parent's own goals and needs.

The content of the intentions suggests that some parents attempt to develop a wide range of skills and attitudes in their children, believing this will enhance their children's career aspirations and thus they will make decisions consistent with those aspirations. Other parents believed that if the child is happy and well adjusted and can engage in satisfactory relationships, then the child's specific career development will be based on important personal characteristics (Young & Friesen, 1992).

Parents are concerned about how their children feel about themselves and want them to be confident about their abilities. Intentions do not necessarily affect actions, but they are part of the counseling process. Parents communicate to their children through intentions, and counselors need to understand how parents use intentions to send messages to their children. "By helping parents and adolescents make intentions more explicit, counselors can begin to unpack the positive and negative baggage that individuals carry to their career lives" (Young & Friesen, 1992, p. 205).

This concludes our discussion about career development for school children. The next chapter focuses on post-secondary education.

10

Career Counseling for Adults

Part I:

Postsecondary Education

and Training

"I won't do work that hurts children."
—A PLEDGE FOR YOUNG PEOPLE TO CONSIDER WHEN
THEY GRADUATE FROM HIGH SCHOOL OR COLLEGE,
AS SUGGESTED BY MARY PIPHER (1996, P. 266).

Chapters 10 and 11 deal with various stages in adulthood. This chapter addresses people who choose to continue their education, and Chapter 11 deals with adult career decisions, changing careers, job displacement, retirement, and other considerations that occur throughout adulthood. This chapter is divided into five sections: (1) vocational/technical schools, (2) community colleges, (3) colleges and universities, (4) career counseling at the post-high school level and (5) a model for a course. Each setting requires a different emphasis or methodology of vocational career counseling.

While reading this chapter, keep in mind the overarching concerns facing adults; the National Career Development Competencies for Adults, published by the NOICC, are presented in Table 10.1.

Facing adult responsibilities can be a challenging time. Young people must make decisions that will affect the rest of their lives. They may obtain jobs that (a) provide focus for future career decisions, (b) allow time to decide career/ family options, or (c) enable a journey of self-discovery. Many post-high school adolescents are leaving home for the first time to be on their own. For some, the

TABLE 10.1 National Career Development Competencies for Adults

SELF-KNOWLEDGE

1. Skills to maintain a positive self-concept.
2. Skills to maintain effective behaviors.
3. Understanding developmental changes and transitions.

EDUCATIONAL AND OCCUPATIONAL EXPLORATION

4. Skills to enter and participate in education and training.
5. Skills to participate in work and lifelong learning.
6. Skills to locate, evaluate, and interpret career information.
7. Skills to prepare to seek, obtain, maintain, and change jobs.
8. Understanding how the needs and functions of society influence the nature and structure of work.

CAREER PLANNING

9. Skills to make decisions.
10. Understanding the impact of work on individual and family life.
11. Understanding the continuing changes in male/female roles.
Skills to make career transitions.

SOURCE: NOICC (1996), pp. 1–8.

major issue becomes survival. For others, this may be a time for idealism to pervade their worldview before the pragmatism of family and daily responsibility modify their perceptions.

VOCATIONAL/TECHNICAL SCHOOLS

The mention of vocational education sometimes triggers strong responses. Arguments for vocational education are based on the premise that "all persons are created equal," but in terms of actual abilities such is not reality. Some students have severe reading and writing difficulties that are often physical or chemical, although they may possess exceptional visiospatial coordination abilities. Ideally, all citizens would learn to read, but the truth is that some will never read well enough to attain standard educational requirements. Yet these persons may excel in mechanical skills that require strong hand–eye coordination. Major criticisms of vocational education generally center around "dumbing down" requirements and abuses in government-supported programs that yield less than effective results.

Different types of vocational education include: (a) high school vocational/technical education, (b) privately funded postsecondary vocational training,

---

Practical Applications

Over half of all high school graduates attend some form of postsecondary educational institution, including four-year colleges, community colleges, or vocational/technical schools. A primary reason for pursuing a college education is to train for a career, but only 60 percent of college graduates report being in their present career as a result of following a conscious plan (Brown & Minor, 1991). Of those adults who either did not finish college or attended a two-year institution, about 43 percent followed a conscious plan into their current careers. Approximately 15 to 20 percent of those who attended some form of postsecondary education had never used any occupational information (Brown & Minor, 1991).

While not every student pursuing postsecondary education is preparing for a career, many expect this will be the result of their education. The career development needs of these students need to be met. Nearly 60 percent of college graduates would seek more information about careers if they could do it over again, and only about 55 percent of those who graduated from college or received some college training feel that their skills are being well used in their current job (Gallup, 1989). Finally, while the number of jobs requiring a college degree is expected to increase, unemployment and underemployment among college graduates will also increase due to the oversupply of graduates and the mismatch between the education received and the actual demands of the workforce (Johnston & Packer, 1987).

(c) special education aimed at vocational rehabilitation, (d) publicly funded vocational education (which prepares people to acquire additional skills within their present job setting and/or community), and (e) other types of vocational education that vary depending on particular needs. Most practitioners do not hesitate to recommend training or education to prepare individuals for their respective roles in the workplace, but many are uncertain which type of vocational education is most appropriate. "Because of the vocational nature of these programs, students often select an area of study at the time of entry and pursue it to completion. In many instances the necessity to make an early decision has led to mistakes" (Isaacson & Brown, 1993, p. 289).

In a report to the U.S. Department of Education, the Accrediting Council for Continuing Education and Training (ACCET) (1991) noted that the schools eligible for financial aid through federally funded programs constitute the largest segment of postsecondary vocational education in the United States. The written documentation required to meet the federal regulations makes them easy to research. Most of these privately owned, accredited, postsecondary schools serve over 3,000,000 students per year at a cost of $12 to $15 billion in federally funded programs. This figure does not include student fees and fees paid to vocational schools ineligible to receive federal financial aid. Much of this money is in the form of student loans, which are to be repaid. But with defaults running as high as 70 percent in many areas, it is basically a grant program (Hall, Hayes, Morris, Rendón & Zepeda, 1993).

People entering vocational school range in age from seventeen to twenty-five. The majority of these people have no idea what to expect from vocational school. Many do not have a high school diploma and will be working on their General Education Diploma (GED) while involved in vocational training. These persons know they must do something to learn a trade, find a job, and become self-supporting.

Hall et al. (1993) compiled a list of questions that a person should ask before enrolling in a vo-tech school. The questions include:

1. What are the programs offered? (e.g., length, certificate or degree, options).

2. Is it accredited (e.g., agency, date, current standing, including temporary or provisional)?

3. How much does it cost (e.g., differences for each program, available financial assistance)?

4. What is the default rate and how is it calculated?

5. Who is on the faculty and what are their credentials?

6. What is the placement profile (e.g., specific companies who have hired graduates [ask for a list]; which programs place best, worst; how placement rates are calculated)?

7. Are career development, résumé preparation, and interview skills training offered?

8. Are tours of the school offered when students are present (e.g., apparent satisfaction of the students, conversations with students)? Ideally, information from students before seeing the campus may give more ideas of questions to ask.

9. What is the interview procedure (e.g., what is promised, allowing time for decision-making, professionalism of the personnel)?

10. What other types of information can you send (e.g., brochures or literature, commission or salary for the admissions people, appearance of facilities and size of classrooms, retention programs in existence, if equipment is current in sufficient numbers, and enrollment fluctuation)?

CASE EXAMPLE

A young woman attended a court reporting school for two years but had not graduated because she had not yet attained the speed required for a certificate. She continued attending class several hours each week and was steadily improving her speed. One day she went to the school to find all the doors were locked and a sign reading "School is Closed." There was no indication of whom to call or what to do. The school never reopened, and the other court reporting school in the city would not accept any of the credits she had earned. She lost two years of her life and was $10,000 in debt.

Usual academic requirements of a vocational instructor include a bachelor's degree. Professional experience and/or certifications may be considered in lieu of this requirement. The instructor must relate well with students and other faculty, maintain poise and a professional perspective when classroom discipline needs to be imposed, have a professional attitude at all times in the classroom, and adhere to the school's policies and procedures (Hall et al., 1993).

Since many of the vocational training schools are privately owned and often are relatively new in the community, it is a "buyer beware" situation.

COMMUNITY COLLEGES

In addition to vocational programs, many community colleges have certification or two-year associate degree programs to train people for specific occupations. The American Association of Community Colleges (AACC, 1996) reports that "community colleges have emerged as vanguard institutions in preparing workers and their companies for the challenges ahead" (p. 1). To remain competitive in the global economy, "frontline workers will be expected to have essentially the same broad set of skills previously required only of supervisors and managers" (p. 1) (all levels of workers will require advanced skills) and community colleges offer programs and certificate to gain these skills.

Three AACC Councils—COMBASE, the National Council for Continuing Education & Training, and the National Council for Occupational Education—have completed the National Workforce Development Study of employers/consumers and community college providers of workforce development programs. This National Workforce study includes the following findings: (1) Businesses of all types and sizes are served by community colleges in the United States, with concentrations in industry/manufacturing, government/public services, and health services. (2) Technological changes have increased the need for workforce development, especially computer skills. (3) Employers also desire "basic communication and computational skills, . . . , enterprise-specific skills, the ability to work with others in solving problems, and strong work ethics" (AACC, 1996, pp. 2–3). (4) Employers value community colleges for cost-effective, customized, and convenient training programs. (5) Most employers—95 percent—would recommend community colleges.

Practical Applications

Career counseling is a major role of community college counselors. Nyre and Reilly (1987) conducted a study of career counseling programs at several different community colleges in California and found that most students consider career counseling a valuable asset of the college. Unfortunately, the results of the study also showed that many students are not properly informed about what is available to them in terms of career counseling, or their expectations differ from what the actual career counseling programs have to offer. Another service of community college counseling centers is career courses, which include specific information for displaced workers, undecided majors, job search skills, students with special abilities, returning students, those who plan to go on to a college/university, and those who are seeking to go directly into jobs (Robinson, 1996).

Community colleges often have a vocational/technical component along with a college transfer program. In many states the college transfer program allows students to transfer to four-year institutions without losing credits. Students select community colleges for a variety of reasons, including (a) financial concerns, (b) remedial study, (c) the desire to determine whether post-high school study is for them, and (d) because they can earn a degree in two years. Students who have academic difficulty may also regain their eligibility to reenroll in four-year institutions by demonstrating their competencies in community college. A remarkable aspect of community colleges is their open-door admissions policy, which enables students to begin at their academic competency level and advance their education. However, this open-door policy does not extend to all programs offered in these institutions. Vocational-technical programs and nursing, accounting, and other programs have established admission standards (Isaacson & Brown, 1993).

Continued

Continued

Some major state universities have reached their capacity in the number of students they can serve and need to limit the number they admit. Some are requesting potential students to attend a community college for two years prior to transferring into the university. As a rule, if students are able to maintain a "B" average, they will be admitted to the four-year school.

Career development programs in community colleges can assist in student retention, especially those with low career maturity (Smith, 1987). Academic advisors in each department or division can identify incoming students in need of special career planning services and refer those students to the career center.

Men usually hold higher status jobs than women while in community college, and the more challenging students' college work experience is the more it affects their grades (Healy & Mourton, 1987). Higher level jobs during community college can complement course work in developing career skills and in networking. Gender differences in attempts to find jobs indicate that women might not recognize as well as men how jobs held during college relate to career development. If paid employment during college studies is important to career progress, women need to consider placing more emphasis on finding paid work while in college.

COLLEGES AND UNIVERSITIES

As a rule, colleges and universities are more selective in the students they admit. While career counseling practices are similar in all educational settings, the differences in the services offered have more to deal with the type of students in the institution and the differences in occupational goals which individuals may possess.

Nationally, an estimated 77 percent of all freshmen and sophomores are in the process of declaring an academic major (Rayman, 1993). These students need particular help to decide major fields of study. Students graduating with bachelor's degrees may need special services to determine job placement, interviewing skills, portfolio development, and other job-seeking skills. Decisions regarding graduate schools may also be involved.

Elwood (1992) proposes a pyramid model as a tool in career counseling with university students (see Figure 10.1).

To understand Figure 10.1, view the pyramid from above and look down on it. The base of the pyramid is a triangle with the three sides representing interests, abilities, and personality traits. The three ridges or edges of the pyramid that lead to the center (the self) are emotionality, intellectuality, and sexuality. Using material from Samples (1976), Elwood suggests that the intellectual ridge rep-

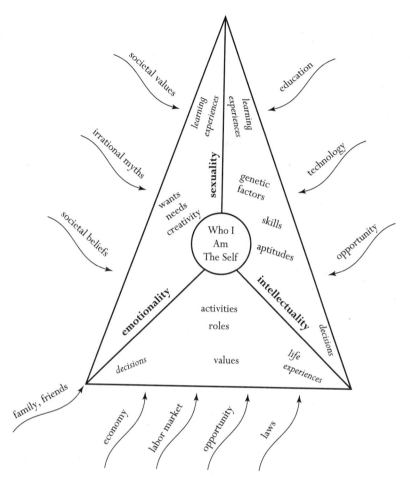

FIGURE 10.1 The Model of Career Counseling University Students
SOURCE: *Elwood, 1992, p. 52.*

resents the activities of the brain—inventing, thinking, verifying. Feeling is represented by the emotionality line. Sexuality is the holistic part of the figure with motivation that involves the whole body. Influences are pictured on all sides. The strength of the model is that all parts support the sense of self.

CAREER COUNSELING AT THE POST-HIGH SCHOOL LEVEL

While the needs of students may vary in each educational setting, vocational practitioners will need to fulfill certain duties and responsibilities in order to provide services to benefit students. Olson and Matkin (1992) provide a comprehensive list of activities which career counselors in postsecondary education and training institutions should consider.

1. Assesses people's needs.
2. Administers and/or interprets interest, personality, skills, and values assessments to persons.
3. Provides values clarification.
4. Administers and/or interprets achievement and ability assessments to individuals.
5. Counsels individuals about their personal problems.
6. Explains the roles that lifestyle and leisure play in career development.
7. Assists persons in exploration of their occupations of interest.
8. Helps persons understand the world of work.
9. Aids persons on computerized guidance programs.
10. Broadens awareness of nontraditional career opportunities.
11. Provides information on current and future job market trends.
12. Provides persons with the skills necessary to understand the interrelatedness of their career decisions and life roles.
13. Teaches persons decision-making skills.
14. Provides persons with goal-setting information.
15. Assists special populations (women, minorities, handicapped, disadvantaged, adults, etc.) in their unique career development needs.
16. Teaches skills necessary for acquiring employment.
17. Coordinates a job placement program.
18. Provides for job adjustment counseling.
19. Advises persons on study skills.
20. Provides academic advising.
21. Provides workshops on study skills.
22. Refers persons to learning center, if necessary.
23. Refers persons to in-depth personal counseling, if necessary.
24. Teaches career awareness and exploration classes.
25. Conducts group counseling for individuals in career planning.
26. Supervises career center activities.
27. Establishes program goals and objectives.
28. Coordinates the career guidance program.
29. Coordinates the purchase of occupational information.

30. Coordinates the purchase of labor market information.

31. Evaluates the effectiveness of specific career guidance activities and services.

32. Writes and distributes a career center newsletter.

33. Plans and conducts career fairs and seminars.

34. Develops and implements a public relations system.

35. Serves as a liaison between educational and community resources.

36. Conducts career workshops for staff, administrators, and teachers.

37. Consults teachers and administrators on the skills necessary to assist students in indirect career guidance.

38. Provides information on educational trends, as well as state and federal legislation that may influence career counseling.

39. Understands the process of human growth and development.

40. Understands career development theories. (pp. 332–333)

While all these activities may be related to various aspects of career counseling, not all are applicable in every setting. However, this long list begins to develop a perspective about the range of responsibilities entailed in the job, as well as the training needed to assume such a position.

Selected Findings and Applications for Career Counselors in Postsecondary Educational Institutions

Zagora and Cramer (1994) conducted a study of client/treatment interaction in a group career-counseling situation with community college students. The authors have found that when groups were homogeneous (for instance, all undecided), the learning for the participants was somewhat more effective than when they were involved in a group with mixed levels of vocational identity. In other words, it is incumbent upon the counselor to be aware of the within-group differences between students and their particular needs to best serve them.

Healy and Reilly (1989) found that older students in community colleges have fewer career needs than do younger students. Thus, different information is needed for different groups of students. Adults over thirty requested more assistance in securing work-related experiences (volunteering, networking), rather than learning decision-making skills. With an increasing number of experienced adults returning to school, counselors must be aware of their needs. At present this trend is seen more in community colleges than other postsecondary education settings, but it will likely extend into four-year institutions.

Savickas (1990) designed and tested a career exploration course that attempted to develop the following attitudes and concepts in students:

- become involved now
- choose based on how things look to you
- work: a problem or an opportunity
- conceptualize career choice
- use four aspects of self as choice bases
- explore your future
- control your future
- view work positively
- base your choice on yourself
- clear up career choice misconceptions

The course generally had a positive impact on a student's ability to engage in career decision-making and on his or her long-term perspective. Students who completed the course had more of a future time orientation.

A series of career/life planning modules developed at the University of Calgary facilitate students' concept of themselves as **active agents** in the career planning process. One of the modules, "Translating a degree into an occupation," helps graduating students identify the unique skills and personal attributes they bring as a potential employee. Liberal arts students have participated extensively in this workshop. The following principles provide the basis for the workshop:

[1.] Career planning is a developmental process that will occur throughout the lifetime of an individual. . . .

[2.] Students will understand that career development occurs during their postsecondary program as they face three major career decisions over that time, namely: choosing a program of studies, choosing occupational fields, and choosing a job. . . .

[3.] Career planning skills are necessary life skills because career development is ongoing throughout the individual's lifetime. . . .

[4.] Career planning is lifestyle planning. . . .

[5.] Clients are viewed as and assisted to become "active agents" in the process of career planning. (Crozier, 1991, pp. 100–101, quotations in original)

These modules are designed to be taken sequentially during a student's four-year university program. Although this is not a requirement, students may, with the assistance of a counselor, choose to do later modules without having completed the earlier workshops. The module format offers the presentation of sepa-

---

Career/Life Planning Model for University Liberal Arts Students

---

Module 1: A Beginning

1st & 2nd year Undergraduates	3rd & 4th year Undergraduates & Graduate Students	3rd & 4th year Undergraduates & Graduate Students
Choosing an Educational Program	Choosing Occupational Fields	Choosing a Job

---

Module 2: Exploring Yourself	Module 4: Translating a Degree into an Occupation	Module 5: Résumé Writing
Module 3: Career Research & Decision-Making		Module 6: Interview Skills/Job Search Techniques

FIGURE 10.2 An Overview of Crozier's Modules and Their Sequencing

SOURCE: *Crozier, S. D. (1991). Empowering the Liberal Arts Students with Personal Flexibility for the World of Work.* Canadian Journal of Counselling, 25, (2), p. 102.

rate units of content that are designed to meet students' needs and time requirements. An overview of the modules is shown in Figure 10.2.

The University of Calgary has also begun a mentorship program that is useful to liberal arts students. Students identify occupational areas to do an information interview. The student is then paired with an alumnus who has previously agreed to the interview. This university also has a volunteer center to place students in experiences that will suit their interests and offer them opportunities to develop skills (Crozier, 1991).

Bradley and Mims (1992) blend family systems and birth order dynamics to develop a college course for career planning entitled "Decision-making for Career Development." A brief summary of the exercises follows:

(1) A lecture on family structure with questions such as "Whom do you turn to when faced with making an important decision?" and "How has your family influenced your career/occupational choice?"

Assignment: construct a genogram of your family; identify messages, boundaries, roles, myths, rules, and relationships; share your genogram in a small group.

(2) A lecture on birth order and the Adlerian concept of striving for significance.

> Assignment: list siblings by sex from oldest to youngest, noting age spacing between each; identify what thing each sibling did best in the family. If an only child, discuss how the lack of siblings affected you.

McAuliffe and Fredrickson (1990) compared two group career decision-making courses with a comparison group on factors such as occupational certainty and satisfaction, appropriateness, and information-seeking behavior. Results were mixed, but generally participants favored the twenty-session course. The courses were based on a seven-step, decision-making model: (1) make a commitment to decision-making, (2) complete a self-assessment, (3) generate alternatives, (4) seek information, (5) choose an occupation, (6) make plans, and (7) take action.

The short-term class covered only the first four steps. The long-term treatment added explicit choosing, planning, and action strategies and further emphasized social learning and behavioral counseling principles. Both courses used the Strong-Campbell Interest Inventory (SCII) (Strong, Campbell & Hansen, 1981), values clarification activities, skills identification, and exploration of printed materials for generating career options and information. On the first and last days of class, the following were measured: (a) certainty about occupational and educational plans, (b) congruence of occupational preference, (c) frequency of information seeking, and (d) knowledge of decision-making. Thus, subjective and objective, cognitive and behavioral, and content and process measures were used.

Generally, this study confirms the value of career planning groups, as evidenced by both treatment groups' significant gains on certainty, satisfaction with plans, and information-seeking behavior. This contrasts with the absence of gains from the control group. These results parallel previous research, which has shown group career counseling to have a positive impact on career decision makers and these findings encourage the continued development of group career counseling models (McAuliffe & Fredrickson, 1990).

Luzzo's (1996) study examined "the relationship between perceived occupational barriers and the Career Decision Making (CDM) attitudes, knowledge of CDM principles, and CDM Self-Efficacy of college students." He used his study as a way of building on previous research in order to clarify "the role that perceived barriers play in the CDM process" (p. 240). Results of his study show that college students who think they will have to overcome many obstacles in the future have more problems in the CDM process because they have less confidence in their ability to make effective decisions than the students who do not see as many barriers. Interestingly, those who "perceive they have overcome family-related barriers in the past have developed more mature CDM attitudes and . . . [have gained more] confidence in their ability to make effective career decisions" (p. 246). Luzzo suggests that discussing ways to overcome occupational barriers may be helpful to students, and refers to two "psychometrically

---

Practical Applications

By asking clients to indicate the specific barriers they believe they have successfully overcome, practitioners might emphasize such accomplishments to help clients recognize that many perceived occupational barriers are surmountable. Increased awareness might help clients develop higher levels of self-efficacy for overcoming similar occupational barriers. Practitioners might also help clients identify potential barriers to future occupational goals. Practitioners can raise student awareness regarding the difference between real and perceived barriers in the workplace.

---

sound instruments for measuring perceived barriers[:] . . . the Perceived Barriers Scale (McWhirter, 1994) and Swanson and Tokar's (1991) Career Barriers Inventory . . . " (p. 247).

Relevance for Multicultural and Diverse Populations Most existing assessment tools reflect the dominant culture of American society (Heppner & Johnston, 1993). When used with ethnic or cultural minority groups, such assessment may produce false or misleading results. Bingham and Ward (1994) report that African-American women tended to have Social as their highest Holland code through paper-and-pencil assessment, but this may simply reflect the structure of occupational opportunity rather than the types of occupations most suitable for them. The need for instruments that are free of cultural biases and stereotypical presentations is obvious and has long been recognized. Card sort techniques allow the counselor to observe the process of the client responding to the assessment (Heppner & Johnston, 1993). Focusing on the process gives the counselor more opportunity to intervene during the actual assessment (Heppner & Duan, 1995). Career counseling professionals need to become advocates for individuals and groups who face possible bias and discrimination in their pursuit of careers (Sue & Sue, 1990).

A MODEL FOR A COURSE

Drawing on experience in both community college and university settings, Nadene Peterson designed a model for a course in a community college setting. While designed for that situation, it can provide the basis for a class in any postsecondary education and training institution.

Career/Occupational Exploration The following is an example of how to begin Career Exploration using the concepts of WHO, WHY, WHAT, WHERE, and WHEN. (Counselor's note: The steps are followed by suggested assessments and tasks.)

WHO involves self-exploration

1. Interests—The Strong Interest Inventory, Self-Directed Search, Kuder DD, or Career Assessment Inventory, depending on the age or experience of the students.
2. Values—The Life Values Inventory, Rokeach Values Survey, or Values Scale.
3. Skills—Haldane's Motivated Skills Chart, *The Quick Job Hunting Map* (Bolles), Campbell Interest and Skills Survey.
4. Personal Traits—Myers-Briggs Type Inventory/Introduction to Type and Careers, *Please Understand Me* (Computer Assisted), Sixteen Personality Factor/Personal Career Development Profile, Adjective Checklist, Adjective Self-Description.
5. Life Goals—Life Goals Inventory (three different forms).

WHY involves exploring family and social influences

1. Family influences—fill out a genogram; study family relationships, such as parents, siblings, blended families, etc.
2. Social influences—use the Career Beliefs Inventory discussed in Chapter 7.

WHAT involves occupational exploration

1. Nature of work—taken from RIASEC and types of jobs, computer assisted programs, Dictionary of Occupational Titles.
2. Requirements
   a. Training
   b. Education
   c. Skills
3. Potential for Advancement
4. Employment Outlook
5. Salary and Benefits

WHEN involves decision making:

1. Using Gelatt's Decision Making model in Chapter 8,
   a. Identify alternatives
   b. List consequences for each alternative
   c. Make choice that best matches your person and environment
2. Develop a plan of action with timelines and specific goals to be met

Up to this point we have discussed "exploration," which is Phase I. Phase II takes us to entering the field (i.e., How to get a job). This involves:

1. Résumé writing/developing a portfolio
2. Interviewing skills
3. Research into the organization
   a. Identifying key personnel
   b. Learning philosophy and mission of the organization
4. Making initial contacts/using networking
5. Communicating clearly how your traits and skills match with the organization's needs and mission

Working with students who are applying for jobs requires that the practitioner as well as the client understand the parameters of this search. Locating a job may be the result of the above process, but it is also important to prepare for the role of happenstance, networking, and sheer luck or lack thereof. Realizing that career shifts are part of life is basic to keeping the flexibility that makes changes possible.

As we will see in the continuation of our look at the types of changes for which adults need to be prepared, the perspective given during the first "real job" seeking experience can prepare the young adult for the realities of the developments that shape our lives.

Career Counseling for Adults

Part II:

Career Transitions

No sooner had I learned to tell time,
than I began to arrive late everywhere.

—EDITH ANN

(WAGNER, 1994, P. 11)

Most of us constantly try to fit more time-based projects and activities into our lives than there is time. Often, the result is being slaves to deadlines and not being proactive and planning for the future. Faced with quick changes and unexpected transitions, people lack the time and energy to effectively adapt to situations. Many times, people are unaware of the problems, issues, and factors that affect the decisions they are or will be making.

In this chapter we first look at workplace issues, including gender, sexual harassment, ageism, and other concerns relevant to most jobsites, regardless of the type of work. Second, we highlight values differences between workers entering the job market and those of earlier generations. Third, we address stress at work and career burnout, which can occur when a person's work ethic creates an unexpected imbalance between work and leisure. Fourth, as the number of people to fill jobs diminishes with the new generation, ideas about retirement, older workers, and government support for aging people will become part of a national dialogue. Our hope is to further the discussion of these changes facing adults.

Consider the facts of the population. Seventy-six million babies were born in the United States between 1946 and 1964; 59 million babies will be born in the next twenty years (Schatz, 1997). Since it takes approximately 3.2 workers to support each retired person, simple math indicates that retirement as the older generation knows it will have to be rethought.

Another factor is an adequate number of people to maintain the workforce. Babyboomers will still need services for many years. Although technology has taken over many jobs once performed by people, the number of job openings will be greater than the next generation can fill. Who will do these jobs? Many babyboomers likely will be asked to continue working and provide a major resource for employers. How will this work out? What will happen to the retirement age? When the retirement age was set at age 65 in the 1930s, the average life span was 61.7 years; now the average person lives to be an octogenarian.

A third factor is the difference in values between older adults and the next generation. As a rule, the new workers are not willing to commit themselves to company loyalty at the level their parents did.

The babyboomer generation has had an incredible impact on society. How this group will affect the picture of retirement remains to be seen. Responsible occupational practitioners need to be aware of the changes and the concomitant needs of the people involved in these developments.

WORKPLACE ENVIRONMENT

Common workplace issues that affect workers' ability to operate efficiently include gender differences, sexual harassment, career plateauing and resiliency, and career development and ageism. Practitioners may assume several roles, including an outside-the-work-environment therapist, an employee assistance program team member, and/or a career development specialist within industry. Such roles require awareness of how these issues impact the workplace.

Gender Differences

During middle childhood, when considerable portions of social play time are spent in segregated groups of one's own sex, the distinctive interaction styles of all-boy and all-girl groups have implications for same-sex and cross-sex relationships that people form as they enter adolescence and adulthood (Maccoby, 1990). Different interactive styles develop in same-sex groups. Girls tend to be more concerned with issues of cooperation to maintain group functioning, so verbal exchanges serve largely to establish linkages and sustain social bonds. Boys tend to be more concerned with issues of dominance to maintain group functioning, so verbal exchanges serve largely to establish hierarchies and to protect an individual's turf. For girls, the main concern tends to be maintaining intimacy; for boys, it tends to be maintaining independence (Tannen, 1990).

These gender differences are not absolute, but a matter of degree. For the most part, males are socialized into *doing* together, females into *being* together. Considerable evidence shows that the interactive patterns found in same-sex dyads or groups in adolescence and adulthood are very similar to those that prevailed in the gender-segregated groups of childhood (Maccoby, 1990). It is difficult to identify the point in the developmental cycle at which the interactional style of girls and boys begins to diverge, or to identify the forces that cause them to diverge. Of interest here is how such behaviors carry over into the workplace (Tannen, 1994).

Men and the Success Element

"Next to the negative injunction, 'don't be like a girl'"—which in itself has misogynist undertones—"no other element is as important and universal for defining a male's role as the one that positively charges him to be a SUCCESS" (Doyle, 1989, p. 167, capitals in original). The traditional role of the male being a good provider as the primary success element for men arises from socialization into a competitive worldview. From the time most men are small boys, they are encouraged to be the best at something (e.g., the most talented academically, the most gifted athletically, the most accomplished aesthetically). A boy who is the best class clown receives at least a grudging measure of respect from his classmates, despite his disruptive behavior. Being a winner is very masculine. To be winners, most men have been socialized into the belief that they must compete.

The Competitive Worldview

Competition occurs when two or more people seek a reward that can only be achieved by one (Doyle, 1989). Young boys learn that competition is an important feature of life. Beating out the other guy becomes vital, especially because losers are not loved. A major problem with the emphasis on competition arises when men begin to see everything in their world solely in terms of competition.

This distorted worldview has at least three assumptions about what the world is really like. First, an impaired competitive spirit forces men to think that everything of worth or value in the world is limited or comes in fixed quantities. Thus, a man's masculinity can be measured as if it were a quantifiable element. In the workplace, many men translate their sense of masculinity into how much money they earn, the size and decor of their office, their job title, the number of workers they manage, and the cost and model of the car. Second, if valued things are limited, then there are just so many of them to go around. This often creates a problem in male-male relationships, where every other man becomes a potential rival for the limited and available proofs of success. Many men quickly learn ways to make their own track record look better than other's. Third, most men assume that competition is always good, never bad or neutral. Whether on the playground or in the classroom, the good thing is to be a competitor who wins. This distorted competitive spirit becomes even more warped when men believe that competitiveness and winning are exclusively male characteristics.

Many men make the mistake of believing that women do not have the same drive or ambition to succeed that men supposedly have (Doyle, 1989; Krebs, 1994). In the minds of these men, action and achievement are more likely to be synonymous with masculinity. The belief that men are competitive and that women, therefore, are cooperative, produces another problem: many men may feel that their own cooperative attempts will be perceived by others as unmanly, while many women may think that their own competitiveness will diminish their femininity in others' eyes. Some men, motivated by the fear of losing their male coworkers' respect, denigrate cooperation as a viable way of solving problems or gaining valued goals.

The Male Provider Role

Given most men's belief about being a good provider, pressures can build, particularly if that man bases his masculinity on how successfully he contributes to his family's material well-being. Throughout most of prerecorded history, men and women apparently shared provider responsibilities, and there is some evidence that, at times, women's contribution was more important than men's (Doyle, 1989). For countless centuries there was little distinction between producers and consumers of goods. Men and women lived and worked in close proximity in open fields, cottages, and small shops. Work environments were similar. However, with the advent of the Industrial Revolution, they became more divided in their lifestyles. Specialization became commonplace. The distinction between producers and consumers became more pronounced. The factory and its centralized location forced most men to leave their homes and journey some distance to work. New gender role definitions evolved as a result of separate work environments for men and women.

The **male provider role** dates from this period. Being a good provider became a prominent standard among men for achieving success. Many men began to equate their manhood with the amount of money they earned. The value placed on material goods received more emphasis. Many women were placed in a vulnerable position because their contributions to the family in either goods or services were not reimbursed. The male provider role was solidly embedded in the U.S. national psyche by the beginning of the twentieth century.

The Great Depression of the 1930s precipitated a form of psychological emasculation for millions of men whose loss of a job equaled a loss of self-respect and a loss of the primary means for validating their masculinity. Although World War II returned a sense of masculinity to countless men, the women who substituted as laborers in jobs vacated by men at war illustrated their innate competencies and capacities. Though women returned to the home during the Baby Boom years, there was a realization that they were valuable workforce members whose skills could qualify them for previously unavailable employment opportunities. Women's entry into the workforce has been unprecedented over the past fifty years. Changes in societal values have since reduced support for the male provider role. For men who wholeheartedly embraced the male provider role as the image of masculine success, questions have arisen about the value of success at all costs and about alternative bases for self-respect.

Women's Vocational Development

By 2005, thirty-nine million people will be trying to get jobs (Perryman, 1996). Women are a growing proportion of that number. Traditionally, twenty-five to forty-four-year-old women have made up about half of the women who work in the U.S. Although the proportion of women in the total workforce is growing, the actual number of women entering the job market in recent years has declined. The U.S. Department of Labor expects the number of women job seekers to increase slowly. More older women are expected to enter the workforce. Increases are projected at 6 percent labor participation for women ages forty to fifty, 8 percent for women ages fifty-five to sixty-four.

New explanatory concepts account for women's vocational behavior (Betz & Fitzgerald, 1987; Laird, 1994; Krebs, 1994; Morrison, White & Velsor, 1987; Nichols, 1994; Silver, 1994; Walsh & Osipow, 1994). Forrest and Mikolaitis (1986) review three trends in the development of theories explaining and predicting women's vocational development. Initially, evidence about women's career development that contradicted prevailing theories was either ignored or not explored further; the trend was to apply to women the well-established vocational theories developed for men without recognizing the limitations of such a strategy. A second trend assumed that theories developed for men could not be applied to women and that new theories were needed to explain women's career development. A third trend has been the attempt to incorporate concepts that explain career development for both women and men. Forrest and Mikolaitis write that one concept which provides useful direction for this third trend is self-in-relation theory (e.g., Chodorow, 1978; Gilligan, 1982). The tendency has been for women

Practical Applications

Assessing the connected voice and separate voice orientations of women and men and the interaction of such orientations with vocational difficulties allows practitioners to conceptualize career issues in a new framework (Forrest & Mikolaitis, 1986). Any models of career development that fail to address how women and men blend career and relationship domains in their lives do not accurately represent people's realities (Cook, 1993). Practitioners need to (1) be aware of how varied people can be, including marital status, sexual orientation, and parenthood status; (2) avoid steering clients towards one voice or the other; (3) recognize and value clients' need for connection, (4) remember that career decisions can be affected when clients' care for others results in a lack of care for themselves (Hotelling & Forrest, 1986); (5) consider the gendered context of the work environment more seriously in preparing clients for career transitions; and (6) examine how their own gender lens may distort the possibilities open to others (Cook, 1993).

We propose contextualizing these two voices with multicultural clientele: for us, the separate voice sometimes appears to characterize much of the English-speaking, U.S. mainstream experience, regardless of gender. In contrast, the connected voice sometimes appears to characterize much of the ethnic, racial, and linguistic minority experience. A willingness to relocate for career progress, for example, may be more readily evident in a client with dominant cultural values than for a client from a minority background who may be rooted to family and a culturally hospitable community.

Practitioners need to ask themselves and their clients some hard questions about our society's work values, especially about the myth of rugged individualism (Cook, 1993). The men who explored and settled the wild American frontier could never have done so without the women who journeyed beside them, the other men who agreed to join them, and the indigenous peoples they encountered along the way. Along with Cook, we question the psychological health implications of perpetuating the rugged individualist myth.

Practitioners must be open to exploring the dynamics of dominant-subordinate relationships between men and women in clients' workplaces. Many avenues merit examination, such as how both genders benefit from workplaces that reinforce traditional gender roles, or how clients often have contradictory expectations of how the genders should behave on the job. Practitioners' gender biases also need to be acknowledged and confronted on a regular basis.

to be socialized into defining themselves, in large part, through their connection with and responsiveness to others. This tendency refers to the "connected voice" orientation. In contrast, the tendency has been for men to be socialized into defining themselves, in large part, through their differentiation from others in terms of abilities and attributes. This tendency refers to the "separate voice" orientation.

Building on these two orientations, Cook (1993) makes two major points. First, through the socialization process, women and men tend to develop different orientations with respect to occupational achievement and interpersonal relationships. These differences interact with broader sociocultural norms for the sexes' behavior that produce disparate lifestyle opportunities and demands, especially where home and career intersect. Second, work environments are gendered, embodying accepted sociocultural assumptions and expectations for the sexes. This gendered work context markedly influences the daily choices and expectations that the sexes face, including daycare policies, norms about work for men, discrimination against women, and sexual harassment.

Sexual Harassment

In the workplace, sexual harassment is both an issue and a stress factor that affects women more than men (Barnett & Rivers, 1996; Gutek, 1985; Solomon, 1998; Webb, 1991). As many as 88 percent of working women and 15 percent of working men have experienced some form of sexual harassment (Webb, 1991). The problem occurs in all jobs, at all salary levels, in all age and racial groups, and in both the private and public sectors. More than 95 percent of all sexual harassment cases involve men as the offenders. Working women who are married or widowed seem to be less likely to be harassed than working women who are divorced, separated, or never married (Gutek, 1985). Male harassers are usually older, predominantly married, and less physically attractive than other male coworkers. The male initiator tends to behave the same way towards younger and older female coworkers as well.

Since the issue of sexual harassment burst upon the U.S. public's awareness in 1991 with Anita Hill's challenges at Clarence Thomas's confirmation hearings for the Supreme Court, complaints to the Equal Employment Opportunity Commission (EEOC) have more than doubled—to 15,549—while monetary awards have more than tripled (Yang, 1996). However, the underfunded EEOC is struggling to stay on top of a heavy caseload, with a backlog of 97,000 cases. Sexual harassment cases often boil down to a matter of credibility, pitting the accuser against the accused. Vindication through the two best avenues available for help—law enforcement agencies and the courts—entail many delays. Maremont and Sassen (1996) write that few women have the fortitude or finances to blow the proverbial whistle.

Behavioral and Legal Definitions

Behavioral Definition. The behavioral definition of sexual harassment is "deliberate and/or repeated sexual or sex-based behavior that is not welcome, not asked for, and not returned" (Equal Employment Opportunity Commission, *Guidelines on Discrimination Because of Sex,* 1980, cited in Webb, 1991, pp. 25–26). Three key elements of the definition are that it is

1. sexual in nature or sex-based;

2. deliberate and/or repeated;

3. not welcome, not asked for, and not returned (Webb, 1991).

There are also two qualifiers of the definition of sexual harassing behavior:

1. the more severe the behavior is, the fewer times it needs to be repeated before reasonable people define it as harassment; the less severe it is, the more times it needs to be repeated

2. the less severe the behavior is, the more responsibility the receiver has to speak up (because some people like this kind of behavior); the more severe it is, the less responsibility the receiver has to speak up, because the initiator of the behavior should be sensitive enough in the first place to know that it is inappropriate (Webb, 1991).

Sexual harassment may be verbal, nonverbal, or physical. Verbal harassment includes jokes, wisecracks, comments, and remarks; these behaviors constitute most complaints and investigations. Nonverbal harassment includes whistles, innuendoes, and staring (Gutek, 1985), certain kinds of looks, gestures, leering, ogling, photographs, or cartoons (Webb, 1991). Physical harassment includes touching, pinching, rubbing, or "accidentally" rubbing against someone's breasts or buttocks; these behaviors are the most severe form of harassment and can involve criminal charges.

Legal Definition. The legal definition of sexual harassment entails that it

1. occurs because of the person's sex,

2. is unwelcome, not returned, not mutual,

3. affects the terms or conditions of employment, including the work environment itself.

Finally, sexual harassment is a power trip. The harasser either thinks or knows, consciously or unconsciously, that he or she has more power in the workplace than the harassee. Otherwise, there would be no harassment, because the harasee could turn to the harasser and demand that it stop and there would be no issue (Webb, 1991).

CASE EXAMPLE

Maremont and Sassen (1996) report on sexual harassment at Astra U.S.A., a Swedish pharmaceutical company. Although there were several perpetrators, the chief executive officer was the primary abuser of power. In many instances the alleged harassment was witnessed or experienced by more than one person at a time. One female sales representative was told by two longtime female managers who witnessed her harassment, "That's the way it is . . . and you'd better get used to it" (p. 87). The sheer number of complaints centering on the same male executives, and the widely held view among both current and former employees that the work environment was generally hostile to women, suggested that a serious problem existed at the company. Those who did complain about sexual harassment at Astra allege that they were targeted for retaliation. Economic need meant that workers put up with behavior that they felt was degrading. Many current and former employees interviewed said they feared complaints would only result in a reputation as a troublemaker, something that would haunt them in the job market.

The atmosphere that allowed harassment to flourish was autocratic, controlling, and dominating. Those male executives who were the main perpetrators used their power and authority to suggest that their victims would not have a job if they did not go along with what was happening. Most of the women harassed were in their mid-twenties, and Astra was their first or second job after college. Female employees who filed harassment complaints found that their own careers became stifled, or they became targets for dismissal. While many of the women subjected to the worst harassment have left the company, an abrupt departure often has made finding another job difficult. Repeated denials of the alleged harassment on the part of the company were also reported.

More than 50 percent of working women will experience sexual harassment on the job (Barnett & Rivers, 1996). In a poll of 1,300 members of the National Association for Female Executives, 53 percent said they were sexually harassed by people who had power over their careers. Of those, 64 percent did not report the harassment, and more than half of those who did report it say the problem was not resolved to their satisfaction (Webb, 1991). In the most extensive survey to date in the United States, involving 23,000 federal employees, 42 percent of women describe experiencing some form of sexual harassment. A

United Nations survey reveals that as many as one in twelve women in the industrialized world are forced out of jobs by sexual harassment (*Boston Globe,* December 1, 1992). In Japan, a survey by the Santama Group to Consider Sexual Discrimination at Work disclosed that 70 percent of Japanese women say they have experienced some type of sexual harassment on the job, and 90 percent said they were sexually harassed while commuting to and from work (Webb, 1991).

Such harassment is not confined to females in the workplace. When young women in high school were targets of sexual harassment from members of a young men's athletic team, coaches and administrators were slow to respond (Ratcliffe, 1996). The antiwoman atmosphere that pervaded the annual Tailhook Association Conventions of the U.S. Navy—an enormous corporation with assets equal to those of the first seven Fortune 500 corporations—created a climate where sexual assaults on women occurred at several of the yearly meetings, with subsequent attempts to cover up the incidents (Vistica, 1995). In both the high school and the U.S. Navy instances, the women who blew the whistle on the abuse experienced reprisals and repercussions, including attempts to discredit them. In both instances, media publicity forced those in authority to respond by confronting the harassers and dealing with them in an appropriate manner.

Ageism

Older workers sometimes feel inadequate in the job market. Discrimination is a common experience for people over forty. Ageism affects both men and women, blue-collar worker and executive, and shows little regard for educational level (Jordan, 1997). Since the number of senior level jobs is smaller than the number of midlevel managers, a move up the career ladder is difficult. And even though older workers may have more job experience, the skills they possess may no longer be in demand. Many younger workers face a different problem. They lack sufficient experience with little opportunity to obtain the needed skills that experience teaches. Regardless of the reasons, it is illegal to discriminate against someone on the basis of age.

The American Association of Retired Persons (AARP) conducted several studies of perceptions of employers toward older employees. Sicker (1997) reported two sets of stereotypes that evolved: one stating that older workers were stable, reliable, responsible, trustworthy, in possession of a strong work ethic, and serious about work commitment; the other that older workers were inflexible, noninnovative, technologically inferior, and unable to work in teams (p. 1). The results of these stereotypes suggest that the positive attributes are excellent for low-pay, low-skill jobs, while the negative perceptions inhibit employers from

---

Practical Applications

Vocational practitioners need be aware of discrimination laws and practices to help older workers market themselves. Practitioners can establish communication with employers to challenge the myths and stereotypes connected with older workers. Jordan (1997) suggests that in assisting older workers to combat ageism in the workforce, it is necessary to (a) commit to a strong work ethic; (b) be able to work with teams as well as individually; (c) practice excellent interpersonal skills; (d) be able to adapt to change in the workplace, including willing-ness to learn new technology and to continue education and training experiences; (e) improve written and oral communication skills; (f) avoid talk of retirement plans; and (g) maintain excellent health and wellness.

While these issues in the work-place are real, concerns about change and transitions are common whether inside the company or outside the corporate setting. These issues involve values, attitudes, and coping abilities. Intergenerational differences in value systems form the next part of the chapter.

---

hiring or retraining older workers who are in higher paying jobs. In either situation, the older worker is relegated to a less important place in the workforce, which the author suggests needs to be confronted.

Since half of the workforce is now forty or older, employers need to rethink their strategies by contracting for settlement with an acceptable severance package, working with supervisors to rank which jobs should be cut, and averaging the age of the layoffs so that no one group is disproportionately cut (Armour, 1997).

Policies and practices that an organization can incorporate to combat ageism include recognition, gradual and incrementally based changes, appropriate rewards, guidance to meet expectations, short-term and specific goals, encouraging plateaus, job rehearsal, and promoting acceptance of change (Kelly, 1990).

INTERGENERATIONAL DIFFERENCES IN VALUES

Adults, Ages 18 to 35

This group has been labeled the "Babybusters" (Deutschman, 1990), "Generation X," and the "Slacker Generation" (Filipczak, 1994), which is in direct conflict with the Yuppies of the 1980s, who work hard to purchase expensive "toys"

Practical Applications

Due to the worldviews, beliefs, and realities of the babybuster generation, vocational practitioners must be able to accommodate this new work ethic. Practitioners need to be aware of their own biases and work values that may conflict with those of this generation, thus interfering with the counseling process.

---

such as BMWs and cell phones. The "'X' in Generation X is the signature of a group that feels it has no identity, or at least no identity that anyone else cares about" (Filipczak, 1994, p. 22).

This generation has little interest in the excessive materialistic notions of the babyboomers. Though "slacker" describes the career ethics of this generation, this is an ageist, unfair label since young people entering the workforce today are facing a much different atmosphere than that of their predecessors. "They have few heroes, no anthems, no style to call their own. They crave entertainment, but their attention span is as short as one zap of a TV dial" (Gross & Scott, 1990, p. 57). However, the ability to be flexible is also shown in their short attention span, and can be a valuable trait in a fast-changing world. These twenty to thirty year olds are not striving to be the most successful, but work their forty-hour weeks, do a good job, and have a life. This worldview is in direct conflict with the babyboomers' workaholic values.

"Today's young adults want to stay in their own backyard and do their work in modest ways" (Gross & Scott, 1990, p. 57). Youth of today crave simplicity in life and would rather be "the generation that is going to renovate America. We are going to be its carpenters and janitors" (p. 57). They want to accomplish less, but want to be able to live in comfort. Deutschman (1990) observes that "many of the obligations of adulthood seem to set in much later these days" (p. 47). Marriage is delayed, "men 25 to 29, 46% have never married [in 1990], compared with 19% in 1970. For women the change has been even greater: 30% vs. 11%" (p. 47).

Due to the declining birthrate, fewer young adults are entering the workforce than ever before. Companies need to rethink their recruiting policies. The demand is larger than the supply, which leaves this generation open to bargaining more effectively with companies. What these employees want includes flexibility in the job, more power to make decisions, and a strict forty-hour work week. Rather than dread evaluations, younger workers want feedback from supervisors, suggesting they need more encouragement in actual quantifiable ways.

They expect regular promotions which can be upward or lateral and allow for "new challenges" (Filipczak, p. 24). Going from one job to another allows workers to develop multiple skills and abilities and become more marketable for future employment opportunities.

Adults in Transition

The world of work is a world of starts and stops, of accelerations and waiting periods. . . . Thinking about adult career development as a *transition process* of moving in, through and out of the workforce helps explain what is, in essence, a highly fluid process. The length of time someone stays in each phase depends on the person, and his or her . . . career plan, and available and perceived options. Each individual's needs, along with appropriate interventions, will differ depending on where the person is in the system. (Schlossberg, 1996, p. 93, italics in original)

Job Change One of the most significant times in a person's life can involve job change. Super (1990) discusses these transitions at length, but he acknowledges that not all changes are planned transitions. Some job changes are sudden—per-

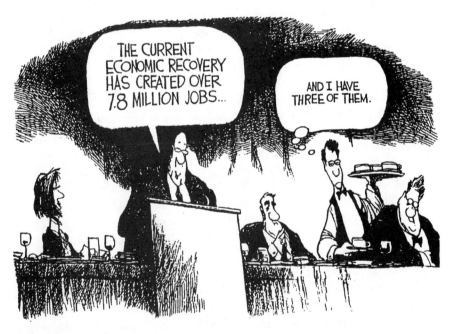

The truth about new jobs

© 1995 MacNelly—*Chicago Tribune*. Reprinted with permission.

sonal problems or corporate changes can result in a lost job, lost sense of security, and profound upheaval, both physically and emotionally. Other job changes are more planned and can result in a change of job or moving up a career ladder. This time of transition is often when the practitioner is sought out to help intervene in the situation. Much of the information in earlier chapters regarding models, assessment, computer systems, and life planning is applicable to this group of people.

Zunker (1998) suggests a counseling program for adults in career transition that synthesizes many theories of vocational counseling. Several ideas broaden the perspective for this particular population: a values-based approach to dealing with career change (Brown, 1996), an integrated life planning model (Hansen, 1997), a community career center (Loeb, 1994), effectiveness of career services for the "educationally disadvantaged" (Champagne, 1987), a model for effective continuous adult learning (MacKinnon-Slaney, 1994), and the role of leisure (McDaniels, 1996).

A new and promising assessment instrument for adults in transition is the Career Transition Inventory (CTI), developed by Heppner (1991). It was designed specifically to "assess and understand internal, dynamic psychological processes that may get in the way of the career transition process" (p. 220). Five basic factors that the instrument attempts to assess are: readiness, confidence, perceived support, control, and decision independence. The CTI is available from Mary Heppner, Ph.D., 305 Noyes Hall, University of Missouri, Columbia, MO, 65211.

Goodman (1994) proposes a "dental model" in which clients plan to make "regular checkups" and accomplish more "routine maintenance" to learn adaptability. Since most adults will report career/life transitions several times in their lives, learning the process and learning to be adaptable are keys to continued employment. She urges practitioners to understand the process of transition, stating "they need to be able to determine which adults need information, which need motivation, and which perhaps need adaptability training. They then need to know how to deliver that training" (p. 83).

Unemployment Losing one's job is a devastating experience. Psychological ramifications of unemployment include high stress levels that can lead to poor health and major depression. When an individual returns to the workforce, his/her mental as well as physical health improves dramatically (Aubrey, Tefft & Kingsbury, 1990; Peregoy & Schliebner, 1990; Wanberg, 1995; Wanberg, Watt & Rumsey, 1996). Adams, Hayes, and Hopson (1977) developed an effective model to describe the mood across time for a person who loses a job (see Figure 11.1).

This model is particularly useful for adults who are fired, forced to resign, downsized, or laid off due to company closure. The seven-phase model identifies the initial shock and elation and minimalization, where a person denies the

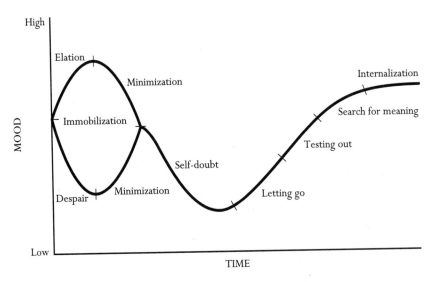

FIGURE 11.1 A Seven-Phase Model of Stages Accompanying a Transition

source: Understanding and Managing Personal Change, *by J. Adams, J. Hayes, and B Hopson. Copyright 1977 by Sage Publications, Inc., p. 38.*

change is happening. Then self-doubt sets in regarding one's ability to provide for self and others. Once the person starts to let go of the anger, frustration, resentment, and fear, energy builds to start the process of searching for meaning. Internalization occurs when the person has changed values and lifestyle and developed new coping skills. The model is still appropriate today.

Career Development in Organizations Hall (1996) offers a relational approach to career development in organizations. "Models based on notions of organizations as pyramids and careers as regular progressions through ladder-like job sequences seem as outdated as the organizational forms on which they were based" (p. 1). Rather than focusing on moving up in a career, Hall suggests focusing on the importance of relationships to one's career growth. "The object of growth in the relational model is not individual mastery but rather interdependence" (p. 2). Hall believes that while resources are declining in the work world, relations between workers are at their best.

People are looking for meaning in their lives, and hence, in their work. Since the workplace is constantly reinventing itself, a person must be able to adapt to the changing environment, which means that they must be able to adjust their skills and learn new ones to fit into the new situations. "This sense of meaning and purpose, along with good opportunities for continuous learning

Practical Applications

Job Search Groups and Job Clubs can be effective interventions for the unemployed. Amundson and Borgen (1988) studied job search group experiences in an attempt to find the most beneficial effects of the intervention. These benefits were: (a) mutual support and encouragement; (b) job search strategies; (c) instruction in resumes and correspondence; (d) a positive outlook; (e) interview practice and preparation; (f) telephone technique; and (g) belonging (p. 109). Stidham and Remley (1992) developed a Job Club methodology based on the U.S. Department of Health and Human Services Guide for Group Job Seeking Programs. The program was designed specifically for welfare recipients in order to help them experience a feeling of success by developing a more positive self-esteem, readiness for training and employability. "Job Club methodology ensures that clients understand the expectations of them through instruction, behavioral rehearsal and practice. The problems of fear, guilt and lack of motivation are addressed by positive reinforcement and support within the group" (p. 74). The Job Club technique could prove itself useful to state agencies as they attempt to help people move from welfare to work.

Pavot, Diener, Colvin, and Sandik (1991) found that life satisfaction as a global evaluation of one's life was relatively unaffected by unemployment and reemployment. Therefore, the effective use of life planning or narrative model of a life story is an important tool in helping an individual develop a satisfactory life.

Mallinckrodt and Fretz (1988) found that most people who took new jobs at the same level or higher found more job satisfaction due to better opportunities for advancement and development. But people who were in less satisfactory jobs experienced poorer mental health (Wanberg, 1995). Occupational practitioners will have to use a variety of skills when working with the unemployed, especially those who are not voluntarily out of work. The possible emotional effects are myriad and need to be addressed by the practitioner.

Peregoy and Schliebner (1990) have developed a Personal Employment Identity Model (PEIM) to assist practitioners in selecting appropriate interventions based on four types of vocational ego identity problems that unemployed persons exhibit.

1. The person whose identity was tied to the job and who now has lost a sense of self. These people are likely to be strongly affected by loss of income and loss of emotional involvement.
2. The person whose identity was tied to the challenge of the job. These people usually have a strong sense of failure and loss of status,

Continued

Continued

experiencing self-rejection, dissatisfaction, and helplessness.

3. The person who has lost identity due to the strain of being unemployed. These people often experience sadness, frustration, and apathy.

4. The person who had little investment in his/her last job. These people express concern with their economic situation and their lack of hope in finding a new job, and often personalize their job rejections, lack information about alternatives, have confusion about their skills, and demonstrate symptoms of hopelessness by exhibiting poor motivation or burnout in the process of job-seeking.

Identifying which type of vocational ego-identity problems the client presents can assist practitioners in asking appropriate questions and getting the necessary information from past employment to work effectively towards reemployment.

To move from unemployment to reemployment, Eby and Buch (1995) propose that job loss can result in career growth. Their study of the victims of downsizing resulted in several practical suggestions. (1) Provide psychological counseling to deal with the negative effects of job loss and to build optimism and self-efficacy. (2) Help clients use support mechanisms around them and to maintain an active daily schedule with various helpful routines. (3) For women, it appears that a flexible, adaptive family is important, and encouraging communication with family members is likely to be helpful. (4) For men, problem-focused and emotion-focused interventions are important.

A recent development is a nonprofit organization called the Talent Alliance, an agency organized by several of the largest companies in the United States to help with the ebb and flow of available jobs in the large companies. Spearheaded by AT&T, the Alliance is composed of such companies as GTE Corp., Lucent Technologies, NCR Corp., TRW Inc., Union Pacific Resources Group, Unisys Corp., and United Parcel Service of America Inc. Services will include things such as job postings between companies, a Futures Forum to explore new ways of thinking and doing that is based on research findings, training and education services, and career growth centers. The Talent Alliance is headquartered in Morristown, New Jersey.

and development, has become the new corporate contribution to the contract, replacing job security" (Hall, 1996, p. 5). Continuous learning and the ability to change and "to redirect one's life and career " are essential, and the energy to produce becomes the primary motivation in the workplace today. "Fewer people are pursuing the external 'carrot' (be it power, money, or security) because in today's flatter organization and lower-paying wage structure, it simply doesn't exist" (p. 6).

CASE EXAMPLE

General Electric in Cincinnati had a vocational counseling center where all the employees' résumés, continuing education hours, and career plans were on file. At the facility eighty classes were offered each semester that could be taken for college credit or continuing education. Employees were reimbursed for their continued education. Each time an employee would complete a program, two-year or four-year degree or graduate work, a vocational counselor would make an appointment with him/her and ask if they were getting what they needed at General Electric. If they wanted to make a lateral or upward move, or change departments, a job/career plan was on file and the infor-mation updated. All job openings in the company were available to all employees with specific skills and qualifications listed. This program would seem applicable to most companies today, and was extremely innovative for the 70s. Now, Jack Welsch, CEO of General Electric has developed a revolutionary process for managerial leadership called WorkOut, which is transforming his organization (Tichy & Sherman, 1993). Some organizations have an on-site work force development center that assists employees in job/career changes, upgrading skills, and reevaluating career path goals. Others contract career development services out to career specialists in the area.

With this new perspective of career in the corporate workplace, a holistic approach that includes personal identity and work identity is necessary. "Viewing the career as a personal quest also implies finding influences on development that are uniquely equipped to promote personal development" (Hall, 1996, p. 7). Rethinking the meaning of career, how it functions with personal life, reframing employer/employee relationships, understanding and using flexibility at work, and adjusting the work environment to reduce **stress** and promote a sense of security are all part of the holistic approach to intervention. While all of this is the ultimate, the reality is that not all employees are capable of learning new skills and adapting to the changing work environment.

Career Plateau/Career Resiliency/Career Renewal With the ongoing threat of corporate downsizing, career plateauing has become a concern for managers and other employees. "The pyramidal shape of most organizations dictates that virtually all careers will level out before an employee reaches top of the institution, agency, or corporation" (Tan & Salomone, 1994, p. 291). Ferrence, Stoner, and Warren (1977, cited in Tan & Salomone, 1994) define career plateauing as "the point in a career when the likelihood of additional hierarchical promotion is very low" (p. 292). This definition follows the attitude of the business world regarding career plateauing as no chance for movement. Organizations can help with career plateauing by "(a) education and candor [about the realities of the situation], . . . (b) alternative work forms and reward systems, . . . (c) second career expectations, . . . and (d) encouraging further education (Tan & Salomone, 1994, pp. 298, 299). Interventions that practitioners may make on an individual level concern the areas of "career goal reassessment, . . . refocused learning goals, . . . and loss and transition" (pp. 299, 300).

One way to survive the changing workplace is to develop career self-reliance (Collard, Epperheimer & Saign, 1996) or **career resiliency** (Waterman, Waterman & Collard, 1994). Career resilience characterizes a person who is (a) self-aware, (b) values-driven, (c) dedicated to continuous learning, (d) future-focused, (e) connected, and (f) flexible (Collard et al., 1996).

Basic assumptions of career development have been transformed. In traditional patterns there were stable economic patterns; in career resilience there is no economic stability. Hierarchy was basic to traditional thinking, but "flattened organizations" are the new reality. Single jobs have become contract/outsourcing and temporary situations with few distinct roles and the use of teams. Being a dependent employee has now become an interdependent partnership, or instead of a child-parent relationship, it is now an adult-adult relationship. Rather than thinking of careers as job matching, upward movement, linear in direction, and management directed, career resiliency is a lifelong process that is proactive, based on values and their effect on work, nonlinear, self-directed, with horizontal moves as important as upward steps (Collard et al., 1996, p. 9).

Career renewal is "a transitional stage that takes place for people generally at the end of the establishment stage and the beginning of the maintenance stage of a job or career" (Beijan & Salomone, 1995, p. 52). It is often related to what is commonly known as midlife transitions and was not included in Super's lifespan events. This process usually includes rethinking (a) career goals, (b) commitment, (c) self and work, and (d) potential changes or adjustments that reflect one's current situation, (e) values, and (f) changes in the work environment. Leisure counseling is included in the process to encourage individuals to find sources other than work to fulfill needs and meet personal goals.

As Engels (1995) states,

the information age and the pending communication age call for career development that emphasizes life-long career resilience and renewal predicated on self understanding, learning to learn, self respect, respect for others, lifelong learning and other knowledge skills highlighted in the competencies designated by the Secretary's Commission on Achieving Necessary Skills (SCANS, 1992), as being essential for success in a global economy (p. 83).

Hudson (1991) describes commitments in life as cyclical. They encompass traits developed in the twenties and thirties: (a) personal identity, (b) intimacy, (c) achievement at work, (d) play and creativity, (e) search for meaning, and (f) compassion and contribution. In midlife, these commitments need to be examined and rethought. The primary cycles that affect adult life are the change cycle and the life cycle. The cycle of change "requires living creatively with the flow of internal and external change " (p. 48). In a person's life cycle the "sense of purpose shifts with the changes of aging, social forces and self-development" (p. 48). Hudson's model of self/career renewal is seen in Figure 11.2.

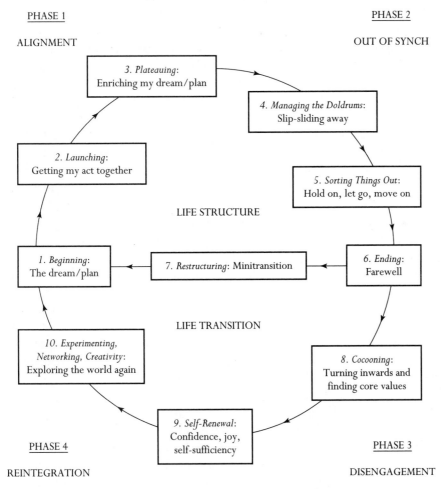

FIGURE 11.2 The Cycle of Change: Ten Personal Skills That Empower Adults Through Life Structures and Transitions

SOURCE: The Adult Years: Mastering the Art of Self-Renewal *by F. M. Hudson, 1991, p. 53. Copyright by Jossey-Bass Inc.*

Practitioners need to be aware of these life structures and transitions in adult development to effectively assist these clients in times of reevaluation. We have explored how career specialists can assist adults while in the job. Our concerns now go to those services available for employees who are being displaced, replaced, or let go.

Outplacement As companies have downsized, reorganized, or closed, many have provided job search services for employees affected by the changes. Companies can hire a team to provide services to employees, and encourage employees to participate by reimbursing them for the time spent in the program or by giving them time from work. Outplacement services have grown exponentially from $50 million in 1980 to $650 million in 1994 (Kirk, 1994). The job of the outplacement counselor is considered to be one of the "hot jobs" in the 1990s by *Newsweek* magazine. "Outplacement services differ widely. They range from providing laid-off workers job search, access to company telephones, computers, and secretarial help to comprehensive relocations packages that cover all moving expenses" (Kirk, 1994, p. 10). Career planning and the ancillary help of resume writing and portfolio preparation often are provided as well. There are many reasons why companies provide these services, including (a) maintaining a positive public image, (b) helping the morale of those remaining, and (c) lessening the potential for legal actions. Kirk (1994) and Pedersen, Goldberg and Papalia (1991) have proposed models for outplacement programs. Pedersen et al. use a "3-stage sequence based on increased *a*wareness of assumptions, *k*nowledge of relevant information, and *s*kill in taking appropriate action (AKS)" (p.74). While there are national organizations that provide this type of counseling service, the authors believe this model can make effective use of local resources and practitioners. Kirk's model is seen in Figure 11.3.

Kirk's (1994) Holistic Outplacement Model consists of three functional elements. The first is called regaining equilibrium, and deals with job grief, loss of income, the affect on self esteem, and stress. This leads to a future orientation that can go two directions and can move laterally between these elements. One concerns career development, including self-assessment, career exploration, decision-making and taking action while the other focuses on job hunting, which involves networking, influencing and negotiating.

Mentor Relationships According to *Bullfinch's Mythology* (1978), in ancient Greece, when Odysseus went off to fight in the Trojan War, he left his son Telemachus in the care of Mentor, a wise and trusted friend. Later, after Telemachus grew to young manhood, the goddess Athena assumed Mentor's identity when Telemachus departed in search of his father. Thus, mentoring originally has both a Western and masculine tradition. Nowadays, one definition of a **mentor**

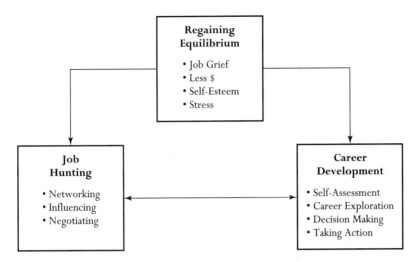

FIGURE 11.3 Holistic Outplacement Model

SOURCE: "Putting Outplacement in its Place," by J. J. Kirk, Journal of Employment Counseling, 31, p. 11.

is "an experienced, productive . . . [senior worker] who relates well to a less experienced employee and facilitates his or her personal development" (Karsten, 1994, p. 117). Both men and women can benefit from understanding what an appropriate mentor-protégé relationship is and is not (Edwards, 1991). Murphy and Ensher (1997) provide a cross-cultural perspective to mentoring.

Since today's professional milieu is so complex and everchanging, few adults can effectively mentor adult workers/professionals. The second author of this text is mindful that "mentoring moments" can occur when more experienced professionals informally are consulted, without the tensions and competitiveness that a more formal mentor-protégé relationship often contains (Levinson, 1978). Hudson (1991) suggests a model to train professional adult mentors with an understanding of (1) change cycle, life cycle of adults, (2) life/career planning, (3) coaching, (4) leadership training, and (5) networking and referrals. The mentor would not function as a clinician but more as a role model, resource, and coach. Adult mentors need to be aware of adult developmental psychology, human systems management, career, leisure, and work-family issues. They also need to know what educational resources for training are available in the geographic area and need to have some knowledge of financial and retirement planning.

Another resource for adult mentoring information is Cohen (1995). He describes core mentor behavioral functions such as relationship, information, facilitation, confrontation, motivation, and encouragement. The Principles of the Adult Mentoring Scale (PAMS) is discussed as well.

Practical Applications

To deal with the rage, anger, and depression that many laid-off and fired workers experience, vocational practitioners can provide support groups and job clubs to give these people a place to deal with these feelings without letting them affect their job interviewing or job search skills.

Outplacement career counseling is about helping people who have lost their jobs due to mergers and downsizing. People need to be able to make well-informed and positively motivated decisions about how they will continue their career after a layoff or a firing. This involves encouraging individuals to perceive that: (a) it is their decision, (b) they will have their own strengths and weaknesses to consider, (c) they will have transferable skills, and (d) there may be a number of opportunities open to them of which they are not aware. To make the most of these opportunities certain skills, such as research and self-marketing skills, may need to be developed (Murray, 1993).

Individuals need guidance to make the right choices with regard to education and employment. Oftentimes they do not know how to make a positive match between their personal traits and the job environment. The mismatching of employee and employment leads to greater stress. There is a definite link between mental and physical stress and unemployment, with increased rates of murder, suicide, cirrhosis of the liver, and heart disease occurring among the unemployed population. Counseling can help people to face unemployment more positively and/or choose a more appropriate career path to follow. People are then better able to accept advice and endure less anxiety about making decisions (Murray, 1993).

Assessments Used with Adults

- Ball Aptitude Battery
- Career Anchors: Discovering Your Real Values, Rev. Ed. 1990
- Career Attitudes and Strategies Inventory: An Inventory for Understanding Adult Careers
- Career Exploration Inventory
- Career Mastery Inventory
- Career Values Card Sort
- Life Space Analysis Profile

Older Workers

As we progress into the new century, our attitudes towards older workers will be altered. Instead of being no longer useful, they will be considered to have valuable experience, able to learn new skills, and have the ability to be flexible. While the Senate Select Committee on Aging (1986) found that older workers tended to remain unemployed longer than younger workers, this too may change as the workforce ages. The United States Senate Special Committee on Aging (1986) discovered that older workers tend to remain unemployed longer than younger workers, thus leaving them without unemployment benefits. To combat the problem of fewer jobs available to older workers, Rife (1989) suggests Job Club placement interventions that can help workers obtain employment and consequently lead to improvement in their overall mental health.

If unemployed workers over the age of 50 have positive support from their social systems, they are more motivated to find a job (Rife & Belcher, 1993). Interestingly, older workers react more positively to the support of unemployed friends than to the support of family and friends who are retired and not actively looking for employment. This confirms the need for Job Club programs to include older workers since the social system is so crucial to their remaining optimistic about finding employment.

Older workers cannot be stereotyped. They come from highly diverse backgrounds (e.g., life experience, education level, cultural identity). When counseling older workers, the practitioner must be aware of characteristics that can be generalized to fit the needs of older workers. For purposes of definition, Lefkovich (1992) cites Kelly's (1990) five subgroups that categorize workers by age.

1. *Midlife career changers.* These are younger-older workers ages 50–62. They have most likely changed jobs due to a midlife transition and are interested in reaping the benefits of experience, such as pay raises, job advancement, and health care and retirement benefits.

2. *Displaced workers aged 62 and younger.* These people have most likely lost jobs due to the changes in corporate structure (downsizing, mergers, acquisitions). They may not have any income, or may be living on a limited severance pay. This group is looking for work that has health and retirement benefits. If they go very long without being hired, they begin to believe their job skills no longer have value and can easily develop a strong sense of hopelessness and helplessness.

3. *Retirees aged 62 and younger.* These people are receiving some health coverage and benefits as a result of accepting an early retirement package. They often find themselves with too much leisure and not enough income.

4. *Retirees aged 62 to 69 who are receiving social security.* Even though this group receives social security benefits, they often are not ready to quit working, either for financial or sense-of-meaning issues. Most, however, will not

Practical Applications

Jensen-Scott (1993) cites several barriers when counseling older adults. "First, although a number of older adults apparently feel highly dissatisfied with their current situation, the counselor may have difficulty reaching those persons most in need of intervention. . . . A second barrier is the potential difficulty in establishing a counseling relationship. . . . A third barrier concerns the tendency for assessment to be difficult with this population. . . . A final barrier concerns possible lack of job and volunteer opportunities available for older adults" (pp. 264–65).

Practitioners need to understand some key elements when working with adults: (a) a perspective on aging, (b) a transitional life-events framework for counseling, and (c) teaching coping skills (Schlossberg, 1990). How the practitioner concep-

tualizes aging determines the choice of the intervention strategy (Gatz, 1985). Aging is a time when significant losses take place, and has positive and negative transitions and experiences. One's choices depend on the knowledge and values one holds. Practitioners need to observe when an older adult is experiencing (a) transitions, (b) life events, (c) stresses, and (d) pleasures, as well as (e) biological, (f) personal, (g) physical, (h) psychological, and (i) social changes. Ask how any change affects the client's self-perception. "The more the event or nonevent alters an [older] adult's roles, routines, assumptions, and relationships, the more the person will be affected by the transition and have to cope with it" (Schlossberg, 1990, p. 9).

Mastering change can be broken down into three major steps. (1)

want to work full time, and are somewhat insecure about their health and ability. They also worry about how potential employers will see them and their ability. Flexible work hours are important to this group.

5. *Retirees aged 70 or older who are on social security.* While often less able to work, these people may be similar to the group above, with more emphasis on part-time work.

Lefkovich (1992) suggests that the following are incentives for people to work: "(a) age, (b) career status, (c) economics, (d) health, (e) family responsibilities, (f) education, (g) the need for health and medical coverage, (h) future family and retirement planning, (i) social interests, (j) the need for personal interactions, or (k) for the intellectual stimulation and challenge" (Lefkovich, 1992, p. 64).

Approaching change—teach adults to look at the changes in their lives and determine how extensive they are. (2) Taking stock of one's resources—teach adults to identify their potential and decide what needs strengthening. (3) Taking charge—teach adults ways to turn a low resource into a high resource (Schlossberg, 1990).

Forced retirement actually may exacerbate the negative attributes which many older people face (Cahill & Salomone, 1987). Practitioners' ability to understand or be sensitive to the values, aspirations, ideals, and beliefs of older clients is essential. Group counseling can help older persons with these issues. Practitioners can help change society's perceptions about older people, including (a) find ways to educate the public; (b) help promote legislation which will help older people with work opportunities; (c) work within corporations to educate personnel officers; and (d) assist in establishing programs that are designed to pro-mote work possibilities for this popu-lation. "Rather than helping people adjust to their environment or, as some suggest, changing the environ-ment to fit the person, counselors can best serve as mediators, integrat-ing the needs of both the person and the environment" (Cahill & Salomone, 1987, p. 195).

Washington (1993) observed specific differences that practitioners need to be concerned with when working with the more experienced client. (1) Older clients know more what they *don't* want. (2) Older clients have more work experience so have developed more work con-tent skills. (3) Older individuals need to identify job families and all the individual occupations connected to that particular family of occupa-tions. (4) Older clients do not want to take major pay cuts. (5) Older clients need to develop a results-oriented portfolio and during inter-views learn to tell stories that make a convincing case for their job skills.

While corporate managers are usually somewhat older people themselves, it has been the practice of companies to enact policies that urge older people to leave their job, often to be replaced by a younger person. While this may appear to be the natural order of things, changing demographics may slow this process.

Group Counseling for Older Workers Many studies address the effectiveness of group counseling in conducting a job search with older adults (Amundeson & Borgen, 1988; Gray & Braddi, 1988; Stidham & Remley, 1992; Rife & Belcher, 1993). Zimpfer and Carr (1989) suggest some reasons for using groups. Groups (a) are efficient, (b) provide social context, (c) have potential for reality testing, and (d) have demonstrated effectiveness. The authors offer some recommendations for consideration for groups for adult workers. These include (a) assessment instruments that are more sensitive to the changes in self concept that take place with adults, (b) follow-up interventions are important, and (c) test outcomes that involve generalizable skills versus specific job-finding skills need to be developed.

STRESS AT WORK/CAREER BURNOUT

Two common workplace occurrences that can be personally experienced but socially negated are stress and **burnout.** One's work ethic and balance between work and leisure can unexpectedly go haywire. Stress at work and career burnout can then happen. The ever-increasing baseline tempo of life in the U.S. has been called, "a harried, Lucy Ricardo-in-the candy-factory level of frenetic activity that's impossible for anyone to sustain except in a state of mental and physical overload" (Sharp, 1996, p. 1). Stress can be both good and bad—depending on its nature, duration, and resources available to respond to it. A **stress experience** occurs when a person is confronted by a demand that is perceived to exceed the emotional or physical resources available to effectively respond to it (Zacarro & Riley, 1987). Events perceived as a threat to one's well-being are handled ineffectively (Klarreich, 1988). The term stress connotes feelings of anxiety, a sense of powerlessness, and sometimes alienation and burnout. Most individuals in all occupations will experience job-related stress to some extent. Stress is a part of life and work. When stress changes from a positive motivator into negative feelings about work or abilities, or feelings of depression and burnout, it becomes a serious problem.

Stress at Work

Shore (1992) classifies stress at work into three categories: (1) biochemical, (2) physical, and (3) psychosocial. Biochemical stress refers to the exposure to chemical and biological substances that interfere with normal body functioning. The mysterious illnesses that afflict thousands of Desert Storm veterans may be due to exposure to chemical agents in the Persian Gulf (Gannett News Service, 1996). Physical stress includes noise, ventilation, heat, pace of production, time of shift (Shore, 1992). Nurses who work on rotating shifts increase their risk of heart disease, and those who work them for more than six years are as much as 50 percent to 70 percent more likely to have serious cardiac problems, including heart attacks (Schieszer, 1996). Psychosocial stress occurs as a result of a potential or actual conflict between a worker and some aspect of the worker's company. This includes conflicting job demands, negative patterns of supervision and communication, lack of respect, and recognition, racism, and sexism.

Barnett and Rivers (1996) summarize previous research and identify seven factors related to work stress.

1. Skill discretion—job complexity and challenge, extent to which a worker can control use of his or her own skills.

2. Decision authority—the extent to which a worker can control authority or use of resources to get her or his job done.

3. Schedule control—the extent to which a worker has control over hours worked.

4. Job demands—the number of tasks to perform, time allowed, number of conflicting demands placed on one's time.

5. Pay adequacy—how much one earns compared to others doing similar work.

6. Job security—one's perception of the likelihood of being fired, laid off, downsized.

7. Relations with supervisor—how well one gets along with one's boss.

Issues related to skill discretion and job demands have a significant negative impact on mental health for both men and women (Barnett & Rivers, 1996). The most unhealthy combination is a tedious job—that is, a lack of variety and challenge—with heavy demands. Employees who experience threats to their reputations with their supervisors or managers are likely to experience emotional distress that goes home with them from work (Doby & Caplan, 1995). Work stress can impinge on the familial domain (M. S. Richardson, 1993).

Do organizations cause stress? Klarreich (1988) asserts:

We often believe . . . the work environment produce[s] our problems. . . . [B]ut we can largely determine what will be stressful, and how much it . . . interfere[s] with our lives, by the views we uphold, irrespective of what goes on in the workplace. . . . [I]f conditions within the organization caused all stress, then all employees in that environment would suffer. . . . And this just does not happen. Certain employees think one way and experience difficulties . . . [;] other employees think another way and undergo minimal discomfort. So to say that a company is "doing us in" is incorrect. We do ourselves in. . . . [C]ertain work conditions . . . [may] require change, but this is a separate issue. . . . [T]o reduce their distress employees must first examine . . . [themselves]. Then they can look at their particular work environment, and decide what changes to go for. (pp. 23–24)

Eustress is the exhilarating feeling of accomplishment that results from effectively coping with stress. **Distress** occurs when a person experiences too many stressors, or when they continue for too long ("Mastering stress," 1987). Work conditions may overstimulate the body's rapid mobilization. Employees are left vulnerable to infection, physical illness, and disease. Stress-related illness costs the U.S. $300 billion a year in medical costs and lost productivity (Sharp, 1996).

Type A Behavior Stress is induced by **Type A behavior** (Friedman & Rosenman, 1975). Type A behavior consists of five components. (1) It is a continuous struggle, an unremitting attempt to accomplish or achieve more or participate in more events in less time, frequently in the face of opposition—real or imagined—from other persons. (2) The Type A personality is dominated by covert insecurity of status, hyperaggressiveness, or both. (3) Struggle eventually fosters a sense of time urgency, a distortion of the Puritan legacy of improving the time. Polonsky (1997) calls time urgency being tyrannized by the clock. (4) Hyperaggressiveness usually shows itself in the easily aroused anger called free-floating hostility. (5) If the struggle becomes severe enough and persists long enough, it may lead to a tendency toward self-destruction. **Type B behavior** refers to an absence of these five components.

Of Type A behavior's five components, hostility has the greatest influence on cardiovascular disease (Barefoot, Larsen, von der Leith & Schroll, 1995; Burg, 1995; Deary, Fowkes, Donnan & Housley, 1994; Smith, 1992). Psychophysiologically, chronic vigilance and arousal contributes to high blood pressure, or hypertension. Health and wellness behaviors can become adversely affected. Symptoms include (a) increases in consumption of food, cigarettes, caffeine, and/or alcohol; and (b) decreases in physical activity and exercise. Interpersonal environments can become more taxing. Affective features may include anger, resentment, annoyance, and contempt. Behavioral manifestations may include antagonism, uncooperativeness, verbal and sometimes physical aggression. Cognitions may include attributions of hostile intent by others and cynicism regarding others' motives.

Sometimes the term **workaholism** is used interchangeably with Type A behavior. Workaholism has been addressed in an incomplete and fragmentary matter (Seybold & Salomone, 1994). It has many definitions: (a) an addiction to work, (b) an escape from the unpleasantries of life, (c) competitiveness caused by a craving for constant stimulation and an overabundance of energy, (d) the result of compensating for a self-image damaged in childhood, and (e) behavior learned from parents and other role models. Workaholism can harm one's health, personal life, and work environment. "Workaholics surely need the assistance of career and mental health counselors to achieve [the] balance [between meaningful productive work and recreative leisure activities for life satisfaction and mental health]" (Seybold & Salomone, 1994, p. 8). One question is whether workaholism is independent enough (i.e., orthogonal) of similar concepts to allow for adequate empirical research and instrument development. Currently, workaholism closely resembles features of obsessive–compulsive disorder and/or Type A behavior.

Two Case Examples of Work Stress

CASE EXAMPLE 1

Police Work

Police officers have received a bad rap in the past several years due to many incidents that have received high-profile media attention. Symptomatic drinking by police officers is most directly effected by level of stress (Violante, Marshall & Howe, 1985). The indirect effect of job demands (e.g., emotional dissonance) mediated by stress and coping (e.g. cynicism) is approximately four times greater than its direct effect. Stress, job demands, and coping all have a meaningful effect on police officer alcohol abuse. Killing someone in the line of duty and experiencing a fellow officer being killed are the top two of 60 ranked stressors for police officers (Violanti & Aron, 1994). Seven organizational/administrative stressors rank among the top twenty stressors: shift work, inadequate department support, incompatible partner, insufficient personnel, excessive discipline, inadequate support by supervisors, and inadequate equipment. Racial conflicts rank last among police stressors. Organizational stressors mediated by job satisfaction and organizational orientation are a source of stress for police officers approximately 6.3 times greater than the inherent stressors related to the dangers of police work (Violanti & Aron, 1993). Officers dealing with organizational stress have lower job satisfaction. Ambiguous, conflicting organizational goals also decrease job satisfaction. These organizational stressors remain largely unknown to the general public and those considering police work. Entrenched attitudes and practices in the upper ranks are "hidden stressors" that contribute to the job stress experienced by police officers and these have a cumulative effect greater than the inherent dangers of the job.

CASE EXAMPLE 2

Full-time Female Homemakers

Barnett and Rivers (1996) summarize why full-time female homemakers score higher on stress indexes than women who work outside the home: (a) long hours of monotonous, boring, repetitive housework; (b) being on-

Continued

Continued

call twenty-four hours a day; (c) the isolation and loss of freedom when home alone with young children; (d) the myth that housework is not really work; and (e) the low status of housework ("just a housewife") contributes to high rates of depression and other symptoms of psychological distress. Permanently dropping out of the workforce after the birth of a child can be more harmful to a woman's health than being employed full time. Women who lose earned income can also lose a sense of entitlement (see also, McKenna, 1997) that decreases mental and physical health. Involvement in activities that give a homemaker a sense of independence, autonomy, and respect from others diminishes the tedious nature of housework and boosts her self-regard.

Violence in the Workplace Violence in the workplace is increasing and is becoming a greater source of stress than ever before. In *The Gift of Fear: Survival Signs that Protect Us from Violence* (1997), Gavin de Becker describes **pre-incident indicators** that can be detected before violence in the workplace occurs. "Stepping on the first rung of a ladder is a significant pre-incident indicator to reaching the top; stepping on the sixth [rung] even more so. Since everything a person does is created twice—once in the mind and once in its execution—ideas and impulses are pre-incident indicators for action" (p. 18). Pre-incident indicators are part of systematized intuition that de Becker's company uses to advise workplaces about managing employees who are likely to act out violently. A unique stressor about workplace violence is that the worksite is the main place where most people have to interact with others whom they may not otherwise have chosen to include in their everyday life. Violence in the workplace can be predicted (de Becker, 1997). Too often, warning signs are ignored and tragedy occurs. Ironically, many people usually are in a position to notice such warning signs. A clear sign of trouble in any context, workplace or not, is the refusal to take "no" for an answer, and eleven elements of prediction can be measured (de Becker, 1997, Appendix 6, pp. 315–319).

Employee emotion is a force to be reckoned with in the age of takeovers, mergers, and downsizing. Problems begin when a job applicant is hired without an extensive check of references and work background. Many employees are managed in ways that bring out the worst in them (de Becker, 1997). Often, managers and bosses receive no training in leadership and decision-making skills, and can show an appalling lack of character and ethics themselves. Job loss can be as painful as the death of a loved one, and support is rarely forthcoming.

The effects of domestic violence also are spreading into the jobsite (Burney, 1995). Domestic violence is not supposed to be a workplace problem, yet violence at home is costing businesses between \$3 billion and \$5 billion a year in lowered employee productivity, increased absenteeism, and higher employee turnover. People are reluctant to tell their employer when they are victims of domestic violence, partly from years of conditioning by employers that they should keep their personal problems outside the workplace, and partly from a realistic fear of being fired because their employer does not want the hassle of dealing with the problem.

According to Linda Osmundson, executive director of CASA, a Pinellas County, Florida, woman's shelter, employers can help fight domestic violence in at least five ways (cited in Burney, 1995): (1) make employees aware that employers know domestic violence is a problem; make brochures from local spouse-abuse shelters available to employees, and publicly support domestic-abuse shelters; (2) make it an explicit policy not to fire victims of domestic-abuse; (3) review and consider the increase in security at the business and in its parking lot; (4) if the employer suspects that an employee is being abused, ask her or him if there is something in their personal life that the employer should know about. The "her or him" is crucial here: victims of domestic abuse range from top executive women down to male assembly line workers. Employers are encouraged not to "accuse" the employee of being abused; it's the employee's choice to make that revelation; and (5) offer support for employees who say they are being abused—this can be as simple as walking them to their car or giving a picture of the abuser to security guards. While workplace politics can definitely hinder employee self-disclosures of domestic abuse, management that is genuinely respectful and responsive to an abused employee will find that others will feel safe enough to come forward with the same issue.

Warning Signs and Sources of Job Stress Some workers experience stress to a slight degree; others may be incapacitated. Warning signs include: intestinal distress; frequent illness; insomnia; persistent fatigue; irritability; nail biting; lack of concentration; increased use of drugs and alcohol; and a hunger for sweets (Miller et al., 1988). Other signs include: resistance to going to work everyday; lackluster job performance; procrastination on minor tasks; avoiding discussion of work with coworkers; preoccupation with petty aspects of the job; feelings of guilt and inadequacy; working late; and frequent physical illness or accidents ("Mastering stress," 1987). When one's identity is largely based upon work, losing a job through downsizing leads many people to stress-induced illnesses (Uchitelle & Kleinfield, 1996).

Sometimes stress can have a positive effect on an employee group, especially if it is a cohesive group, and can lead to a higher overall performance and meeting quotas and deadlines. Other times the strain caused by the stress can lead to: (1) psychological reactions (job dissatisfaction, depression, burnout, anxiety), (2) physiological reactions (high blood pressure, exhaustion, headaches), or (3) be-havioral reactions (smoking, drug and alcohol abuse). Affected individuals are less capable of responding to work demands. Job strain reduces motivation and the work performance. Individuals try to escape from the situation through tardiness and absenteeism (Drummond & Ryan, 1995).

Sources of career stress in organizations take many forms: role conflict, task overload, role ambiguity, discrimination and stereotyping, marriage/work conflicts, interpersonal stress, feelings of inadequacy, discordant values, and lack of progress towards career goals (Hirschorn, 1988). Another stressor is sexual harassment (Barnett & Rivers, 1996). Sexual harassment places an unendurable burden particularly on working women, and has been associated with anxiety, depression, headaches, sleep disturbance, gastrointestinal disorders, weight loss or gain, nausea, sexual dysfunction, and costs a typical Fortune 500 company nearly $7 million per year (Barnett & Rivers, 1996).

Depending upon the structure of organizations and how closed or open they may be, threats and psychological injuries to workers are a part of work life. How stressful or problematic they become is dependent on the personality characteristics of the workers, previous experience, the nature of the psychological boundaries that exist in a work setting, and other factors. Frequently, workers perceive that work entails risk, and risks are experienced psychologically as threats that must be aggressively met, contained, and ultimately transformed into challenges and opportunities (Hirschhorn, 1988).

Anxiety becomes a precursor of a more serious problem as it progresses or persists (Herr & Cramer, 1996). Feelings of anxiety are the fundamental roots of distorted or alienated relationships at work. A work group manages its anxiety by developing and deploying a set of social defenses: people can (a) retreat from role, task, and organizational boundaries; (b) manage their anxiety by projection of blame; (c) bureaucratize their work, (d) resort to excessive paperwork to reduce face-to-face communications, or (e) engage in excessive checking and monitoring of their work to reduce the anxiety of making difficult decisions. Social defenses may depersonalize relationships at work and distort the worker's capacities to accomplish primary work tasks. Potential individual-organizational pathologies can arise and spiral in complexity towards more difficult physical and mental reactions, leading to distortions of the meaning of work or, indeed, to various forms of mental distress or illness (Hirschorn, 1988). One obvious distortion of meaning: millions in the U.S. work when they are sick because corporate cost-cutting has provoked extreme anxiety among employees who feel they can no longer take time off (Genasci, 1995). Not all employees are afraid of losing their jobs. Many say loyalty is the main reason they work when they are sick. An increasing number of workers feel that, with so many coworkers lost to cutbacks, there are no extra bodies to fill in if they take a sick day.

Practical Applications

Practitioners can help workers understand how work stress affects them by (a) getting them to analyze and identify the parts of their job that are sources of stress, (b) helping them learn their own stress reactions, and (c) helping them determine what they can do about job stress (Shore, 1992). Long-range strategies for dealing with stress need to be developed as workers and the work environment change. Stress can be reduced when the organization (a) defines the work roles and responsibilities more clearly, (b) provides career development and counseling services, (c) provides social support systems, (d) encourages meaningful stimulation, (e) redesigns jobs to allow workers to use their skills, (f) reduces work loads, (g) rethinks work schedules, and (h) involves workers in decision-making (Drummond & Ryan, 1995).

To counteract the stress brought on by the changing shape of the job market, Nadene Peterson (Pedrotti, 1990) recommends workers do three things. First, develop a portfolio of transferable skills. Second, learn to network within a given career field. And third, be prepared to market yourself to prospective employers.

Most companies, big or small, are working with fewer staff. Over the last decade, the nation's largest companies eliminated 4.7 million positions, or one-quarter of their workforce. The perception is that managers, increasingly looking at the bottom line, prefer to have people in the office even if they are sick. Worries about job security have brought employees into work during blizzards, even after employers have told them to stay home (Wilde, 1996).

Conscientiousness can become overcompensation for lack of satisfaction in other areas of life (Cobble, 1996). An employee spending too much time on the job may show disinterest in family, friends, and leisure time. Lunch frequently is skipped and only a small amount is eaten at one's desk to maintain a consistent level of frenzied activity. These employees may perceive their work environment to be so competitive they feel they have to outperform each other and work twice as long to keep up, sacrificing their health.

Tension between work and family life is a major source of stress for many workers. Productivity drops when employees have difficulty with dependent care. Bank Street College found that problems with child care caused absenteeism and unproductive time (Solomon, 1991). In a study conducted by the Families and Work Institute in New York City, employees who have latchkey children missed 13 days of work per year as compared to an average of 7 to 9 days for the other workers. Another survey conducted found that more than half of men and women report being interrupted at work because of elder care responsibilities (Solomon, 1991).

Career Burnout

If stressors continue in the workplace with no hope of change, burnout can eventually happen. A person may no longer care about work performance outcome. Burnout is not a single event but a process of gradual change in behavior, eventually reaching intense reactions and often leading to a crisis, if left unresolved. Burnout has been associated with (a) role conflict, (b) work overload, (c) repetitious work tasks, (d) boredom, (e) ambiguity, (f) lack of advancement opportunities, and (g) shortage of time. Excessive work with very disturbed people is highly correlated with burnout (Emener & Rubin, 1980; Farber & Heifetz,

---

Practical Applications

Training programs (e.g., teacher education, the mental health professions, nursing, law) that adopt a tone of moral communities, not just service delivery systems, can also help to prevent burnout. "Helping professionals are less likely to burn out when they are committed to a transcendent set of moral beliefs, and when they work in a community based on those beliefs" (Cherniss, 1995, p. 186).

A singular, unique feature of burnout is that most workers do not realize until too late that they have passed the threshold of their capacities and tolerance. Burnout prevention in the workplace needs greater emphasis. To prevent burnout, a client must be able to recognize what in their work environment causes stress. The client can act to either change the situation within the organization so that the stressors are less acute, or consider a job change. Feelings of helplessness emerge when a client perceives no options, leading to depression and burnout. Often when clients become aware of the problem they will take action (Zunker, 1995). To facilitate this action, Pines and Aronson (1988) have a four-step plan for dealing with career burnout: (1) recognize the symptoms, (2) activate a plan for solving the causes, (3) distinguish between what can be changed and what cannot be changed, (4) develop new coping skills and refine old ones.

Anticipating stressful times of the year can help workers in certain

1981). Off-the-job stress should also be evaluated with clients who exhibit symptoms of burnout (Pardine, Higgins, Szeglin, Berres, Kravitz & Fotis, 1981).

Cherniss (1995) studied 26 human services professionals (7 high school teachers, 6 public health nurses, 7 mental health practitioners, and 6 lawyers) at two points in time. Initially, stressors faced by these new professionals and their coping efforts were examined as they ended their first year on the job. Unstructured interviews obtained the most penetrating information on the work experiences of research participants. Unstructured, follow-up interviews were conducted twelve years later on all the original participants. The following discussion is based on the findings by Cherniss.

After completing their educational preparation, several sources of stress characterized the first-year professionals' work. (1) New professionals often experienced crises of confidence and feelings of inadequacy. They did not know how to handle their job demands. Unrealistic expectations about their jobs were frequently coupled with inadequate formal schooling. Many first-year professionals

occupations to reduce the risk of burnout. Examples of these acute times of inevitable stress are: (1) for accountants, certified public accountants, and tax lawyers—tax season; (2) for retailers and choir directors at schools and churches—Christmas season; (3) for florists—Mother's Day and Valentine's Day; (4) for students, teachers, and professors at colleges and universities—final exam week. Knowing the busiest times of the year can help employees mentally prepare for unavoidable onslaughts.

Cherniss (1995) suggests several antidotes for burnout: (1) A combination of autonomy and support from bosses. (2) Professionals with a history of individual coping effectiveness during their early adult years are less likely to suffer burnout. Those who do not directly enter graduate or professional school after their undergraduate years are less likely to experience burnout. (3)

Early development of career insight, such as (a) self-knowledge of strengths, weaknesses, and preferences; and (b) a clear and accurate idea of what one likes to do best and what one can do best; with (c) periodic testing of other possibilities. (4) Improving organizational negotiation skills, such as (a) avoiding or resolving stressful interpersonal conflicts, (b) overcoming bureaucracy, and (c) obtaining support for meaningful and innovative projects helps professionals regain commitment to and satisfaction with their work. (5) Maintaining a balance between one's work life, personal life, and leisure. When family life and relaxation are just as important as work, recovery from burnout becomes easier. (6) "Doing" less and "being" more enhances more realistic goals about what can be accomplished at work. Burnout can be avoided, and recovery improved, when the need to achieve is moderated by other goals.

were left scrambling to prevent failure and humiliation. Original work values of altruism, compassion, and motives of idealism became less of a priority. (2) Independence and autonomy attracted many to human service professions but worksites limited these motivations. Professionals' academic training had not prepared them for the organizational craziness that awaited them in the real world. Bureaucratic obstruction laid the groundwork for the stress and burnout. (3) Difficult clients tested these new professionals' sense of competence. Dishonest, manipulative clients were the worst. Initial enthusiasm dwindled in the face of uncooperative, unappreciative clients. Uncertainty about competence only served to facilitate feelings of frustration, demoralization, and disillusionment of new professionals. (4) Boredom and routine occurred more than hoped-for meaningful and interesting work. Amounts of clerical work were a shocker. Intellectual stimulation during their educational preparation vanished at their jobs. (5) A lack of collegiality left many new professionals feeling alone and vulnerable at their worksites. Expected communities of like-minded coworkers did not materialize. Lack of information and feedback from more experienced colleagues meant that new professionals' needs for stimulation, encouragement, and affirmation of their competence was not forthcoming. Bureaucracy, social ambivalence towards supporting human service programs, and political and economic changes which have shrunk available resources were part of the social context in which these professionals' feelings of frustration took place.

By the end of their first year of work, many new service professionals became less caring and committed. They (a) adopted more modest goals, (b) blamed others for failure, (c) liked their clients less, (d) looked out for themselves more, and (e) withdrew psychologically from work. What started as a vocation and a calling ended up being just a job. Unremitting stress and constant frustration evolved into burnout.

At the twelve-year follow-up, only 10 of the 26 original research participants remained in the helping professions (1 was permanently disabled, 2 were caring for young children at home full time, 13 had left public service). Those who left public service did so to (a) achieve greater financial rewards, (b) obtain more intellectually stimulating work or higher-status employment, (c) become self-employed, or (d) work with less difficult clients. Those who remained in public service did so because of family obligations, economic considerations, or because a career change was too stressful to contemplate.

PRERETIREMENT AND RETIREMENT

Older adults, an increasingly larger percentage of the population, "face a major challenge in the adjustment to retirement" (Jensen-Scott, 1993, p.257). Career counseling is integral to the success of older workers, since they face ageism.

Retirement is one of the transitions that occur at this stage and, due to the societal importance of occupation/career, retirement can become a period of upheaval and stress in a person's life. However, since people react very differently to the issue of retirement, career counseling must take on a more individualized approach that meets the needs of each individual rather than retirees as a whole. With structured counseling, retirement can become a positive transition in a person's life.

Bolles (1978) describes the traditional way of living one's life: education, work, and leisure/retirement, which should be continuous over one's adult life. Krain (1995) recognizes the loss of boundaries when looking at the transition from work to retirement. He suggests that education needs to continue as well as some involvement in work and leisure activities. He states the following social policy objectives to facilitate changes and alleviate problems for older people: (1) distribute the available work to as many as possible, (2) extend income to those out of work, (3) extend work life of older workers, (4) redesign education to be directed as much to adults and the elderly as to youth and children, (5) base retirement decisions on the assessment of worker fitness, (6) reform the private pension system, and (7) popularize appropriate models of successful integration of education, work and leisure.

In an annual review of vocational behavior research, Brown, Fukunaga, Umemoto, and Wicker (1996) looked at issues of social class and retirement. Individuals of higher income and education tend to engage in activities that involve travel and reading, while those of lower income and education tend to be involved more in arts and crafts hobbies and watching television. Lower-income people tend to live in mobile homes, higher-income people in planned communities with more elaborate homes and social and sports amenities. Adjustment to retirement appears to be affected by previous occupational status, education, and income. Lower-income persons tend to retire earlier and for different reasons than those of higher-income people. Carter and Cook (1995) study the influence of social and work roles on retirement adjustment. They developed a model to demonstrate their results, as seen in Figure 11.4.

Those individuals who do not derive their major source of identity from the work role have "low work role attachment" (p. 72). For many retirees, nonwork roles become more important than work roles. If one has a strong work ethic and his/her personal identity and worth has been attached to a job, then leaving a job may bring feelings of deprivation which can lead to dissatisfaction in retirement. "Leaving the workforce may involve role redefinition or expansion. The success of role redefinition may be determined by one's social roles, work roles, and the internal resources needed to negotiate role changes" (p. 79).

Jensen-Scott (1993) developed a list of tasks for dissatisfied retirees and offered suggestions for interventions to aid them. These are seen in Table 11.2.

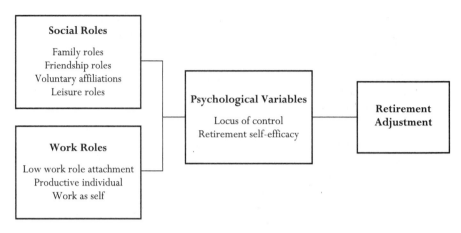

FIGURE 11.4 Roles and Psychological Resources as Determinants of Adjustment

SOURCE: *Carter & Cook (1995), p. 73.*

TABLE 11.2 Possible Tasks of Dissatisfied Retirees and Suggested Interventions

CLIENT'S DISSATISFACTION	TASK	INTERVENTION
Difficulty with change	Adjustment to change	Exploring feelings about retirement, meaning of job and retirement, function of job, and perspectives on aging Provide information
Job is low in hierarchy	Provision of information	Provide information
Job is moderately high or low in hierarchy	Reorder the hierarchy	Values clarification Self-esteem building Decision-making skills Considerations of lifestyle options Communication skills building Provide information
Job is high in hierarchy and job-related goals are met	Reorder the hierarchy	See previous suggestions
Job is high in hierarchy and job-related goals are not met	Acquisition of job or substitute	Explore interests, abilities Research job market Consider volunteer opportunities Provide information
Job is high in hierarchy and goals are not met and unable to obtain job	Reorder the hierarchy	See previous suggestion

SOURCE: Jensen-Scott, (1993), p. 262.

Practical Applications

Jensen-Scott (1993) cautions practitioners to be aware of the specific needs of retirees. First, they are difficult to reach and the counselor needs to go where they are since mental health services are underused by older adults. Second, they are more hesitant to develop a counseling relationship. Third, there are few assessment instruments developed for older adults. Fourth, there is a lack of job and volunteer opportunities for retirees.

For many individuals, part-time employment is a positive option if they find retirement activities to be unsatisfying. Cahill and Salomone (1987) encourage management to support older workers if they want to pursue part-time employment. Kelly (1990) cited a poll by the American Association of Retired Persons, which found that 10 million retirees were sitting at home who wanted to work, but could not find jobs. Practitioners need to be an advocate for the older worker with management, corporations, agencies and schools.

Simon and Osipow (1996) offer a description of a counseling technique for older workers as they approach retirement. Using vocational scripts and life reviews, they propose that the process use three distinct tasks to develop a way to prepare for meaningful retirement. "The first entails helping people define the connections among their various life events and personality changes" (p. 159). A second task "encourages people to define their work experiences as a career" (p. 159), developing themes, areas of expertise and preferred activities, rewards, both inner and outer, and responses to these ideas. The third task focuses on the future, with emphasis on "perseverance and developing autonomy within roles and relationships"(p. 160). Practitioners can be involved as "good coaches, explaining modeling, encouraging, and reinforcing development of the career definition into a vocational script" (p. 160).

New ideas are being proposed about the relationship of career to leisure, where McDaniels (1996) suggests the Career = Work + Leisure. How we view leisure in relationship to our work lives and our retirement years is important to consider. This is an area to be explored.

The life planning/career path throughout adulthood rarely follows a straight path. There are many turns in the road, adaptations that need to be made, and flexibility which is the hallmark of resiliency. With the technological advances that have been made, information about jobs and careers is readily accessible. The places that can provide comprehensive services to help read the roads that unfold as we go down them will play an increasingly important role in our lives.

12

Developing an Occupational Counseling and Information Center (OCIC)

Technology has had a powerful impact on vocational psychology and career guidance services. It has allowed information that was complex and difficult to obtain to become available immediately with easy search systems. Because it has made information easy to update, technology also makes it possible to track changes taking place in job descriptions and titles, which jobs are being eliminated, and where the current job market is shifting. Jobs that were never imagined twenty years ago are being created today.

The use of computers is flourishing, with various systems and approaches to career guidance increasingly becoming part of the tools practitioners may want to have available for their practice. Furthermore, the Internet is a rich source of information that is accessible to anyone. Among our tasks as practitioners will be to help clients access information, on the Internet and other computer-assisted programs, in an efficient and helpful manner, but still allow for interpersonal interaction, which will always be an integral part of vocational counseling.

This chapter is divided into four major sections. First, types of computer-assisted career guidance systems are discussed and examined. Second, online information systems are considered. Third, we describe a multimedia approach for the implementation of an Occupational Counseling and Information Center (OCIC). Fourth, sources of occupational information are listed. As discussed in Chapters 1 and 2, we use the word *occupation* instead of *career* because of the limited focus *career* has developed.

COMPUTER-ASSISTED CAREER
GUIDANCE SYSTEMS

The use of computers in vocational counseling has been a major development for practitioners. While there are limitations, computers can offer efficiency and accuracy when processing complex information, and can lead users to a wider variety of resources with which to conduct searches. The benefits computers provide include:

1. a more efficient use of time for practitioners
2. immediate access to assessments results
3. accuracy of administration and scoring
4. efficient sequential steps that can be guided by the client
5. adaptation to specific vocational theories
6. opportunities for research
7. popularity with students

However, potential problem areas include:

1. loss of client/practitioner interaction
2. assumption of a certain level of cognitive functioning
3. potential loss of privacy
4. allowance for client idiosyncrasies

Self-motivated individuals may be better candidates for using computer-assisted career guidance systems (CACG) (Kivlighan, Johnston, Hogan & Mauer, 1994). Using the Superiority and Goal Instability scales of the Self-Expression Inventory (Robbins & Patton, 1985), Kivlighan et al. found that those who rated high on the Superiority scale and low on the Goal Instability scale were more satisfied with the computer-assisted vocational search program than those who rated low on the Superiority scale and high on the Goal Instability scale. These latter individuals appeared to benefit much more from the interpersonally oriented treatment approach than from computer-assisted applications. Practitioners will have to know the client's needs when deciding what technology to use in the process.

With this as background, we will discuss the two major CACG systems and then focus on some of the research findings on the systems. While these systems have been upgraded and expanded, there are other systems available as well. The two major interactive CACG systems in use are **DISCOVER**, marketed by ACT, Inc. (formerly American College Testing Program) and **SIGI and SIGI PLUS**, marketed by Educational Testing Service (ETS).

Led in its development by Jo Ann Harris-Bowlsbey, DISCOVER released a multimedia version in 1997, which is available in English and French and adapted for use in Canada and Australia using occupational information relevant to those countries. DISCOVER has five versions representing various ages and groups. These include (a) junior high/middle school, (b) high school, (c) college and adults, (d) organizations, and (e) retirement planning for older adults. Each version contains the following modules:

1. Beginning the career journey

2. Learning about the world of work

3. Learning about yourself

4. Finding occupations

5. Learning about occupations

6. Making educational choices

7. Planning next steps

8. Planning your career

9. Making transitions

Though the modules are set up in a sequential order, it is possible to access one module without completing all the previous ones.

The system is designed to be interactive, so users are given exercises that help them gain self-knowledge, identify their interests and abilities, prioritize their values, and inventory life work experiences. Within the DISCOVER system, the user can access the results of each inventory/assessment immediately and be provided with a list of occupations to explore, based on the information the personal profile contains. These results are then placed in the context of the World-of-Work Map, which organizes occupations into clusters, regions, and families. For more information on the use of DISCOVER for college students and adults, see chapter 8 in *Vocational Models for Diverse Populations.*

The System of Interactive and Guidance Information (SIGI and SIGI PLUS), developed by Martin Katz, was designed to assist college students to clarify values, identify occupational options, and develop rational career decision-making (CDM) skills. The five SIGI subsystems include:

1. Values

2. Locate

3. Compare

4. Planning

5. Strategy

SIGI PLUS was developed to include adults and organization needs. It has nine components:

1. Introduction
2. Self-Assessment
3. Search
4. Information
5. Skills
6. Preparing
7. Coping
8. Deciding
9. Next Steps

Katz (1993) discusses the functions of the SIGI systems. The domains of self-understanding include needs, values, interests, temperaments, and aptitude. Needs may be considered as basic motivating forces for which satisfaction is sought. "To the extent that needs reside below the level of consciousness, they are best handled in guidance through their outer manifestations and expressions, as values" (p. 105). Values order, arrange, and unify the interactions of psychological and social forces in the process of career decision-making, as well as allow for the expression of culturally influenced needs. Interests relate to the means by which a goal that represents values may be met. Temperaments define and can be subsumed in values and interests. Aptitude "appears to mean whatever a given developer decides it is to mean" (p. 144).

Skills are further elaborated in SIGI PLUS. Occupational information, strategies for decision-making, and turning decisions into actions are expanded by separating out the Preparing component. This element uses what is typically required for entry into an occupation by defining steps and listing resources, such as time, money, the ability to cope with difficulties, and motivation. Coping is designed to deal with the special needs of adults in transition, whether going into a new occupation, or reentering the labor force after a period of unemployment, or changing occupations. For more information about these systems and their development, Katz (1993) is a good resource.

Which of these two systems is better? There appears to be no clear answer. In a study by Kapes, Borman, and Frazier (1989), undergraduate students and counselors who were being trained rated both systems highly. We found that outcome data indicate that using these systems as part of a thorough career development counseling can be beneficial and helpful. Garis and Niles (1990) found that students responded more favorably to SIGI than to DISCOVER, but the same study indicated that the most effective treatment was a career-planning course

without the use of a CAGC. A study of the impact of SIGI and SIGI PLUS by
Reardon, Peterson, Sampson, Ryan-Jones, and Shahnasarian (1992) indicates that
while both were generally satisfactory to students in analysis, synthesis, and computer effect, more individuals preferred SIGI PLUS than SIGI. Since SIGI PLUS
allows greater flexibility or control of the system functioning by the user, the
amount of time spent on the program by individuals was often less.

Recent research on the effectiveness of CAGC systems has shown several
findings. Sampson et al. (1992) studied these two major CACG systems in terms
of Social Influence Theory (Strong, 1968; Strong & Matross, 1973), which states
that the social power of the counselor in the counseling relationship is a major
factor in the ability to effect behavioral change. Corrigan, Dell, Lewis, and
Schmidt (1980) and Heppner and Dixon (1981) found that clients responded to
expertness, attractiveness, and trustworthiness in the counselor. Dorn (1988)
described these: "Perceived expertness emerges as a result of the counselor's
credibility and reputation in the community, specialized training, and ability to
dispute the client's opinions with knowledgeable arguments. Perceived counselor trustworthiness evolves from the client's realization that the counselor is
working for the client's benefit. Perceived attractiveness of the counselor results
from his or her compatibility, similarity, and positive regard for the client" (p.
270). Applying these standards to the two CACG systems, Sampson et al. (1992)
found that

> the implication is that although CACG systems are comparable to coun-
> selors in providing expert information, they are not so in engendering
> perceptions of attractiveness and trustworthiness. Thus, we can infer that
> the involvement of a counselor in the career exploration process becomes
> exceedingly important. (p. 82)

Research targeting the primary criticisms of CACG systems include issues
such as (a) clients using the systems to answer career-related questions the systems were not designed to answer; (b) lack of comparability with similar paper-
and-pencil measures; (c) ethical concerns; and (d) the pseudo-factual impressions
computers often foster (Garis & Niles, 1990; McKee & Levinson, 1990).

Garis and Niles (1990) further suggest that the parts of a CACG system
should be examined more carefully, rather than just looking at the system as a
whole. Certain assessments might be more effective when combined with other
instruments or used in a defined sequence. CACG systems should be tailored for
the setting they will be used in order to increase the effectiveness of the system.
In addition, the different components of the CACG must be scrutinized as
closely as paper-and-pencil tests have been. Johnston, Buesher, and Heppner
(1988) added that counselors need to examine the contents of the system carefully in order to ensure that they are appropriate to the setting. The system

should not be used as a replacement to counselor intervention as an unstructured intervention.

Gati (1994) sees four problems with CACG systems: the database, the decision-making process, the interactive dialogue, and the context on which the system is built. With occupational information, Gati suggests there is an "image of accuracy" in computerized information, even though human judgment plays a critical role in the information and is subject to unintentional biases. Another concern with the database is how to present "within occupational variance" without being overwhelmed. Regarding the decision-making process, Gati suggests five problematic subareas: eliciting aspirations while encouraging compromise, increasing the number of considered alternatives, the validity of the idea that some alternatives are better or as good as others, whether to rank alternatives in some descending order, dealing with uncertainty. Effective interactive dialogue needs to provide relevant information, be sophisticated rather than simplistic, be flexible instead of constrained, and design the interface to be attractive. It is essential that practitioners familiarize themselves with CACG systems to use them effectively and adapt useful features into the occupational counseling process (Gati, 1994).

Other Computer-Assisted Career Guidance Systems

CHOICES is designed to help high school students make informed and educated decisions about their future, whether it be to attend a university or begin a career. CHOICES offers information about everything from vocational technical schools to financial aid, and its services include:

1. a career interest checklist that helps students relate their interests to occupations,

2. a college letter writer that writes letters for catalogues or more information from selected colleges, and

3. a financial aid letter writer that generates letters to sources of financial aid for more information.

Information is also available regarding occupations, state and local information, education and training, and financial aid.

Career Decisions Software Solutions (CDSS) (Cognito Press, 1994) assists a person in making career decisions by providing accurate career information from an office or career center or a computer at home. This software includes the most recent career information in the United States and cuts down on the research that one used to have to do in a library. CDSS also provides a person with a list of occupations that matches their characteristics or the characteristics of their desired vocation.

The SDS-Computerized Version is an adaptation of Holland's (1985) paper-and-pencil assessment, The Self-Directed Search. This computer version was developed by Reardon and Psychological Assessment Resources (Schinka, 1988), and includes My Vocational Situation, a true-false scale used to identify individuals in need of vocational counseling, and the items and instructions for completing the instruments that are identical to those included in the 1985 paper-pencil version of the SDS. McKee and Levinson (1990) suggest considering the cost—the SDS-CV is more costly, there are fewer errors on the computer version, and the client receives thorough information and feedback without the assistance of a professional. On the other hand, little research has been done to determine the technical adequacy of the computerized version, and we know that the best combination is assessment and consulting with a vocational practitioner.

Selecting and Using Computer-Assisted Career Guidance Systems

A benefit of CACG systems is their flexibility and accessibility across programs. Most systems offer

- occupational information
- armed services information
- information about post-secondary institutions
- information on technical/specialized schools
- financial aid information
- interest inventories
- decision-making skills

Other common components include

- local job information files
- ability measures
- value inventories
- predictions of success in college
- job-search strategies
- how to prepare a resume
- information on job interviewing
- components for adults (Zunker, 1994, pp. 126–127).

Practitioners should take these steps when using CACG systems:

1. Assessment of needs—understand each individual's needs in order to determine which parts of the program should be used.

2. Orientation—explain the purpose and goals of the program provided with a clear understanding of the mechanics of the system.

3. Individualized programs—assist when needs are determined.

4. Practitioner intervention—assist when necessary to help the user work towards occupational choice.

5. Online assistance—assist when different stages are explored during the process.

6. Follow-up—encourage, motivate, set goals, and interpret outcomes before he/she leaves (Zunker, 1994, pp. 133–34).

When selecting a CACG system, it is important to obtain information from colleagues, see a demonstration of the system and evaluate its products, understand the cost to install and to run, and survey equipment needs to determine what can best meet the needs given the available budget. It is important to know what system will be used before selecting hardware to assure a good and adequate fit. Sampson (1994a) also emphasizes

1. integrating the CACG system into the career services center;

2. using hands-on training for the staff to ensure (a) acceptance and involvement with the CACG, (b) ability to operate the system with ease, and (c) a clear understanding of the role of the system in the context of the counseling process; and

3. building in evaluative processes to monitor the effectiveness of the CACG system continually.

Technical Concerns for Choosing the Appropriate CACG System

Aside from the advantages and disadvantages of computers versus paper-and-pencil tests, there are technical concerns that are an entirely unique factor when using computers. Certain expectations must be met when choosing a computerized system, including flexibility, accuracy, usability, and readability. Flexibility is an important part of a computerized system, as the user must be allowed to change his/her answers after they have been entered into the system. Without this, mistakes cannot be rectified. Aside from flexibility, the information must be accurate, easy to understand, and comparable to standard career guides such as *The Occupational Outlook Handbook*.

When purchasing a computerized system it is imperative to address possible technical difficulties and service issues with the program's manufacturer. Several areas should be discussed with the manufacturer before a purchasing decision is made. These include: having the number of the service department as well as some of the centers that are currently using the program, knowledge of the possible defects in the program and how these problems can be corrected, and the types and lengths of the warranty offered. As part of the purchase, the manufacturer should either instruct or setup the program initially so that all of the required hardware and software is loaded correctly onto the system (Johnson, Buescher & Heppner, 1988). If a counselor addresses these issues first, the chances of choosing the best system will be greatly improved.

Ethical Issues One possibility facing vocational counseling is the issue of stand-alone CACG systems. There are serious concerns about the ability of these systems to adequately provide satisfactory service. However, the cost effectiveness of them makes them attractive, and the sophistication of their development may overcome many of the objections. According to Sampson (1997) the issues of making available a stand-alone CACG system and the decision about the type and amount of staff assistance provided to clients should be important when picking and integrating a CACG system. "The need for counselor intervention is ultimately a function of two factors, the characteristics of the CACG system and the characteristics of the user" (p. 5).

Most CACG systems are not meant to be stand-alone systems and should be accompanied by the proper support of a counselor; however, the ethical dilemma arises over how much time a staff member should provide for a client who is using a CACG system. Both overhelping and underhelping a client is detrimental to the client's career decision-making process, and a counselor must be able to differentiate between the client who is able to appropriately use a CACG and requires little help, and the client who is struggling with the system. The information provided by a CACG does not always mean that the client is getting the needed services. He proposes a model that screens to ascertain if the client and the CACG are compatible, providing orientation as may be necessary for the client, and follow-up to determine the effectiveness of the intervention.

Another ethical dilemma arises in the expectations of a client when using a CACG system. Sampson (1997) states "inappropriate expectations about using a computer-assisted career guidance system may limit critical thinking and exploratory behaviors necessary for effective career decision-making" (p. 3).

Herr (1997) notes that "the *ethical obligations* of counselors to clients (e.g. respect, dignity, confidentiality, disclosure, prevent harm, do not harm) change very little . . . but the *roles* of counselors change as new technologies and scientific knowledge bases expand to modify what counselors do" (p. 2). He recommends that to work within ethical guidelines, practitioners see CACG systems as part of the process for all clients, and must "work to demysticize technology" (p. 4).

Practical Applications

With the increasing use of technology in vocational psychology and its practice, it is essential that practitioners be trained to access the systems and sort through the plethora of information available. The amount of data can be overwhelming and users will need assistance to prioritize and take action.

In a conversation between Nadene Peterson and K. Richard Pyle, an employee of ACT, Inc., and the DISCOVER program, Pyle reported about his work facilitating in-service training of counselors to assist them in learning the elements of occupational/career groups as an adjunct to CACG systems. From these groups the students can (a) determine which occupations they want to pursue and the educational/training requirements involved; (b) identify traits, interests and values; (c) respond to subjective aspects of that information and obtain feedback from peers; (d) explore the "fit" of occupational information with personal traits; and (e) suggest opportunities for shadowing, mentors, advisors, work experience, and volunteer activities. This information is an update of his earlier article (Pyle, 1985). (See also, Chapter 11 of Peterson and González, *Career Counseling Models for Diverse Populations*.)

The advantages of group counseling are that more students can be serviced at one time and students have an excellent opportunity to learn from each other. It encourages commitment to plans by requiring them to report each week what they have learned and accomplished. If completing a CACG program is a requirement for high school students, this can provide services to a wider variety of students, not just those who are college-bound.

For more information about various topics concerning CACG systems, how to install and operate them, and how to be aware of current practices, the Center for the Study of Technology in Counseling and Career Development at Florida State University is an excellent source.

Currently Used Computer-Assisted Career Guidance Systems

Table 12.1 lists the names, publishers, and information about currently used computer-assisted career guidance systems.

TABLE 12.1 Computer-Assisted Career Guidance Systems

SYSTEM	DEVELOPER
Career Information Delivery Systems (CIDS)	National CIS University of Oregon Eugene, OR 97403

A comprehensive survey of various career-information formats.

CHOICES	ISM Information Systems
DECISIONS	Management, Inc.

Offers current information about occupations, colleges, majors, financial aid with steps to making decisions, programs designed for children and for adults; DECISIONS helps identify at-risk students.

Coordinate Occupational Information Network (COIN)	Dr. Rodney Durgin COIN Career Guidance Products 3361 Executive Parkway, #302 Toledo, OH 43606

Sources of general occupational information.
Designed for five different groups and age levels, English and French (Canadian) versions with occupational information for Canada and Australia as well as the United States.

Guidance Information Systems (GIS)	Houghton Mifflin Co. Educational Software Div. Box 683 Hanover, NH 03755

DISCOVER	ACT, Inc.
Systems of Interactive Guidance and Information (SIGI) and SIGI PLUS	SIGI Office. Educational Testing Service Princeton, NJ 08541

Guidance through making career choices.

ONLINE SERVICES

The explosion of information available through online systems and the Internet have made it nearly impossible to keep pace with developments. Herr (1997) poses several concerns with this expansion of information:

1. the accuracy, relevance, and timeliness of information

2. adequate preparation for the user to know how to process the information

3. opportunity for follow-up to correct or confirm the information

4. confidentiality and privacy

5. the potential for violation of copyright law

6. ethical exchange of information between sites and users

7. lack of training of counselors with the technology

8. conduct of research with concomitant issues such as informed consent, trust, protecting the identity of participants

We want to emphasize the concern mentioned in the above list about practitioner preparation. Most practitioners probably have not had much opportunity to keep up with the new types of information, let alone current information. As technology changes and develops so rapidly, it is imperative for practitioners to keep abreast of the websites for career and vocational information and to be able to check the accuracy and credentials of the sources of information.

Use of the Internet

The fastest-growing source of information about careers, jobs, and related areas is on the Internet. While a comprehensive listing is beyond the scope of this book, and since e-mail addresses are subject to change, we have chosen to list areas of interest and some major sources. Terms to look under in search engines include: careers, jobs, job search, career development, career guidance, career information, and career counseling.

Some major sources include:

- The National Occupational Information Coordinating Committee (NOICC) for information and the State OICC for area resources. http://www.profiles.iastate.edu/idid/ncdc

- Department of Labor http://www.dol.gov

- Career Counseling Resources http://www.hawk.igs.net/employmentplanning/

- Career Counselors Consortium http://www.careercc.org

- School-to-Career and Career Resources for Counselors http://www.azstartnet.com/~rjm/index.htm

- National School to Work Learning Center http://stw.edu/gov

- Resources for Minorities http://www.vjf.com/pub/docs/jobsearch.html

- ADA Information Center http://www.idir.net/~adabbs

DESIGNING AN OCIC

The Top Ten Reasons to Visit Your Career Center

1. Your friends are sick of hearing that you don't know what to do with the rest of your life.

2. You can have something to tell your parents when they ask you (again) what you're doing about finding a job.

3. Career counselors get lonely when you don't visit them.

4. Once school is finished, you will never be able to get unlimited, free, professional career advice again.

5. Some career centers will videotape you in a practice interview. You can take the tape home and watch it over and over again.

6. Find out who's recruiting on campus before all the interview slots are filled.

7. Get your resume reviewed by an expert so you don't look like an amateur.

8. You'll feel better when you see how many other people don't know what they want to do with their lives.

9. You've already seen the cafeteria, registrar's office, admissions hall, and other campus highlights.

10. Hey, it's something everyone has to do before they graduate.
    —Village, Inc.

Although the top ten reasons to visit an OCIC are a humorous take on these resources, there is a ring of truth in each statement. Unfortunately, many students pass through high school and college without ever being aware of or properly trained to use these centers. The OCIC is an invaluable tool, and if set up correctly should provide a vast array of knowledge of the world of work—whether one is graduating from high school or college or is an alumnus/alumna making a job transition.

Rationale and Services

Several areas must be considered before attempting to design an OCIC. These are primary to a successful and effective delivery of services that will be both attractive to users and thorough in its perspective. They can be organized around four major factors: (1) philosophy of purpose, including major client base; (2) theoretical basis; (3) design of service delivery; and (4) evaluation of outcomes.

The rationale for a center is to provide occupational and career-design services for clients using the vast array of information available. Defining the major client base is basic to any design that may be instituted. Peterson, Sampson, and Reardon (1991) suggest considering the level of the clients, the complexity of the intervention that will typically need to be made, and the competencies needed by staff to properly meet the needs.

The theoretical foundation is important, since many of the programs, computer-assisted guidance systems, and assessment instruments should be chosen with a predominant theory in mind. It is probably wise to be somewhat eclectic theoretically, since many of the tools can be used with more than one theory. However, when initiating a center, it is advisable to begin with a consistent approach to the intervention.

Elements of the design of a center are described in Figure 12.1. A careful systematic approach to organization of the actual space will avoid problems of accessibility, functioning, and loss of interest by the user. Using the services of a systems organizer or observations of other centers will be most helpful in designing a center.

It is imperative to build into the center's activities and functions a means of tracking product outcomes. This can be on both an immediate and a longitudinal basis. Effectiveness in the delivery of services is important to know to make improvements and to justify the existence of the center. Evaluating the usefulness of the services to the user is imperative. For a more thorough discussion of the development of a center, a recommended resource is Peterson, Reardon, and Sampson (1991).

Figure 12.2 outlines the evaluation system developed at Florida State University.

High School OCIC's focus is on life after high school, which for some includes college and for the majority involves vocational/technical school, apprenticeship programs, or working. The OCIC offers students a place to locate the information needed to be prepared for life after graduation. This center should be located in a place that is accessible to all students, and an orientation for incoming high school freshmen should be required. Exposure to the center early in their high school experience can alleviate the concern or fear of exploration. It is the school counselor's responsibility to inform students and faculty about the resources, and it is the responsibility of the OCIC's director to coordinate with the teachers the opportunity for each student to visit the center each year of high school to complete a specific assignment. Ideally, each student will have visited the center a minimum of four times during high school.

Though most high school OCICs focus on students who plan to enter college, the reality is that on the average, only 40 percent attend college and only 25 percent earn a bachelor's degree (Gray & Herr, 1995). Therefore, high school OCICs need to focus on serving those students who are not going to college, whatever the reason. In order to make the center user-friendly for all individuals,

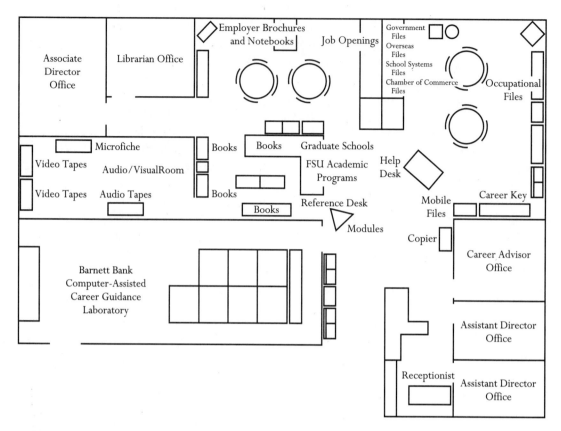

FIGURE 12.1 Floor Plan of the Career Center at Florida State University

SOURCE: Peterson, Sampson & Reardon (1991), p. 383.

procedures must be available which will help them feel comfortable and hopeful by using the services provided.

We propose that a high school OCIC have two tracks from which students can choose. One is the School-to-Work Track. This track is to prepare those students to enter the job market upon graduation. The second track is the School-to-School Track. This one is adapted to those students who plan to further their education upon graduation. While some of the services overlap, there is a particular emphasis that needs to be developed for each track. The School-to-Work Track services will include resources for:

- Identifying interests, aptitudes, abilities, and achievement levels
- Identifying occupational awareness and possibilities based on interests, etc.
- Building decision-making skills
- Locating information about jobs, and how to apply
- Providing opportunities for shadowing, firsthand observations

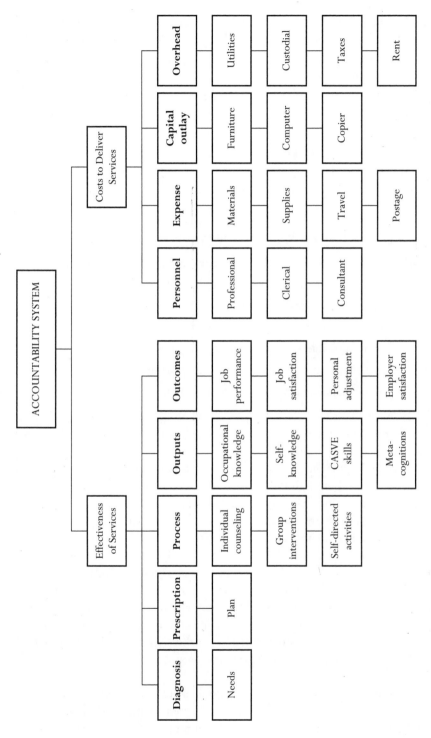

FIGURE 12.2 The Components of an Accountability Model Based on Cognitive Information Processing

SOURCE: Peterson, Sampson, and Reardon (1991), p. 396.

- Teaching basic Job-Seeking Skills, including appearance and attitude, practice interviewing, things to avoid, socially acceptable and expected behaviors
- Teaching work behavior skills, including punctuality, attitude, attempting to ascertain expectations on the job, dealing with hierarchy, and accountability
- Teaching social skills in the work setting, including understanding boundary issues, employer and supervisor relations, peer relations, and the interaction of personal responsibility and self-protection
- Developing résumé and portfolio organization
- Networking and correct uses of it

The School-to-School Track services will include resources for:

- Identifying interests, aptitudes, abilities, and achievement levels
- Identifying occupational awareness and possibilities, based on interests, etc.
- Building decision-making skills
- Identifying college/voc tech/community college interests
- Surveying possible schools and programs
- Learning application process to various colleges and universities
- Providing financial aid availability and application process assistance

An adaptation of these tracks needs to be made for special needs students as well. Other information may need to be sought, with special assessments of aptitudes, abilities, and job possibilities as part of the services the OCIC offers.

Springfield High School in Vermont has an exemplary career resource center that can be accessed through the Internet. The school begins the career counseling process with the incoming freshman and concludes it with the graduating seniors. The center's resources encompass more than providing information; there are also counselors who are available to the students to answer questions and aid in the career/job/college search. Aside from the materials that need to be a part of every career resource center, the setup of the center is of equal importance. Springfield High School's resource center is organized in such a way that many students can access different parts of the center at the same time. Obviously, in order for a high school to offer even the minimum career guidance services, there needs to be a strong commitment from the school board and administration to hire trained staff and provide the necessary space and equipment.

College/University At the college and university level, OCICs should be an integral part of a student's education. More often than not, these centers are underfunded, understaffed, and given little prominence on the campus.

A college career center should focus on life after graduation. The special services for this OCIC should include both a School-to-Work Track and School-to-School Track. School-to-Work Track services to provide are:

All the ones listed as general to all OCICs

Special emphasis on using alumni to mentor/advise

Extensive use of networking with alumni

On-campus recruiting services

Information on jobs and study abroad

School-to-School Track services to provide include:

A complete listing of catalogues with graduate programs

Preparation materials for the GRE, MAT, and other entrance examinations

Application information and assistance

Financial aid, internship, fellowship, and other types of aid

Advice on networking through departments and faculty

Information of study abroad

Another function these OCICs can provide is that of operating work-study programs on campus and training work-study students (Routh, Chretien & Rakes, 1995). The center can provide the necessary occupational decision-making skills to help place these students in appropriate work-study positions, some of whom can be trained to work in the OCIC (Pharr & Glover, 1995).

Adults OCICs for adults feature a different focus. These deal much more with people who are in career transition, job change, loss of job or career, and affected by change in health or abilities. While many of the same programs apply, there is a different emphasis. Oftentimes this will have to do more with immediate job placement. For this the job listings on the SOICC and other job data banks will be primary. Careful determination of the reason for the change is part of an interview process. If the change is due to factors outside the individual's control, then job placement may be the major consideration. However, if there are other factors involved, then more involved assessment procedures may be necessary. Creating a résumé/portfolio is primary and using networking skills and job databases will also be important. If attitude is problematic, practice with interviewing skills may be helpful. If the need for further training becomes obvious, then a different approach will be needed. Adult development is a relatively new area of concern. Super's Salience Inventory, Values Scale, and Adult Career Concerns Inventory each may be helpful with this population, as will Holland's Self-Directed Search and/or the Strong Interest Inventory. If a change of career is desired or necessary, then CACGs may be helpful.

A job club can meet weekly or biweekly to share the information each has found to keep current on job listings and experiences in job seeking. Offering mutual support is a strong component of this group. Equipment should be available to develop cover letters/résumés/portfolios. Videotaping practice interviews can be helpful. These can also be effective with people who have been injured who are seeking to return to the workforce. Work hardening and rehabilitative services can be part of the function of a job club. For more information on these services, see chapters 10, 14, 15, 16, and 19 in Peterson and González, *Career Counseling Models for Diverse Populations: Hands-on Applications by Practitioners.*

OCICs within Industries Within industries, OCICs are yet other types of centers. These centers usually have two emphases in their services. One is the Workforce Development emphasis, which deals with employees who are not functioning at a satisfactory level, need additional training and skills in order to stay on the job, or need to be assessed for a possible lateral move within the organization. The goal is to upgrade skills, abilities, and competencies to avoid a downward move or dismissal. The other emphasis is to provide services for those looking to advance or move to a different type of job, including management and supervision within the organization. Oftentimes, personality inventories, interest inventories, and aptitude measures will be most helpful in these settings, and person/environment fit considerations become especially important.

There are many books that deal with how the business environment is changing: business skills, job exploration and management, management development, and personal growth and development that should be part of the OCIC.

Practical Applications

The focus will be on the similarities that exist in establishing an OCIC in a variety of settings and also to meet specific developmental needs of the users in terms of age, ethnicity, religion, education, gender, and special needs populations. Many of these ideas are the result of Nadene Peterson's experience establishing two career resource centers.

A center can be housed in a high school, community college, college or university, or a community center such as an occupations/employment one-stop center, or a workforce development center. Space requirements, furniture, hardware, software, online capabilities, media equipment, and library resources (e.g., standard reference books, periodicals, job-related books, interviewing, resume writing) and personnel are similar regardless of its location.

Space requirements include modules for each of the activities available, office space for individual counseling, library resources, study and work areas, assessment and testing areas, an area for groups and small classes, and storage area. Basic equipment needs are computer hardware, VCRs, videotaping materials for practice interviews, word processors, and study and work stations with appropriate furniture.

Software needs include computer-assisted career guidance systems (CACGs), online abilities to access databases, and resume writing and interviewing techniques. Testing and assessment materials can be on software or completed as paper-and-pencil tasks.

Staffing needs are similar for all centers, regardless of size. The management and staff of the center should be thoroughly trained as career/vocational counselors. National Certified Career Counselors (NCCCs) specialize in career counseling and are highly recommended for a Director position. Paraprofessional (career facilitators) also have specific training in career counseling. Each staff member needs to be thoroughly familiar with the systems, equipment, location of information, and all the resources contained in the center. Training and effectiveness of the staff is crucial to the success of the center. This is an ongoing process, as new information, sources, and programs are acquired. Staff must be aware of new resources and how to access them, as well as be able to teach classes in vocational decision-making, resume writing, interviewing techniques, job-seeking skills, networking strategies, and orientation to the center.

Marketing the OCIC is a staff responsibility that includes: coordinating career fairs, finding alumni to serve as mentors/advisors, organizing internships, scheduling visits by new students on campus, making presentations to community groups, meeting with academic counselors on campus, and building career services into the curricula. All of these tasks need to be managed and accomplished.

Services that can be provided are: assessment and testing, counseling, resume writing and interviewing skills, a program of firsthand observations of people working in various jobs, a program of mentoring/advising, an internship placement service, contacts with businesses, information via software programs and the Internet, as well as hard copy reading materials.

Figure 12.2 presents a floor plan from the career center at Florida State University.

Each area of the center needs to be clearly identified, and a list of resources should be given to newcomers. Stations/modules around the center may include:

1. Testing and assessment. These tests include values, personal traits, interests inventories, and skills assessments. These tests and assessments can be paper and pencil tests or computer administered.
2. Computer software and Internet access. These can include the CACG systems and other programs.

Continued

Continued

3. Career games, kits, workbooks on career planning, and goal setting. These can include guided career choice and dealing with indecision and uncertainty.

4. Accessing state career information systems, including occupational information listed by state (SOICC) and by NOICC. Specific books and periodicals can include the O*NET—the replacement for the Dictionary of Occupational Titles—and other information sources.

5. Accessing information about colleges/universities, community colleges/technical training, school-to-work programs as well as various information sources regarding financial aid and scholarships.

6. Local employment opportunities

for various educational and experience levels.

These modules should be sequential, although a client may start at any of the modules depending on his or her level of occupational knowledge and needs. Clients should first be interviewed briefly by a trained occupational specialist who can assist them in starting at the station most appropriate for their situation.

Although every OCIC is similar, there are differences depending upon the age group being targeted, and the space available for the center. The next section delineates categories of high school, college, and adult OCICs with specific information that needs to be included in each. Specific resources are listed at the end of this chapter.

SOURCES OF OCCUPATIONAL INFORMATION

Basic Library Resources

- *Occupational Outlook Handbook*
- *Dictionary of Occupational Titles*
- *Enhanced Guide for Occupational Exploration*
- *Dictionary of Holland's Occupational Codes*
- *Peterson's Guides and Directories*
- *Careers in the Non-Profit Sector*
- *The Complete Guide to Public Employment*
- *National Trade and Professional Associations*
- *Global Employment Guide*
- *Directory of Special Programs for Minority Group Members*
- *Directory of Special Opportunities for Women*

Periodical Subscriptions

- *Occupational Outlook Quarterly*
- *Career Opportunities News*
- *Federal Jobs Digest*

Since books and sources of information are regularly updated, we have chosen to list some basic sources. No list can be exhaustive and new ones come into being on a regular basis. Table 12.2 lists basic sources of information.

TABLE 12.2 Basic Sources of Information

GOVERNMENTAL AND BASIC ORGANIZATIONS

National Occupational Information Coordinating Committee (NOICC)
2100 M Street NW, Suite 156
Washington, DC 20037
202/653-5665
The NOICC provides information about CIDS, individual state SOICCs, programs for career development, standards for services, goals for the nation.

O*NET
U.S. Department of Labor Office of Policy and Research/ETA/O*NET
200 Constitution Avenue, NW, Mail Stop N5637
Washington, DC 20210
202/219-7161, Fax: 202/219-9186
For information on the O*NET replacement of the *Dictionary of Occupational Titles,* the
O*NET's website is: www.doleta.gov/programs/onet
The webpage has the latest developments of the O*NET and the timetable for availability of its components.
Other Department of Labor information can be accessed through: www.dol.gov
The Bureau of Labor Statistics has a webpage for information about employment projections that is related to the *Occupational Outlook Handbook*. The URL is: http://stats.bls.gov/emphome.htm

U.S. Government Printing Office
710 N. Capitol Street, NW
Washington, DC 20401
202/512-1800; Fax: 202/512-1355
U.S. Government Bookstores (24) have the latest government information.
These are located in Atlanta, GA; Birmingham, AL; Boston, MA; Chicago, IL; Cleveland, OH; Columbus, OH; Dallas, TX; Denver, CO, Detroit, MI; Houston, TX; Jacksonville, FL; Kansas City, MO; Laurel, MD; Los Angeles, CA; Milwaukee, WI; New York, NY; Philadelphia, PA; Pittsburgh, PA; Portland, OR; Pueblo, CO; San Francisco, CA; Seattle, WA; Washington, DC.

Continued

TABLE 12.2 Basic Sources of Information *(continued)*

GOVERNMENTAL AND BASIC ORGANIZATIONS

National Career Development Association
5999 Stevenson Avenue
Alexandria, VA 22304
703/823-9800
The NCDA maintains a homepage for information: http://ncda.org.
It is possible to download the NCDA Guidelines for the Use of the Internet for Provision of
Career Information and Planning Services.
The NCDA maintains a listserve for people who wish to contact others on the list with questions, ideas, etc.

The Center for Education and Work
University of Wisconsin
964 Educational Sciences Building
1025 W. Johnson Street
Madison, WI 53706-1796
800/446-0399 for U.S. & Canada
95.800.446.0339 for Mexico
Fax: 608/262-9197
E-mail: cewmail@soemadison.wisc.edu
Website: www.cew.wisc.edu

The Center for Technology in Counseling and Career Development
Florida State University College of Education
Department of Human Services and Studies
Tallahassee, FL 32301
904/644-6431

The MU Career Center
110 Noyes Hall
Columbia, MO 65211
573/882-6801; Fax: 573/882-5440
Website: www.missouri.edu/~cppcwww/main.html
The University of Missouri-Columbia maintains an extensive database of information about
work, careers, jobs, etc. as well as helpful guides for job-seeking activities.

Academic Innovations (school)
3463 State Street, Suite 219A
Santa Barbara, CA 93105
805/967-8015; Fax: 805/967-4357

AGS (American Guidance Service) (school)
4201 Woodland Road
P.O. Box 99
Circle Pines, MN 55014-1796
800/328-2560; Fax: 612/786-0907
E-mail: ags@skypoint.com
Website: www.agsnet.com

TABLE 12.2 Basic Sources of Information *(continued)*

GOVERNMENTAL AND BASIC ORGANIZATIONS

Cambridge Career Products
P.O. Box 2153, Dept. CC18
Charleston, WV 25328-2153
800/468-4227

RESOURCES FOR ALL-LEVEL CAREER COUNSELING

Career Development Systems
5225 Verona Road, Building #3
Madison, WI 53711-4495
888/237-9297
Website: www.cdsways.com

Career Planning & Adult Development NETWORK
P.O. Box 611930
San Jose, CA
800/888-4945; Fax: 408/441-9101

Career Research & Testing
P.O. Box 611930
San Jose, CA 95161
800/888-4945
Jump Start Your Job Skills—creates a personal data base of skills, résumés
Achieving Your Career—an interactive approach to define the job-search process
Building Your Job Search Foundation—key questions that strengthens job search
Computerized DOT, Résumé Maker

Career Track (for all ages)
MS20-13
P.O. Box 18778
Boulder, CO 80308-1778
800/334-1018; Fax: 800/622-6211
Website: http://www.careertrack.com

Careerware: STM Systems Corporation
955 Green Valley Crescent
Ottawa, ON K2C 3V4
CANADA
800/267-7095

Chronicle Guidance Publications, Inc. (CGP) (for all ages)
P.O. Box 1190
Moravia, NY 13118-1190
800/622-7284; Fax: 315/497-3359
E-mail: 101565.1244@CompuServe.com

Continued

TABLE 12.2 Basic Sources of Information *(continued)*

RESOURCES FOR ALL LEVEL CAREER COUNSELING

CFKR Career Materials (school)
11860 Kemper Rd Unit 7
Auburn, CA 95603
800/525-5626; Fax: 800/770-0433

The Cress Company (school)
10 West Elm Street
Chicago, IL 60610
800/637-2449
E-mail: eric@cressco.com
Interactive CD-ROMs for students

Consulting Psychologists Press, Inc.
3803 East Bayshore Road
P.O. Box 10096
Palo Alto, CA 94303
800/624-1765; 415/969-8901
Website: www.cpp-db.com

ASSESSMENTS AND BOOKS FOR ALL AGES

Curriculum Innovations Group (school)
Weekly Reader Corp.
3001 Cindel Drive
Delran, NJ 08370
800/446-3355

EdITS (for K–12)
P.O. Box 7234
San Diego, CA 92167
619/222-1666; Fax: 619/226-1666
Provides a variety of assessment instruments, including Career Occupational Preference System (COPS)

Ferguson Publishing Company (school)
200 West Madison Street, Suite 300
Chicago, IL 60606
800/306-9941

International Quality & Productivity Center (IQPC)
150 Clove Road
P.O. Box 401
Little Falls, NJ 07424-0401
800/882-8684; 973/256-0211
Fax: 973/256-0205
E-mail: info@iqpc.com
Website: http://www.iqpc.com
Business and Organizational Information and Workshops

TABLE 12.2 Basic Sources of Information *(continued)*

ASSESSMENTS AND BOOKS FOR ALL AGES

JIST (school and college)
720 North Park Avenue
Indianapolis, IN 46202
800/648-JIST; Fax: 800/JIST-Fax
Sound, color descriptions of jobs in *Occupational Outlook Handbook*

Kidsway Entrepreneur Club Product Catalog
Kidsway, Inc.
5585 Peachtree Road
Chamblee, GA 30341
888/KIDSWAY

Live Wire Media (school)
3450 Sacramento Street
San Francisco, CA 94118
800/359-KIDS

MAR-CO Products, Inc. (school)
Dept. 596
1443 Old York Road
Warminster, PA 18974
800/448-2197

Meridian Education Group (school)
Dept. CG-97
Bloomington, IL 61701
800/727-5507

The National Center for School to Work Training (NIMCO, Inc.)
P.O. Box 9
102 Highway 81 North
Calhoun, KY 42327-0009
800/952-6662
Website: www.nimcoinc.com
Provides information on school-to-work programs, training, funding, and resources

National Employer Leadership Council
1001 Connecticut Ave., NW, Suite 3109
Washington, DC 20036
800/360-NEIC
Website: http://www.neic.org

National TeleLearning Network, Inc.
5801 River Road
New Orleans, LA 70123-5106
800/432-3286

Continued

TABLE 12.2 Basic Sources of Information *(continued)*

ASSESSMENTS AND BOOKS FOR ALL AGES

NCS Assessments
5605 Green Circle Drive
Minnetonka, MN 55343
800/627-7271; Fax: 612/939-5199
Website: www.ncs.com
Assessments for all age groups.

The New Careers Center, Inc. (school)
1515 23rd Street
P.O. Box 339-SK
Boulder, CO 80306
800/634-9024; Fax: 303/447-8684

New Concepts Corp. (school)
Career Development Programs
2341 S. Friebus Avenue
Tucson, AZ 85713
520/323-6645; 800/828-7876
Fax: 520/325-5277

ORYX (school)
4041 N Central Avenue, Suite 700
Phoenix, AZ 85012-3397
800/279-6799

Psychological Assessment Resources, Inc.
P.O. Box 998
Odessa, FL 33556
800/331-TEST; Fax: 800/727-9329
Website: http://www.parinc.com
Assessment instruments for children and adults.

Rosen Publishing Company (school)
29 East 21st Street
New York, NY 10010
800/237-9932
Hardcover books written for teens. Excellent for school libraries.

Sigma Assessment Systems, Inc.
P.O. Box 610984
Port Huron, MI 48061-0984
800/265-1285; Fax: 800/361-9411
E-mail: sigma@mgl.ca
Website: http://www.mgl.ca/-sigma
Computer-assisted guidance programs.

TABLE 12.2 Basic Sources of Information *(continued)*

ASSESSMENTS AND BOOKS FOR ALL AGES

Southern School Media
415 Park Row, Dept. S
Bowling Green, KY 42101-2242
800/736-0288
Films, videos, and resources.

Sunburst Communications (school)
101 Castleton Street
Pleasantville, NY 10570
914/769-2109
Films, videos, and other materials.

The Education ConneXtion
12118 Elysian Court
Dallas, TX 75230
972/991-5252; 800/991-2460
Fax: 972/991-5261
A thorough collection of all types of materials for all school ages.

VGM Career Books (for all ages)
4255 West Touhy Avenue
Lincolnwood, IL 60646-1975
800/323-4900; 847/679-5500
Fax: 847/679-2494

Wintergreen/Orchard House Career Services (school)
P.O. Box 15899
New Orleans, LA 70175-5899
800/321-9479

Chuck Eby's Counseling Resources is an example of a self-maintained site.
Website: www.cybercom.net/~chuck/guide.html

Gail Hackett at Arizona State University also maintains a list of helpful sites.
Website: www.seamonkey.ed.asu.edu/~gail/career.htm.

13

Multicultural and
Diversity Issues

"If we all spoke Esperanto, we wouldn't know who the foreigners were."
—CLIFF CLAVIN, *CHEERS*

Throughout this text we have considered how vocational psychology is relevant to multicultural and diverse populations. In this chapter we take a more in-depth look at multicultural and diversity issues not addressed elsewhere in this text. First, ethnicity, acculturation and assimilation, and affirmative action are discussed. Second, we explore the role of work in the lives of African Americans. Third, the state of vocational psychology for Hispanics is addressed. Fourth, the available information on the occupational development of Asian Americans is presented. Fifth, the limited information on Native Americans' occupational development is mentioned. Sixth, we give an overview of the relatively recent literature pertaining to the work lives of gay, lesbian, and bisexual persons. Finally, the diverse workplace needs of persons with disabilities are examined.

ETHNICITY, ACCULTURATION AND ASSIMILATION, AFFIRMATIVE ACTION

Any consideration of a multicultural and diversity perspective in vocational psychology requires at least a working knowledge of definitions and issues related to being non-White in the workplace. Equal access to occupational opportunities for racial and ethnic minorities will be essential in the future. These matters are no longer a subspecialty within vocational psychology; demographic and technological trends have transformed these concerns from moral imperatives into a matter of survival in the global economy. The challenge for vocational psychology is to become relevant for all current and future members of the workforce.

Ethnicity

Ethnicity is an imprecise concept. It relies on various criteria for definition, including race, language, and region (Petersen, 1980). "Ethnicity patterns our thinking, feeling, and behavior in both obvious and subtle ways. It plays a major role in determining what we eat, how we work, how we relax, how we celebrate holidays and rituals, and how we feel about life, death, and illness" (McGoldrick, 1982, p. 4). Ethnicity includes patterns of values, social customs, perceptions, behavioral roles, language usage, and rules of interactions that group members share (Rotheram & Phinney, 1987).

Practical Applications

While ethnicity likely influences occupational adjustment, it is difficult to distinguish how facets of ethnicity explain differences in career choice or relate to correlates of career choice: self-efficacy, interest inventories, skills, and life aspirations (Brown, 1995). Ethnic-specific approaches to both outreach and intervention are recommended for diverse populations to increase the perception of relevance and potential helpfulness of career development services offered (Leong & Gim-Chung, 1995).

A practitioner can informally and qualitatively assess clients' beliefs about how their ethnicity is relevant at work by asking several questions. Do workers of a given ethnic background believe they need to remain independent because they: (a) are the only non-Whites on the job? (b) need to show that they are qualified for the job without performance standards being lowered for them? (c) are vigilant against being co-opted by insecure, threatened White coworkers? (d) have an inbred mistrust of Whites? or (e) have, if not a mistrust, then a simple (or pronounced) difference in values from their White coworkers?

Similar questions can be asked when workers of a given ethnic background believe they must become interdependent. Do they need: (a) to show themselves as team players? (b) to position themselves politically even if they would prefer not to be around certain ethnically

Continued

Continued

different coworkers? (c) need mentoring? or (d) need to learn the work ways of their White coworkers? The list of possible questions is infinite. Practitioners may find that independence and interdependence are contextual matters that vary by worker and situation, even by work assignment. Likewise, *both* individual *and* familial selves (Roland, 1994) are likely to manifest themselves in a client. It can be useful to help clients sort through times when individual and familial ways of doing things are both a help and a hindrance in the workplace (Weinberg & Mauksch, 1991). For clients from strongly collectivistic backgrounds, disclosure of their private selves in a clinical setting is a good indication that the practitioner is truly entering the world as the client sees it.

Inevitably, a practitioner will have a strongly collectivistic client who appears to put the needs of others first so often that the client seems to be shortchanging himself or herself. The practitioner's individualistic orientation may be aroused, and an ethical dilemma will ensue, revolving around how directive the practitioner should become, with an awareness that the practitioner's own values are likely to be imposed onto the client. The challenge will be to honestly and respectfully tell the client that he or she appears to be getting the short end of the stick, especially in work-related situations where the client is unassertive and refrains from speaking his/her mind. Pros and cons of a collectivistic-oriented client becoming individualistic in certain occupational contexts will have to be explored. There are no easy answers for such a clinical occurrence. The practitioner's task will be to explore all possible avenues of conduct for a collectivistic-oriented client being taken advantage of by individualistic workplace politics. Ultimately, the final decision on how to proceed will be up to the client.

Acculturation and Assimilation

Acculturation Acculturation has been variously defined over the past several decades (Redfield, Linton & Herskovitz, 1936; Social Science Research Council Summer Seminar, 1954). Rotheram and Phinney (1987) define acculturation as "an acceptance of both one's own group and another group; through contact, conflict, and finally adaptation, elements of each ethnic group are included in the culture. This occurs at both personal and group levels" (p. 12).

Assimilation Assimilation and acculturation are sometimes used interchangeably, but these two constructs are not synonymous. **Assimilation** refers to "the processes that lead to greater homogeneity in society" (Abramson, 1980, p. 150).

Practical Applications

In examining the relationship between acculturation and career variables for Hispanics, both generational status and acculturation level should be taken into account (Arbona, 1995; Fouad, 1995). With African Americans, part of any career intervention should consider acculturation level or identification with and acceptance of the dominant cultural system (Bowman, 1995). Landrine and Klonoff (1996) discuss acculturation as a nonracist framework for examining cultural differences among African Americans. Cultural values may underlie occupational values for some Asian Americans (Leong & Gim-Chung, 1995), and therefore acculturation is a useful variable to formally assess. Native Americans are more likely to make sound career decisions if values associated with family, tribal traditions, homeland, and community living are explored in a thorough and comprehensive manner (Martin, 1995).

Practitioners can informally and qualitatively assess their clients' level acculturation through five questions adapted from Marín, Sabogal, Marín, Otero-Sabogal, and Pérez-Stable (1987): (1) In general, what language do you read and speak? (2) What was the language you used as a child? (3) What language do you usually speak at home? (4) In what language do you usually think? (5) What language do you usually speak with your friends? In Chapter 3 we advocated using valid and reliable acculturation measures with multicultural populations who are participants in career-related research projects generally and in the renorming of vocational assessment instruments specifically. Several acculturation measures are described in Dana (1993).

Rotheram and Phinney (1987) further define assimilation as "a situation in which a minority ethnic group" gradually loses its distinctiveness and becomes part of the majority group (p. 12). The idea of a newer group becoming completely absorbed into a larger host group was first articulated by Robert Park (1950). Whenever two ethnic groups come together, assimilation is presumed to occur inevitably. Milton Gordon (1964) disagrees that assimilation is inevitable. In the case of the United States, Gordon does not see that minority groups have to conform to the White, host group's values and behaviors. We contend that immigrant cohort/generational status can influence the nature of the pressure to

TABLE 13.1 Gordon's Seven Subprocesses of Assimilation

1. cultural assimilation	newer/minority group's acceptance of host/dominant group's language, religion, and customs
2. structural assimilation	newer/minority group's large-scale entry into host/dominant group's cliques, clubs, and institutions
3. marital assimilation	newer/minority group's large-scale intermarriage into host/dominant group
4. identificational assimilation	newer/minority group's development of a sense of peoplehood based exclusively on host/dominant group
5. attitude receptional assimilation	host/dominant group's absence of prejudice towards newer/minority group
6. behavioral receptional assimilation	host/dominant group's absence of discrimination towards newer/minority group
7. civic assimilation	host/dominant group's absence of value and power conflict with newer/minority group

SOURCE: adapted from Gordon (1964)

assimilate and conform. Persons who immigrated or who were born in the early 1900s experienced a qualitatively different pressure to assimilate and conform than more recent cohorts/generations.

Gordon (1964) divides assimilation into seven processes, shown in Table 13.1.

Affirmative Action

Similar to acculturation and assimilation, affirmative action has hardly been considered in vocational development theories. Congresswoman Eleanor Holmes Norton, who chaired the U.S. Equal Employment Opportunity Commission (EEOC) under President Jimmy Carter, writes, "Affirmative action is a weak legal concept grounded in strong law. The term is not found in the statute" (1996, p. 40). Bergmann (1996) explains that "affirmative action is planning and acting to end the absence of certain kinds of people—those who belong to groups that have been subordinated or left out—from certain jobs and schools" (p. 7). Affirmative action may be characterized as more of an era (S. L. Carter, 1991) than as a particular law. Most relevant for our discussion here are the Civil Rights Acts of 1964 and 1991 (Hagan & Hagan, 1995).

Practical Applications

Increased attention to the seven subprocesses of assimilation (Gordon, 1964) can add a valuable dimension to the role of work in multicultural and diverse people's lives. Understanding Gordon's (1964) seven subprocesses of assimilation can help racial and ethnic minority clients to decide for themselves when, where, and how much to assimilate. Our experience with graduate students and clients indicates that they focus mainly on perceived pressures to culturally assimilate without knowingly considering the other subprocesses.

Assimilation has most often been applied to immigrants to the United States. But there is plenty of potential application to the occupational development of multicultural and diverse clientele. Here are four examples:

1. First-generation college students of any racial or ethnic background face challenges to structurally assimilate into their educational institutions. Structural assimilation can be harder for those whose parents, siblings, or other close friends and relatives have not attended a college or university.

2. The Texaco scandal of 1996, where executives were tape-recorded in the act of ridiculing minorities (Bacon, 1998) is a blatant example of workplace practices that hinder attitude receptional and behavioral receptional assimilation. A court-created oversight panel reports that Texaco has since made significant gains in diversifying its workforce. Roberts (1998) recounts her experience as an African American employed at Texaco during the scandal.

3. Prevention of structural assimilation is reported by Trillin (1998), who chronicles the history of the Mardi Gras celebrations in New Orleans over the past forty years. Clubs and cliques of old-money White families have the most exclusive Carnival celebrations in that predominantly African-American city. Adjustments to this disenfranchising practice began only in the early 1990s. Attempts to multiculturally integrate the old-line "classic Carnival" events (p. 40) have been overshadowed by commercialization. Meanwhile, the long-term effects of social exclusion on disenfranchised groups is incalculable.

4. The issue of adultery in the military, with the public's perception of one standard for men and another for women (Associated Press, 1997b; Knight-Ridder News Service, 1997) points to gender differences in (a) cultural assimilation—especially customs, (b) structural assimilation—especially into cliques, (c) attitude receptional assimilation, and (d) behavioral receptional assimilation. These differential barriers to assimilation directly impact promotion within the ranks.

The **Civil Rights Act of 1964** was intended to remedy discrimination in housing, public accommodation, and education (Hagan & Hagan, 1995). Title VII of the Civil Rights Act of 1964, as amended in 1972 (Eastland, 1997), prohibits discrimination in employment on the basis of race, color, religion, sex, and national origin. Hagan and Hagan (1995) explain that liability under Title VII can occur for two reasons: disparate treatment and disparate impact.

Disparate treatment refers to instances when an employee is subject to adverse treatment because of the employee's race, color, religion, sex, or national origin. Employment discrimination must be initially established by a plaintiff/employee through prima facie evidence. That is, the employer/defendant must be shown to have discriminated against the plaintiff in one of four ways. The plaintiff (1) belongs to a protected class, (2) has applied for and was qualified for a job, (3) has been rejected for a job in spite of being qualified, (4) the job position also has remained open and the employer continues to seek job applicants. If prima facie evidence has been established, the employer/defendant must provide a legitimate, nondiscriminatory reason for rejecting the plaintiff. Then, the employee must show that the employer/defendant's reason is a pretext for discrimination. "Pretext means that the employer's reason was either insubstantial or not the true reason for treating the employee adversely" (Hagan & Hagan, 1995, p. 4).

In contrast to disparate treatment, **disparate impact** is "discrimination caused by the consequences of a particular practice used by the employer" (Hagan & Hagan, 1995, p. 5). Employment discrimination must be initially established by a plaintiff/employee through prima facie evidence in one of three ways. (1) The plaintiff applied for a job opening with an employer. (2) The plaintiff was rejected for a job because of an employer's particular practice. (3) The employer's particular practice had a discriminatory effect on the employee/plaintiff's protected class. If prima facie evidence has been established, the employer/defendant must show their particular practice is required by business necessity or has a manifest relationship to the business. Then the employee must show that an alternative business device would be less discriminatory yet serve the employer's business necessity.

Both disparate treatment and disparate impact were altered by the Civil Rights Act of 1991 (Hagan & Hagan, 1995). The employer/defendant now has a greater burden of proof for showing why an employee was rejected. The employee/plaintiff can also treat an employer's decision-making process as a single, particular practice without the plaintiff having to show which requirement resulted in the discrimination. The 1991 Act also prohibits **race norming** of any employment or aptitude test results. Race norming refers to "adjusting the scores or using different cut-offs based on the race of the person who takes the test" (Hagan & Hagan, 1995, p. 6).

Affirmative action has its adherents and opponents. Among adherents, Bergmann (1996) notes that "private companies with less than fifty employees are exempt from affirmative action regulations. . . . Larger employers are seldom if ever called to account for their staffing patterns by a government agency . . . " (p. 8). Furthermore, "while the government officially promotes affirmative action, it is not an exaggeration to say that its application has been largely voluntary. As a result, desegregation of employment by race and sex has been uneven" (pp. 8–9). G. D. Richardson (1997) writes, "one would have to be either in complete denial or just plain dishonest to dispute . . . [the racial] inequities in most of the lucrative business and career opportunities in America" (p. 15A). She adds, "there is a real hypocrisy in calling for an end to racial preferences without putting the largest and most obvious preference [enjoyed by Whites] on the table for debate" (p. 15A). Others have become concerned that race-based admissions policies at public universities in Texas and California will decrease the enrollment numbers of African Americans and Hispanics (Associated Press, 1997a, 1997d; "Segregation anew," June 1, 1997).

Affirmative action opponents contend that Title VII's intent of nondiscrimination has been distorted by a push for numerical affirmative action that results in quotas and racial preferences, which was never explicitly defined in Title VII, but came about through judicial interpretation of the law (Eastland, 1997). Affirmative action has benefited ethnic and racial minorities from middle-class backgrounds, with lower-income, inner-city minorities hardly affected (S. L. Carter, 1991; Rodriguez, 1982). Steele (1990) observes that affirmative action has served as an excuse for racial minorities to avoid personal responsibility for admitting to fear of all-out competition with Whites. He uses the term **race-holding** to define "any self-description that serves to justify or camouflage a person's fears, weaknesses, and inadequacies" (p. 26). Race is used as an excuse to keep one from seeing something unflattering in oneself, which prevents self-esteem from developing apart from race. At the end of the next section on African Americans, we discuss those who did not allow race to become an obstacle to their occupational success.

AFRICAN AMERICANS

Affirmative action resulted in part from the civil rights movement of the postwar years that peaked in the 1960s. By 1994, African Americans numbered an estimated 33 million persons, or 12.7 percent of the total U.S. population (Bennett & DeBarros, 1995). By the year 2000, African Americans are projected to number 35.5 million, or 12.8 percent of the total population. Since 1980, 84 percent of the increase in the African-American population has been due to natural increase, with 16 percent of the increase accounted for by immigration. In the remaining part of this section, we consider the social and economic realities of African Americans, research on college students and women, and the psychology of Black success.

Social and Economic Realities

African Americans have largely been confined to (a) blue collar occupations, which are mainly a means of making a living rather than careers; (b) college majors in education, social work, and the social sciences—which have led to **"protected" careers** where less racial discrimination is thought to occur; and (c) positions for African-American women where workplace racism and sexism is presumed to be minimized (Murry & Mosidi, 1993). The social and economic realities of African Americans are vividly illustrated in Asante and Mattson (1992). Much of their data are derived from the 1980 Census through 1988, which in no way diminishes the value of their compilation because few dramatic differences have resulted since the 1990 Census. Relevant to our current discussion are Asante's and Mattson's presentation of data on employment, wages, and unemployment. A few examples of such data are given below.

Employment Employment percentages for African Americans have always differed from Whites in various regions of the U.S. (Asante & Mattson, 1992). For example, the Southeast has the highest percentage of African Americans in the workforce, at 19 percent. Due to the great disparity in wages between African Americans and Whites, the former do not earn 19 percent of the income in that region. While informative, statistics need to be interpreted appropriately. **Labor force representation** refers only to those individuals who are eligible and seeking jobs. Persons are not counted in the labor force for various reasons (e.g., military, prison, medical disabilities). Thus, to say that 91 percent of African Americans in the labor force of a given region are employed is not the same as saying 91 percent of all African-American individuals in the region are employed.

Wages For more than twenty years the wage gap between White and African-American workers has steadily increased (Asante & Mattson, 1992). Wage disparity will probably remain a factor in the economic underdevelopment of African Americans for the foreseeable future. Structural elements of the overall U.S. economy are presumed to control economic conditions for African Americans. Median earnings of year-round, full-time workers 25 years old and over, by educational attainment, sex, and race are presented in Table 13.2.

Table 13.2 shows African-American women with a high school diploma earn 80 cents to the dollar compared to African-American men and 83 percent

**TABLE 13.2 Median Earnings of Year-Round, Full-Time Workers
25 Years Old and Over, by Educational Attainment, Sex, and Race**

	AFRICAN AMERICANS			WHITE, NON-HISPANIC		
	Both Sexes	*Males*	*Females*	*Both Sexes*	*Males*	*Females*
High School Graduate	$18,640	$20,580	$16,460	$24,120	$28,370	$19,850
Bachelor's Degree or More	$32,360	$35,850	$31,160	$41,190	$47,180	$32,920

SOURCE: adapted from Bennet & DeBarros (1995), p. 44.

of comparable White, non-Hispanic women (Bennett & DeBarros, 1995). Among college graduates, African-American women earn 87 percent of comparable African-American men and 95 percent of comparable White, non-Hispanic women. African-American men at both the high school and bachelor's degree levels earn roughly 75 percent of comparable White, non-Hispanic men.

Unemployment A person is said to be in the workforce when that person is either employed or unemployed but has sought a position within the past six months (Asante & Mattson, 1992). The unemployment rate is the rate of people employed to the total number of people in the workforce. For African-American males aged 17 to 24, the unemployment rate is 26.1 percent; for females in the same age group, the rate is 22.7 percent. The awesome social price of these staggering figures represents one of the greatest ongoing challenges to the practical application and utility of vocational psychology and career counseling (see also Brown, 1995; D'Andrea & Daniels, 1992).

African-American College Students

As of 1994, 13 percent of African Americans aged 25 and over had obtained at least a bachelor's degree; this compares with 4 percent in 1970 and 8 percent in 1980 (Bennett & DeBarros, 1995). These changing demographics require career counselors in colleges and universities to become aware of the need for additional and nontraditional intervention strategies, assessment techniques, and counseling practices (Hendricks, 1994). "If career centers of the future are committed to enhancing the career development of students, changes in the way services are delivered . . . [and] cases are conceptualized . . . [are] necessary" (p. 118). Career counseling frameworks that have traditionally worked for White students may be of limited applicability to African-American students' life experiences for

---

Practical Applications

Hendricks (1994) argues that college and university career counselors need to acknowledge and consider how race, gender, economic class, and sociopolitical history impact African-American college students' career aspirations and vocational development. We believe practitioners perform a disservice to their clients if these issues are not examined, but some non-African-American practitioners fail to see the need to explore these issues. Yet, African-American females in college aspire to less prestigious professions than their male counterparts (Grevious, 1985). Thus, even African-American women who gain access to higher education may aim lower than their own capabilities.

---

at least three reasons. (1) Most models implicitly assume that equal opportunities exist for attaining career goals. (2) Traditional career theories and models have been based on White behavior with the attempted generalization of concepts and constructs to ethnic and economic subgroups. Even the commonly used, RIASEC-based Strong Interest Inventory has little psychometric validity with African Americans (Bowman, 1995; R. T. Carter & Swanson, 1990). (3) Several career development theories assume that an occupation provides a person with intrinsic satisfaction and opportunities for self-expression (Hendricks, 1994). But a substantial number of African Americans work in blue collar occupations as a means of making a living (Murry & Mosidi, 1993), not because they seek avenues for self-expression or personally meaningful employment.

African-American Women

Racism and Sexism In choosing a career, African-American women may be influenced by perceived racism and sexism in various occupations (Evans & Herr, 1991; Richie, 1992). Perceived opportunity structure can impact aspirations. Anticipation of racial and/or sexual bias can contribute to avoidance by African-American women of certain careers. These women seem to aspire to traditionally female-dominated careers with minimal racism and sexism.

Nontraditional Professions Barriers to career success are reported significantly more often by African-American women in nontraditional professions than in traditional ones (Burlew & Johnson, 1992). Nontraditional professions (law, medicine, engineering, science) are those fields in which fewer than 30 per-

Practical Applications

Avoidance, modification of lifestyles, and redirection of ambitions and goals may be some of the coping strategies African-American women use to survive the dual effects of racism and sexism in the workplace (Evans & Herr, 1991). Practitioners can explore the extent to which attitudes associated with these biases are internalized by their clients, and whether such biases negatively affect career aspirations. Also, practitioners should determine if clients' self-esteem and self-confidence have deteriorated as a result of racist and sexist perceptions about certain careers. Practitioners might ask themselves if they blame any African-American woman for refraining from knowingly exposing herself to racist and sexist work environments.

Additional recommendations derived from Richie (1992) stimulate further conceptual work in this area. (1) Help the client explore the extent to which her socioeconomic circumstances are truly limiting. (2) Broaden career aspirations of African-American female clients. Help them to see how racism and sexism have conspired to limit their field of vision. (3) If need be, assist African-American women to develop appropriate problem-focused strategies, as opposed to emotion-focused ones, to use selectively in workplace conflicts. Such clients may be more likely than others to modify their strategies based on their appraisal of discrimination in the environment. Emotion-focused strategies (primarily cognitive restructuring) are useful in situations where one needs to accept an outcome beyond one's control. Problem-focused strategies are useful in situations where one believes one can affect the outcome.

(4) The African-American female client with extensive social networks could be encouraged by the practitioners to use that as a support system for career information. (5) Even problem-focused strategies may be ineffective at times. Clients would benefit from a practitioner who aids in preparing them for this possibility. An emphasis on situational specificity that places the focus on the context minimizes the fault of the individual woman. (6) Each individual practitioner will have to decide for herself or himself the extent to which their professional role will expand to that of advocate for individual clients and against classism, racism, and sexism in our society that contribute to work-related problems.

---

cent of the professionals in the field are women. Traditional professions (social work, teaching, and counseling) are those fields in which more than 60 percent of the professionals in the field are women. Racial and gender discrimination are

---

Practical Applications

African-American women in nontraditional professions can develop coping strategies for managing the situational barriers they may encounter (Burlew & Johnson, 1992). Increased role conflict in meeting the combined demands of work and family is another issue; when one demand is assessed as a presenting issue, it might be useful to assess the other demand as well. Organizational consultation could assist employers in identifying forces that work against the advancement of African-American women in nontraditional fields. Access to political clout, for example, is often made possible through a relationship with a mentor. This mentor is typically an older, more powerful figure within the workplace. African-American women in nontraditional fields may lack this type of support.

A practitioner should not automatically assume that decreases in (a) self-esteem, (b) self-confidence, or (c) aspirations for careers in certain fields will appear in their African-American female clients. Bronzaft (1991) reports African-American female freshmen's occupational preferences did not fit the stereotype of "protected" careers. Her research participants' first choice is business (accounting, computers, communications). Their second choice is academic life (teacher, doctor, dentist, lawyer). The overwhelming majority of these young women (83 percent) also envision themselves as having a career and being married with children. These young women would benefit by increased awareness of work-family issues facing dual-career couples.

---

among the impediments that African-American women encounter in nontraditional careers. Additional obstacles include limited opportunities to develop political clout and colleagues' doubt about their competence. African-American women in nontraditional professions report significantly more barriers to career success because of family obligations and marital discord.

The Multiple Self-Referent Model for Career Counseling The multiple self-referent model (Brown-Collins & Sussewell, 1986, cited in Gainor & Forrest, 1991) is adaptable for counseling and career decision-making of African-American women. Three major self-referents comprise the model. (1) The psychophysiological referent concerns the African-American woman's relational self-concept of herself as a woman and includes the nurturing self, caring self, and maternal self. (2) The African-American referent concerns "the socio-

Practical Applications

The multiple self-referent model is helpful to understanding the African-American woman's occupational self-concept (Gainor & Forrest, 1991). Variable emphasis on the three major self-referents can still lead African-American women into the same occupation. The practitioner's task is to emphasize clients' strengths within each self-referent, regardless of the nature of the job position sought or currently held. When the psycho-physiological referent is strongest, care and connection to others will be foremost. When the Afro or Black referent is strongest, racism and its effect on African Americans' educational attainment and occupational achievement will be foremost. When the Euro or White referent is strongest, accommodations to the dominant culture will be foremost. When the myself referent is strongest, advocacy and support of other African-American females will be foremost. A practitioner's exploration of each self-referent can assist an African-American female client to integrate and prioritize unique aspects of her self-concept as she decides the role of work in her life. The developmental nature of the multiple self-referent model is clearly evident; less obvious is the model's contextual nature—in different job positions or geographical locations one self-referent or another can predominate.

political context within which the African-American woman's self-concept develops" (Gainor & Forrest, 1991, p. 262) and consists of (a) the Afro or Black referent and (b) the Euro or White referent. The Afro or Black referent concerns the African-American woman's sense of collectivism and belongingness in the Black community. The Euro or White referent concerns the African-American woman's sense of individualism and perceptions about her from the White majority culture. (3) The myself referent concerns the African-American woman's unique personal history and includes "the religious self, the sexual self, the light-skinned self, and the natural-hair self" (Gainor & Forrest, 1991, p. 264).

The Psychology of Black Success

In *Children of the Dream: The Psychology of Black Success,* Edwards and Polite (1992) describe African Americans who do not allow race to be an obstacle to their occupational success. Among those profiled by the authors, there is no race-holding (Steele, 1990).

Common Features of Successful African Americans A common feature of successful African Americans is a strong patriarch and, in the absence of that, a loving and supporting family where a sense of responsibility predominates (Edwards & Polite, 1992). A second feature is a strong sense of race and an affirming sense of power, defined here as "the ability to provide for and get things done" (p. 187). A third feature is knowledge of how to interact with Whites—and the ability to distinguish which Whites are willing to be open (also known, bluntly, as White people skills). Successful African Americans have discerned the hidden rules of the White middle class (Payne, 1995), and in some cases, the wealthy class. Another key ingredient to success is risk-taking, a perception many White men have not had of African Americans in the world of work (Edwards & Polite, 1992).

Drawbacks to Success for African Americans Occupational success for African Americans has several drawbacks. (1) "Even as blacks integrate into mainstream occupations and professions historically denied them, real corporate power remains elusive" (Edwards & Polite, 1992, p. 58). (2) The very sense of community that originally set the foundation for success so many years ago, and that bolstered the self-confidence of these African Americans and their willingness to persist in their struggles, appears to be mostly absent nowadays. (3) Salary discrimination persists (see Table 13.2 above). (4) Then there is the matter of being qualified:

> Unlike whites, for whom success is frequently a matter of contacts, connections, family combinations, and in the end simply the circumstance of being born white, black success seems always to carry certain prerequisites, chief among them the requirement that a black first prove he or she is "qualified" for achievement. The very notion of becoming qualified, of course, assumes an element of deficiency, a lacking of the skills, training, values, talent, or intellect that ordinarily renders one fit for accomplishment. . . .
>
> As the decline in American productivity has proven, being white does not necessarily equate with being qualified. (p. 77)

The idea of becoming qualified is a psychological assault on African-American occupational aspirations and is used by opponents of affirmative action to discount equal opportunity. Each generation of African Americans has faced the struggle of proving oneself, of being counted as qualified. As an unnamed, African-American Harvard law professor tells Edwards and Polite (1992), the struggle to be counted as worthy for holding his job position is "a presumption against my competence" (p. 200).

Successful African-American Men When an African-American man experiences "a presumption against my competence," White men in the world of work question his ability to perform well in something other than athletics or the entertainment field (Edwards & Polite, 1992). African-American males between the ages 15 to 24 are the most vulnerable. This age group is most at risk for dropping out of school, fathering an out-of-wedlock child, enduring unemployment, running into trouble with the law, or becoming a victim of homicide (see also Muwakkil, 1988; Parham & McDavis 1987).

Historically, the African-American male in the U.S. has been denied power. Yet, the African-American male is confronted with the task all men in the U.S. face in terms of exercising their power: working, earning money, taking care of the women and children in their lives, leading their communities, determining their own destinies (Edwards & Polite, 1992). Successful African-American males know that gaining power threatens White men, who fear that what will be done to them is what they have done to African-American men. Successful African-American men are not threatened by the power of successful African-American women. An instinctive understanding of the nature of power characterizes many successful African-American men. They know power can be denied. It can also be assumed and seized. Power is not finite or ordained. It can be elusive and fleeting, resulting from an act of courage as much as from exercising will. For the African-American male to be a success, he must balance self-regard—that hard-won self-knowledge and centered sense of knowing who one is (Pipher, 1996)—with an awareness of the impression he makes on others. And he must realize that natural power can neither be masked nor denied.

The narratives in Edwards and Polite (1992) closely resemble the kind of ethnographic, qualitative research sorely needed in vocational psychology. These first-person accounts of successful African-American women and men are a valuable source of information for any person striving to overcome seemingly insurmountable odds.

HISPANICS

We use the term Hispanic to refer to persons of full or partial Spanish ancestry or origin who now live in the U.S. A variety of terms describe this cultural group. Some contend that "Hispanic" is a term imposed by outsiders (e.g., the U.S. Government) and prefer the term Latino instead (see also, Flores-Hughes, 1996). We find it pragmatic to conceive of Hispanic as an umbrella term to cover a variety of ethnic groups and nationalities.

The ancestry or origin of Hispanic Americans is 64.3 percent Mexican, 13.4 percent Central and South American, 10.6 percent Puerto Rican, 4.7 percent

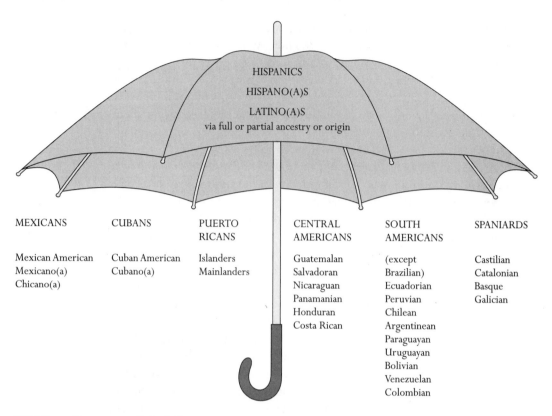

FIGURE 13.1 Hispanics as an Umbrella Term

Cuban, and 7 percent Other Hispanic (del Pinal, 1995). Hispanics may be of any race. Some Hispanics have both indigenous and European backgrounds; these persons are sometimes called mestizos. *Mestizos* vary in complexion from dark brown to olive to fair-skinned, reflecting their ancestral genetic mix.

Educational attainment of Hispanics is lower than the remainder of the population (del Pinal, 1995). The unemployment rate for Hispanics was 11.9 percent in 1993, compared to 6.1 percent for non-Hispanic Whites. Hispanics, like African Americans, earn less than non-Hispanic Whites in comparable full-time, year-round employment positions.

In 1993, 29.6 percent of Hispanics were under 15 years old, compared with 20.4 percent of non-Hispanic Whites (del Pinal, 1995). Median age of Hispanics was about 9 years less than the non-Hispanic White population, 26.7 years to 35.5 years, respectively. Another example of within-group differences is the median age of various Hispanic ethnic groups: in 1993, the median age was 43.6 years for Cubans, 28.6 years for Central and South Americans, 26.9 years for

Practical Applications

Ask Hispanic clients (a) how they identify themselves in terms of ethnicity, race, and/or nationality, and (b) to what extent they believe this has anything to do with the world of work. As with African Americans, ask if complexion (Edwards & Polite, 1992; Harvey, 1995; Hughes & Hertel, 1990; Keith & Herring, 1991), sometimes called **phenotype**, influences a Hispanic's perceived availability of educational and occupational opportunities

(Arce, Murguia & Frisbie, 1987). Like darker-complected African Americans, darker complected, *mestizo*-looking Hispanics are less likely to match the educational attainment and occupational achievement of lighter complected, European-looking Hispanics. In the U.S., Mexico, and in those Central and South American countries with darker complected *mestizos* and indigenous peoples, racism is both an historical and current reality.

Puerto Ricans, and 24.6 years for Mexican Americans. As of 1992, 39.9 percent of Hispanic children under age 18 were living in poverty, compared with 13.2 percent of non-Hispanic Whites. Thus much of the Hispanic population in the U.S. is young and poor. Vocational psychology research has to take these two factors into consideration, and be mindful of within-group differences, when selecting research participants.

The State of Vocational Psychology and Career Counseling Research with Hispanic Populations

In an extensive review of the literature of career counseling research with Hispanics, Arbona (1990) notes that the body of knowledge is fragmentary and lacks a theoretical foundation. She reviews four areas: occupational aspirations, vocational interests, on-the-job behavior, and educational attainment.

Most career research with Hispanics is about occupational aspirations (Arbona, 1990). Hispanic youth have high occupational aspirations. Parental values do not hinder their children's aspirations. But Hispanics have lower expectations than their White peers of reaching their goals; White youth have fewer doubts that economic, educational, and discrimination barriers will hinder their occupational aspirations.

Practical Applications

Practitioners can ask the following questions about occupational aspirations: "(a) What are the obstacles perceived by Hispanics in achieving their aspirations? (b) How does the perception of these obstacles impact their decision-making process? (c) How may career counseling help Hispanics to overcome these obstacles?" (Arbona, 1990, p. 305). For Hispanics, little has been done "to empirically measure *perceived occupational opportunity* or *perceived barriers to occupational attainment* " (Arbona, 1990, p. 316, italics in original). Broader social and economic contexts need further exploration with regard to occupational aspirations (Arbona & Novy, 1991).

Holland's RAISEC hexagon is the most researched model of vocational interests with Hispanics, and appears to be applicable to high school and college populations (Arbona, 1990). Sample sizes of student-research participants are small, mainly populations of convenience. Socioeconomic status, which may operate as a moderator variable, is a missing variable in vocational interest research (Arbona, 1990).

Acculturation may be related to on-the-job behaviors and career progression for Hispanic white-collar workers (Arbona, 1990). Similar to the psychology of Black success (Edwards & Polite, 1992), practitioners can assess Hispanic professionals' knowledge of the hidden rules (Payne, 1995) of the White middle class. The paucity of research on job satisfaction and on occupational values (Arbona, 1990) prohibits a summary of these topics.

Practical Applications

In addition to socioeconomic status, acculturation may be another moderator variable in research on Hispanic vocational interests. Arbona (1990) calls for additional research on (1) "the predictive validity of . . . Spanish and English versions of career interest inventories," (p. 306), (2) gender differences, and (3) applying the RIASEC model to Hispanics in specific occupations—the last of which would diminish reliance on populations of convenience.

Educational Attainment

A major determinant of Hispanics' disadvantaged position in the labor market is their low educational attainment (Arbona, 1990). **Discrimination** in the schools (i.e., grade delay, minimal basic resources such as library holdings and teaching staff, tracking into dead-end general or vocational programs as opposed to college prep or honors programs) is the experience of many Mexican-American and Puerto Rican students. Widespread poverty in Hispanic households negatively impacts academic performance. Small sample sizes in research on Hispanic women's educational attainment impedes generalizations about barriers and facilitators of educational and occupational progress. Information on Hispanics' career decision-making is sparse.

Practical Applications

A huge gap in the vocational psychology literature is the role of family influence on Hispanics' occupational development. An organized body of knowledge remains to be produced on this topic. On a related subject, Sosa (1998) writes of the "Latino disconnect"—a lack of awareness of one's roots and history—which impedes Latino success in business and in life in the United States. He suggests that the values taught by a Latino's family and church need to be more closely scrutinized.

Another largely unexamined area is the role of work in the lives of Hispanic immigrants. The immigration issue raised its ugly head during the 1996 U.S. presidential campaign. Politics being what it is, false and exaggerated accusations were made about immigrants coming to the United States to freeload off of welfare and Medicaid (Marquez, 1996). Expediency often dictates ignoring the positive impact immigrant workers have had on their host societies (see, for example Sowell, 1994, chapter 2). Many U.S. high technology companies—which are among "the most powerful and fastest growing companies in the country . . ." (Associated Press, 1996, p. A2)—voiced concern that hostility toward immigration would bring fewer graduate students from abroad. Immigration reform threatened to prevent the hiring of such foreign-born, U.S.-educated science and engineering talent. The "better sort" of immigrant is always welcome, however, especially to that U.S. presidential candidate who vowed to build a security fence across all 2,000 miles of the U.S.-Mexico border, "and we'll say,

Continued

Continued

'Listen, José, you're not coming in!' "
(New York Times News Service,
1996, p. A1).

Several big U.S. industries—including construction companies, nurseries, and fruit growers—rely on low-wage labor from Mexico and Central America and often knowingly hire these undocumented workers/illegal immigrants (Hedges, Hawkins & Loeb, 1996). We wonder how José will be kept out of the United States when meatpacking plants in the Midwest aggressively recruit thousands of Mexicans and Central Americans to perform their dirty, dangerous jobs (Hedges et al., 1996). Some meatpacking companies advertise for prospective employees on Spanish-language radio stations along the Texas-Mexico border. "Meatpacking has the highest injury rate of all U.S. industries; 36 percent of employees are seriously injured each year" (Hawkins, 1996, p. 40). Needless to say, health insurance and other benefits are sometimes lacking for these workers.

Little vocational psychology research exists on immigrants to the United States, be they Hispanic or otherwise. Valuable information awaits in the stories to be told about the role of work in undocumented Latino workers' lives (see, for example, Langewiesche, 1998, below).

CASE EXAMPLE

Langewiesche (1998) writes, "Five million people live illegally in the United States. Two million live in California alone. More than half of those are Mexican, and by the standards they left behind almost all are doing well" (p. 138).

The author goes on to tell the story of Jesús Ruíz. Jesús Ruíz is a 22-year-old Zapotec Indian from the mountain village of Santa Ana Yareni in the Mexican state of Oaxaca [pronounced: whoh-háh-cah]. His primary language is Zapateco. Like many of the Indians in southern Mexico, Jesús has not culturally assimilated into that society. He speaks very little Spanish. He speaks no English.

It is the winter of 1997–98. Jesús is living in a makeshift shack in a ravine located in the craggy mountains above Escondido (San Diego County), California. The undocumented workers living in the brushy, trash-strewn ravine have named it *Los Olvidados*—"the forgotten ones"—because its hundred or so residents live there like unseen ghosts. Jesús's shack is made

of plywood and corrugated plastic, patched with black plastic sheeting, and held together with nails, branches, and the frame of a wheelbarrow, which had been wedged into the dirt. . . . The center of the shack [is] a roofed but open-sided living area, which [looks] out over the ravine below; it [is] joined at one end to a three-walled kitchen, with rough shelving and a gas burner on a plywood table, and at the other end to a windowless sleeping room about the size of a big mattress. The sleeping room [has] a door that [can] be locked with a bicycle cable. (p. 138)

Like the others living in *Los Olvidados,* Jesús is a day laborer. He finds jobs by knocking on doors or standing on the streets. Usually he works as a gardener.

Jesús first came to *el norte* in 1991. He has gone home to Oaxaca four times, preferring the five-hour plane flight from Tijuana to the eight-day bus ride. Like any other working person, Jesús's time is worth money. He sees no point in a prolonged, round-trip bus journey.

Jesús's home village of Santa Ana Yareni first became connected to the U.S. labor market in 1984, when a California flower grower recruited workers for his farm an hour north of Los Angeles. The Zapotec men from Jesús's village who ventured north were taken by train to Tijuana, smuggled across the border, and then were virtually enslaved when they arrived at the flower grower's. The Zapotecs were forced to work sixteen-hour days and were threatened with being turned in to the Border Patrol if they did not cooperate. In 1990, some of the Zapotecs sought legal recourse. The flower grower was indicted by a federal grand jury in Los Angeles on charges of slavery, but he plea bargained and was charged in- stead with corporate racketeering and labor and immigrant violations. The Zapotecs managed to make their way to *Los Olvidados,* where a small group from Santa Ana Yareni had established themselves. The day-to-day job op- portunities that presented themselves to the Zapotecs of *Los Ovidados* were preferable to the enforced servitude of the flower grower's farm. Jesús had not yet come north at the time of the flower grower's incident, but he still felt the impact from that event. He remains in *Los Olvidados* because of the horror stories he has heard about life outside the ravine.

On one of his trips home, Jesús married Juana. They are now the par- ents of three young children, the lat- ter two born in the United States. Juana worked part time cleaning houses while other women in *Los Olvidados* watched her babies. Then the Border Patrol raided *Los Olvidados* in November 1997. Juana and a visit- ing cousin shut themselves in the shack, but the crying babies led them to be found by Border Patrol agents. When the agents heard that the babies were U.S. citizens, the family was left in peace.

El Niño was ultimately responsible for driving the family apart. Unusu- ally heavy rains made life in *Los Olvidados* too hard for Juana and the babies. Jesús bought his wife and chil- dren one-way plane tickets to Mexico City, where they went to live with a relative. There is nothing for them back at Santa Ana Yareni. Jesús has abandoned his extended family obli- gations back home and he is no longer welcomed there.

Continued

Continued

Jesús dreams of one day buying a piece of land on the outskirts of Mexico City and building a one-room house with money saved from his work in the United States. In addition to gardening, Jesús and the other Zapotec men of *Los Olvidados* take jobs house painting, cement laying, house moving, and fence building. The Zapotecs have learned to claim expertise in any job a customer needs, to negotiate the wage in advance, and to get paid in cash if possible. The contrast between Jesús's lifestyle and the wealthy people he works for does not escape him. He attributes a higher-income lifestyle to the fact that both husband and wife work.

Jesús and his fellow Zapotecs are slowly becoming Americanized. They have learned enough English phrases to negotiate jobs and wages. Some of the men have learned the public transit routes. Others among the men have joined church parishes. Two of the younger Zapotec men have even taken up surfing.

Jesús's primary concern is his wife and children in Mexico City. He quietly admits that a difficult future in the United States is less daunting than his impossible dream of life in Mexico. He has no time to worry about projected increases in Border Patrol budgets to add more agents that will make it harder to cross into the United States. While Jesús is unlikely to ever gain U.S. citizenship status, he has no retreat. He lives a marginalized existence as he looks forward to the day when he can bring his wife and children back to the United States.

ASIAN AMERICANS

Many well meaning counselors may unintentionally restrict the career choices of Asians in the social sciences because of the stereotypic notions that Asians are good in the physical sciences and poor in people relationship areas. An explanation offered for the higher representation of technical majors among Asian Americans is that less discrimination and more objective evaluation of skills and abilities occurs in technical areas. Where verbal skills or assimilation of Western values are less likely choices, careful exploration of all possible fields must be presented to Asian-American students. (D. Sue & D. M. Sue, 1995, pp. 77–78)

Asian Americans are stereotyped as a "Model Minority" (Butterfield, 1990, p. 4; Suzuki, 1989, p. 13) who have "made it" (D. W. Sue & D. Sue, 1990, p. 190) in American society. This social construction of the "Model Minority" has functional value to those who hold power in American society for at least three reasons:

First, these stereotypes reassert the erroneous belief that any minority can succeed in a democratic society if the minority-group members work hard enough. Second, the Asian–American success story is seen as a divisive concept used by the Establishment to pit one minority group against another by holding one group up as an example to others. Third, the success myth has short-changed many Asian–American communities from receiving the necessary moral and financial commitment due them as a struggling minority with unique concerns. (D. W. Sue & D. Sue, 1990, p. 192)

Asian Americans continue to experience inequity in both employment and income (Suzuki, 1989). The poverty rate for Asian and Pacific Islander families—14 percent in 1993—was higher than the 8 percent poverty rate for non-Hispanic White families (Bennett & Martin, 1995). Existing vocational psychology research does not confirm the "model minority" stereotype. Asian-American career development lacks a coherent theoretical framework (Leong & Serafica, 1995), with inadequate attention given to moderating variables such as generational status, acculturation, ethnic identity, socioeconomic status, and perceived minority status. Career assessment issues with Asian Americans have not been completely addressed. The interdisciplinary approach advocated by Leong and Serafica, "one that combines psychological, sociological, and economic theories" (p. 87) is not something that vocational psychology in general has largely espoused (M. S. Richardson, 1993).

Racism

"Since there are no Asian Americans touched by racism in the United States to use as a control group, the relationship of racism to psychological development becomes a complex issue that cannot easily be resolved" (D. Sue & D. W. Sue, 1993, p. 203). We do think it unfeasible to even attempt to resolve the relationship of racism to occupational development for U.S. workers of Asian ancestry. The undoubted persistence of racism is all the more reason to attend to "the wider social milieu in which behavior and identity originate" (D. W. Sue & D. Sue, 1991, p. 193).

Family Influence on Occupational Development

Asian Cultural Values   Confucianism, Buddhism, and **Taoism** have influenced Asian cultural values (Axelson, 1993), with Confucianism having dominated Chinese culture for nearly twenty-five centuries (Yang, 1991). In Confucianism, "patriarchal ideas are embraced and a formal relationship system emphasizes humility, politeness, and respect" (Axelson, 1993, p. 438). In

Practical Applications

Hsia and Hirano-Nakanishi (1989) write:

> With the exception of scholars, bureaucrats, and political activists, Americans of Asian ancestry rarely think of themselves first and foremost as "Asian American." Most ethnic Asians, particularly newcomers, are more likely to identify with their specific national or regional identities: Vietnamese, Korean, Hmong, Punjabi Sikh, Cantonese or Taiwanese, Visayan or Ilocano. (p. 24)

Asian Americans also come from India, Pakistan, Sri Lanka, Bangladesh, Cambodia, Thailand, Burma, Laos, Japan, China, Hong Kong, the Philippines, Indonesia, and Malaysia; Pacific Islanders come from Hawaii, Samoa, Guam, and Tonga (Brandon, 1991; Chow, 1987). In countries like India and China, ethnic and regional differences are extensive. Thus, in the same way that social constructions of the "model minority" are inaccurate, use of the term "Asian American" by vocational psychologists may not be helpful, either. Practitioners will hardly get an accurate sense of who their clients are if practitioners already have a preconceived notion of how clients identify themselves. Within-group differences among U.S. workers of Asian ancestry are vast, even more so than among Hispanics. It may not be useful to persist in using the term "Asian American," especially if the people to whom it refers do not embrace the term themselves. Given that vocational psychology lacks a cohesive framework for working with U.S. workers of Asian ancestry, continued use of a term irrelevant to the people it purportedly refers to will only muddy the waters even more.

Literature on counseling so-called Asian Americans states that an active, directive practitioner style is most effective (Exum & Lau, 1988, cited in Baruth & Manning, 1991; D. W. Sue & D. Sue, 1990; Yagi & Oh, 1995). Ivey (1988) notes that giving advice, providing information, and focusing on a specific problem are frequently used in vocational planning. Ostensibly, then, some U.S. workers of Asian ancestry should be highly amenable to occupational guidance interventions. But the available empirical evidence is disjointed (Leong & Gim-Chung, 1995; Leong & Serafica, 1995). While case studies can be immensely useful (Chen & Leong, 1997; Cook, 1997; Fouad & Tang, 1997; Shanasarian, 1997), "educators, counselors, and pupil personnel workers often do not have enough knowledge of the Asian-American experience to make enlightened decisions" (D. W. Sue & D Sue, 1990, p. 202). This knowledge base could be expanded by increasing the use of contextual interpretivism as a research methodology.

Practical Applications

More consideration needs to be given to broader, external structural factors—such as **institutional racism** and **cultural racism**—that influence occupational development of U.S. workers of Asian ancestry. Institutional racism refers to "social policies, laws, and regulations whose purpose it is to maintain the economic and social advantage of the racial/ethnic group in power" (J. Jones, 1972, cited in Atkinson, Morten & Sue, 1993, p. 11). Cultural racism refers to societal "beliefs and customs that promote the assumption that the products of the dominant culture (e.g., language, traditions, appearance) are superior to other cultures" (J. Jones, 1972, cited in Atkinson et al., 1993, p. 11). An unwillingness to address issues of racism, among other forms of oppression, can look like privileged complacency on the part of practitioners. Practitioners' receptivity to exploring the unique cultural history of their clients of Asian ancestry means reducing a reliance on published articles and chapters that have failed to capture the within-group differences of the group that scholars have broadly labeled "Asian Americans." Given that, "since 1990, the Asian and Pacific Islander population has grown about 4.5 percent per year . . . ." with immigration to the U.S. accounting for 86 percent of this growth (Bennett & Martin, 1995, p. 48), anti-immigration political sentiments—of which racism is admittedly part—also need incorporation into the occupational development of some Asian subgroups. These Asian immigrant subgroups probably need occupational guidance more desperately than many Asian-American college students.

Buddhism, "self-improvement can be found through doing good work and study and through the control of undesirable emotions; optimism, calmness, and harmony are valued" (p. 438). In Taoism, "ancestor worship provides guidance and advice for present living. . . . Traditionally, followers of Taoism are attached to burial sites (location) of ancestors, where they can go to pray, meditate, and pay respects before the graves of the ancestors" (p. 438). Many refugees who were accustomed to visit their ancestors' graves are apt to feel lonely in the U.S. and unable to make decisions without the advice of their forebears.

Acculturation will moderate family influence on occupational development of U.S. workers of Asian ancestry (Leong, 1993; Leong & Tata, 1990; Yang, 1991). Strength of **filial piety**—that is, the child's sense of allegiance and obligation to

Practical Applications

Recent discussion of ethnic identity among Asians in the United States is found in Sodowsky, Kwan, and Pannu (1995). We suggest that practitioners assess the extent to which traditional Asian cultural values are present in their clients' lives, without automatically assuming that such values are uniformly present for clients (see, for example, Mizokawa & Rychman, 1990). Very likely, the presence of traditional Asian cultural values is going to be contextual in nature, contingent upon such things as ethnic subgroup and birth order. A second- or third-born son may feel less family pressure and perceive greater occupational possibilities

than a first-born son. For others, partial cultural assimilation may occur, with native language (Chen & Leong, 1997), religion, and customs predominating at home, but English predominating at school and in the workplace. Structural assimilation may be difficult in cases where large numbers of Asian students in a university's freshman class (Butterfield, 1990) result in college admission quotas (Chen & Leong, 1997). Marital assimilation may occur among more educated, higher-income Asian Americans (Chen & Leong, 1997), but not for those who are less educated, lower income.

parents (D. Sue & D. W. Sue, 1993)—also will vary by acculturation. So will the interdependence of family members, the restraint of potentially disruptive emotions, the tradition of patriarchy, and the inculcation of guilt and shame.

Career Awareness Workshops for Parents Given that less acculturated Asian-American families are more likely to influence their children's occupational development, career awareness workshops for parents can be useful. Evanoski and Tsu (1989) report on such workshops for 2,553 Chinese and Korean parents. The aim is to inform these parents about "the wide range of career possibilities offered by the American educational system to both young women and men" (p. 472). Bilingual role models of similar cultures and backgrounds use their prestige and knowledge to inform parents of career opportunities and available community college and academic and career programs. The role models are required to have several years' professional experience, be good public speakers, and be willing to volunteer to serve the community through their presentations. Occupations represented by the role models include accountancy, law,

---

Practical Applications

The career awareness workshops for Chinese and Korean American parents were successful for several reasons. (1) Use of parents' natural language by the bilingual role models established workshop credibility. (2) Workshops were designed to respect parents' decision-making role in the family. (3) Speakers were concrete and explicit in their presentations. (4) Workshops were held in parents' neighborhoods. (5) Workshops were publicized ahead of time in the Chinese and Korean communities through relevant media, organizations, and at pertinent festivals. These ethnic-specific tailored programs can be replicated in other locales with other ethnic groups, especially with written materials in parents' native language and linkages with influential community organizations. The need for an alliance between parents and occupational development practitioners cannot be overemphasized.

---

engineering, science, medicine, architecture, nursing, physical therapy, social work, advertising, and civil service.

Ten separate workshops, each about three hours long, were presented to Chinese and Korean communities in Queens, New York, over a two-year-period. Fully 95 percent of the parents reported learning more about new job possibilities for their children and themselves. Better information about occupational outlook and anticipated earnings were reported by 86 percent of the parents. Increased awareness of educational requirements for various occupations were reported by 85 percent of the parents. Increased awareness about college financial aid were reported by 94 percent of the parents. Bilingual role models were strongly appreciated by the parents, who preferred the use of native language for the presentations. More career information literature in the parents' native language was also a frequent request.

Asian-American College Students

In comparison to White college students, Asian-American college students have (a) a significantly more dependent decision-making style, with a characteristic denial of personal responsibility, and (b) significantly lower levels of career maturity (Leong, 1991). White college students' occupational stereotyping of Asian Americans has been rationalized as a legitimate research venture because these

Practical Applications

College students as research participants have been called populations
of convenience (Reid, 1993) because
they are statistically nonrepresentative samples whose research results
have extremely limited generalizability. In the same way that research methods borrowed from the
White, dominant culture have not
produced an organized body of
knowledge about the occupational
development of multicultural populations, resorting to the use of populations of convenience likewise
undermines the accumulation of
solid minority scholarship. We question how the "limited knowledge
base on the career development of
Asian Americans" (Leong, 1991, p.
229) is enhanced by the persistent
use of nonrepresentative populations
of convenience.

students "will eventually enter the labor force and assume the majority of positions as administrators, supervisors, and employers of both Asians and Asian
Americans" (Leong & Hayes, 1990). Research participants in these two studies
were obtained from undergraduate psychology classes.

Gender and Socioeconomic Status

In the vocational research on U.S. workers of Asian ancestry, gender differences
have received minimal interest, socioeconomic status next to none (Leong &
Gim-Chung, 1995). Educational attainment of Asian-American women has
been found to be significantly higher than Asian-American men (Brandon,
1991). Chinese women who are immigrants or children of recent immigrants
show significantly higher educational attainment than Chinese men. The same
pattern is found for Filipina women over Filipino men.

Chow (1987) investigated the relationship between sex role identity, occupational achievement, self-esteem, and work satisfaction of 161 Asian-American
working women in the Washington, D. C., area. Most research participants were
employed full time and identified themselves as Chinese, Japanese, Korean, or
Filipino. A weighted, stratified random sampling design was used to ensure that
the sample was representative and the results were generalizable. Sex-role identity
was found to relate significantly to occupational achievement. Asian-American
women who scored as masculine or androgynous on the Bem Sex Role Inventory (BSRI) show significantly higher occupational achievement than women

---

Practical Applications

Gender-related factors are likely mediated by acculturation; this may be more salient for recent Asian immigrants and low-acculturated women (Leong & Gim-Chung, 1995). The task for practitioners is to assess this in a way that does not impose the issue on clients, and to be on the lookout for signs that this issue is pertinent for the client. Socioeconomic status—particularly economic difficulty among recent Asian immigrants—when combined with the presence of traditional Asian cultural values, can have significant implications for occupational development. It is not uncommon to see the sacrificing of some family members to provide opportunities for another family member whose success benefits the entire family. Furthermore, while education is highly emphasized in Asian and Asian-American families, this is not a universal phenomenon.

---

who score as feminine or undifferentiated. Androgynous Asian-American women showed significantly higher self-esteem and greater work satisfaction than masculine, feminine, and undifferentiated women. Occupational achievement was also significantly related to both self-esteem and work satisfaction.

NATIVE AMERICANS

Several areas await further research and practical applications for vocational psychology and career counseling among Native Americans.

Collectivism and Individualism

To the extent that collectivism rather than individualism "forms the normative base of Native American [individual's] culture" (Pedigo, 1983, p. 274), then client occupational concerns will need to be considered "within the context of a larger family and community social system" (LaFromboise, Trimble & Mohatt, 1990, p. 642). "Many Indian people view family, home, and community as the center of their existence rather than a job or career" (Martin, 1991, p. 275). Given likely within-group differences, qualitative and ethnographic research approaches may more effectively address these nuances than quantitative approaches on populations of convenience. Practitioners can also use an informal, qualitative assessment of acculturation to help clients contextualize individualistic and collectivistic choices in their lives.

Vocational Assessment

In the psychological evaluation of Native Americans generally (Horan & Cady, 1990), and in vocational assessment particularly, more research, case studies, and the development of practical applications are needed. Conceptual-based articles and chapters risk the appearance of mere academic exercises. A more pressing issue is the kind of research methodology to be used. The limited information on the occupational development of Native Americans is unlikely to be substantially augmented by logical positivism alone. Contextual interpretivism merits closer scrutiny to move forward the knowledge about Native American work lives, including the persistence of **career myths.**

Career Myths

Herring (1990) defines career myths as "irrational attitudes about the career-development process. These irrational attitudes most often are generated from historical, familial patterns of career ignorance and negative career-development experiences" (p. 13). Native American youth particularly are vulnerable to career myths.

Three common influences on career myths have been identified (Herring, 1990). First, research on Native American occupational development emphasizes populations on Western reservations. Historical and sociological perspectives predominate, and most research has been conducted by non–Native Americans, which can "lack both cultural and ethnic perspectives" (p. 15).

Second, continued negative stereotyping by the media and by "school materials (e.g., textbooks . . .) need to be purged of any inadvertent illustrations, photographs, and references that inaccurately depict Native Americans" (p. 15). Practitioners can help clients determine how negative stereotyping overlapped into myths about occupational development.

Third, a lack of career information and related training requirements can impede occupational development of Native American youth. These misconceptions can adversely affect aspirations, decision-making, and job satisfaction.

Herring (1990) concludes:

To attain the desired goal of the elimination of barriers to the successful career development and the subsequent restoration of rational career thinking will require a multifaceted intervention, which will entail improving counseling techniques (individual and family) and improving the current, unequal career opportunity structure and poor educational systems that created the disparity in achievement and the low expectation levels of Native American students. (p. 17)

We note how occupational development cannot be artificially separated out from external structural factors that impinge upon the role of work in people's lives.

GAY, LESBIAN, AND BISEXUAL PERSONS

Through the end of the 1980s, sexual or affectional preferences were seldom considered or systematically investigated in the career counseling literature (Hetherington, Hillerbrand & Etringer, 1989; Hetherington & Orzek, 1989). Within less than a decade, matters appear to be changing. Gelberg and Chojnacki (1996) write:

Sexual orientation is inextricably connected to the career and life planning process. It affects career choices; the ways in which the job search is conducted; the development of work-related interests, values, experiences, and skills; the nature of personal and professional relationships; and the degree of stress experienced at work and at home. (pp. 4–5)

The authors define **sexual orientation** in the broadest sense of the word, to refer not only to sexual behaviors but also to sexual attractions, emotional preferences, social preferences, sexual fantasies, lifestyle choices, and sense of identity (Klein, Sepekoff & Wolf, 1985). Avoiding polarized thinking about sexual orientation—that is, not classifying people as only gay/lesbian/bisexual or heterosexual—Gelberg and Chojnacki write that the calculations of anywhere from 5 to 25 million gay, lesbian, and bisexual persons in the U.S. are low estimates. When each aspect of sexual orientation is viewed as a distinct factor, an almost limitless number of possible combinations are created. Consequently, distinctions between sexual orientations blur.

Nevertheless, most people in the U.S. are profoundly ignorant about the actual experience of gay/lesbian/bisexual persons (Mohr, 1988). Societal heterosexism and homophobia prevail. Heterosexism refers to the culturally conditioned bias that heterosexuality is intrinsically superior to homosexuality (Rochlin, 1985). Homophobia refers to an irrational dread and loathing of homosexuality and homosexual people (Weinberg, 1972, cited in Rochlin, 1985). Heterosexist social attitudes and practices harm gay, lesbian, and bisexual persons and have a much greater overall harmful impact on society than is usually realized (Mohr, 1988). Many workplaces are heterosexist: they structurally and ideologically promote a particular model of heterosexuality that forces invisibility on gay, lesbian, and bisexual professionals, socially validate heterosexual

Practical Applications

"Lesbians and gay men represent a challenge to some of our most entrenched ideas about the separation of work and sexuality; their mere presence seems to upset our conventional beliefs about privacy, professionalism, and office etiquette" (Woods, 1994, p. 5). For all the eagerness of gay, lesbian, and bisexual employees to detach sexuality from work, the task becomes difficult because work is largely a social activity and personal and professional roles become as firmly intertwined as they do for heterosexual people. As sexual creatures—regardless of one's orientation—humans cannot help that social interactions are colored by sexual possibilities, expectations, and constraints. In dress and in self-presentation, in looks and in flirtations, in jokes and in gossip, in secret affairs and in dalliances, even in the range of coercive behaviors known as sexual harassment, sexuality is al-

luded to, both implicitly and explicitly, in the countless interpersonal exchanges that combine to constitute "work."

Parents and Friends of Lesbians and Gays, Inc. (PFLAG) have a series of supportive, educational, and informational publications that may be especially helpful for practitioners and their clients, particularly when it appears that the exploration of vocational issues might benefit from integration with concerns about sexual orientation. A good place to start is Sauerman (1996). Another PFLAG publication aimed at gay, lesbian, and bisexual youth is *Be Yourself* (1994), with numerous resources provided at the end of the booklet. Two PFLAG publications are aimed at parents: *About Our Children* (1995) includes some sections translated into Chinese, French, Japanese, and Spanish. *Our Daughters and Sons* (1995) is available in English only. Practitioners who do not

mating rituals, reinforce the masculine nature of bureaucratic organizations, and tolerate antigay commentary and imagery that circulates through company channels (Woods, 1994).

Heterosexism is a political and social reality. Nowhere in the U.S. are there legal protections for gay/lesbian/bisexual persons with regards to workplace discrimination. Consequently, gay, lesbian, and bisexual persons (a) may be fired for their sexual orientation; (b) may be denied employment or promotion because of their sexual orientation; (c) are denied the right to file joint income tax returns; (d) may be physically or verbally harassed, or both, on and off the job; (e) may be denied health insurance for their partner; (f) may find that social ac-

specialize in gay, lesbian, and bisexual clientele would also find these PFLAG publications useful reading (see also, Thompson, 1994).

A book aimed more towards adults is *A Family and Friend's Guide to Sexual Orientation* (Powers & Ellis, 1996). Especially relevant are stories from the workplace (Powers & Ellis, 1996, pp. 155–89) and the authors' view that a "Don't Ask, Don't Tell" work environment creates "a tremendous and negative impact on the bottom line" (p. 155), with workplace performance deterioration. Managers who send out signals that it is not okay to be gay/lesbian/bisexual in the workplace negatively impact performance and force such employees to closet themselves. Excluded sexual minorities are less likely to devote the extra energy needed to make the organization successful. When these issues are ignored in the workplace, productive work relationships can be destroyed and top-notch performance of all workers can be undermined.

Another resource is *Straight Jobs, Gay Lives* (Friskopp & Silverstein, 1995). This book examines the role of work in the lives of professional gay men and lesbian women who are alumni of the Harvard Business School. All of the issues discussed in this section on gay, lesbian, and bisexual persons are touched upon in the authors' qualitative-based research.

Practitioners also need to be aware of **heterosexual privilege** (Gelberg & Chojnacki, 1996). Heterosexual privilege allows (a) heterosexual partners to publicly display affection without fear of comment or attack by others, (b) inheritance rights, (c) access to a partner in a hospital, (d) the legal right to marry, and (e) the ability to adopt children. Such rights and freedoms are taken for granted by many heterosexuals. Practitioners have to become knowledgeable about the absence of rights for gay, lesbian, and bisexual persons because these rights can impact career development and work-related behaviors (Curry, Clifford & Leonard, 1996).

tivities at work assume that employees are heterosexual; and (g) may conduct differing types of job searches, depending on how "out" they are in the workplace (Gelberg & Chojnacki, 1996; Woods, 1994).

Most gay/lesbian/bisexual people live in hiding, also known as "in the closet" (Mohr, 1988). "Coming out of the closet" often becomes a central fixture in the life experiences of gay, lesbian, and bisexual persons, and can become intertwined with career decision-making. Woods (1994) defines being "in the closet" as misrepresenting one's sexuality to others by encouraging (or at least permitting) others to draw a conclusion that one knows is false. He likens closets to dark and cramped spaces in which one can hide but where nobody wants to live. Closets conceal those articles that seem unfit for display in larger, more important rooms. A gay/lesbian/bisexual person who is hiding in a closet is invisible to those outside of it; working in a closet allows one little room to move about.

Gay Men

Woods (1994) presents the following scenario about what a gay man must deal with as he begins a new job:

> Entering the workplace, a gay man faces a host of decisions. The head of personnel wants to know what kind of guy he is: How does he spend his time? What sort of skills and interests will he bring to the company? Will he get along with the others who work there? His officemates will invite him to the local tavern, to the baseball game, or to the Monday morning chat about their weekend conquests. As he climbs the corporate ladder, those above will want to know if he shares their values, if he faces the same demands from home and family, if he can be trusted. (p. 25).

The heterosexual mindset most gay men encounter in the workplace mitigates against the creation of a diverse work environment. Nor can he be easily assimilated into the workers' circle if he cannot be who he is. Yet, he can take some heart in knowing that many married men are to some extent putting on a façade, even with each other, about the quality of their marriages and family lives, and they cannot be who they are either.

Lesbians

Through the end of the 1980s, few empirical studies focused on the career decision-making process of lesbian women. While gender may be more significant than sexual orientation in explaining differences in career choice and life planning, lesbian women may be affected differently than heterosexual women by sex-role attitudes which can powerfully influence career decision-making (Hetherington & Orzek, 1989). The stage of a client's lesbian identity, plus her particular stage of career decision-making, interact in an imprecise manner regarding a timetable for duration or age appropriateness. These interactive processes are unique for each individual woman.

As with other multicultural and diverse populations, Sophie's (1985/86) research shows within-group differences in lesbian identity development. Clearly, modernist assumptions about lesbian occupational development are inappropriate. Given the historical context that impacts development or changes in sexual orientation, contextual interpretivist methodologies are underutilized with research on the role of work in lesbian women's lives.

Practical Applications

Practitioners will have to decide the extent to which they will become an advocate for gay men (Hetherington et al., 1989). Gelberg and Chojnacki (1995; 1996) use the term **ally** to refer to heterosexuals who are professionally and personally affirmative to gay, lesbian, and bisexual persons. Practitioners with no real understanding of their own homophobia, however well-intentioned they might be, may be offering fear and confusion which masquerades as healing (Markowitz, 1991; Woolley, 1991). Buhrke (1989) provides a useful resource guide for incorporating lesbian and gay issues into both counselor training generally and career counseling particularly. Practitioners have a professional responsibility to assist gay/lesbian/bisexual clients in overcoming as much discrimination, prejudice, and oppression as possible. Practitioners also have an ethical and moral obligation to work with such clients in an affirmative manner (Buhrke & Douce, 1991). Gelberg and Chojnacki (1996) provide an excellent appendix of career counseling resources that, for gay men, includes gay identity development, materials for career centers, organizations and agencies, and more.

Lesbian Vocational Development Fassinger (1996) summarizes barriers and facilitators to lesbian women's career choice, implementation, and adjustment. Barriers to career choice are related to "coming out of the closet." (1) Lesbians involved in their sexual identity development may neglect occupational decisions and tasks. This hold-up in vocational development tasks, long after peers have addressed these issues, risks being internalized as individual inadequacy rather than normalized as a developmental delay. (2) Occupational stereotyping can interact with "coming out." Some career options may be eliminated because they are perceived as inhospitable toward lesbians "or, conversely, are associated with lesbians" (p. 163). Christie (1997) profiles lesbians in a variety of jobs which can expand the vision occupational opportunities. (3) When many lesbians "come out of the closet," their families may withdraw financial and psychological support, which can impede vocational planning. (4) Lesbians whose self-esteem and self-confidence decrease during the "coming out" process can have their career decision-making constrained. (5) Bias in vocational assessment and (6) on the part of practitioners are two final barriers related to "coming out."

Practical Applications

In view of the sampling of representative literature on the role of work in lesbians' lives (Fassinger, 1996; Sophie, 1985/86), practitioners can prepare themselves to work with lesbian women in several ways (Hetherington & Orzek, 1989). (1) Work to consciously eliminate personal homophobic attitudes. (2) Develop an understanding of the gender issues for women.(3) Learn about lesbian identity development. (4) Help lesbian clients to overcome internalized negative stereotypes. (5) Provide self-exploration assistance in the form of informational interview questions specific to lesbian concerns. Among such questions (Milburn, Eldridge & Hetherington, 1988, cited in Hetherington & Orzek, 1989): (a) Is this career available to me as an "out" lesbian? (b) Had I determined how "out" I wanted to be before I chose this career? (c) Are there any work environments in this career that are more open to lesbians? (d) Is my sexual identity pertinent to this career area? (e) Will my sexual orientation affect being accepted in graduate school?

(6) Develop a list of job search strategies that lesbian clients may use. Among such strategies (Milburn, Eldridge & Hetherington, 1988, cited in Hetherington & Orzek, 1989): (a) learning which companies have non-discrimination policies, (b) learning about the attitudes regarding homosexuality in local communities where a lesbian may consider living, (c) communicating on one's résumé the lesbian and gay activities in which one has been involved, (d) handling the situation in which the presence of a spouse is considered beneficial, (e) handling dual-career issues, (f) learning about companies who are sensitive to lesbian concerns. (7) Provide a list of professional associations and resources for lesbian clients.

Lesbians' career choice has several facilitators (Fassinger, 1996). (1) In making work-related decisions, lesbians are less likely than heterosexual women to be encumbered by "accommodating men or conforming to traditional gender roles" (p. 164). (2) Lesbians are also less likely than heterosexual women to "anticipate depending on men for financial stability" (p. 165). (3) Financial independence between partners is more likely in a lesbian relationship, partially due to laws and company policies that inhibit legal and economic dependence. (4) Lesbians appear more certain and satisfied with career choices than gay men. (5) A strong focus on career planning and preparation may buffer the "coming out" process.

Fassinger (1996) also addresses lesbian women's occupational implementation and adjustment. One set of issues revolves around workplace discrimination, which occurs in the form of

> hiring, wage inequities, legal prohibitions, retention and promotion problems, [sexual] harassment and abuse, surveillance, poor work evaluations, underutilization of abilities . . . , hate crimes and violence, social and collegial ostracism, hostile work climate, limitation of future options, and dual public-private identities. (p. 166)

A second set of issues revolves around identity management. Lesbians closeted in the workplace may use silence, invisibility, "passing," and keeping their work and private lives sharply separated. Secrecy can become a debilitating strain, negatively impact work, and undermine self-confidence.

A third set of issues in lesbian women's occupational implementation and adjustment revolves around dual-career families and work-family issues (Fassinger, 1996). Nearly three-fourths of lesbians are in an intimate relationship at any given time. Out of the need to survive financially or because of commitment to a career, both partners in the relationship are likely to be employed. Large discrepancies in earnings can disrupt an egalitarian relationship. Unwillingness to admit to a potential employer about a dual-career job search can impinge on negotiations. For women willing to admit their dual-career job search to prospective employers, "the institutional supports . . . available for the placement of heterosexual partners in dual-career job searches are less likely to exist for lesbians" (pp. 168–169). Similarly, for those lesbians who are mothers, work-family issues often receive less external support than that received by heterosexual women.

PERSONS WITH DISABILITIES

> People with disabilities represent a very diverse population. There are many different types of disabilities (e.g., cerebral palsy, multiple sclerosis, low vision, deafness, mental retardation), all of which have substantial variation in possible degrees of severity and functional limitations. Even within specific disabilities, there is great variation in resultant functional limitations. . . .
>
> [L]ike race and ethnicity, disability is multifaceted, and cannot be examined in isolation in its impact on career development. (Szymanski, Hershenson, Enright & Ettinger, 1996, p. 70)

An estimated 49 million U.S. citizens have a disability (McNeil, 1995). Of these, 24 million are severely disabled, unable to perform one or more activities and roles. Among those between the ages of 15 and 64 who are disabled, 9.6 percent are Asian and Pacific Islander, 16.9 percent are Hispanic, 17.7 percent are White, 20.8 percent are African American, and 26.9 percent are American Indian, Eskimo, and Aleut. Disability is associated with lower levels of income and an increased likelihood of living in poverty. Chances for employment are reduced among the disabled.

A major reason for reduced employment opportunities among persons with disabilities is an historically negative attitude towards such persons. Magiera-Planey (1990) writes:

> Attitudes regarding disabled persons . . . as a group have a long and illustrious history. In the early days of mankind the disabled were often left behind or eliminated if the group needed to be mobile or if there was a lack of food. In later civilizations many of the disabled and deformed were systematically eliminated as a means of improving the society. These negative attitudes soon included the belief that the disabled individual was being punished for some injustice that he/she had committed. (pp. 45–46)

We detect both a "blaming the victim" and "belief in a just world" mentality in the historical view of persons with disabilities. In the West, from medieval times through the Industrial Revolution, persons with disabilities were consistently devalued (Magiera-Planey, 1990). "Unfortunately disabled persons as a group are still viewed as nonparticipants in society [and in the workforce]" (p. 46). Atkinson and Hackett (1998) present an up-to-date examination of the oppression of persons with disabilities.

The Americans with Disabilities Act

Title I of the Americans with Disabilities Act of 1990 (ADA) took effect on July 26, 1992, for employers for twenty-five or more employees (U.S. Equal Employment Opportunity Commission, 1991b, 1992). The ADA took effect for employers with fifteen or more employees exactly two years later. The ADA prohibits private employers, state and local governments, employment agencies and labor unions from discriminating against *qualified individuals with disabilities* in all employment practices. A person is said to have a "disability" if she or he has "a physical or mental impairment that substantially limits one or more major life activities, has a record of such an impairment, or is regarded as having such an impairment" (U.S. Equal Employment Opportunity Commission, 1992, p. 1). Prohibited discrimination in employment practices includes the following: (a) job application procedures, (b) hiring, (c) firing, (d) advancement, (e) compensation, (f) job training, (g) and other terms, conditions, and privileges of em-

Practical Applications

The U.S. Equal Employment Opportunity Commission's pamphlets on the employment rights of an individual with a disability (1991a, 1991d) and on employer responsibilities (1991c, 1991e) are useful for practitioners and clients.

Reasonable accommodation is vitally needed in postemployment services to promote job retention and job satisfaction (Roessler & Rumrill, 1995). Title I of the ADA says it is up to the employee to (1) identify needed barrier reductions, (2) initiate requests for an employer's reasonable accommodation, and (3) implement such accommodations in collaboration with employers. Rehabilitation counselors in the Rehabilitation Services Administration are often pressured by large caseloads and limited resources to close the file of a disabled client who holds a job successfully for 60 days. Yet, for most people with disabilities, interruptions in employment largely occur after the 60-day employment period. Access to postemployment services are clearly needed for a longer period of time.

An ongoing need for postemployment services includes help with (a) the costs of devices that assist, (b) change of jobs in the same company due to disability-related problems, (c) access to fringe benefits on the job, (d) pay and treatment equal to other workers, and (e) long-term services to maintain employment (Roessler & Rumrill, 1995). Career adjustment and advancement become threatened when employees fail to devise integrative responses to on-the-job barriers. Mindful that most postemployment services are needed after 60 days, practitioners can play a crucial role in assisting persons with disabilities when such services are needed. Syzmanski, Hershenson, Ettinger, and Enright (1996) call for a reexamination of rehabilitation agency polices to ensure that persons with disabilities receive timely service when they need it, and not according to some arbitrary time frame that has no empirical basis. Several types of reasonable accommodation are presented in Brodwin, Parker and DeLaGarza (1996).

ployment. Employment nondiscrimination requirements also apply to: (h) recruitment, (i) advertising, (j) tenure, (k) layoff, (l) leave, (m) fringe benefits, and (n) all other employment-related activities.

A qualified individual with a disability is a person who meets legitimate skill, experience, education, or other requirements of an employment position that he or she holds or seeks, and who can perform the essential functions of the position with or without reasonable accommodation (U.S. Equal Employment Opportunity Commission, 1992).

> Reasonable accommodation is any modification or adjustment to a job or the work environment that will enable a qualified applicant or employee with a disability to participate in the application process or perform essential job functions. Reasonable accommodation also includes adjustments to assume that a qualified individual with a disability has rights and privileges in employment equal to those of employees without disabilities. (p. 5)

Reasonable accommodation can include, but is not limited to: (a) making existing facilities used by employees readily accessible to and usable by persons with disabilities; (b) job restructuring, modifying work schedules, reassignment to a vacant position; (c) acquiring or modifying equipment or devices; adjusting or modifying examinations, training materials, or policies; and (c) providing qualified readers or interpreters. Requiring the ability to perform essential functions assures that an individual with a disability will not be considered unqualified simply because of inability to perform marginal or incidental job functions. If an individual is qualified to perform essential functions except for the limitations created by a disability, then the employer must consider whether the individual could perform these functions with reasonable accommodation. Employers are required to make reasonable accommodation to qualified individuals with disabilities if no **undue hardship** is imposed on the operation of businesses. Undue hardship refers to

> an 'action requiring significant difficulty or expense' when considered in light of a number of factors . . . [including] . . . the size, resources, nature, and structure of the employer's operation. Undue hardship is determined on a case-by-case basis. (p. 7)

Thus, the ADA pertains to an individual job applicant or employee.

Career Counseling for People with Disabilities

Employers are frequently reluctant to hire disabled workers because of unfounded myths and false assumptions regarding (a) nonproductivity, (b) high rates of absenteeism, (c) high risks for accidents, and (d) increased costs through higher insurance rates and special accommodations (Bolles, 1991; Delsen, 1989). Providing career guidance to people with disabilities presents a hurdle (Curnow, 1989), in part because of the limited availability of career development literature as a resource for practitioners. The following is a summary of Curnow's well-referenced article.

Misleading assumptions towards individuals with disability that have restricted the application of vocational development theory include (a) the idea that career options for the disabled are limited, (b) career development is unimportant, arrested, or retarded for individuals with disability, and (c) the career development of people with disabilities are influenced by chance. The rationale for the restricted application of vocational development theories to the disabled is based on the faulty premise that, in comparison with their nondisabled peers, the special needs of people with disabilities preclude the relevance of current theories of vocational development. A contrasting assumption is that current theories may be applicable to individuals with disability if practitioners consider their unique problems and needs that require specialized services.

Disabling Conditions and the Curtailment of Career Development. Disabling conditions can impede career development because of limitations in early opportunities to engage in vocational exploration, few chances for successful experiences in decision-making, and depreciative experiences that may be a common occurrence to individuals with disability which can adversely effect one's self-concept.

Limited Early Opportunities to Engage in Vocational Exploration. Individuals with reduced mobility or who require special medical treatment can miss out on opportunities to engage in vocational exploration that is crucial for later vocational growth and decision-making. Childhood experiences are often limited for the individual with a precareer disability, which can restrict the range of options perceived by people with disabilities. Insufficient experiences related to the acquisition of interests, competencies, self-perceptions, and knowledge about occupational environments can result in maladaptive development.

Few Chances for Successful Decision-making Experiences. Decision-making ability improves with practice. From a developmental perspective, limitations in early experiences have a later detrimental effect on decision-making ability. Individuals with disability who have had few chances for successful experiences in decision-making may lack competence in making decisions. This can be manifested by the inadequate acquisition of vocational information, the insufficient use of resources in vocational planning, and a failure to generate enough career options because of personal limitation. Thus, career decision-making can be negatively impacted.

Depreciative Experiences and Self-Concept. Social attitudes and stereotypes towards disability can be as important as the disability itself. Depreciation from others plays a part in shaping the life role of the individual with disability. Low social status and the prejudicial attitudes of others may be a common occurrence to

Practical Applications

Curnow (1989) describes strategies to facilitate the vocational development of the disabled.

1. *Cultivation of a systematic approach.* Career assessment and counseling in a planned, sequential manner are indispensable to the vocational development of individuals with disability. Individualized education plans (IEPs), individual written rehabilitation plans (IWRPs), and individual service plans (ISPs), among others, can include systematic career development components for students with disability.

2. *Early exposure to vocational and social experiences.* To reduce patterns of delayed and impaired vocational development, establish early goals and objectives (i.e., opportunities to explore varied vocational environments; exposure to appropriate role models; development of decision-making skills by increased attention to the knowledge, experiences, competencies, values, and attitudes already acquired in the client's life). Evaluative criteria determines the effectiveness of goals and objectives.

3. *Supportive counseling and developing decision-making skills.* Efforts to assist clients to cope with their feelings and attitudes about their disability can be productive. Exploring client strengths and limitations promotes realistic vocational aspirations or decisions. Throughout the counseling process, encouraging client involvement and responsibility can (a) enhance social maturity, (b) reduce overprotectiveness and personal dependency, and (c) provide the foundation for clients to learn and practice decision-making skills. Regarding point (b), including family members and other key persons can be vital, especially to ensure that counseling interventions are not working at cross-purposes with messages and expectations the client receives from home, school, and workplace.

The feasibility of employing persons with disabilities is demonstrated in a video by Attainment Productions, *Every One Can Work* (1995).

individuals with disability. Distortions in the client's perception of self or of the occupational world can arise. These individuals are vulnerable to maladaptive career development. Unrealistic vocational aspirations or decisions become vital to assess.

College Students with Disabilities

Overview of Career-related Issues Disability impacts career development in several ways (Enright, Conyers & Syzmanski, 1996). Decision-making ability may be hindered by parental overprotectiveness, high personal-dependency needs, and cognitive impairment—which can affect confidence or competence to make career decisions. Self-concept is apt to differ among college students with congenital disabilities or younger age of onset disabilities than students with older age of onset disabilities. Type of disability is another issue for practitioners to consider, especially the disabled student's perception of his or her disability. Likewise, gender issues merit attention, since employment rates and income are lower for disabled women than for disabled men.

Disability also impacts participation in postsecondary education (Enright et al., 1996). Transition from high school to college can be fraught with challenges (increased academic demands, decreased contact with instructors, changes in social support, nontraditional status for older disabled students, physical and emotional adjustments for recently disabled students). Adjustment to college life is an integral factor for college students with disabilities. Quality of social interactions with peers and responsiveness of faculty to disabled students' needs are critical. Entry into the world of work is another obstacle to overcome. Selecting careers, obtaining a first job, and later job changes are issues for many college students with disabilities.

Accessibility and accommodation of career services, plus the appropriateness of vocational assessment procedures, are a third set of career concerns for college students with disabilities (Enright et al., 1996). Accessible parking, meeting places, and bathrooms are essential. Vocational assessment procedures may need to be modified to include administration in an oral, large print, or Braille format. Extra time or additional breaks may be necessary during assessment procedures, which may need to be conducted in an individual versus group format. Responses may need to be recorded through an interpreter, word processor, or nonwritten methods. Adjustable desks that accommodate wheelchairs may be needed. Interpretation of assessment results can be a problem because of test administration modification or a norm-referenced test that lacks persons with disabilities in the normative sample.

Overcoming Barriers to Employment Increasing numbers of college students with disabilities are entering the competitive job search. A practical and expedient plan to assist students with disabilities in their transition from college graduate to employment is presented by Thompson and Hutto (1992). This employment counseling model was developed—without funds—by a master's student in rehabilitation counseling to meet an internship requirement. Twelve

Practical Applications

No one theory of vocational psychology completely applies to college students with disabilities (Syzmanski et al., 1996). Unique combinations of life experience, interests, resources, and personality traits will mean that no two persons will react the same way to the same degree of disability (Bolles, 1991; Brodwin et al., 1996; Magiera-Planey, 1990). "A counselor will need to evaluate what makes sense given a [disabled] student's individual circumstances" (Enright et al., 1996, p. 105). Practitioners can explore several contextual factors with clients: (a) the nature of the student's disability, (b) how it has been incorporated into the student's self-concept, (c) whether the disabil-

ity is visible, (d) whether the student is informed about the merits and drawbacks of disclosing the disability, and (e) whether the student is informed about the ADA. "The aim in providing guidance should be to assist students in managing their own career development" (Enright et al., 1996, p. 105). Smith (1991), in discussing the feasibility of college for the learning disabled, writes "the learning disabled can achieve almost anything they want, as long as they work harder than other people and use strategies appropriate to their own needs and abilities" (p. 252). She offers 88 strategies for college students with learning disabilities (chapter 15), and 66 more for dealing with everyday life.

students, severely disabled with visible disabilities, served by support services at Mississippi State University, took part in this model. The participants required accessible environments, transportation, adaptive equipment, and technology in the pursuit of their professional careers.

Other Disabilities

Persons with Mental Retardation The major goal of most services provided to individuals with mental retardation is the acquisition of independent living skills to enable successful community adjustment (Levinson, Peterson & Elston, 1994). Acquiring and maintaining employment is a vital prerequisite for attaining such a goal. Employment provides individuals with mental retardation with (a) economic self-sufficiency to function independently in the community, and (b) a sense of worth and purpose in life, which is a common fulfillment need for many workers. Historically, vocational counseling has been a main component

Practical Applications

Thompson and Hutto (1992) present several useful counseling strategies. Students with vocational disabilities are taught ways to reduce the negative impact their disability might have on a potential employer. Students with visual disabilities are made aware of special problems that might limit their effectiveness in an interview situation. Students who use wheelchairs receive advice about the alterations for improved clothing fit while in the seated position. Students are encouraged to seek student work while taking classes. The counselor assists the student in planning alternative strategies in the event that suitable employment was not obtained upon graduation.

The no-cost and minimal-staffing requirements, with an internship level practitioner coordinating the project through her academic department and the student support services office, make this model extremely attractive and feasible. Those who take issue with the directive approaches used are invited to propose viable alternative means of assisting students with disabilities in their transition from college to employment.

of programs that provide comprehensive services (assessment, training, and placement) for persons with mental retardation.

Adults with Attention Deficit Disorder (ADD) The greatest demands placed on an individual for planning, memory, organization, teamwork, and precision occur in the workplace. Consequently, the manifestations of attention deficits in adults often become most apparent in the workplace environment (Nadeau, 1995). Little empirical evidence exists to guide practitioners who serve newly diagnosed adults with attention deficit disorder (ADD). Recognition of ADD in adults is recent and not yet widespread. The population of adults who seek assistance for ADD tends to be skewed toward the high functioning end of the continuum. These persons are likely to be relatively well educated, have read articles or viewed television documentaries, and/or attended presentations about ADD in adults. A large percentage of adults with ADD are likely to be found among prison populations, various subgroups of substance abusers, and among the unemployed or marginally employed. These persons may not be aware of ADD in adults nor have access to treatment.

Practical Applications

Vocational Training

The practitioner who works with persons with mental retardation "should have a commitment to the community integration of [such] persons. . . . This includes a belief that persons with mental retardation, both mild and severely disabled, should have opportunities for interactions with nondisabled persons in integrated settings" (Levinson et al., 1994, p. 277). Ideally, integrated settings will involve activities at home, at work, and in the community, with the ratio of persons with and without disabilities mirroring the community as a whole. Persons with mental retardation benefit by taking as much responsibility as possible in work choices and decision-making. Vocational training goals are tailored to clients' individual needs. Treatment success is enhanced with the positive involvement of parents and other family members. Two extremes need to be avoided when assisting a person with mental retardation to process information for decision-making and to simplify and clarify options. First, practitioners and family members "may encourage a person with mental retardation to accept options in which the individual is not interested" (p. 277). Second, "individuals may . . . flounder and . . . select options that are clearly unrealistic in light of local resources and opportunities" (p. 277). This is where localized knowledge of the community can benefit the practitioner. Ongoing postemployment services are also required for a person with mental retardation.

Vocational Placement

The ultimate goal of all vocational services for persons with mental retardation is job placement (Levinson et al., 1994). Employment options are expanding for persons with mental retardation and include competitive employment, supported employment, and sheltered employment. *Competitive*

Essentially, the central issues that affect the employment success of learning disabled (LD) adults are the very issues associated with adults with ADD (Nadeau, 1995). Due to the very recent recognition of ADD in adults, the greater emphasis has been placed upon learning disabilities. The attentional problems and cluster of problems commonly associated with ADD are presumed to be a subset of the larger group of issues that are typically considered to be features of learning disabilities. Poor academic performance is often the tip of

employment occurs in regular community jobs without support and—with appropriate selection, training, and opportunities—can include such positions as beauty shop assistant, soda fountain clerk, nursery assistant, mechanic's helper, and fast food worker. *Supported employment* is a recent innovation for those with more severe retardation and entails job coaches and ongoing post-employment support services.

Several varieties of supported employment exist. (a) *Individual supported jobs* entail intensive one-on-one, on-the-job training by a job coach whose services eventually fade out as on-site job supervisors and coworkers take over the training and supervision. Ongoing postemployment support services are retained, however. (b) *Enclave-in-industry jobs* entail small group placement of persons with mental retardation within a regular industry or business with supervision most often provided by a rehabilitation or other service agency. When workers meet certain production, quality, and behavioral standards, hiring into a regular work setting is possible.

(c) *Work crews* are more mobile than enclaves and move from place to place to perform their job tasks (i.e., lawn maintenance, janitorial work crews). Like enclaves, work crews allow the person with mental retardation to interact with non-disabled workers during work time and break time. (d) *Clustered part-time employment* entails negotiating single-skill jobs for a specific individual. Sometimes this work is unpaid or extended training, sometimes unpaid employment. This type of work can provide valuable work experience for a persons with mental retardation as long as no undue exploitation occurs. *Sheltered employment* is a third major option for persons with mental retardation and is usually available through human service agencies to employ persons with disabilities to perform service or small contract work. See Levinson et al. (1994) for a further discussion of placement of persons with mental retardation through job seeking skills training, job matching and referral services, job modification, and community-based training.

the iceberg, and attention, memory, and social interaction are seen as playing a greater role than previously thought.

Common Work Patterns of Adults with ADD. Research on the full range of work patterns of adults with ADD is limited (Nadeau, 1995). Available information indicates that hyperactive and impulsive ADD adults have a work pattern with a wide array of short-lived jobs. Less hyperactive and impulsive adults are likely

---

Practical Applications

Nadeau (1995) summarizes the reasonable accommodations employers can provide for adults with ADD, and recommends workplace strategies to adults with the disorder.

---

to present themselves for career-related counseling upon promotion to a position whose demands are beyond their organizational or managerial capacity (Lucius, 1991, cited in Nadeau, 1995). Another work pattern is seen among chronic underachievers, who may possess talent and intelligence, but whose wavering motivation, disorganization, and/or procrastination tendencies permanently relegate them to job tasks below their apparent capability.

Persons with Autism "Historically, . . . appropriate educational, residential, and vocational services . . . for people with autism have been either nonexistent or inadequate" (Smith, Belcher & Juhrs, 1995, p. 6). Only gradually are service delivery systems evolving to provide incentives for supported employment of persons with autism. A young person with autism loses educational entitlements in public school systems at age 21. There are no stable funding sources that assist in the transition to adult services.

The characteristics of autism impact vocational choice and development in various ways (Smith et al., 1995). For example, an *impairment in verbal and non-verbal communication* calls for a job with limited communication requirements, and a job coach to train a person with autism in communication skills. *Deficits in socialization* call for a job with limited social skill requirements, and a job coach to train a person with autism in specific social skills (i.e., contact with the general public, non-solitary job duties). *Abnormal responses to sensory stimulation* (i.e., noise, tactile sensations) call for jobs "that either provide preferred stimulation or avoid nonpreferred stimulation" (p. 9). *Difficulty in handling change* calls for a job with daily stability and predictability, and a job coach to teach behavior management skills in dealing with changes, especially unexpected changes. *Enhanced visual-motor skills* call for jobs where such assets are required (e.g., small component manufacturing and printing for someone with fine motor skills, warehouse stock management for someone with gross motor skills). *Mental retardation* in persons with autism calls for jobs that mirror one's adaptive and cognitive abilities, with a job coach to provide job skill training as needed. *Behavior problems* call for jobs where such problems pose no danger to coworkers and customers and are not job threatening, with a job coach to initiate a behavior program and to manage difficult behaviors. *Savant and splinter skills* (excellent reading skills despite poor spoken language; ability to match stock numbers to packing lists; good rote memory for visual information; arithmetic skills) are sometimes superior to a person with autism's overall level of functioning, and call for jobs that capitalize on such skills. *Ritualistic and compulsive behavior* call for jobs that are repetitive in nature, or that require an attention to detail and exactness that would otherwise bore and demoralize nondisabled counterparts of workers with autism.

Depending on the severity of the characteristics of a person with autism, jobs can be found in manufacturing, retailing, printing and bulk mailing, food service, warehousing, recycling and delivery, and in government (Smith et al., 1995). Funds for training and supporting a job coach are essential for the employment of persons with autism to be viable. Many entry-level jobs can be performed by persons with autism under the supervision of a job coach.

Synopsis

Without ample and continuously available funding, job skills training, job placement, and job retention of persons with disabilities is extremely difficult. All the laws passed to assist persons with disabilities mean nothing if adequate financial resources are not consistently accessible to back up governmental resolutions. "Empirical research on the impact of disability on careers is at a relatively early stage (Syzmanski et al., 1996, p. 115). Methodological weaknesses in much of the existing research literature (Hagner, Fesko, Cadigan, Kiernan & Butterworth, 1996) are problematic. Calls for qualitative research (Syzmanski et al., 1996) along the lines of contextual interpretivism is a largely unexplored option.

I4

Preparing for the
21st Century

Job growth and job skills are increasing concerns of our . . .
political and business leaders. Herewith some food for thought.
The arts, humanities and allied fields will be the brightest sectors of the
next century's economy, and the only fields to see sustainable job growth.
Here's why: As technology has improved productivity, fewer and fewer people
have been needed for the routine labor of assembling and distributing
industrial products, food, clothing and shelter. That trend will continue. . . .
We're accustomed to regarding progress as synonymous with increasingly
rational ways of making, distributing, organizing and knowing.
But we are entering an era in which progress will be gauged by
derationalization, a time in which peculiarly human, imaginative, ruminative,
unstandardizable pursuits and products weigh ever heavier in the economy,
because those things are what people want. . . .
I mean that both labor and leisure, for so long confined in
the starched uniform of rationalization, will increasingly
depend on the creative abilities of more and more people,
and less on by-the-book skills or drudge labor.
Creative work will be more widely dispersed through the workforce.
We will require imaginative labor from architects, from line technicians,
as well as the director of product development.

> But the future of the economy will see the biggest growth
> in demand for artists, designers, musicians and dancers,
> for philosophers and historians and poets.
> Our physical needs can be met by fewer and fewer people.
> But the mind has an infinite thirst for wonder and delight, for beauty
> and provocation, for questioning and stimulation, Wow! and Aha!
>
> —GREENBERG, 1997

As Greenberg states, creative activities and technology will be hallmarks of the twenty-first century. How these help us meet our intellectual, spiritual, and esthetic needs—whether through labor or leisure—is vital to how we will live in this changing world. We begin this chapter with an overview of the influences shaping the twenty-first century. Second, we address cultural diversity and postmodernism in vocational psychology. Third, we discuss the rethinking of jobs and work. Fourth, we argue for a rethinking of the role of work in people's lives to include a balance of training, work, and leisure. Fifth, we cite the changing role of the vocational practitioner and the applied skills that will be required. Finally, we dare to project what occupational guidance will be like in the year 2010.

INFLUENCES SHAPING THE 21ST CENTURY

Cascio (1995) summarizes the changes that have occurred in this century and contrasts them with changes that will happen after the millenium:

> As citizens of the 20th century, we have witnessed more change in our daily existence and in our environment than anyone else who has walked the planet. But if you think the pace of change was fast in this century, expect it to accelerate in the next one. The 21st century will be even more complex, fast paced, and turbulent. (p. 928)

To help deal with the whirlwind of alterations in the next century, Diebold (1994) offers the following rules of thumb about technology and change:

- It is hard to change old patterns of perception.
- Just because something is technologically possible doesn't mean it will necessarily happen.
- Preconditions are often needed.
- Things usually take much longer to happen than one expects them to.
- You cannot anticipate what people will do with a new technology. (pp. 10–11)

Bohl, Luthans, Slocum, and Hodgetts (1996) suggest that employers will rediscover "the importance of people as a firm's only sustainable competitive advantage" (p. 7). Even though the complexity of "finance, marketing, technological processes, and information systems" (p. 8) may appear overwhelming, they draw attention to the work of Boulding and his hierarchy of systems complexity. "Cybernetic systems (today's information systems) are below the cell (the simplest living organism). Then, in increasing complexity, come plants, animals, humans, and human organizations. The complexity culminates in transcendental systems (deities, time machines, and the secrets of the universe)" (p. 8).

There is a "growing paradox" in the United States economy; an increasing sense of isolationism is occurring at the same time there is a growing globalization in the market place. In Chapter 1 we identified the global economy as a primary contributor to the transformation of vocational psychology.

> The shift from military to economic competition is fundamental. It means that the business firm is now the key to global economic competition. Government, to be sure, can help or hinder, and in a major way. The basic initiative in the global market place has shifted to private enterprise. (Weidenbaum, 1996, p. 36)

The cutback on military spending has allowed the growth of the global market, and domestic production is being overshadowed by the immensity of the international trade. Weidenbaum further posits the following eight points, which apply to the changes in the public sector as well as the private sector:

1. Americans do not have to do anything or change anything to be part of the global marketplace.

2. Employees, customers, suppliers, and investors in U.S. companies are increasingly participating in the international economy.

3. The transitional enterprise is on the rise.

4. Some overseas markets are more profitable than domestic sales, but high risk and high rewards tend to go together.

5. The rise of the global marketplace provides a vast new opportunity for Americans to diversify their investments and—of course—to broaden business risk.

6. The rise of China and Southeast Asia is a new and durable force in the world economy that Americans will have to recognize.

7. Despite the military and political issues that divide Western Europe, the economic unification is continuing full force.

8. The American economy is still the strongest in the world and our prospects are impressive. We are not a weak or declining nation in the world marketplace. (pp. 37–43)

From Weidenbaum's perspective, the United States should not become iso-lationist to deal with the increasing competition from other countries, but rather should become more productive and competitive to be effective in the global marketplace. "The ingredients are well known—tax reform, regulatory reform, and a modern labor policy" (p. 44).

We add a few words about Weidenbaum's (1996) sixth and seventh points above. Regarding Weidenbaum's sixth point: while China may continue to rise, Southeast Asia may not (for more on China, see Bernstein & Munro, 1997; De Mente, 1994). John Naisbitt's (1997) *Megatrends Asia*, which forecast the eco-nomic dominance and unprecedented prosperity of Asia, did not anticipate the debt crisis that brought about "the [financial] collapse of the world's biggest growth zone" (Bremner, Engardio, Foust, Capell & Einhorn, 1998, p. 27). The ripple effect is evident as we go to press. Latin America is now being affected as another round of currency devaluations occurs in Asia (Bremner et al., 1998). Thus far, the "Latin American economies [with the exception of Cuba], leavened by free trade and privatization, have rebounded from the 'lost decade' of the 1980s with eight years of robust growth, averaging 5 percent per year" (Larmer, 1998, p. 44, quotations in the original). As to how the United States will be af-fected, "America's industries are inextricably linked to Asia, which now accounts for one-third of global trade" (Bremner et al., 1998, p. 30). As for products manu-factured in Asia, the extent to which U.S. consumers benefit from Asian workers' slave labor conditions is only beginning to come to light (Saporito, 1998). Rarely have human rights considerations been part of trade negotiations and treaties.

Miller (1997) explains that, "In many ways, Asian nations are victims of their own success. The go-go growth that their economies enjoyed in recent years bred complacency and overconfidence. Banks lent recklessly, with little regard for the credit-worthiness of their borrowers" (p. 2B). Part of the reason the Asian economic collapse was not foreseen by many is that—in one distortion of the **Confucian work ethic**—the subtleties of communication in business are such that Asians "don't tell you if there is a problem" (Ruperto C. González IV, per-sonal communication, April 12, 1998). Singapore's Lee Kuan Yew further clari-fies the role of Confucian values in the Asian debt crisis:

> The difference between being a trustee and being an owner is a funda-mental one. You owe a duty to your family and loyalty to your friends, to help and support them. But you must do that from your private resources, not public resources. That's Confucianism. But this value is degraded when you use public resources through your official position to do your duty to your family and be loyal to your friends. That is wrong. (McCarthy, 1998, p. 40).

Lee Kuan Yew adds that the "incestuous system where banks are owned by con-glomerates and lend money to another section in the group without proper feasibility studies" (p. 40) occurred because of a lack of open rules, which enables a tolerance for corruption.

While the International Monetary Fund may bail out some of the Southeast Asian governments, American and European bankers will definitely pressure their Asian counterparts to adopt international (i.e., Western) standards of accounting and banking, especially an implementation of accountability and transparency. Consequently, "Asian nations will have little choice but to change if they want to compete successfully in the 21st century" (Miller, 1997, p. 1B). It will be interesting to see how much of a Puritan work ethic can be infused into Asian business practices and how this will influence the rest of international business.

Which leads us to Weidenbaum's (1996) seventh point above regarding the economic unification of Western Europe: the European Monetary Union became effective on January 1, 1999. Eleven countries from Portugal to Finland have adopted one currency, the euro (Cassidy, 1998). Economically speaking, Euroland now comprises 300 million people, compared to 270 million in the United States. The two economies are about the same size. Economists who used the term "Eurosclerosis" to describe backward conditions in Europe (Cassidy, 1998, p. 13, quotations in the original) are having to revise their social constructions of reality. "If, as seems likely, Britain, Denmark, Greece, and Sweden join the monetary system during the next few years, Euroland will economically dwarf the United States, Canada, and Mexico combined" (p. 14). It remains to be seen if Europe will develop a "savage capitalism"—a term the French have used to refer to American-style capitalism (Bellah, Madsen, Sullivan, Swidler & Tipton, 1992, p. 91). The European Monetary Union is also likely to facilitate the preeminence of a reunited Germany.

The proliferation of popular magazines reflects the rise of the global economy. Some of these magazines are listed in Table 14.1.

The list of magazines in Table 14.1 show a wide range of geographic emphases—Russia, Latin America, India, Mexico, Vietnam—where U.S. business interests are increasing. This worldwide emphasis is yet to be matched by the widespread application of vocational counseling theories. For example, what will be vocational psychology's practical application to the role of work in people's lives in (a) Russia and the former Soviet Union, (b) China, (c) India, (d) Southeast Asia, (e) Euroland, (f) Mexico and Latin America, and (g) Africa? In the twenty-first century, the global relevance of vocational psychology will become more pressing than ever before.

We believe that, rather than fear the global market as a threat to the U.S. economy, we should embrace the possibilities for increased opportunities. Thus, we believe that the current English-only and the antibilingual education sentiments in the United States are particularly ill-timed. As with any change, there are both positives *and* negatives; those who pursue the positive will be ahead of

**TABLE 14.1 Some Magazines that Reflect
the Rise of the Global Economy**

MAGAZINE	PUBLISHERS' ADDRESS
1. Business in Russia	Press Contact Ul. Bolshaya Polyanka 13, str. 1 Moscow 109180, Russia (7-095) 238-07-11 Fax: (7-095) 238-60-58
2. Hispanic Business	Hispanic Business, Inc. 360 S. Hope Ave, Ste. 300C Santa Barbara, CA 93105 (805) 682-5843 Fax: (805) 687-4546 www.HispanStar.com
3. International Business	New Media Productions 10711 Burnet Road, Suite 305 Austin, TX 78758 (512) 873-7761 Fax: (512) 873-7782 www.internationalbusiness.com
4. Latin Trade, Your Business Source for Latin America	Freedom Magazine International First Union Financial Center 200 South Biscayne Boulevard Suite 1150 Miami, FL 33131 (305) 358-8373
5. Siliconindia	SILICONINDIA, INC. 50 Broad St., Suite 430 New York, NY 10004 (212) 271-9691 Fax: (212) 271-9855 www.siliconindia.com
6. US/Mexico Business, The Magazine of the NAFTA Workplace	Hemisphere Publishers' Group, Inc. 5858 Westheimer, Suite 701 Houston, TX 77057 (713) 266-0861 Fax: (713) 266-0980 *or* Prado Norte 530 Primer Piso 11000 México, D. F. (5) 520-09-78 Fax: (5) 202-24-11

Continued

**TABLE 14.1 Some Magazines that Reflect
the Rise of the Global Economy** *(continued)*

7. The Vietnam Business Journal	VIAM Communications Group, Ltd. 114 East 32nd, Suite 1010 New York, NY 10016 (212) 725-1717 Fax: (212) 725-8160 *or* 27 Ly Thai To, Suite 320 Hanoi, Vietnam (844) 825-4589 Fax: (844) 825-4572 www.viam.com
8. World Trade, for the Executive with Global Vision	Freedom Magazines, Inc. 17702 Cowan, Suite 100 Irvine, CA 92614 (714) 798-3500 Fax: (714) 798-3501 (800) 640-7071 web edition: www.worldtrademag.com

the crowd, and those who fight change will be among those who will be left behind. We hope vocational psychology and career counseling will more explicitly emphasize sociopolitical factors in the twenty-first century and not be left behind.

According to Friedman (1996) the economic world is changing rapidly into three distinct economies:

1. The *Networked*—"consists of densely packed concentrations of entrepreneurs and companies in urbanized areas that generate virtually all the nation's globally competitive, high-wage industries" (p. 52).

2. The *Kluge*—consists of "the concentration of public-sector bureaucracies, universities, and closely aligned private companies in government related industries like utilities or defense—exists virtually side by side with the networked economy" (p. 52).

3. The *Provincial*—"self-consciously styles itself as a more moral, less 'Klugey' alternative for Networked businesses and is driven by the deployment of less competitive business and offers America a 19th century answer for 21st century competition" (p. 54).

Kluge is a slang term used by computer programmers to describe a "code that is an ill-assorted collection of poorly matching parts, forming a distressing whole" (p. 52). The Kluge is the least productive of the three economies. The combination of the Kluge and Networked economies account for 50 million jobs, "of which 15% to 18% are directly accounted for by the government" (pp. 52–53).

With this type of global thinking as a background, we want to provide a culmination of the perspective we have attempted to build in this book. This final chapter deals with the convergence of thinking that appears to be shaping the events of the next few years. We began our text with a call for a transformation of vocational psychology to keep pace with the often painful and always profound shifts in the role of work in people's lives. Part of this transformation concerns future trends. Until now, the relevance of vocational psychology for women, racial and ethnic groups, people with disabilities, gay/lesbian/bisexual people, lower-income groups, the permanent underclass, and international populations has been limited at best. In the twenty-first century, primary attention needs to be given to diversity issues.

Cultural Diversity and Postmodernism

Cultural Diversity In the United States, it behooves us to take advantage of the diversity of our population to remain competitive in the global marketplace, for economic motives if not for moral reasons. Sometimes the urgency of this issue appears to escape many people in a position to make a difference. Thomas (1990) projects that by the year 2000, White males will make up only 15 percent of the increase in the workforce during the preceding decade; White males, while still dominant in the workplace, will actually be a statistical minority. By 1990, racial and ethnic minorities, women, and immigrants were already more than 50 percent of the workforce. In the ensuing decade, the so-called mainstream will have become almost as diverse as U.S. society at large. The challenge for the future will be to maximize the potential of women, minorities, and immigrants, which will require an increase in supervisors' abilities to manage diversity so that all kinds of people—including White males—can contribute to workplace productivity.

In a workplace where competence will matter more than ever before, Thomas (1990) suggests ten ways in which individual differences are not merely tolerated, but celebrated:

1. *Clarifying motivations.* Legal compliance, community relations, fulfilling social and moral responsibilities, placating an internal group or pacifying an outside organization are usually good reasons for learning to manage diversity. From a strictly business perspective, the long-term motivation will be sustained only if learning to manage diversity makes a workplace more competitive. And most workplaces are already diverse or soon will be.

2. *Clarifying vision.* If an attitude is conveyed by management that the human resource potential of every member of the workplace is going to be tapped, the White male culture is more likely to give way to respecting differences and individuality and less likely to cling to a vision—consciously or unconsciously—that leaves them in the driver's seat.

3. *Expanding focus.* With an overall objective of creating a dominant heterogeneous culture, this minimizes the traditional affirmative action pattern that required the structural assimilation of women, minorities, and immigrants into a dominant White-male culture workplace.

4. *Auditing workplace culture.* This is often impossible to do without outside help because of hidden rules, unspoken assumptions, unexamined values, and unfounded mythologies that will have created a workplace culture in the first place. Likening workplace culture to a kind of tree, where roots are assumptions about both the workplace and the world, and where branches, leaves, and seeds are behavior, the leaves will not be changed without changing the roots. Nor will peaches grow on an oak tree. Thus, if one wants to grow peaches, then the tree's roots have to be peach-friendly.

5. *Modifying assumptions.* The work culture tree has root guards that turn out in full force whenever a basic assumption is threatened. The challenge is to define belonging "in terms of a set of values and a sense of purpose that transcend the interests, desires, and preferences of any one group" (Thomas, 1990, p. 116).

6. *Modifying systems.* Performance appraisals, promotions, and mentoring are among such systems. For example, the unexamined practices and patterns of performance appraisal has had pernicious effects on women and minorities in the past. Accurate performance feedback often came through the grapevine and differed substantially from official performance appraisals, which made it difficult for women and minorities to correct or defend their alleged shortcomings. In many worksites, obtaining promotion has often required a personal advocate, yet mentors have historically been unwilling to sponsor people too much unlike themselves.

7. *Modifying models.* Most often, this means allowing employees to do the job they have been hired to do, with supervisors supporting and empowering their subordinates.

8. *Helping employees pioneer.* With no one tried and true solution to diversity management, this means there are also multiple barriers that face any workplace, and that supervisors and employees will be judged as pioneers who travel uncharted territory and therefore will make mistakes.

9. *Applying the special consideration test.* This can be answered by one question: "Does this program, policy, or principle give special consideration to one

group?" (Thomas, 1990, p. 117). If the answer is yes, a given workplace is not on the road to managing diversity.

10. *Continuing affirmative action.* Affirmative action is vital for creating and maintaining a diverse workplace. Yet, affirmative action does not address root causes such as prejudice and inequality and does little to maximize the potential contributions of each woman and man in the workplace. Therefore, the goal of diversity management is to increase the capacity to accept, incorporate, develop, and empower the multiple human talents that make the United States the most diverse nation on the earth.

Thomas (1990) concludes by stating that diversity is our reality and it needs to become our strength. This means that vocational psychology will have to admit just how much it is a sociopolitical activity, with interfaces "between personal and societal needs, between individual aspirations and opportunity structures, between private and public identities" (Watts, 1996, p. 229).

We appreciate Thomas's (1990) conciliatory and practical tone. But affirming diversity threatens the vested interests of many White males. For years—if not generations—entrenched White males have occupied positions of authority without possessing the requisite talents and abilities to exercise the power for which their jobs allow. The future vocational counseling needs of those who are not White males cannot be swept under the carpet. We limit our discussion here to three diverse populations: (1) women and children, (2) gay, lesbian, and bisexual persons, and (3) persons with disabilities.

Women and Children. The late Bella Abzug, former member of Congress and founder of the Women's Environment and Development Organization, summarized the plight of women worldwide as the twentieth century came to a close:

[By 2005] more than half the world's population will live in cities, including millions who will swell "megacities," those with populations of more than 10 million. Those cities and megacities create problems, and those problems will hurt women more than others, because 70 percent of the world's 1.3 billion poorest people are female.

[As of 1996,] women account for only 10 percent of legislators worldwide, a pittance of mayors and only 1 percent of executives in corporate and financial board rooms. . . .

According to a [United Nations] estimate, women perform about 60 percent of the world's work but earn just 1 percent of the world's income.

Women and girls migrating to the cities are particularly vulnerable to economic exploitation and hazardous working conditions. Some of the worst offenders are multinational firms whose overseas operations don't comply with U.S. laws. (Abzug, 1996, p. 8A)

Abzug added, "Women need political power to fight poverty and inequality" (p. 8A).

It remains to be seen if vocational psychology can articulate a global perspective on the role of work in women's lives. Certainly, the universality of knowledge claims about occupational development derived from scientific objectivity have yet to be extensively confirmed in international research populations, be they women or men. New paradigms and a multidisciplinary approach could enact a metamorphosis in the way women's work lives are understood. The question is whether scholars and researchers can rise to the occasion and provide practical applications for intervening in women's and girls' occupational development on an international scale (see also Mays, Rubin, Sabourin & Walker, 1996). A reconceptualization of the discipline of vocational psychology will have to occur before global relevance can happen. Until such time, only a miniscule portion of women's—much less men's—occupational development will be explained through the persistent use of largely American research participants, which we believe is an unbecoming, insular worldview. While we do not believe that a White upper-class, intellectualized brand of feminism is appropriate for conceptualizing the occupational development of all women, we do believe in giving full "value [to] the female voice" (Myss, 1996, p. 108).

Consequently, vocational psychology will have to continue to become less androcentric in the twenty-first century before discussions of theoretical convergence can be anything more than an academic exercise. Likewise, classism in vocational psychology will be reduced when greater attention is given to populations who have no choice but to work from an early age. Figure 14.1 shows the photograph of six-year-old Angie Elizabeth Hernández, a little girl in present-day Mexico City. She is the member of a family where everyone works to earn a living, if that. Her weekend job is to be dressed as a clown who entertains motorists at a stoplight with a juggling act. "Out of half-opened windows hands offer small coins before the traffic starts up. An average day brings about ten dollars" (Parfit, 1996, p. 43). In the background are Angie Elizabeth's mother Gabriela, baby sister Sara Nayeli, and uncle José. "'Necessity taught us how to entertain people this way,'" explains Gabriela (p. 43).

Girls as child laborers are nothing new. However, vocational psychology has virtually ignored this phenomenon. For example, the sexploitation of girls as young as eight is an international industry that generates $5 billion a year internationally (Abzug, 1996) and has been called "the underside of the global economy that is rarely seen" (New York Times News Service, 1996, p. 12A). Research methods that would further clarify the role of work in women's and children's lives are discussed below in the section on postmodernism.

Gays, Lesbian, and Bisexual Persons. It took a woman to make cultural history by calling attention to same-sex relationships for millions of television viewers as

FIGURE 14.1 Photograph of Angie Elizabeth Hernández at Age 6,
Child Laborer (Street Juggler/Clown) in Mexico City

SOURCE: *Stuart Franklin, photographer.*

never before: actress and comedienne Ellen DeGeneres "came out" as a lesbian
in life and on her situation comedy, "Ellen," in Spring 1997:

> At a time when an acknowledgment of homosexuality has entered all
> aspects of popular culture, when diversity and acceptance are the words of
> the day but by no means entirely the deeds, and when more and more of
> the sizeable population of homosexual men and women working in the
> entertainment industry today are weighing the risks of coming out them-
> selves, DeGeneres allowed herself to become a poster girl—not for lesbi-
> anism, but for honesty. She volunteered to serve as a test case for whether
> a likable woman with a gentle, clean comedy act can flaunt a sexy girl-
> friend and still win friends, influence people, and maintain healthy
> Neilsen ratings. DeGeneres risked her professional reputation for personal
> freedom. And she pulled it off. (Schwarzbaum, 1997/1998, p. 18)

It is no exaggeration to assert that millions of other gay, lesbian, and bisexual
persons are daily confronted with the question of whether to publicly identify
their sexual orientation and to come out on the job. Sexual identity development and its interaction with occupational development still requires clarification with respect to gay/lesbian/bisexual persons. Fassinger (1995) writes:

> none of the existing [sexual] identity development models sufficiently
> take environmental context into account. Perhaps because lesbian and gay

identity theories are built (implicitly or explicitly) on early work in the development of Black racial and political consciousness, the models tend to imply that fully integrated and mature identity necessitates full public disclosure and political activism. Such a stance ignores the cultural location, life choices, and environmental constraints of lesbians and gay men diverse in age, historical context, geographic location, race and ethnicity, class, religion, and other forms of demographic diversity that exert a profound impact on the identity development process. Resultant models are thus subtly homophobic in their common view of nonpublic, non-politicized behavior as developmental arrest, in that they blame the victim for her or his own inability to come to terms with an oppressed identity. (p. 152)

In addition to the need for more adequate, less pathologizing models of sexual identity development, Fassinger notes "relatively little empirical research [on] actual counseling interventions . . . related to vocational concerns . . . [of lesbians and gays]" (p. 164). Sexual identity concerns are inextricably bound with occupational development, and traditional vocational assessment may be of little value.

Broadly speaking, Prince (1995) notes that "current theories of men's career development ignore altogether the impact of sexual-identity formation as a moderating variable and offer little guidance for understanding such influences" (p. 170). In reference to gay men, "career development theory is equally lacking in its attention to [both the early career development and] the later career development stages of gay men" (p. 172). Other unanswered research questions include (a) how stages of relationship development influence gay men's career development, and (b) overall psychological adjustment on career choice.

Empirical research on the career decision-making of gay, lesbian, and bisexual persons is still lacking (Chung, 1995). Nor have adherence to traditional work values "(e.g., achievement, status, stability)" (p. 182) or the relation between sex role socialization and the development of vocational skills been explored.

"There is not a body of empirical research of sufficient breadth and depth to identify which practices are most important and effective [with gay and lesbian clients]" (Pope, 1995, p. 191). A review of fifteen articles published between 1940 and 1994 on recommended career counseling interventions for gays and lesbians revealed the following three themes. First, counselors were encouraged to focus on themselves. Included here were counselors' learning about sexual identity development, examining one's own biases, using special assessment procedures, and affirming the gay/lesbian/bisexual lifestyle. Second, specific counseling activities were mentioned. These included "openly discussing coming out in the workplace, openly discussing employment discrimination, working with both individuals in the couple on dual-career couple issues, and helping clients overcome internalized negative stereotypes" (Pope, 1995, p. 201). Third, interventions were directed at social-community action. Included here was practitioners "supporting and encouraging gay and lesbian professionals as role models" (p. 201). The author of the article concludes by stating, "Much research remains to be done on the types of special career counseling interventions that are empirically justified for lesbian and gay populations" (p. 202).

People with Disabilities. Like women and children and like gay, lesbian, and bisexual persons, people with disabilities do not fit traditional, androcentric models of career development. Stodden (1998) suggests five ways that persons with disabilities can be better served in their occupational development needs. There is a need to

1. ... [coordinate] education and work preparation programs and services implemented under a unified vision and purpose.... Currently, policy, legislation, and funding streams for special programs within education, transition, work preparation, rehabilitation, and special education are separate and autonomous, and often have conflicting purposes and overlapping initiatives.

2. ... build consensus concerning use of the term 'all' when referring to the participation of children and youth with special needs in education and training programs.

3. ... refocus resources and program agendas from an arena of dependency (i.e., welfare, social work, social services) to the arena of independence ... (i.e., improved education and training programs) ...

4. ... focus on student results from, and satisfaction with, participation in education and training programs.

5. ... capture excellent practices and supports that have been generated through ... separate needs programs and the transition initiative to ensure that such practices ... improve general education curriculum sequences and generic work preparation programs. (pp. 74–75)

People with disabilities, like women and children and like gay, lesbian, and bisexual persons, can benefit immensely by increased attention from vocational psychology. Postmodern approaches to work are one means of attending to these populations.

Postmodernism and the Technologies of Social Saturation The narrative viability of multiple perspectives espoused by postmodernism is upheld by R. A. Neimeyer (1995b):

nearly any model of psychotherapy can be a legitimate resource for the postmodern practitioner, as long as it is interpreted as a historically and culturally bounded set of provisional metaphors and guidelines rather than as an applied science that compels only a certain conceptualization of the problem and only a single approved form of intervention. (p. 16)

Postmodern approaches to work offer some exciting and innovative ways for clinical practitioners to consult with clients regarding work-related issues in clinical practice—provided such approaches are used in a scrupulous manner and not as a cover for deceit and dishonesty. Experience has taught us that social constructionism is hardly immune to misrepresentations of reality and half-truths. It will be recalled that modernism's lineage is based on logical positivism, a twentieth-century philosophical movement that asserts that all knowledge can be discovered through use of the scientific method. The use of observation and experiment (i.e., empiricism) are respected as the only valid means for adding to the knowledge base. Reality is held to be objective in nature and awaiting to be discovered, hence the use of the term scientific objectivity. Furthermore, objective reality is presumed to exist independently of a person and must be detected by the person in order to be known (Burr, 1995). In other words, rules or structures are presumed to already exist and merely await detection. From a modernist perspective, these "hidden structures" can be discovered through the use of reason and rationality.

Postmodernism's rejection of the tradition that the real world has underlying rules and hidden structures is also known as **poststructuralism** (Burr, 1995). Thus, postmodern architecture can seem to disregard all the conventional wisdom that make for a good building design. Postmodern art repudiates the idea that "pop" art is any less equal to the works of the great masters. In the field of literary criticism, the postmodern perspective is reflected in the assertion that there cannot be a "true" reading of a novel or poem, that each reader's interpretation of a piece of literature was equally valid, and that the original author's intended meaning cannot be discerned. From a cultural standpoint, postmodernism becomes evident in the rise of multiculturalism and diversity (González, 1994, 1997, 1998).

Limitations and Strengths of Postmodernism in Clinical Practice. The shortcomings and promises of postmodernism in clinical practice cannot be examined without first addressing postmodernism in the social sciences. Postmodernism in the social sciences can take on either an extreme or moderate tone (Rosenau, 1992). To us, extreme postmodernism appears like preposterous nihilism lacking any sort of coherence that fails to offer any useful alternatives to that which it deconstructs. Extreme postmodernists strain their credibility, undermine their integrity, and can end up resembling members of a lunatic fringe with their self-contradictory claims that all perspectives are valid. In our view, moderate postmodernism resists "throwing the baby out with the bath water" but allows the baby to have several different bubble baths from which to choose. Moderate postmodernism is more likely to include modernism as one broadly agreed-upon view, while also allowing for originality and creativity in devising solutions to problems.

For postmodernism to remain viable in the social sciences, extreme postmodernists will have to be vigilant about positioning themselves into ideological apartheid. Extreme postmodernists can become too hobbled by their own language to be able to exercise the spirit of reconceptualizations about how we explain and experience the world around us (Minuchin, 1991). Rosenau (1992) states that part of the problem is that some postmodernists "do not extend themselves to use words precisely" (p. 178). She points out seven contradictions within postmodernism.

Some postmodern deconstructions of modern science appear unsubstantiated. Science never presumed to include mystical, spiritual, and metaphysical dimensions of human existence, yet is deconstructed in part for not having done so. When modern science is deconstructed in part for not providing adequate guidance for the purposes to which scientific knowledge should be put, the existence and purpose of bioethics is ignored. When science is deconstructed in part for posing as the only legitimate truth, there is a disregard for modern scientists who staunchly adhere to "the *probability* of verifying, not so much as discovering, knowledge or truth" (Earl Jennings, personal communication, February 28, 1995, italics added). Verification instead of discovery via quantitative methods has a moderate postmodern spirit. *Both* quantitative *and* qualitative approaches may benefit the social sciences (see Light & Pillemer, 1982; Polkinghorne, 1984, 1991; Reichardt & Cook, 1979, for discussions on moving beyond the either/or dichotomy). The complete exclusion of one research method in favor of the other is inconsistent with postmodernists' claims to respecting multiple views. Nevertheless, extremists who use postmodernism as a cover for antimodernism risk deconstructing themselves and/or dismissal by others.

The contradictions of postmodern approaches to clinical practice have been soundly criticized. Minuchin (1991) challenges postmodern therapists who deny the legitimacy of their own clinical expertise to avoid the appearance of control, thereby anointing themselves as the new crew of experts. He warns that postmodern therapists risk clinical irrelevance by getting too wrapped up in abstractions about the subjectivity of all truths. Furthermore, he points out the ethical issue of impairment among postmodern therapists, "wounded healers" who, like some of their modernist practitioner counterparts, often are reluctant to seek help for themselves and their relationships. Efran and his colleagues (1988) caution against using postmodernism as a means of trifling with established words and meanings: "those who make their living being experts on the implications of language ought to think twice before taking too many liberties with it" (p. 34).

Practical Applications

Postmodernism challenges vocational psychology to examine how its theories are historically, socially, and culturally bound. The modernist approaches we presented in Chapters 4 through 8 are going to be hard-pressed to move from abstract—and some would add, inert—theorizing to a demonstration of the real-life consequences of their interventions (see also, Greenfield, 1998). Doubtless, many modernist-trained vocational psychology scholars and career counseling practitioners are disconcerted by postmodernism. But modernism has had its chance at articulating the occupational development of persons, and the caliber of scientific objectivity used has left much to be desired. For example, a methodological critique of eight years of research articles on multicultural career development published in three leading career journals was conducted by Koegel, Donin, Ponterotto, and Spitz (1995). Some of the results are as follows:

- Number of articles published in *Journal of Employment Counseling, Journal of Vocational Behavior,* and *The Career Development Quarterly,* from 1985 to 1992:
$$n = 884$$
- Number and percentage of articles that emphasized multicultural concerns:
$$n = 116 \;\; (14\%)$$
- Number and percentage of multicultural concerns that were

(a) quantitative, empirically based studies: $n = 68$ (59%)

(b) conceptual nondata-based reports: $n = 45$ (39%)

(c) quantitative empirical investigations: $n = 3$ (2.5%)

- Most commonly used sample populations:
—high school students $\quad n = 14$
—college undergraduates and graduates $\quad n = 19$
—professionals and semi professionals $\quad n = 5$
—veterans $\quad n = 2$
—others $\quad n = 28$

In evaluating these results, Koegel et al. (1995) write that the

overreliance on student samples is troubling in two respects. First, questions can be raised about how representative student populations are of the community at large. Second, questions can also be raised about the appropriateness of using a population whose dominant environment is academe to investigate career- or work-related behaviors. Thus, the results of nearly one half of the reviewed multicultural career articles may have limited generalizability to the larger population. (pp. 59–60)

Reid (1993) refers to student samples as populations of convenience. An overreliance on such research participants, whether in vocational psychology generally or in multicultural vocational concerns specifically, has provided post-modernists with the premise they need to question the reliability and validity of the modernist enterprise in vocational psychology. Journal editors and their review boards must bear some of the responsibility for allowing a proliferation of research publications comprised of social science with extremely limited generalizabily. (1) We propose broadening the research base in vocational psychology research so that populations of convenience, especially college student samples, are used less and non-professional adult workers, students at technical and vocational schools, and non-college-bound populations are used more.

We are not, however, calling for the elimination of quantitative research in vocational psychology, only for more sophisticated research designs and sampling techniques. Sociologist William Julius Wilson (1996), for instance, uses a stratified probability sample (n = 2,490) of African American, non-Hispanic White, Mexican, and Puerto Rican parents ages 18 to 44 to produce *When Work Disappears: The World of the New Urban Poor*. His findings on the attitudes towards work and welfare among Chicago poverty-tract parents by race or ethnic/immigrant status (see Wilson, 1996, Table 4, p. 251) provide a deeper level of understanding of within-group differences than any population of convenience could ever provide. We respect his efforts to discern work attitudes among less privileged populations.

Logical positivism has yet to convincingly verify through observation and experiment—empiricism—the universal truths about the role of work in people's lives. The scientific method has been misapplied in much of the vocational psychology research. Knowledge claims about occupational development have inaccurately and incompletely reflected the experience of multicultural and diverse populations (Gelberg & Chojnacki, 1996; Leong, 1995). The overuse of modernist objectivity has yet to successfully discover the universal meaning presumed to underlie the occupational development of persons not of the dominant culture in the United States, much less elsewhere. Postmodern contextual interpretativism merits consideration as a valid alternative in vocational psychology, especially in view of the unprecedented impact of the global economy and the social saturation of the self wrought by technology (Gergen, 1991b). In many respects, the meaning of work is socially legitimated in particular communities through localized or situated knowledge. We see no contradiction in the duality of existence of *both* logical positivism *and* contextual interpretivism in vocational psychology. *Both* universality *and* particularity are relevant to the role of work in people's lives.

The "technologies of social saturation" of which Gergen (1991b) writes are another persuasive argument for integrating more of a postmodern perspective into vocational psychology. A "business as usual" approach will simply not

Continued

Continued

work anymore. Theories of occupational development are not keeping pace with advances in telecommunication that impact the role of work in a global economy. Rather than taking an either/or position, we espouse *both* modernism *and* postmodernism in the research and practice of vocational psychology. In a modification of Savickas (1993), reality is *both* objective *and* subjective. Language *both* reflects *and* produces reality. Meaning is *both* discovered *and* invented. Moreover, meaning resides *both* in the world *and* in the word. As much as possible, clients receive a combination of *both* predefined services *and* are active and independent agents in interpreting and shaping their own lives. For the field of vocational psychology to be relevant for the twenty-first century, we agree with Richardson (1993) that career counseling becomes a subspecialty within vocational psychology. We also suggest that future research (a) gives more attention to both the conceptual and technical aspects of instrument development, (b) studies the occupational behavior of multicultural and diverse populations in a more coherent fashion than what has happened up to now, (c) studies people other than those facing occupational decisions during the entry and early years of work life, and (d) evaluates the effectiveness and utility of vocational interventions (for generic examples of postmodern program evaluation, see Mabry & Stake, 1997).

Efran and Clarfield (1992) contend that the postmodern idea that hierarchy can be eliminated in therapy is absurd and counterproductive. "To act as if all views are equal and that we—as therapists—have no favorites among them undercuts the very sort of frank exchange we want and expect to have with our clients" (p. 208).

González (1997) notes that postmodernists can resemble some of their modernist counterparts in their lack of basic "people skills" and a failure to practice what they preach, the latter of which does not prevent the disparagement of those not of their ideological clique. Another concern González (1998) raises is whether postmodern paradigms are foisted onto unsuspecting clients without their informed consent. Practitioners can easily "manipulate naive clients' realities under the guise of co-construction" (p. 369). Without a system of checks and balances, so-called conversational artistry can readily degenerate into "con artistry" (Efran & Fauber, 1995). Postmodernists are challenged to squarely and courageously face this underside of themselves or risk a rigid paradigmatic stratification, or segregation, that is the antithesis of postmodernism.

Postmodern advocacy without honoring diverse viewpoints can appear as ludicrous posturing. An indispensable point is made by Anderson and Goolishian

(1991): "Keep in mind that negative connotation, or the invalidation, of any major participant (including one's colleagues) is destructive to the process of opening space for conversation" (p. 7). The perpetual challenge is for postmodernists of any ilk to contain the tendency to assume a totalizing view within themselves. Totalizing is the assumption of "a totality, a total view. By extension this rejects other perspectives. Postmodernists criticize totalizing theories" (Rosenau, 1992, p. xiv). Credibility is enhanced when advocates of emerging postmodern paradigms strive to espouse the tenets of these paradigms interpersonally, professionally, and organizationally. Such striving will be a life-long effort.

RETHINKING JOBS AND WORK

Unwanted and unexpected change can be a debilitating experience for many people. When a person loses a job, he or she is forced into a situation in which they must find something new. It may not seem like it at the time, but job loss can bring about positive changes since it forces a person into a new and possibly more fulfilling situation. Many people who have gone through losing their jobs have discovered that there is "life after work." The greater the repertoire of work-related skills a person has, the greater the likelihood of rejuvenation in the marketplace.

Borchard (1995) describes it this way: "**career death** can actually awaken us to intriguing new possibilities—to a rebirth experience" (p. 8, boldface added). He points out that we are not only experiencing career loss and death as we have known it, but also the death of an era.

> We have come to the end of life in the Mass Production Era. Our rebirth as individuals and as a collective society depends upon letting go of old paradigms and embracing a new, but foggy reality. The major issue of life and work in the twentieth century may well be the challenge associated with letting go of familiar lifestyle structures. (pp. 8–9)

With the combination of workplace changes and more focus on adult psychological development, practitioners will need more than ever to (a) stay current, (b) anticipate the next changes, and (c) be able to make appropriate interventions. The emphasis will be more on self-development.

> Neither fun nor passion was afforded much credibility as a career planning orientation in the past. Passion in this content refers to a very personal and energizing interest in some kind of activity or cause. In the new era, there are far more choices available to more individuals than ever before, and there are far more opportunities to create new enterprises. . . .

Pursuing a uniquely personal passion may well be the best antidote to the stress of these chaotic times. (Bourchard, 1995, p. 10)

Individuals also experience change in their mental, emotional, and spiritual well-being which have their own career ramifications. Some of these concerns have to do with aging, burnout, values shifts, spiritual awakening, and personal meaning crises (Borchard, 1995; Myss, 1996). Table 14.2 summarizes where we have been (Mass Production Era) and where we are going (Knowledge-Service Era).

As the necessary skills change for most jobs, there will be people left unemployed and/or underemployed. The global changes which are now happening in the workforce increase the necessity of a vocational practitioner who is knowledgeable about the different types of unemployed as well as the emotional effects on the individual and the family unit. "A simplistic or unidimensional view of unemployment tends to cause counselors to contend that their profession will reduce unemployment" (Herr, 1992, p. 278). This leads to the belief that practitioners must understand what counseling can accomplish as well as make it clear to their clients that they are not in the position to create jobs.

Vonk and Hirsch (1992) use the term **"free agent,"** which has always been associated with baseball, to describe employees who have decided to manage their own careers. "Free agent managers have chosen to proactively manage their own careers, scanning opportunities, both within the organization and across firms and industries, maintaining knowledge of their own market value while at the same time taking every opportunity to increase that value as they perform the functions of their job" (p. 151). Through counselor intervention, an employee can use this concept to further his or her career. A counselor can teach an employee to find work that looks good on their résumé while staying away from assignments that decrease the employee's marketability (Jones, 1996).

On a related matter, Hamilton, Baker, and Vlasic (1996) describe the office design of the future. They state that "project teams have become an increasingly desired part of the workforce; however, individuals still need a private place in order to gather their thoughts as well as accomplish solo projects. Office designers are attempting to provide for both the team environment as well as the solo environment by creating **"cave and commons"** environments by grouping private work areas around larger communal team space" (p. 29). The future office design is growing in two different directions: (1) reorganizing the space of the employees, who are going to still work in the office and (2) outsourcing other services. "For people involved in product innovation or development, for example, cutting cycle time is key. The need for speed makes it imperative for employees to team up and share information" (Hamilton et al., 1996, p. 109).

Another alternative for management of office space is by **"hoteling."** This space would be available for office meetings, team meetings and in-services but other times the individual would be operating primarily from his/her car or

TABLE 14.2 Career Development: Then and Now

STRUCTURAL CHARACTERISTICS	MASS PRODUCTION ERA (1865–1980s)	KNOWLEDGE SERVICE ERA (1980s AND BEYOND)
Economic reality: job-creating forces	Huge manufacturing industries oriented to the national economy	Knowledge-service enterprises, competing in a global market
Job-market structure/dominant job types	Two-tiered factory: *blue collar *white collar	Multitiered (no tiered) mixed technical, professional, executive
Occupational characteristics	A few stable, clearly classifiable types	Many rapidly evolving and amorphous types
Career preparation	Complete your education and then get a job	Continual working, learning, keeping pace with ongoing education
Career choice: how you enter and pursue a career	Luck, happenstance, what you happened to know about or fall into	Decision making aided by a professional and ongoing attention
How you get jobs	Blue collar: family work ties White collar: resumes, classified ads, placement services	Skill/competency based on self-definition and ongoing networking
Primary employment targets	*Fortune* 500 companies	Smaller companies, skill-contracting agencies, self-employment
Who controls your career	The organization	The individual (with the aid of professionals)
Career development objectives	Climbing prescribed organizational ladders	Personal development in areas of expertise
Employment source	One organization for entire career	Series of organizations and contracting agents
Primary employment concerns (rewards)	Salary, benefits, leave, promotions, titles	Developing potentials, pursuing work interests
Major career limitations	Restrictions based on sex, race, age, religion	Skills, knowledge, and job development savvy
Retirement financing	Company retirement and Social Security	Portable, personal retirement programs
Retirement considerations	40 years—gold watch and no need to work ever again. Relax, play, travel, die	Ongoing balance in self, developing work, leisure, and learning

SOURCE: Bouchard (1995).

home. Other companies are designing workstations that are mobile. All furniture and equipment are on wheels and walls are portable, such as in companies like Procter and Gamble, Haworth and Fallon-MCelligott.

With the increasing technological advances, workers are able to do their job just about anywhere.

> Laptops, fax machines, cellular phones, networks, e-mail, and voice mail are making **telecommuting** a way of doing business that satisfies strategic goals of spending more time with customers, and using commute time better. After all, does it matter whether a critical voice-mail message you received was sent from a client's office, airport, or a traffic jam? (Hamilton et al., 1996, p. 117, boldface added).

Jayson (1993) conducted an interview with Max Messmer, John Challenger, and Donald DeCamp regarding their predictions specifically for management accountants regarding the work environment, hiring, downsizing, and job areas that are growing. Even though they addressed the accounting profession, it is clear that their recommendations are applicable to other career areas. Messmer stated that the workforce of the 1990s is "much more mobile and volatile than in previous years. While the [19]80s merger and acquisition activity has slowed, it has been replaced with a different type of turmoil: massive layoffs due to increased global competition, more advanced technology, and a more cost conscious approach to staffing" (p.16). DeCamp observed that managers are supervising more and more people as downsizing has eliminated many middle-management positions. He states, "We are returning to decentralization and empowering our people" (p. 16).

When asked about their recommendations for succeeding in the new workforce, DeCamp, Messmer, and Challenger had diverse opinions. Challenger sees interviewing as the key to finding a job, Messmer attributes success to flexibility and creativity, while DeCamp sees specialization as important. It seems that success in the future will require all of these skills and attributes.

When asked for their predictions of the workforce in ten years, these people offered several opinions: there will be (a) less commitment and loyalty to a company, (b) more hiring through temporary agencies, and (c) fewer positions in management. DeCamp states that the employer can benefit through better quality service, and the employee will benefit by developing crucial skills (Jayson, 1993).

Corporate anorexia is a term used to describe the massive downsizing that is occurring in the workforce. However, it seems that some companies have gone too far in their cutbacks and have been left without enough employees to continue their rate of production, thus those that are left are working long stressful hours. However, even as the economy grows, the downsizing will continue. "Even after the economy improved in 1994 and created 3 million new jobs, layoffs continued at a pace only slightly below 1993, leaving another half million workers without jobs" (Stamps, 1996, p. 33).

As an illustration of a different approach to the way labor unions are thinking, the United Automobile Workers (UAW) voted in March 1996 to renew a contract with the Saturn plant that exchanges pay and job security for a voice in the operations of the company. This was in the light of shrinking sales and a fear of loss of jobs. The standard union bargaining position has been to guarantee pay and jobs, but in this situation, the workers are willing to make potential short-term sacrifices so the company, General Motors, can adapt more easily to market demands (Lippert, 1997).

According to Cascio (1995), "In this emerging world of work, more and more organizations will focus carefully on their core competencies and outsource everything else. They will be characterized by terms such as *virtual*, *boundary-less*, and *flexible*, with no guarantees to workers or managers" (p. 930, italics in original).

As we mentioned earlier in Chapters 1, 2, and 12, the changes that are happening in organizations are effecting both white-collar manager and blue-collar workers. The autocratic hierarchical management approach is outmoded. For organizations to survive, they must be able to respond quickly to the changing markets both nationally and internationally. This requires vision, using a collaborative team approach and empowering workers to be both creative and productive (Cascio, 1995). Bohl et al. (1996) propose that organizational change must involve the individuals in the organization. They suggest "individuals need empathy to repair relationships caused by intricate webs of people who have diverse values and experiences" (p. 13). This will help them learn from their coworkers, customers, and other business associates. They further emphasize that "Employees need to focus on the totality of their experiences and not compartmentalize these" into a box (p. 13).

Barney (1991, cited in Cascio, 1995) suggests three human resource requirements if organizations are going to sustain a competitive edge: (a) the workers must add positive economic benefits, (b) employees' skills need to be clearly distinguishable from other competitors, and (c) these skills are not easily duplicated (p. 931).

The pace of change will greatly affect the world of work including: (a) global competition, (b) information technology, (c) reengineering business processes, (d) networks of specialists, (e) smaller companies employing fewer people, and (f) shifting from making a product to providing a service. Most of all, "there is an emerging redefinition of work itself: growing disappearance of the job as a fixed bundle of tasks, along with an emphasis on constantly changing work" that is based on what customers want (Cascio, 1995, p. 937).

The California Department of Education has produced a video series entitled "The Changing Culture of the Workplace," which was mentioned in Chapter 12, and Chapter 11 refers to the SCANS report for necessary skills. Another concern we have deals with employee benefits. Medical plans in which individuals can participate when working as an independent contractor are a crucial issue which needs to be addressed. Vocational psychology will also need to learn how to assist individuals in preretirement and retirement planning as aging Baby Boomers create more elderly persons than ever before.

As of 1995, "Baby Boomers (those persons born from 1946 to 1964) . . . [accounted for] . . . 30.3 percent of the total [U.S.] population" (Deardorff & Montgomery, 1995, p. 6).

Technology and Its Impact on Job Security

We agree with Gergen (1991b) that the technology of social saturation affects every aspect of the workplace, although we are not ardent social constructionists. As more technological advances are made, the necessary skills for a worker to function in the workplace are changing quickly. Technology also creates new economic conditions that change commerce and ultimately affect the job market. "Often these changes result in new approaches to lifestyles, home designs, and the use of natural resources" (Mosca, 1989, p. 98).

The workplace of today requires one to be literate in technology in order to remain employed. Brainpower is replacing manual labor due to the technical advancements that are changing jobs. Future workers must continually educate themselves and increase their skills in order to maintain their value in the workplace. As automation becomes more prevalent in the world of work, a person can be without a career almost overnight as automation makes some tasks obsolete. The effectiveness of career development in relation to the changing workforce needs constant scrutiny. According to Feller (1991), "Finding, attracting, and developing quality workers will remain a priority throughout the 1990s [and into the twenty-first century] as employers try to combat labor shortages, meet changing worker expectations, upgrade their work force, and build innovation and creativity into internationally competitive organizations" (p. 13).

Diebold (1994) further believes that the problems we are continuing to face are more conceptual than theoretical, and that our inability to conceptualize keeps us from making the best use of the **"infostructure"** (his word for information-based infrastructure) that is already in place. He projects that major growth will be centered in "real-time data collection, database storage of historical and current information, communications working, and service-providing software for the users and support staff of the infostructure" (p. 14).

Organizations cannot rely on automation to replace workforce planning since it is essential for a company to accomplish its objectives and goals. Behind all of the automation is a human element that needs to be a part of the company plan. With careful planning, a company can meet both the needs of the business and the individual. Ripley (1995) states that "skill-gap and surplus information projected during the workforce planning process enable any organization to do a better job in such areas as career counseling, training, recruiting, diversity and retraining—both for employees' needs and for tailoring such programs to the specific needs of the organization and its business units" (p. 13).

Ripley (1995) suggests an eight-step process for developing a workforce plan:

- Lay out a plan and a schedule.
- Perform a staffing assessment.
- Develop demand data.
- Develop supply data.
- Compare demand and supply data.
- Develop the workforce plan.
- Communicate and implement the workforce plan.
- Evaluate and update the plan. (pp. 13–14)

It is imperative that vocational practitioners be prepared to deal with job losses brought on by technology and the potential tidal waves of change this is creating. We need to also be prepared to consult with business and industry to develop workforce plans and career development centers.

CASE EXAMPLE

While in the process of completing this chapter, a friend called us to say her employer, a major insurance company, just experienced its third downsizing in three years. Before, there had been a warning. This time her unit of thirty employees was summoned to a meeting and there they were informed that they needed to eliminate half of their staff. Those eliminated would be given the option of providing the work they had been doing on an outsource basis. She was one of the people who stayed on the job, but she was given the responsibility for managing these outsource operations. She has had no experience with outsourcing, but because she has kept her skills updated, has been able to adapt them to new situations and has taken a leadership role at critical times. It appears her job is secure for the immediate present. This example highlights the need for flexibility and leadership on the part of those who remain valued employees.

BALANCING TRAINING, WORK, AND LEISURE

Watts (1996) proposes five ways in which vocational psychology can perform a practical, enhanced social role:

1. Make vocational counseling available to individuals throughout their life-span in order to enhance occupational development, especially in coordination with training/education and employers.

2. Strengthen the role of career education in the schools by providing a foundation for lifelong occupational development.

3. Vocational psychology needs to become more constructivist in its approach to help workers develop a subjective career narrative. Clients can take authorship of the role of work in their lives by narrating "a coherent, continuous, and credible story" (p. 233).

4. Occupational development services can support individuals by helping them record their achievement, identify their skills, and develop a plan of action and goal setting.

5. Establish closer links between vocational, financial, relationship and stress counseling. (pp. 233–34)

As the Baby Boomers age, occupational development becomes more crucial as a life-span approach rather than a concern primarily of young adults. This means that practitioners need to be trained to work with older workers who are wanting to change careers or merely obtain new skills in their present career/occupation. As the necessary skills change for the workforce of the future, workers will need to be able to adapt to these changes in order to continue to be employed. This changing workforce places pressure on practitioners to be able to effectively intervene with workers in transition. Feller (1991) states that

> Such turbulent times magnify the counselor's complex task even though the call to 'automate, innovate, or evaporate' has been in the headlines for some time. Although years of experience, seniority, and the union's ability to preserve one's career proved worthy in the past, workers today must realize that their only security is being able and willing to understand and adapt to change. (p. 4) He further suggests that practitioners will need to help clients "integrate new rules, consider new foundations, and constantly assess the gaps between what is needed and what is available" (p. 19).

Figure 14.2 illustrates Feller's chart of the implications for learning, work, and career development.

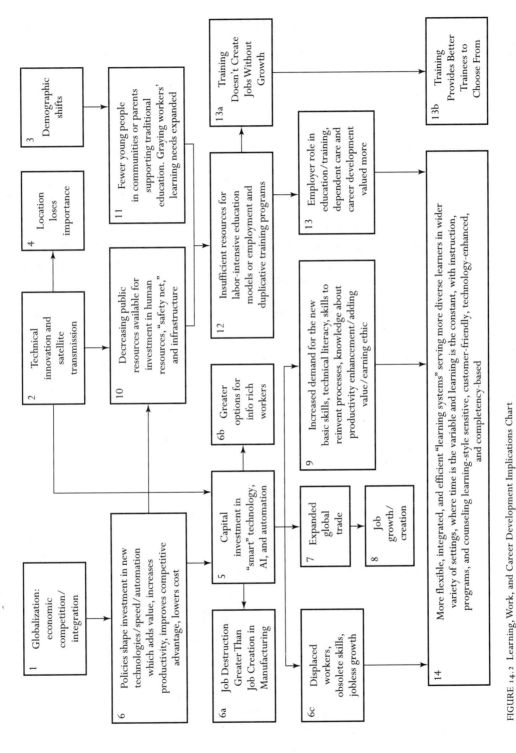

FIGURE 14.2 Learning, Work, and Career Development Implications Chart

source: "Redesigning 'Career' During the Work Revolution" by Rich Feller (1996). In R. Feller & G. Walz, Eds., Career Transitions in Turbulent Times. Copyright 1996 ERIC Counseling and Student Services Clearinghouse.

The Pitfall of "McJobs"

As we have stated earlier, the greatest challenge facing career/occupational specialists in high school, post-high school and adult years are the individuals who do not get specific training and end up with jobs that Ritzer (1996) calls "McJobs."

> It is important that we see McJobs for what they are . . . low-status, poorly paid and dehumanized jobs . . . that tend to offer dead-end careers that serve to a large degree as impediments to one's ability to acquire the higher-status, higher-paying, more complex and more human post-industrial jobs. (p. 211)

Ritzer goes on to recommend that students be advised to avoid McJobs and give more attention to their educational and creative abilities. "The skills acquired in McJobs are not likely to prepare one for, help one to acquire, or help one to function well in the foremost desirable post-industrial occupations" (p. 215).

As clearly presented above, workers in the next century will need to rethink their lives, balancing work and family (Stoltz-Loike, 1992), and work and leisure (Solomon, 1991) with spirituality (Myss, 1996). To help integrate training, work and leisure, Popcorn (1996) suggests attributes that successful people in the twenty-first century will possess. She organizes these into the acronym CLICK.

C is for courage

L is for letting go

I is for insight

C is for commitment

K is for know-how.

Clicking onto technological awareness, flexibility, acceptance of change and embracing its positive aspects, and working independently will help individuals deal with the changing world of work. Her book can be useful to practitioners and clients to help understand current trends.

THE CHANGING ROLE OF THE VOCATIONAL PRACTITIONER

Theories Revisited

In a time of change, theorists are rethinking, restating, or expanding current practices and ideas that are shaping our lives. Some of these are considered below to indicate future trends in the how we work as career specialists.

Savickas Rethinks Adler Savickas (1989, pp. 289–320) adapts generic Adlerian counseling into occupational guidance. Adlerian counseling can enhance the matching of persons to environments by including considerations of belongingness and ability to contribute and cooperate. Such enhancement adds to the dimension of making social contributions rather than simply earning personal success and satisfaction. Another addition of Adlerian techniques is an emphasis on the uniqueness of the individual. "Clients' goals and means reveal their uniqueness more than do interest inventory profiles" (p. 294).

Instead of focusing on interests, the life goals of a person determine the interests (Savickas, 1989). Therefore, the career path is important to understand, since the career decision-making process is more important to the Adlerian practitioner than the specific occupation chosen. Clients have evolved a private logic to deal with life, and the practitioner must be attuned to that logic.

Rather than the usual test batteries, Adlerian practitioners use another set of interests to begin the counseling process. The career-style interview consists of eight stimulus questions geared to elicit life goal and lifestyle information (Savickas, 1989): (1) role models—concentrating on what the client admires; (2) favorite books; (3) magazines the client reads; (4) leisure activities; (5) how the client did in various school subjects—to obtain a type of work environment to which the client responds; (6) mottoes and sayings the client uses and likes; (7) ambitions parents had for the client and which the client has; and (8) decisions as examples of strategies used. This information gives the practitioner the basis of assessment.

The seven assessment steps are: (1) Review the responses to the role model question, assessing problems and interests that will help resolve the problem. (2) Review the leisure question to determine actual interests and the types of "roles, functions and rewards that intrinsically attract the client" (Savickas, 1989, p. 306). (3) Magazine questions help identify the types of people, things and ideas that the client values. (4) School questions help identify a client's response to work environments and demonstrate reasons for success and failure he/she has experienced. (5) Occupational fantasies, parental expectations and the client's own ambitions describe self-images. (6) By now, the practitioner may have some clear ideas about a client's career style. This step can begin the process of identifying occupational possibilities. (7) It is now time to begin a more formal procedure that may involve the use of Holland's occupational codes and other tools. The process moves on to counseling with a focus on career style and path, decision-making obstacles, interests, occupational prospects, and choice barriers (Savickas, 1989).

> Ironically, the thing that people crave most—meaning is the one thing that science hasn't been able to give them.
>   —Eleanor Arroway, *Contact*

Based on our survey of the field of vocational psychology, and using Hansen's (1993) conclusions as a basic guide, we believe the following need to be considered.

1. The changes in the workplace are permanent. Therefore, vocational practitioners need to be able to assist individuals in the change process.

2. The vocational counseling process must be revised and reinvented to meet the changes in the workplace, in values, and in the actualities of the shift in the age of major population groups.

3. Occupational development programs need to be integrated continuously into the regular curriculum and classroom. School counselors, parents, and teachers need to be involved in helping students develop both short- and long-term plans.

4. More specific strategies are needed to deal with the "underserved, underrepresented, deprived populations" (Hansen, 1993, p. 20), using such techniques as mentoring, shadowing, work cooperatives and on-the-job training.

5. Vocational practitioners will need to be aware of the technological tools available as aids, and know how to use and process the information obtained with students/clients.

6. Occupational decision-making needs to include logical, rational, intuitive, personal, family, and spiritual processes in order to integrate life/work planning.

7. Developmental-contextual and integrative vocational approaches will become more appropriate treatment modalities. Working people in general will be forced to rethink the role of work in their lives.

8. It is the duty of policymakers, economists, business leaders, educators, and occupational development professionals to work together to be proactive in planning for this next century, and that these plans be incorporated into services for youth and adults.

9. Occupational development specialists will need to have training in the psychology of work, family roles and work, career/life planning, theoretical advances and applications, educational/information systems, and vocational/educational assessment.

10. Vocational psychology scholars and researchers will need to interface more with other academic disciplines, including but not limited to: (a) international business, (b) management, (c) political science, (d) sociology, (e) women's studies, (f) gay and lesbian studies, (g) social psychology, (h) developmental psychology, (i) gerontology, and (j) anthropology. Ethnographic

and other constructivist research methods will also need greater incorporation into vocational psychology as never before.

11. The role of work in people's lives needs to be emphasized more in the fields of teacher education (including special education and bilingual education), educational leadership, social work, clinical psychology, rehabilitation counseling, marriage and family therapy, and pastoral counseling.

Counselor education, in particular, needs to be expanded to include training on all levels. Certification of vocational practitioners needs to be rethought with emphasis on the knowledge base that is needed to make effective interventions. It is not enough to deal solely with career and job issues, when that is often the "tip of the iceberg." The need to be prepared for the gamut of problems that arise or to know when to refer one to another therapist are part of the necessary training of occupational counselors. A model for training programs is described in Osborne and Usher (1994) with a description of programs that include undergraduate, graduate, and doctoral students.

Miller-Tiedeman Revisits Miller-Tiedeman Ann Miller-Tiedeman's thinking about life and career posits the belief differences between traditional career and her LIFECAREER®.

TABLE 14.3 Belief Differences

TRADITIONAL CAREER	**LIFECAREER®**
Career as job	Career as life
Support career theorists	Believes that each person is his or her own best theorist
Emphasis on self-concept	Emphasis on self-conceiving theory
Control of life—make it happen	Cooperation with life
Suggests parts equal the whole	The whole organizes the parts
Knowing where you're going is a first condition to getting there	Learn as you go
Focus on right and wise decisions	Honor decisions that go right as well as those that do not work out
Trends and former patterns guide	The understood life from personal experience
Career is made	Career is lived in the moment, and becomes the path you leave behind

SOURCE: Adapted from Miller-Tiedeman (1996), pp. 109–110.

Krumboltz Extends Social Learning John Krumboltz (1998) recommends that practitioners be open to the possibility of serendipity. A logical extension of his social learning theory, his ideas indicate how unplanned events and situations also influence a client and become part of his/her own reality. Rather than follow the path of "true reasoning," Krumboltz suggests that when clients refuse to predict their own future, practitioners should consider the idea of openmindedness rather than labeling them as undecided or indecisive. He further recommends teaching that unplanned events are a normal part of the career process, even to the point of encouraging them to understand their part in creating these serendipitous happenstances.

McDaniels Combines Work and Leisure After thirty years of studying the work/leisure relationship, McDaniels has devised the concept that Career = Work + Leisure for the following reasons:

1. Combining Work and Leisure is More Holistic.

2. Combining Work and Leisure is Life Span Oriented.

3. Combining Work and Leisure is Future Oriented.

4. Combining Work and Leisure is Ever Present. (McDaniels, 1996, pp. 53–54)

Hansen Integrates Theories and Strategies L. Sunny Hansen (1997) makes a strong case for Integrative Life Planning as "a complex, comprehensive process of examining critical themes influencing our lives and identifying patterns and strategies which can help us to understand, manage, and perhaps even shape those influences" (p. 23). Practitioners and all clients are seen as agents of change in her positivistic and carefully outlined conceptual framework.

Brown Revisits Values Duane Brown (1996) uses a newly developed Life Values Inventory (Crace & Brown, 1996) to rethink the role of values in the life planning process. The LVI has "both quantitative and qualitative dimensions that require the client to consider which values are important for satisfaction in various life roles" (Brown, 1996, p. 361).

OCCUPATIONAL GUIDANCE SERVICES 2005

As we have attempted to distill all the information we have gathered, looked at the predictions, the directions, and the hopes for the future, we would like to formulate a look at the workforce of the future and propose some specific occupational guidance services.

The Workforce

The changes in the workforce and attitudes towards education, work, and leisure are likely to undergo substantive changes. The incredible increase of workers who are aging and dealing with retirement, combined with fewer available workers in this new generation to fill the needs of the job market, will make an older workforce inevitable. Added to this mixture is the change in the values of commitment to the job in terms of time and loyalty on the part of the new generation of workers. Bolles's (1978) vision of the future still holds with the "three boxes of life—education, work and leisure," less associated with a specific time of life, but rather seen as activities which are undertaken throughout the life span. Retirement will be redefined and rethought. How that will develop is not clear—what is clear is that retirement will not be what it was for the parents and grandparents of the Baby Boomers.

K–12 *The American people* will be made aware of the directions of employment opportunities through a campaign via media and other sources to alter the emphasis on college-bound postsecondary education to more technical preparation, in order to meet the projected needs in the world of work. In addition, the need for flexibility and the use of technological aids to work in various environments will be considered basic tools for work success.

Educational associations, starting at the state level and moving down through independent school district boards, will be more informed about current employment information, will work to mandate changes in educational requirements, and will motivate schools to develop programs that will reflect the realities of the needs of the work force.

Administrators and teachers will be fully aware of the relationship of work and the curriculum, with programs that motivate students as much as possible in the academic pursuits as well as help them envision themselves as productive workers in occupations. Especially challenging will be dealing with involuntary minorities (Ogbu, 1992) who view educational attainment as trying to be too much like White people. Teacher education in a global society (Gutek, 1993) is inextricably related to occupational education in the schools.

School counselors will be able to provide a comprehensive career guidance program for students from K–12 to become familiar with the world of work, the possibilities for themselves, and begin the process of elimination of possibilities through various assessments in order to focus planning and training. In addition, counselors will be able to provide basic job seeking skills at the level they are needed for each individual student.

Post-High School Adults *Those who go on to higher education* will be primarily of two types. The individuals who get a two-year vo-tech, specialized skill training will be filling approximately 60 percent of the jobs (Handy, 1995). This will be the single largest group in the workforce. The creation of these types of training programs is paramount and many community colleges, four year colleges, and universities will find themselves cooperating with local industries to provide education and training for the personnel the industry projects it will need. There will be an emphasis on these types of programs.

The second group will be the traditional professional training of four-year and graduate college studies. The predictions indicate that there is less need for highly trained professionals than is currently being offered. This will result in downsizing or consolidating programs, higher entrance standards, higher performance requirements, and extended training. The best schools will be at the forefront of these changes.

Adults in transition will need a variety of services offered. Among the services will be job clubs, career development services in industry and programs for special populations. In addition, good entrepreneurs will develop one-stop centers ("Occupational Guidance in a Box" career centers, similar to the "Doc in a Box" medical clinics) that serve people in easily accessible places, providing basic services apart from highly specialized offices. These career centers will be located in shopping malls and various other places where people gather. The centers will have computer programs, access to the government Internet services such as the O★Net, state and local statistical information regarding work, and contacts with the business community. They will need *trained personnel* who are certified occupational counselors and specialists. The services provided will include more than simply matching people and jobs; but, on a much larger scale, services will involve life and work planning and individual counseling services for situations that relate to obtaining, maintaining and increasing job productivity. These centers will also provide services for those of retirement age who want to continue to remain involved with a productive life.

Feller (1991) concludes that the next twenty-five years will demand that vocational practitioners "integrate new rules, consider new foundations, and constantly assess the gaps between what is needed and what is available. Only then will a client's employment and career development be better served in a world of change" (p. 19)

Appendix 1

Code of Fair Testing Practices
in Education

The Code of Fair Testing Practices in Education states the major obligations to test takers of professionals who develop or use educational tests. The Code is meant to apply broadly to the use of tests in education (admissions, educational assessment, educational diagnosis, and student placement). The Code is not designed to cover employment testing, licensure or certification testing, or other types of testing. Although the Code has relevance to many types of educational tests, it is directed primarily at professionally developed tests such as those sold by commercial test publishers or used in formally administered testing programs. The Code is not intended to cover tests made by individual teachers for use in their own classrooms.

The Code addresses the roles of test developers and test users separately. Test users are people who select tests, commission test development services, or make decisions on the basis of test scores. Test developers are people who actually construct tests as well as those who set policies for particular testing programs. The roles may, of course, overlap as when a state education agency commissions test development services, sets policies that control the test development process, and makes decisions on the basis of the test scores.

The Code presents standards for educational test developers and users in four areas:

A. Developing/Selecting Tests
B. Interpreting Scores
C. Striving for Fairness
D. Informing Test Takers

The Code has been developed by the Joint Committee on Testing Practices, a cooperative effort of several professional organizations, that has as its aim the advancement, in the public interest, of the quality of testing practices. The Joint Committee was initiated by the American Educational Research Association, the American Psychological Association, and the National Council on Measurement in Education. In addition to these three groups, the American Association for Counseling and Development/Association for Measurement and Evaluation in Counseling and Development, and the American Speech-Language-Hearing Association are now also sponsors of the Joint Committee.

This is not copyrighted material. Reproduction and dissemination are encouraged. Please cite this document as follows:
Code of Fair Testing Practices in Education. (1988) Washington, D.C. Joint Committee on Testing Practices. (Mailing Address: Joint Committee on Testing Practices, American Psychological Association, 1200 17th Street, NW, Washington, D.C. 20036.)

Organizations, institutions, and individual professionals who endorse the Code commit themselves to safeguarding the rights of test takers by following the principles listed. The Code is intended to be consistent with the relevant parts of the *Standards for Educational and Psychological Testing* (AERA, APA, NCME, 1985). However, the Code differs from the Standards in both audience and purpose. The Code is meant to be understood by the general public, it is limited to educational tests, and the primary focus is on those issues that affect the proper use of tests. The Code is not meant to add new principles over and above those in the Standards or to change the meaning of the Standards. The goal is rather to represent the spirit of a selected portion of the Standards in a way that is meaningful to test takers and/or their parents or guardians. It is the hope of the Joint Committee that the Code will also be judged to be consistent with existing codes of conduct and standards of other professional groups who use educational tests.

DEVELOPING/SELECTING APPROPRIATE TESTS*

Test developers should provide the information that test users need to select appropriate tests.

Test users should select tests that meet the purpose for which they are to be used and that are appropriate for the intended test-taking populations.

Test Developers Should:

1. Define what each test measures and what the test should be used for. Describe the populations for which the test is appropriate.

2. Accurately represent the characteristics, usefulness, and limitations of tests for their intended purposes.

3. Explain relevant measurement concepts as necessary for clarity at the level of detail that is appropriate for the intended audiences.

4. Describe the process of test development. Explain how the content and skills to be tested were selected.

5. Provide evidence that the test meets its intended purpose(s).

Test Users Should:

1. First define the purpose for testing and the population to be tested. Then, select a test for that purpose and that population based on a thorough review of the available information.

2. Investigate potentially useful sources of information, in addition to test scores, to corroborate the information provided by tests.

3. Read the materials provided by test developers and avoid using tests for which unclear or incomplete information is provided.

4. Become familiar with how and when the test was developed and tried out.

5. Read independent evaluations of a test and of possible alternative measures. Look for evidence required to support the claims of test developers.

*Many of the statements in the Code refer to the selection of existing tests. However, in customized testing programs test developers are engaged to construct new tests. In those situations, the test development process should be designed to help ensure that the completed tests will be in compliance with the Code.

6. Provide either representative samples or complete copies of test questions, directions, answer sheets, manuals, and score reports to qualified users.

7. Indicate the nature of the evidence obtained concerning the appropriateness of each test for groups of different racial, ethnic, or linguistic backgrounds who are likely to be tested.

8. Identify and publish any specialized skills needed to administer each test and to interpret scores correctly.

6. Examine specimen sets, disclosed tests or samples of questions, directions, answer sheets, manuals, and score reports before selecting a test.

7. Ascertain whether the test content and norms group(s) or comparison group(s) are appropriate for the intended test takers.

8. Select and use only those tests for which the skills needed to administer the test and interpret scores correctly are available.

INTERPRETING SCORES

Test developers should help users interpret scores correctly.

Test users should interpret scores correctly.

Test Developers Should:

9. Provide timely and easily understood score reports that describe test performance clearly and accurately. Also explain the meaning and limitations of reported scores.

10. Describe the population(s) represented by any norms or comparison group(s), the dates the data were gathered, and the process used to select the samples of test takers.

11. Warn users to avoid specific, reasonably anticipated misuses of test scores.

12. Provide information that will help users follow reasonable procedures for setting passing scores when it is appropriate to use such scores with the test.

13. Provide information that will help users gather evidence to show that the test is meeting its intended purpose(s).

Test Users Should:

9. Obtain information about the scale used for reporting scores, the characteristics of any norms or comparison group(s), and the limitations of the scores.

10. Interpret scores taking into account any major differences between the norms or comparison groups and the actual test takers. Also take into account any differences in test administration practices or familiarity with the specific questions in the test.

11. Avoid using tests for purposes not specifically recommended by the test developer unless evidence is obtained to support the intended use.

12. Explain how any passing scores were set and gather evidence to support the appropriateness of the scores.

13. Obtain evidence to help show that the test is meeting its intended purpose(s).

STRIVING FOR FAIRNESS

Test developers should strive to make tests that are as fair as possible for test takers of different races, gender, ethnic backgrounds, or handicapping conditions.

Test users should select tests that have been developed in ways that attempt to make them as fair as possible for test takers of different races, gender, ethnic backgrounds, or handicapping conditions.

Test Developers Should:

14. Review and revise test questions and related materials to avoid potentially insensitive content or language.

15. Investigate the performance of test takers of different races, gender, and ethnic backgrounds when samples of sufficient size are available. Enact procedures that help to ensure that differences in performance are related primarily to the skills under assessment rather than to irrelevant factors.

16. When feasible, make appropriately modified forms of tests or administration procedures available for test takers with handicapping conditions. Warn test users of potential problems in using standard norms with modified tests or administration procedures that result in noncomparable scores.

Test Users Should:

14. Evaluate the procedures used by test developers to avoid potentially insensitive content or language.

15. Review the performance of test takers of different races, gender, and ethnic backgrounds when samples of sufficient size are available. Evaluate the extent to which performance differences may have been caused by inappropriate characteristics of the test.

16. When necessary and feasible, use appropriately modified forms of tests or administration procedures for test takers with handicapping conditions. Interpret standard norms with care in the light of the modifications that were made.

INFORMING TEST TAKERS

Under some circumstances developers have direct communication with test takers. Under other circumstances, test users communicate directly with test takers. Whichever group communicates directly with test takers should provide the information described below.

Under some circumstances, test developers have direct control of tests and test scores. Under other circumstances, test users have such control. Whichever group has direct control of tests and test scores should take the steps described below.

Test Developers or
Test Users Should:

17. When a test is optional, provide test takers or their parents/guardians with information to help them judge

Test Developers or
Test Users Should:

19. Provide test takers or their parents/ guardians with information about rights test takers may have to obtain

whether the test should be taken, or if an available alternative to the test should be used.

18. Provide test takers the information they need to be familiar with the coverage of the test, the types of question formats, the directions, and appropriate test-taking strategies. Strive to make such information equally available to all test takers.

copies of tests and completed answer sheets, retake tests, have tests rescored, or cancel scores.

20. Tell test takers or their parents/guardians how long scores will be kept on file and indicate to whom and under what circumstances test scores will or will not be released.

21. Describe the procedures that test takers or their parents/guardians may use to register complaints and have problems resolved.

Note: The membership of the Working Group that developed the Code of Fair Testing Practices in Education and of the Joint Committee on Testing Practices that guided the Working Group was as follows:

Theodore P. Bartell
John R. Bergan
Esther E. Diamond
Richard P. Duran
Lorraine D. Eyde
Raymond D. Fowler
John J. Fremer
  (Co-chair, JCTP and Chair,
  Code Working Group)

Edmund W. Gordon
Jo-Ida C. Hansen
James B. Lingwall
George F. Madaus
  (Co-chair, JCTP)
Kevin L. Moreland
Jo-Ellen V. Perez
Robert J. Solomon
John T. Stewart

Carol Kehr Tittle
  (Co-chair, JCTP)
Nicholas A. Vacc
Michael J. Zieky
Debra Boltas and Wayne
  Camara of the American
  Psychological Association
  served as staff liaisons

Appendix 2

National Career Development Association Ethical Standards (Revised 1991)

These Ethical Standards were developed by the National Board for Certified Counselors (NBCC), an independent, voluntary, not-for-profit organization incorporated in 1982. Titled "Code of Ethics" by NBCC and last amended in February 1987, the Ethical Standards were adopted by the National Career Development Association (NCDA) Board of Directors in 1987 and revised in 1991, with minor changes in wording (e.g., the addition of specific references to NCDA members).

PREAMBLE

NCDA is an educational, scientific, and professional organization dedicated to the enhancement of the worth, dignity, potential, and uniqueness of each individual and, thus, to the service of society. This code of ethics enables the NCDA to clarify the nature of ethical responsibilities for present and future professional career counselors.

SECTION A: GENERAL

1. NCDA members influence the development of the profession by continuous efforts to improve professional practices, services, and research. Professional growth is continuous through the career counselor's career and is exemplified by the development of a philosophy that explains why and how a career counselor functions in the helping relationship. Career counselors must gather data on their effectiveness and be guided by their findings.

2. NCDA members have a responsibility to the clients they are serving and to the institutions within which the services are being performed. Career counselors also strive to assist the respective agency, organization, or institution in providing the highest caliber

of professional services. The acceptance of employment in an institution implies that the career counselor is in agreement with the general policies and principles of the institution. Therefore, the professional activities of the career counselor are in accord with the objectives of the institution. If, despite concerted efforts, the career counselor cannot reach agreement with the employer as to acceptable standards of conduct that allow for changes in institutional policy that are conducive to the positive growth and development of clients, then terminating the affiliation should be seriously considered.

3. Ethical behavior among professional associates (e.g., career counselors) must be expected at all times. When accessible information raises doubt as to the ethical behavior of professional colleagues, the NCDA member must make action to attempt to rectify this condition. Such action uses the respective institution's channels first and then uses procedures established by the American Counseling Association, of which NCDA is a division.

4. NCDA members neither claim nor imply professional qualifications which exceed those possessed, and are responsible for correcting any misrepresentations of these qualifications by others.

5. NCDA members must refuse a private fee or other remuneration for consultation or counseling with persons who are entitled to their services through the career counselor's employing institution or agency. The policies of some agencies may make explicit provisions for staff members to engage in private practice with agency clients. However, should agency clients desire private counseling or consulting services, they must be apprised of other options available to them. Career counselors must not divert to their private practices, legitimate clients in their primary agencies or of the institutions with which they are affiliated.

6. In establishing fees for professional counseling services, NCDA members must consider the financial status of clients and the respective locality. In the event that the established fee status is inappropriate for the client, assistance must be provided in finding comparable services of acceptable cost.

7. NCDA members seek only those positions in the delivery of professional services for which they are professionally qualified.

8. NCDA members recognize their limitations and provide services or only use techniques for which they are qualified by training and/or experience. Career counselors recognize the need, and seek continuing education, to assure competent services.

9. NCDA members are aware of the intimacy in the counseling relationship, maintain respect for the client, and avoid engaging in activities that seek to meet their personal needs at the expense of the client.

10. NCDA members do not condone or engage in sexual harassment which is defined as deliberate or repeated comments, gestures, or physical contacts of a sexual nature.

11. NCDA members avoid bringing their personal or professional issues into the counseling relationship. Through an awareness of the impact of stereotyping and discrimination (e.g., biases based on age, disability, ethnicity, gender, race, religion, or sexual preference), career counselors guard the individual rights and personal dignity of the client in the counseling relationship.

12. NCDA members are accountable at all times for their behavior. They must be aware that all actions and behaviors of a counselor reflect on professional integrity and, when inappropriate, can damage the public trust in the counseling profession. To protect

public confidence in the counseling profession, career counselors avoid public behavior that is clearly in violation of accepted moral and legal standards.

13. NCDA members have a social responsibility because their recommendations and professional actions may alter the lives of others. Career counselors remain fully cognizant of their impact and are alert to personal, social, organizational, financial, or political situations or pressures which might lead to misuse of their influence.

14. Products or services provided by NCDA members by means of classroom instruction, public lectures, demonstrations, written articles, radio or television programs, or other types of media must meet the criteria cited in Sections A through F of these Ethical Standards.

SECTION B: COUNSELING RELATIONSHIP

1. The primary obligation of NCDA members is to respect the integrity and promote the welfare of the client, regardless of whether the client is assisted individually or in a group relationship. In a group setting, the career counselor is also responsible for taking reasonable precautions to protect individuals from physical and/or psychological trauma resulting from interaction within the group.

2. The counseling relationship and information resulting from it remains confidential, consistent with the legal obligations of the NCDA member. In a group counseling setting, the career counselor sets a norm of confidentiality regarding all group participants' disclosures.

3. NCDA members know and take into account the traditions and practices of other professional groups with whom they work, and they cooperate fully with such groups. If a person is receiving similar services from another professional, career counselors do not offer their own services directly to such a person. If a career counselor is contacted by a person who is already receiving similar services from another professional, the career counselor carefully considers that professional relationship and proceeds with caution and sensitivity to the therapeutic issues as well as the client's welfare. Career counselors discuss these issues with clients so as to minimize the risk of confusion and conflict.

4. When a client's condition indicates that there is a clear and imminent danger to the client or others, the NCDA member must take reasonable personal action or inform responsible authorities. Consultation with other professionals must be used where possible. The assumption of responsibility for the client's behavior must be taken only after careful deliberation, and the client must be involved in the resumption of responsibility as quickly as possible.

5. Records of the counseling relationship, including interview notes, test data, correspondence, audio or visual tape recordings, electronic data storage, and other documents are to be considered professional information for use in counseling. They should not be considered a part of the records of the institution or agency in which the NCDA member is employed unless specified by state statute or regulation. Revelation to others of counseling material must occur only upon the expressed consent of the client; career counselors must make provisions for maintaining confidentiality in the storage and disposal of records. Career counselors providing information to the public

or to subordinates, peers, or supervisors have a responsibility to ensure that the content is general; unidentified client information should be accurate and unbiased, and should consist of objective, factual data.

6. NCDA members must ensure that data maintained in electronic storage are secure. The data must be limited to information that is appropriate and necessary for the services being provided and accessible only to appropriate staff members involved in the provision of services by using the best computer security methods available. Career counselors must also ensure that electronically stored data are destroyed when the information is no longer of value in providing services.

7. Data derived from a counseling relationship for use in counselor training or research shall be confined to content that can be disguised to ensure full protection of the identity of the subject/client and shall be obtained with informed consent.

8. NCDA members must inform clients, before or at the time the counseling relationship commences, of the purposes, goals, techniques, rules and procedures, and limitations that may affect the relationship.

9. All methods of treatment by NCDA members must be clearly indicated to prospective recipients and safety precautions must be taken in their use.

10. NCDA members who have an administrative, supervisory, and/or evaluative relationship with individuals seeking counseling services must not serve as the counselor and should refer the individuals to other professionals. Exceptions are made only in instances where an individual's situation warrants counseling intervention and another alternative is unavailable. Dual relationships with clients that might impair the career counselor's objectivity and professional judgment must be avoided and/or the counseling relationship terminated through referral to another competent professional.

11. When NCDA members determine an inability to be of professional assistance to a potential or existing client, they must, respectively, not initiate the counseling relationship or immediately terminate the relationship. In either event, the career counselor must suggest appropriate alternatives. Career counselors must be knowledgeable about referral resources so that a satisfactory referral can be initiated. In the event that the client declines a suggested referral, the career counselor is not obligated to continue the relationship.

12. NCDA members may choose to consult with any other professionally competent person about a client and must notify clients of this right. Career counselors must avoid placing a consultant in a conflict-of-interest situation that would preclude the consultant's being a proper party to the career counselor's efforts to help the client.

13. NCDA members who counsel clients from cultures different from their own must gain knowledge, personal awareness, and sensitivity pertinent to the client populations served and must incorporate culturally relevant techniques into their practice.

14. When NCDA members engage in intensive counseling with a client, the client's counseling needs should be assessed. When needs exist outside the counselor's expertise, appropriate referrals should be made.

15. NCDA members must screen prospective group counseling participants, especially when the emphasis is on self-understanding and growth through self-disclosure. Career counselors must maintain an awareness of each group participant's welfare throughout the group process.

16. When electronic data and systems are used as a component of counseling services, NCDA members must ensure that the computer application, and any information it contains, is appropriate for the respective needs of clients and is nondiscriminatory. Career counselors must ensure that they themselves have acquired a facilitation level of knowledge with any system they use including hands-on application, search experience, and understanding of the uses of all aspects of the computer-based system. In selecting and/or maintaining computer-based systems that contain career information, career counselors must ensure that the systems provide current, accurate, and locally relevant information. Career counselors must also ensure that clients are intellectually, emotionally, and physically compatible with the use of the computer application and understand its purpose and operation. Client use of a computer application must be evaluated to correct possible problems and assess subsequent needs.

17. NCDA members who develop self-help, stand-alone computer software for use by the general public, must first ensure that it is initially designed to function in a stand-alone manner, as opposed to modifying software that was originally designed to require support from a counselor. Secondly, the software must include program statements that provide the user with intended outcomes, suggestions for using the software, descriptions of inappropriately used applications, and descriptions of when and how counseling services might be beneficial. Finally, the manual must include the qualifications of the developer, the development process, validation data, and operating procedures.

SECTION C: MEASUREMENT AND EVALUATION

1. NCDA members must provide specific orientation or information to an examinee prior to and following the administration of assessment instruments or techniques so that the results may be placed in proper perspective with other relevant factors. The purpose of testing and the explicit use of the results must be made known to an examinee prior to testing.

2. In selecting assessment instruments or techniques for use in a given situation or with a particular client, NCDA members must evaluate carefully the instrument's specific theoretical bases and characteristics, validity, reliability, and appropriateness. Career counselors are professionally responsible for using unvalidated information with special care.

3. When making statements to the public about assessment instruments or techniques, NCDA members must provide accurate information and avoid false claims or misconceptions concerning the meaning of psychometric terms. Special efforts are often required to avoid unwarranted connotations of terms such as IQ and grade-equivalent scores.

4. Because many types of assessment techniques exist, NCDA members must recognize the limits of their competence and perform only those functions for which they have received appropriate training.

5. NCDA members must note when tests are not administered under standard conditions or when unusual behavior or irregularities occur during a testing session and the results must be designated as invalid or of questionable validity. Unsupervised or inadequately supervised assessments, such as mail-in tests, are considered unethical. However, the use of standardized instruments that are designed to be self-administered and self-scored, such as interest inventories, is appropriate.

6. Because prior coaching or dissemination of test materials can invalidate test results, NCDA members are professionally obligated to maintain test security. In addition, conditions that produce most favorable test results must be made known to an examinee (e.g., penalty for guessing).

7. NCDA members must consider psychometric limitations when selecting and using an instrument, and must be cognizant of the limitations when interpreting the results. When tests are used to classify clients, career counselors must ensure that periodic review and/or retesting are conducted to prevent client stereotyping.

8. An examinee's welfare, explicit prior understanding, and agreement are the factors used when determining who receives the test results. NCDA members must see that appropriate interpretation accompanies any release of individual or group test data (e.g., limitations of instrument and norms).

9. NCDA members must ensure that computer-generated assessment administration and scoring programs function properly, thereby providing clients with accurate assessment results.

10. NCDA members who are responsible for making decisions based on assessment results, must have appropriate training and skills in educational and psychological measurement—including validation criteria, test research, and guidelines for test development and use.

11. NCDA members must be cautious when interpreting the results of instruments that possess insufficient technical data, and must explicitly state to examinees the specific purposes for the use of such instruments.

12. NCDA members must proceed with caution when attempting to evaluate and interpret performances of minority group members or other persons who are not represented in the norm group on which the instrument was standardized.

13. NCDA members who develop computer-based interpretations to support the assessment process must ensure that the validity of the interpretations is established prior to the commercial distribution of the computer application.

14. NCDA members recognize that test results may become obsolete, and avoid the misuse of obsolete data.

15. NCDA members must avoid the appropriation, reproduction, or modification of published tests or parts thereof without acknowledgment and permission from the publisher.

SECTION D: RESEARCH AND PUBLICATION

1. NCDA members will adhere to relevant guidelines on research with human subjects. These include:
   a. *Code of Federal Regulations*, Title 45, Subtitle A, Part 46, as currently issued.
   b. American Psychological Association. (1982). *Ethical principles in the conduct of research with human participants.* Washington, DC: Author.
   c. American Psychological Association. (1981). Research with human participants. *American Psychologist, 36,* 633-638.
   d. Family Educational Rights and Privacy Act. (Buckley Amendment to P. L. 93-380 of the Laws of 1974)
   e. Current federal regulations and various state privacy acts.

2. In planning research activities involving human subjects, NCDA members must be aware of and responsive to all pertinent ethical principles and ensure that the research problem, design, and execution are in full compliance with the principles.

3. The ultimate responsibility for ethical research lies with the principal researcher, although others involved in research activities are ethically obligated and responsible for their own actions.

4. NCDA members who conduct research with human subjects are responsible for the subjects' welfare throughout the experiment and must take all reasonable precautions to avoid causing injurious psychological, physical, or social effects on their subjects.

5. NCDA members who conduct research must abide by the following basic elements of informed consent:
   a. a fair explanation of the procedures to be followed, including an identification of those which are experimental.
   b. a description of the attendant discomforts and risks.
   c. a description of the benefits to be expected.
   d. a disclosure of appropriate alternative procedures that would be advantageous for subjects.
   e. an offer to answer any inquiries concerning the procedures.
   f. an instruction that subjects are free to withdraw their consent and to discontinue participation in the project or activity at any time.

6. When reporting research results, explicit mention must be made of all the variables and conditions known to the NCDA member that may have affected the outcome of the study or the interpretation of the data.

7. NCDA members who conduct and report research investigations must do so in a manner that minimizes the possibility that the results will be misleading.

8. NCDA members are obligated to make available sufficient original research data to qualified others who may wish to replicate the study.

9. NCDA members who supply data, aid in the research of another person, report research results, or make original data available, must take due care to disguise the identity of respective subjects in the absence of specific authorization from the subject to do otherwise.

10. When conducting and reporting research, NCDA members must be familiar with, and give recognition to, previous work on the topic, must observe all copyright laws, and must follow the principles of giving full credit to those to whom credit is due.

11. NCDA members must give due credit through joint authorship, acknowledgment, footnote statements, or other appropriate means to those who have contributed significantly to the research and/or publication, in accordance with such contributions.

12. NCDA members should communicate to others the results of any research judged to be of professional value. Results that reflect unfavorably on institutions, programs, services, or vested interests must not be withheld.

13. NCDA members who agree to cooperate with another individual in research and/or publication incur an obligation to cooperate as promised in terms of punctuality of performance and with full regard to the completeness and accuracy of the information required.

14. NCDA members must not submit the same manuscript, or one essentially similar in content, for simultaneous publication consideration by two or more journals. In addi-

tion, manuscripts that are published in whole or substantial part in another journal or published work should not be submitted for publication without acknowledgment and permission from the previous publication.

SECTION E: CONSULTING

Consultation refers to a voluntary relationship between a professional helper and help-needing individual, group, or social unit in which the consultant is providing help to the client(s) in defining and solving a work-related problem or potential work-related problem with a client or client system.

1. NCDA members acting as consultants must have a high degree of self-awareness of their own values, knowledge, skills, limitations, and needs in entering a helping relationship that involves human and/or organizational change. The focus of the consulting relationship must be on the issues to be resolved and not on the person(s) presenting the problem.

2. In the consulting relationship, the NCDA member and client must understand and agree upon the problem definition, subsequent goals, and predicted consequences of interventions selected.

3. NCDA members must be reasonably certain that they, or the organization represented, have the necessary competencies and resources for giving the kind of help that is needed or that may develop later, and that appropriate referral resources are available to the consultant.

4. NCDA members in a consulting relationship must encourage and cultivate client adaptability and growth toward self-direction. NCDA members must maintain this role consistently and not become a decision maker for clients or create a future dependency on the consultant.

5. NCDA members conscientiously adhere to the NCDA Ethical Standards when announcing consultant availability for services.

SECTION F: PRIVATE PRACTICE

1. NCDA members should assist the profession by facilitating the availability of counseling services in private as well as public settings.

2. In advertising services as private practitioners, NCDA members must advertise in a manner that accurately informs the public of the professional services, expertise, and counseling techniques available.

3. NCDA members who assume an executive leadership role in a private practice organization do not permit their names to be used in professional notices during periods of time when they are not actively engaged in the private practice of counseling.

4. NCDA members may list their highest relevant degree, type, and level of certification and/or license, address, telephone number, office hours, type and/or description of services, and other relevant information. Listed information must not contain false, inaccurate misleading, partial, out-of-context, or otherwise deceptive material or statements.

5. NCDA members who are involved in partnership or corporation with other professionals must, in compliance with the regulations of the locality, clearly specify the separate specialties of each member of the partnership or corporation.

6. NCDA members have an obligation to withdraw from a private-practice counseling relationship if it violates the NCDA Ethical Standards; if the mental or physical condition of the NCDA member renders it difficult to carry out an effective professional relationship; or if the counseling relationship is no longer productive for the client.

PROCEDURES FOR PROCESSING
ETHICAL COMPLAINTS

As a division of the American Counseling Association (ACA) the National Career Development Association (NCDA) adheres to the guidelines and procedures for processing ethical complaints and the disciplinary sanctions adopted by ACA. A complaint against an NCDA member may be filed by any individual or group of individuals ("complainant"), whether or not the complainant is a member of NCDA. Action will not be taken on anonymous complaints.

For specifics on how to file ethical complaints and a description of the guidelines and procedures for processing complaints, contact:

ACA Ethics Committee
c/o Executive Director
American Counseling Association
5999 Stevenson Avenue
Alexandria, VA 22304
(800)347-6647

Appendix 3

Tests and Publishers

MAJOR PUBLISHERS

American College Testing
2201 North Dodge Street
PO Box 168
Iowa City, IA 52243
(800) 498-6065

CFKR Career Materials, Inc.
P.O. Box 439
Meadow Vista, CA 95722
(800) 525-5626

Consulting Psychologists Press (CPP)
3803 E. Bayshore Road
P.O. Box 10096
Palo Alto, CA 94303
(800) 624-1765

CTB McGraw-Hill
20 Ryan Ranch Road
Monterey, CA 93940
(708) 392-3380

Educational and Industrial Testing Services (EdITS)
PO Box 7234
San Diego, CA 92107
(619) 222-1666

Institute for Personality and Ability Testing (IPAT)
1801 Woodfield Drive
Savoy, IL 61874
(217) 352-4739

NCS Assessments (NCS)
P.O. Box 1416
Minneapolis, MN 55440★
(612) 939-5000

Psychological Assessment Resources, Inc. (PAR)
P.O. Box 998
Odessa, FL 33556
(800) 331-8378

The Psychological Corporation (PSYCORP)
555 Academic Court
San Antonio, TX 78204-2498
(800) 228-0752

Research Psychologists Press, Inc. (SIGMA)
P.O. Box 610984
Port Huron, MI 48061-0984
(800) 265-1285

Vocational Psychology Research
University of Minnesota
Elliot Hall N620
75 East River Road
Minneapolis, MN 55455-0344
(612) 625-1367

Western Psychological Services (WPS)
12031 Wilshire Boulevard
Los Angeles, CA 90025-1251
(310) 478-2061

ABILITY TESTS	PUBLISHER
American College Testing (ACT)	American College Testing
Armed Services Vocational Aptitude Battery (ASVAB)	Department of Defense Defense Manpower Data Center Personnel Testing Division 99 Pacific Street, Suite 155A Monterey, CA 93940 (408) 583-2400
APTICOM	Vocational Research Institute 1528 Walnut Street #1502 Philadelphia, PA 19102 (215) 875-7387
Differential Aptitude Test (DAT)	PsyCorp
General Aptitude Test Battery (GATB)	Western Assessment Research and Devel. Ctr. 140 East Third Street Salt Lake City, UT 84111

INTEREST TESTS	PUBLISHER
Campbell Interest and Skills Survey (CISS)	NCS
Career Assessment Inventory (CAI)	NCS
Copsystem Interest Inventory (COPS)	EdITS
Explore the World of Work (EWOW)	CFKR Career Materials, Inc.
Ideas, Determination, and Assessment System (IDEAS)	NCS
Jackson Vocational Interest Inventory (JVII)	SIGMA
Kuder Occupational Interest Survey (KOIS)	CTB McGraw-Hill (All Kuder Instruments)
Minnesota Satisfaction Questionnaire (MSQ)	Vocational Psych. Research
My Vocational Situation (MVS)	CPP
Rockwell Occupational Approval Grid (ROAG)	Taylor Rockwell, Brownlee Dolan Stein Associates, Inc. 90 John Street New York, NY 10038 Phone number not available
Self-Directed Search (SDS)	PAR
Strong Interest Inventory (SII)	CPP
Vocational Interest Inventory (VII)	WPS
Vocational Preference Inventory (VPI)	WPS
Wide Range Interest, Opinion Test (WRIOT)	Riverside Publishing Co. 425 Spring Lake Drive Itasca, IL 60143-2070
World of Work (WOW)	World of Work, Inc. 2923 North 67th Place Scottsdale, AZ 85251 (602) 946-1884
Work Attitudes Questionnaire (WAQ)	Marathon Consult. and Press P.O. Box 09189 Columbus, OH 43209-0189 (614) 235-5509

PERSONALITY TESTS	PUBLISHER
Adjective Checklist (AC)	CPP
California Psychological Inventory (CPI)	CPP
Edward's Personal Preference Schedule (EPPS)	PsyCorp
Eysenck Personality Inventory (EIP)	EdITS
Millon Clinical Multiaxial Inventory (MCMI)	NCS
Minnesota Multiphasic Personality Inventory (MMPI)	NCS
Myers-Briggs Type Indicator (MBTI)	CPP
Neuroticism, Extroversion, and Openness Personality Inventory—Revised (NEO-PI-R)	PAR
Sixteen PF Personal Career Development Profile (16F)	IPAT

VALUES TESTS	PUBLISHER
Family Environment Scale (FES)	CPP
Minnesota Importance Questionnaire (MIQ)	Vocational Psych. Research
Rokeach Value Survey (RVS)	CPP
Salience Inventory (SI)	CPP
Values Scale (VS)	CPP
Work Values Inventory (WVI)	Houghton Mifflin Company 1 Beach Street Boston, MA 02107

CAREER DEVELOPMENT INVENTORIES TESTS	PUBLISHER
Adult Career Concerns Inventory (ACCI)	CPP
Assessment of Career Decision Making (ACDM)	WPS
Career Adjustment and Development Inventory (CADI)	Dr. J. W. Pickering Old Dominion University Norfolk, VA 23529

Career Attitudes and Strategies Inventory (CASI)   PAR

Career Beliefs Inventory (CBI)   CPP

Career Confidence Scale (CCS)   CPP

Career Decision Scale (CDS)   PAR

Career Decision Profile (CDP)

Lawrence K. Jones
North Carolina State Univ.
Box 7801
Raleigh, NC 27695
(919) 515-6359

Career Development Inventory (CDI)   CPP

Career Maturity Inventory (CMI)

Crites Career Consultants
5460 White Place
Boulder, CO 80303
(303) 447-1639

Career Thoughts Inventory   PAR

Geriatric Depression Scale (GDS)

T.L. Brink
1103 Church Street
Redlands, CA 92374
(909) 793-8288

Harrington O'Shea Career Decision Making System Revised (CDMS-R)

American Guidance Service
4201 Woodland Road
Circle Pines, MN 55014
(800) 328-2560

Occupational Stress Inventory (OSI)   PAR

Work Environment Scale (WES)   CPP

Glossary

A

ability—the inherent skills one possesses.

ability tests—"measure skills in terms of speed, accuracy, or both" (Kaplan & Saccuzzo, 1997, p. 11).

acculturation—the process of accepting both one's original group values and the values of at least one other group (Olmedo, 1979); and the accumulation and incorporation of the beliefs and customs of at least one alternative culture (Mendoza & Martínez, 1981).

achievement tests—measure previous learning.

active agents—individuals responsible for one's own career planning.

adaptive skills—a set of skills needed to survive in the world of work including the following: skills of problem recognition and definition, handling evidence, analytical skills, skills of implementation, human relations, [and] learning skills (The U.S. Congress Office of Technology Assessment, pp. 131, 132).

AFDC (Aid to Families with Dependent Children)—see **House Rule (HR) 3734,** the Personal Responsibility and Work Opportunity Reconciliation Act.

affirmative action—the "planning and acting to end the absence of certain kinds of people—those who belong to groups that have been subordinated or left out—from certain jobs and schools" (Bergman, 1996, p. 7).

African Americans—descriptive term used by the U.S. Bureau of the Census to refer to persons of African ancestry or origin now living in the United States.

Afrocentrism—the idea that behaviors based on an African cultural heritage account for differences between Black and White student behaviors.

agentic behavior—interpreting and shaping one's own life through action and independence.

ally—heterosexuals who are professionally and personally affirmative to gay, lesbian, and bisexual persons.

androcentric—the focus on white male standards to define normality.

Anglo—a misnomer used to refer to White persons of various ethnic ancestries that presumes English cultural uniformity.

anti-Semitism—anti-Jewish **prejudice** and **discrimination.**

anxiety—one of several factors that can be part of career indecision. These factors are: (a) anxiety, (b) external locus of control, (c) problems in self-perception, (d) interpersonal difficulties and dependency, (e) interests, (f) ability levels, and (g) cognitive styles (Newman, Fuqua & Seaworth, 1989).

aptitude tests—the potential for acquiring a specific skill.

Archway Model—Super's (1990) graphic representation of the synthesis of theories and models of life-span, life-space approach to career counseling.

Artistic type—this development of an Artistic pattern of activities, competencies, and interests creates a person who is predisposed to exhibit the following behavior:

1. Prefers artistic occupations or situations in which one can engage in preferred activities and competencies and avoid the activities demanded by conventional occupations or situations.
2. Uses artistic competencies to solve problems at work and in other settings.
3. Perceives self as expressive, original, intuitive, nonconforming, introspective, independent, disorderly, having artistic and musical ability, and ability in acting, writing, and speaking.
4. Values aesthetic qualities (Holland, 1992, p. 20).

These demands, opportunities, and Artistic people create a characteristic atmosphere that operates to produce the following outcomes:

1. It stimulates people to engage in artistic activities.
2. It fosters artistic competencies and achievements.

3. It encourages people to see themselves as expressive, original, intuitive, nonconforming, independent, and as having artistic abilities (acting, writing. and speaking). It encourages people to see the world in complex, independent, unconventional, and flexible ways.

The Artistic person possesses is apt to be:

Complicated	Imaginative	Intuitive
Disorderly	Impractical	Nonconforming
Emotional	Impulsive	Original
Expressive	Independent	Sensitive
Idealistic	Introspective	Open

(Holland, 1992, p. 21)

Asian American/Pacific Islander—descriptive term used by the U.S. Bureau of the Census to refer to persons of Asian ancestry or origin now living in the United States.

assessment—a procedure used to evaluate an individual in terms of current and future functioning (Kaplan & Saccuzzo, 1997).

assessment tool—another name for **test**.

assimilation—the merging of cultural traits from previously distinct cultural groups (Random House Dictionary, 1979).

associative learning experiences—occur when an individual pairs a situation that has been previously neutral with one that is positive or negative. Two types of associative learning experience are: (1) observation, and (2) classical conditioning. This is an extension of the classical conditioning paradigm.

avocational activities—activities pursued systematically and consecutively for their own sake; the objective is for other than monetary gain, which may incidentally occur (Super, 1976).

avocational pursuits—hobbies.

B

babybusters—people who are in their twenties and are making an impact on the world of work.

basic academic skills—the ability to read, follow directions, and use mathematics.

basic skills—reading, writing, arithmetic, and mathematics, speaking and listening (U.S. Department of Labor, Special Commission on Achieving Necessary Skills, 1991).

behavior—overt actions such as driving a car or playing a guitar (Van Hoose & Paradise, 1979).

behavior-based conflict—see **work-family conflict.**

belief in a just world—the tendency for laypeople to view victims as the cause of their own misfortune.

between-group differences—differences that occur between two or more racial or ethnic groups; cross-cultural comparisons.

birth order—the order of a child's birth, which is thought to affect the child's place in his/her family and on a larger scale, the child's future placement in society.

Black Cultural Learning Style (BLS)—an example of attempts to use cultural values as a primary explanation for behaviors that benefit or impede educational attainment and its related occupational development for African Americans.

blaming the victim—an ideological process which stigmatizes the victim by accounting for their victimization by locating the malignant nature of poverty, injustice, slum life, and racial difficulties as located within the victim. (Ryan, 1971).

Buddhism—cultural value where self-improvement can be found through doing good work and study and through the control of undesirable emotions; optimism, calmness, and harmony are valued (Axelson, 1993, p. 438).

burnout—a process of gradual change in behavior, eventually reaching intense reactions and often leading to a crisis, if left unresolved.

C

calculus—the relationship within and between types or environments that can be ordered according to the hexagonal model for defining Holland's typology. Types adjacent to each other on the hexagonal model are presumed to be most similar. Types opposite each other are presumed to be most dissimilar.

Calvinism—ideas put forth by Protestant reformer John Calvin (e.g., the fulfillment of duties through work is the highest form of moral activity an individual can assume).

career—the "sequence of occupations in which one engages" (Tolbert, 1980, p. 31).

career adaptability—a construct which Super and Knasel (1979) proposed to describe the balance an individual attempts to maintain between the work world and personal environment.

career counseling—"planning and making decisions about occupations and education" (Tolbert, 1980, p. 32). The term has evolved into being most applicable to those of the professional class.

career death—job loss which may force a person into a situation in which they must find some new work.

career development—"the lifelong process of developing work values, crystallizing a vocational identity, learning about opportunities, and trying out plans in part-time, recreational, and full-time work situations" (Tolbert, 1980, p. 31); used interchangeably with **occupational development** and **vocational development**.

career decision-making self-efficacy—beliefs about one's ability to decide on an appropriate career choice.

Career Decisions Software Solutions (CDSS)—a computer program that assists a person in making career decisions by providing accurate career information from an office or a computer. It provides a list of occupations that matches the person's characteristics or the characteristics of the desired vocation.

career first, then family—observations that Richter, Morrison, and Salinas (1991) make about ways to deal with the issue of dual careerism in which the couple must deal with the issues of (a) the biological time clock for women, (b) men's physical degeneration and lowering of stamina, (c) age differences in child raising, and (d) ambivalence/reality testing.

career indecision—the "state of being undecided about a career" (Newman, Fuqua & Seaworth, 1989).

career maturity—a hypothetical construct of a constellation of physical, psychological, and social characteristics; psychologically, it is both cognitive and affective. It includes the degree of success in coping with the demands of earlier stages and substages of career development and especially with the most recent.

career myths—"irrational attitudes about the career-development process. These irrational attitudes most often are generated from historical, familial patterns of career ignorance and negative career-development experiences" (Herring, 1990, p. 13).

Career Navigator—a Computer-Assisted Career Guidance System that places more emphasis on job search assistance than on self-exploration.

career plateauing—"the point in a career when the likelihood of additional hierarchical promotion is very low" (Ferrence, Stoner & Warren, 1977).

casual register—language that is (a) used between friends, (b) with a general, nonspecific word choice, (c) dependent upon nonverbals for assistance in conveying meaning, and (d) that often uses incomplete syntax.

career renewal—a transitional stage that takes place for people generally at the end of the establishment stage and at the beginning of the maintenance stage of a job or career (Beijan & Salomone, 1995, p. 52).

career resiliency—one who is: (a) self-aware; (b) values driven; (c) dedicated to continuous learning; (d) future-focused; (e) connected; and (f) flexible (Collard, Epperheimer & Saign, 1996).

career search self-efficacy—the "individual's degree of confidence that they can successfully perform a variety of career exploration activities, including their judgments about their ability to successfully explore personal values and interests, effectively network with professionals in a field of interest, [and] successfully interview for a job" (Solberg, Good, Fischer, Brown & Nord, 1995, p. 448).

Career Transition Inventory—an assessment instrument for adults in transition. It was designed specifically to "assess and understand internal, dynamic psychological processes that may get in the way of the career transition process" (p. 220). Five basic factors the instrument attempts to assess are (a) readiness; (b) confidence; (c) perceived support; (d) control; and (e) decision independence (Mary Heppner, 1991).

CASVE Cycle—a cycle of generic career-problem-solving and decision-making skills which includes: (1) communication—understanding the external demands and internal states that signal the need to begin problem-solving; (2) analysis—clarifying or obtaining knowledge about self, occupations, decision-making, or metacognitions; (3) synthesis—elaborating and synthesizing alternatives; (4) valuing—prioritizing alternatives and making tentative primary and secondary choices; and (5) execution—formulating a plan for implementing a tentative choice that includes a preparation program, reality testing, and employment seeking. "The cycle is a recursive process, in which individuals move backward and forward through the cycle in response to their emerging decision needs and the availability of information resources" (Sampson et al., 1992 p. 68).

caves and commons—environments arranged by grouping private work areas around larger communal team space.

chance processes—capitalizing on chance and unforeseen events.

character—that within an individual which makes wise and kind (i.e., moral) choices (Pipher, 1996).

childcare options—observations Richter, Morrison and Salinas (1991) make about ways to deal with the issue of dual careerism, in which the couple must deal with the options of (a) parental care—staggered hours, (b) care by extended family member, (c) family daycare, (d) group care, (e) full-time babysitter/housekeeper/nanny, (f) two parents who can dovetail their work schedules, (g) taking a child to work, (h) parent cooperative, (i) children in charge of themselves, (j) drop-in centers, (k) working from home, and (l) a combination of the above.

child time—a pace that is flexible and mainly slow. It entails patiently making allowances for "oversee[ing] the laborious task of tying a [child's] shoelace, [tolerating] a [child's] prolonged sit on the potty, [and listening] to the scrambled telling of a tall tale" (Hochschild, 1997, p. 5).

classism—the pathological labeling of behavior patterns that differ from middle-and upper-class norms. Often, such alternative behavior patterns may be functional in a lower socioeconomic class person's community (Payne, 1995).

CHOICES—a Computer-Assisted Career Guidance Systems intended for high school students to assist them in making informed and educated decisions about their future, whether it be to attend a university or begin a career.

Code of Fair Testing Practices in Education—a valuable resource for comprehending the uses and abuses of assessment procedures written for the general public, especially test-takers and/or their parents or guardians.

cognitive career/vocational counseling—an approach that helps clients challenge their irrational vocational beliefs so that they can attain their career and personal goals.

Cognitive Information Processing (CIP)—perspective used by Sampson, Peterson, Lenz, and Reardon (1992) to describe the career development of individuals.

collectivism—"in-group norms and role relations provide both the motivating force that drives the individual and the compass from which the individual takes direction" (Ross & Nisbett, 1991, p. 181).

commitments—an individual's ability to act on one's values when it is neither convenient nor easy (Pipher, 1996).

competence assumption—a political view of human nature, as described by Lawrence W. Mead in *The New Politics of Poverty* (1992), shared by both conservative and liberal political thinkers when discussing poverty in America. The competence assumption takes for granted "that the individual is willing and able to advance his or her own economic interests. . . . Americans are in motion toward economic goals" (p. 19).

Conduct—when a person voluntarily chooses between alternative courses of action.

Confucianism—cultural value where patriarchal ideas are embraced and a formal relationship system emphasizes humility, politeness, and respect (Axelson, 1993, p. 438).

Confucian work ethic—teaches children that they are required to do well because they owe it to their parents (Butterfield, 1990).

congruence—the process of an environment fit to the person; different personality types requiring different model work environments.

connected voice—describes women's orientation with respect to occupational achievement and interpersonal relationships, due to being socialized into defining themselves through their connection with and responsiveness to others.

consequentiality—an act cannot be labeled occupationist unless it is potentially harmful or helpful to a person's interests, which is termed consequentiality. "The effects of occupationist acts may be either harmful or beneficial to an individual's interests, depending on the circumstances" (Carson, 1992, p. 492).

consistency—the degree of relatedness between personality types or between model work environments.

consolidation—a period of establishment in a career by advancement, status, and seniority (Zunker, 1994).

constructive developmental theory—an individual's meaning-making framework, for career transitions.

constructive developmentalism—an approach to career counseling where life is viewed as a learning process and, from experience, one constructs one's own reality and meaning. The approach promotes the development of self-awareness, meaning-making, and choices, helping people lead more "self-directed, decision-guided" lives.

constructivism—a theory of clinical practice in which individuals actively construct their personal realities and create their own representational models of the world (Meichenbaum & Fong, 1993).

constructivist epistemologies—the conceptualization of human beings as "active agents who, individually or collectively, co-constitute the meaning of their experiential world" (R. A. Neimeyer, 1993a, p. 222).

content bias—occurs when test items are more familiar to one racial or ethnic group than another. (The second author of this text's experience as a multicultural fairness reviewer of tests has shown that content bias also includes familiarity of objects and terms can based upon one's geographical region).

contexual interpretation—the understanding of people's behavior as embedded in the context of their lives (Savikas & Walsh, 1996, pg. 352). Meaning is invented with the goal of attaining that which is socially useful, relevant, and viable.

Conventional type—this development of a Conventional pattern of activities, competencies, and interests creates a person who is predisposed to exhibit the following behavior:

1. prefers conventional occupations or situations in which one can engage in preferred activities and avoid the activities demanded by artistic occupations or situations,
2. uses conventional competencies to solve problems at work and in other situations,
3. perceives self as conforming, orderly, and as having clerical and numerical ability, and
4. values business and economic achievement (Holland, 1992, p. 22).

These demands, opportunities, and Conventional people create an atmosphere that produces the following goals and outcomes:

1. It stimulates people to engage in conventional activities, such as recording and organizing data and records.
2. It fosters conventional activities and competencies.
3. It encourages people to see themselves as conforming, orderly, nonartistic, and as having clerical competencies; it encourages them to see the world in conventional, stereotyped, constricted, simple, dependent ways.
4. It rewards people for the display of conventional values: money, dependability, and conformity (p. 40).

The conventional person is apt to be:

Careful	Inflexible	Persistent
Conforming	Inhibited	Practical
Conscientious	Methodical	Prudish
Defensive	Obedient	Thrifty
Efficient	Orderly	Unimaginative
(p. 23)		

corporate anorexia—a term that describes the massive downsizing occurring in the workforce.

correspondence—when the individual and the environment are attuned and when work meets the needs of the individual and the individual meets the demands of the work environment. Correspondence is an everchanging process because both the needs of the individual and the demands of the job change. However, if the correspondence continues, job tenure is extended.

countertransference—when a boss or coworker reacts toward a person in a manner similar to a sig-

nificant person in the boss's or coworker's past or present life.

crystallization—a cognitive process period of formulating a general vocational goal through awareness of resources, contingencies, interests, values, and planning for the preferred occupation (Zunker, 1994).

cultural inversion—a process whereby certain behaviors, events, symbols, and meanings which involuntary minorities are apt to consider as inappropriate for themselves because these characterize White Americans.

culturally deprived—see **culturally disadvantaged.**

culturally disadvantaged—the term "culturally deprived" suggests an absence of culture, while "culturally disadvantaged" refers to a person who lacks the cultural background formed by the dominant social and political structure (Atkinson, Morten & Sue, 1993, chapter 1).

culturally learned expectations and values—these make behavior meaningful from a multicultural perspective and promote a tolerance for a varied and complex **worldview.**

cultural racism—societal "beliefs and customs that promote the assumption that the products of the dominant culture (e.g., language, traditions, appearance) are superior to other cultures" (J. Jones, 1972, cited in Atkinson, Morten & Sue, 1993, p. 11).

criterion-referenced test—describes the specific types of skills, tasks, or knowledge of an individual relative to a well-defined mastery criterion.

D

decided-decisive client—clients classified thus could be treated through support since this is not a diagnosable problem.

decided-undecided state—temporary indecision which accompanies many decision-making tasks.

decided-indecisive client—clients in this state are in self-conflict. They have formed a temporary decision, but are unable to make an actual choice. They are in conflict as they want to pursue one career, but have interest in a dissimilar career (adapted from Miller, 1993).

decision-making skills—understanding and mastering the decision-making process.

decisive-indecisive trait—a more permanent trait that is part of decision-making tasks.

deconstruction—"a postmodern method of analysis. Its goal is to undo all constructions. Deconstruction tears a text apart, reveals its contradictions and assumptions" (Rosenau, 1992, p. xi).

defense mechanisms—coping strategies to fend off unpleasant ideations and/or feelings.

developmental perspectives—presumes that how people see themselves changes over time as a consequence of age and life experience.

developmental tasks—a new accomplishment or responsibility to be faced at a certain point in an individual's life, the successful achievement of which leads to happiness and success.

dialogic community—where language is the primary vehicle for creating meaning in the workplace.

differential validity—the extent to which a test has different meanings for different groups of people, such as a test that may be a valid predictor of college success for White students but not Black students.

differentiation—the degree to which a person or an environment is well-defined.

discourse—"a system of statements, practices, and institutional structures that share common values" (Hare-Mustin, 1994, p. 19).

DISCOVER—a Computer-Assisted Career Guidance Systems released in a multimedia version in 1997, which is available in English and French, and is adapted for use in Canada and Australia, using occupational information relevant to those countries.

discriminability—occurs when people make judgments based on the relative position of a person's occupation within "an almost universally agreed upon" occupational "prestige hierarchy" (Krumboltz, 1991b, p. 310).

discrimination—"treatment or consideration of or making a distinction in favor of or against a person or thing based on the group, class, or category to which that person or thing belongs rather than on individual merit" (Random House Dictionary, 1979).

disparate impact—"discrimination caused by the consequences of a particular practice used by the employer" (Hagan & Hagan, 1995, p. 5).

disparate treatment—instances when an employee is subject to adverse treatment because of the employee's race, color, religion, sex, or national origin.

dispositionism—the belief "that individual differences or traits can be used to predict how people will behave in new situations" (Ross & Nisbett, 1991, p. 3).

distress—when there are too many stressors or when they continue for too long.

diversity—a broad term which considers gender, age, culture, ethnicity, disabilities, sexual orientation, etc.

dominance—when one option is better than another in at least one aspect and is at least as good as the other for each of the other relevant aspects (Gati, 1990).

downsizing—job losses incurred by higher-paid, white collar workers.

dual-career couple—a relationship in which both partners are employed; usually in different occupations.

dual-career families—a major factor altering the family for years to come; see also, **dual-career couple.**

dynamics of dominant-subordinant relationships—the development of a cultural identity that determines clinician and client attitudes toward (a) self, (b) others of the same group, (c) others of a different group, and (d) the White, dominant cultural group.

E

early recollections—one's childhood memories, usually those from before the age of eight, which coincide with the individual's pattern of lifestyle and the manner in which they are retained is purposeful and deliberate. Early recollections are an integral part of a lifestyle's maintenance.

educational attainment—the highest level of formal schooling one has obtained.

emic—a perspective which is culture-specific and examines behavior using criteria related to the internal characteristics of the culture, presumably from a position within that culture (Dana, 1993).

emotional resources—the ability to exercise self-control and stamina to weather negative situations and feelings and, most importantly, to move up from one class to the other.

empiricism—the belief that observation and experiment are the only valid means for adding to the knowledge base.

enterprising type—this development of an enterprising pattern of activities, competencies, and interests creates a person who is predisposed to exhibit the following behavior:

1. Prefers enterprising occupations or situations in which one can engage in preferred activities and avoid the activities demanded by investigative occupations and situations.
2. Uses enterprising competencies to solve problems at work and in other situations.
3. Perceives self as aggressive, popular, self-confident, sociable, possessing leadership and speaking abilities, and lacking scientific ability.
4. Values political and economic achievement (Holland, 1992, p. 22).

These demands, opportunities, and Enterprising people create a characteristic atmosphere that operates to produce the following goals and outcomes:

1. It stimulates people to engage in enterprising activities such as selling, or leading others.
2. It fosters enterprising competencies and achievements.
3. It encourages people to see themselves as aggressive, popular, self-confident, sociable, and as possessing leadership and speaking ability. It encourages people to see the world in terms of power, status, responsibility, and in stereotyped, constricted, dependent, and simple terms (p. 39).

The Enterprising person is apt to be:

Acquisitive	Energetic	Flirtatious
Adventurous	Exhibitionistic	Optimistic
Agreeable	Excitement	Self-confident
Ambitious	Seeking	Sociable
Domineering	Extroverted	Talkative (p. 21)

entrepreneurial skills—job skills needed to operate a full or part-time business out of the home as an alternative to the corporate world.

environmental conditions—refers to (a) the number and nature of job opportunities; (b) the number and nature of training opportunities; (c) social policies and procedures for selecting trainees and workers; (d) rate of return for various occupations; (e) labor laws and union rules; (f) physical events such as earthquakes, droughts, floods, and hurricanes; (g) availability and demand for natural resources; (h) technological developments; (i) changes in social organization; (j) family training, experiences, and resources; (k) educational systems; (l) neighborhood and community influences, and other social, cultural, political, and economic considerations.

environmental constructs—the physical nature of the workplace (e.g., architectural design, job accommodation).

epistemology—the origin, structure, and methods of knowing, and the standards of judging and validating knowledge about the world (Dervin, 1994; Peterson, 1970).

equal access to occupational opportunities—determined by external, structural factors.

equity theory—job satisfaction based on what is obtained, such as, justice, equity, personal fairness, versus what is desired, such as pay and working conditions.

ethics—represent an objective inquiry about behavior.

ethnic identity development—"one's sense of belonging to an ethnic group and the part of one's thinking, perceptions, feelings, and behavior that is due to ethnic group membership" (Rotheram & Phinney, 1987, p. 13).

ethnicity—an imprecise concept which relies on various criteria for definition, including race, language, and region (Petersen, 1980).

ethnocentrism—where one culture's values matter more than those of another culture (Atkinson et al., 1993).

etic—a perspective which emphasizes universal behaviors of human beings where many cultures are examined and compared, presumably from a position outside those cultures (Dana, 1993).

eustress—the exhilarating feeling of accomplishment which results from effectively coping with stress.

existential approach—existentialism is rooted in the philosophy that humans control their destiny. When applied to career counseling, the client's growth is based upon his or her chosen philosophy, which can be altered. Each person has a unique view of life through which he or she tries to understand the world through an interpretation of his or her experiences.

external locus of control—the sense that events are outside one's control.

extraversion (E)—in the extraverted attitude (E) of the **MBTI**, attention seems to flow out, or to be drawn out to the objects and people of the environment.... [The following are] characteristics associated with extraversion: awareness and reliance on the environment for stimulation and guidance; an action-oriented, sometimes impulsive way of meeting life; frankness; ease of communication; or sociability.

extreme postmodernism—"is revolutionary; it goes to the very core of what constitutes social science and radically dismisses it" (Rosenau, 1992, p. 4).

F

face validity—the extent to which items on a test appear to be meaningful and relevant. Face validity is actually not a form of validity, since it is not a basis for inference (Kaplan & Saccuzzo, 1997).

face visibility—judging workers on their actual amount of time present in the workplace, regardless of **productivity.**

familism—the inclusion of biological and nonbiological members into a family.

family first, then career—observations Richter, Morrison and Salinas (1991) make about ways to deal with the issue of dual careerism is which the couple must deal with the issues of (a) less affluence, (b) less money, (c) fewer options for having material things, (d) shorter or lessened career opportunities, (e) fewer guilt feelings for neglect of family-oriented values, (f) more marital satisfaction if the person is oriented to family values, and (g) one staying at home for a few years while the other works, then then trading off.

family-in-relation—a contextual understanding of the family used by **MCT**.

family systems—an analysis of roles, boundaries, values, traditions, and messages, within a family.

family systems approaches—an approach to clinical practice which focuses on the interactions between individuals within a family.

fantasy—stage of career development of childhood (before age 11) characterized by purely play orientation in the initial stage; near the end to this stage, play becomes work oriented.

feeling (F) —one of four basic mental functions or processes. Feeling (F) is the function by which one comes to decisions by weighing the relative values and merits of the issues. Feelings rely on an understanding of personal and groups values; thus, it is more subjective than thinking. . . . [P]ersons making judgments with the feeling function are more likely to be attuned to the values of others . . . [have] a concern with the human as opposed to the technical aspects of problems, a need for affiliation, a capacity for warmth, a desire for harmony, and a time orientation that includes preservation of the values of the past (Myers & McCaulley, 1985, p. 12).

first-order change—"any change in a system that does not produce a change in the structure of the system" (Lyddon, 1990, p. 122).

financial resources—having money and purchasing power.

flex-time—an opportunity for a worker to adjust the hours on the job to a schedule that is suitable for other concerns, such as family responsibilities.

floating family—a blurring of boundaries with traditional family units related by blood, common residence, and shared surnames (Gergen, 1991a), and resulting in a family which consists of relationships that can be in a more continuous state of flux than with one's family of origin. Floating family networks are based on affectional ties of choice rather than blood ties of chance, and often occur when traditional family members withdraw from the family's orbit through connections established by the technologies of social saturation.

folkways—"the normative structure of values, customs and meanings that exist in any culture" (Fischer, 1989).

formal register—language which is used (a) in work and school, (b) with a specific word choice, and (c) with complete sentences and standard syntax.

formative evaluation—program-evaluation activities that are conducted during the course of a program. Formative evaluation is somewhat more flexible in that adjustments and corrections can be made to evaluation procedures during their ongoing activities.

formed family—evolves for those persons who do not have access to a supportive biological family or for those who prefer a community of friends to the families into which they were born. The staying power of a formed family is contingent upon whether its members stay together despite disagreements, lend each other money when one member loses a job, or visit one another in a convalescent center after one has been paralyzed in a car crash (Pipher, 1996).

free agent—describes employees who have decided to manage their own careers.

fundamental attribution error—the failure to recognize the power of the situation.

G

Gelatt decision-making model—a type of decision-making model which provides: (a) a framework from which methods and techniques can be derived and used as guidelines in career-counseling programs; (b) a system to determine values as a significant part of the decision-making process; and (c) a concept of a series of decisions—immediate, intermediate, and future—pointing out that decision-making is a continuous process.

gender role analysis—assesses the potential coasts and benefits for women and men in terms of adopting traditional and nontraditional gender role behavior.

gender stratification—"the hierarchical distribution by gender of economic and social resources in a society" (Andersen, 1983, p. 77).

generational poverty—families who have lived in poverty for two or more generations.

genetic endowment—the innate aspects rather than those which are learned. These include: (a) physical appearance, (b) race, (c) sex, (d) physical appearance, (e) intelligence, (f) musical ability, (g) artistic ability, (h) muscular coordination, and (i) predisposition to certain physical illnesses.

genogram—a format for drawing a family tree that records information about family members and their relationships over at least three generations. Genograms display family information graphically in a way that provides a quick gestalt of complex family patterns and a rich source of hypotheses about how a clinical problem may be connected to the family context and the evolution of both problem and context over time (McGoldrick & Gerson, 1985, p. 1).

global competition—see **global economy.**

global economy—the increasing interdependence of trade and commerce that links economics across the globe.

grand narrative—a legacy of the Puritan work ethic, where one's work and career is central. The grand narrative of the twentieth century emphasizes new advances in human productive capacities founded upon reason and freedom.

group tests—tests given to more than one person at a time (Kaplan & Saccuzzo, 1997).

H

healthy paranoia—can characterize any individual or subgroup that has experienced extreme oppression.

hermeneutic activity—career counseling principal where the interpretation of the meaning of a client's story becomes primary.

heterosexism—the culturally conditioned bias that heterosexuality is intrinsically superior to homosexuality (Rochlin, 1985).

heterosexual privilege—the rights and freedoms taken for granted by many heterosexuals which include: (a) heterosexual partners to publicly display affection without fear of comment or attack by others, (b) inheritance rights, (c) access to a partner in a hospital, (d) the legal right to marry, and (e) the ability to adopt children.

hidden rules—see **knowledge of hidden rules.**

Hispanic—descriptive term used by the U.S. Bureau of the Census to refer to persons of at least partial Spanish ancestry or origin now living in the United States.

historical context—past events with enduring effects in the present.

Hmong—an ethnic group originally from the mountains of southwest China, where many remain. They migrated to Southeast Asia, in the northern parts of Laos, Vietnam, and Thailand, with small groups in Burma (Tapp, 1993).

homophobia—irrational dread and loathing of homosexuality and homosexual people.

hoteling—an alternative for management of office space. Space would be available for office meetings, team meetings and in-services, but at other times the individual would be operating primarily from his/her car or home.

House Rule (HR) 3734, the Personal Responsibility and Work Opportunity Reconciliation Act—so-called welfare reform actually refers to House Rule (HR) 3734, the Personal Responsibility and Work Opportunity Reconciliation Act, passed by both Houses of Congress in August 1996. HR 3734 replaced (1) AFDC—Aid to Families with Dependent Children which expired in October 1996, (2) JOBS—the Job Opportunities and Basic Skills training program, (3) Emergency Assistance programs, and (4) ended entitlements to cash assistance (Hard & Schoenmakers, 1997). TANF—Temporary Assistance for Needy Families was created in October 1996 and replaced the AFDC and JOBS programs. Block grants are provided to each state in the form of cash assistance and employment services for TANF.

human ability tests—an assessment of achievement, aptitude, and intelligence (Kaplan & Saccuzzo).

I

identification—relating to another person or idea by taking on aspects of the object to which one is relating.

identity—an estimate of the clarity and stability of a person's identity or a model work environment's identity.

Ikhwàn al-Safá—a group of five to ten Muslim reformers who are thought to have lived in the Basra region of what is now southern Iraq, who collectively called themselves Ikhwàn al-Safá to hide their individual identities for fear of reprisal by Islamic fundamentalists. They wrote the text, Rasa'il Ikhwàn al-Safá wa-Khulln al-Wafa (commonly translated as **Treatises of the Brothers of Purity**, also known as the TBP).

implementation—completing training for vocational preference and entering employment (Zunker, 1994).

index person—the individual who is the primary focus of a **genogram.**

individual psychology (IP)—conveys an awareness of the human being as indivisibly embedded in the social world. IP regards the person's movement in response to the challenges of the life tasks to be self-determined and purposeful in every expression of thought, feeling, and action. IP considers each individual's lifestyle as based on convictions and attitudes initially assumed in childhood and rehearsed and refined thereafter in an unself-conscious manner.

individual tests—can be given to only one person at a time by a test administrator; group tests can be given to more than one person at a time (Kaplan & Saccuzzo, 1997).

individualism—"an emphasis on personal goals, interests, and preferences. Social relationships are dictated by commonality of interests and aspirations and are therefore subject to change as those interests and aspirations shift over time" (Ross & Nisbett, 1991, p. 181).

industrialism—the rise of industries that manufactured products, particularly by the assembly line method.

inequality—see **inequity**.

inequity—unequal treatment in hiring, education, job pay and promotion; often occurs on the basis of gender or racial/ethnic groups.

inference—logical deductions made from evidence about something that one cannot observe directly.

information and planning—a competence dimension concerning specificity of information individuals have concerning future career decisions and past planning accomplished.

information competencies—includes acquiring and evaluating data, organizing and maintaining files, interpreting and communicating, and using computers to process information (U.S. Department of Labor, Special Commission on Achieving Necessary Skills, 1991).

infostructure—information-based infrastructure.

institutional racism—"social policies, laws, and regulations whose purpose it is to maintain the economic and social advantage of the racial/ethnic group in power" (J. Jones, 1972, cited in Atkinson, Morten & Sue, 1993, p. 11).

instrumental learning experiences—occur when the individual acts upon the environment in such a way as to produce desirable consequences. An instrumental learning experience has three components: antecedents, behavior, and consequences.

intelligence tests—tests measure the potential to (1) solve problems, (2) adapt to changing circumstances and (3) profit from experiences (Kaplan & Saccuzzo, 1997).

Interactive Life Planning (ILP)—a model of career planning based on a holistic view of adult life with career and work as part of a life plan, combining aspects of traditional career planning with a more philosophical approach and focusing on the person as a whole (Sunny Hansen, 1997).

interest inventories—usually result in a profile where clients' responses to questions about interests in activities, competencies, and occupations are matched with interests of persons already working in various occupations who self-report that they enjoy the work they do. Interest inventories do not tell clients what to do for a living.

internal structure bias—pertains to the relationship among items of a test, and the manner in which test-takers perceive the items.

interpersonal skills competencies—working on teams, teaching others, serving customers, leading, negotiating and working well with people from culturally diverse backgrounds (U.S. Department

of Labor, Special Commission on Achieving Necessary Skills, 1991).

introversion (I)—in the introverted attitude (I), energy is drawn from the environment, and consolidated within one's position. The main interests of the introvert are in the inner world of concepts and ideas. . . . [Introverts have the following] characteristics associated with introversion: interest in the clarity of concepts and ideas; reliance on enduring concepts more than on transitory external events; a thoughtful, contemplative detachment; and enjoyment of solitude and privacy (Myers & McCaulley, 1985, p. 13).

intuitive (N)—one of four basic mental functions or processes as measured by the **Myers-Briggs Type Indicator.** Intuition (N) refers to perception of possibilities, meanings, and relationships by way of insight. . . . Intuition permits perception beyond what is visible to the senses, including possible future events. Thus, persons oriented towards intuitive perception may become so intent on pursuing possibilities that they may overlook actualities. They may develop the characteristics than can follow from emphasis on intuition and become imaginative, theoretical, abstract, future-oriented, or creative.

Investigative type—this development of an Investigative pattern of activities, competencies, and interests creates a person who is predisposed to exhibit the following behavior:
1. Prefers occupations or situations in which one can engage in preferred activities and competencies and avoid activities demanded by enterprising occupations and situations.
2. Uses investigative competencies to solve problems at work and in other settings.
3. Perceives self as scholarly, intellectual, having mathematical and scientific ability, and lacking in leadership ability.
4. Values science. (Holland, 1992, p. 20)

These demands, opportunities, and Investigative people create a characteristic atmosphere that operates to produce the following outcomes:
1. It stimulates people to perform investigative activities.
2. It encourages scientific competencies and achievements.
3. It encourages people to see themselves as scholarly, as having mathematical and scientific ability, and as lacking leadership ability; it encourages them to see the world in complex, abstract, independent, and original ways.
4. It rewards people for the display of scientific values (p. 37).

The Investigative person is apt to be:

Analytical	Helpful	Responsible
Cooperative	Idealistic	Sociable
Patient	Empathetic	Tactful
Friendly	Kind	Understanding
Generous	Persuasive	Warm (p. 20)

invisible daddy track—means that, while men are not vocal about childcare concerns, the public is quite unaware of the strain placed on fathers (Hall, 1989).

involuntary minorities—immigrants to a country through enforced slavery, political expulsion from their homelands, or other economic or military developments beyond their control (Triandis, 1993) and are inclined to secondary cultural differences.

irrational beliefs—errors in thinking (e.g., dichotomous thinking, overgeneralization, personalization, magnification) which Albert Ellis's RET calls irrational beliefs and which Aaron T. Beck's cognitive therapy calls cognitive distortions.

J

jingoism—a pronounced chauvinism and nationalism marked by a belligerent foreign policy.

job—"a group of similar positions in a business, industry, or other place of employment" (Tolbert, 1980, p. 31).

JOBS (the Job Opportunities and Basic Skills training program)—see **House Rule (HR) 3734**, Personal Responsibility and Work Opportunity Reconciliation Act.

job satisfaction—the result of an appropriate match of personality traits, interests, and work environment.

job sharing—two people accomplishing one job by dividing the hours required by the job.

job shock—changes caused by downsizing, layoffs, and restructuring of corporations, forcing many well-paid, highly skilled, white-collar workers into unemployment (Dent, 1995).

job stress—anxiety caused by a mismatch of job, skills, interests and work environment, or a work overload.

judging (J)—in the judging attitude (J), a person is concerned with making decisions, seeking closure, planning operations, or organizing activities. For thinking-judging (TJ) types the decisions and plans are more likely to be based on logical analysis; for feeling-judging (FJ) types the decisions and plans are more likely to be based on human factors. But for all persons who characteristically live in the judging (J) attitude, perception tends to be shut off as soon as they have observed enough to make a decision. . . . Persons who prefer J often seem in their outer behavior to be organized, purposeful, and decisive. . . . It is important to make sure it is understood that judgment refers to decision-making, the exercise of judgment, and is a valuable and indispensable tool (Myers & McCaulley, 1985, p. 14).

K

Kluge—a distinct economy which consists of the concentration of public-sector bureaucracies, universities, and closely aligned private companies in government-related industries, and which exists virtually side by side with the networked economy.

knowledge of hidden rules—having an awareness of the unspoken understandings and cues that allow an individual to fit into a certain group—which is essential if one wishes to survive in a particular socioeconomic class.

L

labor force representation—refers to those who are eligible or actively seeking jobs.

learning experiences—"One's career preferences are a result of her or his prior learning experiences. An individual may have millions of prior learning experiences that will eventually influence his or her career decision" (Sharf, 1997, p. 328).

leisure—activities intended as a relaxation from work demands; leisure time is often stolen by habitual television viewing and "happy hour" activities.

Life-Career Rainbow—a model used by Super (1990) to describe the various roles one plays during his/her life.

life space—the major roles in an individual's life.

life span—the course of an individual's life.

lifestyle—a coherent, consistent and unitary perceptual adaptational set, which serves as a stable frame of reference for the individual, providing a method for both organizing and interpreting internal and external events (Watkins, 1984, p. 29).

life theme—Csikszentmihalyi and Beattie (1979) define life theme as "an affective and cognitive representation of existential problems which a person wishes to resolve. It becomes the basis for an individual's fundamental interpretation of reality and a way of coping with that reality" (p. 45).

localized knowledge—awareness about how the world of work is differentially manifested in various communities.

location of study—or **situated knowledge**, is "a point of view, a perspective of the knower in relation to what is known" (Richardson, 1993, p. 427).

logical positivism—a twentieth-century philosophical movement that contends that all genuine knowledge can be discovered through the use of the scientific method.

loss of face—humiliation of one who is already socialized to behave with humility; pertains to **Asian Americans.**

M

maintaining face—inhibited expression of undesirable emotions; pertains to Asian Americans.

male provider role—for many men the male provider roles means his sense of self-worth is derived from occupational status and income.

marginalization—a political practice that overtly and covertly prevents the full participation in life-enhancing opportunities of individuals from social categories that have been labeled as inferior or deviant.

MCT—see **multicultural counseling and therapy**.

mean—is the arithmetic average of a set of scores on a variable.

mechanistic models—aim to scientifically discover the processes which can describe the true mechanisms that explain a given phenomena (Flew, 1984).

median age—the age where half of a population are below and half are above a given age.

median income—the income level where half earn below and half earn above a given amount.

mental resources—having the abilities and skills (e.g., reading, writing, computing) to process information and use it to negotiate daily life—is an advantage that lends itself to self-sufficiency.

metacognitions—self-talk, self-awareness, and the monitoring of cognitions.

metatheory—a "theory of theories" (Sue, Ivey & Pedersen, 1996, p. 12).

Mirror of Human Life—one of the earliest comprehensive compilations of occupational descriptions, Speculum Vitae Humanae (Mirror of Human Life), published by Bishop Rodrigo Sánchez de Arévalo in 1468, the late Spanish medieval period which immediately preceded the joint reigns of King Fernando of Aragón (reigned 1479-1516) and Queen Isabel of Castile (reigned 1474-1504).

mission—according to the Random House Dictionary, is "an assigned or self-imposed duty or task." Synonyms are *calling* and *vocation*.

model minority—an inaccurate **stereotype** of Asian Americans.

moderate postmodernism—encourages substantive redefinition and innovation in the social and behavioral sciences (Rosenau, 1992).

modernism—see **logical positivism**.

morality—morality concerns itself with action that is purposeful and for the good of all. The goodness or badness of a behavior is the provenance of morality; choosing wisely and decently how one will be in the universe (Pipher, 1996) broadly defines morality.

multicultural counseling—a specialized aspect or subfield of clinical practice.

multicultural counseling and therapy (MCT)—is a **metatheory** that forms a means of understanding the numerous helping approaches developed by humankind by considering the totality and interrelationships of experiences (individual, group, and universal) and contexts, such as, individual, family, and cultural milieu (Sue, Ivey & Pedersen, 1996).

multicultural perspective—a philosophical orientation that encompasses the entire field of multicultural clinical practice beyond all previously used terms (e.g., minority group counseling, pluralistic counseling, cross-cultural counseling).

multiculturalism—(1) Pedersen's multicultural perspective in clinical practice that includes demographic, ethnographic, status, and affiliation variables; (2) Sue, Ivey and Pedersen's multicultural counseling and therapy metatheory.

multiculturation—the accumulation and incorporation of the belief and customs of one's own racial or ethnic group and the elements of several other groups.

multiple helping roles—the one-to-one encounter approach used by **MCT** aimed at remediation in the individual, larger social units, systems intervention, and prevention—developed by many culturally different groups and societies.

multiple role realism—may be defined as "the recognition that multiple role involvement is a complex and potentially stressful lifestyle, paired with awareness of the need for careful planning and consideration of the interface between work and family roles (Weitzman, 1994, p. 16).

Myers-Briggs Type Indicator (MBTI)—based on a theory of personality devised by Swiss psychologist and psychiatrist Carl Gustav Jung [1875–1961], and for career purposes, the instrument is used primarily with interests and aptitude assessments. The MBTI manual (Myers & McCaulley, 1985) lists work environments in which various types of people labor, suggesting that the MBTI can apply to career adjustment as well.

myth of rugged individualism—the legacy of the Backcountry people that pervades the work ethic in the United States today.

N

narcissism—self-absorption and self-preoccupation (Pipher, 1996).

narrative approaches—an approach to clinical practice which focuses on the stories clients tell about themselves and others in attempts to make sense out of the world around them (Penn, 1991; Sarbin, 1986).

narrative approaches to career counseling—an approach which focuses on the stories clients tell about themselves and others as a way of making meaning of the world, which can also help clients address the subjective experience of their careers (Savickas, 1992).

narrative viability—means the newly emergent story (**personal narrative**) has to cohere into the larger system of personally and socially constructed realities into which it is incorporated (Granvold, 1996).

National Career Development Association (NCDA)—sets standards and goals for career counseling.

National Career Development Guidelines—a handbook of information for anyone responsible for career development in any setting for any age group. The purpose of the handbook is "to strengthen and improve comprehensive, competency-based career counseling, guidance and education programs" (p. i).

National Certified Career Counselors—have passed NCOA exam on standards and goals for career counseling.

negotiation—an important "art" in the dual-career marriage.

networked—densely packed concentrations of entrepreneurs and companies in urbanized areas that generate virtually all the nation's globally competitive, high-wage industries.

normative sample—see **standardization sample.**

norms—summarize the performance of a group of individuals on which a test was standardized, and usually include the mean standard deviation for a reference group and information on how to translate a raw score into a percentile rank.

norm-referenced tests—evaluates each individual relative to a normative group (Kaplan & Saccuzzo, 1997) or standardization sample.

O

objective personality tests—see **structured personality tests.**

occupation—"a definable work activity that occurs in many different settings" (Tolbert, 1980, p. 31).

occupational development—see **career development.**

occupational knowledge—information about individual occupations and a schema for organizing occupations.

occupational segregation—an overrepresentation of specific population groups in some occupations while being underrepresented in others (Leong & Serafica, 1995).

occupationism—discrimination against individuals based solely on their occupation.

oppressed groups—groups of persons who are deprived of some human right or dignity where such persons are (or perceive that they are) powerless to do anything about it (Goldenberg, 1978).

oppression—see **oppressed groups.**

organization-in-relation—a contextual understanding of the organization used by **MCT.**

organizational transference—where a boss or coworker reminds an employee of an important family member (Weinberg & Mauksch, 1991).

orientation to vocational choice—an attitudinal dimension determining if the individual is concerned with the eventual vocational choice to be made.

outcome constructs—job satisfaction, work adjustment, job stress, discrimination, and prejudice.

P

paradigm—"a central overall way of regarding phenomena . . . [and] may dictate what kind of explanation will be found acceptable" (Flew, 1984, p. 261).

parental intentions—Young and Friesen (1992) describe ten categories of parental intentions:
(1) skill acquisition;
(2) acquisition of specific values and beliefs;
(3) protection from unwanted experience;
(4) increase independent thinking or action;
(5) decrease sex role stereotyping;
(6) moderation of parent–child relationships;
(7) facilitation of human relationships;
(8) enhancement of character development;
(9) development of personal responsibility; and
(10) achievement of parent's personal goals.
The parent's side of the parent–child interaction sequence is particularly appropriate to the study of parental influence in the career development of their children. It was the parent who interacted with the child or intervened on the child's behalf and whose action had intention.

parenting issues—observations Richter, Morrison, and Salinas (1991) make about ways to deal with the issue of dual careerism is which the couple must deal with the need to decide (a) how it will be done, (b) who is going to do it, (c) who is going to be responsible for discipline, and (d) what are the shared responsibilities—quality time with children, physical needs, security, recreation/ leisure time, allowing autonomy for children, delegation of household chores.

percentile ranks—the proportion of scores that fall below a particular score.

perceptive (P)—in the perceptive attitude (P) of the **MBTI,** a person is attuned to incoming information. For sensing-percepting (SP) types the information is more likely to be the immediate realities. For intuitive-perceptive (NP) types the information is more likely to be new possibilities. But for both SP and NP types the perceptive attitude is open, curious, and interested. Persons who characteristically live in the perceptive attitude seem in their outer behavior to be spontaneous, curious, and adaptable, open to new events and changes, and aiming to miss nothing.

Personal Employment Identity Model (PEIM)—a career/job decision model developed by Peregoy and Schliebner (1990) to assist practitioners in selecting appropriate interventions based on four types of vocational ego-identity problems unemployed persons exhibit.

personal qualities skills—individual responsibility, self-esteem, sociability, self-management and integrity (U.S. Department of Labor, Special Commission on Achieving Necessary Skills, 1991).

Person by Environment (PxE) Fit—trait-factor theory **personality tests**; measure overt and covert traits, temperaments, and dispositions (Kaplan & Saccuzzo, 1997).

person-centered approaches—in person-centered approaches to career counseling and vocational guidance, the practitioner does not assume responsibility from the client nor lead or direct the client to make a choice the practitioner may believe is best for the client. The client is the center of the process, and the determiner of the content of the process and its outcome.

phenomenological perspective—a clinical counseling perspective which "seeks to comprehend the meaning of clients' interests and abilities as part of a life pattern" (Savickas, 1992, p. 337).

phenotype—an individual's physical appearance, especially their complexion.

physical resources—being able-bodied and mobile—like mental resources—is another advantage that lends itself to self-sufficiency.

population of convenience—student samples used in research.

position—a "group of activities, tasks, or duties performed by one person" (Tolbert, 1980, p. 32).

positive uncertainty—A "whole-brained approach to planning your future" (p. vi). "Uncertainty describes the condition of today's river of life. The successful decision maker navigating the river needs to be understanding, accepting, even positive about that uncertainty" (Gelatt, 1991, p. 1).

postmodernism—the belief that there are many beliefs, multiple realities, and a profusion of worldviews.

poststructuralism—postmodernism's rejection of the tradition that the real world has underlying rules and hidden structure.

potential biases in career assessment instruments—can lead to the dissemination of misleading information to minority clients at best, or potentially damaging information at worst.

poverty rate—the number of persons living below an income level set by the government.

power—"the capacity to influence for one's own benefit the forces that affect one's life space and/ or as the capacity to produce desired effects on others" (Pinderhughes, 1995, p. 133).

predictive validity—the extent to which a test forecasts scores on the criterion at some future time.

pre-incident indicators—part of systematized intuition that de Becker's company uses to advise workplaces about managing employees who are likely to act out violently.

prejudice—"the emotional aspect of racism" (Axelson, 1993, p. 168).

privileged complacency—a lack or awareness and respect for **oppression, discrimination, racism,** sexism, **classism,** an ageism.

productivity—judging workers on the excellence of their job performance.

projective personality tests—a personality test which provide ambiguous test stimuli where response requirements are less clear. "Rather than being asked to choose among alternative responses, as in structured personality tests, the individual is asked to provide a spontaneous response" (Kaplan & Saccuzzo, pp. 10–11).

protected careers—occupations where other members of the African-American community tend to congregate, such as, education, social work, and the social sciences—where less racial discrimination is perceived to occur (Murry & Mosidi, 1993).

Protestant Reformation—religious movement begun by Martin Luther in Germany in 1517 that inadvertently resulted in a split from the Catholic Church and gave rise to the Protestant churches.

Protestant work ethic—teaches that work should be the main, if not defining, focus of one's life, and presumes that everyone has equal access to occupational opportunities.

provincial—an economy which self-consciously styles itself as a moral alternative for networked businesses and is driven by the deployment of less competitive business and offers America a nineteenth-century answer for twenty-first-century competition.

Psycho-Clarity Process—the goal of self-understanding is reached through engaging clients in the Psycho-Clarity Process (Powers & Griffith, 1987, cited in Powers & Griffith, 1993). The purpose of the Psycho-Clarity Process is to assist clients in understanding (a) what they are doing; (b) what their purpose is in doing these things; (c) what costs are involved in doing as they do; and (d) what else is open to them to do in whatever situations they find themselves.

Puritan work ethic—the belief that work is virtuous, that poverty is the result of one's lack of moral centeredness, and that persons lacking virtue require charity (e.g. welfare) (Whitmore, 1971).

Q

quality time—the attempt to improve the time spent with one's family to compensate for work's encroachment into the familial domain. It presumes that the time workers devote to family relationships can be separated from ordinary time, with the hopes that scheduling intense periods of family togetherness will compensate for the lost time devoted to work, in the belief that parent–child relationships will suffer no loss of quality.

R

race norming—"adjusting the scores or using different cut-offs based on the race of the person who takes the test" (Hagan & Hagan, 1995, p. 6).

race-holding—"any self-description that serves to justify or camouflage a person's fears, weaknesses, and inadequacies" (Steele, 1990, p. 26).

racial and ethnic role models—provide influential motivational information crucial for the career decision-making of racial and ethnic minorities.

racism—"the belief that some races are *inherently* superior to others" (Axelson, 1993, p. 168, italics in original).

Rational-Emotive Therapy (RET)—RET posits an A-B-C model where emotional, behavioral, and physiological disturbances are most likely the results of beliefs about the activating event.

realistic—stage of career development of middle adolescence (seventeen to young adulthood) marked by an integration of capacities and inter-

ests: further development of values; specification of occupational choice; crystallization of occupational patterns; as proposed by theorists Ginzberg, Ginsburg, Axelrad, and Herma (1951).

Realistic type—

1. Prefers realistic occupations or situations— electrician—in which one can engage in preferred activities and avoid activities demanded by social occupations or situations.
2. Uses realistic competencies to solve problems at work and in other settings.
3. Perceives self as having mechanical and athletic ability and lacking ability in human relations.
4. Values concrete things or tangible personal characteristics—money, power, and status (Holland, 1992, p. 19).

The demands, opportunities and people of the realistic type, create a characteristic atmosphere that operates in the following way:

1. It stimulates people to perform realistic activities such as using machines and tools.
2. It fosters technical competencies and achievements.
3. It encourages people to see themselves as having mechanical ability and lacking ability in human relations; it encourages them to see the world in simple, tangible, and traditional terms.
4. It rewards people for the display of conventional values and goods, money, power, and possessions (pp. 36–37).

The Realistic person is apt to be:

Asocial	Materialistic	Self-effacing
Conforming	Natural	Inflexible
Frank	Normal	Thrifty
Genuine	Persistent	Uninsightful
Hard-headed	Practical	Uninvolved
(p. 19)		

reality of rugged collectivism—the collective, community-based values that contributed to the settling of the frontier.

reasonable accommodation—any modification or adjustment to a job or the work environment that will enable a qualified applicant or employee with a disability to participate in the application process or perform essential job functions. Reasonable accommodation also includes adjustments to assume that a qualified individual with a disability has rights and privileges in employment equal to those of employees without disabilities (U.S. Equal Employment Opportunity Commission, 1992).

recursive process—a cycle in which individuals move backward and forward through the process in response to their emerging decision needs and the availability of information resources (Sampson et al., 1992).

reliability—"the accuracy, dependability, consistency, or repeatability of test results. In more technical terms, reliability refers to the degree to which test scores are free of measurement error" (Kaplan & Saccuzzo, 1997, p. 12).

responsible stewardship—an opportunity and a challenge to make use of the God-given resources, both in oneself and in the environment (see **work**).

Roe's eight occupational groups—

1. Service: occupations concerned with catering to and serving the personal tastes, needs, and welfare of other people. Occupations include social worker, guidance/career counselor, domestic and protective services (e.g., house manager, executive housekeeper, waiter, waitress.)

2. Business Contact: occupations concerned with sale of commodities, investments, real estate, and services with persuasion as a basic task.

3. Organization: occupations concerned with organization and efficient functioning of commercial enterprises and governmental agencies, such as administrative and management positions.

4. Technology: occupations concerned with production, maintenance, and transportation of commodities and utilities, including engineering, crafts, machine and tool operators, transportation, and communication.

5. Outdoor: occupations concerned with cultivation, preservation and gathering of items which grow in the earth's environment for food and use in other products. These include farmers, fishermen, foresters, harvesters of all kinds.

6. Science: occupations concerned with scientific theory and its application. These include natural scientists, social scientists, physical scientists, physicians, psychologists, chemists, and physicists.

7. General Culture: occupations concerned with preservation and transmission of cultural heritage, with interest in human activities rather than individuals. These include educators, journalists, law specialists, religious functionaries, linguists, and people who function in the humanities.

8. Arts and Entertainment: occupations concerned with the use of special skills in the creative arts and entertainment. These include painters, writers, musicians, dancers, poets, entertainers, etc. (Roe & Lunneborg, 1990, adapted from Roe & Klos, 1972).

Rokeach Values Survey—an assessment tool used to evaluate values.

role flexibility—the inconstant in who is the head of the family or parental figure.

role models—knowing and having access to adults who are nurturing and appropriate in their behavior towards children, and who do not demonstrate habitually self-destructive behavior—are particularly helpful in teaching one how to emotionally live one's life.

S

salience—the importance of a role in a person's life.

secondary cultural differences—"arose after two populations came into contact or after members of a given population began to participate in an institution controlled by the dominant group, such as the schools controlled by the dominant group" (Ogbu, 1992, p. 8).

second-order change—"a type of change whose occurrence alters the fundamental structure of a system" (Lyddon, 1990, p. 122); change that occurs "when the generations can shift their status relations and reconnect in a new way [so that] the family can move on developmentally" (Carter & McGoldrick, 1989, p. 14).

selection bias—occurs when a test's predictive validity is differential across groups.

self-concept—self-definition.

Self-Directed Search—an assessment tool used to evaluate interests.

self-efficacy—perceived judgments of one's capacity to successfully perform a given task or behavior (Bandura, 1977, 1984, 1986).

self-esteem—the value one places upon oneself.

self-knowledge—knowledge of one's own values, interests, and skills.

self-in-relation—a contextual understanding of the individual used by **MCT**.

self-regard—When one behaves according to one's own value system, he or she shows character through self-regard. Self-regard implies hard-won self-knowledge (Pipher, 1996).

self-serving bias—whereby laypeople invoke situational causes to justify their own conduct, especially in circumstances viewed negatively by others, with a minimization of traits and dispositional causes.

sensing (S)—one of four basic mental functions or processes of the **MBTI**. Sensing (S) refers to perceptions observable by way of the senses. Sensing establishes what exists. Because the senses can bring to awareness only what is occurring in the present moment, persons oriented towards sensing perception tend to focus on the immediate experience and often develop characteristics associated with this awareness such as enjoying the present moment, realism, acute powers of observation, memory for details, and practicality.

separate voice—describes men's orientation, with respect to occupational achievement and interpersonal relationships, with emphasis on differentiation from others.

sequential elimination approach—Gati's decision-making model which used the idea that each occupational alternative has a series of aspects and that at each stage of the selection process, the importance of the aspect becomes the criterion for keeping or eliminating the alternative. It is considered to be a rational manner to approach career decision-making, especially when many alternatives are present.

sexual orientation—sexual behavior including: sexual attractions, emotional preferences, social preferences, sexual fantasies, lifestyle choices, and sense of identity (Klein, Sepekoff & Wolfe, 1985).

share career and family together—observations Richter, Morrison, and Salinas (1991) make about ways to deal with the issue of dual careerism in which the couple must deal with the issues of (a) both sharing the problem of task overload and emotional overload, and (b) both sharing in the best of both worlds.

SIGI—a Computer-Assisted Career Guidance Systems designed to assist college students to clarify values, identify occupational options, and develop rational **career decision-making (CDM) skills**.

SIGI PLUS—an expansion of **SIGI** developed to include adults and organization needs.

situated knowledge—see **localized knowledge**.

situationalism—the belief that the ability to predict how people will react in certain situations is actually quite limited (Ross & Nisbett, 1991).

social constructionism—"maintains that individuals' sense of what is real—including their sense of the nature of their problems, competencies, and possible solutions—is constructed in interaction with others as they go through life" (De Jong & Berg, 1998, p. 226); a clinical practice which views meanings and understandings of the world as developed through social interaction (Gergen, 1985).

social saturation—an accelerating social connectedness marked by the technological advances of the late twentieth century—computers, electronic mail, satellites, faxes—that is leading to a state of multiphrenia, where the individual is split into a multiplicity of self-investments. (Kenneth J. Gergen, 1991b).

Social type—this development of a Social pattern of activities, competencies, and interests creates a person who is predisposed to exhibit the following behavior:

1. Prefers social occupations and situations in which one can engage in preferred activities and competencies and avoid the activities demanded by realistic occupations and situations.
2. Uses social competencies to solve problems at work and in other settings.
3. Perceives self as liking to help others, understanding others, having teaching ability, and lacking mechanical and scientific ability.
4. Values social and ethical activities and problems (Holland, 1992, p. 21).

These demands, opportunities, and Social people create a characteristic atmosphere that operates to produce the following goals and outcomes:

1. It stimulates people to engage in social activities.
2. It fosters social competencies.
3. It encourages people to see themselves as liking to help others, understanding of others, cooperative, and sociable; it encourages them to see the world in flexible ways.
4. It rewards people for the display of social values (p. 38).

The Social person is apt to be:

Ascendant	Helpful	Responsible
Cooperative	Idealistic	Sociable
Patient	Empathetic	Tactful
Friendly	Kind	Understanding
Generous	Persuasive	Warm (p. 21)

situational poverty—families who have lived in poverty for a shorter time due to circumstances such as death, illness, or divorce.

specification—a period of moving from tentative vocational choices towards a specific vocational preference (Zunker, 1994).

spiritual resources—believing in a higher power that provides guidance and understanding for life's purpose, which helps see oneself not as hopeless but as capable, worthy, and valuable.

stabilization—a period of confirming a preferred career by actual work experience and use of talents to demonstrate career choice as an appropriate one (Zunker, 1994).

standardized administration—see **standardization sample**.

standard deviation—the square root of the average deviation around the mean, and is used as a measure of variability in a distribution of scores. Standard deviation squared equals the variance.

standard error of measurement—tells how much a score varies on the average, from a true score. The standard deviation of an observed score and the reliability of the test are used to compute estimates of the standard error of measurement.

standardization sample—a comparison group consisting of individuals who have been administered a test under standard conditions; the instructions, format, and general procedures are usually outlined in the test manual for the standardized administration of a test (Kaplan & Saccuzzo, 1997). Also known as a normative sample.

Standards for Educational and Psychological Testing—a discussion of the ethical issues involved in educational and psychological testing by the joint committee of the American Education Research Association, the American Psychological Association, and the National Council on Measurement in Education.

strain-based conflict—see **work-family conflict.**

structured personality tests—personality tests based on self-report statements where the test-taker answers "true" or "false" or "yes" or "no."

stress experience—a process that occurs when a person is confronted by a demand that is perceived to exceed the emotional or physical resources available to effectively respond to it (Zacarro & Riley, 1987).

sublimation—substituting hostile, aggressive, or sexual impulses into a more socially accepted form.

summative evaluation—program evaluation activities that are conducted at the end of a program.

support systems—having friends and family who have valuable knowledge to share and who will back up a person in times of need.

systems competencies—understanding social, organizational and technological systems, monitoring and correcting performance, and designing or improving systems (U.S. Department of Labor, Special Commission on Achieving Necessary Skills, 1991).

T

TANF (Temporary Assistance for Needy Families)—TANF aims to: (1) provide in-home care for children of needy families; (2) end government dependency by promoting job preparation, work, and marriage; (3) prevent out of wedlock pregnancies; and (4) encourage two-parent families (Hard & Schoenmakers, 1997).

Taoism—cultural value where ancestor worship provides guidance and advice for present living. Traditionally, Taoists are attached to burial sites (location) of ancestors where they can go to pray, meditate, and pay respect before the graves of their ancestors (Axelson, 1993, p. 438).

task approach skills—understanding how an individual approaches a task is one of the most important parts of career decision-making. Task approach skills include: (a) goals setting, (b) value clarification, (c) generating alternatives, and (d) obtaining career information. Interactions among genetic endowment, environmental conditions, and learning experiences lead to skills in doing a variety of tasks (Sharf, 1997).

technology competencies—selecting equipment and tools, applying technology to specific tasks, and maintaining and troubleshooting technologies (United States Department of Labor, Special Commission on Achieving Necessary Skills, 1991).

telecommuting—a way of doing business using laptops, fax machines, cellular phones, networked computers, e-mail, and voicemail which satisfies a goal of spending more time with customers, and using commute time more efficiently.

tentative—the stage of adolescent career development (ages 11 to 17) marked by gradual recognition of work requirements; recognition of interests, abilities, work reward, values, and time perspectives; as proposed by theorists Ginzberg, Ginsburg, Axelrad, and Herma (1951).

test battery—a collection of tests whose scores are used together to appraise an individual.

test bias—see **content bias**, **internal structure bias**, and **selection bias.**

tests—measurement instruments that quantify behavior.

Theory of Work Adjustment (TWA)—the theory is that work adjustment is a "continuous and dynamic process by which a worker seeks to achieve and maintain a correspondence with a work environment" (Dawis & Lofquist, 1984, p. 237).

The Quick Job Hunting Map (Richard Bolles)—an assessment tool used to evaluate skills.

The SDS-Computerized Version—a computer program adaptation of Holland's (1985) paper-and-pencil assessment, the Self-Directed Search.

The Survey of Career Development (SCD)—a computerized system that can be used with **DISCOVER**. Recently, this program has been used to measure the effectiveness of career planning and computerized guidance systems.

thinking skills—thinking creatively, making decisions, solving problems, imagining, and knowing how to learn and reasoning (U.S. Department of Labor, Special Commission on Achieving Necessary Skills, 1991).

time-based conflict—see **work-family conflict.**

time ways—"attitudes toward the use of time, customary methods of time keeping, and the conventional rhythms of life" (Fischer, 1989, p. 9).

traits—learned interests, special aptitudes, and scholastic aptitudes.

trait-factor theory—the matching approach to vocational psychology using assessment to match the individual to training programs or occupations.

transference—a client reacting towards a boss or coworker in a manner similar to a significant person in the client's past or present.

Treatises of the Brothers of Purity—the text, Rasa'il Ikhwàn al-Safá wa-Khulln al-Wafa (also known as the TBP), written around 955 A.D. by what is believed to be a group of five to ten Muslim reformers who lived in the Basra region of what is now southern Iraq. The initial goal of the authors of the TSB was to compile all the known sciences into one work, regardless of the cultural origins of such knowledge.

two-by-four process—a decision-making process offered by Gelatt (1991) which includes two attitudes and four factors. The attitudes are: (a) accept the past, present, and future as uncertain; and (b) be positive about uncertainty. The four factors to consider are: (a) what you want; (b) what you know; (c) what you believe; and (d) what you do (Gelatt, 1991, p. 6).

Type A behavior—Type A behavior consists of five components. First, it is above all a continuous struggle, an unremitting attempt to accomplish or achieve more and more things or participate in more and more events in less and less time, frequently in the face of opposition—real or imagined—from other persons. Second, the Type A personality is dominated by covert insecurity of status, or hyperaggressiveness, or both. Third, struggle eventually fosters a sense of time urgency. Fourth, as the struggle continues, the hyperaggressiveness (and also perhaps the status insecurity) usually shows itself in the easily aroused anger termed free-floating hostility. Fifth and finally, if the struggle becomes severe enough and persists long enough, it may lead to a tendency toward self-destruction. Type B behavior refers to an absence of these five components.

Type B behavior—see **Type A behavior.**

U

unconscious motivation—the mechanism that determined human behavior as posited by Freud. Unconscious motivation presumably occurs out of one's awareness but is revealed clinically through free association and in daily life through behaviors such as slips of the tongue and the jokes one finds funny.

undecided-decisive client—clients in this state merely need more information and would most benefit from assessment and/or career counseling.

undecided-indecisive client—clients in this state are experiencing choice anxiety. These clients suffer from anxiety, low self-concept, immaturity and other negative personality traits that impair career counseling. Personal and career counseling are recommended.

undue hardship—an "action requiring significant difficulty or expense" when considered in light of a number of factors...[including]...the size, resources, nature, and structure of the employer's operation. Undue hardship is determined on a case-by-case basis.

unjustifiability—occurs when "a property of occupationism is related to the degree of knowledge an individual has of the quality of work performed by another" (Carson, 1992, p. 492).

unspoken cues—see **knowledge of hidden cues.**

V

validity—"the meaning and usefulness of test results ... [and] the degree to which a certain inference or interpretation based on a test is appropriate" (Kaplan & Saccuzzo, 1997, p. 12).

value-indicator—denotes a value in the process of "becoming."

values—(a) worth in terms of usefulness (a principle), (b) that which is of importance to the possessor (a standard), and (c) utility or merit (a quality). As a verb, value means to regard highly, to esteem, or to prize.

Values-based model—a career/job decision process developed by Duane Brown (1996) for dealing with people in transition, whether the change was planned or unplanned.

values clarification activities—help clients prioritize what is important for them, usually based on the seven standards for constructing a value (Raths, Harmin & Simon, 1966).

variance—see **standard deviation.**

vocational development—see **career development.**

vocational irrational beliefs—see **irrational beliefs.**

vocational psychology—a social and behavioral science that attempts to explain, predict, and control how people choose their initial occupations and pursue their ongoing careers.

voluntary minorities—immigrants who go to a country voluntarily to improve their economic situation (Traindis, 1993) and are inclined to primary cultural differences.

W

wavering—entails movement towards meaning and a life-shaping decision that can alter the course of a person's life.

weekend warriors—individuals (more often men than women) who engage in athletic activities for which they are not in shape are risking physical injury.

White people skills—knowledge of how to interact with Whites—and the ability to distinguish which Whites are willing to be open.

will—an individual's ability to act on one's values (Pipher, 1996).

within-group differences—differences that occur within one racial or ethnic group; intercultural comparisons.

Women of Color—racial and ethnic minority adult females.

work—"purposeful mental, physical, or combined mental-physical activity that produces something of economic value . . . [and] may produce a service to others as well as a material product" (Tolbert, 1980, p. 32).

work adjustment—see **Theory of Work Adjustment.**

workaholism—a cluster of behaviors which may include: (a) an addiction to work, (b) an escape from the unpleasantries of life, (c) competitiveness caused by a craving for constant stimulation and an overabundance of energy, (d) the result of compensating for a self-image damaged in childhood, and (e) behavior learned from parents and other role models.

work ethic—the principles of conduct that govern a person's work-related behaviors.

workers' productive use of resources competencies—allocating time, money, materials, space, and staff (U.S. Department of Labor, Special Commission on Achieving Necessary Skills, 1991).

work-family conflict—
(1) time-based conflict—time can only be spent on one role which neglects the other roles;
(2) strain-based conflict—stress from one role effects all areas of performance; and
(3) behavior-based conflict—behavioral styles are not compatible throughout all roles (Greenhaus & Beutell, 1985).

workforce—a person is said to be in the workforce when that person is either employed or unemployed but has sought a **position** within the past six months (Asante & Mattson, 1992).

work ways—"work ethics and work experiences; attitudes toward work and the nature of work" (Fischer, 1989, p. 9).

worldview—"the frame of reference through which one experiences life. It is the foundation for values, beliefs, attitudes, [and] relations" (Fouad & Bingham, 1995, p. 335).

Z

zone of applicability—Pipher's (1996) term for the limits of time, place, occupation, gender, and income that constrict any clinical approach.

References

Chapter 1

Ajgaonkar, S. M. T. (Ed.). (n.d.). *Mahatma: A golden treasury of wisdom—thoughts and glimpses of life*. Mumbai [formerly Bombay], INDIA: India Printing Works.

Arbona, C. (1995). Theory and research on racial and ethnic minorities: Hispanic Americans. In F. T. L. Leong (Ed.), *Career development and vocational behavior of racial and ethnic minorities* (pp. 37–66). Mahwah, NJ: Lawrence Erlbaum Associates, Inc.

Armendariz, Y. (1997, April 11). Today women's pay catches up to men's. *El Paso Times*, p. C1.

Asante, M. K., and Mattson, M. T. (1992). *Historical and cultural atlas of African Americans*. New York: Macmillan Publishing.

Asian population doubles, Census Bureau reports. (1991, March 11). *San Antonio Express-News*, p. 2A.

Associated Press. (1996a, November 23). China replaces Japan as U.S. trade challenge. *El Paso Times*, p. 8E.

Associated Press. (1996b, November 23). Chinese imports flood U.S. stores. *El Paso Herald-Post*, p. A15.

Associated Press. (1996c, September 1). Teaching force grays while enrollment grows. *El Paso Times*, p. 1A.

Associated Press. (1996d, March 7). There's no signs of slowing merger mania: Corporate bosses predict more buyouts in U.S. and abroad. *El Paso Times*, p. 5D.

Associated Press. (1996e). University tuition rates skyrocketing. *El Paso Herald-Post*, p. A2.

Associated Press. (1997a, February 21). China could soon top world's economy. *El Paso Times*, p. 11A.

Associated Press. (1997b, February 22). Hawkers cash in on Deng's demise. *El Paso Herald-Post*, p. A3.

Axelson, J. A. (1993). *Counseling and development in a multicultural society* (2nd edition). Pacific Grove, CA: Brooks/Cole Publishing.

Ayles, E. (1993, January–February). Breaking away. *World Watch*, 10.

Baruth, L. G., and Manning, M. L. (1991). *Multicultural counseling and psychotherapy: A lifespan perspective*. New York: Macmillan.

Barnett, R. C., and Rivers, C. (1996). *She works, he works: How two-income families are happier, healthier, and better off*. HarperSanFrancisco.

Bellah, R. N., Madsen, R., Sullivan, W. M., Swidler, A., and Tipton, S. M. (1992). *The good society*. New York: Vintage.

Bennett, A. (1990). *The death of the organizational man*. New York: William Morrow and Company, Inc.

Bennett, C. E., and Martin, B. (1995). The Asian and Pacific Islander population. In U.S. Bureau of the Census, Current Population Reports, Series P23–189, *Population Profile of the United States: 1995* (pp. 48–49). Washington, D.C.: U.S. Government Printing Office.

Berg, I. K., and De Jong, P. (1996). Solution-building conversations: Co-constructing a sense of competence with clients. *Families in Society: The Journal of Contemporary Human Sciences, 77* (6), 376–391.

Blossfeld, H.-P., and Shavit, Y. (1993). Persisting barriers: Changes in educational opportunities in thirteen countries. In Y. Shavit and H.-P. Blossfeld (Eds.), *Persistent inequality: Changing educational attainment in thirteen countries* (pp. 1–23). Boulder, CO: Westview Press.

Boroughs, D. L., Guttman, M., Mallory, M., McMurray, S., and Fischer, D. (1996, January 22). Winter of discontent: With wages frozen, American workers find themselves out in the cold. *U.S. News & World Report,* pp. 47–52, 54.

Bradford, Z. B., Jr. (1996, March 8, 1996). Downsizing: The trashing of America's soul; Military suffers, too. *The New York Times,* p. 30A.

Bragg, R. (1996a, March 5). More than money, they miss the pride a good job brought. *The New York Times,* p. A17–A18.

Bragg, R. (1996b, March 5). Big holes where the dignity used to be. *The New York Times,* pp. A1, A16, A18.

Bridges, W. (1994). *Job shift: How to prosper in a workplace without jobs.* Reading, MA: Addison-Wesley.

Brown, L., Flaven, C., and Postel, S. (1992, May–June). A planet in jeopardy. *The Futurist,* 10.

Carter, S. G. (1996, March 14). Should downsizing lead to a new system? Blacks and insecurity. *The New York Times,* p. 22A.

Dawis, R. V. (1992). The individual differences tradition in counseling psychology. *Journal of Counseling Psychology, 39* (1), 7–19.

De Jong, P., and Berg, I. K. (1998). *Interviewing for solutions.* Pacific Grove, CA: Brooks/Cole Publishing.

del Pinal, J. (1995). The Hispanic population. In U.S. Bureau of the Census, Current Population Reports, Series P23–189, *Population profile of the United States: 1995* (pp. 46–47). Washington, D.C.: U.S. Government Printing Office.

Dent, H. (1995). *Job shock.* New York: St. Martin's Press.

Dervin, B. (1994). Information-Democracy. An examination of underlying assumptions. *Journal of the American Society for Information Science, 45* (6), 369–85.

Deutschman, A. (1990, August 27). What 25 year olds want. *Fortune,* 42–48.

Downsizing and its discontents. (1996, March 10). *The Sunday New York Times,* Section 3, p. 14.

Drummond, R., and Ryan, C. (1995). *Career counseling: A developmental approach.* Englewood Cliffs, NJ: Merrill.

Feller, R. (1996). Redefining "career" during the work revolution. In R. Feller and G. Walz (Eds.), *Career transitions in turbulent times: Exploring work, learning, and careers* (pp. 143–161). Greensboro, NC: ERIC Counseling and Student Services Clearinghouse.

Frank, R., and Cook, P. (1995). *Winner take all society: How more and more Americans compete for ever fewer and bigger prizes, encouraging economic waste, income inequality, and an impoverished cultural life.* New York: Martin Kessler/Free Press.

Freire, P. (1993). *Pedagogy of the oppressed.* (Rev. ed.) (M. B. Ramos, Trans.) New York: Continuum. (Original work published 1970)

Gaskell, J., and Willinsky, J. (Eds.). (1995). *Gender in/forms curriculum: From enrichment to transformation.* New York: Columbia University Teachers College Press.

Gilligan, C., and Noel, N. (1995, April). *Cartography of a lost time: Women, girls, and relationships.* Workshop sponsored by the Austin Women's Psychotherapy Project, Austin, TX.

Goldenberg, I. I. (1978). *Oppression and social intervention.* Chicago: Nelson-Hall.

González, R. C. (1997). Postmodern supervision: A multicultural perspective. In D. B. Pope-Davis and H. L. K. Coleman (Eds.), *Multicultural counseling competencies: Assessment, education and training, and supervision* (pp. 350–386). Thousand Oaks, CA: Sage Publications.

González, R. C. (1998). A technically eclectic blend of paradigms and epistemologies for multicultural clinical relevance. In C. Franklin and P. S. Nurius (Eds.), *Constructivism in practice: Methods and challenges* (pp. 349–735). Milwaukee, WI: Families International, Inc.

Greenwald, J. (1997, January 20). Where the jobs are. *Time,* 54–59, 61.

Hall, D. T., and Associates. (1997). *The career is dead—long live the career.* San Francisco: Jossey-Bass.

Helms, J. E., and Richardson, T. Q. (1997). How "multiculturalism" obscures race and culture as differential aspects of counseling competency. In D. B. Pope-Davis and H. L. K. Coleman (Eds.), *Multicultural counseling competencies: Assessment, education and training, and supervision* (pp. 60–79). Thousand Oaks, CA: SAGE Publications.

Hernandez, R. (1998, August 21). Poverty opens computer gap. *El Paso Times,* p. 11A.

Herr, E. L., and Cramer, S. H. (1996). *Career guidance and counseling throughout the lifespan* (5th edition). New York: Harper Collins Publishers.

Hirschhorn, L. (1988). *The workplace within: Psychodynamics of organizational life.* Cambridge, MA: MIT Press.

Hispanic population nears 30 million. (1998, August 7). *El Paso Times,* p. 6A.

Hollinger, R. (1994). *Postmodernism and the social sciences: A thematic approach.* Thousand Oaks, CA: SAGE Publications.

Holmes, S. A. (1996, June 20). Income disparity between poorest and richest rises. *The New York Times,* pp. A1, A18.

Johnson, K. (1996, March 7). In the class of '70, wounded winners. *The New York Times,* pp. A1, A20–A22.

Kadlec, D., and Baumohl, B. (1997, April 28). How CEO pay got away. *Time,* 59–60.

Kleinfield, N. R. (1996, March 4). The downsizing of America: In the workplace musical chairs; the company as family, no more. *The New York Times,* pp. A1, A12–A14.

Koss-Chioino, J. D., and Vargas, L. A. (1992). Through the cultural looking glass: A model for understanding culturally responsive psychotherapies. In L. A. Vargas and J. D. Koss-Chioino (Eds.), *Working with culture: Psychotherapeutic interventions with ethnic minority children and adolescents* (pp. 1–22). San Francisco: Jossey-Bass.

Kozol, J. (1991). *Savage inequalities: Children in America's schools.* HarperPerennial.

Kramer, M. (1997, January 20). Job training has to be reworked. *Time,* 62.

Krannich, R. (1989). *Careering and recareering for the 1990s.* Manassas, VA: Impact Publications.

Leong, F. T. L., and Gim-Chung, R. H. (1995). Career assessment and intervention with Asian Americans. In F. T. L. Leong (Ed.), *Career development and vocational behavior of racial and ethnic minorities* (pp. 193–226). Mahwah, NJ: Lawrence Erlbaum Associates.

Leong, F. T. L., and Serafica, F. C. (1995). Career development of Asian Americans: A research area in need of a good theory. In F. T. L. Leong (Ed.), *Career development and vocational behavior of racial and ethnic minorities* (pp. 67–102). Mahwah, NJ: Lawrence Erlbaum Associates.

Loesch, L. C. (1995). Preparation for helping professionals working with diverse populations. In N. A. Vance, S. B. DeVaney, and J. Wittmer (Eds.), *Experiencing and counseling multicultural and diverse populations* (3rd edition, pp. 339–61). Bristol, PA: Accelerated Development.

Madrick, J. (1996). *The end of affluence: The causes and consequences of America's economic dilemma.* New York: Random House.

Mendoza, R. H., and Martínez, J. L. (1981). The measurement of acculturation. In A. Barón, Jr. (Ed.), *Explorations in Chicano psychology* (pp. 71–82). New York: Praeger.

Mercer, M. (1992 December/1993 January). On "savage inequalities": A conversation with Jonathan Kozol. *Educational Leadership,* 4–9.

Michelozzi, B. (1996). *Coming alive from 9 to 5* (5th edition). Mountain View, CA: Mayfield Publishing.

Morrison, P. (1990, March–April). Applied demography. *Futurist,* 9–15.

Newman, K. (1988). *Falling from grace: The experience of downward mobility in the American middle class.* New York: Free Press.

New York Times News Service. (1996, December 29). Study says minority progress in classroom shows reversal. *San Antonio Express-News,* p. 16A.

New York Times News Service. (1997, January 27). College moves further from reach of poor. *El Paso Herald-Post,* p. A1.

Olmedo, E. L. (1979). Acculturation: A psychometric perspective. *American Psychologist, 34,* 1061–1070.

Orenstein, P. (1994). *School girls: Young women, self-esteem, and the confidence gap.* New York: Anchor Books.

Osipow, S. H., and Fitzgerald, L. F. (1996). *Theories of career development* (4th edition). Boston: Allyn and Bacon.

O'Toole, P. (1993, November). Redefining success. *Working Woman,* 49–55, 96–97.

Payne, R. K. (1995). *A framework for understanding and working with students and adults from poverty.* Baytown, TX: RFT Publishing.

Pedersen, P. (1990). The multicultural perspective as a fourth force in counseling. *Journal of Mental Health Counseling, 12,* (1), 93–95.

Perryman, M. R. (1996, March 21). Number of working moms expected to rise. *El Paso Herald-Post,* p. C5.

Peterson, J. A. (1970). *Counseling and values: A philosophical examination.* Scranton, PA: International Textbook Company.

Pipher, M. (1994). *Reviving Ophelia: Saving the selves of adolescent girls.* New York: G. P. Putnam's Sons.

Pipher, M. (1996). *The shelter of each other: Rebuilding our families.* New York: Ballantine Books.

Poole, G. A. (1996, March 7). Revolution of computers in schools has two faces: Students in private schools have advantages over kids in public schools when it comes to technology. *El Paso-Herald Post,* pp. C5, C6.

Prospect Centre. (1991). *Growing an innovative workforce.* Kingston upon Thames: Prospect Centre.

Reingold, J. (1997, April 21). Executive pay. *Business Week,* 58, 60, 62, 64, 66.

Richardson, M. S. (1993). Work in people's lives: A location for counseling psychologists. *Journal of Counseling Psychology, 40,* 425–33.

Rifkin, J. (1987). The clocks that make us run. *East-West Journal,* 44.

Rimer, S. (1996, March 6). A hometown feels less like home. *New York Times,* pp. A1ff.

Roberts, S. V., Friedman, D., Sieder, J. J., Schwartz, D. A., and Sapers, J. (1996, January 22). Workers take it on the chin. *U.S. News & World Report,* 44–46.

Roberts, S. V., Thornton, J., Gest, T., Cooper, M., Bennefield, R. M., Hetter, K., Seter, J., Minerbrook, S., and Tharp, M. (1995, February 13). Affirmative action on the edge. *U.S. News & World Report,* 32ff.

Rochlin, M. (1985). Sexual orientation of the therapist and therapeutic effectiveness with gay clients. In J. C. Gonsiorek (Ed.), *A guide to psychotherapy with gay and lesbian clients* (pp. 21–29). New York: Harrington Park Press.

Rodriguez, M. A. (1994). Preparing an effective occupational information brochure for ethnic minorities. *The Career Development Quarterly, 43,* 178–84.

Rosenau, P. M. (1992). *Post-modernism and the social sciences: Insights, inroads, and intrusions.* Princeton, NJ: Princeton University Press.

Ross, L., and Nisbett, R. E. (1991). *The person and the situation: Perspectives of social psychology.* New York: McGraw-Hill.

Rotheram, M. J., and Phinney, J. S. (1987). Introduction: Definitions and perspectives in the study of children's ethnic socialization. In J. S. Phinney and M. J. Rotheram (Eds.), *Children's ethnic socialization: Pluralism and development* (pp. 10–31). Newbury Park, CA: Sage Publications.

Sadker, M., and Sadker, D. (1995). *Failing at fairness: How our schools cheat girls.* New York: Touchstone.

Sanger, D. E., and Lohr, S. (1996, March 9). A search for answers to avoid the layoffs. *The New York Times,* Section 1, pp. 1ff.

Savickas, M. L. (1994). Vocational psychology in the postmodern era: Comment on Richardson (1993). *Journal of Counseling Psychology, 41,* 105–7.

Savickas, M. L. (1995). Current theoretical issues in vocational psychology: Convergence, divergence, and schism. In W. B. Walsh and S. H. Osipow (Eds.), *Handbook of vocational psychology* (2nd edition, pp. 1–34). Mahwah, NJ: Lawrence Erlbaum Associates.

Schwartzbeck, C. (1997, January 20). Foreign ways: Cultural family differences require counseling changes. *El Paso Herald-Post,* p. D2.

Scott, D. (1995, November 18). Retailers move early to foil yule grinch. *Christian Science Monitor,* p. 31.

Solomon, C. (1991, August). 24-hour Employees. *Personnel Journal,* 56–63.

Stein, H. (1989, June). Problems and nonproblems in American economy. *AEI Economist,* 56–70.

Sue, D. (1992). The challenge of multiculturalism: The road less traveled. *American Counselor, 1,* 6ff.

Sue, D. W., Ivey, A. E., and Pedersen, P. B. (1996). *A theory of multicultural counseling and therapy.* Pacific Grove, CA: Brooks/Cole Publishing.

Sue, D. W., and Sue, D. (1990). *Counseling the culturally different: Theory and practice* (2nd edition). New York: John Wiley & Sons.

Super, D. E., and Hall, D. T. (1978). Career development: Exploitation and planning. *Annual Review of Psychology, 29,* 333–72.

Suzuki, H. (1989, November/December). Asian Americans as the "Model Minority": Outdoing Whites? Or media hype? *Change,* 13–19.

Tagliabue, J. (1996, June 20). In Europe, a wave of layoffs stuns white-collar workers. *The New York Times,* pp. A1ff.

Tapp, N. (1993). Hmong. In P. Hockings (Ed.), *The encyclopedia of world cultures* (Vol. 5, pp. 92–95). New York: G. K. Hall and Company.

Taylor, J. M., Gilligan, C., and Sullivan, A. M. (1995). *Between voice and silence: Women and girls, race and relationships.* Cambridge, MA: Harvard University Press.

Tinsley, H. E. A. (1994). Construct your reality and show us its benefits: Comment on Richardson (1993). *Journal of Counseling Psychology, 41,* 108–11.

Toffler, A. (1970). *Future shock.* New York: Bantam Books.

Tolbert, E. L. (1980). *Counseling for career development* (2nd edition). Boston: Houghton Mifflin.

Tolchin, S. (1996). *The angry American: How voter rage is changing the nation.* Boulder, CO: Westview Press.

Uchitelle, L., and Kleinfield, N. R. (1996, March 3). On the battlefield of business, millions of casualties. *The New York Times,* Section 1, pp. 1ff.

United Way Strategic Institute. (1990, July–August). Nine forces reshaping America. *Futurist,* 9–16.

Valdez, D. W. (1995, December 22). Companies don't save bad news for new year. *El Paso Times,* pp. 8E, 5E.

Vidueira, J. R. (1996, August). Loss of language? What does the lack of Spanish fluency among young Hispanic Americans mean for their future—and the future of America? *Vista, 11* (12), 16.

Walberg, M. (1996, March 4). Workplace security can start at home. *El Paso Herald-Post,* p. B4.

Wilde, A. D. (1996, January 14). Earning it; Who's really essential? In a blizzard, it's a blur. *The New York Times,* Section 3, p. 10.

Yates, R. (1995, October 29). Workers' anger grows as layoffs continue to rise. *San Antonio Express News,* p. 6J.

Young, C. (1989). Psychodynamics of coping and survival of the African-American female in a changing world. *Journal of Black Studies, 20,* 208–23.

Zunker, V. (1994). *Career counseling: Applied concepts of life planning* (4th edition). Pacific Grove, CA: Brooks/Cole Publishing.

Chapter 2

Abramson, H. J. (1980). Assimilation and pluralism. In S. Thernstrom (Ed.), *The Harvard encyclopedia of American ethnic groups* (pp. 150–60). Cambridge, MA: Belknap Press.

Andersen, M. L. (1983). *Thinking about women: Sociological and feminist perspectives.* New York: Macmillan Publishing.

Anderson, H. D., and Goolishian, H. A. (1991, January). *New directions in systemic therapy: A language systems approach.* Symposium presented at the Texas Association of Marriage and Family Therapy, Dallas, TX.

Andreski, S. (1983). Introduction. In S. Andreski (Ed.), *Max Weber on capitalism, bureaucracy, and religion: A selection of texts* (Trans. by S. Andreski) (pp. 1–12). London: Allen & Unwin.

Ashley, M. (1980). *The house of Stuart.* London: J. M. Dent & Sons, Ltd.

Associated Press. (1997, February 19). Clinton hears from critics of welfare reform. *El Paso Times,* p. 5A.

Atkinson, D. R., and Hackett, G. (Eds.) (1993). *Counseling diverse populations.* Madison, WI: Brown & Benchmark.

Atkinson, D. R., Morten, G., and Sue, D. W. (1993). *Counseling American minorities: A cross-cultural perspective* (4th edition). Madison, WI: Brown & Benchmark.

Baxandall, R., and Gordon, L. (1995). *America's working women: A documentary history, 1600 to the present* (revised and updated). New York: W. W. Norton & Company.

Becvar, D. S., and Becvar, R. (1996). *Family therapy: A systemic integration* (3rd edition). Boston: Allyn & Bacon.

Berger, P. (1990). *The human shape of work.* New York: Macmillan Publishing.

Bolles, R. (1981). *Three boxes of life.* Berkeley, CA: Ten Speed Press.

Borow, H. (1973). Shifting postures toward work: A tracing. *American Vocational Journal, 48,* 28–29, 108.

Bowman, S. L. (1995). Career intervention strategies and assessment issues for African Americans. In F. T. L. Leong (Ed.), *Career development and vocational behavior of racial and ethnic minorities* (pp. 137–164). Mahwah, NJ: Lawrence Erlbaum Associates.

Bragg, R. (1996a, March 5). More than money, they miss the pride a good job brought. *The New York Times,* p. A17–A18.

Bragg, R. (1996b, March 5). Big holes where the dignity used to be. *The New York Times,* pp. A1, A16, A18.

Buenning, M., and Tollefson, N. (1987). The cultural gap hypothesis as an explanation for the achievement patterns of Mexican-American students. *Psychology in the Schools, 24,* 264–272.

Burr, V. (1995). *An introduction to social constructionism.* London, England: Routledge.

Butterfield, F. (1990, January 21). Why they excel. *Parade,* 4–6.

Carter, R. T. (1991). Cultural values: A review of empirical research and implications for counseling. *Journal of Counseling and Development, 70,* 164–173.

Corey, G. (1996). *Theory and practice of counseling and psychotherapy* (5th edition). Pacific Grove, CA: Brooks/Cole Publishing.

Corey, G., and Corey, M. S. (1997). *I never knew I had a choice* (6th edition). Pacific Grove, CA: Brooks/Cole Publishing.

Corey, G., Corey, M. S., and Callanan, P. (1993). *Issues and ethics in the helping professions* (4th edition). Pacific Grove, CA: Brooks/Cole Publishing.

Cose, E. (1996, September 9). No work, no workfare. *Newsweek,* 46–47.

Dawis, R. (1984). Job satisfaction: Workers aspirations, attitudes, and behavior. In N. C. Gysbers (Ed.), *Designing careers, counseling to enhance education, work, and leisure* (pp. 65–90). San Francisco: Jossey-Bass.

Dawis, R. V. (1992). The individual differences tradition in counseling psychology. *Journal of Counseling Psychology, 39* (1), 7–19.

Dervin, B. (1994). Information-Democracy. An examination of underlying assumptions. *Journal of the American Society for Information Science, 45* (6), 369–385.

Doherty, W. J. (1991, September/October). Family therapy goes postmodern. *Family Therapy Networker, 15* (5), 37–42.

Dosick, W. (1995). *Golden rules: The ten ethical values parents need to teach their children.* HarperSanFrancisco.

Efran, J. S., and Fauber, R. L. (1995). Radical constructivism: Questions and answers. In R. A. Neimeyer and M. J. Mahoney (Eds.), *Constructivism in psychotherapy* (pp. 275–304). Washington, D.C.: American Psychological Association.

Farmafarian, R. (1989, November). "Worksteading: The new lifestyle frontier." *Psychology Today,* 37–44.

Feixas, G. (1990). Approaching the individual, approaching the system: A constructivist model for integrative psychotherapy. *Journal of Family Psychology, 4* (1), 4–35.

Festinger, L. (1957). *A theory of cognitive dissonance.* Stanford, CA: Stanford University Press.

Festinger, L., Schacter, S., and Back, K. (1950). The spatial ecology of group formation. In L. Festinger, S. Schacter, and K. Back (Eds.), *Social pressure in informal groups* (pp. 33–59). New York: Harper.

Fischer, D. H. (1989). *Albion's seed: Four British folkways in America.* New York: Oxford University Press.

Fitzgerald, L. F., and Nutt, R. (1985). The Division 17 principle concerning the counseling/psychotherapy of women: Rationale and implementation. *The Counseling Psychologist, 14,* 180–216.

Flew, A. (1984). *A dictionary of philosophy* (2nd edition, revised). New York: St. Martin's Press.

Foucault, M. (1970). *The order of things.* New York: Random House.

Fouad, N. A., and Bingham, R. P. (1995). Career counseling with racial and ethnic minorities. In W. B. Walsh and S. H. Osipow (Eds.), *Handbook of vocational psychology: Theory, research, and practice* (2nd edition) (pp. 331–365). Mahwah, NJ: Lawrence Erlbaum Associates.

Frisby, C. L. (1993). One giant step backward: Myths of Black cultural learning styles. *School Psychology Review, 22* (3), 535–557.

Frymier, J., Cunningham, L., Duckett, W., Gansneder, B., Link, F., Rimmer, J., and Scholz, J. (1995, September). *Values on which we agree.* Bloomington, IN: Phi Delta Kappa International.

Frymier, J., Cunningham, L., Duckett, W., Gansneder, B., Link, F., Rimmer, J., and Scholz, J. (1996, September). Values and the schools: Sixty years ago and now. *Research Bulletin; Phi Delta Kappa; Center for Evaluation, Development, and Research, 17.* 1–4.

Fuentes, C. (1992). *The buried mirror: Reflections on Spain and the New World.* Boston: Houghton Mifflin.

Gergen K. J. (1985). The social constructionist movement in modern psychology. *American Psychologist, 40,* 266–275.

Gergen, K. J. (1994). *Realities and relationships: Soundings in social construction.* Cambridge, MA: Harvard University Press.

Gilbert, D. T., and Jones, E. E. (1986). Perceiver-induced constraints: Interpretation of self-generated reality. *Journal of Personality and Social Psychology, 50,* 269–280.

Goren, A. A. (1980). Jews. In S. Thernstrom (Ed.), *The Harvard encyclopedia of American ethnic groups* (pp. 571–598). Cambridge, MA: Belknap Press.

Graziano, L. (1988, Winter). I'm optimal, you're optimal: An economist's way of knowledge. *Propaganda Review, 36.*

Hackman, J., and Oldham, G. (1981). Work redesigned: People and their work. In J. O, Toole, J. Sheiber, and L. Wood (Eds.), *Working changes and choices* (pp. 173–182). Sacramento, CA: The Regents of the University of California.

Hare-Mustin, R. T. (1994). Discourses in the mirrored room: A postmodern analysis of therapy. *Family Process, 33,* 19–35.

Herz, F. M., and Rosen, E. J. (1982). Jewish families. In M. McGoldrick, J. K. Pearce, and J. Giordano (Eds.), *Ethnicity and family therapy* (pp. 364–392). New York: The Guilford Press.

Herzberg, F. (1966). *Work and nature of man.* New York: The World Publishing.

Herzberg, F., Mausner, B., and Snyderman, B. (1959). *The motivation to work.* New York: John Wiley & Sons.

Hochschild, A. R. (1997). *The time bind: When work becomes home and home becomes work.* New York: Henry Holt and Company.

Hsia, J., and Hirano-Nakanishi, M. (1989, November/December). The demographics of diversity: Asian Americans and higher education. *Change,* 20–27.

Ibrahim, F. A., (1991). Contribution of a cultural worldview to generic counseling and development. *Journal of Counseling and Development, 20,* 13–19.

Jones, E. E. (1979). The rocky road from acts to dispositions. *American Psychologist, 34,* 107–117.

Kadlec, D., and Baumohl, B. (1997, April 28). How CEO pay got away. *Time,* 59–60.

Kirschenbaum, H. (1977). *Advanced value clarification.* La Jolla, CA: University Associates.

Koh, H. H. (1994, Fall). Bitter fruit of the Asian immigration cases. *Constitution,* 68–77.

Lessnoff, M. H. (1994). *The spirit of capitalism and the Protestant ethic: An enquiry into the Weber thesis.* Brookfield, VT: Edward Elgar Publishing.

Licht, W. (1988, February). How the workplace has changed in 75 years. *The Monthly Labor Review,* 19–24.

Lipset, S. (1990, Winter). The work ethic: Then and now. *Public Interest,* 61–69.

Lofquist, L., and Dawis, R. (1969). *Adjustment to work: A psychological view of man's problems in a work-oriented society.* New York: Appleton-Century-Crofts.

Luethy, H. (1970). Once again: Calvinism and capitalism. In D. Wrong (Ed.), *Makers of modern social science: Max Weber* (pp. 123–134). Englewood Cliffs, NJ: Prentice Hall.

Lyddon, W. J. (1995). Forms and facets of constructivist psychology. In R. A. Neimeyer and M. J. Mahoney (Eds.), *Constructivism in psychotherapy* (pp. 69–92). Washington, D.C.: American Psychological Association.

Macoby, M., and Terzi, K. (1981). What happened to the work ethic? In J. O'Toole, J. Scheiber, and L. Wood (Eds.), *Working changes and choices* (pp.162–171). Sacramento, CA: The Regents of the University of California.

Maylunas, A., and Mironenko, S. (1997). *A lifelong passion: Nicholas and Alexandra, their own story* (D. Galy, Trans.). New York: Doubleday.

McAuliffe, G. J. (1993). Constructive development and career transition: Implications for counseling. *Journal of Counseling and Development, 72,* 23–28.

McGeeney, P. (1987). *The limitations of contemporary work in providing meaning.* (Unpublished manuscript).

McKenna, E. P. (1997). *When work doesn't work anymore: Women, work, and identity.* New York: Delacorte Press.

Meichenbaum, D. and Fong, G. T. (1993). How individuals control their own minds: A constructive narrative approach. In D. W. Wegner and J. W. Pennebaker (Eds.), *Handbook of mental control* (pp. 473–490). Englewood Cliffs, NJ: Prentice Hall.

Michelozzi, B. (1996). *Coming alive from nine to five: The career search handbook* (5th edition). Mountain View, CA: Mayfield Publishing.

Miller, S. M. (1971). Introduction. In S. M. Miller (Ed.), *Max Weber* (pp. 1–17). New York: Thomas Y. Crowell.

Morrow, L. (1981, May 11). *Time,* 94.

Neimeyer, R. A. (1993). An appraisal of constructivist psychotherapies. *Journal of Consulting and Clinical Psychology, 61,* 221–234.

Neimeyer, R. A. (1995a). Client-generated narratives in psychotherapy. In R. A. Neimeyer and M. J. Mahoney (Eds.), *Constructivism in psychotherapy* (pp. 231–246). Washington, D.C.: American Psychological Association.

Nisbett, R. E., and Ross, L. (1980). *Human inference: Strategies and shortcomings of social judgment.* Engelwood Cliffs, NJ: Prentice Hall.

Osipow, S. H., and Fitzgerald, L. F. (1996). *Theories of career development* (4th edition). Boston: Allyn and Bacon.

O'Toole, J. (Ed.). (1973). *Work in America.* Cambridge, MA: MIT Press.

O'Toole, P. (1993, November). Redefining success. *Working Woman,* 49–50, 52–53, 96–97.

Packer, J. I. (1990). *A quest for godliness: The Puritan vision of the Christian life.* Downers Grove, IL: Crossway.

Penn, P. (1991). Letters to ourselves. *Family Therapy Networker, 15* (5), 43–45.

Peterson, J. A. (1970). *Counseling and values: A philosophical examination.* Scranton, PA: International Textbook Company.

Pipher, M. (1997, August 14). *Homes without walls.* Luncheon presentation sponsored by Loretto Academy, El Paso, TX.

Pritchard, R. (1969). Equity theory: A review and critique. *Organizational Behavior and Human Performance, 4,* 176–211.

Raths, L. E., Harmin, M., and Simon, S. B. (1966). *Values and teaching: Working with values in the classroom.* Columbus, OH: Charles E. Merrill Publishing.

Reich, R. (1997, June 13–15). Being a dad: Rewarding labor. *USA Weekend,* 10–11.

Richardson, T. Q. (1993). Black cultural learning styles: Is it really a myth? *School Psychology, 22* (3), 562–567.

Rokeach, M. (1973). *The nature of human values.* New York: Free Press.

Rosenburg, M. (1957). *Occupations and values.* Glencoe, IL: Free Press.

Ross, L., and Nisbett, R. E. (1991). *The person and the situation: Perspectives of social psychology.* New York: McGraw Hill Publishing.

Ryan, W. (1971). *Blaming the victim.* New York: Random House.

Saracho, O. N. (1989). Cultural differences in the cognitive style of Mexican-American students. In B. J. Robinson Shade (Ed.), *Culture, style, and the educative process* (pp. 129–136). Springfield, IL: Charles C. Thomas.

Sarbin, T. R. (Ed.). (1986). *Narrative psychology: The storied nature of human conduct.* New York: Praeger.

Savickas, M. L. (1993). Career counseling in the postmodern era. *Journal of Cognitive Psychotherapy: An International Quarterly, 7* (3), 205–215.

Savickas, M. L. (1995a). Constructivist counseling for career indecision. *The Career Development Quarterly, 43,* 363–373.

Savickas, M. L. (1995b). Current theoretical issues in vocational psychology: Convergence, divergence, and schism. In W. B. Walsh and S. H. Osipow (Eds.), *Handbook of vocational psychology* (2nd edition) (pp. 1–34). Mahwah, N.J.: Lawrence Erlbaum Associates.

Schor, J. (1991). *The overworked American: The unexpected decline of leisure.* New York: Basic Books.

Sears, S. (1982). A definition of career guidance terms. A National Vocational Guidance Association perspective. *The Vocational Guidance Quarterly, 31,* 137–143.

Segall, M., Dansen, V., Berry, J., and Poortinga, V. (1990). *Human behavior in a global perspective: An introduction to cross-cultural psychology.* New York: Pergamon Press.

Severy, M. (1983, October). The world of Luther. *National Geographic,* 418–463.

Simon, S. B., Howe, L. W., and Kirschenbaum, H. (1995). *Values clarification.* New York: Warner Books, Inc.

Smith, L. B. (1971). *This realm of England: 1399–1688* (2nd edition). Lexington, MA: D. C. Heath and Company.

Spindler, G. (Ed.). (1955). *Education and culture.* Stanford, CA: Stanford University Press.

Steers, R., and Porter, L. (1975). *Motivation and work behavior.* New York: McGraw-Hill.

Stone, E., and Taylor, P. (1991, November–December). The overworked American. *New Age Journal,* 34–43, 101–104.

Strong, R. (1992). *Royal gardens.* New York: Pocket Books.

Super, D. (1976). *Career education and the meaning of work.* Monographs on Career Education. Washington, D.C.: The Office of Career Education, U.S. Office of Education.

Sverko, B., and Vizek-Vidovic, V. (1995). Studies of the meaning of work: Approaches, models, and some findings. In D. E. Super and B. Sverko (Eds.), *Life roles, values, and careers: International findings of the work importance study* (pp. 3–21). San Francisco: Jossey-Bass.

Tawney, R. H. (1958). Forward. In M. Weber (1958). *The Protestant ethic and the spirit of capitalism* (T. Parsons, Trans.), pp. 1–11. New York: Charles Scribner's Sons.

Terkel, S. (1975). *Working.* New York: Avon Books.

Texas Education Agency. (1996). *Building good citizens for Texas. Character education resource guide.* Austin, TX: Author.

Van Hoose, W. H., and Paradise, L. V. (1979). *Ethics in counseling and psychotherapy.* Cranston, RI: The Carroll Press.

Vecchio, R. (1980). The function and meaning of work and the job. Morse and Weiss (1955) revisited. *Academy of Management Journal, 23,* 361–67.

Weber, M. (1976). *The agrarian society of ancient civilizations* (R. I. Frank, Trans.) (pp. 37–67). London: New Left Books. Reprinted in S. Andreski (Ed.) (1983). *Max Weber on capitalism, bureaucracy, and religion* (pp. 30–58). London: Allen & Unwin. (Original work published in 1891)

Weber, M. (1958). *The Protestant ethic and the spirit of capitalism* (T. Parsons, Trans.). New York: Charles Scribner's Sons. (Original work published in 1904-5)

Whitmore, H. (1971). Horrible conspiracies (R. Graham, Director). In R. Graham (Producer), *Elizabeth R.* London: British Broadcasting Corporation.

Will, G. (1997, February 20). Enjoyable film showed Jefferson's good, bad sides. *El Paso Times*, p. 6A.

Williams, G. (1989, September). Tomorrow in America. *American Legion Magazine*, 21ff.

Wilson, W. J. (1996). *When work disappears: The world of the new urban poor.* New York: Alfred A. Knopf.

Wrong, D. (1970). Introduction: Max Weber. In D. Wrong (Ed.), *Makers of modern social science: Max Weber* (pp. 1–76). Englewood Cliffs, NJ: Prentice Hall.

Yankelovich, D. (1979). Work values and the new breed. In C. Kerr and J. Rosow (Eds.), *Work in America: The decade ahead* (pp. 3–26). New York: Van Nostrand Reinhold.

Yankelovich, D. (1982). *New rules: Searching for self-fulfillment in an upside down world.* New York: Bantam Books.

Zinam, O. (1989, January). Quality of life, quality of the individual, technology, and economic development. *American Journal of Economics and Sociology*, 55–68.

Zucchino, D. (1997). *Myth of the welfare queen.* New York: Scribner.

Zytowski, D. (1994). A Super contribution to vocational theory: Work values. *The Career Development Quarterly, 43,* 25–31.

Chapter 3

American Association of School Counselors. *Get a life: Your personal planning profile.* Alexandria, VA: Author.

American College Testing (1988). *ACT assessment program: Technical manual.* Iowa City, IA: Author.

American Education Research Association, American Psychological Association and National Council on Measurement in Education. (1985). *Standards for educational and psychological testing.* Washington, D.C.: American Psychological Association.

Associated Press. (1996a, December 27). Jackson reconsiders Ebonics plan. *El Paso Herald-Post*, p. A7.

Associated Press. (1996b, December 25). Recognizing Black English troubles U.S. education chief. *El Paso Times*, p. 9A.

'Black English' is stumbling block for black children. (1996, December 27). *El Paso Herald-Post*, p. A4.

Bloch, D. (1992). The application of group interviews to the planning and evaluation of career development programs. *The Career Development Quarterly, 40,* 340–350.

Blustein, D. (1992). Toward the reinvigoration of the vocational realm of counseling psychology. *The Counseling Psychologist, 20,* 4, 712–23.

Brown, D., Brooks, L. and Associates. (1991). *Career choice and development.* San Francisco: Jossey-Bass.

Butcher, J., Dahlstrom, W., et al. (1989). *Manual for the restandardized MMPI/MMPI 2: An administrative and interpretive guide.* Minneapolis, MN: University of Minnesota Press.

Campbell, D., Strong, E. K., and Hansen, J–I. C. (1985). *Strong Interest Inventory.* Palo Alto, CA: Consulting Psychologists Press.

Cattell, R. (1949). *Sixteen Personality Factor Questionnaire: Manual for forms A and B.* Champaign, IL: Institute for Personality and Ability Testing.

Cervantes, R. C., and Acosta, F. X. (1992). Psychological testing for Hispanic Americans. *Applied & Preventive Psychology, 1,* 209–19.

Clark, G. M., Kolstoe, O. P. (1995). *Career development and transition education for adolescents with disabilities* (2nd edition). Boston: Allyn and Bacon.

Code of Fair Testing Practices in Education. (1988). Washington, D.C.: Joint Committee on Testing Practices.

Conger, D., Hiebert, B., and Hong-Farrell, E. (1993). *Career and employment counseling in Canada.* Ottawa, Ontario, Canada: Canadian Labor Force Development Board.

Crites, J. (1981). *Career counseling: Models, methods, and materials.* New York: McGraw-Hill.

Curnow, T. C. (1989). Vocational development of persons with disability. *The Career Development Quarterly, 37,* 269–278.

Dana, R. H. (1993). *Multicultural assessment perspectives for professional psychology.* Boston: Allyn and Bacon.

Educational Testing Service. (1992). *ETS Test collection catalogue* (Vol. 6). Phoenix, AZ: Oryx Press.

Engels, D. (Ed.). (1994). *The professional practice of career counseling and consultation: A resource document* (2nd edition). Alexandria, VA: National Career Development Association.

Flynn, R. (1994). Evaluating the effectiveness of career counselling: Recent evidence and recommended strategies. *Canadian Journal of Counselling, 28,* 77–90.

Fouad, N. A. (1993). Cross-cultural vocational assessment. *The Career Development Quarterly, 42,* 4–13.

Fouad, N. A. (1995). Career behavior of Hispanics: Assessment and career intervention. In F. T. L. Leong (Ed.), *Career development and vocational behavior of racial and ethnic minorities* (pp. 165–191). Mahwah, NJ: Lawrence Erlbaum Associates.

Fretz, B. R. (1981). Evaluating the effectiveness of career interventions [monograph]. *Journal of Counseling Psychology, 28,* 77–90.

Gelberg, S., and Chojnacki, J. T. (1996). *Career and life planning with gay, lesbian, and bisexual persons.* Alexandria, VA: American Counseling Association.

Gough, H. (1957). *California Psychological inventory manual.* Palo Alto, CA: Consulting Psychologists Press.

Gough, H. (1990). The California Psychological Inventory. In C. Watkins, Jr., and V. Campbell (Eds.), *Testing in counseling practice* (pp. 37–62). Hillsdale, NJ: Lawrence Erlbaum Associates.

Grieger, I., and Ponterotto, J. G. (1995). A framework for assessment in multicultural counseling. In J. G. Ponterotto, J. M. Casas, L. A. Suzuki, and C. M. Alexander (Eds.), *Handbook of multicultural counseling* (pp. 357–374). Thousand Oaks, CA: SAGE Publications.

Gysbers, N., Hughey, K., Starr, M., and Lapan, R. (1992). Improving school guidance programs: A framework for program, personnel, and results evaluation. *Journal of Counseling and Development, 70,* 565–570.

Hackett, G., and Lonborg, S. D. (1993). Career assessment for women: Trends and issues. *Journal of Career Assessment, 1* (3), 197–216.

Hanson, F. A. (1993). *Testing testing: Social consequences of the examined life.* Berkeley: University of California Press.

Hathaway, S. and McKinley, J. (1943). *Minnesota Multiphasic Personality Inventory.* Minneapolis, MN: National Computer Scoring Systems.

Heppner, M, O'Brien, K., Hinkelman, J., and Flores, L. (1996). Training counseling psychologists in career development: Are we our own worst enemies? *The Counseling Psychologist, 24,* 1, 105–125.

Herr, E. L., and Cramer, S. H. (1996). *Career guidance and counseling throughout the lifespan* (5th edition). New York: Harper Collins Publishers.

Hiebert, B. (1994). A framework for quality control, accountability, and evaluation: Being clear about the legitimate outcomes of career counselling. *Canadian Journal of Counselling, 28,* 344–345.

Hutchinson, N. (1995). Using performance assessments to evaluate career development programs. *Guidance and Counselling, 11* (3), 3–7.

Ivey, A. E., and Gluckstern, N. B. (1984). *Basic influencing skills.* North Amherst, MA: Microtraining Associates.

Ivey, A. E., Gluckstern, N. B., and Ivey, M. B. (1982). *Basic attending skills.* North Amherst, MA: Microtraining Associates.

Johansson, C. (1982). *Manual for the Career Assessment Inventory.* (2nd edition). Minneapolis, MN: National Computer Systems Interpretive Scoring System.

Jones, E. E., and Thorne, A. (1987). Rediscovery of the subject: Intercultural approaches to clinical assessment. *Journal of Consulting and Clinical Psychology, 55,* 488–495.

Kapes, J., Mastie, M., and Whitfield, E. (1994). *A counselor's guide to career assessment Instruments.* Alexandria, VA: National Career Development Association.

Kaplan, R., and Saccuzzo, D. (1997). *Psychological testing: Principles, applications, and issues* (4th edition). Pacific Grove, CA: Brooks/Cole Publishing.

Kellett, R. (1994). The evaluation of career and employment counseling: A new direction. *Canadian Journal of Counselling/Revue canadienne de counseling, 28,* 4, 346–352.

Killeen, J., and Kidd, J. (1991). *Learning outcomes of guidance: A review of recent research* (Research paper No. 85). London, England: National Institute for Careers Education and Counseling.

Killeen, J., White, M., and Watts, A. (1993). *The economic value of careers guidance.* London, England: Policy Studies Institute.

Kirschner, T., Hoffman, M., and Hill, C. (1994). Case study of the process and outcome of career counseling. *Journal of Counseling Psychology, 41,* 216–226.

Krug, S. (1991). The Adult Personality Inventory. *Journal of Counseling and Development, 69,* 266–274.

Krumboltz, J., Mitchell, A., and Jones, G. (1976). A social learning theory of career selection. *The Counseling Psychologist, 6,* 71–81.

Kuder, F. (1991). *Kuder Occupational Interest Inventory.* Monterey, CA: CTB McGraw-Hill.

Lapan, R., Gysbers, N., Hughey, K., and Arni, T. (1993). Evaluating a guidance and language arts unit for high-school juniors. *Journal of Counseling and Development, 71,* 444–51.

Levinson, E. M., Peterson, M., and Elston, R. (1994). Vocational counseling with persons with mental retardation. In D. C. Strohmer and H. L. Prout (Eds.), *Counseling and psychotherapy with persons with mental retardation and borderline intelligence* (pp. 257–304). Brandon, VT: Clinical Psychology Publishing Co., Inc.

Lowman, R. L. (1991) *The clinical practice of career assessment: Interests, abilities, and personality.* Washington, D.C.: American Psychological Association.

Martin, W. E., Jr. (1995). Career development assessment and intervention strategies with American Indians. In F. T. L. Leong (Ed.), *Career development and vocational behavior of racial and ethnic minorities* (pp. 227–248). Mahwah, NJ: Lawrence Erlbaum Associates.

Millon, T. (1987). *Millon Clinical Multiaxial Inventory—II (Manual).* Minneapolis, MN: National Computer Systems.

Missouri Department of Elementary and Secondary Education. (1989). *Comprehensive guidance program standards and indicators* (draft standards). Jefferson City, MO: Author.

Multon, K., and Lapan, R. (1995). Developing scales to evaluate career and personal guidance curricula in a high school setting. *Journal of Career Development, 21,* 293–305.

Myers, I., and McCauley, M. (1985). *Manual: A guide for the Myers-Briggs Type Indicator.* Palo Alto, CA: Consulting Psychologists Press.

Nathan, R., and Hill, L. (1992). *Career counseling.* London: SAGE Publications.

Nadeau, K. G. (1995). ADD in the workplace: Career consultation and counseling for the adult with ADD. In K. G. Nadeau (Ed.), *A comprehensive guide to attention deficit disorder in adults* (pp. 308–334). New York: Bruner/Mazel.

National Career Development Association. (1991). *The nuts and bolts of private practice career counseling.* Alexandria, VA: Author.

Nevo, O. (1990). Career counseling from the counselee perspective: Analysis of feedback questionnaires. *Career Development Quarterly, 38,* 314–24.

Paniagua, F. A. (1994). *Assessing and treating culturally diverse clients: A practical guide.* Thousand Oaks, CA: SAGE Publications.

Parsons, F. (1909). *Choosing a vocation.* Boston: Houghton Mifflin.

Rochlin, M. (1985). Sexual orientation of the therapist and therapeutic effectiveness with gay clients. In J. C. Gonsiorek (Ed.), *A guide to psychotherapy with Lesbian and Gay clients* (pp. 21–29). New York: Harrington Park Press.

Rogers, C. (1946). Psychometric tests and client-centered counseling. *Educational and Psychological Measurements, 6,* 139–144.

Sattler, J. M. (1988). *Assessment of children* (3rd edition). San Diego, CA: Author.

Savickas, M. L. (1992). New directions in career assessment. In D. H. Montross and C. J. Shinkman (Eds.), *Career development: Theory and practice* (pp. 336–351). Springfield, IL: Charles C. Thomas.

Spokane, A. (1991). *Evaluating career intervention.* Englewood Cliffs, NJ: Prentice Hall.

Subich, L. (1994). Annual review: Practice and research in career counseling and development—1993. *The Career Development Quarterly, 43,* 114–145.

Super, D. (1955). Transition: From vocational guidance to counseling psychology. *Journal of Counseling Psychology, 2,* 3–9.

Suzuki, L. A., and Kugler, J. F. (1995). Intelligence and personality assessment: Multicultural perspectives. In J. G. Ponterotto, J. M. Casas, L. A. Suzuki, and C. M. Alexander (Eds.), *Handbook of multicultural counseling* (pp. 493–515). Thousand Oaks, CA: SAGE Publications.

Texas evaluation model for professional school counselors (TEMPSC). (1991). Austin, TX: Texas Counseling Association.

U.S. Department of Defense. (1992). *Armed services vocational aptitude battery forms 18/19.* Monterrey, CA: Defense Manpower Data Center.

U.S. Office of Technological Assessment. (1992). *Testing in American schools: Asking the right questions.* Washington, D.C.: Author.

Walsh, W. B. (1990). Putting assessment in context. *The Counseling Psychologist, 18,* 261–65.

Walsh, W. B., and Betz, N. (1990). *Tests and assessments* (2nd edition). New York: Prentice Hall.

Warnke, M., Kim, J., Koeltzow-Milster, D., Dauser, P., Dial, S., Howie, J., and Thiel, M. (1993). Career counseling practicum: Transformations in conceptualizing career issues. *The Career Development Quarterly, 42,* 180–85.

Watkins, E. (1992). Historical influences on the use of assessment methods in counseling psychology. *Counseling Psychology Quarterly, 5,* 177–88.

Woods, J. D. (1994). *The corporate closet: The professional lives of gay men in America.* New York: The Free Press.

Zunker. V. G., and Norris, D. S. (1997). Using assessment results for career development (5th Edition). Pacific Grove, CA: Brooks/Cole Publishing.

Zytowski, D. (1985). 1984 Division 17 presidential address: Frank, Frank, where are you now that we need you? *The Counseling Psychologist, 13,* 129–35.

Zytowski, D. (1994). Tests and counseling: We are still married and living in discriminant analysis. *Measurement and Evaluation in Counseling and Development, 26,* 220–23.

Chapter 4

American College Testing. (1988). *ACT assessment program: Technical manual.* Iowa City, IA: Author.

Bennett, G. K., Seashore, H. G., and Wesman, A. G. (1991). *Differential Aptitude Test with the Career Interest Inventory Counselor's manual.* San Antonio, TX: The Psychological Corporation.

Betz, N. E. (1994). Basic issues and concepts in career counseling for women. In W. B. Walsh and S. H. Osipow (Eds.), *Career counseling for women* (pp. 1–41). Hillsdale, NJ: Lawrence Erlbaum Associates.

Betz, N. E., and Fitzgerald, L. F. (1987). *The career psychology of women.* Orlando, FL: Academic Press, Inc.

Bolles, R. N., (1998). *What color is your parachute? A practical manual for job hunters and career changers.* Berkeley, CA: Ten Speed Press.

Brown, M. T. (1995). The career development of African Americans: Theoretical and empirical issues. In F. T. L. Leong (Ed.), *Career development of and vocational behavior of racial and ethnic behaviors* (pp. 7–36). Mahwah, NJ: Lawrence Erlbaum Associates.

Butcher, J., Dahlstrom, W., et al. (1989). *Manual for the restandardized MMPI: MMPI-2: An administrative and interpretive guide.* Minneapolis: University of Minnesota Press.

Campbell, D. P. (1992). *Campbell Interest and Skill Survey manual.* Minneapolis: NCS Assessments.

Campbell, D. P., Strong, E. K., and Hansen, J–I. C. (1985). *Strong Interest Inventory Manual.* Palo Alto, CA: Consulting Psychologists Press.

Carson, A. D., and Mowsesian, R. (1991). Moderators of the prediction of job satisfaction from congruence: A test of Holland's theory. *Journal of Career Assessment, 1,* 130–44.

Carson, A. D., and Altai, N. M. (1994). 1000 years before Parsons: Vocational psychology in classical Islam. *The Career Development Quarterly, 43,* 197–206.

Cattell, R. B., Eber, H. W., and Tatsuoka, M. M. (1970). *Handbook for the Sixteen Personality Factor Questionnaire (16PF).* Champaign, IL: Institute for Personality and Ability Testing.

Chabussus, H., and Zytoski, D. G. (1987). Occupational outlook in the fifteenth century: Sanchez de Arevalo's *Mirror of human life. Journal of Counseling and Development, 66,* 168–70.

Chartrand, J. M. (1991). The evolution of trait-factor career counseling: A person and environment fit approach. *Journal of Counseling and Development, 69,* 518–24.

Chartrand, J. M., and Bertok R. L. (1993). Current trait-factor career assessment: A cognitive interactional perspective. *The Journal of Career Assessment, 1* (4), 323–40.

Chartrand, J. M., Rose, M. L., Elliott, T. R., Marmarosh, C., and Caldwell, S. (1993). Peeling back the onion: Personality, problem-solving, and career decision-making style correlates of career indecision. *Journal of Career Assessment, 1* (1), 66–74.

Costa, P. T., Jr., and McCrae, R. R. (1985). *The NEO Personality Inventory.* New York: Psychological Assessment Resources.

Dawis, R. V. (1994). The theory of work adjustment as convergent theory. In M. L. Savickas, and R. W. Lent (Eds.), *Convergence in Career Development Theories: Implications for Science and Practice.* Palo Alto, CA: CPP Books.

Dawis, R. V., England, G. W., and Lofquist, L. H. (1964). A theory of work adjustment. *Minnesota Studies in Vocational Rehabilitation, 15.*

Dawis, R. V., Lofquist, L. H., and Weiss, D. J. (1968). A theory of work adjustment (a revision). *Minnesota Studies in Vocational Rehabilitation, 23.*

Dawis, R. V., and Lofquist, L. H. (1969). *Adjustment to work.* New York: Appleton-Century-Crofts.

Dawis, R. V., and Lofquist, L. H. (1984). *A psychological theory of work adjustment.* Minneapolis: University of Minnesota Press.

Dawis, R. V., Dohm, T. E., Lofquist, L. H., Chartrand, J. M., and Due, A. M. (1987). *Minnesota Occupational Classification System III: A psychological taxonomy of work.* Minneapolis: University of Minnesota Press.

Dillon, M., and Weissman, S. (1987). Relationship between personality types on the SCII and MBTI. *Measurement and Evaluation in Counseling and Development, 120,* 68–79.

Dumont, F., and Carson, A. D. (1995). Precursors of vocational psychology in ancient civilizations. *Journal of Counseling and Development, 73,* 371–78.

Edwards, A. L. (1959). *Edwards Personal Preference Schedule manual.* The Psychological Corporation.

Educational Testing Service. (1992). *ETS Test collection catalogue* (Vol. 6). Phoenix, AZ: Oryx Press.

Fouad, N. (1993). Cross-cultural vocational assessment. *The Career Development Quarterly, 42,* 4–13.

Gilbert, D. T., and Jones, E. E. (1986). Perceiver-induced constraints: Interpretation of self-generated reality. *Journal of Personality and Social Psychology, 50,* 269–80.

Gottfredson, G. D., and Holland, J. L. (1990). A longitudinal test of the influence of congruence: Job satisfaction, competency utilization, and counterproductive behavior. *Journal of Counseling Psychology, 37,* 389–98.

Gottfredson, G. D., Jones, E. M., and Holland, J. L. (1993). Personality and vocational interests: The relation of Holland's six interest dimensions to five robust dimensions of personality. *Journal of Counseling Psychology, 40* (4), 518–24.

Gough, H. (1957). *California Psychological Inventory manual.* Palo Alto, CA: Consulting Psychologists Press.

Hackett, G., and Lonborg, S. D. (1993). Career assessment for women: Trends and issues. *Journal of Career Assessment, 1* (3), 197–216.

Hammer, A. L. (1993). *Introduction to type and careers.* Palo Alto, CA: Consulting Psychologists Press.

Hammer, A. L., and Kummerow, J. M. (1992). *Strong-MBTI career development workbook.* Odessa, FL: Psychological Assessment Resources.

Hansen, J. (1992). Does enough evidence exist to modify Holland's theory to accommodate the individual differences of diverse populations? *Journal of Vocational Behavior, 40,* 188–93.

Harrington, T., and O'Shea, A. (1993). *Harrington-O'Shea Career Decision-Making System—Revised (CDM-R) manual.* Circle Pines, MN: American Guidance Service, Inc.

Harris, J. A., and Dansky, H. (1992). *APTICOM.* Philadelphia: Vocational Research Institute.

Helms, S. T. (1996). Some experimental tests of Holland's congruency hypothesis: The reactions of high school students to occupational simulations. *Journal of Career Assessment, 4* (3), 253–68.

Helms, S. T., and Williams, G. D. (1973). *An experimental study of the reactions of high school students to simulated jobs.* (Research Report No. 161). Baltimore: Center for Social Organization of Schools, Johns Hopkins University. (ERIC Document Reproduction Service No. ED 087 882.)

Herr, E. L., and Cramer, S. H. (1996). *Career guidance and counseling through the lifespan: Systematic Approaches* (5th edition). New York: Harper Collins.

Hershensohn, D. (1996). Work adjustment: A neglected area in career counseling. *Journal of Counseling and Development, 74,* 442–46.

Hesketh, B. (1993). Toward a better adjusted theory of work adjustment. *Journal of Vocational Behavior, 43,* 75–83.

Hogan, R., DeSoto, C., and Solano, C. (1977). Traits, tests, and personality research. *American Psychologist, 32,* 255–64.

Holland, J. L. (1973). *Making vocational choices: A theory of careers.* Englewood Cliffs, NJ: Prentice Hall.

Holland, J. L. (1985/1992). *Making vocational choices: A theory of vocational personalities and work environments* (2nd edition). Englewood Cliffs, NJ: Prentice Hall.

Holland, J. (1994). *The Self-Directed Search: Professional manual.* Odessa, FL: Psychological Assessment Resources

Holland, J. L., Daiger, D. C., and Power, P. G. (1980). Some diagnostic scales for research in decision-making and personality: Identity, information and barriers. *Journal of Personality and Social Psychology, 39,* 1191–1200.

Hyland, A., and Muchinsky, P. (1991). Assessment of the structural validity of Holland's model with job analysis (PAQ) information. *Journal of Applied Psychology, 76,* 75–80.

Jackson, D. (1977). *Manual for the Jackson Vocational Interest Survey.* Port Huron, MI: Research Psychologists Press.

Johansson, C. B. (1986). *Manual for the Career Assessment Inventory.* Minneapolis: NCS Assessments.

Johansson, C. B. (1990). *Ideas, Determination and Assessment System (IDEAS) manual.* Minneapolis: NCS Assessment.

Johnson, M. J., Swartz, J. L., and Martin, W. E., Jr. (1995). Applications of psychological theories for career development with Native Americans. In F. T. L. Leong (Ed.), *Career development and vocational behavior of racial and ethnic minorities* (pp. 103–33). Mahwah, NJ: Lawrence Erlbaum Associates.

Kaplan, R., and Sacuzzo, D. (1997). *Psychological testing: Principles, applications, and issues* (4th edition). Pacific Grove, CA: Brooks/Cole Publishing.

Klein, K., and Weiner, Y. (1977). Interest congruency as a moderation of the relationship between job tenure and job satisfaction and mental health. *Journal of Vocational Behavior, 10,* 91–98.

Knapp, R. R., and Knapp, L. (1990). *Career Occupational Preference System Interest Inventory (COPS) manual.* San Diego: EDITS.

Kuder, F. (1991). *Kuder Occupational Interest Survey, Form DD (KOIS): General manual.* Monterey, CA: CTB McGraw-Hill.

Krumboltz, J. D. (1979). A social learning theory of career decision-making. In A. M. Mitchell, G. G. Jame, and J. D. Krumbolz (Eds.), *Social learning and career decision-making* (pp. 19–49). Cranston, RI: Carroll Press.

Meir, E. (1989). Integrative elaboration of the congruence theory. *Journal of Vocational Behavior, 35,* 219–30.

Miller, C. (1974). Career development theory in perspective. In E. Herr (Ed.), *Vocational guidance and human development* (pp. 235–62). Boston: Houghton Mifflin.

Miller, M. (1991). Accuracy of the leisure activities finder: Expanding Holland's typology. *Journal of Vocational Behavior, 39,* 362–68.

Miller, M. (1988). Integrating Holland's typology with the Myers-Briggs Type Indicator: Implications for career counselors. *Journal of Human Behavior, 5,* 25–28.

Miller, M. (1992). Synthesizing results from an interest and a personality inventory to improve career decision making. *Journal of Employment Counseling, 29,* 50–59.

Murray, H. (1938). *Explorations in personality.* New York: Oxford University Press.

Nevill, D. D., and Super, D. E. (1989). *The Values Scale (VS) manual.* Palo Alto, CA: Consulting Psychologists Press.

Osipow, S. H., Carney, C. G., Winer, J., Yanico, B., and Koschier, M. (1987). *Career Decision Scale (CDS) manual.* Odessa, FL: Psychological Assessment Resources, Inc.

Pittenger, D. J. (1993). The utility of the Myers-Briggs Type Indicator. *Review of Educational Research, 63,* 467–88.

Prediger, D., Swaney, K., and Mau, W. (1993). Extending Holland's hexagon: Procedures, counseling approaches, and research. *Journal of Counseling and Development, 71,* 422–28.

Prince, J. P., Uemura, A. K., Chao, G. S., and Gonzales, G. M. (1991, Spring). Using career interest inventories with multicultural clients. *Career Planning and Adults Development Journal,* 45–50.

Rounds, J. B., Jr., Henly, G. A., Dawis, R. V., and Lofquist, L. H. (1981). *Manual for the Minnesota Importance Questionnaire: A measure of needs and values.* Minneapolis: Vocational Psychology Research, University of Minnesota.

Rounds, J., and Tracey, T. (1990). From trait-factor to person-environment fit counseling: Theory and process. In W. B. Walsh and S. H. Osipow (Eds.), *Career counseling: Contemporary topics in vocational psychology.* (pp. 1–44). Hillsdale, NJ: Lawrence Erlbaum Associates.

Savickas, M. (1985). Identity in vocational development. *Journal of Vocational Behavior, 27,* 329–37.

Schwartz, R. (1992). Is Holland's theory worthy of so much attention, or should vocational psychology move on? *Journal of Vocational Behavior, 40,* 170–87.

Sharf, R. (1996). *Applying career development theory to counseling.* Pacific Grove, CA: Brooks/Cole Publishing.

Smart, J. (1989). Life history influences on Holland vocational type development. *Journal of Vocational Behavior, 34,* 69–87.

Spokane, A. (1985). A review of research on person-environment congruence in Holland's theory of careers. *Journal of Vocational Behavior, 26,* 306–43.

Staats, A. W. (1981). Paradigmatic behaviorism, unified theory, unified theory construction methods, and the *zeitgeist* of separatism. *American Psychologist, 36,* 239–56.

Super, D. E. (1970). *Work Values Inventory: Manual.* Boston: Houghton Mifflin.

Tinsley, D. J. (1993). Extensions, elaborations, and construct validity of the theory of work adjustment. *Journal of Vocational Behavior, 43,* 67–74.

U.S. Department of Defense. (1992). *Armed services vocational aptitude battery forms 18/19.* Monterrey, CA: Defense Manpower Data Center.

USES General Aptitude Test Battery (GATB)/USES Interest Inventory (USES II) Manual, user's guide. Salt Lake City: U.S. Employment Service, Wester Assessment Research and Development Center.

Walsh, W. B., and Betz, N. E. (1990). *Tests and assessment* (2nd edition). Englewood Cliffs, NJ: Prentice Hall.

Weiss, D. J., Dawis, R. V., England, G. W., and Lofquist, L. H. (1967). *Minnesota Satisfaction Questionnaire manual.* Minneapolis: Vocational Psychology Research, University of Minnesota.

Williamson, E. G. (1939). *How to counsel students: A manual of techniques for clinical counselors.* New York: McGraw-Hill.

Williamson, E. G. (1950). *Counseling adolescents.* New York: McGraw-Hill.

Williamson, E. G. (1965). *Vocational counseling: Some historical, philosophical, and theoretical perspectives.* New York: McGraw-Hill.

Zytowski, D., and Borgen, F. (1983). Assessment. In W. B. Walsh and S. H. Osipow (Eds.), *Handbook of vocational psychology* (Vol. 2) (pp. 5–40). Hillsdale, NJ: Lawrence Erlbaum Associates.

Zytowski, D., and Warman, R. (1982). The changing use of tests in counseling. *Measurement and Evaluation in Guidance, 15,* 147–52.

Chapter 5

Anderson, H., and Goolishian, H. A. (1988). Human systems as linguistic systems: Preliminary and evolving ideas about the implications for clinical theory. *Family Process, 27,* 371–93.

Beck, A. T. (1993). Cognitive therapy: Past, present, and future. *Journal of Consulting and Clinical Psychology, 61* (2), 194–98.

Berger, P. L., and Luckmann, T. (1966). *The social construction of reality.* New York: Doubleday.

Best, S., and Kellner, D. (1991). *Postmodern theory: Critical interrogations.* New York: Guilford.

Blustein, D. L., and Noumair, D. A. (1996). Self and identity in career development: Implications for theory and practice. *Journal of Counseling and Development, 74,* 433–41.

Bohart, A. C. (1995). The person-centered psychotherapies. In A. S. Gurman and S. B. Messer (Eds.), *Essential psychotherapies: Theory and practice* (pp. 85–127). New York: Guilford.

Bordin, E. (1946). Diagnosis in counseling and psychotherapy. *Educational psychology measurement, 68,* 169–84.

Borman, C., and Dickson, M. (1991). A career counseling model. *Texas Association for Counseling and Development Spring,* 13–21.

Brooks, L., and Forrest, L. (1994). Feminism and career counseling. In W. B. Walsh and S. H. Osipow (Eds.), *Career counseling for women* (pp. 87–134). Hillsdale, NJ: Lawrence Erlbaum Associates.

Brown, D. (1985). Career counseling: Before, after, or instead of personal counseling. *Vocational Guidance Quarterly, 33,* 197–201.

Bruner, J. (1986). *Actual minds, possible worlds.* Cambridge, MA: Harvard University Press.

Cannella, G. S., and Reiff, J. C. (1994). Preparing teachers for cultural diversity: Constructivist orientations. *Action in Teacher Education, XVI* (3), 37–45.

Chusid, H., and Cochran, L. (1989). Meaning of career change from the perspective of family roles and dramas. *Journal of Counseling Psychology, 36,* 34–41.

Coale, H. W. (1992). The constructivist emphasis on language: A critical conversation. *Journal of Strategic and Systemic Therapies, 11,* 12–26.

Cochran, L. (1991). *Life-shaping decisions.* New York: Peter Lang Publishing, Inc.

Corey, G. (1996). *Theory and practice of counseling and psychotherapy* (5th edition). Pacific Grove, CA: Brooks/Cole Publishing.

Csikszentmihalyi, M., and Beattie, O. V. (1979). Life themes: A theoretical and empirical exploration of their origins and effects. *Journal of Humanistic Psychology, 19* (1), 45–63.

Denner, B. (1995). Stalked by the postmodern beast. *American Psychologist, 50,* 390–91.

Doherty, W. J. (1991). Family therapy goes postmodern. *Family Therapy Networker, 15,* (5), 37–42.

Dorn, F. (1992). Occupational wellness: The integration of career identity and personal identity. *Journal of Counseling and Development, 71,* 176–78.

Ellis, A. (1991). The revised ABC's of rational-emotive therapy (RET). *Journal of Rational-Emotive and Cognitive Behavioral Therapy, 9,* 139–72.

Ellis, A. (discussant). (1992, June). In D. Richman (chair), *Cognitive interpretation for employees and their organization.* Symposium conducted at the World Congress of Cognitive Therapy, Toronto, Ontario, Canada.

Feixas, G. (1990). Personal construct theory and systemic therapies: Parallel or convergent trends? *Journal of Marital and Family Therapy, 16* (1), 1–20.

Feixas, G. (1995). Personal constructs in systemic practice. In R. A. Neimeyer and M. J. Mahoney (Eds.), *Constructivism in psychotherapy* (pp. 305–37). Washington, D.C.: American Psychological Association.

Forster, J. R. (1992). Eliciting personal constructs and articulating goals. *Journal of Career Development, 18* (3), 175–85.

Frankl, V. (1967). *Psychotherapy and existentialism: Selected papers on logotherapy.* New York: Washington Square Press.

Franklin, C. (1995). Expanding the vision of the social constructionist debates: Creating relevance for practitioners. *Families in Society: The Journal of Contemporary Human Services, 76,* 395–406.

Franklin, C., and Nurius, P. S. (Eds.). (1996). Constructivism in social work practice [Special issue]. *Families in Society: The Journal of Contemporary Human Services, 77.*

Freeman, S. C. (1990). C. H. Patterson on client-centered career counseling: An interview. *The Career Development Quarterly, 38,* 291–301.

Gergen, K. J. (1985). The social constructionist movement in modern psychology. *American Psychologist, 40,* 266–75.

Gergen, K. J. (1991b). *The saturated self: Dilemmas of identity in contemporary life.* New York: Basic Books.

Gergen, K. J. (1994a). Exploring the postmodern: Perils or potentials? *American Psychologist, 49,* 412–16.

Gergen, K. J. (1995). Postmodern psychology: Resonance and reflection. *American Psychologist, 50,* 394.

Gergen, M. N., and Gergen, K. J. (1984). The social construction of narrative accounts. In K. J. Gergen and M. M. Gergen (Eds.), *Historical social psychology* (pp. 173–89). Hillsdale, NY: Lawrence Erlbaum Associates.

Golan, S. (1988). On second-order family therapy. *Family Process, 27,* 51–65.

Gonçalves, Ó. F. (1995). Cognitive narrative psychotherapy: The hermeneutic construction of alternative meanings. In M. J. Mahoney (Ed.), *Cognitive and constructive psychotherapies: Theory, research, and practice* (pp. 139–62). New York: Springer.

Goodyear, R., Roffey, A., and Jack, L. (1994). Edward Bordin: Fusing work and play. *Journal of Counseling and Development, 72,* 563–72.

Gough, H. (1960). The adjective checklist as a personality assessment research technique. *Psychological Reports, 6,* 107–22.

Gough, H., and Heilbrum, A. (1980). *The adjective checklist manual.* Palo Alto, CA: Consulting Psychologist Press.

Granvold, D. K. (1996). Constructivist psychotherapy. *Families in Society: The Journal of Contemporary Human Services, 77,* 345–57.

Greenson, R. R. (1967). *The technique and practice of psychoanalysis.* New York: International Universities Press.

Guyton, E., and Rainer, J. (Eds.). (1996). Constructivism in teacher education [Special issue]. *Action in Teacher Education, XVIII* (2).

Hackett, G., and Lonborg, S. D. (1993). Career assessment for women: Trends and issues. *Journal of Career Assessment, 1* (3), 197–216.

Harding, S. (1993). Rethinking standpoint epistemology: What is "strong objectivity"? In L. Alcoff and E. Potter (Eds.), *Feminist epistemologies* (pp. 49–82). New York: Routledge.

Held, B. S. (1990). What's in a name? Some confusions and concerns about constructivism. *Journal of Marriage and Family Therapy, 16,* 179–86.

Hoffman, L. (1991). A reflexive stance for family therapy. *Journal of Strategic and Systemic Therapies, 10,* 4–17.

Horvath, A. O., and Greenberg, L. S. (1989). Development and validation of the Working Alliance Inventory. *Journal of Counseling Psychology, 36* (2), 223–33.

Horvath, A. O., and Greenberg, L. S. (1994). *The working alliance: Theory, research, and practice.* New York: John Wiley & Sons, Inc.

Horvath, A. O., and Symonds, B. D. (1991). Relation between Working Alliance and outcome in psychotherapy. A meta-analysis. *Journal of Counseling Psychology, 38* (2), 139–49.

Imbimbo, P. V. (1994) Integrating personal and career counseling: A challenge for counselors. *Journal of Employment Counseling, 31,* 50–59.

Koehn, C. (1986). Meaningless, death, and responsibility: Existential themes in career counseling. *Canadian Journal of Counselling, 20,* 177–85.

Lewis, R., and Gilhousen, M. (1981). Myths of career development: A cognitive approach to vocational counseling. *The Personnel and Guidance Journal, 59,* 296–99.

Lyddon, W. J. (1990). First- and second-order change: Implications for rationalist and constructivist cognitive therapies. *Journal of Counseling and Development, 69,* 122–27.

Manuele-Adkins, C. (1992). Career counseling is personal counseling. *The Career Development Quarterly, 40,* 313–23.

Matre, G., and Cooper, S. (1984). Concurrent evaluations of career indecision and indecisiveness. *The Personnel and Guidance Journal, 62,* 637–39.

McAuliffe, G. (1993). Constructive development and career transition: Implications for counseling. *Journal of Counseling and Development, 72,* 23–28.

McIlroy, J. (1979). Career as a lifestyle: An existential view. *Personal Guidance Journal,* 351–54.

Meara, N. M., and Patton, J. P. (1994) Contributions of the working alliances in the practice of career counseling. *The Career Development Quarterly, 43,* 161–77.

Meichenbaum, D. (1993). Changing conceptions of cognitive behavior modification: Retrospect and prospect. *Journal of Consulting and Clinical Psychology, 61* (2), 202–4.

Melvin, G. V. (1998, July 7). Job, money pressures prevent dad from taking family leave. *San Antonio Express News,* 10E.

Miller, M. (1993). A career counseling diagnostic model: How to assess and counsel career-concerned clients. *Journal of Employment Counseling, 30,* 35–43.

Miller, M. (1988). A client-centered career counseling assessment method. *Person-Centered Review, 3,* 195–212.

Neimeyer, R. A. (1995b). Constructivist psychotherapies: Features, foundations, and future directions. In R. A. Neimeyer and M. J. Mahoney (Eds.), *Constructivism in psychotherapy* (pp. 11–38). Washington, D.C.: American Psychological Association.

O'Hara, M., and Anderson, W. T. (1991). Welcome to the postmodern world. *Family Therapy Networker, 15* (5), 19–25.

Osbeck, L. M. (1991, August). *Social constructionism and the pragmatic standard.* Paper presented at the 99th Meeting of the American Psychological Convention, San Francisco, CA.

Osipow, S. (1983). *Theories of career development.* Englewood Cliffs, NJ: Prentice Hall.

Patterson, C. (1964). Self-clarification and the helping relationship. In H. Borow (Ed.). *Man in a world of work* (pp. 434–59). New York: Houghton Mifflin.

Patterson, C. (1982). Some essentials of a client-centered approach to assessment. *Measurement and Evaluation in Guidance, 15,* 103–6. (With C. F. Watkins, Jr.).

Polkinghorne, D. E. (1988). *Narrative knowing and the human sciences.* Albany, NY: State University of New York Press.

Richman, D. (1993). Cognitive career counseling: A rational-emotive approach to career development. *Journal of Rational-Emotive and Cognitive-Behavior Therapy, 11,* 91–107.

Robins, C. J., and Hayes, A. M. (1993). An appraisal of cognitive therapy. *Journal of Consulting and Clinical Psychology, 61* (2), 205–14.

Rockwell, T. (1986). The Rockwell Occupational Approval Grid (with a Manual for Counselors). (Available from Taylor Rockwell, Brownlee Dolan Stein Associates, Inc., 90 John Street, New York, NY 10038).

Rockwell, T. (1987, Fall). The social construction of careers: Career development and career counseling viewed from a sociometric perspective. *JGPPS, 93*–107.

Rogers, C. (1942). *Counseling and psychotherapy.* Boston: Houghton Mifflin.

Russell, R. L., and Gaubatz, M. D. (1995). Contested affinities: Reaction to Gergen's (1994) and Smith's (1994) postmodernisms. *American Psychologist, 50,* 389–90.

Salamone, P. (1982). Difficult cases in career counseling II: The indecisive client. *The Personnel Guidance Journal, 60,* 496–500.

Sampson, J. P., Jr., Peterson, G. W., Lenz, J. G., and Reardon, R. C. (1992). A cognitive approach to career services: Translating concepts into practice. *The Career Development Quarterly, 41,* 67–74.

Savickas, M. L. (1992). New directions in career assessment. In D. H. Montross and C. J. Shinkman (Eds.), *Career development: Theory and practice* (pp. 336–51). Springfield, IL: Charles C. Thomas.

Segal, S. (1961). A psychoanalytic analysis of personality factors in vocational choice. *Journal of Counseling Psychology, 8,* 202–10.

Sharf, R. S. (1996). *Theories of psychotherapy and counseling: Concepts and cases.* Pacific Grove, CA: Brooks/Cole Publishing.

Simpson, S. (writer, director, and producer). (1987, September 1). *NOVA: Freud under analysis.* Boston: WGBH.

Smith, H. (1989). *Beyond the post-modern mind.* Wheaton, IL: Theosophical Publishing House.

Spence, D. P. (1982). *Narrative truth and historical truth: Meaning and interpretation in psychoanalysis.* New York: W. W. Norton & Company.

Terkel, S. (1974). *Working.* New York: Avon Books.

Vygotsky, L. (1978). *Mind in society: The development of higher psychological processes.* Cambridge, MA: Harvard University Press.

Watzlawick, P., Weakland, J., and Fisch, R. (1974). *Change: Principles of problem formation and problem resolution.* New York: W. W. Norton.

Wolitzky, D. L. (1995). The theory and practice of traditional psychoanalytic psychotherapy. In A. S. Gurman and S. B. Messer (Eds.), *Essential psychotherapies: Theory and practice* (pp. 12–54). New York: Guilford.

Wrenn, C. G. (1988). The person in career counseling. *The Career Development Quarterly, 36,* 337–42.

Yalom, I. D. (1980). *Existential psychotherapy.* New York: Basic Books.

Chapter 6

Archer, S., and Waterman A. (1983). Identity in early adolescence: A developmental perspective. *Journal of Early Adolescence, 3,* 203–14.

Atkinson, D. R., Morten, G., and Sue, D. W. (1989). *Counseling American minorities* (3rd edition). Dubuque, IA: William C. Brown.

Betz, N. (1994). Self-concept theory in career development counseling. *The Career Development Quarterly, 43,* 20–27.

Bordin, E., Nachmann, B., and Siegel, S. (1963). An articulated framework for vocational development. *Journal of Counseling Psychology, 10,* 107–16.

Borgen, F. H. (1991). Megatrends and milestones in vocational behavior: A Twenty-year counseling psychology retrospective. *Journal of Vocational Behavior, 39,* 263–90.

Brown, D., Brooks, L., and Associates. (1996). *Career choice and development* (3rd edition). San Francisco: Jossey-Bass.

Cass, V. C. (1979). Homosexual identity formation: A theoretical model. *Journal of Homosexuality, 4* (3), 219–35.

Erikson, E. (1950). *Childhood and society.* New York: Norton.

Erikson, E. (1959). Identity and the life cycle. *Psychological Issues, 1,* 18–164.

Erikson, E. (1963). *Childhood and society.* (2nd edition). New York: Norton.

Erikson, E. (1968). *Identity: Youth in crisis.* New York: Norton.

Fouad, N. A., and Arbona, C. (1994). Careers in a contextual context. *The Career Development Quarterly, 43,* 96–104.

Freeman, S. (1993). Donald Super: A perspective on career development. *Journal of Career Development, 19,* 255–64.

Gainor, K., and Forrest, L. (1991). African American women's self-concept: Implications for career decisions and career counseling. *The Career Development Quarterly, 39,* 261–73.

Gelatt, H. B. (1991). *Creative decision making using positive uncertainty.* Los Altos, CA: Crisp.

Gelberg, S., and Chojnacki, J. T. (1996). *Career and life planning with gay, lesbian, and bisexual persons.* Alexandria, VA: American Counseling Association.

Ginzberg, E., Ginsburg, S., Axelrad, S., and Herma, J. (1951). *Occupational choice: An approach to a general theory.* New York: Columbia University Press.

Ginzberg, E. (1971). *Career guidance: Who needs it, who provides it, who can improve it?* New York: Columbia University Press.

Goodman, J. (1994). Career adaptability in adults: A construct whose time has come. *Career Development Quarterly, 43,* 74–84.

Gottfredson, L. (1981). Circumscription and compromise: A developmental theory of occupational aspiration. *Journal of Counseling Psychology, 28,* 545–79.

Gottfredson, L. S. (1996). Gottfredson's theory of circumscription and compromise. In D. Brown, L. Brooks, and Associates, *Career choice and development.* (3rd edition). San Francisco: Jossey-Bass.

Hall, D. T. (1986). *Career development in organizations.* San Francisco: Jossey-Bass.

Herr, E. L. (1992). Counseling for personal flexibility in a global economy. *Educational and Vocational Guidance, 53,* 5–16.

Herr, E. L. (1997). Super's life-span, life-space approach and its outlook for refinement. *The Career Development Quarterly, 45,* 238–46.

Herr, E. L., and Cramer, S. H. (1996). *Career guidance and counseling through the lifespan: Systematic approaches* (5th edition). New York: HarperCollins Publishers.

Jepsen, D. A. (1994). The thematic extrapolation method: Incorporating career patterns into career counseling. *The Career Development Quarterly, 43,* 43–53.

Johnson, M. J., Swartz, J. L., and Martin, W. E., Jr. (1995). Applications of psychological theories for career development with Native Americans. In F. T. L. Leong (Ed.), *Career development and vocational behavior of racial and ethnic minorities* (pp. 103–33). Mahwah, NJ: Lawrence Erlbaum Associates.

Leong, F. T. L. (1991). Career development attributes and occupational values of Asian American and White American college students. *The Career Development Quarterly, 39,* 221–30.

Martin, W. E., Jr. (1995). Career development assessment and intervention strategies with American Indians. In F. T. L. Leong (Ed.), *Career development and vocational behavior of racial and ethnic minorities* (pp. 227–48). Mahwah, NJ: Lawrence Erlbaum Associates.

Miller-Tiedeman, A., and Tiedeman, D. (1990). Career decision-making: An individualistic perspective. In D. Brown, L. Brooks, and Associates (Eds.), *Career choice and development: applying contemporary theories to practice* (2nd edition, pp. 308–37). San Francisco: Jossey-Bass.

Osipow, S. H. (1987). Counseling psychology: Theory, research, and practice in career counseling. *Annual Review of Psychology,* volume 38, 257–78.

Osipow, S. H., and Fitzgerald, L. (1996). *Theories of career development.* Needham Heights, MA: Allyn and Bacon.

Osipow, S. H., and Littlejohn, E. M. (1995). Toward a multicultural theory of career development: Prospects and dilemmas. In F. T. L. Leong (Ed.), *Career development and vocational behavior of racial and ethnic minorities* (pp. 251–61). Mahwah, NJ: Lawrence Erlbaum Associates.

Phillips, S. D. (1997). Toward an expanded definition of adaptive decision making. *The Career Development Quarterly, 45,* 275–87.

Pratzner, F. C., and Ashley, W. L. (1984). Occupational adaptability and transferable skills: Preparing today's adults for tomorrow's careers. In C. H. Shulman (Ed.), *Adults and the changing workplace: 1985 yearbook of the American Vocational Association* (pp. 13–22). Arlington, VA: American Vocational Association.

Sastre, M., and Mullet, E. (1992). Occupational preferences of Spanish adolescents in relation to Gottfredson's theory. *Journal of Vocational Behavior, 40,* 306–17.

Savickas, M. (1989). Annual review. Practive and research in career counseling and development, 1988. *The Career Development Quarterly, 38,* 100–34.

Savickas, M. (1994). Measuring career development: current status and future directions. *The Career Development Quarterly, 43,* 54–62.

Savickas, M. (1997). Career adaptability: An integrative construct for life-span, life-space theory. *Career Development Quarterly, 45,* 247–59.

Sharf, R. (1992). Applying career development theory to counseling. Belmont, CA: Brooks/ Cole Publishing.

Seligman, L. (1994). *Developmental career counseling and assessment.* Thousand Oaks, CA: SAGE Publishers.

Stephan, N. (1989). *Finding your life mission.* Walpole, NH: Stillpoint.

Super, D. E. (1974). *Measuring vocational maturity for counseling and evaluation.* Washington, D.C.: National Vocational Guidance Association.

Super, D. E. (1980). A lifespan-lifespace approach to career development. *Journal of Vocational Behavior, 16,* 282–98.

Super, D. E. (1990). A lifespan/lifespace approach to career development. In D. Brown, L. Brooks, and Associates (Eds.), *Career choice and development: Applying contemporary theories to practice* (2nd edition, pp. 197–261). San Francisco: Jossey-Bass.

Super, D. E., and Knasel, E. G. (1979). *Development of a model, specifications, and sample items for measuring career adaptability (vocational maturity) in young blue-collar workers.* Cambridge, England: National Institute for Careers Education and Counselling, and Ottawa, Canada: Canada Employment and Immigration.

Super, D. E., Osborne, W. L., Walsh, D. J., Brown, S. D, and Niles, S. G. (1992). Developmental career assessment and counseling: The C-DAC model. *Journal of Counseling and Development, 71,* 74–83.

Super, D. E., Savickas, M., and Super, C. N. (1996). The life-span, life-space approach to careers. In D. Brown, L. Brooks, and Associates (Eds.) *Career choice and development* (3rd edition, pp. 121–78). San Francisco: Jossey-Bass.

Super, D. E., Sverko, B, and Super, C. N. (Eds.) (1995). *Life roles, values, and careers: International findings of the work importance study.* San Francisco: Jossey-Bass.

Tiedeman, D., and O'Hara, R. (1963). *Career development: Choice and adjustment.* Princeton, NJ: College Entrance Examination Board.

Troll, L. E. (1975). *Early and middle adulthood.* Pacific Grove, CA: Brooks/Cole Publishing.

Vondracek, F. (1990). A developmental-contextual approach to career development research. In R. Young and W. Borgen (Eds.), *Methodological approaches to the study of career.* (pp. 37–56). New York: Praeger.

Vondracek, F. (1992). The construct of identity and its use in career research. *The Career Development Quarterly, 41,* 130–43.

Wagner, J. (1994). *Edith Ann: My life, so far.* New York: Hyperion.

Wrenn, C. G. (1988). The person in career counseling. *The Career Development Quarterly, 36,* 337–42.

Chapter 7

Alter, J. (1997, September 15). Diana's real legacy. *Newsweek,* 59ff.

Associated Press. (1997, September 10). News photographers feel backlash: Diana's death brings heightened sensitivity among public. *El Paso Times,* p. 2A.

Bandura, A. (1977). Self-efficacy: Toward a unifying theory of behavior change. *Psychology Review, 84,* 191–215.

Bandura, A. (1982). Self-efficacy mechanism in human agency. *American Psychologist, 37,* 122–47.

Bandura, A. (1984). Recycling misconceptions of perceived self-efficacy. *Cognitive Therapy and Research, 8,* 231–55.

Bandura, A. (1986). *Social foundations of thought and action: A social cognitive theory.* Englewood Cliffs, NJ: Prentice Hall.

Betz, N. E. (1992). Counseling uses of career self-efficacy theory. *The Career Development Quarterly, 41,* 22–26.

Betz, N. E. (1994). Career counseling for women in the sciences and engineering. In W. B. Walsh and S. H. Osipow (Eds.), *Career counseling for women* (pp. 237–61). Hillsdale, NJ: Lawrence Erlbaum Associates.

Betz, N. E., and Fitzgerald, L. F. (1987). *The career psychology of women.* Orlando, FL: Academic Press, Inc.

Betz, N. E., and Hackett, G. (1981). The relationship of career-related self-efficacy expectations to perceived career options in college women and men. *Journal of Counseling Psychology, 28,* 399–410.

Betz, N. E., and Hackett, G. (1983). The relationship of mathematics self-efficacy expectations to the selection of science-based college majors. *Journal of Vocational Behavior, 23,* 329–345.

Bingham, M., and Stryker, S. (1995). *Things will be different for my daughter: A practical guide to building her self-esteem and self-reliance.* New York: Penguin Books.

Blustein, D. L., Ellis, M. V., and Devenis, L. (1989). The development and validation of a two-dimensional model of the commitment to career choice process. *Journal of Vocational Behavior, 35,* 342–78.

Blustein, D. L., and Phillips, S. D. (1990). Relation between ego identity statuses and decision-making styles. *Journal of Counseling Psychology, 37,* 160–68.

Byrnes, J. P. (1996). *Cognitive development and learning in instructional contexts.* Boston: Allyn and Bacon.

Candrl, K. I., and Heinzen, C. J. (1994). Career Quest: An innovative student organization designed to meet the needs of "deciding" students. *Journal of Career Development, 21,* 141–48.

Carson, A. (1992). On occupationism. *The Counseling Psychologist, 20,* 490–508.

Chartrand, J. M., Robbins, S. B., Morrill, W. H., and Boggs, K. (1990). Development and validation of the Career Factors Inventory. *Journal of Counseling Psychology, 37*, 491–501.

Church, A. T., Teresa, J. S., Rosebrook, R., and Szendre, D. (1992). Self-efficacy for careers and occupational consideration in minority high school equivalency students. *Journal of Counseling Psychology, 39*, 498–508.

Cohen, C. R., Chartrand, J. M., and Jowdy, D. P. (1995). Relationships between career indecision subtypes and ego identity development. *Journal of Counseling Psychology, 42*, 440–47.

Czerlinsky, T., and Chandler, S. L. (1993). *Vocational Decision-Making Interview-Revised, Administration manual*. Dallas, TX: ProPublishing Associates.

Dinklage, L. (1968). *Decision strategies of adolescents*. Unpublished doctoral dissertation, Harvard University.

Eastman, C., and Marzillier, J. S. (1984). Theoretical and methodological difficulties in Bandura's self-efficacy theory. *Cognitive Therapy and Research, 8*, 213–29.

Elium, J., and Elium, D. (1994). *Raising a daughter: Parents and the awakening of a healthy woman*. Berkeley: Celestial Arts.

Gati, I. (1986). Making career decisions: A sequential elimination approach. *Journal of Counseling Psychology, 33*, 408–17.

Gati, I. (1990). Why, when, and how to take into account the uncertainty involved in career decisions. *Journal of Counseling Psychology, 37*, 277–80.

Gati, I. (1994). Computer-assisted career counseling: Dilemmas, problems and possible solutions. *Journal of Counseling and Development, 73*, 51–55.

Gati, I., Fassa, N., and Houminer, D. (1996). Applied sequential elimination approach. *Career Development Quarterly, 43*, 211–21.

Gati, I. and Tikotzki, Y. (1989). Strategies for collection and processing of occupational information in making career decisions. *Journal of Counseling Psychology, 36*, 430–39.

Gelatt, H. (1989). Positive uncertainty: A new decision making framework for counseling. *Journal of Counseling Psychology, 36*, 252–56.

Gelatt, H. (1991). *Creative decision-making: Using positive uncertainty*. San Jose, CA: Crisp Publications.

González, R. C. (1990). *Cognitive assessment in computerized nicotine fading*. Unpublished doctoral dissertation, Stanford University.

Gottfredson, L. S. (1981). Circumscription and compromise: A developmental theory of occupational aspirations. *Journal of Counseling Psychology, 28*, 545–79.

Graham, K. (1997, September 15). A friend's last goodbye. *Newsweek*, 68–69.

Griffith, A. R. (1980). Justification for a Black career development. *Counselor Education and Supervision, 19*, 301–10.

Hackett, G., and Betz, N. E. (1981). Self-efficacy approach to the career development of women. *Journal of Vocational Behavior, 18*, 326–39.

Hackett, G., Betz, N. E., Casas, J. M., and Rocha-Singh, I. A. (1992). Gender, ethnicity, and social cognitive factors predicting the academic achievement of students in engineering. *Journal of Counseling Psychology, 39*, 527–38.

Harrington, T. F. (1991). The cross-cultural applicability of the career decision-making system. *The Career Development Quarterly, 39*, 209–20.

Heppner, M. J., and Heindricks, F. (1995). A process and outcome study examining career indecision and indecisiveness. *Journal of Counseling and Development, 73*, 426–37.

Holland, J. L., Daiger, D. C., and Power, P. G. (1980). *My vocational situation*. Palo Alto, CA: Consulting Psychologist Press.

Holland, J. L., Gottfredson, G. G., and Nafziger, D. H. (1973). *A diagnostic scheme for specifying vocational assistance.* Baltimore: Johns Hopkins University Center for Social Organization of Schools (Report No. 164).

Jones, L. K. (1989). Measuring a three-dimensional construct of career indecision among college students: A revision of the vocational decision scale—The Career Decision Profile. *Journal of Counseling Psychology, 36,* 477–86.

Krumboltz, J. D. (1979). A social learning theory of career decision making. In A. Mitchell, G. Jones, and J. Krumboltz (Eds.), *Social learning and career decision making* (pp. 194–99). Cranston, RI: Carroll Press.

Krumboltz, J. D. (1991a). *Career Beliefs Inventory.* Palo Alto, CA: Consulting Psychologist Press.

Krumboltz, J. D. (1991b). The 1990 Leona Tyler award address: Brilliant insights—platitudes that bear repeating. *The Counseling Psychologist, 19,* 298–315.

Krumboltz, J. D. (1991c). The dangers of occupationism. *The Counseling Psychologist, 20,* 511–18.

Krumboltz, J.D. (1992). The wisdom of indecision. *Journal of Vocational Behavior, 41,* 239–44.

Krumboltz, J., and Hamel, D. (1977). *Guide to career decision making skills.* New York: Educational Testing Services.

LaFromboise, T. D., Trimble, J. E., and Mohatt, G. V. (1990). Counseling intervention and American Indian tradition: An integrative approach. *The Counseling Psychologist, 18,* 628–54.

Lent, R. W., Brown, S. D., and Hackett, G. (1996). Career development from a social cognitive perspective. In D. Brown, L. Brooks, and Associates (Eds.), *Career choice and development* (3rd edition) (pp. 373–421). San Francisco: Jossey-Bass.

Lent, R. W., and Hackett, G. (1987). Career self-efficacy: Empirical status and future directions. *Journal of Vocational Behavior, 30,* 342–82.

Lent, R. W., Larkin, K. C., and Brown, S. D., (1989). Relation of self-efficacy to inventoried vocational interests. *Journal of Vocational Behavior, 34,* 279–88.

Maddux, J., Stanley, M., and Manning, M. (1987). Self-efficacy theory and research: Applications in clinical and counseling psychology. In J. Maddux, C. Stoltenberg, and R. Rosenwein (Eds.), *Social processes in clinical and counseling psychology* (pp. 39–55). New York: Springer-Verlag.

Marone, N. (1988). *How to father a successful daughter.* New York: Fawcett Crest.

Marzillier, J. S., and Eastman, C. (1984). Continuing problems with self-efficacy theory: A reply to Bandura. *Cognitive Therapy and Research, 8,* 257–62.

Mau, W., and Jepsen, D. (1992). Effects of computer-assisted instruction in using formal decision making: Strategies to choose a college major. *Journal of Counseling Psychology, 39,* 185–92.

McAuliffe, G. (1992). Assessing and changing career decision-making self-efficacy expectations. *Journal of Career Development, 19,* 25–36.

McDaniels, R. M., Carter, J. K., Heinzen, C. J., Candrl, K. I., and Weinberg, A. M. (1994). Undecided/undeclared: Working with "deciding" students. *Journal of Career Development, 21,* 135–39.

Mitchell, L., and Krumboltz, J. (1984). Research of human decision making: Implications for career decision makers and counselors. In D. Brown and R. Lent (Eds.), *Handbook of counseling psychology* (pp. 238–80). New York: Wiley.

Mitchell, L. K., and Krumboltz, J. D. (1990). Social learning approach to career decision-making: Krumboltz's theory. In D. Brown, L. Brooks, and Associates. *Career choice and development: Applying contemporary theories to practice* (2nd edition) (pp.197–261). San Francisco: Jossey-Bass.

Newman, J., Fuqua, D., and Seaworth, T. (1989). The role of anxiety in career indecision: Implications for treatment. *Career Development Quarterly, 37,* 221–37.

O'Brien, K. M., Heppner, M. J., Flores, L. Y., and Bikos, L. H. (1997). The Career Counseling Self-Efficacy Scale: Instrument development and training applications. *Journal of Counseling Psychology, 44,* 20–31.

Ogbu, J. U. (1992). Understanding cultural diversity and learning. *Educational Researcher, 21,* 5–14.

Osipow, S. H. (1983). *Theories of career development* (3rd edition). Englewood Cliffs, NJ: Prentice Hall.

Osipow, S. H., and Rooney, R. A. (1989). *Task-specific occupational self-efficacy scale.* Columbus, OH: Authors.

Pickering, J. W., Calliotte, J. A., and McAuliffe, G. J. (1989). *Career Confidence Scale.* (Available from Dr. J. W. Pickering, Old Dominion University, Norfolk, VA. 23529).

Pitz, G., and Harren, V. (1980). An analysis of career decision making from the point of view of information processing and decision theory. *Journal of Vocational Behavior, 16,* 320–46.

Polkinghorne, D. E. (1984). Further extensions of methodological diversity for counseling psychology. *Journal of Counseling Psychology, 31,* 416–29.

Polkinghorne, D. E. (1991). Two conflicting calls for methodological reform. *The Counseling Psychologist, 19,* 103–14.

Reid, P. T. (1993). Poor women in psychological research: Shut up and shut out. *Psychology of Women Quarterly, 17,* 133–50.

Sampson, J., Peterson, G., Lenz, J., and Reardon, R. (1992). A cognitive approach to career services: Translating concepts into practice. *Career Development Quarterly, 41,* 67–74.

Savickas, M. (1990). Annual review: Practice and research in career counseling and development, 1988. *Career Development Quarterly, 41,* 100–34.

Sharf, R. (1997). *Applying career development theory to counseling* (2nd edition). Pacific Grove, CA: Brooks/Cole Publishing.

Solberg, V. S., Good, G. E., Fischer, A. R., Brown, S. D., and Nord, D. (1995). Career decision-making and career search activities: Relative effects of career search self-efficacy and human agency. *Journal of Counseling Psychology, 42,* 448–55.

Solberg, V. S., Good, G., E., Nord, D., Holm, C., Hohner, R., Zima, N., Heffernan, M., and Malen, A. (1994). Assessing career search expectations: Development and validation of the Career Search Efficacy Scale. *Journal of Career Assessment, 2,* 111–23.

Solberg, V. S., O'Brien, K., Villarreal, P., Kennel, R., and Davis, B. (1993). Self-efficacy and Hispanic college students: Validation of the College Self-Efficacy Instrument. *Hispanic Journal of Behavioral Sciences, 15,* 80–95.

Taylor, K. M., and Betz, N. (1983). Applications of self-efficacy theory to the understanding and treatment of career indecision. *Journal of Vocational Development, 22,* 63–81.

Temple, R. D., and Osipow, S. H. (1994). The relationship between task-specific self-efficacy egalitarianism and career indecision for females. *Journal of Career Assessment, 2,* 82–90.

Triandis, H. C. (1993). Comments on "multicultural career counseling." *The Career Development Quarterly, 42,* 50–52.

Tversky, A. (1972). Elimination by aspects: A theory of choice. *Psychology Review, 79,* 281–90.

Wilson, W. J. (1996). *When work disappears: The world of the new urban poor.* New York: Alfred A. Knopf.

Zunker, V. (1990). *Career counseling: Applied concepts of life planning* (3rd edition). Pacific Grove, CA: Brooks/Cole Publishing.

Chapter 8

Associated Press. (1996a, September 17). Anglos receive most welfare, study says. *El Paso Times,* p. 4A.

Associated Press. (1996b, September 11). Fewer workers have health insurance. *El Paso Herald-Post,* p. A2.

Associated Press. (1997a, September 16). Keep families in mind, CEO tells colleagues. *El Paso Times,* p. 5D.

Associated Press. (1997b, December 26). Off welfare and into the work force. *El Paso Times,* p. 4B.

Associated Press. (1997c, June 30). Welfare's old ways at an end. *El Paso Herald-Post,* p. A2.

Associated Press. (1998, August 10). Statistics paint complex picture of U.S. poverty. *El Paso Times,* p. 7A.

Baber, K., and Monaghan, P. (1988). College women's career and motherhood expectations: New options, old dilemmas. *Sex Roles, 19,* 189–203.

Barnett, R. C., and Rivers, C. (1996). *She works, he works: How two-income families are happier, healthier, and better off.* HarperSanFrancisco.

Betz, N. E. (1994). Basic issues and concepts in career counseling for women. In W. B. Walsh and S. H. Osipow (Eds.), *Career counseling for women* (pp. 1–41). Hillsdale, NJ: Lawrence Erlbaum Associates.

Bradley, R. (1982). Using birth order and sibling dynamics in career counseling. *The Personnel and Guidance Journal, 31,* 25–31.

Carter, B., and McGoldrick, M. (1989). Overview: The changing family life cycle—A framework for family therapy. In B. Carter and M. McGoldrick (Eds.), *The changing family life cycle: A framework for family therapy* (2nd edition) (pp. 3–28). Boston: Allyn and Bacon.

Clark, R. M. (1983). *Family life and school achievement: Why poor Black children succeed or fail.* Chicago: University of Chicago Press.

Cose, E. (1996, September 9). No work, no welfare. *Newsweek,* 46–47.

Davies, M., and Kandel, D. (1981). Parental and peer influences on adolescents educational plans: Some further evidence. *American Journal of Sociology, 87,* 363–87.

Derr, C. (1986). *Managing the new careerists: The diverse career success orientations of today's workers.* San Francisco: Jossey-Bass.

Fischer, D. H. (1989). *Albion's seed: Four British folkways in America.* New York: Oxford University Press.

Friesen, J. (1986). The role of family in vocational development. *International Journal for the Advancement of Counseling, 9,* 87–96.

Fulmer, R. H. (1989). Lower-income and professional families: A comparison of structure and life cycle process. In B. Carter and M. McGoldrick (Eds.), *The changing family life cycle: A framework for family therapy* (2nd edition) (pp. 545–78). Boston: Allyn and Bacon.

Gergen, K. J. (1991a). The saturated family. *Family Therapy Networker, 15* (5), 27–35.

Goldenberg, I., and Goldenberg, H. (1985). *Family therapy: An overview* (2nd edition). Pacific Grove, CA: Brooks/Cole Publishing.

Gysbers, N. C., and Moore, E. J. (1987). *Career counseling: Skills and techniques for practitioners.* Boston: Allyn and Bacon.

Hall, D. (1989). Promoting work/family balance: An organization-change approach. *Organizational Dynamics,* 5–18.

Hard, N. L., and Schoenmakers, C. (1997, May). *Common terms and acronyms—care and education of young children.* [hand-out]

Hardy, K. V. (1993). Live supervision in the postmodern era of family therapy: Issues, reflections, and questions. *Contemporary Family Therapy, 15,* 9–20.

Harmon, L. (1989). Longitudinal changes in women's career aspirations: Developmental or historical? *Journal of Vocational Behavior, 35,* 46–63.

Hartung, P. (1992). Balancing work and love: The case of Rosie. *The Career Development Quarterly, 42,* 56–60.

Jones, D., and Belton, B. (1997, September 30). Median income up $410. *USA Today,* p. 3B.

Kaplan, P. (1993). *The human odyssey: Life-span development.* Minneapolis/St. Paul: West.

Kuehr, W. (1997). *Processes and outcomes of mentoring relationships in selected at-risk elementary students.* Unpublished doctoral dissertation, Our Lady of the Lake University.

Loerch, K. J., Russell, J. E. A., and Rush, M. C. (1989). The relationships among family domain variables and work—family conflict for men and women. *Journal of Vocational Behavior, 35,* 288–308.

Los Angeles Times. (1997, October 14). Advocates urge disability cutoff appeals. *El Paso Times,* p. 4A.

MacGregor A, and Cochran, L. (1988). Work as enactment of family drama. *Career Development Quarterly, 37,* (2) 138–48.

Maslow, A. M. (1954). *Motivation and personality.* New York: Harper & Row.

McDaniels C., and Gysbers, N. (1992). *Counseling for career development.* San Francisco: Jossey-Bass.

McGoldrick, M. (1989a). Ethnicity and the family life cycle. In B. Carter and M. McGoldrick (Eds.), *The changing family life cycle: A framework for family therapy* (2nd edition) (pp. 69–90). Boston: Allyn and Bacon.

McGoldrick, M. (1989b). The joining of families through marriage: The new couple. In B. Carter and M. McGoldrick (Eds.), *The changing family life cycle: A framework for family therapy* (2nd edition) (pp. 209–233). Boston: Allyn and Bacon.

McGoldrick, M. (1989c). Women and the family life cycle. In B. Carter and M. McGoldrick (Eds.), *The changing family life cycle: A framework for family therapy* (2nd edition) (pp. 29–68). Boston: Allyn and Bacon.

McGoldrick, M., and Gerson, R. (1985). *Genograms in family assessment.* New York: W. W. Norton & Company.

Mead, L. M. (1992). *The new politics of poverty: The nonworking poor in America.* New York: Basic Books.

Meeks, S., Arnkoff, D., and Glass, C. (1986). Wives' employment status, hassles, communication and relational efficacy: Intra- and extra-relationship factors and marital adjustment. *Family Relations Journal of Applied Family and Child Studies, 35,* (2) 249–55.

Minuchin, S. (1974). *Families and family therapy.* Cambridge, MA: Harvard University Press.

Moon, S., Coleman, V., McCollum, E., Nelson, T., and Jensen-Scott, R. (1993). Using the genogram to facilitate career decisions: A case study. *Journal of Family Psychotherapy, 4,* (1), 45–56.

New York Times News Service. (1997, May 5). Aid for immigrants back in budget. *El Paso Herald-Post,* p. A2.

Okiishi, R. (1987). The genogram as a tool in career counseling. *Journal of Counseling and Development, 66,* 139–43.

Owens, T. (1992). The effect of post-high school social context on self-esteem. *Sociological Quarterly, 33* (4), 553–77.

Penick, N. (1990). *An exploratory investigation of the relationship between measures of family functioning and adolescent career development.* Unpublished doctoral dissertation, University of Iowa.

Pinderhughes, E. (1995, March). Empowering diverse populations: Family practice in the 21st century. *Families in Society: The Journal of Contemporary Human Services,* 131–40.

Powers, R., and Griffith, J. (1993). The case of Rosie: An Adlerian response. *The Career Development Quarterly, 42,* 69–75.

Rabinow, P. (Ed.). (1984). *The Foucault reader.* New York: Pantheon Books.

Rachlin, V, and Hansen, J. (1985). The impact of equity or egalitarianism on dual-career couples. *Family Therapy, 12* (2), 151–64.

Rawlings, S. W. (1995). Households and families. In U.S. Bureau of the Census, Current Population Reports, Series P23–189, Population Profile of the United States, 1995 (pp. 22–23). Washington, D.C.: U.S. Government Printing Office.

Richter, C., Morrison, D. L., and Salinas, A. (1991). *The dual-career family and implications for the career counselor.* Unpublished paper.

Roe, A. (1957). Early determinants of vocational choice. *Journal of Counseling Psychology, 4,* 212–17.

Roe, A., and Lunneborg, P. (1990). Personality development and career choice. In D. Brown, L. Brooks, and Associates (Eds.). *Career choice and development: Applying contemporary theories to practice.* (2nd edition) (pp. 68–102). San Francisco: Jossey-Bass.

Savickas, M. L. (1989). Career-style assessment and counseling. In T. Sweeney (Ed.), *Adlerian counseling: A practical approach for a new decade* (3rd edition). Muncie, IN: Accelerated Development.

Single parents: Career-related issues and needs. (1988). ERIC Digest No. 75. Columbus, OH: Clearinghouse on Adult, Career and Vocational Education.

Spencer, K. I., and Featherman, D. L. (1978). Achievement ambitions. *Annual Review of Sociology, 4,* 373–420.

Srivastva, S., Fry, R. E., and Cooperrider, D. L. (1990). Introduction: The call for executive appreciation. In S. Srivastva, D. L. Cooperrider, and Associates (Eds.), *Appreciative management and leadership: The power of positive thought and action in organizations* (pp. 1–33). San Francisco: Jossey-Bass.

Sullivan, S. (1992). Is there a time for everything? Attitudes related to women's sequencing of career and family. *The Career Development Quarterly, 40,* 234–42.

The Center for Public Policy Priorities. (1997, March 14). *The policy page, 44,* 1–5.

Thomas, R. R., Jr. (1990, March–April). From affirmative action to affirming diversity. *Harvard Business Review,* 107–17.

von Bertalanffy, L. (1968). *General systems theory: Foundation, development, application.* New York: George Braziller.

Voydanoff, P. (1988). Work and family: A review and expanded conceptualization. *Journal of Social Behavior and Personality, 3* (4), 1–22.

Walsh, F. (1989). The family in later life. In B. Carter and M. McGoldrick (Eds.), *The changing family life cycle: A framework for family therapy* (2nd edition) (pp. 311–34). Boston: Allyn and Bacon.

Washington Post. (1996, September 24). 1st conditions of welfare law take effect amid confusion. *El Paso Times,* p. 4A.

Watkins, C. E. (1984). The individual psychology of Alfred Adler: Toward an Adlerian vocational theory. *Journal of Vocational Behavior, 24,* 28–47.

Watkins, C. E., and Savickas, M. L. (1990). Psychodynamic career counseling. In W. B. Walsh and S. H. Osipow (Eds.), *Career counseling: Contemporary topics in vocational psychology* (pp. 79–116). Hillsdale, NJ: Lawrence Erlbaum Associates.

Watts, R., and Engels, D. (1995). The life task of vocation: A review of Adlerian research literature. *Texas Counseling Association Journal,* 9–19.

Weiberg, R. B., and Mauksch, L. B. (1991). Examining family-of-origin influences in life at work. *Journal of Marital and Family Therapy, 17,* 233–42.

Weitzman, L. (1994). Multiple role realism: A theoretical framework for the process of planning to combine career and family roles. *Applied and Preventive Psychology, 3,* 15–25.

Young, R., and Friesen, J. (1992). The intentions of parents in influencing the career development of their children. *The Career Development Quarterly, 40,* 198–205.

Young, R., Friesen, J., and Dillabough, R. (1991). Personal constructions of parental influence related to career development. *Canadian Journal of Counselling, 25,* 183–90.

Chapter 9

Allen, J. M. (1994). School counselors collaborating for student success. *ERIC Digest,* Report No. EDO-CG-94-27. Greensboro, NC: Clearinghouse on Counseling and Student Services.

American Association of University Women. (1991, January). *Shortchanging girls, shortchanging America: Executive summary.* Washington, D.C.: Author.

Atkinson, D., Morten, G., and Sue, D. (1993). *Counseling American minorities: A cross-cultural perspective* (4th edition). Dubuque, IA: Brown and Benchmark.

Belvis, R., Rodriguez, R., and Fellan, E. (1996). Integrating career exploration in the middle school curriculum. Unpublished paper.

Berman, J., and Cosca, T. (1992). The 1990–2005 job outlook in brief. *Occupational Outlook Handbook, 36,* 6–41.

Bingham, M., Edmonson, J., and Stryker, S. (1987). *Choices: A teen women's journal for self-awareness and planning.* Santa Barbara, CA: Advocacy Press.

Bingham, M., and Stryker, S. (1995). *Things will be different for my daughter: A practical guide to building her self-esteem and self-reliance.* New York: Penguin Books.

Brown, D., Minor, C., and Jepsen, D. (1992). Public support for career development activities America's schools: Report of the 1989 NCDA survey. *The School Counselor, 39,* 257–62.

Brzowsky, S. (1998, February 8). Are girls being shortchanged? *Parade Magazine,* 10.

Byrnes, J. P. (1996). *Cognitive development and learning in instructional contexts.* Boston: Allyn and Bacon.

Campbell, C. A., and Dahir, C. A. (Eds.). (1997). *The National Standards for School Counseling Programs.* Alexandria, VA: American School Counselor Association.

Canfield, J., and Wells, H. C. (1994). *100 ways to enhance self-concept in the classroom.* Boston: Allyn and Bacon.

Catherine, L. (1997). *Career education guide: Comprehensive, PK-adult.* San Antonio, TX: East Central Independent School District.

Catlett, J. (1992). The dignity of work: School children look at employment. *The Career Development Quarterly, 27,* 150–54.

Cobb, R. B., and Neubert, D. A. (1998). Vocational education: Emerging vocationalism. In F. R. Rusch and J. G. Chadsey (Eds.), *Beyond high school: Transition from school to work* (pp. 101–26). Belmont, CA: Wadsworth Publishing.

Cochran, L. (1983). Implicit versus explicit importance of career values in making a career decision. *Journal of Counseling Psychology, 30,* 188–93.

Cohen, J. L. (1992). *Tu puedes ser una ingeniera* (J. M. Yáñez, Trans. from English). Culver City, CA: Cascade Pass, Inc.

Cohen, J. L. (1995). *You can be a woman engineer.* Culver City, CA: Cascade Pass, Inc.

Commission of the Skills of the American Workforce. (1990). *America's choice: High skills or low wages.* Rochester, NY: National Center of Education and Economy.

Commission on Precollege Guidance and Counseling. (1986). *Keeping the options open: Recommendations.* NY: College Entrance Examination Board.

Elium, J., and Elium, D. (1994). *Raising a daughter: Parents and the awakening of a healthy woman.* Berkeley, CA: Celestial Arts.

Fairchild, T., and Seeley, T. (1994). Time analysis: Still an important accountability tool. *The School Counselor, 41,* 273–78.

Ferrero, G., and McKenna, A. (1991). Ninth grade students attitudes toward nontraditional occupations. *The Career Development Quarterly, 40,* 168–81.

Freeman, B. (1996). The use and perceived effectiveness of career assessment tools: A survey of high school counselors. *Journal of Career Development, 22,* 185–96.

Gabriel, D. L., and Cohen, J. L. (1993a). *Tu puedes ser paleontóloga* (J. M. Yáñez, Trans. from English). Culver City, CA: Cascade Pass, Inc.

Gabriel, D. L., and Cohen, J. L. (1993b). *You can be a woman palentologist.* Culver City, CA: Cascade Press, Inc.

Ghez, A. M., and Cohen, J. L. (1995). *You can be a woman astronomer.* Culver City, CA: Cascade Press, Inc.

Ginzberg, E. (1952). Toward a theory of occupational choice. *Occupations, 30,* 491–94.

Goldentyer, D. (1994). *Dropping out of school.* Austin, TX: Raintree Steck-Vaughan.

Grant, D. (1997). *Random thoughts and observations re middle school students and career guidance.* Unpublished paper.

Grant, D. (1997). *Report card paycheck program.* San Antonio, TX: Northside Independent School District.

Grotevant, H., and Cooper, H. (1988). The role of family experience in career exploration: A life span perspective. In P. Baltes, D. Featherman, and R. Lerner (Eds.), *Life span development and behavior* (pp. 231–58). London: Lawrence Erlbaum.

Grotevant, H., and Durrett, M. (1980). Occupational knowledge and career development in adolescence. *Journal of Vocational Behavior, 17,* 171–82.

Haggerty, R. (1989). Youth and America's future: The forgotten half. *Developmental and Behavioral Pediatrics, 10,* 321–25.

Hall, A., Kelly, K., and VanBuren, J. (1995). Effects of grade level, community of residence, and sex on adolescent career interests in the zone of acceptable alternatives. *Journal of Career Development, 21,* 223–31.

Hanley-Maxwell, C., Pogoloff, S. M., and Whitney-Thomas, J. (1998). Families: The heart of transition. In F. R. Rusch and J. G. Chadsey (Eds.), *Beyond high school: Transition from school to work* (pp. 234–64). Belmont, CA: Wadsworth Publishing.

Hansen, L. S. (1993). Career development trends and issues in the United States. *Journal of Career Development, 20,* 7–24.

Henderson, P. (1996). *Facilitating students' career development through comprehensive guidance programs: Delivery systems activities.* San Antonio, TX: Northside Independent School District.

Hoare, C. (1991). Psychosocial identity development and cultural others. *Journal of Counseling and Development, 70,* 45–53.

Hoffman, L., and McDaniels, C. (1992). Career development in the elementary schools: A perspective for the 1990s. *Elementary School Guidance and Counseling, 25,* 163–171.

Hoyt, K. B. (1989). *Counselors and career development—A topic in educational reform proposals: A selected review of national education reform documents.* Columbus, OH: Center on Education and Training for Employment, Ohio State University.

Hoyt, K. B. (1994). Youth apprenticeship: American style and career development. *The Career Development Quarterly, 42,* 216–23.

Hoyt, K. B., Hughey, J. K., and Hughey, K. F. (1995). An introduction to the "Counseling for High Skills: Vo-Tech Career Options" project. *The School Counselor, 43,* 10–18.

Interest Determination, Exploration, and Assessment System (IDEAS). (1990). Minneapolis, MN: NCS Assessments.

Kuczynski, L. B. (1997). *Life planning and career assessment: Eighth grade at-risk students model.* Unpublished paper.

Kush, K., and Cochran, L. (1993). Enhancing a sense of agency through career planning. *Journal of Counseling Psychology, 40,* 434–39.

Lichtenstein, S. (1998). Characteristics of youth and young adults. In F. R. Rusch and J. G. Chadsey (Eds.), *Beyond high school: Transition from school to work* (pp. 3–35). Belmont, CA: Wadsworth Publishing.

Lingg, M. A. (1996). Training for job-skills confidence. *Journal of Career Development, 22,* 261–71.

Lopez, F., and Andrews, S. (1987). Career indecision: A family systems perspective. *Journal of Counseling ad Development, 65,* 304–7.

Marcia, J. (1966). Development and validation of ego identity status. *Journal of Personality and Social Psychology, 3,* 551–58.

Marone, N. (1988). *How to father a successful daughter.* New York: Fawcett Crest.

Mau, W.-C. (1995). Educational planning and academic achievement of middle school students: A racial and cultural comparison. *Journal of Counseling and Development, 73,* 518–26.

McCharen, B. (1997). *Career connection and the counselor's role: Providing opportunities and hope for today's students and families.* Paper presented at the Mid-Winter Conference of the Texas Career Guidance Association/Texas Career and Technology Guidance Association, Austin, TX.

McAlary, F., and Cohen, J. L. (1992a). *Tu puedes ser bióloga marina* (J. Yáñez, Trans. from English). Culver City, CA: Cascade Press, Inc.

McAlary, F., and Cohen, J. L. (1992b). *You can be a woman marine biologist.* Culver City, CA: Cascade Press, Inc.

McKenna, A., and Ferrero, G. (1991). Ninth grade students' attitudes toward nontraditional occupations. *The Career Development Quarterly, 40,* 168–80.

Middleton, E., and Loughead, T. (1993). Parental influence on career development: An integrative framework for adolescent career counseling. *Journal of Career Development, 19,* 161–72.

National Occupational Information Coordinating Committee (NOICC). (1996). *The National Career Development Guidelines.* Washington, D.C: NOICC.

Olesky-Ojikutu, A. E. (1986). A career time-line: A vocational counseling tool. *The Career Development Quarterly, 35,* 47–52.

Otto, L., and Call, V. (1985). Parental influence on young people's career development. *Journal of Career Development, 12,* 65–96.

Penick, N., and Jepsen, D. (1992). Family functioning and adolescent career development. *The Career Development Quarterly, 40,* 208–22.

Phipps, B. J. (1995). Career dreams of preadolescent students. *Journal of Career Development, 22,* 20–32.

Post, P., Williams, M., and Brubaker, L. (1996). Career and lifestyle expectations of rural eighth grade students: A second look. *The Career Development Quarterly, 44,* 250– 57.

Prediger, D. J., and Brandt, W. E. (1991). Project CHOICE: Validity of interest and ability measures for student choice of vocational program. *The Career Development Quarterly, 40,* 132–43.

Ramirez, M. (1991). *Psychotherapy and counseling with minorities: A cognitive approach to individual and cultural differences.* New York: Pergamon Press.

Rea-Poteat, M., and Martin, P. (1991). Taking your place: A summer program to encourage non-traditional career choices for adolescent girls. *The Career Development Quarterly, 40,* 182–88.

Redborg, R., and Cohen, J. L. (1996). *You can be a woman cardiologist.* Culver City, CA: Cascade Press, Inc.

Rusch, F. R., and Millar, D. M. (1998). Emerging transition best practices. In F. R. Rusch and J. G. Chadsey (Eds.), *Beyond high school: Transition from school to work* (pp. 36–59). Belmont, CA: Wadsworth Publishing.

Sagor, R. (1993). *At-risk students: Reaching and teaching them.* Swampscott, MA: Watersun.

Siegel, M., and Cohen, J. L. (1992a). *Tu puedes ser una arquitecta* (J. M. Yáñez, Trans. from English). Culver City, CA: Cascade Press, Inc.

Siegel, M., and Cohen, J. L. (1992b). *You can be a woman architect.* Culver City, CA: Cascade Press, Inc.

Siegel, S. (1998). Foundations for a school-to-work system that serves all students. In F. R. Rusch and J. G. Chadsey (Eds.), *Beyond high school: Transition from school to work* (pp. 146–78). Belmont, CA: Wadsworth Publishing.

Szymanski, E. M. (1998). Career development, school-to-work transition, and diversity: An ecological approach. In F. R. Rusch and J. G. Chadsey (Eds.), *Beyond high school: Transition from school to work* (pp. 127–45). Belmont, CA: Wadsworth Publishing.

The William T. Grant Foundation Commission on Work, Family, and Citizenship. (1988, February). The forgotten half: Non-college bound youth in America. *Phi Delta Kappan,* 409–14.

Thompson, V., and Cohen, J. L. (1993). *Tu puedes ser una zoóloga* (J. M. Yáñez, Trans. from English). Culver City, CA: Cascade Press, Inc.

Thompson, V., and Cohen, J. L. (1992). *You can be a woman zoologist.* Culver City, CA: Cascade Press, Inc.

Thurlow, M., and Elliott, J. (1998). Student assessment and evaluation. In F. R. Rusch and J. G. Chadsey (Eds.), *Beyond high school: Transition from school to work* (pp. 265–296). Belmont, CA: Wadsworth Publishing.

Trice, A. (1991). Stability of child career aspirations. *Journal of Genetic Psychology, 152,* 137–139.

Trice, A., Hughes, M., Odom, C., Woods, K., and McClellan, N. (1995). The origins of children's career aspirations: Testing hypotheses from four theories. *The Career Development Quarterly, 43,* 307–22.

Trice, A., McClellan, N., and Hughes, M. (1992). Origins of children's career aspirations II: Direct suggestions as a method of transmitting occupational preferences. *Psychological Reports, 71,* (1) 253–54.

Trice, A., and King, R. (1991). Stability of kindergarten children's career aspirations. *Psychological Reports, 68,* 1378.

Trice, A., and Tillapaugh, P. (1991). Children's estimates of their parents' job satisfaction. *Psychological Reports, 69,* 63–66.

Trusty, J., and Watts, R. E. (1996). Parents' perceptions of career information resources. *Career Development Quarterly, 44,* 242–49.

Trusty, J., Watts, R. E., and Crawford, R. (1996). Career information resources for parents of public school seniors: Findings from a national study. *Journal of Career Development, 22,* 227–38.

United States Department of Labor, Special Commission on Achieving Necessary Skills. (1991). *What work requires of schools: A SCANS report for America 2000.* Washington, D.C.: United States Department of Labor.

Walz, G., and Bleuer, J. C. (1992). *Student self-esteem: A vital element of School Success.* Ann Arbor, MI: Counseling and Personnel Services.

Whiston, S. (1989). Using family systems theory in career counseling: A group for parents. *The School Counselor, 36,* 343–47.

Wood, S. (1990). Initiating career plans with freshmen. *The School Counselor, 37,* 233–37.

Young, R., and Friesen, J. (1992). The intentions of parents in influencing the career development of their children. *The Career Development Quarterly, 40,* 196–207.

Young, J., Thomas, R., Hillard, S., Shaw, H., and Epstein, E. (1996). Anatomy of a career guidance unit. *Elementary School Guidance and Counseling, 30,* 304–12.

Yost, E., and Corbishley, M. (1987). *Career counseling: A Psychological Approach.* San Francisco: Jossey-Bass.

Chapter 10

Accreditation Council of Continuing Education and Training (ACCET) Report. (1991). U.S. Department of Education.

Allyn, D. P. (1989) Application of the 4mat model to career guidance. *The Career Development Quarterly, 37,* 280–88.

American Association of Community Colleges. (1996) *Developing the world's best workforce: An agenda for America's community colleges—Executive summary.* Washington, D.C.: Author.

Bingham, R., and Ward, C. (1994). Career counseling with ethnic minority women. In W. B. Walsh and S. H. Osipow (Eds.), *Career counseling for women* (pp. 165–95). Hillsdale, NJ: Lawrence Erlbaum Associates.

Bradley, R. W., and Mims, G. A. (1992). Using family systems and birth order dynamics as the basis for a college career decision-making course. *Journal of Counseling & Development, 70,* 445–48.

Brown, D., and Minor, C. (Eds.). (1991). *Minorities' perceptions of career planning and work.* Alexandria, VA: National Career Development Association.

Crozier, S. (1991). Empowering the liberal arts student with personal flexibility for the world of work. *Canadian Journal of Counselling and Development, 25,* 97–109.

Elwood, J. A. (1992). The pyramid model: A useful tool in career counseling with university students. *The Career Development Quarterly, 41,* 51–54.

Gallup Organization. (1989). *A Gallup survey regarding career development.* Princeton, NJ: Author.

Hall, C., Hayes, R., Morris, S., Rendón, I, and Zepeda, F. (1993). *Vocational Schools.* Unpublished manuscript.

Healy, C., and Mourton, D. (1987). Career exploration, college jobs, and GPA. *Journal of College Student Personnel, 28,* 27–34.

Healy, C., and Reilly, K. (1989). Career needs of community college students: Implications for theory and practice. *Journal of College Student Development, 30,* 541–45.

Heppner, M., and Duan, C. (1995). From a narrow to expansive world view: Making career centers a place for diverse students. *Journal of Career Development, 22,* 87–100.

Heppner, M., and Johnston, J. (1993). Career counseling: A call to action. In J. Rayman (Ed.), *Contemporary career services.* San Francisco: Jossey-Bass.

Isaacson, L., and Brown, D. (1993). *Career information, career counseling, and career development* (5th edition). Needham Heights, MA: Allyn and Bacon.

Johnston, W., and Packer, A. (1987). *Workforce 2000: Workers and work for the 21st century.* Indianapolis: Hudson Institute.

Kobylarz, L. (Ed.). (1996). *National Career Development Guidelines K-Adult Handbook.* National Occupational Information Coordinating Committee, Stillwater, OK: NOICC Training Support Center.

Luzzo, D. (1996). Exploring the relationship between the perception of occupational barriers and career development. *Journal of Career Development, 22,* 239–48.

McAuliffe, G. J., and Fredrickson, R. (1990). The effects of program length and participant characteristics on group career-counseling outcomes. *Journal of Employment Counseling, 27,* 19–22.

McCarthy, B. (1987). *The 4mat system: Teaching to learning styles with right/left mode techniques* (revised edition). Barrington, IL: Excel.

McWhirter, E. (1994, August). *Perceived barriers to education and career: Ethnic and gender differences.* Paper presented at the Annual Convention of the American Psychological Association, Los Angeles.

Nyre, G., and Reilly, K. (1987). *A study of career/vocational counseling in California community colleges.* Santa Clara, CA: C/VEG Publications.

Olson, T., and Matkin, R. (1992). Student and counselor perceptions of career counselor work activities in a community college. *The Career Development Quarterly, 40,* 324–33.

Rayman, J. (1993). Concluding remarks and career service imperatives for the 1990s. In J. Rayman (Ed.), *The changing role of career services.* (pp. 101–108). San Francisco: Jossey-Bass.

Robinson, C. R. (1996). *Increasing the value of career courses.* Paper presented at the Texas Vocational Guidance Association/Texas Career Guidance Association Mid-Winter Conference, Austin, TX.

Samples, B. (1976). *The metaphoric mind.* Reading, MA: Addison-Wesley.

Savickas, M. (1990). The career decision making course: Description and field test. *Journal of College Student Development, 38,* 275–84.

Smith, G. E. (1987). *A study of the career development characteristics of first-year community college business majors with implications for additional research and a suggested advisement model.* Paper presented at the American Vocational Association Convention, Las Vegas, NM. ERIC ED 290032.

Swanson, J. L. & Tokar, D. M. (1991). Development and initial validation of barriers to career development. *Journal of Vocational Behavior, 39,* 92–106.

Yaegel, J. (1978). Certainty of vocational choice and the persistence and achievements of liberal arts community college freshman. *Dissertation Abstracts International, 38,* 118A.

Zagora, M., and Cramer, S. (1994). The effects of vocational identity status on outcomes of a career decision making intervention for community college students. *Journal of College Student Development, 35,* 239–47.

Chapter 11

Amundson, N. E., and Borgen, W. A. (1988). Factors that help and hinder group employment counseling. *Journal of Employment Counseling, 25,* 104–14.

Armour, S. (1997, October 24). Age-bias case sounds warning. *USA Today,* p. 1B.

Aubrey, T., Tefft, B., and Kingsbury, N. (1990). Behavioral and psychological consequences of unemployment in blue-collar workers. *Journal of Community Psychology, 18,* 99–109.

Barefoot, J. C., Larsen, S., von der Leith, L., and Schroll, M. (1995). Hostility, incidence of acute myocardial infarction, and mortality in a sample of older Danish men and women. *American Journal of Epidemiology, 142,* 477–84.

Beijan, D., and Salomone. (1995). Understanding midlife career renewal: implications for counseling. *The Career Development Quarterly, 44,* 52–64.

Brown, D. (1995). A values-based approach to facilitating career transitions. *The Career Development Quarterly, 44,* 4–11.

Brown, D. (1996). Brown's values-based holistic model of career and life-role choices and satisfaction. In D. Brown, L. Brooks and Associates (Eds.), *Career Choice & Development,* (3rd edition) (pp. 337–72). San Francisco: Jossey-Bass.

Brown, M., Fukunaga, C., Umemoto, D., and Wicker, L. (1996). Annual review, 1990–1996: Social class, work and retirement behavior. *Journal of Vocational Behavior, 49,* 159–89.

Bullfinch's Mythology. (1978). New York: Avenel Books.

Burg, M. M. (1995). Anger, hostility, and coronary heart disease: A review. *Mind/Body Medicine, 1,* 159–72.

Burney, T. (1995, December 11). It's not supposed to be a workplace issue: But the effects of domestic violence are spreading into the workplace. *El Paso Herald-Post,* p. B5.

Cahill, M., and Salomone, P. (1987). Career counseling for work life extension: integrating the older worker into the labor force. *The Career Development Quarterly, 35,* 188–267.

Carter, M., and Cook, K. (1995). Adaptation to retirement: role changes and psychological resources. *The Career Development Quarterly, 44,* 67–83.

Champagne, D. (1987). Disadvantaged adult learners: can career counseling enhance adult education program effectiveness? *Adult Education Quarterly, 37,* 63–77.

Cherniss, C. (1995). *Beyond burnout: Helping teachers, nurses, therapists, and lawyers recover from stress and disillusion.* New York: Routledge.

Chodorow, N. (1978). *The reproduction of mothering.* Berkeley: University of California Press.

Cobble, D. (1996, February 29). Be wary of employees who overwork. *El Paso Herald-Post,* p. A10.

Cohen, N. (1995). *Mentoring adult learners: A guide for educators and trainers.* Melbourne, FL: Krieger Publishing.

Collard, B., Epperheimer, J. S., and Saign, D. *Career resilience in a changing workplace.* Adapted from ERIC Information Series No. 366.

Cook, E. P. (1993). The gendered context of life: Implications for women's and men's career-life plans. *The Career Development Quarterly, 41,* 227–37.

Crace, R., and Brown, D. (1992). *The Life Values Inventory.* Minneapolis: National Computer Systems.

Deary, I. J., Fowkes, F. G. R., Donnan, P. T., and Housley, E. (1994). Hostile personality and risks of peripheral arterial disease in the general population. *Psychosomatic Medicine, 56,* 197–202.

de Becker, G. (1997). *The gift of fear: Survival signals that protect us from violence. Boston:* Little, Brown, and Company.

Deutschman, A. (1990, August 27). "What twenty-five year olds want." *Fortune,* 42–48.

Doby, V. J., and Caplan, R. D. (1995). Organizational stress as threat to reputation: Effects on anxiety at work and at home. *Academy of Management Journal, 38* (4), 1105–1123.

Doyle, J. A. (1989). *The male experience* (2nd edition). Dubuque, IA: Wm. C. Brown.

Drummond, R., and Ryan, C. (1995). *Career counseling: A developmental approach.* Englewood Cliffs, NJ: Prentice Hall.

Eby, L. T., and Buch, K. (1995). Job loss as career growth: Responses to involuntary career transitions. *The Career Development Quarterly, 44,* 26–43.

Educational Testing Service. (1994). SIGI PLUS [computer software]. Princeton, NJ: Author.

Edwards, O. (1991). *Upward nobility: How to succeed in business without losing your soul.* New York: Crown Publishers.

Emener, W., and Rubin, S. (1980). Rehabilitation counselor roles and functions and sources of role strain. *Journal of Applied Rehabilitation Counseling, 11* (2), 57–69.

Engels, D. (1995). Common themes in midlife career transitions. *The Career Development Quarterly, 44,* 83–89.

Farber, B., and Heifetz, L. (1981). The satisfaction and stresses of psychotherapeutic work: A factor analytic study. *Professional Psychology, 12* (5), 621–30.

Ference, T., Stoner, J., and Warren, E. (1977). Managing the career plateau. *Academy of Management Review, 2,* 602–12.

Filipczak, B. (1994, April). It's just a job: Generation X at work. *Training,* 21–27.

Forrest, L., and Mikolaitis, N. (1986). The relational component of identity: An expansion of career development theory. *The Career Development Quarterly, 35,* 76–88.

Friedman, M., and Rosenman, R. H. (1975). *Type A behavior and your heart.* New York: Knopf.

Friedman, M., and Ulmer, D. (1984). *Treating Type A behavior—and your heart.* New York: Knopf.

Gannett News Service. (1996, March 28). Immune system behind gulf illness, expert says. *El Paso Times,* pp. 1A, 6A.

Gates, B. (1997, April 27). Gates outlines 10 attributes of a good employee. *San Antonio Express-News,* p. 6J.

Genasci, L. (1995, December 20). Take two aspirin and get back to work. *El Paso Herald-Post,* pp. B5, B6.

Gilligan, C. (1982). *In a different voice.* Cambridge, MA: Harvard University Press.

Goodman, J. (1994). Career adaptability in adults: A construct whose time has come. *The Career Development Quarterly, 43,* 74–84.

Gross, D. M., and Scott, S. (1990, July 16). Proceeding with caution. *Time,* 56–62.

Gutek, B. A. (1985). *Sex and the workplace: The impact of sexual behavior and harassment on women, men, and organizations.* San Francisco: Jossey-Bass.

Gysbers, N. C., Heppner, M. J., and Johnston, J. A. (1998). *Career counseling: Process, issues and techniques.* Needham Heights, MA: Allyn & Bacon.

Hall, D., and Louis, M. (1988). When careers plateau. *Research Technology Management, 31,* 41–45.

Hall, D. T., and Associates. (1996). *The career is dead long live the career: A relational approach to careers.* San Francisco: Jossey-Bass.

Hansen, L. S. (1997). *Integrative life planning: Critical tasks for career development and changing life patterns.* San Francisco: Jossey-Bass.

Heppner, M. J., Multon, K. D., and Johnston, J A. (1994). Assessing psychological resources during career change: Development of the Career Transitions Inventory. *Journal of Vocational Behavior, 44,* 55–74.

Hirschhorn, L. (1988). *The workplace within: Psychodynamics of organizational life.* Cambridge, MA: MIT Press.

Hotelling, K., and Forrest, L. (1985). Gilligan's theory of sex-role development: A perspective for counseling. *Journal of Counseling and Development, 64,* 183–86.

Hudson, F. (1991). *The adult years: Mastering the art of self-renewal* (1st edition). San Francisco: Jossey-Bass.

Insel, P. M., and Roth, W. T. (1985). *Core concepts in health* (4th edition). Palo Alto, CA: Mayfield Publishing.

Jackson, P. R., Stafford, E. M., Banks, M. H., and Warr, P. B. (1983). Unemployment and psychological distress in young people: The moderating role of employment commitment. *Journal of Applied Psychology, 68,* 525–35.

Jensen-Scott, R. L. (1993). Counseling to promote retirement adjustment. *The Career Development Quarterly, 41,* 257–67.

Jordan, K. (1997, September 11). Ageism in the workplace: Fact or fiction [8 paragraphs]. *Online Solutions* [On-line serial].

Karsten, M. F. (1994). *Management and gender.* Westport, CT: Quorum Books.

Klarreich, S. H. (1988). *The stress solution: A rational approach to increasing corporate and personal effectiveness.* Toronto: Key Porter Books Limited.

Kelly, J. L. (1990, January). What went wrong? *Personnel Journal,* 43–55.

Kirk, J. J. (1994). Putting outplacement in its place. *Journal of Employment Counseling, 31,* 10–18.

Krain, M. A. (1995). Policy implications for a society aging well. *American Behavioral Scientist, 39,* (2), 131–51.

Krebs, N. B. (1993). *Changing woman, changing work.* Aspen, CO: MacMurray & Beck.

Laird, J. (1994). Changing women's narratives: Taking back the discourse. In L. V. Davis (Ed.), *Building on women's strengths: A social work agenda for the twenty-first century* (pp. 179–210). New York: The Haworth Press.

Levinson, D. (1978). *The seasons of a man's life.* New York: Knopf.

Lefkovich, J. (1992). Older workers: Why and how to capitalize on their powers. *Employment Relations Today,* 63–79.

Loeb, L. (1994). Community career services: The past, present, and future. *Journal of Career Development, 21,* 167–69.

Maccoby, E. E. (1990). Gender and relationships: A developmental account. *American Psychologist, 45,* 513–20.

MacKinnon-Slaney, F. (1994). The adult persistence in learning model: A road map to counseling services for adult learners. *Journal of Counseling and Development, 72,* 268–75.

Mallinckrodt, B., and Fretz, B. R. (1988). Social support and the impact of job loss on older professionals. *Journal of Counseling Psychology, 35,* 281–86.

Maremont, M., and Sassen, J. A. (1996, May 13). Abuse of power: The astonishing tale of sexual harassment at Astra U.S.A. *Business Week,* 86ff.

Mastering stress. (1987). Dallas, TX: Human Services, Inc.

McDaniels, C. (1996). Career + Work + Leisure (C = W + L): A developmental/trait factor approach to career development. In R. Feller and G. Walz (Eds.) *Career Transitions in Turbulent Times* (pp. 45–55). Greensboro, NC: ERIC/CASS Publications.

Morrison, A. M., White, R. P., and Van Velsor, E. (1987). *Breaking the glass ceiling.* Reading, MA: Addison-Wesley.

Murphy, S. E., and Ensher, E. A. (1997). The effects of culture on mentoring relationships. In C. S. Granrose and S. Oskamp (Eds.), *Cross-cultural work groups* (pp. 212–33). Thousand Oaks, CA: SAGE Publications.

Murray, P. (1993). Outplacement and careers: Giving your client a feel for work. *Employee Counseling Today, 5* (2), 14–17.

Nichols, N. A. (Ed.). (1994). *Reach for the top.* Cambridge, MA: Harvard Business Review.

O'Donohue, W. (Ed.), (1997). *Sexual harassment: Theory, research, and treatment.* Boston: Allyn and Bacon.

Pardine, P., Higgins, R., Szeglin, A., Beres, J., Kravitz, R., and Fotis, J. (1981). Job stress, worker-strain relationship moderated off-the-job experience. *Psychological Reports, 48,* 963–70.

Pavot, W., Diener, E., Colvin, C., and Sandvik, E. (1991). Further validation of the Satisfaction with Life Scale: Evidence for the cross-method convergence of well-being measures. *Journal of Personality Assessment, 57,* 149–61.

Pedersen, P., Goldberg, A., and Papalia, T. (1991). A model for planning career continuation and change through increased awareness, knowledge and skill. *Journal of Employment Counseling, 28,* 74–79.

Pedrotti. A. (1990, August 24). Change is part of today's job market. *Today's Catholic,* 19.

Peregoy, J. J., and Schliebner, C. T. (1990). Long term unemployment: Effects and counseling interventions. *International Journal for the Advancement of Counselling, 13,* 193–204.

Peregoy, P., and Schliebner, C. (1988, Aug.). *Impasse and sanity: Effects and interventions.* Paper presented at the International Roundtable for the Advancement of Counseling. Calgary, Alberta.

Perryman, M. R. (1996, March 21). Number of working moms expected to rise. *El Paso Herald-Post,* p. C5.

Pines, A., and Aronson, E. (1988). *Career burnout: Causes and cures.* New York: Free Press.

Polonsky, W. (1997, October 6). *Personality, motivation, and health: A seminar for health professionals.* Workshop presented by Mind Matters Seminars, El Paso, TX.

Ratcliffe, K. (1996, July). Five girls fight back. *Seventeen,* 110ff.

Rife, J. (1989). Reducing depression and increasing job placement success of older unemployed workers. *Clinical Gerontologist,* 81–85.

Rife, J., and Belcher, J. (1993). Social support and job search intensity among older unemployed workers: Implications for employment counselors. *Journal of Employment Counseling, 30,* 98–107.

Richardson, M. S. (1993). Work in people's lives: A location for counseling psychologists. *Journal of Counseling psychology, 40,* 425–33.

Ryan, W. (1971). *Blaming the victim.* New York: Random House

Schatz, R. D. (1997). The aging of the workforce. *Working Woman, 22* (5), 64–66.

Schieszer, J. (1996, January 16). Shifts that'll make your stomach turn. *El Paso Herald-Post,* pp. B3, B4.

Schlossberg, N. K. (1996). A model of worklife transitions. In R. Feller and G. Walz (Ed.), *Career transitions in turbulent times* (pp. 93–104). Greensboro, NC: ERIC/CASS Publications.

Sekarian, U., and Leong, F. T. L. (Eds.), *Womanpower: Managing in Times of Demographic Turbulence.* Newbury Park, CA: SAGE Publications.

Seybold, K. C., and Salomone, P. R. (1994). Understanding workaholism: A review of causes and counseling approaches. *Journal of Counseling and Career Development, 73,* 4–9.

Sharp, D. (1996, March 15–17). So many lists, so little time. *USA Weekend,* 1, 4–6.

Shore, L. (1992). Stress. In L. Jones, (Ed.), *The encyclopedia of career change and work issues* (pp. 138–51). Phoenix, AZ: Onyx Press.

Sicker, M. (1997, March). Age discrimination in employment [8 paragraphs]. *Modern Maturity, 40* (2), 77, 79 [On-line serial]. Hostname: http://db.texshare.edu/utexas.

Silver, A. D. (1994). *Enterprising women: Lessons from 100 of the greatest entrepreneurs of our day.* New York: American Management Association.

Smith, T. (1992). Hostility and health: Current status of a psychosomatic hypothesis. *Health Psychology, 11,* 139–50.

Solomon, C. (1991, August). 24-hour Employees. *Personnel Journal,* 56–63.

Solomon, J. (1998, March 16). An insurance policy with sex appeal. *Newsweek,* 44.

Stidham, H. H., and Remley, T. P., Jr. (1992). Job club methodology applied to a workfare setting. *Journal of Employment Counseling, 29,* 69–76.

Simon, J., and Osipow, S. H. (1996). Continuity of career: The vocational script in counseling older workers. *The Career Development Quarterly, 45,* 154–62.

Super, D. (1990). A life-span, life-space approach to career development. In D. Brown, L. Brooks, and Associates (Ed.), *Career choice and development* (2nd edition) (pp. 197–261). San Francisco: Jossey-Bass.

Tan, C., and Salomone, P. (1994). Understanding career plateauing: Implications for counseling. *The Career Development Quarterly, 42,* 291–301.

Tannen, D. (1994). *Talking from 9 to 5.* New York: William Morrow and Company, Inc.

Tannen, D. (1990). *You just don't understand.* New York: Ballantine.

Tichy, N. M., and Sherman, S. (1993, June). Walking the talk at GE. *Training and Development.* 27–35.

United States Senate, Special Committee on Aging. (1986). *Developments in aging. 1985.* Washington, D.C.: U.S. Government Printing Office.

Violante, J. M., and Aron, F. (1993). Sources of police stressors, job attitudes, and psychological distress. *Psychological Reports, 72,* 899–904.

Violante, J., M., and Aron, F. (1994). Ranking police stressors. *Psychological Reports, 75,* 824–26.

Violante, J. M., Marshall, J. R., and Howe, B. (1985). Stress, coping, and alcohol use: The police connection. *Journal of Police Science & Administration, 13,* 106–10.

Vistica, G. L. (1995). *Fall from glory: The men who sank the U.S. Navy.* New York: Simon & Schuster.

Wanberg, C. R. (1995). A longitudinal study of the effects of unemployment and quality of reemployment. *Journal of Vocational Behavior, 46,* 40–54.

Wanberg, C. R, Watt, J. D., and Rumsey, D. J. (1996). Individuals without jobs: An empirical study of job-seeking behavior and reemployment. *Journal of Applied Psychology, 81,* No. 1, 76–87.

Walsh, W. B., and Osipow, S. H. (Eds.). (1994). *Career counseling for women.* Hillsdale, NJ: Lawrence Erlbaum Associates.

Washington, T. (1993, Winter). Career counseling the experienced client. *Journal,* 37ff.

Waterman, R. H. Jr., Waterman, J. A., and Collard, B. A. (1994, July–August). Toward a career-resilient workforce. *Harvard Business Review,* 87–95.

Watson, R. (1997, September 8). Do it, be it, live it. *Newsweek,* 30–57.

Webb, S. L. (1991). *Step forward: Sexual harassment in the workplace.* New York: Master Media, Ltd.

Wilde, A. D. (1996, January 14). Earning it; Who's really essential? In a blizzard, it's a blur. *The New York Times,* Section 3, p. 10.

Yang, C. (1996, May 13). Getting justice is no easy task. *Business Week,* 98.

Yankelovich, D. (1981). The meaning of work. In J. O'Toole, J. Scheiber, and L. Woods (Eds.), *Working: Changes & choices* (pp. 33–34). New York: Human Sciences Press.

Zacarro, S., and Riley, A. (1987). Stress, coping and organization effectiveness. In A. Riley and S. Zacarro (Eds.), *Occupational stress and organizational effectiveness* (pp. 3–47). New York: Praeger.

Zimpfer, D., and Carr, J. (1989). Groups for midlife career change: A review. *Journal for Specialists in Group Work, 14,* 243–50.

Zunker, V. (1998) *Career counseling: Applied concepts of life planning* (5th edition). Pacific Grove, CA: Brooks/Cole Publishing.

Chapter 12

American College Testing. (1985). *DISCOVER for Schools.* Hunt Valley, MD: Author. [computer program]

Career Decision Software System. (1994). San Francisco: Cognito Press.

Career Navigator. (1987). Drake, Beam & Moran, Inc.

Corrigan, J., Dell, D., Lewis, K., and Schmidt, L. (1980). Counseling as a social influence process: A review. *Journal of Counseling Psychology, 27,* 395–441.

Dorn, F. J. (1988). Utilizing social influence in career counseling: A case study. *Career Development Quarterly, 36,* 269–80.

Educational Testing Service. (1984). *System of interactive guidance and information (SIGI).* Princeton, NJ: Author.

Educational Testing Service. (1985). *SIGI PLUS.* Princeton, NJ: Author.

Garis, J. W., and Niles, S. G. (1990). The separate and combined effects of SIGI or DISCOVER and a career planning course on undecided university students. *The Career Development Quarterly, 38,* 261–74.

Gati, I. (1994). Computer-assisted career counseling: Dilemmas, problems, and possible solutions. *Journal of Counseling and Development, 73,* 51–57.

Gray, K. C., and Herr, E. L. (1995). *Other ways to win: Creating alternatives for high school graduates.* Thousand Oaks, CA: Corwin Press, Inc.

Heppner, P. P., and Dixon, D. (1981). A review of the interpersonal influence process in counseling. *The Personnel and Guidance Journal, 60,* 542–50.

Herr, E. L. (1997, January). *Ethical issues in using computers to deliver career services: Counseling intervention, equality of access, and the Internet.* Paper presented at the National Career Development Association Conference, Daytona Beach, FL.

Holland, J. L. (1985). *SDS: Professional manual, 1985 Edition.* Odessa, FL: Psychological Assessment Resources.

Johnston, J. A., Buescher, K. L., and Heppner, M. J. (1988). Computerized career information and guidance systems: Caveat emptor. *Journal of Counseling Development, 67,* 39–41.

Kapes, J. T., Borman, C. A., and Frazier, N. (1989). An evaluation of SIGI and DISCOVER microcomputer-based career guidance systems. *Measurement and Evaluation in Counseling and Development, 22,* 126–36.

Katz, M. R. (1993). *Computer-assisted career decision-making: The guide in the machine.* Hillsdale, NJ: Erlbaum.

Kivlighan, D. M. Jr., Johnston, J. A., Hogan, R. S., and Mauer, E. (1994). Who benefits from computerized career counseling? *Journal of Counseling and Development, 72,* 289–92.

McKee, L. M., and Levinson, E. M. (1990). A review of the computerized version of the self-directed search. *Career Development Quarterly, 38,* 325–33.

Mlekodaj, N. L. (1995). *A baseline study of career information on the Internet and state and land-grant colleges.* Unpublished manuscript.

Osipow, S. H. (1980). *Manual for the Career Development Scales* (2nd edition). Columbus, OH: Marathon Consulting and Press.

Peterson, G. W., Sampson, J. P., Jr., and Reardon, R. C. (1991). *Career development and services: A cognitive approach.* Pacific Grove, CA: Brooks/Cole Publishing.

Pharr, M., and Glover, J. (1995). Training and outcomes for federal college work-study. *Journal of Student Employment, 6,* 6–17.

Pyle, K. R. (1985). "Hi tech-hi touch": A synergy applicable to career development using the computer in group counseling. *Journal of Career Development, 10,* 333–41.

Reardon, R. C., Peterson, G. W., Sampson, J. P. Jr., Ryan-Jones, R. E., and Shahnasarian, M. (1992). A comparative analysis of the impact of SIGI and SIGI PLUS. *Journal of Career Development, 18,* 315–22.

Reardon, R. C. (1987). Development of the computerized version of the SDS. *Measurement and Evaluation in Counseling and Development, 20,* 62–67.

Robbins, S. R., and Patton, M. J. (1985). Self psychology and career development: Construction of the superiority and goal instability scales. *Journal of Counseling Psychology, 32,* 221–31.

Routh, L., Chretien, C., and Rakes, T. (1995). Career centers and work-study employment. *Journal of Career Development, 22,* 125–33.

Sampson, J. P., Jr. (1994a). *Effective computer-assisted career guidance: Occasional paper number 2.* Center for the Study of Technology in Counseling and Career Development, Florida State University.

Sampson, J. P., Jr. (1994b). Factors influencing the effective use of computer-assisted careers guidance: The North American experience. *British Journal of Guidance and Counselling, 22,* 91–106.

Sampson, J. P., Jr. (1997, January). Ethical delivery of computer-assisted career guidance services: Supported vs. stand-alone system use. In R.C. Reardon (Chair), *Ethical Issues in Using Computers to Deliver Career Services: Counseling Intervention, Equality of Access, and the Internet.* Symposium conducted at the National Career Development Association Conference, Daytona Beach, FL.

Sampson, J. P., Jr., Peterson, G. W., Reardon, R. C., Lenz, J. G., Shahnasarian, M., and Ryan-Jones, R. E. (1992). The social influence of two computer-assisted career guidance systems: DISCOVER and SIGI. *Career Development Quarterly, 41,* 75–83.

Schinka, J. A. (1988). *Self-Directed Search: Computer manual for use with Apple computers.* Odessa, FL: Psychological Assessment Resources.

Strong, S. (1968). Counseling: An interpersonal influence process. *Journal of Counseling Psychology, 20,* 25–37.

Strong, S., and Matross, R. (1973). Change process in counseling and psychology. *Journal of Counseling Psychology, 20,* 25–37.

Chapter 13

About our children. (1995, Rev. edition). Los Angeles, CA: Parents and Friends of Lesbians and Gays, Inc. [booklet]

Amundson, N., Firbank, O., Klein, H., and Poehnell, G. (1991). Job link: An employment counseling program for immigrants. *Journal of Employment Counseling, 28,* 167–76.

Anderson, J. D. (1992). Family-centered practice in the 1990s: A multicultural perspective. *Journal of Multicultural Social Work, 1,* 17–29.

Applebone, P. (1997, April 8). Schools see re-emergence of "separate but equal." *New York Times,* p. 10.

Arbona, C. (1990). Career counseling research and Hispanics: A review of the literature. *The Counseling Psychologist, 18,* 300–23.

Arbona, C., and Novy, D. M. (1991). Career aspirations and expectations of Black, Mexican American, and White students. *The Career Development Quarterly, 39,* 231–39.

Arce, C. H., Murguia, E., and Frisbie, W. P. (1987). Phenotype and life chances among Chicanos. *Hispanic Journal of Behavioral Sciences, 9,* 19–32.

Associated Press. (1996, February 28). Immigration reform worries companies. *El Paso Herald-Post,* p. A2.

Associated Press. (1997a, August 28). Drop in minorities worries law school. *El Paso Times,* p. 4B.

Associated Press. (1997b, June 13). Most see two standards in military sex case. *El Paso Times,* p. 6A.

Associated Press. (1997c, January 29). Most segregated cities aren't in South. *El Paso Times,* p. 4A.

Associated Press. (1997d, July 28). [Texas] Tech to have fewer minorities. *El Paso Herald-Post,* p. B2.

Atkinson, D. R., and Hackett, G. (1998). *Counseling diverse populations* (2nd edition). Boston: McGraw Hill.

Atkinson, , D. R., Morten, G., and Sue, D. W. (Eds.). (1998). *Counseling American minorities: A cross-cultural perspective* (5th edition). Boston: McGraw Hill.

Attainment Productions. (1995). *Every one can work* [video]. (Available from Attainment Company, Inc., P.O. Box 930160, Verona, WI 53593, 1-800-327-4269.)

Bacon, J. (1998, January 30). Texaco diversity. *USA Today,* p. 10A.

Belz, J. R. (1993). Sexual orientation as a factor in career development. *The Career Development Quarterly, 41,* 197–201.

Bennett, C. E., and DeBarros, K. A. (1995). The Black population. In U.S. Bureau of the Census, Current Population Reports, Series P23–189, *Population Profile of the United States: 1995* (pp. 44–45). Washington, D.C.: U.S. Government Printing Office.

Bergmann, B. R. (1996). *In defense of affirmative action.* New York: Basic Books.

Be yourself: Questions and answers for Gay, Lesbian, and Bisexual youth. (1994). Washington, D.C.: Parents and Friends of Lesbians and Gays, Inc. [booklet]

Bolles, R. N. (1991). *Job-hunting tips for the so-called handicapped or people who have disabilities.* Berkeley, CA: Ten Speed Press.

Bowman, S. L., and Tinsley, H. E. A. (1991). The development of vocational realism in Black American college students. *The Career Development Quarterly, 39,* 240–50.

Brandon, P. R. (1991). Gender differences in young Asian Americans' educational attainments. *Sex Roles, 25,* 45–61.

Brodwin, M., Parker, R. M., and DeLaGarza, D. (1996). Disability and accommodation. In E. M. Szymanski, and R. M. Parker (Eds.), *Work and disability: Issues and strategies in career development and job placement* (pp. 165–207). Austin, TX: PRO-ED, Inc.

Bronzaft, A. L. (1991). Career, marriage, and family aspirations of young Black college women. *Journal of Negro Education, 60,* 110–18.

Buhrke, R. A. (1989). Incorporating lesbian and gay issues into counselor training: A resource guide. *Journal of Counseling and Development, 68,* 77–80.

Buhrke, R. A., and Douce, L. A. (1991). Training issues for counseling psychologists in working with lesbian women and gay men. *The Counseling Psychologist, 19,* 216–34.

Burlew, A. K., and Johnson, J. L. (1992). Role conflict and career advancement among African-American women in nontraditional professions. *The Career Development Quarterly, 40,* 302–12.

Butterfield, F. (1990, January 21). Why they excel. *Parade Magazine,* 4–6.

Carter, R. T., and Swanson, J. L. (1990). The validity of the Strong Interest Inventory with Black Americans: A review of the literature. *Journal of Vocational Behavior, 36,* 195–209.

Carter, S. L. (1991). *Reflections of an affirmative action baby.* New York: Basic Books.

Chen, S., and Leong, F. T. L. (1997). Case study: The case of Jessica Chang. *The Career Development Quarterly, 46,* 142–47.

Chodorow, N. (1978). *Reproduction of mothering.* Berkeley, CA: University of California Press.

Chow, E. N.-L. (1987). The influence of sex-role identity and occupational attainment on the psychological well-being of Asian-American women. *Psychology of Women Quarterly, 11,* 69–81.

Christie, S. (1997, July/August). Beyond gym teacher: Dyke jobs today. *Girlfriends,* 24–27.

Cook, E. P. (1997). Gender discrimination in Jessica's career. *The Career Development Quarterly, 46,* 148–54.

Croteau, J. M., and Hedstrom, S. M. (1993). Integrating commonality and difference: The key to career counseling with lesbian women and gay men. *The Career Development Quarterly, 41,* 201–9.

Curry, H., Clifford, D., and Leonard, R. (1996). *A legal guide for lesbian and gay couples* (9th national edition). Berkeley, CA: Nolo Press.

D'Andrea, M., and Daniels, J. (1992). A career development program for inner-city Black youth. *The Career Development Quarterly, 40,* 272–80.

Delsen, L. (1989). Improving the employability of the disabled: A practical approach. *International Journal for the Advancement of Counselling, 12,* 125–35.

Eastland, T. (1997). *Ending affirmative action: The case for colorblind justice.* New York: Basic Books.

Edwards, A., and Polite, C. K. (1992). *Children of the dream: The psychology of Black success.* New York: Doubleday.

Enright, M. S., Conyers, L. M., and Szymanski, E. M. (1996). Career and career-related educational concerns of college students with disabilities. *Journal of Counseling & Development, 75,* 103–14.

Evanoski, P. O., and Tse, F. W. (1989). Career awareness program for Chinese and Korean American parents. *Journal of Counseling and Development, 67,* 472–74.

Evans, K. M., and Herr, E. L. (1991). The influence of racism and sexism in the career development of African-American women. *Journal of Multicultural Counseling and Development, 19,* 130–35.

Fassinger, R. E. (1996). Notes from the margins: Integrating lesbian experience into the vocational psychology of women. *Journal of Vocational Behavior, 48,* 160–75.

Flores-Hughes, G. (1996, September). Why the term "Hispanic"? *Hispanic,* 64.

Fouad, N. A., and Tang, M. (1997). Caught in two worlds: Jessica Chang from a cross-cultural perspective. *The Career Development Quarterly, 46,* 155–60.

Friskopp, A., and Silverstein, S. (1995). *Straight jobs, gay lives: Gay and lesbian professionals, the Harvard Business School, and the American workplace.* New York: Touchstone.

Gainor, K. A., and Forrest, L. (1991). African-American women's self-concept: Implications for career decisions and career counseling. *The Career Development Quarterly, 39,* 261–72.

Gelberg, S., and Chojnacki, J. T. (1995). Developmental transitions of gay/lesbian/bisexual-affirmative, heterosexual career counselors. *The Career Development Quarterly, 43,* 267–73.

Gilligan, C. (1982). *In a different voice.* Cambridge, MA: Harvard University Press.

Goldberg, J. R. (1993). Is multicultural family therapy in sight? *Family Therapy News, 24* (4), 1ff.

Gordon, M. M. (1964). *Assimilation in American life.* New York: Oxford University Press.

Grevious, C. (1985). A comparison of occupational aspirations of urban Black college students. *Journal of Negro Education, 54,* 35–42.

Hacker, A. (1992). *Two nations: Black and White, separate, hostile, and unequal.* New York: Charles Scribner's Sons.

Hagan, J. W., and Hagan, W. W., II. (1995). What employment counselors need to know about employment discrimination and the Civil Rights Act of 1991. *Journal of Employment Counseling, 32,* 2–10.

Hagner, D., Fesko, S. L., Cadigan, M., Kiernan, W., and Butterworth, J. (1996). Securing employment: Job search and employer negotiation strategies in rehabilitation. In E. M. Szymanski, and R. M. Parker (Eds.), *Work and disability: Issues and strategies in career development and job placement* (pp. 309–40). Austin, TX: PRO-ED, Inc.

Harvey, V. M. (1995). The issue of skin color in psychotherapy with African Americans. *Families in Society: The Journal of Contemporary Human Sciences, 76,* 3–10.

Hawkins, D. (1996, September 23). The most dangerous jobs. *U.S. News & World Report,* 40–41.

Hedges, S. J., Hawkins, D., and Loeb, P. (1996, September 23). The new jungle. *U.S. News & World Report,* 34–45.

Hendricks, F. M. (1994). Career counseling with African-American college students. *Journal of Career Development, 21,* 117–26.

Herring, R. D. (1990). Attacking career myths among Native Americans: Implications for counseling. *The School Counselor, 38,* 13–18.

Hetherington, C., Hillerbrand, E., and Etringer, B. D. (1989). Career counseling with gay men: Issues and recommendations for research. *Journal of Counseling and Development, 67,* 452–54.

Hetherington, C., and Orzek, A. (1989). Career counseling and life planning with lesbian women. *Journal of Counseling and Development, 68,* 52–57.

Horan, K., and Cady, D. C. (1990). The psychological evaluation of American Indians. *Arizona Counseling Journal, 15,* 6–12.

Hsia, J., Hirano-Nakanishi, M. (1989, November/December). The demographics of diversity: Asian Americans and higher education. *Change,* 20–27.

Hughes, M., and Hertel, B. R. (1990). The significance of color remains: A study of life chances, mate selection, and ethnic consciousness among Black Americans. *Social Forces, 68,* 1105–1120.

Ivey, A. E. (1988). *Intentional interviewing and counseling* (2nd edition). Pacific Grove, CA: Brooks/Cole Publishing.

Keith, V. M., and Herring, C. (1991). Skin tone and stratification in the Black community. *American Journal of Sociology, 97,* 760–78.

Klein, F. Sepekoff, B., and Wolf, T. J. (1985). Sexual orientation: A multivariable dynamic process. *Journal of Homosexuality, 11,* 35–49.

Knight-Ridder News Service. (1997, June 10). General drops effort to lead joint chiefs. *El Paso Times,* p. 1A.

LaFromboise, T. D., Trimble, J. E., and Mohatt, G. V. (1990). Counseling intervention and American Indian tradition: An integrative approach. *The Counseling Psychologist, 18,* 628–54.

Landrine, H., and Klonoff, E. A. (1996). *African-American acculturation: Deconstructing race and reviving culture.* Thousand Oaks, CA: SAGE Publications.

Langewiesche, W. (1998, February 23 and March 2). A reporter at large: Invisible men. *The New Yorker,* 138ff.

Leong, F. T. L. (1991). Career development attributes and occupational values of Asian-American college students. *The Career Development Quarterly, 39,* 221–30.

Leong, F. T. L. (1993). The career counseling process with racial-ethnic minorities: The case of Asian Americans. *The Career Development Quarterly, 42,* 26–40.

Leong, F. T. L. (Ed.). (1995). *Career development and vocational behavior of racial and ethnic minorities.* Mahwah, NJ: Lawrence Erlbaum Associates.

Leong, F. T. L., and Hayes, T. J. (1990). Occupational stereotyping of Asian Americans. *The Career Development Quarterly, 39,* 143–54.

Leong, F. T. L., and Tata, S. P. (1990). Sex and acculturation differences in occupational values among Chinese American children. *Journal of Counseling Psychology, 37,* 208–12.

Lingg, M. A. (1995). Pre-employment training for African-American youth. *Journal of Career Development, 22,* 67–82.

Magiera-Planey, R. (1990). Special populations. In C. Schiro-Geist (Ed.), *Vocational counseling for special populations* (pp. 45–63). Springfield, IL: Charles C. Thomas.

Markowitz, L. (1991, January/February). Homosexuality: Are we still in the dark? *Family Therapy Networker, 15* (1), 26ff.

Marín, G., Sabogal, F., Marín, B. V., Otero-Sabogal, R., and Pérez-Stable, E. J. (1987). Development of a short acculturation scale for Hispanics. *Hispanic Journal of Behavioral Sciences, 9,* 183–205.

Marquez, M. (1996, January 7). Immigrant bashers won't face facts. *El Paso Times,* p. 6A.

Martin, W. E., Jr. (1991). Career development and American Indian living on reservations: Cross-cultural factors to consider. *The Career Development Quarterly, 39,* 273–78.

McGoldrick, M. (1982). Ethnicity and family therapy: An overview. In McGoldrick, M., Pearce, J. K., and Giordano, J. (Eds.), *Ethnicity and family therapy* (pp. 3–30). New York: Guilford Press.

McNeil, J. (1995). Disability. In U.S. Bureau of the Census, Current Population Reports, Series P23–189, *Population Profile of the United States, 1995* (pp. 32–33). Washington, D.C.: U.S. Government Printing Office.

Mizokawa, D. T., and Ryckman, D. B. (1990). Attributions of academic success and failure: A comparison of six Asian-American ethnic groups. *Journal of Cross-Cultural Psychology, 21,* 434–51.

Mohr, R. D. (1988). Gay basics: Some questions, facts, and values. In C. Pierce and D. Van DeVeer (Eds.), *AIDS: Ethics and public policy* (pp. 193–205). Belmont, CA: Wadsworth.

Morgan, K. S., and Brown, L. S. (1991). Lesbian career development, work behavior, and vocational counseling. *The Counseling Psychologist, 19* (2), 273–91.

Murry, E., and Mosidi, R. (1993). Career development counseling for African Americans: An appraisal of the obstacles and intervention strategies. *Journal of Negro Education, 62,* 441–47.

Muwakkil, S. (1988, June 22–July 5). Getting black males off the endangered species list. *In These Times,* p. 7.

National Career Development Association. (1991). *Guidelines for the preparation and evaluation of career and occupational information literature.* Alexandria, VA: Author.

New York Times News Service. (1996, March 4). Keeping José out could cost billions. *El Paso Herald-Post,* pp. A1ff.

Norton, E. H. (1996). Affirmative action in the workplace. In G. E. Curry (Ed.), *The affirmative action debate* (pp. 39–49). Reading, MA: Addison-Wesley.

Our daughters and sons: Questions and answers for parents of gay, lesbian, and bisexual people. (1995). Washington, D.C.: Parents and Friends of Lesbians and Gays, Inc.

Parham, T. A., and McDavis, R. J. (1987). Black men, an endangered species? Who's really pulling the trigger? *Journal of Counseling and Development, 66,* 24–27.

Park, E. R. (1950). *Race and culture.* Glencoe, IL: Free Press.

Pedigo, J. (1983, January). Finding the "meaning" of Native American substance abuse: Implications for community prevention. *The Personnel and Guidance Journal,* 273–77.

Petersen, W. (1980). Concepts of ethnicity. In S. Thernstrom (Ed.), *The Harvard encyclopedia of American ethnic groups* (pp. 234–42). Cambridge, MA: Belknap Press.

Phinney, J. S. (1996). When we talk about American ethnic groups, what do we mean? *American Psychologist, 51,* 918–27.

Powers, B., and Ellis, A. (1996). *A family and friends' guide to sexual orientation.* New York: Routledge.

Redfield, R., Linton, R., and Herskovits, M. J. (1936). Memorandum on the study of acculturation. *American Anthropologist, 38,* 149–52.

Reid, P. T. (1993). Poor women in psychological research: Shut up and shut out. *Psychology of Women Quarterly, 17,* 133–50.

Report of the Secretary's Task Force on Black and Minority Health (Margaret M. Heckler, Secretary). U.S. Department of Health & Human Services, August 1985. Volume I: Executive Summary.

Richardson, G. D. (1997, November 14). Reality is, whites are already preferred. *USA Today,* p. 15A.

Roberts, B.-E. (1998). *Roberts vs. Texaco: The true story of race and corporate America.* New York: Avon Books.

Rodriguez, R. (1982). *Hunger of Memory.* New York: Bantam Books.

Roessler, R. T., and Rumrill, P. D., Jr. (1995). Promoting reasonable accommodations: An essential postemployment service. *Journal of Applied Rehabilitation Counseling, 26* (4), 3–7.

Roland, A. (1994). Identity, self, and individualism in a multicultural perspective. In E. P. Salett and D. R. Koslow (Eds.), *Race, ethnicity, and self: Identity in a multicultural perspective* (pp. 11–23). Washington, D.C.: National MultiCultural Institute.

Sauerman, T. H. (1984). *Read this before coming out to your parents.* Los Angeles: Parents and Friends of Lesbians and Gays, Inc. [booklet]

Schmidtz, T. J. (1988). Career counseling implications with the gay and lesbian population. *Journal of Employment Counseling, 25,* 51–56.

Segregation anew. (1997, June 1). *New York Times,* p. 16.

Shahnasarian, M. (1997). The case of Jessica Chang: A business and industry perspective. *The Career Development Quarterly, 46,* 155–160.

Smith, M. D., Belcher, R. G., and Juhrs, P. D. (1995). *A guide to successful employment for individuals with autism.* Baltimore: Paul H. Brookes.

Smith, S. L. (1991). *Succeeding against the odds: How the learning disabled can realize their promise.* New York: G. P. Putnam's Sons.

Social Science Research Council Summer Seminar. (1954). Acculturation: An exploratory formulation. *American Anthropologist, 56,* 973–1002.

Sodowsky, G. R., Kwan, K.-L. K., and Pannu, R. (1995). Ethnic identity of Asians in the United States. In J. G. Ponterotto, J. M. Casas, L. A. Suzuki, and C. M. Alexander (Eds.), *Handbook of multicultural counseling* (pp. 123–54). Thousand Oaks, CA: SAGE Publications.

Sophie, J. (1985/86). A critical examination of stage theories of lesbian identity development. *Journal of Homosexuality, 12,* 39–51.

Sosa, L. (1998, January/February). The *Americano* dream: How Latinos can achieve success in business and in life. *Hispanic,* 88, 90, 92, 94.

Sowell, T. (1994). *Race and culture: A world view* (chapter 2, pp. 32–60). New York: Basic Books

Steele, S. (1990). *The content of our character: A new vision of race in America.* New York: HarperPerennial.

Sue, D., and Sue, D. M. (1995). Asian Americans. In N. A. Vacc, S. B. DeVaney, and J. Wittmer (Eds.), *Experiencing and counseling multicultural and diverse populations* (3rd edition) (pp. 63–89). Bristol, PA: Accelerated Development.

Sue, D., and Sue, D. W. (1993). Ethnic identity: Cultural factors in the psychological development of Asians in America. In D. R. Atkinson, G. Morten, and D. W. Sue, (Eds.), *Counseling American minorities: A cross-cultural perspective* (4th edition) (pp. 199–210). Madison, WI: Brown & Benchmark.

Szymanski, E. M., Hershenson, D. B., Enright, M. S., and Ettinger, J. M. (1996). Career development theories, constructs, and research: Implications for people with disabilities. In E. M. Szymanski, and R. M. Parker (Eds.), *Work and disability: Issues and strategies in career development and job placement* (pp. 79–126). Austin, TX: PRO-ED, Inc.

Szymanski, E. M., Hershenson, D. B., Ettinger, J. M., and Enright, M. S. (1996). Career development interventions for people with disabilities. In E. M. Szymanski, and R. M. Parker

(Eds.), *Work and disability: Issues and strategies in career development and job placement* (pp. 255–276). Austin, TX: PRO-ED, Inc.

Thompson, A. R., and Hutto, M. D. (1992). An employment counseling model for college graduates with severe disabilities: A timely intervention. *Journal of Applied Rehabilitation Counseling, 23* (3), 15–17.

Thompson, M. (Ed.). (1994). *Long road to freedom: The Advocate history of the gay and lesbian movement.* New York: St. Martin's Press.

Trillin, C. (1998, February 2). New Orleans unmasked. *The New Yorker,* 38–43.

U.S. Bureau of the Census. (1992, November). *1990 Census of population, General population characteristics, United States.* Washington, D.C.: U.S. Government Printing Office.

U.S. Equal Employment Opportunity Commission. (1991a). *La ley para personas con impedimentos: Los derechos laborales de las personas con impedimentos (EEOC-BK-21).* Washington, D.C.: U.S. Government Printing Office.

U.S. Equal Employment Opportunity Commission. (1991b). *La ley para personas con impedimentos, preguntas y respuestas (EEOC-BK-22).* Washington, D.C.: U.S. Government Printing Office.

U.S. Equal Employment Opportunity Commission. (1991c). *Sus responsabilidades cómo empleador (EEOC-BK-20).* Washington, D.C.: U.S. Government Printing Office.

U.S. Equal Employment Opportunity Commission. (1991d). *The ADA, Your employment rights as an individual with a disability (EEOC-BK-18).* Washington, D.C.: U.S. Government Printing Office.

U.S. Equal Employment Opportunity Commission. (1991e). *The ADA, Your employment rights as an employer (EEOC-BK-17).* Washington, D.C.: U.S. Government Printing Office.

U.S. Equal Employment Opportunity Commission. (1992, September). *The Americans with Disabilities Act, Questions and Answers (EEOC-BK-15).* Washington, D.C.: U.S. Government Printing Office.

Weinberg, R. B., and Mauksch, L. B. (1991). Examining family-of-origin influences in life at work. *Journal of Marital and Family Therapy, 17,* 233–242.

Weston, K. (1991). *Families we choose: Lesbians, gays, kinship.* New York: Columbia University Press.

Westwood, M., and Ishiyama, F. I. (1991). Challenges in counseling immigrant clients: Understanding intercultural barriers to career adjustment. *Journal of Employment Counseling, 28,* 130–43.

Woolley, G. (1991, January/February). Beware the well-intentioned therapist. *Family Therapy Networker, 15* (1), 30.

Yagi, D. T., and Oh, M. Y. (1995). Counseling Asian-American students. In C. C. Lee (Ed.), *Counseling for diversity: A guide for school counselors and related professionals* (pp. 61–83). Boston: Allyn and Bacon.

Yang, J. (1991). Career counseling of Chinese American women: Are they in limbo? *The Career Development Quarterly, 39,* 350–359.

Chapter 14

Bernstein, R., and Munro, R. H. (1997). *The coming conflict with China.* New York: Alfred A. Knopf.

Bohl, D. L., Luthans, F., Slocum, Jr., J. W., and Hodgetts, R. M. (1996, Summer). Ideas that will shape the future of management practice. *Organizational Dynamics,* pp. 7–13.

Borchard, D. (1995). Planning for career and life: Job surfing on the tidal waves of change. *The Futurist, 29,* 8–12.

Bremner, B., Engardio, P., Foust, D., Capell, K., and Einhorn, B. (1998, January 26). What to do about Asia. *Business Week,* 26–30.

Brown, D. (1996). Brown's values-based holistic model. In Brown, D., Brooks, L. & Associates, Career Choice & Development, 3rd ed., San Francisco: Jossey-Bass.

California Department of Education. (1995). *The changing culture of the workplace.*

Cascio (1995). Whither industrial and organizational psychology in a changing world of work? *American Psychologist, 50* (11), 928–939.

Cassidy, J. (1998, May 4). Europe reinvented. *The New Yorker,* 13–14.

Chung, Y. B. (1995). Career decision making of lesbian, gay, and bisexual individuals. *The Career Development Quarterly, 44,* 178–190.

Deardorff, K. E., and Montgomery, P. (1995) National population trends. In U.S. Bureau of the Census, Current Population Reports, Series P23–189, *Population Profile of the United States: 1995* (pp. 6–7). Washington, D.C.: U.S. Government Printing Office.

De Mente, B. F. (1994). *Chinese etiquette and ethics in business* (2nd edition). Lincolnwood, IL: NTC Business Books.

Diebold, J. (1994, May–June). The next revolution in computers. *The Futurist, 28,* 34–37.

Efran, J. S., and Clarfield, L. E. (1992). Constructionist therapy: Sense and nonsense. In S. McNamee and K. J. Gergen (Eds.), *Therapy as social construction* (pp. 200–217). London: Sage.

Efran, J. S., Lukens, R. J., and Lukens, M. D. (1988). Constructivism: What's in it for you? *Family Therapy Networker, 12* (5), 27–35.

Fassinger, R. E. (1995). From invisibility to integration: Lesbian identity in the workplace. *The Career Development Quarterly, 44,* 148–167.

Feller, R. (1997, January). *Redesigning "career" during the work revolution.* Paper presented at the meeting of the National Career Development Association, Daytona Beach, FL.

Feller, R. (1991). Employment and career development in a world of change: What is ahead for the next twenty-five years? *Journal of Employment Counseling, 28,* 13–20.

Friedman, D. (1996). Are you ready for a networked economy? *Inc., 18,* 62–65.

Gelberg, S., and Chojnacki, J. T. (1996). *Career and life planning with gay, lesbian, and bisexual persons.* Alexandria, VA: American Counseling Association.

Gergen, K. J. (1991b). *The saturated self: Dilemmas of identity in contemporary life.* New York: Basic Books.

González, R. C. (1994, August). Multiculturalism and social constructionism: An overview. In J. M. Georgoulakis (Chair), *Multiculturalism in therapy: Social constructionist applications.* Symposium presented at the American Psychological Association Annual Convention, Los Angeles, CA.

González, R. C. (1998). A technically eclectic blend of paradigms and epistemologies for multicultural clinical relevance. In C. Franklin and P. S. Nurius (Eds.), *Constructivism in practice: Methods and challenges* (pp. 349–735). Milwaukee, WI: Families International, Inc.

Greenberg, M. (1997, November 2). Mamas, don't let your babies become CPAs. *San Antonio Express News.* p. OH.

Greenfield, M. (1998, April 20). "Paperizing" policy. *Newsweek,* 74.

Gutek, G. L. (1993). *American education in a global society.* New York: Longman.

Hamilton, J., Baker, S., and Vlasic, B. (1996, April 29). The new workplace. *Business Week,* 106–117.

Hansen, L. S. (1993). Career development trends and issues in the United States. *Journal of Career Development, 20,* 7–24.

Held, B. S. (1990). What's in a name? Some confusions and concerns about constructivism. *Journal of Marital and Family Therapy, 16,* 179–186.

Herr, E.L. (1992). Emerging trends in career counselling. *International Journal for the Advancement of Counselling, 15,* 255–288.

Jayson, S. (1993). Career forecast for the '90s. *Management Accounting, 74,* 38–40.

Jones, L. K. (1996). A harsh and challenging world of work: Implications for counselors. *Journal of Counseling and Development, 74,* 453–459.

Koegel, H. M., Donin, I., Ponterotto, J. G., and Spitz, S. (1995). Multicultural career development: A methodological critique of 8 years of research in three leading career journals. *Journal of Employment Counseling, 32,* 50–63.

Krumboltz, J.D. (1998). Serendipity is not serendipitous. *Journal of Counseling Psychology, 45,* 390–92.

Larmer, B. (1998, April 27). A special breed of bandit. *Newsweek,* 44.

Leong, F. T. L. (Ed.). (1995). *Career development and vocational behavior of racial and ethnic minorities.* Mahwah, NJ: Lawrence Erlbaum Associates, Inc.

Light, R. J., and Pillemer, D. B. (1982). Numbers and narrative: Combining their strengths in research reviews. *Harvard Educational Review, 52,* 1–26.

Lippert, J. (1997, March 12). Saturn crew votes to stay unique. *San Antonio Express News,* pp. 2A, 2C.

Mabry, L., and Stake, R. E. (Eds.). (1997). *Evaluation in the post-modern dilemma.* Greenwich, CT: Jai Press.

Mays, V. M., Rubin, J., Sabourin, M., and Walker, L. (1996). Moving toward a global psychology: Changing theories and practice to meet the needs of a changing world. *American Psychologist, 51,* 485–87.

McCarthy, T. (1998, March 16). In defense of "Asian values." *Time,* 40.

McDaniels, C. (1996). Career = Work + Leisure: A developmental/trait factor approach to career development. In Feller, R. & Walz, G. R., *Career Transitions in Turbulent Time: Exploring Work, Learning and Careers.* Greensboro, NC: ERIC/CASS Publications pp. 45–56.

Miller, R. (1997, November 26). Sun sets on crony capitalism. *USA Today,* pp. 1B, 2B.

Miller-Tiedeman, A. (1996). Surfing the quantam: Notes of LIFECAREER Development. In Feller, R. & Walz, G. R., *Career Transitions in Turbulent Time: Exploring Work, Learning and Careers.* Greensboro, NC: ERIC/CASS Publications pp. 105–14.

Minuchin, S. (1991). The seductions of constructivism. *Family Therapy Networker, 15* (5), 47–50.

Mosca, J. (1989). Technology affects careers: A proposal for the year 2000. *Journal of Employment Counseling, 26,* 98–105.

Myss, C. (1996). *Anatomy of the spirit: The seven stages of power and healing.* New York: Three Rivers Press.

Naisbitt, J. (1997). *Megatrends Asia: Eight Asian megatrends that are reshaping our world.* New York: Touchstone.

Neimeyer, R. A. (1995b). Constructivist psychotherapies: Features, foundations, and future directions. In R. A. Neimeyer and M. J. Mahoney (Eds.), *Constructivism in psychotherapy* (pp. 1–38). Washington, D.C.: American Psychological Association.

New York Times News Service. (1996, August 9). Grim look offered at world of child porn. *San Antonio Express-News,* p. 12A.

Osborne, W. L., and Usher, C. H. (1994). A Super approach: Training career educators, career counselors and researchers. *Journal of Career Development, 20,* pp. 219–225.

Parfit, M. (1996, August). Mexico City: Pushing the limits. *National Geographic, 190* (2), 24–43.

Popcorn, F., and Marigold, L. (1996) *Clicking: 16 trends to future fit your life, your work, and your business.* New York: Harper Collins.

Pope, M. (1995). Career interventions for gay and lesbian clients: A synopsis of practice knowledge and research needs. *The Career Development Quarterly, 44,* 191–203.

Prince, J. P. (1995). Influences on the career development of gay men. *The Career Development Quarterly, 44,* 168–77.

Reichardt, C. S., and Cook, T. D. (1979). Beyond quantitative versus qualitative methods. In T. D. Cook and C. S. Reichardt (Eds.), *Qualitative and quantitative methods in evaluation research* (pp. 7–32). Beverly Hills, CA: SAGE.

Reid, P. T. (1993). Poor women in psychological research. *Psychology of Women Quarterly, 17,* 133–50.

Ripley, D. (1995). How to determine future work force needs. *Personnel Journal, 74,* 83–89.

Ritzer, G. (1996). McJobs. In R. Feller and G. Walz (Eds.), *Career transitions in turbulent times: Exploring work, learning, and careers* (pp. 211–17). Greensboro, N.C.: ERIC Counseling and Student Services Clearinghouse.

Russell, J. (1991). Career development interventions in organizations. *Journal of vocational Behavior, 39,* 131–81.

Saporito, B. (1998, March 30). Taking a look inside Nike's factories. *Time,* 52–53.

Schertzer, B. (1985). *Career planning: Freedom to choose.* Boston: Houghton Mifflin.

Schwarzbaum, L. (1997, December 26/1998, January 2). Ellen DeGeneres: Entertainer of the year. *Entertainment Weekly, 411/412,* 16–18.

Solomon, C. M. (1991, April). Twenty-four-hour employees. *Personnel Journal,* pp. 56–63.

Stamps, D. (1996, February). Corporate anorexia: In their obsession to cut costs-and people-have some companies cut too close to the bone? *Training, 33,* 24–30.

Stodden, R. A. (1998). School-to-work transition: Overview of disability legislation. In F. R. Rusch and J. G. Chadsey (Eds.), *Beyond high school: Transition from school to work.* Belmont, CA: Wadsworth Publishing.

Stolz-Loike, M. (1995). Adult career transitions. *The Career Development Quarterly, 44,* 89–93.

Vonk, T.H., and Hirsch, P.M. (1992). Job security: The free agent manager. In L.K. Jones (Ed.), *The encyclopedia of career change and work issues* (pp. 151–52). Phoenix, AZ: Oryx.

Watts, A. G. (1996). The changing concept of career: Implications for career counseling. In R. Feller and G. Walz (Eds.), *Career transitions in turbulent times: Exploring work, learning, and careers* (pp. 229–35). Greensboro, N.C.: ERIC Counseling and Student Services Clearinghouse.

Weidenbaum, M. (1996, February–March). American isolationism versus the global economy. *Executive Speeches, 10,* 18–22.

Index